The History of American Classical Music

The History of American Classical Music

MacDOWELL THROUGH MINIMALISM

by
JOHN WARTHEN STRUBLE

Facts On File®

AN INFOBASE HOLDINGS COMPANY

The History of American Classical Music

Copyright © 1995 by John Warthen Struble

Facts On File, Inc.
460 Park Avenue South
New York, NY 10016

Library of Congress Cataloging-in-Publication Data
Struble, John Warthen.
   The history of American classical music : MacDowell through minimalism / by John Warthen Struble.
      p.   cm.
Includes bibliographical references and index.
ISBN 0-8160-2927-X
   1. Music—United States—History and criticism.   I. Title.
ML200.S95   1995
780'.973—dc20   94-29092

Text design by Mark Safran/Layout by Robert Yaffe
Jacket design by Semadar Megged
Printed in the United States of America

MP FOF 10 9 8 7 6 5 4 3 2 1

This book is printed on acid-free paper.

Contents

Acknowledgments

I would like to acknowledge the generous assistance of the follow-ing individuals, without whose insights, assistance and reactions this book would have been much poorer stuff.

For sharing their firsthand reminiscences and views of their work: the late Stephen Albert, William Bolcom, the late John Cage, the late Aaron Copland, Philip Glass, Alan Hovhaness, Daniel Pinkham, Steve Reich, Terry Riley, the late Virgil Thomson, Christian Wolff, La Monte Young.

For other firsthand information about the lives and works of the composers discussed herein: the late Jorge Bolet, James Bolle, Harry Hay, the late John Kirkpatrick, Jack Larson, Vivian Perlis, Elliott Schwartz, Noel Zahler, Marilyn Ziffrin.

For stimulating my interest in American music generally and for their insights into its history and structure, certain of my former teachers and present colleagues, including: Chris Chafe, John Eaton, Robert Erickson, Cecil Lytle, Gerald Gabel, Thomas Nee, Pauline Oliveros, Juan Orrego-Salas, Paul Paccione, Robert Shallenberg, Bertram Turetzky, Iannis Xenakis.

For their advice on certain technical and historical matters and their willingness to review all or portions of the manuscript, the following scholars of American history and music history: Donna K. Andersen, J. Peter Burkholder, Philip Carlsen, MacDonald Moore, Vivian Perlis, Leigh Rutledge, Marilyn Ziffrin.

For their generous help in the myriad technicalities of researching, interviewing, preparing, proofreading and finalizing the manuscript: my editor Philip Saltz of Facts On File, Inc., Judith Weber of Sobel-Weber Associates, my agent Albert Zuckerman of Writers House, Inc., Gary Schuster of Dunvagen Music, Helene Caan of Outward Visions, Inc., Jim

Steinblatt of ASCAP, Ralph Jackson of BMI, Catherine Philbin, my apprentice Tom Andes, and my friend and associate Donald M. Campbell.

And, most of all, the individual who set in motion the chain of events that led to the writing of this book and who believed in its potentialities from the very beginning, novelist Tom Philbin.

JWS

Foreword

❧

It seems that our American musical culture has been on an endless search for self-identity. With our past firmly rooted in the art and folk music of Europe and Africa, American composers and historians have appeared uncomfortable and unsure about a cultural identity which could be described as autonomous and authentic. In fact our schools and text-books have always emphasized our debt to traditions that flourished be-yond our shores—traditions, we have been reassured, with histories of their own beginning hundreds of years before any thought of an American musical heritage could possibly have been imagined. And not only that. Our educational system has been wholly European. To this day our young composers (myself included among an older generation) have regularly gone to Europe to complete their education, this being considered a special mark of accomplishment.

All of this is, of course, an old story that we need not dwell on here. More and more we have come to acknowledge that Eurocentrism has been the backdrop in front of which our own history has unfolded, and which has marked its identity until now.

The question now arises: What, if anything, has changed now that, at the end of the 20th century, we are able to perhaps look at our musical culture somewhat differently. I would suggest that, in fact, we are experi-encing something now which is no less than a sea-change in the way we view ourselves and our history. There are many reasons that could be brought forward to elucidate this, but I will briefly mention four—geopo-litical, economic, cultural and technological—which have created a climate in which new thinking about American music (John Warthen Struble's book is an excellent example of this) can take place.

These changes became evident after World War II and some quite a bit more recently than that. The emergence of the United States as one of the two "superpowers" dates, of course, from the late 1940s. The establishment of the United Nations in New York City was far more than a mere symbol. It was an acknowledgment on a worldwide scale that the United States had become the de facto power broker in international affairs. For at least the next fifty years no new international arrangements would be made without U.S. involvement on some level. Just as quickly the world economic center shifted to the New World. Not only was "Wall Street" the barometer of the world economy but, as anyone who has traveled abroad extensively can attest, the "dollar" became the closest thing the world would have to an international currency.

American "culture" was not far behind in taking center stage. Movies, food, clothing, popular music as well as so many artifacts of modern life from cars to TV—all were dominated by American inventiveness and style, a style that has been envied and imitated as well as feared and despised around the world. No wonder, then, that the confidence that all this inspired in America in general would eventually find its way into American art making—painting, music, theatre, poetry, sculpture, architecture, dance et al.—producing often a buoyant, sometimes even aggressive American style.

I've saved consideration of the technological revolution for last—a revolution largely promulgated in the United States—because it has contributed so mightily to a new self-awareness of the strength and vitality of what appears now to be an indigenous American culture. It must be noted that the cultural productions of a society are inextricably tied to the technology (we might say "the level" of technology) that produces them. Now, we must look at "technology" in the larger meaning of the word. Technology refers simply to the tools we use to manipulate the world of phenomena and concepts. From this point of view, the history of European art music would not be understandable without knowing something of the history of the technology that produced it. Here I'm referring specifically to the development of the concert grand piano, wind and string instruments *as well* as the whole notational system and the evolution of counterpoint, harmony practice and use of rhythmic structures.

In terms of contemporary music, technological innovation of the last several decades has centered around programmable synthesizers, computers with their companion software, as well as MIDI and sampling systems, to mention a few. This is technology either born and made in the United States or made outside the United States based on home-made concepts and largely for American consumption. This is not to suggest that this is taking place in the United States alone. But clearly the inventiveness and appetite for the new technology have a large American component.

Undoubtedly the music of the next century will be tremendously affected by the emerging technology, and I fully expect American music to be central to developments in music in the coming years. After all, this will inevitably be music that will grow out of this technological revolution, a revolution that has a distinctively American style and origin. As one example, I expect that soon there will hardly be any young composer not using a computer and (as yet) undeveloped software for composing music. Make no mistake about it. Technology and language are inseparable. As our tools change, the language of music will change with it. I fully expect that music written with paper and pencil *and the language that goes with it* will soon become a thing of the past.

Another area already being impacted by the new technology is new and experimental music theatre, where technology specific to theatre has made possible new visions wherein dance, film, opera and theatre are combined.

Another force driving music away from Europe as the home of contemporary art music is the acknowledgment of the importance of "world music"—that is, the great traditions of classical music from India, Africa, Indonesia, Japan, Korea and so on. For this reason I don't expect the dawning of a kind of American musical "jingoism," which, if it occurred, would be most unfortunate. In fact I think 21st century music will be international in character, and future American composers will see themselves as Internationalists first and Americans second, which is how it should be.

So, as to the present book on the history of American art music. When put into the framework I am suggesting, John Warthen Struble's work brings a perception to the subject both long overdue and highly appropriate. Mr. Struble, besides being an able historian, is a composer himself which allows him to bring, I think, a special urgency to this subject. I believe we are entering a new period of reflection and evaluation of American music and we will soon be seeing new research, commentaries and histories as Americans discover their own voice both creatively and critically—a voice which, in fact, it has had all along.

Philip Glass
New York

This book is gratefully dedicated
to the memory of
SERGE KOUSSEVITZKY
(1874–1951)
and
LEONARD BERNSTEIN
(1918–1990)
whose musicianship, scholarship
and passion to communicate
caused much of this history to occur.
As Shakespeare's Marc Antony
said of Caesar:
"When comes such another?"

Introduction

ॐ

Any person who presumes to write history must understand that he himself works within a specific historical context. Thus, every history book actually comprises two historical documents: one consisting of the facts, dates and information it contains, and the other embodying the sum of the perceptions, selections and interpretations reflected by the writer in his own historical milieu. The former gives us useful information; the latter gives us an insight into how the writer's world thought of itself and its predecessors.

Much of the information relating to events prior to 1985 in the present book can be found in other sources, especially the important histories of American music by Louis Elson, John Tasker Howard, Gilbert Chase, H. Wiley Hitchcock, Charles Hamm and Ronald Davis (see bibliography). And a good deal of the information concerning later events can be gleaned from a wide variety of readings of other modern writers on "serious" music. But, while many excellent histories have covered the entire scope of American music, including both classical and vernacular, and many more have discussed American classical music in the context of its role in 20th century world music, no book yet published has dealt exclusively with the history of American classical music in and of itself. The reasons for this are complex and varied. For one thing, many people still do not accept the fact that there is a body of American classical music that has its own history and patterns of development. Others dispute the kind of music literature that should be included in the classification. The distinction, for instance, between that which is merely "art" music—music made to be listened to for its own sake—and that which is "classical" music hinges on that music's ability to reflect the characteristic traits of the whole culture, as well as the music's longevity in purely chronological terms.

The serious assertion, made by a number of African-American intellectuals within the past twenty years, to wit: that jazz is *THE* American classical music, is the most challenging question to have been raised in this regard recently. And, while it is clear that jazz meets any reasonable definition of an "art music" style, it is arguable whether it reflects the essential musical personality of America as a whole in the same way that the "classical music" traditions of other countries embody the characteristic emotional traits of those nations. This is not to say that jazz is not one of several very significant streams of musical thought that enters into the broader spectrum of American classical music. And, as the passage of time gives scholars more perspective on American music generally, it may yet come to pass that jazz, in the broadest sense of the term, is viewed as the classical music of African Americans, while the body of music discussed in the present volume is viewed as the classical music of Euro-Americans. But this also implies a fixed racial division in American classical music styles that seems incompatible with the pluralistic, democratic aspirations of our contemporary American society. And it also fails to account for the important role played by Native American music, Asian-American music and Latin American music in both our vernacular and classical music traditions—or for those "classical" composers who have successfully integrated jazz techniques into their work.

We can look to the histories written by earlier generations of American music scholars and discover not only the important names, dates and events, but also the ways in which those historians perceived the status of American music on the world stage, the implied predictions they made about the future course of its development, and the tacit assumptions underlying their definition of "classical" music in general. In the earliest attempt at a comprehensive history of American music, written by Frédéric Louis Ritter in 1883, the writer assumed that America was, in effect, another European nation partaking of the same cultural values, traditions and artistic objectives as its European contemporaries. Thus, the vital traditions of rural folk music and the important musical subculture of African Americans (not the bastardized parody of it known as "minstrelsy") were given but slight consideration. Ritter assumed the future of American music to be in the hands of now-forgotten imitators of the European Romantic movement such as William Gilchrist, William Henry Fry or George Frederick Bristow. In later histories, such as Howard's scholarly *Our American Music* (1929) or Chase's more concise *America's Music* (1955), our native styles, forms and methods are given much greater consideration, but the distinction between an indigenous "art" music and an indigenous "vernacular" music is still obscured by the equal consideration these later authors tried to give to every branch of the American musical tree, from the popular ballads of Stephen Foster to the serial works of Milton Babbitt. Wilfred

Mellers' *Music in a New Found Land* (1964, 1975) was an influential work which abandoned conventional chronological history and focused instead on the author's deep and controversial interpretation of the various fields of American music. But, although the book received wide acclaim by critics, Mellers qualified virtually every positive statement he made with some chauvinistic aside betraying his tacit assumption that American classical music could only be evaluated by the yardstick of European musical evolution, despite his extensive and penetrating discussions of indigenous forms such as New England psalmody, "blackface" minstrelsy and jazz.

The present book is predicated on the assertion that American classical music does, in fact, constitute a coherent if manifold tradition, a tradition based on a variety of European and non-European antecedents vastly wider in scope than that of any other nation. Moreover, it is my contention that American classical music can only be fairly evaluated by its own standards and criteria, standards and criteria based on the intentions of the men and women who created it. The only cases in which German or French or Italian or English theoretical models of composition are salient guides to the quality of American music occur when the composers in question were specifically trying to work within such European traditions. Admittedly, this was true of most American composers of concert music prior to Charles Ives. But these 19th-century American symphonists and opera composers do not constitute the basis of American classical music today; on the contrary, they represent a blind alley, a necessary period of experimentation, the whole result of which was to demonstrate that *American classical music would never find itself by imitating European models.* Antonin Dvořák stated this idea when he sojourned in the United States from 1892 to 1895. And for a long time it was thought that Dvořák's recommendation—namely that American classical composers turn to what Dvořák supposed to be the music of the American Negro as their most fruitful source of inspiration—fell on deaf ears. But it is significant that one of the first pieces of characteristically American-sounding classical music, music that could not have been written by any European composer, was Edward MacDowell's *Woodland Sketches,* composed only months after Dvořák's return to Europe. Thereafter, the effort to base an American classical tradition purely on imitation of European styles became increasingly outmoded, although the theoretical ideas of significant 20th-century European figures such as Debussy, Schoenberg, Stravinsky, Hindemith, Webern, Boulez and Xenakis continued to influence American composers.

The late works of MacDowell, the music of Charles Ives, the adaptations of Arthur Farwell and Percy Grainger, and the sensitivity to non-Western musical thought of Charles Griffes laid the groundwork for much American classical music during the 20th century, and the flowering of our indigenous classical tradition is almost entirely a product of this same century. But, despite the profoundly original contributions of our native composers, the *institutions* of American musical life have by no means freed themselves from the domination of European practice, optimistic claims to the contrary notwithstanding. The evidence of this is all around us. The repertoire of our own symphony orchestras and public radio stations today (1994) comprises at least 85 percent music by dead European composers as opposed to about 15 percent music by Americans. Music theory, literature and history as they are taught in the vast majority of our colleges, universities and conservatories consist almost entirely of European music of the so-called "common practice period" (roughly 1700–1920). Private music students at the precollegiate level are still consistently trained in the standard European keyboard, vocal and instrumental literature, which is endorsed to the near exclusion of American music by such national organizations as the Music Teachers' National Association, National Association of Teachers of Singing, American String Teachers' Association, Music Educators National Conference and National Guild of Piano Teachers. Such students generally enter college knowing nothing of American music beyond an occasional piece by Gottschalk or Copland. They may be able to distinguish between the Renaissance, Baroque, Classical, Romantic and Modern periods of European music, but generally cannot describe the difference between the periods and esthetics of William Billings and Lowell Mason, or between Samuel Barber and Wallingford Riegger. The bulk of our promising young concert artists ignore American musical literature and prefer to concentrate on the hackneyed repertoire of Europe of the past three centuries. America, in the global culture of the post-World War II era, flatters itself with the delusion that it has achieved overall musical independence from Europe, yet we have still failed to devise a system of music education that seriously integrates American classical models into its curriculum or takes account of our own musical vernacular in any meaningful way.

What is "classical music"? Frequently it is easier to say what it is not. For instance, folksong which serves a utilitarian purpose—such as maintaining the rhythm of some repetitive job that it accompanies—or tunes used for communal singing and dancing are not in themselves "classical music," though they may serve as a basis for later classical works. Music used in religious services or music intended to serve as background for conversation and social occasions generally is not thought of as "classical" when it is created, but may become so with the passage of time, or when it is presented in an exclusively concert format. The serenades, cassations, divertimenti, dance suites, masses and liturgical music of Haydn, Mozart and other composers fall into this category.

In terms of historical musicology it seems apparent that certain conditions must obtain before any given national culture can develop its own classical music literature. Whether one is studying the classical music of Russia, Indonesia, China, India or Europe, one finds that its development has always been preceded by several centuries of folk music and religious music. Secular classical music—written to be listened to and studied for its own sake, apart from any utilitarian function, any accompanying text or any association with labor or worship—is invariably built on such vernacular foundations.

Furthermore, based on the historical record, secular classical music also requires a cultural foundation that includes a written language, well-developed political, economic and social institutions, and a class of affluent patrons (frequently including royalty or aristocrats) who have the leisure and money necessary to promote the fine arts. Not every culture that possessed these social attributes has developed a substantial classical music tradition, but no such tradition has ever emerged in their absence.

The United States, in contrast to older cultures, holds the unusual (if not unique) distinction of having come into being as a nation almost at one stroke. By the very nature of the creation of our country, we Americans have missed the gradual evolution, requiring centuries of time, that characterized the cultures of other great nations. As a nation of immigrants, our folk music roots lie in the polyglot national musics which were imported along with our ancestors. Prior to the Civil War, these different musics tended to be concentrated in different geographical regions. Within its own territory each regional style underwent significant internal evolution, but had little contact with other regional styles. The massive uprooting of peoples caused by the Civil War, and particularly the intermingling of soldiers and former slaves from different parts of the country, created the first significant musical crossfertilization among these regional styles. For music was one of the soldier's few forms of entertainment, and small, easily portable instruments were a common component of every military camp and campfire. Apart from the music of the colonial New England singing masters (see Chapter 1), the ballads of the Civil War became the first American folk music with discernible features that can be considered unique to America: the first "American" sounding music, as distinct from any regional style derived from another country.

It was only a few short decades later that our indigenous classical tradition began to emerge. In the mid-20th century, this already telescoped evolutionary process was further overtaken by the "globalization" of Western culture generally. In the aftermath of World War II, musical nationalism rapidly became a passé idea, and the distinctions between national stylistic traditions were obscured by the rise of serial, electronic and aleatoric music.

This phenomenon led to a situation where composer demographics, such as sex, religious heritage, national origin or ethnic roots, became largely unidentifiable in the classical music created by composers of many nationalities from the 1940s through the 1970s.

Today the assumptions of the classical music world appear to be changing once again, as even the most sophisticated listeners and musicians have begun to grow weary of the abstraction that characterized international classical music of the past three decades. A kind of neo-Romanticism has arisen in the works of such composers as Philip Glass, Stephen Albert, David Del Tredici, John Adams and many others. Although never completely absent from the American classical tradition, this side of our musical thinking is once more in the ascendant.

Classical music in general is at once both a music "of the people" and a music "not of the people." Particularly in its nationalistic manifestations (such as the works of Moussorgsky, Wagner, Grieg, Dvořák, Bartók, Sibelius, Vaughan Williams, Smetana or Ives) it is "of the people" in the sense that it draws on the anonymous folk music traditions of the composer's native country. But the classical music of all nations has also traditionally been more *composer-oriented* than has its vernacular music counterpart. (There are even serious scholars of folk music who maintain that a given song cannot qualify as a true folksong if its composer can be identified, so strong is those scholars' attachment to the ideal of a totally anonymous vernacular tradition.) In classical traditions, however, composers are known and studied as individual musical thinkers. Their personal creative evolutions are traced analytically through the chronological sequence of their works, and their ideas are extended, altered and developed by succeeding generations of other classical composers. Thus, classical music is "not of the people" in the sense that what any given composer of genius does with pre-existing vernacular (as well as classical) traditions inevitably exerts a profound effect on the future course of that country's music, by serving as a model for later composers of the same nationality.

We may also identify certain formal trends in the musical styles and forms of particular countries. If it can be said that Germans tended to be masters of the fugue and sonata-form symphony, that Italians were the masters of opera, that the English were of an oratorio persuasion, that the French owned the short character-piece (*morceau* as well as *chanson*)—if such broad generalities are admitted into the discussion, we might well ask what form has exerted the greatest attraction for American composers and tunesmiths throughout our history?

The likeliest candidate is the 16- or 32-bar sung ballad—originating in the ballad operas of colonial times and the folksongs of Anglo-Celtic immigrants, extended in the songs of Stephen Foster and his contemporaries, and finding later expression as the formal skeleton of instrumental or vocal works of American composers such as MacDowell, Gershwin, Virgil Thomson, Leonard Bernstein and even Philip Glass. This is not to say that all American classical music is based on the ballad or even that a preponderance of it is. But the most successful American composers (in terms of public recognition) have always been those whose music asserted a direct and uncomplicated melodic appeal, even when its other musical parameters have been rooted in more abstract, "high-brow" concepts. This is amply demonstrated by the overwhelming popularity of such works as MacDowell's "To a Wild Rose," Gershwin's *Rhapsody in Blue,* Copland's *Appalachian Spring,* Barber's *Adagio for Strings* and many other such American classical "hits."

Americans mastered the ballad because the rugged conditions of colonial (and later pioneer) life required that music be simple, primarily vocal and generally not calling for any instrument that couldn't be carried on a horse or in a Conestoga wagon. Then, as now, our composers have been inspired to write songs (or at least to write melodically) because songs have always been the most practical mode of musical communication with the American public.

Ultimately, any national classical music tradition, built in part on a foundation of folk music and transformed at the hands of composers of genius, must, like a national epic, reflect the character, values, moods and aspirations peculiar to the people of the nation in question. Today America is a *pluralistic,* not (as Mellers asserted in his aforementioned history) a *polyglot,* nation. And neither jazz nor the European-oriented classical music of many American composers can yet lay *full* claim to this ability. I believe that the works of composers like Gershwin, Bernstein, Copland and Ives have come closest to it thus far, and this seems to be borne out by the relatively greater recognition afforded their music by the general American public than that of more specialized schools, including jazz. But we may also hope that, great as the contributions of American composers have been, we will yet hear greater things to come in the ongoing evolution of our native classical music.

There is clear evidence that the coming decades will see a greater infusion of the works of a growing population of women composers and of composers of non-European ethnic extraction represented in the canons of American classical music. Indeed, it is this author's hope that the very definition of American classical music may change for the better as a result of the as-yet-unrecognized efforts of this more broadly based population of creative minds. Add to that the crucial questions of how serious musicians in the 21st century will deal with changing musical technology, especially in the areas of mass communication and automated music, as well as increasingly conservative audiences and a deeply troubled system of public music education, and it is clear that many fertile fields of exploration remain open to the energetic young musical minds of today.

I hope that the present text will contribute to achieving a historical perspective on these necessary and inevitable changes, for a large part of knowing where we are going is knowing from whence we have come.

John Warthen Struble
Wolfeboro, New Hampshire

1

Forerunners

(1620–1860)

American music prior to the Civil War can be divided into seven distinct "schools" or regional styles. These are: (1) New England psalmody/hymnody, (2) the "genteel" or "cultivated" tradition of the mid-Atlantic cities: New York, Philadelphia, Boston and Charleston, (3) the folk music of the southern Appalachian, Ozark and Blue Ridge Mountains, (4) the Creole and West Indian-influenced music of New Orleans and the Gulf Coast, (5) the music of Native American tribal groups, (6) the music of African-American slaves in the deep south, and (7) the "blackface" minstrel ballads of the 19th century and the closely related popular ballads carried into the southwest by pioneers and cowboys. After the assimilation of Texas, New Mexico, Arizona and California into the United States, these seven domains of musical practice were joined by an eighth, namely, the hybrid Hispano-Indian folk music of Mexico. And, from the late 19th century on, the influence of Asian music was increasingly prominent in California. Virtually every piece of distinctively American classical music created between 1896 and 1950 has some roots in one or more of these vernacular traditions.

New England Psalmody/Hymnody: Composers of the
"First New England School" (1620–1820)

A closer study of the specific history of this era than can be accommodated by the present book will reveal that the debate between conservative and liberal approaches to music is nothing new. In the late 1600s the dominant mode of religious music in New England was the singing of psalms from the *Ainsworth Psalter,* originally published in 1612 at Amsterdam and brought to America with the Pilgrims. This volume included such stately numbers as "Old Hundredth," which has permeated American Protestant church music ever since and is still in use as the standard tune of the doxology. But before very long a livelier tradition of singing grew up in the rural communities, and the Puritan fathers of Boston took pains to discourage what they viewed as wanton, frivolous and sensual ornamentation in the singing of these psalms. Contemporary reports of the style of this vigorous rural psalmody emphasize the individual variations imposed on the tune by each singer, as well as the spontaneous flourishes and ornaments thrown in at will. The result may have been not unlike modern heterophonic gospel singing, especially as practiced in the African-American Baptist tradition although probably lacking modern gospel music's characteristic rhythmic syncopations.

Later in the 18th century, religious composers felt the urge to burst the bonds of the Old Testament texts of the psalms and began to create hymns with original texts or texts based on the New Testament. In 1735, John Wesley, the founder of Methodism, made a trip to Georgia at the invitation of James Oglethorpe; this led to his playing a major role in initiating the movement toward revivalist hymnody. The hymns of Wesley and other writers of the period were generally simpler in structure and closer to the folk music of common people than were the older psalms, but they too underwent a process of invigoration among the poorly educated rural farmers, whose few sources of diversion included Sabbath singing. As with the earlier psalmody, a conservative reaction tried to restore the original simplicity to later hymnody, but without noticeably greater success. It was in the context of this late-18th-century hymnody that there arose a school of itinerant singing masters, of whom the oldest and most significant was William Billings (1746–1800) of Boston. These singing masters, sometimes referred to as the "First New England School," created many of the standard hymns, which are still sung throughout the United States.

In addition to Billings, the principal native composers of the First New England School were: Justin Morgan (1747–1798), Andrew Law (1748–1821), Supply Belcher (1751–1836), Daniel Read (1757–1836), Timothy Swan (1758–1842), Jacob Kimball (1761–1826), Jeremiah Ingalls (1764–1828), Oliver Holden (1765–1844) and John Wyeth (1770–1858). Their numerous collections of hymns, anthems, songs and fuguing tunes have served as a repeated source of inspiration and quotable material for many later composers, notably William Schuman and Virgil Thomson.

Like most of the composers of his generation, William Billings was officially an amateur musician. He was trained as a tanner, but spent most of his life composing and publishing anthems and conducting "singing schools" in his native Boston and its environs. Billings seems to have been a rather repulsive looking individual, although no contemporary portrait of him has been preserved. He is reported to have been lame, blind in one eye and suffering from a withered arm. He was a man of ferocious energy and wholly dedicated to his musical vocation, but was unable to earn a decent living from it and died a pauper. He is buried in an unmarked grave somewhere on Boston Common. Of the many hundreds of songs and anthems he composed or arranged, the most famous is the four-part hymn "Chester," which was adopted by the American troops during the Revolutionary War and reincarnated as a popular march with fife and drum.

An 18th-century American singing school of the type Billings and his colleagues conducted consisted of rudimentary training in pitch matching, solfege (using the four syllable fa-sol-la-mi system current at the time) and the singing of psalms, hymns and secular songs in three- or four-part harmony. One of the characteristic features of these singing schools was that the respective male and female voices were frequently assigned to double their parts in any convenient octave, thus filling out the harmony and, particularly in the original compositions and arrangements of Billings, generating a massive texture of close-position chords that is unlike any sound created in any other European-based culture. This was one of the first characteristically American features of our early music.

As hymnody spread to the southern colonies, in part due to the large number of collections published by the above-named composers, the itinerant singing-school masters struggled to find a notation that would facilitate pitch recognition by their "students" within the fa-so-la-mi tradition. This resulted in the promulgation of "shape note" notation, where a different shape was assigned to each of the four syllables. The prime mover among the shape-note composers was Andrew Law. Later the system was expanded to include seven shapes, one for each of the seven syllables used in modern solfege. While characteristic New England hymnody gradually died out in the north, largely due to the efforts of urban musicians such as Lowell Mason (see below) to suppress it and substitute their own, more "scientific" approach, in the south it continued to thrive well into the 20th century and is still practiced as a historical novelty. But, more importantly, southern hymnody also continued to evolve musically and, in the 19th century, began to assume unique melodic characteristics of its own. Some of the hymns of this region and period, especially those found in Ananias Davisson's *Kentucky Harmony* (1817), William Walker's *Southern Harmony* (1835) and similar collections, continue to be associated with an

"American" melodic sound, even to modern ears. Moreover, the southern recensions of the various New England hymns displayed a remarkable ability to adapt themselves to the independent styles of African-American slave music and Appalachian folksong, which resulted in even more characteristic settings, especially during and after the Civil War.

A number of writers on the subject have criticized what they view as the faulty technique, measured by 18th-century European standards, of the New England singing master composers. But such criticism is only valid if one assumes that the choral models developed between the 12th and 18th centuries in France, Germany, England, Italy and the Netherlands are the only appropriate ones. And one must further assume that it was the *intention* of the New England composers to emulate those models. In fact, there is no evidence to suggest that either of these assumptions is justified. The presence of parallel fifths, octaves and unisons, the crossing of voices and false relations between them are no more conspicuous in the music of these composers than they are in the motets and conducti of the Notre Dame school of Perotin or other examples of early polyphony, where such phenomena are accepted as legitimate elements of the style. A more accurate analysis of this body of music literature would assume that the composers, who regularly heard their music and participated in its performance, knew what effects they wanted and wrote the notes that produced precisely those effects. It may be fair to state that their stage of development was less advanced than their European contemporaries but even this assumes that, had the New England tradition survived, it would have evolved along lines similar to the early choral traditions of European countries. The only possible basis for such an assumption is the chauvinistic belief that the specific course of development of European choral music was, *ipso facto,* the best or only possible one.

The Mid-Atlantic Genteel Tradition (1765–1875)

The music of the urban centers of the Atlantic seaboard was the closest in style and spirit to contemporaneous European music during the colonial and early national period. Because the urban colonists were largely of English origin, their music was particularly similar to the English style of the day, dominated by Georg Friedrich Händel and ballad opera composers such as Samuel Arnold.

The first identifiable composers of this urban colonial tradition were either native gentleman amateurs, such as Francis Hopkinson (1737–1791) of the Philadelphia, or professional instrumentalists and music teachers, many of whom emigrated from England or other countries. The best known works that survive from the colonial and early federal period are those of

Francis Hopkinson *(1737–1791). Lawyer, patriot and a signer of the Declaration of Independence, he became the first citizen of the United States to achieve renown as a "cultivated" composer.*

Hopkinson, Alexander Reinagle (1756–1809), Philip Phile (17?–1793) and the Moravian Johann Friedrich Peter (1746–1813), although these four were by no means the only composers active at the time.

The largest cities in 18th-century America—Boston, New York, Philadelphia and Charleston—were no greater in population or geography than a large American town by today's standards, and the entire population of the United States then was less than that of modern New York City alone. It is difficult to imagine today how truly sparse American society was in the 18th century, but that very sparseness entailed two very important phenomena in early American music-making. One is that the gentry—the political, commercial, religious and economic leaders of each region—were generally acquainted with each other on a personal basis. As a consequence, events which would be lost in the flux of daily news today assumed a larger significance then. For example, Hopkinson's most famous song, "My Days Have Been So Wondrous Free," though competently composed for the period, betrays little or no evidence of the originality expected of a great composer. Its claim to fame rests on the probability that it was the first published art song created in the fledgling United States by a native-born citizen, which was an event of some significance to the movers and shakers of the young nation. (Although Hopkinson himself claimed his *Seven Songs for Harpsichord* as the first composition by a native of the United States in a letter to George Washington dated 1788, it is doubtful that he imagined himself to be the first native of the North American continent to have composed a piece of music. More probably his claim was intended as a tribute to the cultural promise of the new nation that, as a signer of the Declaration of Independence and admiralty judge from Pennsylvania, Hopkinson played a role in founding.)

In a similar manner, the comings and goings of George Washington particularly excited a considerable amount of musical composition, including Hopkinson's "Washington's March," played at a public celebration in Philadelphia on May 1, 1784, and Phile's "The President's March" reportedly played at Trenton Bridge when Washington crossed it on his way to his first inauguration, April 29, 1789. It is often the case that a particular event in American musical history, or a particular composition, is considered important not because of its intrinsic merits (whatever they may or may not be), but because it was the *first* event or composition of its kind in the United States. And this was still true, to some extent, even as late as the 1960s.

The second feature of early American music-making, attributable to the relatively small size of the urban society of the day, was that most musicians survived by practicing several professions. Alexander Reinagle managed a theatre and wrote numerous ballad operas. Hopkinson himself was a lawyer and government official, while Philip Phile apparently made his living as a teacher of several instruments, professional violinist and leader of theatre orchestras. In this regard, such composers were not unlike many small town musicians even up to the present time. While Americans of the late 18th century enjoyed public theatrical performances, ballad operas and at-home amateur music-making, there simply was not sufficient cultural life in the cities, nor any system of aristocratic patronage, to allow any American composer of the period to devote himself to composition as exclusively as a Mozart or a Beethoven. To what extent this may have dampened potentially significant compositional efforts at the time is a question that can no longer be answered with assurance.

The urban genteel tradition was less exclusively vocal than New England psalmody. In 1798 Johann Friedrich Peter composed six string quintets, similar in character to the chamber music of Haydn. Hopkinson, Reinagle and James Hewitt all composed instrumental and keyboard music, often with a programmatic content reflecting some great battle of the

Revolution or other recent event. If most of these efforts display more enthusiasm than quality, it should be noted that even Beethoven had difficulty getting a good piece of music out of a battle symphony. Of the ballad operas of the period, by Reinagle and others, little can be noted with assurance, except their proneness to imitate their English models, because most of the music has not survived. Our best indications of what this music was like come from individual ballads extracted from the scores and published independently in any of the several music journals that thrived in the cities, notably Benjamin Carr's *The Musical Journal,* established in 1800.

The second best documented region of musical America in the 17th and early 18th centuries is rural Pennsylvania, and, although the music of this region was largely religious, it remained much more a part of the cultivated European tradition than did its New England and southern counterparts. The original Quaker settlers of Pennsylvania apparently made little music, but the later Lutherans and Moravians were steeped in the rich musical traditions of the German Reformation and brought those traditions with them, both in authentic and in highly individualized form. Conrad Beissel, founder of the Ephrata Cloister in Lancaster County, encouraged vigorous communal singing among his religious followers, and even developed a highly personalized system of harmonic theory in which he indoctrinated the faithful. We have previously noted the contributions of J. F. Peter, who emerged from the Moravian tradition. And the community of Bethlehem, Pennsylvania, in particular, continues to the present day to play a significant role in the propogation of the Lutheran musical traditions of Bach, Walther, Pachelbel, Buxtehude and their ilk in the United States. But this entire region has always been firmly rooted in its German origins and faithful to them. Despite the wonderful quality of its performances and scholarship, its contributions to the development of an indigenous American classical music have been minimal.

The urban genteel tradition did, however, play a significant role in American religious music, principally through the efforts of Lowell Mason (1792–1872). A native of Boston, Mason devoted his life to what he saw as "improving" American musical practice, particularly in the areas of church music and music education. Mason's ideas involved teaching singers to read the standard notation (as opposed to the shape-notes of the rural New England singing schools), and, more significant for its impact on native art music, the wholesale adaptation of hymn tunes from the works of European masters such as Beethoven, Mozart, Haydn, Schubert and others. Many of his adaptations are still in common use today. Mason also composed many famous original hymns, such as "My Faith Looks Up to Thee" and "Nearer My God to Thee." When adapting tunes from other composers, he usually limited himself to simplifying and/or regularizing the phrase structure, and

Lowell Mason *(1792–1872), music educator and composer of hymns such as "Nearer My God to Thee" and "Watchman, Tell Us of the Night." Almost single-handedly he set in motion the "better music" movement, which virtually destroyed Billings' New England Singing Masters school of composition.*

reducing the harmony to basic diatonic chords—relying on a variety of collaborating poets to produce appropriate religious texts for the tunes in question.

In collaboration with the Boston Handel and Haydn Society and the Boston Academy of Music (which he co-founded), Mason issued about twenty major collections of Protestant church music during his long public career, collections that dominated American hymnology until only very recently. While he succeeded in getting music made part of the primary and secondary school curriculum in Boston (other cities soon following suit), he also used his position of authority to shape the musical taste of most of 19th-century America away from its emerging native tradition and toward a mediocre imitation of the European models he so admired.

Mason founded a musical dynasty. His son, William Mason, studied in Europe and became one of the most prominent pianists of the mid-19th century in America. His grandson, Daniel Gregory Mason, became a well-known if not particularly significant composer of the "Second New England School" (see Chapter 4). The Masons were also involved in publishing and the manufacture of the Mason and Hamlin piano.

It is easy to criticize Lowell Mason's influence and to speculate that, had he not existed, American classical music might have been allowed to develop along the indigenous lines that were emerging from the work of Billings and his contemporaries. However, given the strongly European-ized consciousness of early 19th century urban civilization in America, it is equally possible that "somebody had to be Lowell Mason" (to borrow Arnold Schoenberg's caustic comment on his own fate)—in short, that the appearance of a figure such as Mason was a sociological inevitability of that period in our history. In either case, the damage was done, and the pervasive influence of European music dominated the cultivated musical circles of New York, Boston and Philadelphia throughout the 19th century and well into the 20th.

Our earliest symphonic composers emerged in the eastern cities of the United States, in tandem with the formation of symphony orchestras and opera companies in those cities throughout the 19th century. These composers were consistent followers of European models and included such now-obscure figures as Anthony Philip Heinrich (1781–1861), George F. Bristow (1825–1898), William Henry Fry (1813–1864), William W. Gilchrist (1846–1916), Silas Pratt (1846–1916), Frederick Gleason (1848–1903) and Sydney Lanier (1842–1881), the first three of whom will be dealt with more fully in the next chapter. Of them all, Lanier was the most promising, but his early death prevented the full realization of his musical ambitions. Today he is recognized principally for his substantial contribution to American poetry.

The Folk Music of Appalachia and the Mississippi Valley

The Louisiana Purchase of 1803 opened up vast regions of the modern states of Tennessee, Kentucky, West Virginia and Missouri to exploration and settlement. Much of this land is mountainous and, as a result, many of its communities became geographically isolated prior to the Civil War. (Some remained so even into the 20th century.) A high percentage of the settlers in this region were of Scottish and Irish descent, and they brought with them the rich tradition of folk ballads originating in those countries. Such characteristically Appalachian ballads as "Barbara Allen" or "Black Is the Color of My True Love's Hair" were sung and resung for generations throughout this region, sometimes remaining relatively identical to their

Anglo-Celtic origins, sometimes undergoing a process of evolution unique to the region in which they were sung.

Although no significant names of composers are preserved from this regional style, the style itself became both coherent and distinctive. During the Civil War it was crossfertilized with both northern and southern forms of the popular American ballad and hymn and, in turn, invested these popular songs with a modal character and poignancy derived from Anglo-Celtic folk music, which they previously lacked. This can be heard reflected in certain composed ballads of the Civil War such as "When This Cruel War Is Over," despite the fact that this particular song was written by a New Hampshire Yankee.

Later, the Appalachian style split into several distinct subgenres, especially after becoming intermingled with the black American plantation music that was liberated with the slaves after the war. The two most conspicuous of these subgenres are "bluegrass" and the "rhythm and blues" style that gave birth to the earliest forms of "rock and roll" in the 1950s. Aspects of the old Appalachian style also entered into the popular genre now known as "country and western" music. The city of Nashville, Tennessee, became the center of all these commercial musical activities in the 1920s and has remained so through the present time.

Although later composers, such as Virgil Thomson, Percy Grainger and Aaron Copland made arrangements of Appalachian tunes, and adapted some of them into symphonic music, the music of this region per se has not yet exerted as profound an influence on American classical music as it might.

Music of Native American Tribes

The competition of cultures at different levels of historical development for possession of the same land area has always led to tragic consequences. In the 16th and 17th centuries the first acts of this drama were played out on both the North and South American continents. While the native cultures of Central and South America, the Aztec and the Inca, had evolved to a stage roughly equivalent to that of Homeric Greece or ancient Mesopotamia, the tribes on the northern continent were still very much at the level of late stone-age hunter/gatherers. When confronted with the post-Renaissance military technology of French, Spanish and English invaders, the outcome for these peoples was a foregone conclusion: the less technologically developed culture was obliterated by the superior strength of the invader. To the credit of the North American tribes it may be noted that it required four hundred years for European-based "civilization" to complete its genocidal conquest in the face of unwavering resistance against unequal odds by the tribal peoples, a far greater length of time than it took to conquer the more "developed" cultures of the Central and South American native populations. Perhaps the only observation that can be made to the credit of the conquerors is that some of them had the good grace to feel guilty about the ruthlessness with which they wrested the land from the Indian.

In any case, Amerindian music, along with most other aspects of Amerindian culture, fell victim to the holocaust and, by the time serious efforts were made to document and collect it, little was left to collect. One of the great pioneers of this musicological rescue project was Natalie Curtis Burlin who, at the turn of the 20th century, made exhaustive efforts to transcribe not only the music, but the mythology, folklore and graphic art of some two dozen major and minor tribal groups. Her definitive collection, *The Indians' Book* (first published in 1907) set the standard for all future musicologists in the study of this important body of musical monuments.

The Indians of North America had no classical music as we understand the term, nor had they evolved a secular folk music of any substance. In common with most "primitive" cultures, virtually all of their music was religious in character. It was claimed by some of the Indians with whom Mrs. Burlin interacted that certain songs were of ancient origin, handed down through the oral tradition in unchanged form. And there is no substantive evidence either to prove or dispute this claim. But it is also clear that a great deal of Indian music was (and still is) improvised spontaneously. Song as a means of communicating with God, either directly or in the guise of various spirits or subdeities, was for the Indian the principal mode of what Europeans would term "worship." Indian songs were often personalized to the point of embodying the actual soul of the singer. They were sung as part of mystical rituals, rites of passage and as a means of marshalling and focusing metaphysical power within both the individual and the tribe. The stereotyped "war-dance" is the image perhaps most familiar to white Americans because of its repeated appearance (in forms distorted to the point of parody) in commercial films. But Indian song and dance also served to accompany seasonal festivals, fertility rites, religious sacrifices and other events of significance to the tribe.

In American Indian culture there was no separation between music as an art and everyday life. It has been said that every act in the life of any Native American who had not been assimilated into European-based society, was an act of worship. The Indians of North America lived their religion from moment to moment, in a way that no European or Euro-American outside of a monastery is accustomed to. And music was an integral part of that continual experience of the immediacy of God so characteristic of Indian metaphysics.

The influence of authentic Amerindian music on American classical music in general has been minimal. For one thing, very few American composers have bothered to acquire any systematic or substantial knowl-edge of Amerindian song. And, in tandem with the general inferiorization of Indian culture practiced by United States society for the last two centu-ries, such attempts as have been made have usually been based on grossly distorted stereotypes. It seems, for instance, that every elementary piano method book published in the U.S. contains at least one so-called "Indian" song. These concoctions are usually nothing more than a vehicle to intro-duce repeated harmonic fifths in the left hand, or the (very European) minor mode in the melody, and have absolutely no resemblance to any real Indian music. The musical atrocities committed by Hollywood film composers, many of whom were German, Austrian or Russian immigrants, in the early part of the present century are another demonstration of how poorly European music theory accommodates the vocal music of preliterate cul-tures. Even today, composers who would never dream of reviving the racist "coon songs" of 19th-century blackface minstrelsy seem to feel no qualms about indulging in the equally scurrilous misrepresentation of Indian music when the occasion arises.

Although composers such as Edward MacDowell and Henry F. B. Gilbert made use of Indian themes in their concert music of the late 1890s and early 1900s, the most important American composer of classical music who made an informed and systematic use of authentic Indian material was Arthur Farwell, about whom we will discover more in Chapter 4. Today, the possibilities of integrating American Indian music into our art music tradition, in a manner that does justice to the ethereal beauty and indigenous techniques of the extant literature, still remain a largely unexplored field for composers.

African-American Plantation Music

African slaves were imported into the colony of Virginia by Dutch traders as early as 1619. Thus the history of African Americans actually predates the Pilgrims of the *Mayflower* by one year. Although Africans were kid-napped and sold as slaves by both Europeans and sometimes their own or rival tribes throughout the African continent, the majority came from west African coastal regions. Transported under unspeakable conditions in slave ships, they were sent either directly to the English colonies of North America or brought there via the West Indies.

Like the American Indian, the African slave was a participant in a tribal culture. Both groups shared the enormous religious significance of the bulk of their music, and both lacked a native classical music tradition of their own. (The Arabic classical music of North Africa was *not* a product of sub-Saharan tribal cultures.) But black African culture generally was more prone to what we might term "folksong" than was the Indian, or at least we have more of a record of African folksong not necessarily connected with religious rites and practices. Because many African tribes had developed stable agricultural societies, work songs designed to accompany group labor or to focus the timing of repetitive tasks such as threshing grain had developed to a considerable degree in African culture. Moreover, African culture seems to have evolved a wider variety of instruments than had the primarily vocal music of the American Indian. Native African instruments included a variety of monochords, flutes, xylophones, drums, rattles and the "kalimba" (or "thumb-piano" as it is sometimes called) consisting of flexible strips, fixed over a bridge and resonating chamber, which were tuned and plucked with the fingers.

In addition, native African music of the period seems to have included the practice of call and response singing, where a solo voice articulates a line of song which is then answered by the singing group. This was not unlike the New England psalmodist's practice of "lining out" musical phrases for congregations that lacked the benefit of our modern hymnbooks and may account in part for the ability of later plantation music to synthesize with Anglo-American hymnody, or vice versa.

Furthermore, again in contrast to most Amerindian music, African tribal singing seems to have included some degree of harmony, often in parallel intervals. This would have provided an additional point of connection between the musical habits of early slaves and the hymns of their white masters.

Needless to say, no systematic study of slave music was conducted during the 17th or 18th centuries, and such collections as were made in the 19th century (*vide Slave Songs of the United States* [1867] and the *Negro Singer's Own Book* [1846]) are reflective of an African-American culture already two hundred years old, as distinct from purely African music. It is impossible to describe with certainty exactly what the music of the first slaves was like; at best we can indulge in educated speculation, extrapolating from what is known about the music history of west Africa.

In the early 19th century we encounter the first meaningful documentation of African-American music in the two references cited above. By this time there had already been substantial mixing of African and Anglo-American elements in the music of southern slaves. Many slaveholders encouraged singing and the practice of the Christian religion among their slaves, and the hymnody of the 18th century as transmitted through its southern branch found its way into slave culture. This gave rise to the mournful religious song type known as the "Negro spiritual," perhaps as early as 1800.

After emancipation we encounter the first clear evidence of a spontaneous song type comprised of three, 4-bar phrases. The first two phrases are usually identical, stating a problem or condition in the text and beginning respectively on the implied tonic and subdominant harmonies. The text of the third phrase states some reaction or conclusion to the problem of the first two, and generally begins on the implied dominant harmony. All three phrases tend to cadence on a sustained tonic occupying the third and fourth bar. This distinctive song pattern, probably African in its distant origin and possibly related to the call-response work song, became known as the "blues" around 1910, and played a seminal role in the evolution of jazz, bluegrass music and early rock and roll.

Although the term "blues" was later borrowed by composers such as George Gershwin and Aaron Copland in a variety of art music contexts, very few American classical composers have yet integrated the characteristic structure of the blues into a consistent style (an unexpected exception being Samuel Barber, whose second piano "Excursion" is very specifically based on blues phrase structure). The influence of the blues on American classical music, rather, has been indirect via the jazz styles of the first two decades of the 20th century, which have been copiously adapted by American classical composers. This is not to say that the blues are a dead issue. This style of singing is so pervasive in American culture and possesses such immediacy for the average American listener, white or black, that the possibilities offered by direct integration into classical styles can by no means be said to have been fully explored.

A further significant feature of African music is its complex and highly developed rhythmic dimension. Of all the world's national or regional musical cultures, the music of Africa has carried the study of rhythm to its farthest extremes—far outdistancing any European, Asian, Indonesian, Arabic or Pacific Rim culture. The regular and sophisticated use of multiple syncopations, polyrhythmic and polymetric organizational schemes, even within the performance of a single player, are an integral part of African music. It requires years of study for any Western musician to master even the simplest aspects of this fascinating dimension of African music, and its practice is quite simply beyond the powers of many classically trained musicians whose rhythmic sense has been stunted by too much monorhythmic European repertoire. Moreover, black African culture has exceeded the achievements of every other part of the world in the technology of pitched and unpitched percussion instruments, numbering in the hundreds, and originally created with nothing more than the natural materials at hand.

This highly developed rhythmic dimension of music was undoubtedly imported into North America with the first slaves and has continued to exert a profound and distinctive influence on every branch of American music ever since. It played a particularly conspicuous role in the development of ragtime and the "swing" style of big band jazz from 1920 to 1950, but has also taken African-American gospel music beyond the worst nightmares of the Puritan fathers who sought to suppress free improvisation in early psalm singing. It is impossible to imagine American music today without the rhythmic contribution of African styles. Among all the species of American composer, however, the creators of our classical music have made the least impressive use of this rich rhythmic tradition, probably due to the continued domination of the rhythmically stultified pre-Stravinskyian European tradition in our colleges and conservatories.

Balladry and Minstrelsy

As noted in the Introduction, each nation with a well-developed musical culture seems to have a special affinity for a particular form of music: in Japan, the unaccompanied introspective piece for *koto* or *shakuhachi;* in Indonesia, the extended "gendhing" for gamelan orchestra; in Italy, opera; in India, the sitar "raga"; in Germany, the symphony; in England, the oratorio, and so on. If we accept this admittedly very broad generalization, then there can be no question that the vocal ballad, in all its many forms, is the single most dominant mode of American music-making. The standard 32-bar Broadway or pop song, the 12-bar blues, the 16-bar rock & roll tune are all distinctively American inventions that have been borrowed by other cultures (increasingly since about 1964) and adapted to individual national styles everywhere from England to China. Balladry was not unknown to the New England colonials, and we have already touched on its Appalachian manifestations, but the first great flowering of American balladry (as distinct from mere imitation of the English ballad operas) began in the 1820s and has continued unabated ever since.

The songs of Hopkinson, Reinagle, Henry Russell and other early American "genteel" tunesmiths have been mistakenly credited by some writers as representing the origins of American song generally. In fact, the original hymns of the First New England School composers are a far likelier candidate for that distinction. As these hymns made their way south into Pennsylvania, and later the Carolinas and the rest of the South, they assumed ever more unique characteristics. The style became simplified; four voices retracted to three, then to one. By the early 19th century many southern collections contained only the hymn tunes, without the elaborations so characteristic of Billings and his colleagues. When these southern hymns were further intermingled with Appalachian folksong, they sometimes assumed a starkly modal character or became overtly pentatonic. As the movement toward religious revivalism gained momentum, vividly manifested in the camp meetings that proliferated throughout rural America from about 1820 into the 1940s, these southern hymns branched off in the direction that led to the modern gospel hymn. And when they encountered the plantation-music culture of the slaves, they melded into what is now generally known as the Negro spiritual. All of these subgenres of American vernacular religious music are interrelated, yet each maintains distinct characteristics of its own. The gospel hymn tends to be full-blooded and joyous, while the spiritual inclines toward the mournful and (unless specially adapted for choir) is probably better suited to solo singing. The remnants of original southern hymnody that survive today can partake of either of the above characteristics, but as often as not retain an additional measured restraint and primitiveness in their melodic structure that lends them a somewhat archaic sound, perhaps an echo of their Puritan origins.

In the 1820s, the genteel English-style ballad was still being sung in the increasing numbers of urban locales in America, but it was beginning to grow trite. Many songwriters who emerged from the genteel tradition began to look elsewhere for fresh sources of inspiration. As the political movement toward the abolition of slavery grew, aided by such musicians as New Hampshire's Hutchinson Family Singers, and as more and more free blacks entered the population of the North (and even some southern communities), interest in the music of the American Negro began to awaken. This culminated in the first collection of purely African-American songs, *The Negro Singer's Own Book* (1846), previously noted. Songwriters such as John Hill Hewitt and Stephen Foster began to study what they called "Ethiopian" music and to integrate some of its elements into their productions. As a result of all these influences intermingling, a new kind of distinctively American ballad began to develop.

By the 1850s folksongs such as "My Darling Clementine" and composed songs such as Foster's "I Dream of Jeanie with the Light Brown Hair" reflected this new style. Gone were the stuffy formalities and virtually arrhythmic posturings of Hopkinson's "My Days Have Been So Wondrous Free." In their place came a simpler, less affected sense of melody where ornamental features such as appogiaturas and suspensions were woven into the fabric of the tune, rather than being stuck on to it as an afterthought. Simple syncopations began to appear, possibly in response to the African influence. Song accompaniments focused much more on the clear delineation of meter and harmony, rather than attempting to provide the singer with the musical equivalent of scenery, costume and props. Especially in the hands of Stephen Collins Foster (1826–1864), the American popular art song came into its own and acquired a character uniquely American. It could not be said of Foster's songs (in contrast to Hopkinson's) that they could have been written by any competent English tunesmith.

The following decade ushered in the Civil War, the conflict that dominates American history of the 19th century and defined the American national character (to the extent that there *is* an American national character), together with all of that war's social upheaval and intermingling of previously isolated subcultures. During the Civil War, the songs of Foster and others of his generation would provide the structural models for our first discernibly national folk music, which in turn would lay the necessary groundwork for the beginnings of characteristically American classical music in the 1890s.

Less refined than Foster, but no less reflective of the emerging national character of American music, were the "blackface" minstrel composers that began cropping up throughout the country, beginning in the late 1820s. Principal among these were Daniel Decatur Emmett, Thomas "Jim Crow" Rice and E. P. Christy. The history of American minstrelsy has been amply documented, and there is no need to recapitulate it here. Suffice it to say that the minstrel singer-songwriters were white men who blackened their faces with burnt cork, dressed in outlandish costumes and sang a variety of popular songs in what was then considered "Negro dialect." In our own times, the whole corpus of minstrel shows and songs is generally viewed as racist and degrading to African Americans. Whether it was the conscious intention of Decatur, Rice, Christy and others to ridicule blacks or merely to seize on a popular form of entertainment in order to make their careers, without regard to the question of whom it might offend, the inescapable fact is that this style of performance perpetuated an image of black Americans as ignorant, gullible, superstitious, lazy and indifferent to any of life's concerns beyond their own physical comfort.

Having said that, it must be pointed out that, like it or not, some of the most influential American vernacular songs emerged from the minstrel tradition. Emmett was the composer of such American classics as "Dixie" and "Old Dan Tucker." Christy popularized many of the "Ethiopian" songs of Stephen Foster, such as "Old Folks at Home," "Camptown Races" and "Old Black Joe." Minstrel songs like "Turkey in the Straw" or "O Dem Golden Slippers" are integral to any discussion of the history of American song and have played a significant role in the development of the American classical tradition, particularly in the work of Charles Ives. Gilbert Chase has rightly pointed out as well that not all of the songs and skits of the minstrel shows portrayed blacks in the negative manner mentioned above.[1] In some cases, the black central character was shown to possess elements of a folk hero, such as superior strength or sophistication in dealing with gullible or pretentious whites. Such characters may have been based on

---

[1] *America's Music,* pp. 259–282.

similar heroes of authentic Afro-American folklore, such as High John the Conqueror.

The minstrel shows of the 19th century introduced the banjo into the place it now holds in American musical culture. This instrument, an early form of which is mentioned in the letters of the young Thomas Jefferson, came directly from the antebellum plantation culture of the slaves and was probably derived from one or more African chordophones. In its earliest versions it apparently had only four strings and was played in a melodic, "picking" style. The five-string banjo may have been developed as early as 1830 and was in general use by the 1840s. The banjo music of minstrel shows apparently adhered closely to the picking style of plantation music; the development of elaborate strumming techniques or the virtuoso bluegrass style of an Earl Scruggs only emerged later. It is not a native Appalachian instrument, but came to that branch of the American musical tree via slave and minstrel music.

If the minstrel tradition should serve as a source of shame for anyone, it is certainly not for the blacks who were being made fun of. The existence of the minstrel tradition for seventy years of our history does far more discredit to the white musicians who created it than to the targets of their "humor." In 1915, ragtime composer Scott Joplin spent most of his savings to produce a concert version of his opera *Treemonisha* for a group of potential backers in Harlem. Because the plot of *Treemonisha* openly addressed the issue of Negro superstition and witchcraft and the need for African Americans to rise above such relics of slavery, it made most of the New York black intelligentsia of the time very uncomfortable and failed to receive the necessary support for a production. By 1972, when the opera was finally produced, the question of rural superstitions was not such a sensitive one among American blacks, and *Treemonisha* received its long overdue premiere in the proper context of a historical reference whose time had passed. In a similar manner, we may hope that some day the tradition of American minstrelsy can be studied and evaluated with greater detachment, once the stereotypes it promoted are no longer perceived as threatening to the self-esteem of African Americans generally, because it is a part of our musical history that we ultimately cannot ignore.

It remains to be said that the ballads of the southern American hymn tune writers and of urban minstrels like Emmett and Foster began to make their way west with the European-American and African-American settlers and pioneers of the first half of the 19th century. "Oh! Susanna" became the virtual theme song of the California gold rush of 1849, and many similar ballads infiltrated into the upper Mississippi Valley region, the southwestern desert, Colorado and the Dakotas. To these were added original efforts and new adaptations such as "My Darling Clementine," "The Yellow Rose of Texas," "The Red River Valley" and similar songs of the so-called cowboy tradition. In fact the standard cowboy ballad, with some notable exceptions, is no more distinctive than the general run of American ballads sung prior to the Civil War, but was preserved in the West in its more or less antebellum form for a longer period, as the West was relatively untouched by the crossfertilizing encampments and battles of the war, and has thus come to be more closely associated with the cowboy mythos. As such, these ballads entered into the works of some early 20th-century classical composers, especially Aaron Copland and Roy Harris, as well as their obvious and significant influence on modern country and western music.

Creole and Gulf Coast Music

The city of New Orleans was and is the cultural capital of the United States Gulf Coast, and it is fitting that it produced the first authentically American classical composer in the figure of Louis Moreau Gottschalk (1829–1869). New Orleans had been founded in 1718 by Sieur de Bienville, ceded by the French to the Spaniards in 1762, then back to the French in 1800, and finally acquired by the United States as part of the Louisiana Purchase in 1803. As a southern city it was, of course, slaveholding and contained a highly diverse population of free blacks, whites, mulattos and other peoples of mixed race. A great many of the slaves in New Orleans and Louisiana came from the West Indies, especially Haiti (Santo Domingo). The surrounding bayou

New Orleans born composer and pianist **Louis Moreau Gottschalk** *(1829–1869) as he looked in the 1860s. He became the first American to achieve international fame in the world of classical music.*

country also became the home of French-Canadian immigrants who had been expelled from their northern homeland by the British. These settlers were known as Acadians (Cajuns).

Because of its great ethnic diversity (greater than any other part of the United States in the early 1800s), the music of the New Orleans and Mississippi Delta region was a fascinating reflection of French, Spanish, African, Haitian, Cuban and American influences. Popular dances such as the "bamboula" were common at public gatherings, and the risqué atmosphere of the French Quarter was, even then, a subject of interest to Americans. Moreover, as the principal southern port for the Mississippi River, New Orleans was a clearing house for people, ideas and music all along the course of the river, even up into the Great Lakes Region. Today the music of calypso, Creole songs, Latin American dances, Caribbean steel drum bands and Dixieland jazz are intermingled in the ongoing cultural mix of this great American city.

Gottschalk was born in New Orleans on May 8, 1829. His father was of English descent and his mother a French-speaking Creole. The family was well-off financially and, when Gottschalk displayed an early aptitude for music, found him the best available teachers. By the age of twelve he had exhausted the music education available to him in New Orleans, so the family sent him to France for further study. There, under the tutelage of Camille Stamaty, he blossomed into a virtuoso pianist. In 1845 Stamaty presented him at a concert in the Salon Pleyel, at which Chopin was present. The reports were that Chopin praised Gottschalk and predicted a great future for him. Later encounters with Liszt, Berlioz and other European Romantic composers reaffirmed this initial judgment.

From the outset, Gottschalk centered his compositional efforts on the music of his native region. Early piano pieces, such as *La Bamboula* and *Banjo* reflected not only his interest in, but his exceptional sensitivity to, the native dances and songs of his youthful environs. Of the several hundred works Gottschalk composed for the piano, these dances—derived from ethnic folk music of the Caribbean—form the foundation on which his reputation rests. Of course, Gottschalk composed other kinds of music as well, notably his symphonic Civil War poem for piano, *The Union,* and his hearts-and-flowers elegy, *The Dying Poet,* but these are all too similar to the works of the many lesser composers of piano pieces who were active at the time, and are not representative of Gottschalk's best.

In turning to the ethnic folk music with which he was most familiar, Gottschalk anticipated the advice given American composers by Antonin Dvořák some forty years later when he sojourned in the United States between 1892 and 1895. The significance of Gottschalk's contribution lies in the effectiveness with which he integrated that folk music into the florid pianistic style of the early Romantic era, as developed especially by Liszt and Chopin. However, Gottschalk's position in our classical musical history is more that of an American Glinka, rather than an American Beethoven. Partly this is because of the uneven quality of his work and his manifest limitations as a composer, but it is also attributable in part to the fact that the Caribbean music which Gottschalk so loved was not reflective of the American ethos at large. Despite its charm and exoticism, the varied music of the Mississippi Delta was largely circumscribed by its regional flavor and had little of import to say to New Englanders, mid-Atlantic urbanites or western pioneers. Had Gottschalk been born into a regional culture closer in spirit to the emerging American mainstream and turned his powers in that direction, he might indeed have reversed the negative effects of Lowell Mason's slavish imitation of European styles and given birth to a more broadly American art music.

One suspects that Gottschalk himself may have sensed this, as he spent his last decade wandering ceaselessly through the North American frontier communities, Cuba, Central America and Brazil. During these years of roaming he gave hundreds of concerts, earned and spent lavish amounts of money and dissipated his creative energy. He was a witty and acerbic diarist and perhaps inherently too cynical to believe in the full possibilities of his own compositional talent. In either case, while he was unquestionably the first American superstar of classical music, he missed the distinction of becoming our first truly great composer.

In summary, it is easy to see that the American musical scene before the Civil War was a diverse collection of regional "musics," each with its own set of musical values, its own regional audience and its own implied view of the future of American music generally. At times these regional styles pulled against each other, as with the First New England School and the genteel, "better music" movement founded by Mason. At times they merged to influence each other reciprocally and to form new subgenres, as in the case of southern hymnody and the music of the plantations. Other groups, like the Moravians and some Appalachian communities, remained insular and devoted exclusively to the musical traditions of their ancestors. But, during the decades immediately preceding the Civil War, a clear kind of "American" sound began to emerge in the South, especially reflected in southern hymns, the ballads of Stephen Foster and some of the songs of the minstrel troupes active at the time. When the cataclysm that was the Civil War finally came, it uprooted untold thousands of people from every region of the country, mingled them together and often left them transplanted on "alien" cultural ground. Traumatic as this process was, it provided the crucible needed to forge a characteristically American style of folk music, which later became the partial basis of a serious attempt at a national classical style.

2

Edward MacDowell and the "Second" New England School

ॐ

(1865–1900)

For many historians the Civil War (1861–1865) represents the defining event in American history, the event that, more than any other, forged a unified national consciousness. Historian Shelby Foote has pointed out, for example, that prior to the war it was customary for Americans to refer to "these" United States in everyday discourse, whereas afterward the singular article "the" (United States) became standard. Before the war, Americans had lived primarily in isolated geographical pockets. Regions such as New England, rural Pennsylvania, the mid-Atlantic coastal states, the deep South, the Mississippi Valley and urban centers such as Boston, New York, Philadelphia, Charleston and New Orleans each had distinct social, linguistic and musical characteristics. Social, political and commercial intercourse among these regions was limited by the transportation and communications technology of the day—railroad, steamboat, telegraph and horse—and most of the traveling that was done was done by merchants, evangelists, itinerant laborers and artisans, journalists, politicians and others whose professions caused them to move about the country. A majority of the population of the United States prior to 1860 probably never traveled more than fifty miles from home throughout their lives.

The Civil War changed all of this. Massive numbers of young men on both sides were uprooted from their native regions and moved, along with the respective armies they comprised, up and down the eastern seaboard and far out into the relative wilderness of Texas and the Midwest. And they took their regional folksongs with them, mixing and intermingling during the lulls between the fighting. Thus began the first significant cross-fertilization of American vernacular music styles in our history, reflected in the many hundreds of popular songs spawned by the war.

Looking back from one hundred thirty years' distance, from an age when Americans are often thought to be selfish, cynical and crassly materialistic, it is easy to forget how deeply sentimental and devout were those of our ancestors who fought that brutal conflict. The letters of ordinary soldiers abound in passionate, romantic imagery which idealized home and hearth, mother, wife and country. Allusions to the heroes and events of ancient mythology are not lacking in these documents either and reveal the strong classical bent of such education as was available to Americans at the time.

Of course, the Romantic movement in European art, literature and music was in high gear when the war broke out. But, whatever influence this movement may have had on the attitudes of mid-19th century Americans, the strong strain of sentimentality and romanticism in American life at the time betrays properties of an indigenous cultural trait as well. Perhaps it was inspired by the still-rugged landscape of the country, the idealism of the founding fathers, the influence of fundamentalist religious sects or the emerging pioneer mythos. Perhaps it was all of these things combined. In any case, this sentimental romanticism became a vital element in original American classical music during the latter part of the 19th century and remained so throughout the period of the First World War. It is perhaps the most characteristic common emotional thread among the works of all our native composers prior to Charles Ives.

The Civil War also had profound political, economic and ethnological consequences—all of which had an impact on the development of our classical music. While the war settled, once and for all, the political question of slavery that had plagued America since colonial times, it proved to be only the beginning of the long struggle by African Americans to achieve social and economic parity with their white countrymen, a struggle which has continued to this day. After the assassination of Abraham Lincoln in 1865, the federal government came under the control of a long succession of Republican administrations, many of which were dominated by corrupt political bosses and financiers. The policies of these administrations featured harsh, punitive reconstruction of the southern states' economies and political institutions, increased westward expansion of European-American settlements, *de facto* extermination of the Native American populations in the Great Plains and desert southwest, unbridled exploitation of the country's natural resources, importation of cheap immigrant labor to staff factories in the east and build railroads in the west, and a virtually unrestrained growth of private fiscal speculation in which large private and corporate fortunes were amassed and sometimes lost without any meaningful government involvement or regulation.

The social and economic isolation of African Americans from the mainstream of society during Reconstruction laid the groundwork for the urban black subcultures that began to coalesce when freed blacks gradually migrated into northern cities. The forced collection of urban black populations into ghetto neighborhoods created the social conditions necessary for the emergence of a unique subcultural musical vernacular, derived from earlier slave music and invested with a new vigor by the changing material circumstances in the lives of black Americans. The first clear manifestation of this subcultural African-American idiom was ragtime, which developed during the late 1880s through about 1910. It was followed by the brief period of "classical" blues during the second decade of the 20th century, and finally amalgamated into the collective term "jazz" after 1920.

As the separation of Eurocentric white American culture from African-American culture increased during the late 19th century, the unprecedented growth of private wealth in the hands of "robber barons" such as Andrew Carnegie, J. Pierpont Morgan, John Jacob Astor, the Rockefellers, the Vanderbilts, the Mellons and others made possible new efforts to institutionalize America's love affair with European culture—efforts that dwarfed the achievements of the prewar generations. Great museums were founded and filled with European painting and statuary. Great libraries were established as repositories for hundreds of thousands of books, most of which were written in European languages and dealt with European subjects. Symphony orchestras and concert halls were endowed in the largest cities, devoted to performance of the great European masterpieces. New York, Chicago and San Francisco acquired opera companies capable of performing any existing repertoire in a professional manner. By 1876, when the nation celebrated its first centennial with a year of festivals, fairs and expositions, all the conditions necessary for the emergence of a native classical music had been fulfilled. And the first native composer to achieve a high profile in this milieu stepped onto the national stage in the person of John Knowles Paine.

However, before dealing with Paine, and the generation led by MacDowell for whom he paved the way, some mention should be made of three men who preceded him, briefly noted in the previous chapter, and whose names have all but disappeared even from the awareness of most educated American musicians today. They were Anton (or Anthony) Philip "Father" Heinrich, William Henry Fry and George Frederick Bristow.

Anthony Philip Heinrich was the oldest of this group of precursors. He was born in Bohemia (Czechoslovakia) in 1781 and came to America as an adult, settling in the wilds of Kentucky around 1817. Although the son of a wealthy family, he had lost his fortune early in life as a result of the failure of the bank for which he worked and turned to composing as a vocation. He was a notorious eccentric, and both his life and grandiose musical conceptions fall into the esthetic mold of composers like Berlioz or Alkan.

In his 1848 lecture, "The Poetic Principle," Edgar Allan Poe wrote:

> If, by "sustained effort," any little gentleman has accomplished an epic, let us frankly commend him for the effort ... but let us forbear praising the epic on the effort's account.

Although there is no hard evidence that Poe knew or was referring to Heinrich (though they were both acquainted with a certain Lydia M. Child, a "poetess" and genius enthusiast of the period), this statement might stand as a perfect epitaph for the composer. For Heinrich's effort was indeed sustained, in fact monumental, resulting in two hundred published works and many more in manuscript (now held by the Library of Congress). And his conceptions were of epic proportions. Unfortunately, the judgment of history has been unanimous in its verdict that Heinrich's creative gift was simply not equal to his ambitions. His music is highly repetitious, inordinately florid and dense, and at times formally incoherent. His contemporaries referred to him as the "Beethoven of America," but Heinrich's resemblances to the German master are superficial, never substantial. Today the best we can do is "commend him for the effort."

Heinrich's importance in the history of our classical music lies not in his productions as a composer, but rather in his advocacy of musical "Americanism." In this he was our first great champion. His anthologies and large symphonic works bear such titles as: *The Dawning of Music in Kentucky, or the Pleasures of Harmony in the Solitudes of Nature* (1820), *The Columbiad: grand American national chivalrous symphony* (1837), or *Jubilee: a grand national song of triumph, composed and arranged for a full orchestra and vocal chorus—in two parts, commemorative of events from the landing of the Pilgrim fathers to the consummation of American liberty* (1840). During a public career that spanned forty years and took him across continents, into the presence of monarchs and presidents, as well as slums, garrets and the wilderness, Heinrich beat his many drums and sounded his many trumpets for the cause of an indigenous American classical music. Yet, despite what one is tempted to view as his outright buffoonery, Heinrich was a serious musician whose real contributions included conducting the first documented performance of a Beethoven symphony (during the composer's lifetime, no less) in the United States, the chairmanship of the fledgling New York Philharmonic Society, and his indefatigable propagandizing for the cause of American art music.

Heinrich was not intimidated by the rich and powerful. John Hill Hewitt tells a story, in his autobiography *Shadows on the Wall* (1877), of a meeting between Heinrich and President John Tyler, which he arranged at Heinrich's request in order to enlist Tyler's support for the grandiose *Jubilee* symphony. According to Hewitt, Heinrich proceeded to play, at Tyler's invitation, a piano transcription of his symphony, sweating and straining at the White House piano, sprinkling his performance with comments and explanations of the geographic features portrayed in the music. Midway through this performance, Tyler gently laid a hand on Heinrich's shoulder and asked if he knew any Virginia Reels! The volatile Heinrich then stormed out of the White House in high dudgeon, announcing that Tyler knew no more about music than an oyster, and that the people who elected him should be hanged!

In 1846 Heinrich became the beneficiary of two enormous concerts, consisting entirely of his own music, staged respectively by his admirers in New York (May 5) and Boston (June 13). The aforementioned Lydia Child was instrumental in organizing the New York concert, at which she reportedly distinguished herself by tossing a laurel wreath from the orchestra pit that landed squarely on Father Heinrich's head onstage! While the financial gains from these concerts were virtually erased by their huge cost, and the composer complained about inaccuracies in the performance, the concerts were greeted with tremendous enthusiasm by standing-room-only crowds and considerable publicity in the musical press. It is hard to reconcile today the reports of such enthusiastic support with the complete obscurity of Heinrich's music. Irving Lowens, in *Music and Musicians in Early America*, claims that "the music of worse composers than . . . Father Heinrich is heard today" and compares the scope of Heinrich's conceptions with the tone poems of Richard Strauss, even though Heinrich's works were written decades before the birth of that composer. But Lowens' opinion is distinctly in the minority of those who have heard Heinrich's music. Nevertheless, it is reasonable to state that the works of this colorful, forgotten predecessor of our great modern composers might deserve another hearing, as critical perspectives are prone to change with time.

Of equal importance to Heinrich are the composers William Henry Fry (1813–1865) and George Frederick Bristow (1825–1898), whose names are often paired because of the famous controversy with the New York Philharmonic Society in which they embroiled themselves in 1854. Touched on in the previous chapter, this exchange of heated letters in the New York *Musical World and Times* was provoked by a bad review of Fry's

Santa Claus Symphony by critic Richard Willis, in late December of 1853, which provoked an angry letter of response from Fry. Fry claimed that, in the eleven years since its 1842 founding by Charles Edward Horn, Henry C. Timm, William Scharfenberg and Urelli Corelli Hill, the New York Philharmonic had performed no works by American composers. Bristow jumped into the fray with a letter of his own, noting that Fry had been incorrect: the Philharmonic had played ONE work by an American, namely an overture of his. Philharmonic co-founder Henry C. Timm responded with a list of performances given by the Philharmonic of works by then-living composers. One of the more interesting features of this list is its clear indication that orchestras and other large performance institutions of the day were in the habit of holding public dress rehearsals at which certain works, which may have been considered too risky to program on actual concerts, were given public readings. Many of the examples Timm cited were performed only at these open rehearsals; a total of three native pieces were actually played on concert programs. The controversy is significant today only insofar as it illustrates that the fondness of American symphony orchestras for ignoring emerging talent in our own country is nothing new.

As far as the music of Fry and Bristow is concerned, they share a common problem with all the American composers of their generation, (including Frederick G. Gleason, Silas G. Pratt and Sidney Lanier) and, to some extent, with the later work of Paine and the Second New England School. The problem is a certain lack of original musical vision. Technique they had, often acquired through serious study in European conservatories, but all of their creations come across as pale imitations of European models.

Fry was the elder of the two men, and his passion was opera. He composed three, of which the most notable was *Leonora* (1845; revised 1858). He also wrote four symphonies, two oratorios, a *Mass in Eb* and numerous other choral and orchestral works. *Leonora* was produced in Philadelphia in 1845 and again in New York in 1858, both productions heavily underwritten by Fry himself. The reception was mixed: most critics and educated audience members admiring Fry's skill but decrying his debt to the Italian "bel canto" style, especially that of Bellini. Fry himself was aware of his debt to European music, and of the contradiction entailed in his passionate advocacy of native American composition contrasted with his own European musical mannerisms. In a telling comment from his "Prefatory Remarks" to *Leonora,* he stated:

> The action laid in this country, also, could not be illustrated with national music, *since the original type is wanting.*[2] (emphasis mine)

---
[2]   Cited in Zuck, *A History of Musical Americanism*, p. 19.

William Henry Fry *(1813–1864). The first American composer to seriously attempt operas and symphonies. As early as 1853 he took the New York Philharmonic to task for not playing the music of living American composers.*

Clearly, Fry understood that America had not developed a character-istic classical tradition of her own, but he could not have understood the full extent of the vernacular tradition's fragmentation prior to the Civil War. (In any case, it is unlikely that a composer of Fry's intentions would have turned to *any* vernacular tradition.) But the salient point in Fry's observa-tion is its assumption that an original type of national music would already have to be in place before he could work with it. Apparently it never occurred to him to attempt to forge the beginnings of such a tradition himself, at least not as early as 1845. His later symphonies may point to some glimmer of effort in this direction, but he achieved no substantive success at it.

Fry undertook to present a series of eleven public lectures at Metro-politan Hall in New York City in 1852. Again produced at his own expense, these lectures comprised a comprehensive history of music composition as Fry understood it, including acoustics, esthetics and world music literature. He hired a chorus, soloists, orchestra and a military band to illustrate his presentations, and the whole series became a historical event in its own right. How much lasting effect it may have had on the musical conscious-ness of Fry's auditors is impossible to gauge, but it seems unlikely that the level of music appreciation in New York at the time was any the worse for it. These lectures of Fry's were, in a sense, the precursors of Leonard Bernstein's celebrated "Young People's Concerts," televised with the New York Philharmonic from the late 1950s through the 1960s, and reflect that concern with music education on a grand scale that has been more characteristic of the United States than of any other country prior to the mid-20th century.

Bristow, in contrast to Fry, was a working, practical musician all his life. While Fry, who possessed independent financial means, served as music critic for the New York *Tribune,* Bristow was a violinist and conductor associated for many years with the selfsame New York Philharmonic whose programming policies vis-a-vis American music he criticized. The ongoing controversy caused a rift in Bristow's relations with the orchestra in 1854, but it was soon healed.

Bristow, was probably the better composer of the two, though he also was heavily indebted to European traditions. He composed five symphonies, overtures, chamber music and the "second" opera by an American composer, his *Rip Van Winkle,* to a libretto by J. R. Wainwright based on the Washington Irving story. *Rip Van Winkle* was produced at Niblo's Theatre in New York in 1855, three years before the New York premiere of Fry's *Leonora.* It ran for four weeks at Niblo's and was received enthusiastically, although critics complained about the dryness of Bristow's orchestration. The important difference between the two works is that Bristow's opera is based on an American subject. Apparently he did not share Fry's view, nor assume that an existing model of American classical composition was a necessary prerequisite for such a subject. Bristow's style was less influenced by the bel canto tradition, but otherwise not strikingly more original than Fry's. He outlived the latter by thirty-four years, and died in 1898, more than twenty years after the last significant performance of any of his large works.

The importance of Heinrich, Fry and Bristow probably lies not in their achievements as composers (although, given that no orchestra or opera company has made any serious effort to give their works a rehearing in this century and that copies of their scores are not readily available for study, this may not be a fair statement), rather, their significance is rooted in their passionate advocacy of indigenous classical composition at a time when such an idea was openly scorned in Europe and, at best, grudgingly tolerated in the United States. Through their relentless propagandizing it is a virtual certainty that these three composers significantly raised the awareness of the American musical public of the need to foster native composers of worth. And it is doubtful whether later composers such as Paine,

Chadwick or MacDowell would have found as ready an acceptance as they did had Heinrich, Fry and Bristow not prepared the way for them.

While the works of these three often have American titles, subjects or programs, their characteristic musical idiom is not discernibly American in any way (with the possible exception of some of Heinrich's work). It hardly needs saying that they paid little or no attention to American folk music in any of its forms of the time, nor did they understand how the inherent inflections of folk traditions enter into the process of evolving a classical school associated with a particular national culture. Furthermore, considering the period at which the bulk of their music was written, i.e., before or during the Civil War, it is debatable whether America even possessed a coherent "national culture." But this problem is not unique to Heinrich, Fry and Bristow. Later generations of American composers, even some who wrote the most characteristically American sounding music, also rejected the idea that a "national" music could be based on folk music traditions or that such a music was even a desirable goal to seek. As we shall see below, composers from John Knowles Paine, to Edward MacDowell, to Amy Beach, and even Aaron Copland, have resisted the idea there is any virtue in being labeled an "American" composer or that the conscious use of vernacular musical materials is necessarily the most effective means of establishing such an identity.

John Knowles Paine (1839–1906)

While Heinrich, Fry and Bristow were battling for a hearing, a young man from Portland, Maine, was growing up and developing a formidable technique as a composer and organist. John Knowles Paine was born on January 9, 1839, and, by the age of eighteen, had given his first public recital as a virtuoso organist. He then proceeded to systematic study in Germany, after rejecting the opportunity to work with César Franck in Paris, and finally returned to the United States in 1861, just as the Civil War was breaking out.

The best term to describe Paine's personality, lifestyle and music is "academic Romanticism." Throughout his career he was saturated with the "learned" styles of counterpoint, orchestration, harmony, form and pedagogy. In 1862 he sought and received an appointment as music instructor at the citadel of American higher education, Harvard College, and became the first in a long line of professor-composers that extends right down to the present day.

Because Harvard had no music department as such at the time, and there was considerable resistance to the teaching of music as an academic subject for credit (notably from the prominent historian and novelist

John Knowles Paine *(1839–1906). Father of the*
"New England Classicists" and founder of
Harvard's music department, his music is still
sometimes played today.

Francis Parkman—a force to be reckoned with on the Harvard faculty),
Paine taught his music courses as an unpaid volunteer for thirteen years.
Finally, in 1875, Parkman notwithstanding, he was appointed to a full
professorship and the department was established.

Paine was considered a dry, pedantic teacher by many of his students,
yet he must have brought something special to his curriculum for he
attracted many students, even when the course was an elective offered
without credit. Among his pupils were later composers of note such as
Arthur Foote, Frederick Converse, John Alden Carpenter and Daniel
Gregory Mason (grandson of Lowell Mason).

But, above all, Paine's importance rests on the fact that he was the first
native composer to achieve an international reputation and to receive both
regular professional performances of his works and important commissions. Moreover, his music is generally considered to be far superior both
in technique and originality of conception than that of any of his American
predecessors, with the possible exception of Gottschalk.

Perhaps the most significant public event in Paine's career was the
commissioning and performance of his *Centennial Hymn* for the Philadelphia Exposition of 1876. The year 1876 was a important one in America. It
marked the 100th anniversary of the signing of the Declaration of Indepen-

dence, and the close of the corrupt administration of President Ulysses S. Grant. Money flowed freely as the nation geared itself up for marathon celebrations of its first century of existence, not forgetting the trauma of the Civil War only eleven years in the past. The most prominent conductor of this period, and for many years afterward, was Theodore Thomas. Thomas was a gifted musician who took seriously his obligation to present the work of living composers, though he carried no special brief for American music and preferred eclectic programming policies. Thomas was responsible for commissioning both Paine and the German opera composer, Richard Wagner, to provide special music for the Centennial Exposition. Wagner responded with his *Centennial March,* a work written hastily and of a quality far inferior to his operatic music. Paine's contribution was the *Centennial Hymn,* which, though overshadowed by the greater celebrity afforded Wagner's march, was a better piece and better received.

Paine became the first American composer to take advantage of post-war conditions in a serious way. Without the establishment of large professional orchestras and other performance resources mentioned earlier; without the availability of wealthy patrons to support commissions and underwrite risky performance ventures; and without the surge of patriotism attendant on the 1876 centennial, and the general desire to put the tragedies of war behind and build the new nation—without all these things Paine might have been destined to carry on his work from the lonely and embattled position of his predecessors. As it was, he was able to find the resources he needed to present large scale works in convincing performances, and to establish himself as a professional composer of symphonic music whose work was to be taken seriously, not merely a gifted amateur or anomalous radical.

Among his other works are the *Columbus March and Hymn,* commissioned by Thomas for the Chicago World's Fair in 1892, incidental music for Sophocles' *Oedipus Tyrannus,* an opera *Azara,* symphonic poems on Shakespeare's *The Tempest* and *As You Like It,* a *Mass in D,* an oratorio *St. Peter,* an *Island Fantasy* comprising musical portraits of the Isles of Shoals off New Hampshire's Atlantic coast, two symphonies, four cantatas, two piano sonatas and much choral and chamber music. At its best, Paine's music is as good as that of any number of his European contemporaries, and, like his later colleague from Maine, Walter Piston, his technique is always impeccable. Moreover, the quality of his work was recognized during his lifetime, and he was universally acknowledged as the "dean" of American composers throughout the late 19th century.

One must speculate, in view of all this, as to why Paine's music has fallen into such obscurity in the 20th century. Certainly his accomplishments have been overshadowed by the more memorable efforts of Mac-

Dowell, Ives, Copland, Griffes, Gershwin and others. And he never quite succeeded in establishing a distinctive personal style—one that makes his music immediately recognizable as the work of a particular composer. But these things are true of a great many composers whose works are still performed and broadcast on a regular basis. Part of the problem certainly lies in the failure of American orchestras to program Paine's work regularly in this century. It is entirely possible that, if his works received the same exposure as, for example, the lesser orchestral pieces of Dvořák, Grieg, Schubert, Weber or Saint-Saëns, they might be better known and as much admired as these others. In the final analysis, Paine's music is not of the absolutely first rank nor are his tunes "catchy." But his music has strength and, in its better moments, the power to move audiences. Perhaps his compositions will have to wait for a future time when their historical position alone may gain them the kind of hearings needed to find a new audience.

The "Second" New England School

John Knowles Paine finally achieved what his predecessors—Heinrich, Fry and Bristow—had sought so long and unsuccessfully; namely, the placement of an American composer's name on the list of "important" composers of serious music. Regardless of the merits of his music, the mere fact of his public status established a precedent that enabled the next wave of young composers to be taken seriously. Before Paine, a serious American composer was seen as a cultural oddity; after him, they became the subjects of intense interest and pride.

The generation of American composers that followed Paine, several of whom had been his students, came to be known collectively as the "Second New England School," because the bulk of them lived and worked in close proximity to each other in Boston around the turn of the century. The "first" New England School (in Gilbert Chase's terminology) had been the singing-master composers such as Billings, Holden, Belcher, Swan and Kimball, active in Massachusetts, New Hampshire and Maine during the late 18th century.

The most prominent figures in the Second New England School were George Whitefield Chadwick (1854–1931), Horatio Parker (1863–1919), Arthur Foote (1853–1937), Arthur Whiting (1861–1936) and Amy Cheney Beach (1867–1944, née Amy Marcy Cheney). All of them were born around the time of the Civil War and most lived into the Great Depression era between World Wars I and II. Furthermore, by the end of their lives, all but Parker had lived to see their accomplishments beginning to be eclipsed by the work of Gershwin, Copland, Ives, Roy Harris and even younger

George Whitefield Chadwick *(1854–1931), the leader of the "Second New England School" and a brilliant orchestral composer.*

composers with a much more radical mission. Hence, this group is sometimes referred to as the "New England Classicists."

In our own time only the work of Chadwick and Beach still receives any serious attention. In Chadwick's case this is clearly due to an irrepressible and attractive humor that permeates certain of his orchestral pieces. A native of Lowell, Massachusetts, Chadwick was the son of an amateur musician and displayed an early, if not prodigious, attraction to music. He traveled to Berlin to study in 1877 with Saloman Jadassohn and later with Josef Rheinberger. Returning to the United States in 1880 he established himself as a private teacher in Boston, where Horatio Parker and Arthur Whiting were among his first pupils. Although he wrote three symphonies, five string quartets and a variety of smaller pieces, his principal fame rests on his six concert overtures: *Rip Van Winkle* (1879), *Thalia* (1883), *The Miller's Daughter* (1884), *Melpomene* (1891), *Adonais* (1899), and *Euterpe* (1906), as well as his 1907 *Symphonic Sketches* and the orchestral ballad *Tam O'Shanter* (1917). In these works Chadwick gave full vent to his brilliant command of orchestration and the whimsical, capricious side of his creativity so consistent in spirit with MacDowell's "Will O' the Wisp" or Ives'

"Hawthorne" movement from the *Concord Sonata.* His opera *Judith* was performed with some success, and concert number from it will still show up on a program now and then. But his primary genre was orchestral portraiture, in which he excelled all his contemporaries, including Mac-Dowell.

Amy Cheney Beach, who preferred to be known by her married name of Mrs. H. H. A. Beach, was a child prodigy on the piano and, although her public performances prior to the death of her husband were limited, remained a brilliant pianist throughout her long career. Her piano music and solitary *Piano Concerto* tend toward the virtuoso bravura style of the late Romantic era, while her orchestral music—including her *"Gaelic" Symphony*—explores sometimes subtler dimensions of the post-Romantic palette. A native of Henniker, New Hampshire, she made her concert debut at sixteen and completed her formal musical studies in Boston, rather than Europe. After marrying Dr. Beach in 1885, she stayed largely out of the public limelight, confining her performances mainly to charity events, and

Mrs. H. H. A. Beach *(née Amy Marcy Cheney, 1867–1944), the youngest of the "Second New England School" and the first important woman composer in America.*

concentrated on composition and making a home for her husband. After his death in 1910, she resumed a public career and came into the full flowering of her talent as a composer. In addition to her works in large forms, Mrs. Beach composed more than one hundred and fifty songs, several of which achieved wide popularity during the early years of this century. However, her vocal music suffers from the excessive sentimentality that audiences seemed to demand at the time and rarely rises above the level of the similar productions of an Ethelbert Nevin or an Oley Speaks.

Although she never broke out of the European Romantic tradition, and made no substantially original contributions in style or form, she is still featured prominently in many recitals today because of her status as the first woman composer of significance in America. Although she was not the first American woman to write concert music, nor certainly was she the last, the relatively high stature she attained has made her an inspirational model to many women in music today. She herself disputed the importance of the fact that she was a woman composer, and many would agree with her that sex has little to do with musical ability. But, as will become even clearer in the chapter on Charles Ives, amateur music-making in the United States (for better or for worse) has been largely the province of women since colonial times, and Mrs. Beach became an attraction to many clubs and amateur societies in small communities during her lifetime, especially around her native New England. These have helped to preserve her reputation into the present era.

Among the New England Classicists, Arthur Foote (student of Paine) and Arthur Whiting (student of Chadwick) remain the most obscure today. Though prominent in their own time in the Boston area, their music has fallen into virtually complete obscurity. Foote was born in Salem, Massachusetts, and graduated from Harvard in 1875. He established himself as a private teacher in Boston and produced a steady stream of accessible, even charming music for a wide variety of media. His works included church music, chamber music, piano pieces, songs, a string serenade, a string suite, a symphonic poem on "Francesca da Rimini" and three large choral odes: *The Farewell of Hiawatha* (1886), *The Wreck of the Hesperus* (1888) and *The Skeleton in Armor* (1893). Like many other American composers of his time, including Paine, Parker, Dudley Buck and Ives, Foote was an organist and served in that capacity for thirty-two years (1878–1910) at the First Unitarian Church in Boston.

Whiting, as a composer, was less ingratiating than Foote and wrote music tending to be dryly academic in style. His output was small, dominated by the style of Brahms and heavily influenced by his love of chamber music. After 1907 he made New York City his base and was an active teacher and chamber musician.

The last of this group, Horatio Parker, is perhaps better known today as the founder of the music department at Yale University and principal composition teacher of Charles Ives than as a composer. Born in Auburndale, Massachusetts, and of English descent, Parker followed his teacher Chadwick's example and went to Germany to study with Rheinberger in 1882. After returning to the United States he taught at the National Conservatory of Music in New York, of which Dvořák became the director in 1892. Parker returned to Boston the following year. Whether or not his departure had any relationship to Dvořák's arrival remains unclear. In 1894 he was invited to head the newly formed music department at Yale. Together with Paine, Chadwick and MacDowell, Parker was one of the principal founders of serious music education at the collegiate level in the United States. Each headed the music department of a major institution—Paine at Harvard, Chadwick at the New England Conservatory, MacDowell at Columbia and Parker at Yale—and each made substantial

Horatio Parker *(1863–1919). Another major figure in the "Second New England School" with an affinity for the English choral style of Elgar and Parry. He founded the music department at Yale and taught Ives, Sessions and many others.*

contributions toward developing the highest caliber of curricula at this crucial early stage.

Like his colleagues in the Second New England School, Parker was a thoroughly trained compositional technician and solidly wedded to the European Romantic tradition. His most significant works are in the choral idiom, and his oratorio *Hora Novissima* (1892) is the best known of these. Partly because of his choral predilection, and partly because of his temperament, Parker was highly admired in England and had many performances there. His musical persona is closely allied with that of Edward Elgar in many respects, though he never achieved the striking originality displayed by his English contemporary in works such as the *"Enigma" Variations.* John Tasker Howard favorably compares Parker's opera *Mona* to Strauss' *Salomé* and Debussy's *Pelleas et Melisande,* and there is no question that Parker could write powerful and impressive music. Even Ives, though not sympathetic to Parker's style, admired his strength and creative abilities, and felt that he had profited from the elder composer's enormous grasp of traditional compositional techniques.

Parker cultivated the aura of a dignified gentleman, broadly educated and intolerant of weakness or shoddy work in his students. He became a notable figure in the New Haven community, where he continued his work at Yale until his death in 1919.

Although their work is neither performed nor studied much today, the composers of the Second New England School served an important function in turn-of-the-century America by broadening and consolidating the public acceptance of native American composition initiated by Paine. As teachers, performers and composers they made important contributions to setting American art music on a rigorous foundation which rendered the vulgarities and derivativeness of earlier composers such as Heinrich, Fry and Bristow permanently unacceptable. However, none of them possessed the originality to break free of their own musical educations or to forge a truly individual and significant creative identity. Although they sometimes worked with American subjects, probably none of them would have considered it important to be viewed specifically as American composers. They perceived their objective, first and foremost, to be excellent musical craftsmen with substantial creative ideas. Whether those ideas sprang from indigenous or European roots was a secondary consideration. It remained for Edward Alexander MacDowell to push American music beyond the self-imposed limitations of the Second New England School, a feat that he accomplished in spite of his sharing most of their musical ideals and prejudices.

Edward MacDowell (1861–1908)

Although MacDowell was a New Yorker by birth, he spent much of his creative life in Boston and at his summer home in Peterborough, New Hampshire. He has never been identified by historians as one of the members of the Second New England School, despite his being a contemporary of theirs, because his music does not fall into the "classicist" mold they fostered. He never wrote a symphony, string quartet or opera, and, while he did produce four large-scale piano sonatas and two concertos, most of his work lies in smaller genres—the art song and short character piece for piano.

But the factor that distinguishes MacDowell from his colleagues more than any other is his achievement of a truly distinctive, personal style which has enabled his music to survive into the present day, while theirs has virtually disappeared. The success of MacDowell, in contrast to his contemporaries, lends credence to the idea that something inherent in the composer himself, rather than his training, historical epoch, attitudes or specific professional activities, makes the difference between quality and mediocrity.

In all superficial respects, MacDowell was just like his fellow composers of the period. Like them he was born during the Civil War era; like

Edward MacDowell *(1861–1908) as a young man. The first American after Gottschalk to achieve lasting recognition as a composer. His life and career were shattered by his confrontation with the president of Columbia University.*

them he traveled to Europe to study and was saturated with the European Romantic musical language; like them he made Boston and New York his base of activity; like them he founded the music department of a major American university and laid a rigorous academic foundation for its curriculum, as well as performing conscientiously and successfully as a teacher for many years; like them he disputed the idea that it was important to be known as an "American" composer and considered it far more important to be a "good" composer first; like them he worked in traditional forms and with traditional instrumental and vocal resources. Why, then, is he so unlike his fellows in terms of the success and longevity of his music?

Part of the answer may lie in a personality trait MacDowell shared with his later American colleague, Charles Griffes (see Chapter 4), who also outshone his contemporaries and whose works survive in the standard repertoire today. Both men were extraordinarily, even morbidly, sensitive individuals by temperament. In the case of the nominally heterosexual MacDowell, this sensitivity was manifested in extreme shyness around strangers, intense performance anxiety when appearing as soloist, a tender and very private life partnership with his wife Marian, an exquisite receptiveness to the language and nuance of late-Victorian poetry and an active fantasy life preoccupied with such things as Celtic mythology, landscape portraits and historical subjects. In the case of the overtly homosexual Griffes, this extreme sensitivity took the form of a similar shyness around strangers, his refusal to pursue a public career or even an academic career beyond the limited confines of a prep school in upstate New York, similar obsessions with exotic poetry and things Celtic, as well as a strong interest in Oriental culture. Both men were amateur poets and visual artists as well. And both died young.

Furthermore, as early as 1908 the critic Lawrence Gilman (one of the most discerning musical minds of his day) was writing about the atmosphere of sublimated eroticism inherent in much of MacDowell's work. While similar strains of tormented sexuality are well-documented in the works of composers such as Wagner, Tchaikovsky and Grieg, no one ever accused any members of the Second New England School of writing music lower down than the head (or perhaps the heart, on or off the sleeve). Perhaps this is an additional feature that sets MacDowell apart from his American contemporaries.

Throughout his life, MacDowell shared an exceptional affinity with the Norwegian composer, Edvard Grieg, and the two men, who shared common Scottish ancestral roots as well, were active correspondents, mutual admirers and highly sympathetic spirits, though they never met in person. MacDowell's attachment to Grieg's sensibility is evident as early as his *Second Piano Concerto* in D minor (1885), whose themes are modeled so closely after Grieg's famous A minor *Concerto* that the former piece might profitably be studied as a grand variation on the latter. Grieg was also quite aware of the erotic strain in his own work. Both concerti were written when their composers were young, newly married men. MacDowell and Grieg also died within a year of each other.

It is very likely as well that MacDowell's great emotional sensitivity played a significant role in his early death, which occurred less than four years after he was forced to resign from the faculty of Columbia University after an idiotic controversy between himself and Columbia president Nicolas Butler—a controversy that had been provoked by two irresponsible student journalists. Unlike Paine, Chadwick or Parker, MacDowell lacked the hardy psychological constitution needed to survive a major showdown in the academic political arena—and the seeming failure of his dreams for the Columbia music department preyed incessantly on his mind during the last years of his life, disrupting both his creative and overall mental faculties.

MacDowell was born on December 18, 1861 at 220 Clinton Street, New York City. He was the third son of Thomas and Frances Knapp MacDowell, a middle-class Quaker couple of Scottish and English descent. He received his first piano lessons when he was about eight years old from the Colombian Juan Buitrago, a friend of the family, and later studied with a professional teacher, Paul Desvernine, until the age of fifteen. During these same years he also received sporadic lessons with the brilliant pianist, Teresa Carreño, during her visits to New York.

In 1876 the family decided to send him to France to further his studies. The young musician and his mother left for Paris, where he entered the Conservatoire that autumn as a pupil of Marmontel and Savard. One of his classmates was the young Claude Debussy. MacDowell was not happy at the Conservatoire, was not secure in the French language and, at this time, appeared to be as interested in drawing as he was in music. When his French language tutor happened to notice one of the young man's sketches and showed it to an eminent French artist, it was suggested that MacDowell submit himself to a course of instruction in that art as well. MacDowell himself rejected the suggestion and continued his musical studies, albeit with growing dissatisfaction.

When Nicolas Rubinstein performed the Tchaikovsky Bb minor *Piano Concerto* at the Paris Exposition of 1878, MacDowell was deeply moved and determined that he, himself, could never achieve such technical ability as a pianist in Paris. It was decided then that he should change to the Stuttgart Conservatory, which proved to be equally disappointing. Finally, in 1879, MacDowell's mother returned to the United States and the young musician took up his studies with Joachim Raff at the Frankfurt Conservatory, where he remained for the next two years. It was during this period that he took up private teaching as well; one of his pupils was an American girl, Marian Nevins, whom he later married.

In 1881 MacDowell applied for and received an appointment as piano teacher at the Darmstadt Conservatory and gave private lessons to the children of local nobility at the Erbach-Feurstnau castle. This period saw the composition of his two *Modern Suites* for piano, as well as his first serious reading of English and German poets. Tiring of his arduous teaching chores, MacDowell returned to Frankfurt and, at Raff's suggestion, visited Franz Liszt in Weimar in 1882 with the score of his first piano concerto. MacDowell played this work in two-piano arrangement, together with Eugen d'Albert, and Liszt was visibly impressed. Liszt was always a friend to young composers of merit, and, unlike so many musicians of his stature, usually translated his verbal admiration into action. Upon Liszt's recommendation, the prestigious German firm of Breitkopf and Haertel published MacDowell's two piano suites, and MacDowell, encouraged by this, devoted most of the next two years to more composition, producing works up through his Op.19 *Wood Idylls*.

In 1884 he returned to America and married Marian Nevins, then almost immediately sailed for Europe again with his new bride. The couple lived primarily in Frankfurt and Wiesbaden during the next four years, with frequent trips to other parts of the continent in search of teaching positions or for sightseeing. In 1885 Breitkopf and Haertel brought out MacDowell's first concerto, and he composed the second in D minor as well. In addition to much composing, MacDowell also used these years to deepen his readings among the great poets of Germany and England and to develop his profound attachment to nature in the cultivated countryside of Europe. It was probably this period that transformed an essentially urban young man into the nature poet that MacDowell later became, even to the extent of building his own log cabin in the woods at Peterborough some ten years later. Also during this period MacDowell enjoyed the friendship of George Templeton Strong, Jr., an American composer whose fame has never matched the merits of his music. Strong's father had been a prominent New York attorney, Civil War diarist and patron of the Philharmonic, and the younger Strong's friendship with MacDowell represents an important musical association that has not yet been fully documented.

Throughout the late 1880s, while MacDowell lived the life of an expatriate artist in Europe, his music was gaining a growing reputation at home. Teresa Carreño incorporated his piano pieces into several of her recitals, and his first concerto received its New York premiere under the hands of one B. L. Whelpley in April of 1888, garnering significant praise from critics. Finally, at the urging of many American friends, MacDowell and his wife returned to America in 1888, settling in Boston where the composer took up private teaching to make a living. He premiered his D minor concerto in New York and Boston in 1889 and again at the Paris Exposition of 1889 under the baton of the prominent conductor Frank Van der Stucken. The Paris concert, significantly, consisted entirely of American works. MacDowell shared the program with overtures and art songs by Chadwick, Paine, Foote, Dudley Buck, Henry Huss, Margaret Lang and Van der Stucken himself.

MacDowell remained in Boston until 1896. These were probably the happiest and most productive years of his life. He devoted his time to teaching, performing and composing, and apparently made a reasonably comfortable living at it. But, more significantly, the scope of his compositions deepened considerably. Gradually he began to abandon the slavish, if effective, imitation of European models that characterized his style through the *Second Concerto.* He progressed from his Op.36 *Concert Study* for piano through his *Second Piano Sonata,* the "Eroica" Op.50, composing mainly songs and piano pieces as well as his A minor *Orchestral Suite,* Op.42 and his second or *"Indian" Suite,* Op.48.

The period of the mid-1890s became a turning point in American classical music generally when Antonin Dvořák was invited to head the National Conservatory in New York. Dvořák arrived in 1892 and almost immediately set to work on his *Symphony No. 9, "From the New World."* Dvořák was Bohemian by birth and an ardent nationalist. His nationalism extended into his music, and he was one of the first of a series of Eastern European composers (culminating in Bartók and Kodály) who advocated turning to folk music traditions as a source of both material and formal characteristics in symphonic music. Upon encountering America, Dvořák saw no reason not to apply the same principles and became acquainted with H. T. Burleigh, one of the conservatory's African-American students, who introduced him to the spirituals and minstrel songs of the mid-19th century. Dvořák was deeply moved by Burleigh's vocal renditions of these songs and somewhat precipitously jumped to the conclusion that the folk music of the entire country resided principally in the music of black Americans. By 1895, Dvořák was agitating seriously, in a famous article in the February issue of *Harper's* magazine, that American composers turn to their multi-ethnic folk music in order to form a national style.

Most of the prominent composers of the period, including Chadwick, Parker, Paine and MacDowell, chose to ignore Dvořák's advice and perhaps were offended by the famous foreigner lecturing them on how to create their own national music. Finding little sympathy for his views, Dvořák returned to Europe in 1895. It remained for the next generation of American composers, led by Arthur Farwell and Charles Ives, to respond to Dvořák's challenge in a serious way. But, beyond this, at the risk of sounding repetitious, most of the composers of the period went on record repeatedly insisting that a "national" style was not important to them and was not one of their artistic objectives; MacDowell was no exception.

Nevertheless, MacDowell's music from the *"Indian" Suite* onward became increasingly indebted to American vernacular elements. In May of 1896 he was offered the chair of the newly formed music department at Columbia and made what proved to be the fatal mistake of his life in accepting it. Virtually on the eve of taking up his duties at Columbia, only months after Dvořák's return to Europe, MacDowell created the work that has proved to be his most enduring legacy and the most characteristically American of all his music, the Op.51 *Woodland Sketches*. That same year he purchased an old farm in Peterborough, New Hampshire (perhaps the "Deserted Farm" of the Op.51?), which became his summer home for the remainder of his life, and was eventually transformed into the still-active MacDowell Colony by his widow, Marian.

It is not clear whether MacDowell was writing about his New Hampshire retreat in *Woodland Sketches*. The work was composed while he was still residing in Boston. Perhaps it represented the composer's sense of anticipation at finally having a rural place of his own in which to work. Perhaps the purchase of the farm was stimulated by the suite. Whatever the case, the *Woodland Sketches* contains material and inflections which are so rooted in the musical reflexes of certain subgenres of American folk music that, with this piece, MacDowell achieved what may be considered the first piece of American classical music that could not have been written by a European composer, even Dvořák. These gestures are apparent from the ascending minor third that ends "To a Wild Rose," the first piece of the series, reflecting an inherently American melodic gesture which permeates Appalachian folksong, the songs of Stephen Foster and cowboy ballads alike, to the semi-quotation of the Cornell University college hymn "Far Above Cayuga's Waters," ("Alma Mater") that begins the middle section of "A Deserted Farm." It is not beyond imagining that MacDowell was linking the ideas of his impending academic appointment and purchase of the New Hampshire farm together—in a sort of post-Romantic stream of consciousness—in this remarkably poignant piece.

Woodland Sketches also contains references to American Indian music, as MacDowell understood it, and blackface minstrelsy in the movements entitled "From an Indian Lodge" and "As Told by Uncle Remus," respectively (the latter being a reference to the pseudo-African-American folktales written by Joel Chandler Harris). But its "Americanism" resides in subtler features than these. We have previously noted the strain of sentimentality that runs throughout American vernacular music from the ballads of the Civil War and earlier, right through the so-called art songs of composers such as George Root, Henry Work, Chadwick, Parker, Ethelbert Nevin and Mrs. Beach. MacDowell was certainly not immune to this sentimentality, which peaked in the popular songs of the "Gay '90s" such as "Silver Threads Among the Gold" or Nevin's notorious "The Rosary." Indeed, much of MacDowell's music sounds overly sentimental, even sappy, to modern American ears. But, despite all this, MacDowell skilfully treads a fine line between formal integrity and sheer mawkishness in most of his music, especially in the smaller character pieces—a line of which he himself was conspicuously aware and that he rarely overstepped for more than a few moments at a time. It is this dynamic tension between the banal qualities of so much American popular song and the substantive melodic constructions of a gifted composer that gives *Woodland Sketches,* and all MacDowell's better music, its staying power and continues to make him a composer over whose merits serious musicians disagree even today. And it is a kind of tension whose character, by its very nature, is largely perceptible only to people who have been raised amid the milieu of American popular song of the last one hundred and fifty years.

To suggest that MacDowell had a conscious program of musical commentary on the "American condition" in mind when he wrote this music would extend to him properties of political and social consciousness that he simply did not possess. But, despite his years in Europe, MacDowell clearly and instinctively absorbed the native syntax of late 19th-century American popular music, at least the popular music of middle- and upper-class whites, and incorporated elements of that syntax into his own style in a way that goes beyond the mere quotation of folk material. And he did so without losing a particle of his developed personal language as a composer. This is something that none of his colleagues among the Second New England School ever achieved, with the possible exception of Chadwick, and then only sporadically.

In late 1896 MacDowell took up his duties at Columbia, and he and his wife moved to New York. MacDowell was not merely teaching, however, but was charged with the entire task of developing his own curriculum from the ground up. He created courses in general European music esthetics and history, which he followed from the ancient Greeks up to his present; in form and style, also with a strong historical content; in practical theory including harmony, counterpoint and elementary composition; and in advanced composition, including orchestration. In general, he personally taught five to six different courses per week, with the occasional help of one paid assistant, and had about ninety students enrolled in a peak year. He reportedly spent hours correcting exercise books, lecturing and administering examinations, often by interview with one student at a time. He also entertained students socially and for informal discussions in his home.

Despite this labor, he continued to compose (although he virtually suspended his appearances as a pianist) and completed all his works up through his Op.62 *New England Idylls,* including his third and fourth *Piano Sonatas.* Most of this music was written at Peterborough during the summers.

MacDowell went on sabbatical during the academic year 1902–03, during which the new president of Columbia, Nicolas Butler, reorganized the fine arts curriculum. When MacDowell returned he was upset by the changes Butler had instituted and privately informed the president of his intention to resign in January 1904. MacDowell was basically a guileless man, so when two student journalists interviewed him on the subject of his resignation, he spoke out more forcefully than tactfully on his views of Butler's reorganization. The issue reached the *New York Times,* which quoted MacDowell as saying that his colleagues were "barbarians" and his students largely incompetent. This was followed by a heated exchange of public letters between MacDowell and Butler in which the college president succeeded in portraying the composer as a lazy and negligent teacher. MacDowell was understandably beside himself with fury at the injustice of this characterization and was further insulted by a reprimand from the trustees in their acceptance of his resignation.

He left Columbia at the close of the academic year in June an angry, bitter and depressed man, obsessed by the unfairness of the treatment he had received. He was unable to put the experience behind him and, during the next two years, grew increasingly troubled by insomnia, loss of memory and inability to work. His physicians suspected a brain lesion and, by 1907, his once robust frame had shrunk, his hair had turned white and he had lost the ability to walk or speak coherently for more than a few moments at a time. He spent hours turning over the pages of illustrated Celtic fairy tales and mythology books. Friends solicited funds for his assistance and that of his wife. The musical public grieved over his deterioration. He died in New York City on January 23, 1908, and was buried in Peterborough.

In the years after his death MacDowell's widow Marian, an accomplished pianist in her own right, promoted his work through performances and publications, and finally turned the Peterborough farm into what is now known as the MacDowell Colony, a residence for artists of every discipline to stay and work for several weeks at a time without interruption. Additional cabins were built in the woods surrounding the main house and, in the early years, Mrs. MacDowell herself would bring lunch to the residents, leaving it discreetly outside the door so as not to disturb their work. A great deal of the music of many later composers, including Copland, Harris, Sessions and others was created at the MacDowell Colony, which remains a lasting tribute to the memory of our first world-class composer of serious music.

3

Charles Ives

ॐ

(1874–1954)

The Composer

As a young man growing up in Danbury, Connecticut, in the 1880s, Charles Edward Ives had two consuming interests: music and baseball. Thus, from the very beginning, both the external facts of his life and the internal world of his thoughts drove straight into the heart of one of the most crucial issues in American classical music: the knotty problem of reconciling the rarefied, and sometimes effete, atmosphere of "high art" with the rugged, earthy and masculine character of the broader American cultural mythos, reflected even today by a strong strain of anti-intellectualism in American life. Ives' long, tormented and unique life, and the vast amount of starkly original music that resulted from it, can be viewed as an eighty-year battle to come to terms with this conflict.

A number of distinguished scholars have argued that it is possible to analyze and evaluate the music of Charles Ives apart from any necessary reference to the life and attitudes of the man who composed it. While this may be true of more "objectified" works of the European Baroque, Classical, Neo-classical or Serialist traditions, it is a certain formula for error when attempting to understand Ives' music or the place that it occupies in American music history. Despite Ives' formidable and amply demonstrated academic technique, it would be hard to imagine a more inherently "subjective" composer than he. And, as J. Peter Burkholder has pointed out, a tremendous amount of misunderstanding, both of the composer and his works, has been generated by the failure of theorists, performers and biographers alike to give adequate consideration either to the chronology of his compositions or to the many different creative aims represented in specific pieces.

Ives is probably the most written-about of any American composer. By 1990 his bibliography encompassed approximately twenty books devoted exclusively to him, close to a hundred doctoral dissertations or master's theses and countless articles, in addition to the published writings and music of Ives himself. The range of opinion is enormous. He has been revered as the first truly "great" American composer and vilified as a technically deficient amateur who couldn't hear the results of his own work, even in his mind's ear let alone in actual performance. Historian William Austin, writing in his monolithic *Music in the 20th Century,* dismissed Ives as a faulty craftsman; Stravinsky viewed him as a passing fad; Henry and Sidney Cowell placed him alongside Bartók, Schoenberg and Stravinsky as one of the four most important figures in early 20th-century composition. Like so many great artists of the past, Ives forms a kind of historical prism through which the biases of each commentator are refracted, producing widely varying results. But the core of the artist and his work, the thing that makes Ives Ives, pure and simple, remains as elusive and indescribable as ever.

The composer was born in Danbury on October 20, 1874. The most significant aspect of his childhood, and the prime formative influence on his later musical personality, was his close relationship with his father, George Ives. Later in life Ives would write that he owed more of his musical identity to his father than to any other single influence, although he also gave due credit to his principal teacher, Horatio Parker.

George Ives had been the youngest bandmaster in the Union army during the Civil War. After the war he returned to Danbury, the home of most of his relatives, where he eked out a living working in a bank, teaching music, directing choirs and leading the town band. George was an accomplished musician, but, more important, had what is arguably the most adventurous musical mind in 19th-century America. His curiosity was insatiable, and the young Charles quickly became a party to his father's radical experiments. Some of these included tuning his piano and other instruments to micro-tones, attempting to imitate the acoustical components of a thunderstorm in chord structures or stationing units of the town band at different locations while having them play different pieces to create a collage effect. But the elder Ives also saw to it that his son received a thorough grounding in the fundamentals of traditional harmony, counterpoint and other academic aspects of music.

Charles Ives was a precocious student and, by the age of fifteen, was serving as organist at Danbury's Second Congregational Church. A year earlier his *Holiday Quickstep* had been performed at the local opera house and he was already at work on his whimsical, irreverent *Variations on America* (1891–92). Like his predecessors Paine, Chadwick, Parker, Foote and Dudley Buck, Ives was an accomplished organist. The *Variations* were originally written for that instrument and later orchestrated by composer William Schuman. Even though it is an early work, it nevertheless manifests many of the quirky characteristics that have become inseparable from our concept of Ives' mature style.

Frank Rossiter has pointed out, in his definitive biography of the composer, that Ives was involved in the amateur musical life of Danbury outside his home as well. As in most communities in 19th-century America, this musical micro-world was dominated by genteel local matrons and advocates of "nice" music. Nice music meant the more accessible works of the German masters from Bach through Schubert, as well as liberal doses of the sentimental salon pieces and vocal "potboilers" being produced by minor European and American composers of the day. Ives gleaned everything that was of value from these hometown recitals and musicales and discarded the rest. He also acquired the roots of his later hostility toward any music that he viewed as being too easy, too pretty, too willing to pander to the complacency and limited imaginations of the public.

But the music of Danbury was not limited to such cultivated recitals. The town was also visited by itinerant preachers, and young Charles attended his share of revival meetings. He was equally attracted to the rough, spontaneous singing of manual laborers and, under the influence of his father's ideas, often heard what he considered to be more authentic musical utterances here than in the polite parlors of Danbury's social elite. And, of course, the music of the town band led by his father was always before him, working its way into his blood and bone. A great deal of Ives' later music, particularly works such as the *"Holidays" Symphony* and the "Hawthorne" movement of the *Concord Sonata,* represent idealized, and sometimes literal, reminiscences of these boyhood experiences with the American musical vernacular of the time. One might describe such passages as musical "snapshots," filtered through the somewhat sepia-toned memory of the composer, brought forward from Main Street of the 19th century into the concert halls of the 20th. Such a perspective is probably much closer to Ives' actual intentions in these works than the more pretentious discussions of musical collage, or musical stream-of-consciousness that fill many treatises on Ives.

As a lad of fifteen, Ives was an enthusiastic and admired member of the Danbury "Alerts" baseball team. Photographs of him from this period seem to show the face of an intelligent, handsome, somewhat cocky young man who was probably not prone to "suffer a fool gladly" for any length of time. Throughout his life, Ives' photographs reveal an ever-present intensity in his stare. And later ones, taken after he had retired from the insurance business and grown his now-familiar beard, betray a return to the occasional arch look of his youth. During the years 1889–1892 it was not unusual for Ives to pitch for an Alerts game in the afternoon and play one of his own compositions in a recital that same evening.

In 1893 the eighteen-year-old composer enrolled at the Hopkins Grammar School in New Haven, a preparatory academy for future Yale students. Ives had never been a model student in the conventional sense, although his ability to absorb and recall information and to think creatively about subjects that interested him was enormous. After a year at Hopkins, he entered Yale in the fall of 1894. Only a few weeks later, on November 4, Ives was struck by one of the hardest blows in his life up to that point, the sudden and premature death of his father, George, at the age of forty-nine.

This was a critical juncture in the life of the young man. Charles had idolized his father. Away from home for the first time, perhaps somewhat overawed by the size and prestige of the university, and out of touch with the family life at Danbury, George Ives' death must have devastated his eldest son emotionally, although, with characteristic Yankee reserve about private matters, Ives only briefly hinted at the full impact of this experience in his later public writings.[3]

The sudden absence of the principal masculine anchor in his life caused Ives to seek out the mentoring influence of the older men in his academic circle more than he might otherwise have done. So, while it would be an exaggeration to refer to any of them as surrogate fathers to young Ives, three men in particular assumed a much greater role in his life at this time. In order of importance they were: John Cornelius Griggs, choirmaster at New Haven's Center Church (who had been engaged at the same time that Ives was engaged as organist there, September 1894); Horatio Parker, his principal teacher of composition and music theory; and William Lyon Phelps, his instructor in American literature, especially the literature of the Concord Transcendentalists.

Although only nine years older than Charles, Griggs shared many of George Ives' ideas about music, and seemed to offer the kind of tacit mutual understanding the composer had found with his father. Griggs was particularly interested in the subject of just intonation. He had an excellent baritone voice and was apparently willing to try to sing anything. During the four years that Ives and Griggs shared the historic choirloft at Center Church in New Haven, the latter performed several of Ives' early songs and anthems, including "The Light That Is Felt" and "The All-Enduring." The

---

[3] *Memos*, p. 45.

young composer also played the musical illustrations at several of Griggs's Yale lectures between 1894 and 1898.

Griggs later went on to teach at Vassar College and the Canton Christian College in China. The two remained close friends until Griggs' death in 1932. The importance of Griggs in this critical period of Ives' life was best stated by the composer himself, in a letter to his friend from January, 1930.

> I don't know as you remember, but when I came to Center Church, under and with you, my father had just died. I went around looking and looking for some man to sort of help me fill that awful vacuum I was carrying around with me—the men among my classmates—the tutors program, etc.—and a kind of idea that Parker might—but he didn't—I think he made it worse—his mind and his heart were never around together. You didn't try to superimpose any law on me, or admonish me, or advise me, or boss me, or say very much—but there you were, and there you are now.[4]

Ives' relation to his formal composition teacher, Parker, was somewhat more complex. As discussed in the previous chapter, Parker was a leading member of the Second New England School. He had been trained in Germany and his sympathies were entirely European. Like his colleagues, he paid not the slightest attention to Dvořák's suggestion that American composers look toward their native folk music and remained solidly in the post-Romantic tradition of Sullivan and Elgar throughout his life. In short, he represented that very musical world that young Ives was rebelling against.

But Parker was, nevertheless, a composer of considerable skill and knowledge. Moreover, as the sole regular music faculty at Yale he was, in effect, the "only game in town." So Ives audited his courses as a freshman and later studied composition more formally with him. Ives' principal work from this period, composed more or less under Parker's supervision, was his *Symphony No.1*, the most conservative of his four completed symphonies. Parker objected to the extraordinary freedom with which Ives modulated through and juxtaposed unrelated keys and insisted that the first movement be rewritten, as well as recommending other changes. Ives reluctantly complied, but maintained to the end of his days that the symphony was better as he had originally conceived it.

There were other occasions when the two composers, in the role of teacher and student, butted heads, and the experience of having to modify his musical thinking along Parker's more traditional lines undoubtedly

---

[4] *Memos*, pp. 257–258.

strengthened Ives' command of compositional technique. But the musical world that Horatio Parker offered to Charles Ives ultimately proved to be one to which the younger man could not reconcile himself. Upon graduation from Yale in 1898, young Ives was confronted with the perennial question that faces all young composers: how to make a living.

Ives quite accurately recognized that, in order to survive as a professional composer, he would inevitably have to compromise his innovative ideas and produce music that was more commercially palatable. In those days, commercial success as a classical composer meant writing in the manner of MacDowell, Chadwick, Parker and their colleagues. Even if he were able to do so, he would just as inevitably end up having to teach or perform standard repertoire to supplement his income. Moreover, even if he could learn to live with such accommodations, Ives knew that the best economic success a musician could hope for in the United States offered something less than an affluent standard of living. The periodic financial embarrassments and survival jobs endured by his father were lessons not lost on the young man. If he had any desire to marry and raise a family, ambitions that were almost taken for granted among young men of his age and social class, the life of a professional musician offered at best a grim prospect for supporting dependents. All these factors came together in Ives' historic decision to enter business and compose only in his free time. In pursuing this course he unconsciously set forth a model that many subsequent American composers have followed, and which still presents itself as a challenging option to young composers who find themselves in similar circumstances today.

Before leaving the subject of Ives' Yale years, his important interaction with William Lyon Phelps (1865–1943) requires some attention. Phelps was a major figure on the Yale faculty, was frequently in demand as a guest lecturer and was viewed as one of the foremost authorities on American literature in the country. Though Ives, as has been previously noted, was not a model student, his grades in Phelps' literature courses were among his best while at Yale. Later alumni of Phelps' classes included playwright/novelist Thornton Wilder and poet Stephen Vincent Benét.

Phelps' lecture notes show remarkable parallels to Ives' later tastes in literature, and it is reasonable to infer that Phelps was the primary formative influence on Ives' early views of the Concord Transcendentalists and other literary figures. Phelps was a particular devoté of Ralph Waldo Emerson, Nathaniel Hawthorne and the English poet Robert Browning. The material he collected and wrote on these three is roughly twice the length of his average notes on any other author. Moreover, many of Phelps' comments were later echoed, almost verbatim, by Ives in his *Essays Before a Sonata*, the book he wrote to accompany the second edition of his monumental

Piano Sonata No.2, "Concord, Mass., 1840–1860, commonly known as the *Concord Sonata.* For example, Phelps wrote of Emerson:

> E(merson)'s Essays read as well backwards as forwards: you can begin equally well in the middle . . . A prodigal in thought, an economist in words.

> E(merson) is not a great poet: he is not a great man of letters. He *is* rather "a great man who wrote poetry"—"a great man who wrote essays."[5]

Compare this with Ives' sentiments:

> Emerson wrote by sentences or phrases, rather than by logical sequence. His underlying plan of work seems based on the large unity . . . of a subject, rather than on the continuity of its expression. As thoughts surge to his mind, he fills the heavens with them, crowds them in, if necessary, but seldom arranges them along the ground first.[6]

In their respective discussions of Hawthorne the link between Phelps' ideas and Ives' is even more startlingly explicit.

> His great theme, however, is SIN and conscience . . . He studies with a sad intensity the effect of sin on the heart.—Phelps, ms. lecture notes.

> Any comprehensive conception of Hawthorne, either in words or music, must have for its basic theme something that has to do with the influence of sin upon the conscience.—Ives, *Essays.*

The Yale archives retain manuscript notes prepared by Phelps on Emerson, Hawthorne, Bret Harte, Whitman, Henry James, Poe, Thoreau and various European authors. To Phelps, Emerson was the premier American philosopher and Hawthorne's *The Scarlet Letter* was the greatest American novel up to that time. He related Hawthorne's "Ethan Brand" to Browning's "Paracelsus" (a portion of which was later set as a song by Ives). Clearly he played a major role in shaping Ives' conception of these authors and, by extension, in the important creative use Ives made of them.

In the summer of 1898 Ives secured a job at the Mutual Life Insurance Co. in New York through the assistance of his father's second cousin, Dr. Granville White, medical examiner for the firm. He joined a number of

---

[5] Wm. L. Phelps, ms. lecture notes, Sterling Library: Manuscripts and Archives (Boxes 9–15), Yale University, New Haven, Conn.
[6] *Essays Before a Sonata,* "Emerson."

fellow Yale alumni, most of whom were medical students at Columbia University's College of Physicians and Surgeons, in renting two apartments on the fourth floor of 317 West 58th Street that they collectively christened "Poverty Flat." Ives continued to live with the Poverty Flat collective until his marriage in 1908. Poverty Flat was more of an institution than a location, and was subsequently moved to 65 Central Park West, then (in 1907) to 34 Gramercy Park. Old members of the group left and new ones joined over the years. Ives was one of the few who remained for the duration. In its social organization Poverty Flat was something of a commune. The men pooled resources for rent, meals and other expenses, shared clothing and provided a mutual friendship and support system not unlike a fraternity. There is no evidence that their relationships were anything other than friendships among heterosexual bachelors, most of whom eventually married and moved on.

During his residence at Poverty Flat, Ives produced a substantial portion of his musical canon, including drafts of his *Second* and *Third Symphonies,* the cantata *The Celestial Country,* the *Three Page Sonata, Halloween,* his first two *Violin Sonatas,* the *Washington's Birthday* and *Thanksgiving* movements of his *Holidays Symphony,* the *First Piano Sonata,* a large number of songs and anthems, the chorus *Let There Be Light,* many ragtime dances and piano studies, much chamber music, *Central Park in the Dark, From the Steeples and the Mountains, The Unanswered Question,* and sketches that ultimately led to the *Concord Sonata* and *Three Places in New England.* He had met his future business partner, Julian Myrick, early in his employment at Mutual Life and the two became immediate friends. In 1907 they established their own agency of the Washington Life Insurance Co. under the name "Ives and Co."

Ives had been courting Harmony Twichell for several years and, in June of 1908, they were married by her clergyman father, a close friend of Mark Twain. Ives moved out of Poverty Flat and Myrick promptly moved in to replace him. However, the collective disbanded soon after that (probably for reasons other than Myrick's joining it). Ives and Myrick continued their partnership, with increasing prosperity, until Washington Life was sold to Pittsburgh Life and Trust in late 1908. The two then returned to Mutual Life and formed their own agency under the rubric "Ives and Myrick," the name they retained until their respective retirements.

Through this entire period, and for several years after his marriage as well, Ives truly was an "amateur" composer. Performances of his work were few and far between, and mostly done by friends and fellow amateurs. *The Celestial Country* was performed at Central Presbyterian Church in 1902 and the renowned Kaltenborn Quartet played the *Intermezzo* (from the same cantata) later that year in New Haven. Conductor Walter Damrosch read through part of the *First Symphony* with his orchestra in 1910, but, for the most part, performances of Ives' work were limited to occasional vocal or church recitals during the years 1902–1924. The Iveses lived at various addresses in Manhattan during the peak of his business years, but, by 1912, were sufficiently affluent to afford a country place in Redding, Connecticut. They purchased fifteen acres of land and had a home built there, where they summered for the next seventeen years. After Ives' retirement in 1930 they took up more or less permanent residence there.

The period between 1909 and 1926 comprises the last stage of Ives' active composing. After the creation of his song "Sunrise" in August 1926, Ives completed no more new pieces. The cessation of Ives' original musical work was not sudden, but developed gradually over a period of twenty years. He had had indications of a heart problem as early as 1906. After ten years of building a dynamic, flourishing insurance firm by day, and composing at a vigorous pace in the evenings and on weekends, Ives suffered a severe heart attack in October of 1918. It is possible that his distress over the involvement of the United States in World War I contributed to his illness, because Ives was a thoroughly independent political thinker who combined what would today be considered a basically right-wing temperament with radical anti-nationalism and an abiding belief in direct (as opposed to representative) democracy. He even wrote a pamphlet on the latter subject, entitled "The Majority," in which he advocated nothing short of government by referendum of the entire populace.

The heart attack of 1918 kept Ives away from his office throughout the entire ensuing year. During this time he oversaw the preparation and engraving of the privately printed first edition of the *Concord Sonata* and wrote his accompanying book of prose, *Essays Before a Sonata*. Apparently Ives never completely recovered his health and later developed diabetes and further complications with his heart. He returned to his insurance business in September of 1919, but worked at a somewhat slower pace until his final retirement ten years later.

Throughout the final two decades of his creative activity, roughly 1908 to 1926, Ives developed sketches and ideas dating from the Poverty Flat period into finished compositions, including: *Three Places in New England,* the *Concord Sonata,* the third and fourth *Violin Sonatas,* the second and third *Orchestral Sets,* the *Fourth Symphony* and sketches for a fifth—the so-called "Universe"—symphony, his second *String Quartet,* the remaining movements of the *Holidays Symphony,* numerous choruses, including *The New River, General William Booth Enters into Heaven* (Vachel Lindsay), and *Duty* (Emerson). He also wrote many new songs to texts by a number of authors, among them himself, his wife and their adopted daughter Edith. In 1922 Ives arranged for the G. Schirmer Co. to print, at his own expense, his definitive collection of *114 Songs*, which he then sent around to everyone and anyone he could think of who might be interested, repeating the procedure he had followed with the printed first edition of the *Concord Sonata* in 1921. In his vivid preface to *114 Songs*, Ives referred to the collection as the result of his "having cleaned house," and the eclectic character of the anthology bears witness both to his tremendous range as a composer and the wide variety of purposes reflected in his music. Among the *114 Songs* are conventional potboilers in the late 19th-century mold; seminal works such as "The Cage" and "The Majority," songs that form the bases of later works for expanded resources such as "The Housatonic at Stockbridge," "Lincoln, the Great Commoner," "The Camp Meeting" or "He Is There!"; songs based on hymn tunes and popular tunes; songs in French; songs in German and songs which are frankly so experimental that the composer himself doubted whether they could or should be sung.

As a result of Ives sending out complimentary copies of his songs, essays and the *Concord Sonata*, serious musical minds finally began to pay attention to him in the 1920s. He received and/or developed correspondence with such figures as the writer Henry Bellamann, the theorist Percy Goetschius, pianist E. Robert Schmitz, Nicolas Slonimsky, John Kirkpatrick, Henry Cowell and others during the 1920s, many of whom became enthusiasts of his work. He began to receive some performances and to attract the attention of younger composers such as Aaron Copland and Elliott Carter.

Bellamann and Cowell in particular became devotés and advocates of the aging composer. The former began to give lectures, illustrated with musical excerpts, on the *Concord Sonata* and, in 1927, published the first major scholarly article on Ives in the quarterly journal *Pro Musica*. This was followed by an article by Cowell in the *Aesthete Magazine* (August, 1928) entitled "Four Little-Known Modern Composers," which dealt extensively with Ives' work. Both became close friends and regular visitors at the Ives household.

Charles Ives lived until 1954. The savage irony of his last thirty years is that he only began to see his music receive the recognition it deserved after he had stopped writing it. He devoted the bulk of his time after retirement to revising his scores and putting many of them into shape for publication, receiving visitors and inquiries, attending occasional performances of his own and others' music, writing his autobiographical book *Memos* (edited by John Kirkpatrick) and traveling in Europe.

Perhaps the most significant event in establishing Ives as a force to be reckoned with in the world of concert music was John Kirkpatrick's 1939 premiere of the entire *Concord Sonata* at Town Hall in New York. Kirkpatrick had received a copy of the first edition in 1927, when he was living in Paris. It took him two years to develop a strong interest in the work, but, by the mid-1930s, he was playing "The Alcotts" movement in his solo recitals. By 1938 he had gained sufficient command of the piece to perform it from memory at a private gathering in Cos Cob, Connecticut, which received a favorable review from Paul Rosenfeld in *Modern Music.* The Town Hall recital of the following year, in which Kirkpatrick played only the Beethoven *"Waldstein" Sonata* and the *Concord,* was the first complete public performance of the work. Lawrence Gilman was the influential music critic of the New York *Herald-Tribune*, and, conveniently, had been a close friend and schoolmate of Mrs. Ives' brother, David, in earlier days. Gilman was deeply interested in American music and, as noted in the last chapter, had written the most important biography of Edward MacDowell to that time in 1908. Ives sent him advance copies of the score and the *Essays Before a Sonata,* and Gilman came to Kirkpatrick's recital fully prepared to give the sonata an educated hearing. The result was his historic review, which bluntly stated that the *Concord Sonata* was "the greatest music composed by an American."

Throughout the 1940s Ives' reputation grew steadily and the number of musicians who sought him out, corresponded with him, performed his music and wrote about him increased exponentially. The principal figures among these were Henry Cowell (see Chapter 10) and John Kirkpatrick. Cowell, and his wife Sidney, became close friends of the Iveses and, by 1947, Cowell was proposing to write a book on the composer. Kirkpatrick, though much younger than either Ives or Cowell, became equally close to the family and, after the composer's death, became his musical executor and curator of the vast collection of his papers and music manuscripts housed at Yale. Indeed, it is largely thanks to Kirkpatrick's lifelong dedication to the task of organizing, editing and publishing Ives' works in all media that present and future generations will have available the authenticated manuscripts of our first acknowledged "great" composer.

The greater recognition afforded Ives during the last decade of his life culminated in 1947, when he was awarded the Pulitzer Prize for his *Third Symphony.* In typical fashion, Ives sent the money from the prize to Dr. John J. Becker (see next chapter), an academic composer and family friend who had orchestrated *General William Booth.* Another significant event occurred in February of 1951 when Leonard Bernstein conducted the *Second Symphony* at Carnegie Hall in a concert broadcast on nationwide radio. Ives did not attend this landmark performance of his fifty-year-old symphony, possibly due to his or his wife's ill health but more probably because, at this stage of his life, he had become embittered by the years of

Charles E. Ives *(1874–1954) in old age. The first American classical composer to exert a worldwide influence on music itself. He became an insurance executive and, frustrated by lack of appreciation, had ceased composing by the time his music won recognition.* (Photo by Frank Gerrantano, courtesy of BMI.)

official neglect of his music. He did, however, reportedly listen to the broadcast.

Death finally came for Charles Ives on May 19, 1954 in New York City, just six months short of his eightieth birthday. He did not live to see the publication of the Cowells' book on him later the following year, nor the final chapter, devoted to him, of Gilbert Chase's important history, *America's Music*, also published in 1955. He was buried in West Redding.

If Gottschalk and Paine were the first American composers to achieve international reputations, and Edward MacDowell was the first to create music of an enduring character, Charles Ives was our first composer of classical music to have a profound influence on music itself, worldwide. In this respect he is the likeliest candidate for the label of America's first "great" composer, for whatever that label might be worth.

Reaction to Ives' work during its first half century of public exposure (roughly 1930–1980) was deeply divided. His approach to composition was so fundamentally original to himself, and the sound of the music that resulted was so often incredibly dense and dissonant, that both serious musicians and the public were reluctant to commit themselves to a full appreciation of his achievement. Much nonsense and much distortion appeared in print during those years, largely as a result of incomplete information about Ives and less than full access to the entire body of his work.

The Cowells' book was well-intentioned and cogently written, serving as a necessary first attempt to comprehend the Ives phenomenon. But, as Burkholder has noted, the Cowells were writing from a perspective that looked backward over Ives' life and were not in full possession of important material relating to his early music and activities. Thus, for example, they give a more far-reaching significance to the role played by the Concord Transcendentalist authors in Ives' thinking than it actually had. And they attempted to create a unified picture of Ives' stylistic identity, when in fact Ives could be many different composers at different times and for different purposes.

We have previously noted the ambivalent attitudes toward Ives of commentators such as William Austin and Igor Stravinsky, attitudes shared by the academic establishment for many years. Furthermore, many American composers of Aaron Copland's generation, including Copland himself, experienced an early enthusiasm for Ives which seemed to cool later in their careers. None, with the possible exception of Lou Harrison, embraced the totality of Ives' musical esthetic for any substantial length of time, and most gravitated more toward the European conventions of form, orchestration and harmonic theory that Ives had long since transcended. But, for younger composers (those born approximately between 1915 and 1935), Ives assumed a much greater significance. Composers as different as John Cage, Leonard Bernstein and Steve Reich all share certain influences originating in diverse aspects of Ives' work. In the case of Cage and other aleatorists, this influence may be seen stemming from the random juxtapositions of instrumental choirs, meters, tempi and tonalities that occur in many of Ives' mature orchestral works. In the case of Bernstein and other "Americanist" composers, the influence can be traced in the specific techniques Ives used to deploy and vary vernacular melodies throughout his orchestral textures. In the case of Reich and other "minimalists," Ives can been seen smiling behind their use of rhythms with simultaneous, contradictory metric implications. There are many other examples as well.

No other single American composer has exerted such a variety and depth of influence on such a great number of his successors as has Ives. And his influence continues to be felt up to the present day. Indeed, if anything, his stature seems to be increasing while that of contemporaries such as Schoenberg and Stravinsky is beginning to wane.

The Music

The major creative periods of Ives' life fall into four broad categories. These are: (1) the Danbury, Yale and early Poverty Flat years, (2) the years between 1902 and his marriage in 1908, (3) the first fifteen years following his marriage, and (4) the period from around 1922 until his death, including the cessation of his active composing. Speaking in very broad generalities, the music of these periods can be characterized as follows.

(1) The Period Before 1902: including such works as the *Variations on America, Country Band March, Harvest Home Chorales, The Celestial Country,* the first *String Quartet* and first two *Symphonies,* reflects Ives' view of himself as a serious student composer. He wrote music for performance occasions, music that was accessible to his limited public, music that occasionally experimented with techniques derived from his father, and finally, music that attempted to integrate the more formal techniques acquired both from George Ives and Horatio Parker. A good deal of this was publishable by the standards of the time; a good deal of it was church music. And there is every indication that Ives intended to pursue a musical career up until his senior year at Yale.

Furthermore, though his decision to enter business was highly significant, both for him personally and for the historic precedent it set for other composers, it was not arrived at overnight. Between 1898 and 1902 Ives seemed to be wavering between viewing his insurance job as a survival occupation, a stopgap in his musical career, and as his chosen profession. After 1902, when he made the decision to (in his own words) "give up music," that is, to give up the idea of pursuing music professionally, his composition assumes a much more experimental character.

(2) The Period from 1902 to 1908: includes the *Third Symphony,* the *Three-Page Sonata,* numerous piano studies and ragtime pieces, overtures on various subjects (not all of which are complete), the *First Piano Sonata, Central Park in the Dark, The Unanswered Question, Thanksgiving* for orchestra, the first *Violin and Piano Sonata* and part of the second, as well as a variety of chamber works. Once Ives began to view his music as an avocation, and removed himself both from regular employment as a church musician and the regular critical appraisal of musically literate colleagues, his music began to focus more deeply on exploring experimental relationships in harmony, rhythm/meter, orchestration and form. Much of it was written in a joking, satirical vein, and he seemed much less concerned about finishing sketches or preparing readable scores. When he resigned as organist at Central Presbyterian Church in New York in June of 1902, he left behind a large number of anthems and organ music which he had created for services over the years, very little of which was recoverable later on. He began to write more for the piano after that, and for the piano in combination with other instruments—groupings which had previously played little role in his work.

(3) The Period from 1908 to 1922: includes most of Ives' major works. Among these are the *Holidays Symphony,* the *Second String Quartet, Three Places in New England,* the *Fourth Symphony,* the *Concord Sonata,* the second, third and fourth *Violin Sonatas,* the *Second Orchestral Set,* and a number of secular choruses. This was a period of consolidation and achievement for him, which might not have been possible without the deeply committed relationship he shared with his wife, Harmony, and her unshakable confidence in his genius. He suffered occasional periods of self-doubt, during which she restored his sense of the rightness of his musical vision, even though she herself was not sufficiently versed in music to read or auralize his scores. Harmony Ives, who deserves a biography of her own, was the daughter of a prominent Hartford family, had been educated as a registered nurse, had done medical work in settlement houses and wrote a great deal of poetry, some of which Ives set to music. She was a woman of great inner strength and provided a calm central anchor for Ives' hectic life and excitable temperament.

(4) The Period after 1922: As Ives' health deteriorated and his compositional activity began to slow down, his attention turned to repairing and correcting the gaps in his earlier work. After 1922 he wrote mostly in smaller forms, producing two complete movements and part of another for his *Third Orchestral Set,* a *Largo and Allegro* for two pianos tuned in quarter-tones (for a discussion of this tuning technique in Ives see pp. 276–277) and a group of eleven songs, not included in the *114 Songs* he had published in 1922. In 1926, shortly after he had purchased his permanent New York home at 164 East 74th Street, he came downstairs one evening with tears in his eyes, telling Harmony that he just couldn't find the way to compose anymore, that nothing seemed to come out right. Thereafter, he wrote no new music but devoted himself to organizing, revising and promoting his existing works. It was also during these latter years that Ives produced most of his prose writing, and began to develop his extraordinary sexual invective against "nice" or "pretty" music to a previously unknown degree.

Rossiter has speculated that Ives was increasingly unwilling to accept the technological and lifestyle changes occurring in American society during the 1930s, 1940s and 1950s. That he retreated into nostalgia is clear from his writings, and Kirkpatrick believed that Harmony encouraged him to do so. He consistently began to refer to composers of highly accessible music with effeminate adjectives and pronouns. While this was not a new practice for him, it clearly became excessive in his later years. His use of terms like "pussies," "pansies," "sissies," and "ladies," when discussing the attitudes of critics, conductors, certain other composers and audiences betrays an extreme homophobia, rather than contempt for women. To what extent this originated in the dynamics of the Ives family household in Danbury, and his intensely close relationship to his father, remains unclear and can probably not be determined with any assurance. It is possible that the experience of being coddled as something of a musical prodigy by the matrons of Danbury had an effect on the formation of these attitudes, and it is not inconceivable that Ives' obsession with baseball and other sports was motivated as much by a desire to be viewed as masculine (despite his interest in music) as it was by an intrinsic interest in the games. It is instructive to remember that, in English-speaking countries during the 19th century, the adjective "musical" was applied to young men as an explicit euphemism for "homosexual."

In a sense, the whole issue of masculinity in music is relevant to American culture in a way it has never been to European music. As Elliott Carter has pointed out, part of Americans' attitude toward art music undoubtedly stems from the education and economic backgrounds of the European and other immigrants who chose to settle here, passing those attitudes along to future generations.[7] Those who were comfortable with European art and life, presumably, stayed in Europe for the most part. In addition, the American pioneer mythos has always exaggerated tradition-ally masculine qualities of roughness, physicality and a somewhat suspicious attitude toward anyone or anything that smacked of too much sophistication. To the extent that all American males invest their sense of masculinity in these qualities, art music can seem a very unmasculine profession to some. This is no less true today than it was in Ives' boyhood, and the problem is not made any easier by the number of significant American composers who have been overtly bisexual or homosexual men, including Charles Griffes, Aaron Copland, Virgil Thomson, Samuel Bar-ber, Henry Cowell, Leonard Bernstein, Marc Blitzstein, Ned Rorem, Lou Harrison, John Cage and others.

As Theodor Timreck's excellent film, *A Good Dissonance Like a Man* (1976), makes clear, Ives associated dissonant harmony, complex rhythmic structures, clashing tonalities and other features of his work with his cherished sense of rugged masculinity. What is difficult to determine is the extent to which his predilection for such features was a psychological

---
[7] Allen Edwards, *Flawed Words and Stubborn Sounds*, pp. 13–18.

defense against implications of effeminacy he inferred in less radical music, versus the extent to which masculinity became a justification for his pre-existing musical interests. Had he not associated musical convention with effeminacy in his own mind, a very real question exists as to whether he would have evolved in the musical direction he took.

Thus, his specific canon of work touches upon issues in the American (male) character that penetrate to a deeper psychological level than any theorist has yet discussed in print. In this respect, Ives is not unlike Ernest Hemingway as a uniquely American artist. For the time being, however, we must wait for a fuller and more informed discussion of this issue, both in terms of Ives' own work and his influence on succeeding generations of American composers to appear in the literature of our first indisputable American master composer.

4

Other American Composers of the Early 20th Century

ॐ

All of the important American composers of classical music prior to World War I at times seemed to share a certain youthful optimism and exuberance that directly reflected the forward-looking view America had of itself during its first century and a half. This is especially apparent in the dance-derived pieces of Gottschalk, the enthusiasms and pomposities of Heinrich, the mercurial overtures of Chadwick and piano idylls of MacDowell, and the irrepressible, bursting-at-the-seams vigor of Ives' instrumental works, to say nothing of the ragtime of Scott Joplin and other vernacular styles. Even the horrors and dislocations of the Civil War had not repressed this side of the American spirit for long, although the experience of the war seemed to deepen and mature it somewhat. This can, perhaps, be seen in the differing levels of mythic consciousness reflected by prewar writers such as Washington Irving or Fenimore Cooper, when contrasted with the post-war sensibilities of a Mark Twain or a Henry James.

American composers, like most American intellectuals of the time, were conspicuously aware of this optimistic attitude and saturated with its innate assumptions about American life and the future of the country. MacDowell wrote:

> What we must arrive at is the youthful optimistic vitality, and the un-daunted tenacity of spirit that characterizes the American man. This is what I hope to see echoed in American music.[8]

---

[8] Cited in J. Machlis, *American Composers of Our Time*, p. ix.

In a 1915 article entitled "The American Composer," Henry F. B. Gilbert wrote:

> Meanwhile we have already developed a strong and distinctive American *spirit.* As compared with that of Europe it is the spirit of youth in contrast to the spirit of age. We are filled with a glorious will for accomplishment, an impatience of restraining bonds of tradition, and a buoyant and incontrovertible optimism.[9]

These sentiments are typical and are echoed and re-echoed by almost all the composers at the turn of the 20th century. Moreover, this youthful spirit, though damaged by World War I, survived into the 1920s and played a significant role in the music of George Gershwin, which dominated that era. Echoes of it can even be heard in some American music as late as the works of Copland and Leonard Bernstein from the 1930s, 1940s and 1950s. But, beginning in the 1920s and continuing through the age of the Cold War and the atom bomb, this freshness and naive enthusiasm diminished significantly. While its remnant may be inferred from the energetic *labors* of mid-to-late-century composers, this exuberant spirit becomes increasingly more difficult to identify in the actual *music* they wrote.

The entry of the United States into World War I was not merely a milestone of American political history. It exerted profound and irreversible effects on American culture. Before World War I, we were basically an isolated, self-satisfied people content to tend our own business and leave international affairs to the tycoons of commerce. The mass, mechanized slaughter and protracted trench warfare that was experienced at firsthand by so many young Americans in France and the low countries of Europe after 1916, however, changed all that. A major portion of our innocence was irretrievably lost, and, from that point on, it became clear that the United States was going to have to assume a much larger position in world affairs.

The period of America's participation in the war effort and its aftermath (officially from 1917–1918, though actually closer to 1915–1919) saw many changes on the American musical scene. The last of the old generation of 19th-century symphonic composers, William Gilchrist and Silas Pratt, died in 1916. Scott Joplin, depressed over the failure of his plans to produce his ragtime opera *Treemonisha,* died in 1917; and ragtime, for all practical purposes, died with him. Horatio Parker died in 1919, and the survivors of the Second New England School, though they lived on for a couple of decades, fell into increasing obscurity and irrelevance. Ives, after completing a coherent draft of the *Concord Sonata,* suffered his first serious heart attack in 1918, and was never quite the same. Charles T. Griffes, after a

---

[9]   G. Chase, *The American Composer Speaks,* pp. 96–97.

frustrating and difficult attempt to establish himself as a recognized composer, succumbed to empyema in 1920 at the age of thirty-six. The next generation both of serious composers and popular songwriters, including Henry Cowell, George Gershwin, Irving Berlin and W. C. Handy, were just beginning to achieve some recognition. The blues became a coherent and recognized form in American vernacular music and the term "jazz" began to show up more frequently. Copland, Thomson, Harris and their generation were late-adolescent music students. The composers who would shape the American classical music world of the 1950s and 1960s (John Cage, Leonard Bernstein, Elliott Carter, Gian-Carlo Menotti, Milton Babbitt, Alan Hovhaness, Samuel Barber et al.) were for the most part newborn babes or toddlers.

American classical music during the period between 1900 and 1920 evolved in a kaleidoscopic variety of directions. By then it had become reasonably clear that slavish adherence to European models was a dead end for American composers, and the search for a means to develop a characteristically American school of serious composition intensified accordingly. One of these directions involved the first systematic attempt to base American classical composition on American ethnic and folk music.

As has been mentioned in earlier chapters, Antonin Dvořák had been invited to head the National Conservatory of Music in New York in 1892, and almost immediately began agitating for American composers to turn to their folk music roots for inspiration. Dvořák leapt to the conclusion, consistent with the views of historians of the period such as Ritter and Elson, that American ethnic music resided chiefly in plantation spirituals and the songs of Indian tribes and lobbied American composers to attempt the deliberate creation of a national style by basing it on these specific ethnic musics.

But, there is a difference between realizing that the classical music of a given national culture is rooted in its more ancient folk-music traditions and attempting self-consciously to create an art music from oral-tradition songs. In the former case, one looks at a body of completed classical works and discovers that features such as the vocal inflections appropriate to the language of the song, the characteristic rhythmic and metric patterns, and the intervallic predilections of melody and its modal bases have parallels and apparent antecedents in the older body of oral-tradition folk music. But this in an analytical process, carried out "after the fact" as it were, and serves principally to explain why, for example, French composers of all historical epochs share a certain "Frenchness" of sound that simply cannot be found among their German or Italian contemporaries.

Dvořák attempted to reverse this process. If it were possible to discern the identifying traits of a national classical style in a country's folk music roots, he reasoned, it should be equally possible to synthesize such a style, taking folk music as the starting point. This idea had a certain appeal, perhaps because it dovetailed with the American passion for new, practical approaches to old problems (reflected in our early propensity for mechanical inventions and later obsession with high technology). But such a simplistic view of musical evolution fails to account for many other, far less tangible factors, such as the ineluctable role played in the formation of musical styles by social conventions, culture-specific prejudices and values, and even modes of thinking fostered by the specific linguistic habits of the indigenous language.

One of the clearest examples of why Dvořák's approach failed, when adopted by the younger composers whom he influenced, emerges when we realize that Dvořák was raised in a society that was racially, if not ethnically, homogenous. Whatever experience he may have had of the ethnic divisions and rivalries between Czechs, Slovaks, gypsies and other groups in his native Bohemia, he clearly had little appreciation for the depth of the ingrained racism that divided blacks and whites in the United States after the Civil War.

Throughout the late 19th century, emancipated blacks began a long process of migration from the Deep South to the urban centers of the North, in search of better opportunities. The reaction of middle- and upper-class northern whites, most of whom were still of Anglo-Saxon heritage at this point, was to insulate themselves from these new arrivals (as well as from the hordes of European immigrants being imported by the boatload to staff the industrial factories of the North). This process peaked in the 1890s, a period when the white genteel (and Gentile) population ensconced itself in tree-shaded, segregated suburbs filled with massive Victorian houses, in summer retreats or in small, settled towns outside of the major urban centers. And it continues to some extent even today in some communities, under the sociological label "white flight." American blacks and European immigrants in the late 19th century were herded into ghetto neighborhoods in the cities, where they often lived under conditions of extreme poverty, squalor and social repression.

Composers such as MacDowell, Parker, Chadwick and others of the Second New England School were all members of the white upper-middle class, and, while they may not have been as bigoted as their less refined peers, were nonetheless products of the value system then operative. For a foreigner such as Dvořák, then, to inject himself into the American musical scene and start telling these people their only hope for achieving a substantive art of their own lay in embracing the music of the most despised and downtrodden elements of the American population (i.e., blacks and Indians) was ludicrous to many musicians of the time.

But, beyond the social issues, Dvořák's theories were as naive as might be expected, given the infant status of the science of musicology at the time. His personal application of them, in the *"New World" Symphony,* merely resulted in a very well-crafted European symphonic work, based on certain melodic and rhythmic patterns that happen to occur in American folk music and not even particularly black American folk music (Burleigh notwithstanding). The success of the *"New World" Symphony* probably owes much more to the fresh inspiration Dvořák himself acquired from his personal experiences in America than from any inherently American musical features it might contain.

The best-known American composers of the time, whatever their social attitudes, probably sensed this problem and definitely maintained a skeptical reserve. Many articles and speeches were written, and continued to be written during the next twenty years, disputing the notions that: (a) an "American" classical music was necessarily a desirable thing, and/or (b) that it could be achieved merely by quoting folk tunes in symphonic or other European-music contexts. Horatio Parker deserted the faculty of National Conservatory shortly after Dvořák arrived, and the other Boston classicists steadfastly ignored Dvořák's ideas.

Nevertheless, the ideas took hold in some quarters. MacDowell, while maintaining serious ideological reservations, flirted periodically with the use of Indian and "Negro" themes in his piano suites, increasingly after Dvořák's departure. Composers such as Arthur Farwell and Charles Wakefield Cadman made sincere attempts to integrate American Indian themes into their early works, using the pioneering collections of this rapidly disappearing material that were just coming into print at the time, and even occasional first-hand research. But, perhaps more significant than Dvořák's advocacy of specific ethnic source materials was the new spirit of inquiry his ideas seemed to generate among younger American composers. Charles Ives, of course, already had this spirit in abundance, captured from the early training provided by his father, and was making far more sophisticated use of vernacular musical processes than Dvořák and Co. ever dreamed of. But nobody was listening to Charles Ives before 1930.

As far as *public* musical activity was concerned, the mantle fell to composers such as Farwell, Griffes, Cadman, Carpenter, Edward Burlingame Hill, Edgar Stillman Kelley, and a list of figures we might whimsically call the Henry's, the Harry's and the Harvey's: Henry Eichheim, Harvey Worthington Loomis, Henry Hadley, Henry F. B. Gilbert and Harry Lawrence Freeman. Each of these pursued the quest for a new, and sometimes specifically "American" sound in his own unique way. And each contributed significantly to the myriad profiles of American classical music prior to the emergence of George Gershwin.

Before examining the ideas of the above composers, however, it may be useful to identify the different lines of exploration which were available to them at the time. Chapter 1 outlined those strains of specifically American music that were already established by the 1890s. In addition to these, a variety of Asian musics began to influence the thinking of American composers (especially Griffes and Eichheim), who built on the efforts of the French composer, Claude Debussy, after 1900 to integrate Asian concepts into Western music. Moreover, as traditional ragtime and blues began to coalesce into coherent jazz styles, these vernacular idioms became yet another subject for integration into classical music models.

Furthermore, there was a clearly discernible tendency for the musical cultures of France and the United States to influence each other reciprocally, especially in the areas of ragtime and jazz, beginning around 1905. Increasingly, American composers who chose to study abroad gravitated toward French, rather than German, teachers, and World War I accelerated this process by bringing large numbers of French and American musicians together in Paris between 1917–1918.

Debussy had been attracted to the ragtime of Joplin as early as his *Golliwog's Cakewalk* (1908), and the emergence of jazz captured the imagination of the French more than any other European culture. (Of course this Franco-American affinity has antecedents going back to Baudelaire's obsession with the works of Poe, and later reached its zenith in the mutual admiration society formed by Ravel-Gershwin-Milhaud, as well as the enormous number of American composers who studied with Nadia Boulanger.)

So, the field of inquiry potentially open to Farwell, Griffes and other composers of their generation included the songs of the New England psalmodists; American Indian music; African-American ragtime, minstrelsy, blues and jazz; Caribbean and Creole folk music; Appalachian and southwestern folk music; the cultivated European-American symphonic, operatic and chamber music traditions; and, increasingly, the newly available sounds of a variety of Asian musics. Of these, all but the New England and Appalachian traditions were extensively, if not completely, explored by various American composers in the first two decades of the 20th century. It remained for the later efforts of Copland and his generation to reevaluate and adapt the more specifically Anglo-Saxon vernacular music traditions.

Arthur Farwell (1872–1952)

Forty years after his death, Arthur Farwell remains a controversial, challenging and, unfortunately, rather neglected figure among American composers. He is principally remembered as the founder and guiding spirit of the Wa-Wan Press, a publishing enterprise based in Newton Center, Massachusetts, between 1901 and 1912, which devoted itself to promoting the works of about forty American composers living at the time. Despite his having created more than one hundred major original compositions, including a variety of highly progressive instrumental pieces during his later years, Farwell is often considered to have been more an arranger of Indian tunes and other kinds of folk music than a composer of original pieces.

He was born in St. Paul, Minnesota, on April 23, 1872 and spent the first eighteen years of his life there. Although he was given violin instruction as a child, he displayed little interest in music until he began studies in engineering at the Massachusetts Institute of Technology in 1890. At MIT Farwell came under the influence of one Rudolph Gott, usually described as an "eccentric musician" by Farwell's biographers. Gott apparently aroused Farwell's interest in music to such a feverish pitch that it was all the young man could do to complete his engineering degree in 1893. After his graduation, Farwell began studies with the French-trained theorist Homer Norris (1860–1920) in Boston and also took some lessons from Chadwick. But Chadwick's formal, pedantic approach to music pedagogy alienated Farwell and, with encouragement from MacDowell, the young composer sailed for Germany, where he studied with Engelbert Humperdinck (who also taught Griffes) and Hans Pfitzner (an early rival of Mahler and Schoenberg) from 1897 to 1899. He also studied briefly with the organist-composer Alexandre Guilmant in Paris.

Upon returning to the United States in May of 1899, Farwell applied for a lectureship at Cornell University, where he stayed for the next two years. But academic teaching was not to Farwell's taste and, in 1901, he resigned from Cornell, determined to find another way to support himself. His parents had moved to Newton Center, near Boston, and this became Farwell's home base for the next several years.

Although he was only eleven years younger than MacDowell and five years younger than Amy Cheney Beach, Farwell was at least a generation removed from the Boston Classicists in his musical thinking. In a letter to a young composer, published in the September, 1907 issue of *The Wa-Wan Press Monthly*, Farwell wrote:

> I cannot uphold you in sympathizing with *all* that is being done in
> Boston, for despite so much that is truly worthy in its achievement, I
> believe that much that is being done here is in direct opposition to
> what America must eventually affirm and maintain.

Farwell had not merely absorbed Dvořák's point of view about basing original art music on indigenous ethnic sources. His vision of a specifically

American classical music extended into the sociological dimension as well, and he perceived a need to integrate a high calibre of native musical culture into the everyday life of everyday Americans. In effect he became the first radical "Americanist" composer since Anthony Philip Heinrich in the 1850s. And his first effort to achieve this ideal in practical reality took the form of the Wa-Wan Press, which he founded at the family home in Newton immediately after his resignation from Cornell.

The term "Wa-Wan" is the name of an important ceremony of the Omaha Indians, a ceremony, according to Gilbert Chase, of "peace, fellowship and song." Farwell established the offices at his family home in Newton Center and personally oversaw the editorial, business and clerical details of the operation. The design, engraving and printing of issues were "farmed out" to professional printers in Boston and Newton. Originally subscribers were offered two volumes each quarter, one comprised of vocal and the other of instrumental music. After 1906, the publications were issued monthly. All the editions were liberally bolstered with essays and program notes by Farwell and the other composers represented and were beautifully and painstakingly designed with original artwork. In 1909 Farwell became the chief music critic for the Boston area for *Musical America* and found it increasingly difficult to keep the Wa-Wan Press in operation. Finally, in 1912, he turned the plates over to G. Schirmer on a royalty basis.

Among the thirty-seven composers published by the Wa-Wan Press were Carlos Troyer (1837–1920), Arthur Shepherd (1880–1958), Edgar Stillman Kelley (1857–1944), Harvey W. Loomis (1865–1930), William Schuyler (1855–1914), Ernest R. Kroeger (1862–1934), Frederick Ayres (1876–1926), John Parsons Beach (1877–1953), Henry F. B. Gilbert (1868–1928), Natalie Curtis (Burlin) (1875–1921) and, of course, Farwell himself. For the most part, these were the "young Turks" of turn-of-the-century American classical music. They had rejected the desiccated classicism of Chadwick, Parker, Foote, Paine and others of the Second New England School and were committed to the development of an "American" art music. Farwell and Curtis were the leaders in the research and adaptation of American Indian music, but the entire range of composers represented went far beyond the "Indianist" movement. Wa-Wan publications included art songs and piano pieces, sometimes with instrumental obbligati, based on mainstream American and European poetry as well as "pure music," i.e., music without cross-cultural references or extra musical programs. A complete, five volume reprint of all the music published by the Wa-Wan Press was issued by the Arno Press and the *New York Times* in 1970 under the editorship of Vera Brodsky Lawrence and remains one of the most important documents of this period of American music history today.

Farwell's early arrangements of Indian music were simplistic and rooted in conventional European harmonic practice. But, as he matured as a composer, he became more daring and was able to base his ideas more on the inherent qualities of the Indian source material itself. The gradually increasing sophistication of his settings first becomes apparent with his *Impressions of the Wa-Wan Ceremony of the Omahas*, Op.21 in 1905 for piano, and continued throughout the remainder of his creative life. He went on to teach at the University of California at Berkeley (1918–1919) and at Michigan State College (1927–1939).

In the 1930s Farwell began to move away from conventional European harmonic practice in his non-Indian works as well and started to develop a strikingly original style. The beginning of this trend can be noted in his 1930 piano solo *Vale of Enithharmon*, Op.91 and continued in his twenty-three polytonal etudes for piano, Op.109 (1940–1952) and his single-movement, 13-minute *Piano Sonata*, Op.113 (1949). Farwell was also deeply concerned with getting indigenous classical music into the lives of Americans through community music-making activities and, to this end, wrote a large number of community chorus pieces, masques and pageants. His pioneering attempts to involve the audience in these activities anticipated the later work of John Cage, Terry Riley, Robert Ashley and other avant-garde composers of the 1960s and 1970s.

Arthur Farwell died in New York City on January 20, 1952, three months short of his eightieth birthday. While he is not especially honored today as a great American composer, certainly not to the extent of Ives or Griffes, his legacy permeates the entire fabric of American classical music after 1900 in both subtle and obvious ways. And his work is ripe for revival.

Charles T. Griffes (1884–1920)

Twelve years younger than Farwell, and ten years younger than Ives, Charles Tomlinson Griffes was the most important American composer of this period whose works were professionally published and performed during his own creative lifetime. But these achievements did not descend upon Griffes as a result merely of his genius. He worked hard and relentlessly at promoting his music and getting it into the hands of the right people. At his premature death in 1920, *Musical America* ran an obituary bemoaning the relative neglect afforded Griffes by the classical music mainstream in America, and letters of condolence arrived from figures as important as Prokofiev, Leopold Stokowski and Pierre Monteux.

Griffes was born on September 17, 1884, in Elmira, New York. He was raised in a middle-class atmosphere by a father who was a frustrated intellectual compelled to work at business from an early age, and a quiet,

Charles T. Griffes *(1884–1920) around 1915. Oppressed by his duties as a schoolteacher, he nevertheless began to achieve major success shortly before his premature death. His exotic post-Impressionist style explored the early influences of Asian music as well.* (Photo courtesy of ASCAP.)

artistically inclined mother who was dominated by her own, socially prominent, religiously fundamentalist mother. As a boy, Griffes was fond of painting and amateur theatrics. He was the middle of five children, including three sisters and one brother. He was particularly sensitive to color, both in nature and in art, and later came to associate, like his Russian predecessor, Alexander Scriabin, specific shades and hues with specific tonalities and sonorities. This artistic predilection helped make the work of Debussy and other "Impressionists" far more congenial to Griffes than to other American composers of the time. He also tried his hand at photography, which remained a lifelong hobby.

At about the age of eleven, Griffes contracted typhoid fever and was kept in bed for several months. During this time he regularly heard his elder sister, Katharine, practicing Beethoven and other European classics at the piano. He conceived a passionate desire to learn music and began to take some lessons from her. His progress was astonishing and, at thirteen, he had exhausted everything his sister could teach him. It was then that the young

Griffes was introduced to his first, and perhaps most important, professional teacher, Mary Selena Broughton.

Miss Broughton was a native of New Zealand, of English descent, who immigrated to the United States in 1891. She had been a pupil of Karl Klindworth (student of Liszt and colleague of Hans Von Bülow) and had fled to the United States to escape a frustrated love affair in which she had been thwarted by her elder sisters. She remained a spinster for the rest of her life, and threw all her energies into her teaching.

She recognized Griffes' gifts at once and began to devote extraordinary attention to his musical education. She became his friend, benefactor and mentor, and remained so for the rest of the composer's short life. Griffes, in turn, became her protégé and her special project. He took his lessons from her at Elmira College, and practiced and performed at the local YMCA, perhaps in an attempt to make friends during an otherwise insulated adolescence.

Griffes was homosexual and acknowledged this fact to himself relatively early in life, certainly by his fifteenth year. Considering the sexually repressive, Victorian atmosphere in which he was raised, his frankness in acknowledging his sexual orientation was remarkably courageous and free of neurotic guilt complexes for its time. His homosexuality was apparently obvious to his boyhood companions, according to his earliest biographer, Edward Maisel, but there is no evidence of overt physical relationships either with his peers or with the older men in his milieu at the time. After his subsequent period of study in Europe and return to the United States, Griffes had become adept at concealing any outward signs of effeminacy or erotic attraction to other men, unless he chose to reveal his feelings. He was a regular member of the faculty of the Hackley School for Boys in Tarrytown from 1907 until his death, and suffered no controversy or scandal during that time. Apparently, even if he experienced a romantic attraction to any of his students—and there is little evidence that he did—he wisely elected to keep his professional life strictly segregated from his personal liaisons.

By 1903, Miss Broughton had decided that young Griffes needed more advanced musical instruction. Recognizing that travel to Europe was beyond the means of the large household of Wilber and Clara Griffes, she resolved to send him there at her own expense. Accordingly, he set sail on August 13 of that year, destined for Germany. He arrived in Berlin on August 25, where Miss Broughton—who was summering in Europe—met him. Visiting the Zoölogical Garden the following week, he was fascinated by the appearance of a pure white peacock, an image that later found expression in one of his best-known works. He enrolled at the Stern

Conservatory and began studies of piano with Ernst Jedliczka, composition with Phillipe Rufer and theory with Max Loewengard.

Griffes was fluent in German and had a good reading knowledge of French. He associated with both visiting Americans and native students, and his letters from the period are filled with the enthusiasms of a young man abroad for the first time. In particular, during his first year in Berlin, Griffes developed an attachment to one Konrad Wölcke (Edward Maisel's pseudonym for Emil Joël), a tall, blond, twenty-eight-year-old neighbor of his and fellow student. Wölcke was an ardent chauvinist for Germany and German music and influenced his younger friend increasingly more toward composition than piano studies. There can be little doubt that Griffes was in love with Wölcke, and that Wölcke felt more than a casual friendship for young Charles. Griffes kept the older man's picture with him throughout his life. The two became almost constant companions, and Wölcke assisted Griffes in getting tickets to concerts and operas at reduced rates. Gradually, Wölcke became the most important intellectual influence in Griffes' life at that time and guided his young friend's education with considerable insight. During the four years he spent at Wölcke's side in Berlin, Griffes studied vast amounts of music and literature and encountered such prominent figures in the musical world as Ferruccio Busoni, Edvard Grieg, Richard Strauss, Isadora Duncan, Enrico Caruso and Engelbert Humperdinck. The last of these became his composition teacher in late 1905, accepting Griffes as a private student without fee.

On November 10, 1905, Griffes' father died of pleurisy complicated by pneumonia and a weak heart. Like Charles Ives, Griffes had lost his father at the tender age of twenty, but, unlike Ives' intense emotional reaction to this event, for Griffes it seemed somehow distant and unreal. The relationship between Charles and Wilber Griffes had never been as close as that between Charles and George Ives, nor had the elder Griffes played any significant role in the formation of his son's musical personality. It was not until Griffes sat by his friend Wölcke during the final illness of the latter's mother the following year that the reality of death came home to him. But, despite his emotional distance from Charles, Wilber Griffes' death was to have a serious impact on the future course of his son's career, as it became necessary for Charles to contribute to the support of his mother and siblings after his return to America in 1907.

In the summer of 1906 it became clear that Miss Broughton's funds could not support another year abroad for Griffes. After considerable tension over the gloomy prospect of having to return home before he felt his studies were complete, Konrad Wölcke came to the young composer's rescue by providing him with the bulk of the necessary money, supplemented by the few private pupils Griffes could find and occasional contributions from home. He continued intermittent studies with Humperdinck through April of 1907, interrupted periodically by the elder composer's travel and creative projects, and finally said his goodbyes to Konrad and Germany in June.

Upon returning to America, Griffes obtained a job as music instructor at the newly founded Hackley School for Boys in Tarrytown, New York. Hackley, at that time, was a small prep school primarily geared toward remedial studies for a few less-than-scholarly sons of the very rich, hoping to gain admission to Harvard, Princeton or Yale. Music was not part of the regular curriculum, and Griffes' duties consisted primarily of giving private lessons to those students who wanted them, playing the organ for morning chapel and Sunday services, arranging occasional concerts by visiting artists, conducting the school choir and playing accompaniments for various school functions. He had hoped that the Hackley engagement would be a short-lived stepping-stone to bigger and better things. As it happened, he remained there for the rest of his life.

Griffes was frequently unhappy with his job at Hackley. He rightfully felt that his abilities far exceeded his role as a schoolteacher. His salary was only just sufficient for his needs, and he set aside nearly half of it for the support of his mother. His students were often indifferent dabblers, and his work was not considered in any sense central to the school's mission. In spite of all this, however, he earned enormous personal respect both from the students who knew him and from those faculty colleagues who had an appreciation for art and culture generally. Many pitied him for being called upon to perform tasks far below his gifts, and all marveled at his exceptional skills as a pianist. Neither the homosexual side of his personality nor his achievements as a composer attracted any significant attention at the school.

During his first few years at Hackley, Griffes succeeded in getting G. Schirmer in New York to publish a number of his early songs, set to German texts. These were written before Griffes' distinctive personal style was fully developed, and were therefore more comprehensible to the conventional, commercial sensibilities of that publisher. But, as Griffes' work began to grow more individual and original, he began to meet with closed doors in the New York music publishing establishment—a story all too often told in the lives of significant American composers.

Griffes attracted the attention of Arthur Farwell, who made extraordinary efforts on behalf of the younger composer. But, by 1912, Farwell had turned the Wa-Wan Press's operations over to Schirmer and had no more success persuading them to publish Griffes' music than had Griffes himself. However, Farwell continued to be interested in his younger colleague's development, and the two remained friends and consultants until Griffes' death.

Beginning around 1914, Griffes' fortunes took a slight turn for the better, and the last six years of his life were his most productive and most successful. He intensified his efforts at making the rounds of musicians and publishers in New York and, little by little, became a more familiar figure in that city. In late 1914 Schirmer accepted five new songs for publication, and, the following year, Griffes submitted six of his most famous piano pieces composed during the previous five years: the *Three Tone Pictures*, Op.5 and the *Fantasy Pieces*, Op.6. With the vigorous endorsement of Busoni, who was visiting New York and with whom Griffes had renewed his earlier acquaintance, Schirmer accepted these as well.

In the meantime, Griffes had met the man who, more than any other in his life, was to be his principal companion and confidant. This was a New York City policeman, identified by Maisel by the pseudonym "Dan C. Martin." Martin was seven years older than Griffes, married and the father of two children. They managed their relationship in such a way that it did not interfere with Martin's home life, and Griffes even became something of a friend of Martin's family. Martin provided a stabilizing influence throughout the rest of the high-strung composer's life and used his private study of law to assist Griffes with advice on royalty and contractual matters.

Besides Farwell and Busoni, during the next two years, Griffes met and interacted with other prominent musicians in the New York scene, including Edgard Varèse, Leo Ornstein, Arthur Whiting, Percy Grainger, Ernest Hutcheson and Marion Bauer. He became interested in labor politics as a result of his friendship with Laura Moore Elliot, a gifted amateur musician who was a prominent feminist, socialist and labor activist of the time. Mrs. Elliot encouraged Griffes and exerted herself on behalf of his music. Farwell was, at that time, becoming increasingly interested in community music projects and increasingly skeptical that there was any real future for American composers in the concert music establishment. He and Mrs. Elliot both attempted to enlist Griffes' efforts in the direction of creating pageants and community choruses. The result was *These Things Shall Be*, a unison chorus to a text by John Addington Symonds that reflected Griffes' own social philosophies.

In 1916 Griffes collaborated with a group of New York artists on the larger of his two extant music theatre pieces, *The Kairn of Koridwen*, which ran for twelve performances in early 1917. This work (which was first published in 1993) attracted much approbation, despite a flawed performance and a production schedule beset by problems of many kinds. Griffes, like MacDowell, had always been interested in exotic subjects. But, unlike the earlier composer, Griffes made serious attempts to integrate non-Western musical ideas into his compositions after 1915. He lacked the benefit of the thorough or systematic education in these non-Western musics that became available to American composers later in the century, but compensated for this deficiency by intense private study of Asian musical, literary and artistic source materials. While Griffes' interest in non-Western musics was predated by Henry Eichheim's efforts (see below), he nevertheless made a significant contribution to opening the ears of educated American listeners to the new possibilities offered by this body of music literature.

He was encouraged and assisted in these efforts by the soprano Eva Gauthier (who was also to play a role in Gershwin's career). Gauthier had sojourned extensively in the Orient, especially in Java and Japan, collecting examples of native folksongs. Griffes made instrumental settings of Japanese folksongs and, in 1919, set three Javanese texts to music. He also experimented with setting Chinese poems in a characteristic idiom and, in 1916, made a vocal setting of Rupert Brooke's poem "Wai Kiki" which suggested the Polynesian music of Hawaii. Gauthier was instrumental in introducing many of these works to the public. Griffes' interest in Asian music also influenced his most important composition for full orchestra, *The Pleasure-Dome of Kubla Khan,* composed between 1912 and 1917, inspired by Samuel Taylor Coleridge's poem.

Kubla Khan marks the beginning of the final period of Griffes' composition, the period in which he produced his masterpieces and worked himself into an early grave. Among these last works were the *Poem for Flute and Orchestra* (1919), the *Piano Sonata* (1918) and an incomplete set of *Five Pieces for Piano* which were published in 1967 as *Three Preludes.*

The entry of the United States into World War I altered the musical scene in the East Coast cities considerably. On January 22, 1918, a Boston patroness of the Boston Symphony Orchestra (BSO) sent a letter to the orchestra demanding the dismissal of its German conductor, Karl Muck, which led to Muck's eventual replacement by Pierre Monteux. The New York Philharmonic declared a moratorium on the performance of works by living German composers (which probably cost them little enough grief as the only living German composers taken at all seriously at the time were the controversial Richard Strauss and the plodding Max Reger). Percy Grainger (see Chapter 10) enlisted in the military and began giving concerts for the troops, along with many other prominent musicians of the time. A host of composers, publishers, performers and performance institutions jumped on the patriotic bandwagon and produced patriotic songs and concerts by the long ton. Although Griffes' earlier labor song, "These Things Shall Be," was published in the *National Song Book of the Soldiers and Sailors,* the fundamentally apolitical composer refused to participate in all the flag-waving and ballyhoo. Indeed, he seemed entirely indifferent to the war except as it posed a certain danger that he might be drafted. Communication with his many friends and correspondents in Germany, especially Konrad Wölcke, was virtually suspended, and Griffes grew more conservative in his associations.

But, beyond everything else, the reason for Griffes' seeming indifference to the world situation unfolding around him was the increasing intensity of his compositional efforts and the increasing depth of his musical conceptions. In July of 1917 he composed the ballet *Sho-Jo, or—the Spirit of Wine—A Symbol of Happiness* for his close friend, choreographer Adolph Bolm. The ballet was conceived as a vehicle for the Japanese dancer Michio Ito, then associated with Bolm. Although it remains unpublished today, *Sho-Jo* represented the final, distilled essence of Griffes' attempts to integrate non-Western music into his personal style. In a statement sent to the critic Frederick H. Martens, Griffes himself provided the key to understanding his treatment of Asian musics.

> It (*Sho-Jo*) is *developed* Japanese music—I purposely do not use the term "idealized." [Charles Wakefield] Cadman and others have taken American Indian themes and have "idealized" rather than "developed" them in Indian style. There is really nothing in them save themes; the harmonization, etc., might have come from Broadway. Modern music tends more and more toward the archaic, especially the archaism of the East. The ancient Greek modes, the pentatonic scales of China and Japan are much used, and there is little difference between the whole-tone and one of the Chinese scales. There is a striving for harmonies which suggest the quarter-tones of Oriental music, and the frequent employ of the characteristic augmented second, as well as of the organ point common to both systems. In the dissonance of modern music the Oriental is more at home than in the consonance of the classics. And all this I have borne in mind in the development of the *Sho-Jo* music.[10]

By modern standards of ethnomusicology the above reads as naive, but it is significant in terms of its historical period. Here Griffes showed himself to be firmly engaged in the kind of studies being pursued contemporaneously by Henry Cowell and Henry Eichheim, and later developed in the work of American composers from Lou Harrison, Harry Partch and Alan Hovhaness to La Monte Young and Steve Reich.

Perhaps as a way of "backing-off" from the intensity of his experiments with non-Western influences, Griffes turned to the composition of two abstract pieces in late 1917 and 1918. The first of these was his one-movement *Piano Sonata*, begun in December of 1917 and premiered by Griffes himself on February 26, 1918 at a concert devoted exclusively to his works, sponsored by the MacDowell Club in New York. All but one

---

[10]   Cited in Maisel, *Charles T. Griffes: The Life of an American Composer*, p. 205.

of the reviews of this important work were unfavorable, but the prominent Swiss pianist, Rudolph Ganz, gave a public interview shortly thereafter in which he praised the *Sonata* as being "free from all foreign influences," thus assisting in creating a more tolerant atmosphere for the work at subsequent reception.

The *Sonata* ranks as one of Griffes' most significant achievements in terms of pure composition. Its thematic development and harmonic design reach far beyond the "impressionistic" character of his earlier works and reap the benefits of the intellectual discipline engendered in composing his Asian pieces. It remains the most respected of his works among academic composers today.

The *Poem for Flute and Orchestra* resulted from a request for such a piece by Griffes' friend, flutist George Barrère, for performance in 1919. Griffes spent the summer of 1918 happily based in New York City and traveling around for visits and performances, when not working on the *Poem.* He was increasingly concerned about the likelihood of being drafted and took steps to insure that he could use his knowledge of German to get into the Army's corps of interpreters. He was on the verge of enlisting, certain that his call-up was imminent, when the Armistice was declared in November of that year.

Throughout 1919 Griffes worked incessantly on revisions of the *Poem,* the *Sonata* and *Kubla Khan.* He had also taken on the chore of preparing easy arrangements of popular songs for Schirmer in 1918, using the pen name "Arthur Tomlinson," and continued to sell these outright as a way to supplement his income from Hackley, which was still no greater than $1,700 per year. His royalties were insignificant, and supplemental work of this sort was essential to finance his growing travel commitments, hiring of copyists and other expenses. He continued producing songs of rare craftsmanship and beauty, especially the *Three Poems by Fiona Mac-Leod,* Op.11 of 1918.[11]

Griffes continued and expanded his visits, recitals and conferences with prominent musicians of the day and became acquainted with Sergei Prokofiev, Darius Milhaud, Artur Rubinstein, Harold Bauer, Walter Damrosch, Pierre Monteux, Leopold Stokowski and a large number of singers, instrumentalists, choreographers and others who championed his music. His press notices grew more frequent and more favorable, leading to the night of November 16, 1919, when the *Poem* was premiered by

---

[11] "Fiona MacLeod" was a pen name used by the Celtophile English poet William Sharp, who adopted the feminine pseudonym as an expression of the androgynous side of his consciousness. His work was a major influence on both Griffes and MacDowell, as well as many other early 20th-century English and American composers.

Barrère and the New York Symphony under Damrosch. The performance was an unmitigated triumph for Griffes, who was called back seven times by the enthusiastic audience. It was the first unconditional, major public success of his career. A mere twelve days later, on November 28, Monteux conducted *The Pleasure Dome of Kubla Khan* with the Boston Symphony Orchestra. Its success exceeded even that of the *Poem* in New York, and the reviews were unanimous in their approbation.

Griffes had finally achieved the unequivocal recognition of the East Coast musical establishment, and his major works, from that point on, made their way into the standard repertoire. But this recognition came at the eleventh hour for Griffes. He was already suffering from severe chest congestion and digestive problems, aggravated by the strain of overwork and the continued drudgery of his duties at Hackley. His physique had thinned noticeably; he coughed too much and deep lines had become etched in his face. In December 1919, he collapsed at Hackley and was taken to the headmaster's house to convalesce. What at first had seemed to be a bad cold or influenza grew worse. His mother was summoned to stay with him, and it was feared he had developed either pneumonia or tuberculosis. When his condition failed to improve he was removed, in the dead of winter, to the Loomis Sanatorium in the Catskills. His old friend Laura Elliott inundated him with Christian Science tracts and endless letters, which his mother and doctors took pains to divert. Still, he continued to decline and, in March, was transferred by train to New York Hospital. Emergency surgery was performed on April 5, to clear the infection from his lungs, but he died early on the morning of the 8th. The final diagnosis was empyema, or abscesses of the lungs, which no medical treatment available at the time would have been able to cure.

The musical world was shocked by Griffes' death. Many of his friends had not even known he was ill. Tributes and appreciations appeared in all the major publications, and the inevitable comparisons to the last days of Mozart and Schubert were circulated by many of the publishers and journalists who had been willing enough to ignore him during his lifetime.

The importance of Griffes' contribution to American classical music has been seriously underestimated by most historians. As recently as a decade ago, Charles Hamm devoted only an single sentence to him in *Music in the New World*.[12] Many other commentators have dismissed him, after superficial examination of a few select pieces, with the facile label of an "American Impressionist" despite the manifest differences between his work and that of Debussy or Ravel, and his own stated reservations about

---

[12] Hamm, p. 456.

the later style of Debussy. Much of what is known about Griffes today is due to the superlative biography—*Charles T. Griffes; The life of an American Composer*—by Edward Maisel, first published in 1943 and updated to coincide with the composer's centennial in 1984.

In fact, Griffes was one of the few composers of his generation who wrote substantive music in a highly original idiom which found its way into both print and performance during his lifetime and stayed there after his death. He was one of the pioneers in the effort to intergate non-Western musical ideas into Western symphonic, vocal and instrumental genres; and his work in this area is at least as impressive as that of Henry Cowell, though very different in purpose and effect. But, above all, while he laid the unacknowledged groundwork for a great many later composers, Griffes created and maintained an entirely personal voice in music. He neither led nor followed any stylistic "movement" or trend, and absolutely transcended the epidemic of derivativeness, whether from European or "Americanist" sources, that characterizes so much of the music of his contemporaries.

Much of Griffes' music has been rescued from oblivion through the determined efforts of Professor Donna K. Anderson, one of the leading contemporary Griffes scholars, editor of the bulk of his posthumously published music and author of a recent biography (*Charles T. Griffes: A Life in Music*) of the composer. Still, a significant amount of his music remains inaccessible to the general public, and we can only hope for the day when the works of this major American composer become fully available.

Apart from the preëminent figures of Ives, Farwell and Griffes, the other American composers of symphonic, chamber and operatic music born (approximately) between 1865 and 1890 can be divided loosely into two groups: (1) those who continued the conservative, Europhilic tradition of the Second New England School and (2) those who branched out into new directions, especially directions that sought a specifically "American" idiom. While some kept one foot in each camp, none of these lesser creative voices achieved a lasting impact on American music. But, like the composers of the Mannheim school in the 1750s, each contributed to the conditions that finally permitted the emergence of later masters, such as George Gershwin, Aaron Copland, Virgil Thomson, Roy Harris and others of the developed "Americanist" modes in the 1920s, 1930s and 1940s.

The most prominent and/or important among the minor composers of this period were John J. Becker (1886–1961), whose work was admired by Ives and to whom Ives donated the cash award from his Pulitzer Prize of 1947, the previously mentioned Marion Bauer (1887–1955), Ernest Bloch (1880–1959), Charles Wakefield Cadman (1881–1946), John Alden Carpenter (1876–1951), Henry Eichheim (1870–1942), Percy Grainger (1882–

1961), Charles Martin Loeffler (1861–1935), Daniel Gregory Mason (1873–1953), Leo Ornstein (b. 1895) Wallingford Riegger (1885–1961), Carl Ruggles (1876–1971) and Deems Taylor (1885–1966).[13] Still others included Felix Borowski (1872–1956), Frederick Converse (1871–1940), Harry Lawrence Freeman (1869–1954), Henry F. B. Gilbert (1868–1928), Rubin Goldmark (1872–1936), Louis Gruenberg (1884–1964), Henry K. Hadley (1871–1937), Edward Burlingame Hill (1872–1960), Edgar Stillman Kelley (1857–1944), Harvey Worthington Loomis (1865–1930), Arthur Nevin (1871–1943, younger brother of the songwriter Ethelbert Nevin), John Powell (1882–1963), Bernard Rogers (1893–1968), Carlos Salzedo (1885–1961), Bertram Shapleigh (1871–1940), Arthur Shepherd (1880–1958), David Stanley Smith (1877–1949) and Emerson Whithorne (1884–1958), as well as the first prominent American women composers after Amy Beach: Gena Branscombe (1881–1977), Mabel Wheeler Daniels (1878–1971), Ethel Glenn Hier (1889–1971), Mary Howe (1882–1964) and Mary Carr Moore (1873–1957). Within a scant sixty years of the time when Heinrich, Bristow and Fry had to fight for a hearing, native and immigrant American classical composers were proliferating throughout the country.

The composers who held to the conservative lines of the Boston Classicists included Goldmark, Kelley, Hadley, Mason, Smith, Hill and Shepherd. The more progressive element was reflected in the work of Becker, Bauer, Eichheim, Gilbert, Gruenberg, Ornstein and Whithorne. Composers like Cadman, Carpenter, Loeffler, Taylor and Converse maintained an eclectic posture, writing accessible music that occasionally incorporated some mildly experimental elements, usually in the orchestration.

The conservatives remained centered around New England, New York and the Ivy League colleges: Harvard, Yale, Princeton, Columbia, Dartmouth. **David Stanley Smith,** a prize pupil of Horatio Parker and teacher of Quincy Porter, assumed Parker's position at Yale in 1919 and continued the Parker tradition until his retirement in 1940. Among his list of works is a *Fête Gallante* (1920) for flute and orchestra, also premiered by Georges Barrère but far inferior to the Griffes *Poem,* and a *Sonatina* (1932) for junior string orchestra that reflected the growing concern among academic composers to provide substantive material for young instrumentalists (cf. Marion Bauer's *American Youth Concerto).* By contrast to Smith, Edward Burlingame Hill (who taught at Harvard and became Leonard Bernstein's composition teacher) was a lively composer in the mercurial spirit of his teacher, Chadwick. Hill had a wide variety of interests and produced symphonies, chamber music, two orchestral suites after the

---

[13]   The importance accorded to Bloch, Riegger and Ruggles today outshines that of the other names on this list, and they will be discussed in subsequent chapters.

poems of Robert Louis Stevenson and a tone poem on Poe's *The Fall of the House of Usher.* But he was also interested in early jazz and created a set of *Jazz Studies* for two pianos (1924–1935) that may have influenced Bernstein's later interest in that idiom as well.

Among the academics, the most interesting figure is perhaps **Frederick S. Converse,** taught at the New England Conservatory and Harvard. He holds the distinction of having been the first American composer to have had an opera produced at the Metropolitan Opera in New York (*The Pipe of Desire,* 1910) and created other symphonic and chamber music including two orchestral pieces on specifically American themes: *California* (1928) and *American Sketches* (1929). But his most important work is the orchestral suite *Flivver Ten Million* (1927), portraying various aspects of the introduction of the automobile into American life. Among the timbral devices he used in this piece were muted Ford automobile horns, factory whistles and anvils, placing him alongside Antheil, Varèse, Gershwin and a number of European composers in the effort to integrate "noise" elements (however ornamental) into symphonic music.

The most vociferous and, in his lifetime, the most influential of the conservatives was **Daniel Gregory Mason,** grandson of the same Lowell Mason who so thoroughly quashed the efforts of the singing-master composers from Billings onward. While Daniel Gregory Mason's music has faded into utter oblivion today, only forty years after his death, he is still remembered for his many books and polemics, which attempted to uphold the "cultivated" tradition in the face of new musical influences. Mason saw himself as the last standard-bearer of the white, Anglo-Saxon, upper-middle-class New England tradition against the onrush of black American, immigrant and other musics during the early part of the 20th century. His writings are overtly racist and anti-Semitic, and his music, modeled on the works of Brahms, Vincent d'Indy and the post-Romantic European composers is consistently dull. He not only railed against ragtime and jazz, but saw in the works of second generation Russian Jews (such as Gershwin, Copland, Louis Gruenberg, Leo Ornstein, Irving Berlin and Bernstein) the imminent downfall of the cultivated, Europhilic ideals inherited from his father, uncle and grandfather.

As MacDonald Moore has pointed out in a lucid study of this era,[14] Mason's attitudes were strangely allied with Ives' philosophical stance, despite the polar opposition of their musical styles. Both believed that the culture of New England was the fountainhead from which all things truly "American" flowed. But, where Ives had a deep affinity for the intellectual traditions of New England and its innate spiritual qualities, Mason stood

---

[14] *Yankee Blues.*

for the more superficial, and sometimes less admirable, social aspects of the northern Anglo-Saxon heritage. Because Mason lacked Ives' grasp of the inner substance of this heritage, he was far less tolerant of new ideas, new influences and new music. And he was far less adventurous in his own work.

Edgar Stillman Kelley and **Henry K. Hadley** were also among the more conservative composers of the time. Of the two, Kelley is the more impressive. He was one of the oldest composers (born in 1857) to be published by Farwell's Wa-Wan Press; he had a puckish penchant for tone poems on literary subjects. Among his best are *The Pit and the Pendulum* (after Poe), his *"Gulliver" Symphony,* and his *Alice in Wonderland* orchestral suite. The last of these was the first in a long series of American works portraying Lewis Carroll's unforgettable characters, a tradition which culminated in David Del Tredici's series of "Alice" orchestral works, one of which received the Pulitzer Prize in 1980 (see Chapter 12). Hadley, on the other hand, devoted as much of his time to conducting as to composing, but still managed to produce five symphonies, five operas, overtures, tone poems and other works mainly for orchestra. He founded the National Association for American Composers and Conductors, and served as its director until his death in September, 1937.

Still another conservative from this period, **Rubin Goldmark**, who had studied with the pianist Raphael Joseffy and Dvořák, taught privately in New York and numbered among his later pupils both Gershwin and Copland. His compositional work remains undistinguished, with the exception of a *Requiem* inspired by Lincoln's Gettysburg Address, which may have had an influence on Copland's later orchestral narrative, *A Lincoln Portrait.*

Among the more progressive composers during the first thirty years of the 20th century, John J. Becker stands out conspicuously. Unlike many of his contemporaries who were born in the central part of the country and later moved to the Eastern seaboard to pursue their careers, Becker remained a Midwesterner all his life. Aesthetically he belonged to the camp of Charles Ives and Carl Ruggles (see Chapter 10), and, considering the attention that has been devoted to those composers in recent years, it is remarkably strange that Becker remains such an obscure figure today. He studied at the Wisconsin Conservatory and in Berlin, then returned to the United States where he became music director at the University of Notre Dame in Indiana and later at the College of St. Scholastica and Barat College of the Sacred Heart in Illinois. Unlike Ives and Ruggles, Becker worked largely within conventional forms, and had a special interest in religious music and early Baroque polyphony. Yet he remained an uncompromising modernist in his personal compositional style and incorporated innovative

John J. Becker *(1886–1961). Ives admired Becker's music so much that he gave him the cash award from his 1947 Pulitzer Prize. A composer whose works merit revival.* (Photo from the collection of Don Gillespie, courtesy of C.F. Peters Corp.)

percussion effects into his *Third Symphony* (1929) and dance piece *Obongo* (1933) at the same time that Cowell, Partch, Varèse and Cage were engaged in similar studies. Perhaps Becker's current obscurity is attributable in part to the small quantity of his music that has been published to date, or to his having divided his time between composition and academic work. Of the "Credo" from one of Becker's masses Charles Ives said, "It is one of the finest, high-moving, stirring pieces of music of its kind I have ever heard. It is the expression of a big man with something great to say and not afraid to say it."[15] If for no other reason than the above comment, Becker's work clearly mandates revival and rehearing by modern audiences.

While an important figure in the history of this period and an important example for American women composers, **Marion Bauer** was only perceived as a progressive until about 1935. Her style leans heavily toward impressionism, even more so than that of her friend and colleague, Charles

---

[15]   Cited by J. T. Howard in *Our Contemporary Composers*, p. 183.

Griffes. But, unlike Griffes, she did not undergo substantial evolution during her later years, when impressionism had ceased to be considered innovative. While certain of her works have attracted considerable attention such as the *Viola Sonata,* the *Dance Sonata for Piano, Sun Splendor* (for orchestra), her incidental music to *Prometheus Bound* and her *American Youth Concerto,* the principal part of her legacy for American classical music may lie in three important books she wrote in her advocacy and assistance to other composers of the time, including Griffes and Copland. The books are *How Music Grew* (1925) and *Music Through the Ages* (1932) (both co-authored with Ethel Peyser), and the landmark *20th Century Music,* one of the first serious histories of modern music published during the 1930s. In addition, she managed the (New York) League of Composers' "Young Composers' Concerts" for many years, introducing works by Copland, Antheil, Křenek, Bernard Rogers and others to the public.

The work of **Leo Ornstein** parallels that of Marion Bauer in certain respects. Like her, he was a friend and promoter of Griffes' music between ca. 1914–1920, and was a prominent figure in the New York scene. Ornstein was a gifted pianist whose experiments with tone-clusters and exotic devices resemble those of Henry Cowell from the same general period. But, like Bauer, he also became more conservative in later years, eventually retiring into the teaching of piano in Philadelphia, at the expense of his composition. His works include *The Wild Man's Dance* and *À la Chinoise* for piano, a *Piano Concerto* (1923), chamber music, instrumental sonatas and the *Noctourne and Dance of the Fates* for orchestra (1936).

Louis Gruenberg and **Emerson Whithorne** were also important figures among the lesser-known progressive composers during the early part of the century. Gruenberg was an electric experimenter whose teachers included Busoni. He was particularly interested in attempting to free American jazz from the formal rigidities of the time, and to integrate it into symphonic works. Ideologically he asserted the primacy of melody in music, but his actual compositions often fell short of his ideals in this regard. Although he wrote symphonies, piano concertos and chamber music, he is best remembered for his operas: *The Emperor Jones* (after Eugene O'Neill, 1933), *Jack in the Beanstalk* (libretto by John Erskine, 1931) and *Green Mansions* (after the novel by W. H. Hudson, 1937). He also composed a *Jazz Suite* for orchestra, *The Daniel Jazz* for voice and instruments, and a setting of James Weldon Johnson's classic sermon in verse, *The Creation,* also for voice and chamber ensemble.

Emerson Whithorne, by contrast, resisted the "jazz" label even though his works are characterized by consistent use of highly syncopated rhythms. Having studied with James H. Rogers in his native Cleveland, Ohio, Whithorne went to Europe for further studies with Leschetizky and

Robert Fuchs, then spent several years in London as critic for the *Pall Mall Gazette* (1907–1915). Returning to the United States after the outbreak of World War I, he attracted attention with his orchestral suite *New York Days and Nights,* then went on to compose a *Poem* for piano and orchestra (premiered by Walter Gieseking and the Chicago Symphony in 1927) and numerous orchestral tone poems, including: *The Dream Pedlar* (1931), *Moon Trail* (1933) and *Fata Morgana.* In addition he produced symphonies, chamber music and songs on poems of the African-American poet Countee Cullen. He also participated in the move to incorporate Asian music with his incidental music for the play *Marco's Millions,* in which he made a serious effort to utilize Chinese themes and to reproduce the sound of Chinese instruments with the conventional orchestra.

However, despite the efforts of Griffes, Cowell, Whithorne and others to use Asian materials in their music, the label of pioneer clearly belongs to **Henry Eichheim.** Born in Chicago in 1870, Eichheim started out as a professional orchestral violinist. It was only after he retired from the Boston Symphony in 1912 that he turned his full attention to composition. He made five trips to Southeast Asia in 1915, 1919, 1922, 1927 and the mid-1930s. Here he was free to indulge the interest in Asian musics that had occupied him since around 1905. The first tangible results of his studies came with his *Oriental Impressions* of 1918–1922. Scored originally for piano, these were later adapted for chamber ensemble and then for full orchestra. By 1924, *Oriental Impressions* had been performed by major orchestras in Philadelphia, New York, Paris, Washington and Denver. In 1923 Eichheim moved to Montecito, California. He became a close friend of Leopold Stokowski, who conducted many of his works and traveled with him to Bali in 1928.

Among Eichheim's later works were the orchestral pieces *Java* (1929) and *Bali* (1933), in which he used native gamelan instruments together with the standard orchestra. He also collected many Asian instruments, which were given to the University of California, Santa Barbara after his death in 1942.

Eichheim was the first American composer actually to travel to the Far East and make a systematic study of the techniques and instruments later incorporated into his works. Before him, all such interpolations and efforts, including those of Griffes, were derived from second-hand sources. He set the standard for all subsequent efforts to integrate Eastern and Western musics by American composers, and foreshadowed the later work of Hovhaness, Harrison, Reich and others.

If all the other composers of the time danced around Dvořák's advice to look to the African-American folk culture for inspiration, at least one took him literally. This was **Henry F. B. Gilbert,** quoted at the beginning of this chapter. Gilbert was the first to use authentic Negro spirituals and ragtime in concert orchestral works. He had also been the first American student of MacDowell after the latter's return to the United States in 1888, and his music was published by the Wa-Wan Press. Gilbert had been born in Somerville, Massachusetts, adjacent to Boston, in 1868 and was closely associated with the New England Conservatory and Harvard. By rights he should have been one of the later members of the Second New England School. But his sympathies lay elsewhere. He had a catholic interest in music of all kinds, and, as a young man, supported himself with odd jobs in order to be free of the academic establishment. Although a skillful orchestrator and adventurous harmonist, Gilbert's conceptions of both African-American life and music were naive, and his works reflect a sometimes stereotypical vision. Nevertheless, he represents the first serious outreach from the white musical establishment to black American idioms, and his work is pioneering in that respect. Among his better-known compositions are the *Comedy Overture on Negro Themes* (1911), the *Negro Rhapsody* (1913) and the *Dance in Place Congo* (1918), which harks back to Gottschalk's use of the "bamboula" in his piano pieces of the 1850s. In many respects, Gilbert represents a bridge between the early Romanticism of Gottschalk and the later adaptation of African-Americanisms and Caribbean music by Gershwin.

The composers who were considered to be the "great" American moderns in the 1920s and 1930s, at least as far as general audiences were concerned, did not include Ives, Farwell or Griffes. Nor did the list include conservatives like Mason or innovators like Eichheim. The really "great" composers, in the minds of their countrymen, were the middle-of-the-road creators of light, accessible, often humorous works for the stage or concert hall. Principal among these were Charles Wakefield Cadman, John Alden Carpenter and Deems Taylor, with the French-born Charles Martin Loeffler adding a bit of esoteric spice to the pantheon.

Loeffler, the eldest of the group, was also the most serious. He was an orchestral violinist of considerable skill and reputation, raised in Europe and saturated with the post-Romantic idiom, especially the mystical music of Alexander Scriabin. His music is very impressionistic and never achieves any spirit that is peculiarly American. After his retirement from playing he became a reclusive mystic, ensconced on his farm in Medfield, Massachusetts, preoccupied with Celtic studies and occult subjects. Although historian David Ewen attached extraordinary importance to Loeffler's work, his music has largely faded from public attention today. His most notable works were the *Pagan Poem* for orchestra, the *Hora Mystica* (1916), and the *Canticum Fratris Solis,* based on the writings of St. Francis.

John Alden Carpenter was the oldest, and probably the best, of the three native-born Americans on the list of public musical giants at the time. Born in Park Ridge, Illinois, in 1876, Carpenter was the son of a wealthy industrialist and traced his ancestry back to his famous Pilgrim namesake. He studied with Paine at Harvard and took his degree in 1897. Like Ives, he then went into business, in this case the family shipping firm. He later traveled to England for a brief period of study with Elgar in 1906.

Carpenter also kept his compositional efforts going while functioning as an executive during the day, but, unlike Ives, he wrote in a highly accessible idiom and enjoyed many performances of his works during his creative years. An early *Violin Sonata* (1911), was followed by his first major success, *Adventures in a Perambulator* (1914), an orchestral suite that humorously portrayed a child's-eye view of the world. The music was ingratiating and pleasant, and it achieved an instant success. Ives, of course, living at the time in frustrated obscurity in New York and Redding, was galled by the public reception afforded Carpenter's work and would later refer specifically to *Perambulator* in one of his invectives.

John Alden Carpenter *(1876–1951). Born in the year of Custer's defeat at Little Big Horn, he became a success-ful businessman (like Ives) and was a much better known composer during his lifetime. His jazzy ballet scores influenced Gershwin and are still occasionally played today.* (Photo courtesy of ASCAP.)

In 1915 Carpenter composed his *Concertino* for piano and orchestra and began to show an interest in using elements of the popular music of Tin Pan Alley current at the time. Becoming acquainted with the same choreographer, Adolph Bolm, who had been the motive force behind Griffes' ballet *Sho-Jo,* Carpenter created the musical pantomime *Krazy Kat,* based on a popular comic strip of the day, for Bolm in 1921. *Krazy Kat* was an instant success, due in no small measure to its brilliant orchestration, with which Gershwin no doubt familiarized himself before writing his *Concerto in F* or *An American in Paris.* The success of *Krazy Kat* led Ballet-Russe impresario Serge Diaghilev to ask for an American ballet from Carpenter, to be produced at Monte Carlo. For this Carpenter wrote *Skyscrapers* (1923–1924), but Diaghilev's production never materialized, so the second ballet received its premiere at the Metropolitan Opera in February 1926. From this point on Carpenter's reputation was made and has not yet entirely disappeared, although performances of his work are very rare today. He went on to compose two symphonies, a violin concerto, many songs, and tone poems including *Patterns* (1932), *Sea Drift* (1933), *Danza* (1937) and *The Anxious Bugler* (1943). Carpenter died in Chicago on April 26, 1951.

As referenced in the quotation from Griffes above, **Charles Wakefield Cadman** wrote primarily "idealized" versions of American Indian music throughout his life. His style was conservative and his ideas competent, but limited. Most of his studies were private, with prominent musicians of the day, and he became a professional accompanist and conductor early in his career. In 1909 Cadman developed an interest in Indian music and spent the summer collecting source materials on the Omaha and Winnebago reservations. Earlier that year he had produced four arrangements of Indian songs, from which the tune "From the Land of Sky-Blue Water" became and instant and enormous success. He also produced the non-Indian potboiler "At Dawning," which remained a bourgeois Romantic favorite for many years.

For several years Cadman toured with a series of lecture-performances on American Indian music, finally settling in Los Angeles in 1916. He then devoted himself primarily to the composition of operas on Indian and other American subjects. The best-known of these were *Shanewis* (1918), *The Witch of Salem* (1926) and *The Garden of Mystery* (1925) based on Nathaniel Hawthorne's short story, "Rappaccini's Daughter." Though very famous in his lifetime, Cadman's work has fallen into even greater obscurity than Carpenter's since his death in 1946.

The youngest of the early 20th-century American musical moderates was **Deems Taylor,** born in New York in 1885. Taylor was an enormously energetic man of diverse talents who not only composed prolifically, but

Americanist **Charles Wakefield Cadman** *(1881–1946). Despite his having written songs in the "potboiler" tradition, he was a serious composer who explored Amerindian music and later turned to operas on American themes.* (Photo courtesy of ASCAP.)

wrote, edited and produced radio commentary on music throughout his life. He was a director of ASCAP, advisor to Walt Disney on the film *Fantasia,* an editor of *Musical America* and a member of many boards and committees involved with the musical world. It is likely that his public voice in musical matters had as much influence on the fame of his compositions as did any musical qualities they might have possessed, and their relatively quick demise after his death would seem to bear this out. Even during their heyday, Taylor's works met with consistently mixed reviews. He knew how to play to his audiences and gave them what they seemed to want. But the consensus of critical opinion was that his music was facile, derivative and too often shallower than the subjects he addressed.

Taylor the composer was principally known for two of his operas: *The King's Henchman* (1926) and *Peter Ibbetson* (1930). The first of these was the better of the two and remained in the repertoire of the Met for three seasons. The latter opera was much more poorly received and was the first in what has become a long history of second-rate works commissioned by the Met from American composers. It is unlikely that this has to do with any lack of gifted American composers, but rather has more to do with the

Met's criteria for commissioning and the conditions it places on the resulting work.

Taylor also composed choral settings of the poems *The Chambered Nautilus* and *The Highwayman,* as well as yet another "Alice" piece, the orchestral tone poem *Through the Looking Glass* (1919). He died in 1966.

The first two or three decades of the 20th century were a period of experimentation and creative ferment in American classical music. On the one hand, many talented composers devoted their creative lives to prolonging the death agonies of the Second New England School, while others engaged in the protracted, piecemeal search for a specifically American musical identity. Still others tried to do both. Little by little, the academic establishment gained a strength it had never known in the days of Mac-Dowell, Chadwick and Parker. But, as original creative effort in music became more and more respectable, it also became more stilted. None of the most powerful musical voices of the time maintained any serious, lifelong connection to academia, and none of the second generation of academic composers succeeded in establishing a lasting musical presence. As we will see in subsequent chapters, this phenomenon eventually became a pattern in all serious American music of this century.

The one characteristic shared by all American classical composers up to about 1920 was that they approached the problem of creating American classical music from the standpoint of musicians trained in conventional European musical concepts and techniques. This was as true of Ives and Griffes as it was of MacDowell and Chadwick, and would later be of Copland, Harris and Thomson. No matter how deeply they delved into the musical vernacular of our country, they did so through the tinted lenses of European musical reflexes.

The first composer to approach the issue of symphonic music from the native milieu of a popular tunesmith, and the first to achieve modern superstar status as result, was George Gershwin. It is to his unique synthesis that we turn in the next chapter.

5

George Gershwin's New Synthesis

❧

Of all the names in American classical music, none is more immediately recognized than that of George Gershwin. He is by far the best-known and most popular American composer who ever essayed symphonic works and operas. His approach to the problem of creating serious works was as unprecedented and unique as the music that resulted from it, and, while his public achievement has been approached by other composers since, it has never been duplicated. So great is the Gershwin name and legend today, it is difficult to remember that his entire life encompassed a mere thirty-nine years, and that there are still some people alive as of this writing who were born before him.

One factor, more than any other, distinguishes Gershwin from all the major American composers who preceded him: He was the first to approach classical music from the perspective of a popular songwriter. Had Stephen Foster attempted to write symphonic poems or concertos, Gershwin might have had an antecedent. As it is, Gershwin was the first of his kind. The popular tunes of Broadway and Tin Pan Alley were the music he was weaned on, despite a lifelong habit of intermittent private study with traditional teachers. These songs comprised his native musical language, the baseline and frame of reference from which he attacked all compositional projects. And while composers such as MacDowell, Ives, Griffes and Farwell certainly were exposed in their youth to American folk and vernacular music, none of them was, like Gershwin, a seasoned professional popular songwriter before attempting his first serious works. Nor is it likely that any of these earlier composers could have contemplated a career as a Tin Pan Alley tunesmith without major psychological adjustments and a sense of acute self-consciousness. Gershwin, on the other hand, was not only unashamed of his popular music origins, but considered his popular song writing to be an equal or greater expression of his creativity than his symphonic works. And he continued producing the enormously popular show tunes and scores that make up the vast majority of his work right up until the year of his death.

It has often been asserted that Gershwin achieved his unique synthesis by combining jazz with symphonic forms and styles. This is a superficial and problematical analysis, demonstrated by the fact that neither classical musicians nor jazz musicians are entirely comfortable with the inclusion of Gershwin in their ranks. From the classical side, the problem arises mainly from the manifest deficiencies in Gershwin's formal technique as a "serious" composer, at least when judged by the criteria of European classical music. On the popular side, much of the difficulty stems from the differing definitions of the word "jazz" that have been used over the years. Jazz is not a single style, but rather a stylistic idiom that has undergone significant evolution from the early days of ragtime to the present. Gershwin's use of jazz, per se, can only be discussed intelligently in the context of those specific musical features that defined jazz in his own time (i.e., before 1935).

But, understanding Gershwin's music requires an even deeper search into other branches of the American musical tree, including the music of the Yiddish theatre in turn-of-the-century New York, the music of vaudeville, the piano music of Scott Joplin and other ragtime giants, music of the Gullah people from the islands off the coast of South Carolina, Latin American (especially Cuban) music, the Anglo-American art songs of the 1890s, the early Tin Pan Alley hits of Irving Berlin and Jerome Kern, the operetta style of Friml, Romberg and Herbert, as well as the post-Romantic and impressionist music of European composers such as Ravel, Prokofiev, Schoenberg and Stravinsky. All of these played a role in the formation and development of Gershwin's concert music style.

Before going into the specifics of Gershwin's life and work, it may be helpful to have some background on the American social and musical context of the years surrounding World War I. After the great period of European immigration which started in the 1870s, ethnicity became an issue in American life to a degree unprecedented in our history. Throughout the 19th century the principal ethnic groups in the United States had been white Anglo-Saxons (or Anglo-Celts), African Americans, American Indians, Irish, Germans, French Canadians in the northeast, Creoles in the Gulf Coast, Mexicans in the southwest and Asians in the Far West. By 1900, the major Eastern cities were teeming with a new flood of Russians, Poles, Italians, Portuguese, Greeks, Scandinavians, Hungarians and other national groups.

A high percentage of these immigrants were Jews. Jews had been systematically persecuted by most European societies (especially those of eastern Europe) for centuries and possessed, therefore, an even greater stake in the opportunities for religious toleration offered by the New World than had other immigrants who suffered merely economic privations at home. Moreover, as the more intelligent, enterprising, creative and vocal elements of any population have historically formed the most obvious targets for political persecution at home, it is possible that this group formed a large proportion of the new immigrants. Elliott Carter, among others, has speculated that this may account in part for the extraordinarily practical, entrepreneurial spirit for which Americans have been famous over the years.[16]

At the turn of the century the ethnic groups of this newly industrialized "melting pot" had coalesced into their own urban neighborhoods, preserving the language, culture and traditions of their homelands. Each had its own folklore and musical traditions as well, which continued to be celebrated within these ethnic enclaves without, however, becoming integrated into the more generalized American folklore and folk music established after the Civil War. Perhaps because Jewish (or more precisely, Yiddish) culture was in a sense *pan-national,* cutting across purely geographical categories of European origin, its folklore and music gained a foothold in New York that smaller ethnic groups were not able to achieve. Thus, the Yiddish theatre became one of the most important artistic institutions in the city at that time, supported by thousands of enthusiastic patrons. And the Yiddish theatre, together with the pre-existing tradition of American stage minstrelsy, became the fountainhead from which sprang both vaudeville and Tin Pan Alley.

Starting around 1913, American music as a whole began to divide into the multiplicity of styles, genres and factions that continue today, each with its own creative figures, star performers, promotional institutions and devoted audiences. Initially, these divisions were not merely a matter of differing esthetic tastes, but were very specifically keyed to racial, ethnic and economic class divisions in American society of the time. One has merely to list the great names in American classical music, versus the great names in jazz, versus the great names in American musical theatre to see these divisions vividly displayed. Almost all our great classical composers have been white males of Anglo-Saxon, Russian-Jewish or other European extraction. Almost all the great jazz composers have been African Americans. And almost all the great names in American musical theatre, at least prior to 1940, were ethnic Jews. Unlike any of his predecessors, and in direct contradiction to the attitudes of composers like Ives or Daniel Gregory Mason, Gershwin partook of all three traditions, partly as a result of his

---

[16]   Allen Edwards, *loc. cit* pp. 15–17.

birth heritage and partly by conscious choice, while refusing to become exclusively identified with any one of them.

Gershwin was born Jacob Gershvin, second son of Rose and Morris Gershvin (né Gershovitz) at 242 Snediker Avenue, Brooklyn, New York on September 26, 1898. His parents had both emigrated from Russia in the early 1890s and were married in New York in 1895. George's elder brother (and future lyricist) Ira, had been born two years earlier.

Like many immigrants from non-English-speaking countries, Morris Gershovitz had probably had his name involuntarily changed to Gershvin by an immigration official upon arrival, and he simply kept the new spelling. It was George himself who later changed the spelling to "Gershwin," and the family followed suit. Similarly, although the family had given Hebrew first names to all their children, each was known by an American name at home, thus "Jacob" became "George." There were also two younger siblings, a brother, Arthur, and sister, Frances.

Many romantic tales have been told of the Gershwin family's poverty during George and Ira's childhood. In fact the Gershwins were of respectable, middle-class merchant stock and, although Morris engaged in a variety of entrepreneurial ventures, the children were reasonably well provided for. George was neither a "latch-key kid" nor a street urchin, but, like many children in the city, got around on his own and spent a great deal of time on the street playing with friends, visiting arcades and nickelodeons and indulging in other urban childhood pursuits. Although the family moved several times during the boys' childhood, George and Ira grew up principally in the predominantly Jewish Lower East Side of Manhattan.

While Ira was the shy, bookish type, young George was an active and headstrong boy who reveled in physical activity. Prior to 1910 he had displayed some curiosity about music by attempting to reproduce tunes by ear on a friend's piano. In that year, the Gershwins acquired a piano of their own with the intention of giving Ira music lessons. But it was George who took over the instrument and made it his own. After two years of trying out various teachers, the young Gershwin was finally introduced to Charles Hambitzer by a pianist friend. Hambitzer became Gershwin's first serious teacher, and was one of his most important musical mentors until his death in 1918. Under Hambitzer's influence, George acquired a more solid grounding in conventional piano technique and acquired a passing acquaintance with the works of the great European masters (including Debussy and Ravel). Hambitzer was a gifted musician who had received rigorous training as both a composer and pianist, and inflamed his young protégé with his own passion for music of all kinds. He encouraged Gershwin to attend orchestral concerts, after which the teenager would go home and attempt to reproduce what he had heard at the keyboard.

In 1913, Gershwin had progressed sufficiently to land a job as a pianist at a summer resort in the Catskills. His salary was $5.00 per week. His predilection for the embryonic style then coming to be known as jazz, and for popular songs, was already evident, and he was trying his hand at composing songs of his own. He had developed a passion for the songs of Irving Berlin, especially "Alexander's Ragtime Band," which had swept the nation that year and signaled the death knell of the authentic ragtime pioneered by Joplin. Berlin was ten years Gershwin's senior (although he outlived him by 52 years). Despite the manifest inferiority of his songwriting, when compared to Gershwin's, Berlin remained one of Gershwin's idols and closest colleagues throughout the latter's life.

In 1914, young Gershwin dropped out of high school and became a professional "piano pounder" at the publishing firm of Jerome H. Remick on West 28th Street. At that time the entire length of 28th Street between Broadway and Fifth Avenue was lined with music publishing houses specializing in popular songs. It became known as Tin Pan Alley.

The role of individual sheet music editions of popular songs then was analogous to the role of recordings today in determining the success of any given tune. Because sound recording technology was still in its infancy, most American homes lacked even the primitive gramophone then available. Radio had not yet been adapted to commercial music broadcasts on any mass scale. Amateur music-making was still largely a matter of buying sheet music and hammering it out on the upright piano that graced most middle-class parlors. Thus, sheet music sales were tracked in the tens of thousands, and, in the case of exceptional hits, in the millions—equivalent to a modern recording "going gold." The job of selling as many copies of his employer's product as humanly possible fell to the "song plugger" and the "piano pounder."

A variety of tactics were employed in service of this objective. Young Gershwin spent most of his time at the fundamental task of sitting in a piano cubicle at Remick's, playing any Remick song upon request for any passing patron who happened to ask for it or accompanying staff pluggers who sang it for the patron. More experienced pluggers and pounders also attended theatrical and music hall performances to arouse enthusiasm among the audience for given songs, buttonholed singers anywhere and everywhere to push a certain tune, and even resorted to outright bribery.

Apart from the firsthand knowledge of the commercial ins and outs of the music publishing industry that Gershwin's years at Remick gave him, the principal result in terms of his own musicianship was an enormous development in his capacities as a keyboard improviser and transposer. He was regularly called upon to play any song in any key the customer might want, to adapt to all the vagaries of amateur singers attempting to render the song at sight and somehow to convey the essence of the tune, despite his limited music-reading skills. Undoubtedly his Tin Pan Alley apprenticeship equipped Gershwin with the tremendous keyboard facility that was his trademark, and to some extent his curse. To the end of his life, Gershwin could sit for hours and improvise on his own and others' tunes, usually developing new rhythmic aspects and novel harmonic combinations in the process. He did this in private for his own amusement, at parties and during the process of evolving his compositions in both serious and popular media. He was a composer chained to the piano; his very musical thinking was instinctively and inescapably pianistic. And, perhaps more significantly, that pianistic musical thought was relentlessly improvisatory. The result was that he never fully developed the capacity to master long-range formal considerations in extended pieces. When he ran out of ways to vary a given idea, he was all too-prone simply to abandon it and take up a different one.

During his years at Remick, Gershwin also began to develop his highly individualized style of shaping melodic and rhythmic ideas. He became acquainted with a diverse array of Broadway figures, including the young Fred Astaire, journalist Max Abramson, lyricist Irving Caesar and songwriters Jerome Kern and Berlin. These individuals, as well as his fellow song pluggers, were impressed with the originality and inventiveness of Gershwin's improvising. David Ewen quotes Gershwin's colleague at the time, Harry Ruby, as saying: "Sometimes when he spoke of the artistic mission of popular music, we thought he was going highfalutin . . . (his piano playing) was far and beyond better than the piano playing of any of us . . . and we did not completely understand it at the time."[17]

Kern, who later composed the musical *Showboat,* which included his most famous song "Old Man River," seems to have been a particular model for Gershwin at the time. Gershwin later said of his attachment to Kern's music, "I followed Kern's work and studied each song he composed. I paid him the tribute of frank imitation, and many things I wrote at this period sounded as though Kern had written them himself."[18]

In 1916, Tin Pan Alley publisher Harry von Tilzer issued the first song on which Gershwin's name appeared as composer, although not the first song Gershwin had written. This was "When You Want 'Em You Can't Get 'Em," with lyrics by Murray Roth. The legendary vaudeville singer Sophie Tucker admired this song and was instrumental in persuading von Tilzer to publish it. She continued to be an advocate of Gershwin's music for many years.

---

[17] Ewen, *George Gershwin, his journey to greatness,* p. 26.
[18] *Ibid* p. 29.

But, the more important early piece by Gershwin to emerge in 1916 was his piano rag *Rialto Ripples* (written in collaboration with one Will Donaldson and published by Remick in 1917). *Rialto Ripples* demonstrates an absolute mastery of the ragtime idiom as inherited from Joplin et al. Assuming that the bulk of the piece is Gershwin's own conception, it represents a remarkable and atypical product from the future composer of *Rhapsody in Blue*. Later popularized by the comedian Ernie Kovacs as the theme song of his early 1960s television show, *Rialto Ripples* remains one of the most novel instrumental pieces to emerge from Gershwin's pen and contains the germinal motif of the composer's third *Piano Prelude,* written some ten years later.

Gershwin—like many pianists of the day including Griffes, Joplin and many of the great names in European classical music—also began to record piano rolls in 1916. Unlike the recordings of his "high brow" contemporaries, however, Gershwin's rolls were mainly of other people's music, made for hire. A player piano roll is made of punched paper scrolls, which can be played back by the specially designed mechanism of the instrument. This was the nearest thing to mass-produced, commercially recorded music available in the home prior to the improved phonographs which began to appear in the 1920s. Gershwin recorded rolls for the Perfection and Universal labels, using both his own name and pseudonyms such as Bert Wynn, Fred Murtha and James Baker.

In 1915 Gershwin had begun theory lessons with violinist-composer Edward Kilyeni, at the instigation of his piano teacher Hambitzer. He continued to study intermittently with Kilyeni for about the next five years, and the Hungarian-born composer remained a close friend and mentor throughout Gershwin's life. While Hambitzer and Kilyeni were Gershwin's most important teachers, at various times Gershwin also took lessons from a number of prominent composers, including Rubin Goldmark, Henry Cowell and Wallingford Riegger. There is also evidence that Gershwin, in later life, approached both Maurice Ravel and Arnold Schoenberg for private instruction. But, while both composers professed to be admirers of Gershwin's mature works, neither would accept him as a pupil.

Gershwin seems to have had an obsession with the ongoing study of classical forms and techniques. But his biographers disagree radically over his seriousness as a music student. Those, like David Ewen, who seem anxious to avoid portraying Gershwin in any but the most favorable light, insist that he was a diligent student who devoted long hours to passionate study of harmony, counterpoint, form and orchestration. More critical observers, such as Charles Schwartz, point to the rather rudimentary and careless exercises in Gershwin's extant sketch books and his propensity to flit from teacher to teacher as evidence of a less than scholarly attitude, suggesting that Gershwin was more interested in enhancing his musical prestige through *association* with great teachers, rather than actually doing the work they would have demanded. The bulk of the evidence seems to favor the latter view.

A particularly telling episode concerns Gershwin's *Lullaby* for string quartet. This 1919 single-movement composition (first published in 1968) was reportedly submitted to Goldmark in 1923 to satisfy a composition assignment Gershwin had failed to complete on time. When Goldmark praised the piece, claiming that Gershwin was already showing improvement as a result of his lessons, Gershwin decided it was not worth studying with a man who could be so easily fooled. Both the shabbiness of the hoax and the unjustifiable conclusion Gershwin drew from it demonstrate something less than the attitude of a serious music student.[19]

By early 1917, Gershwin felt he had gained everything he could from working at Remick and set his sights on the career of a Broadway composer. The musical life of Broadway at that time was a very mixed bag of music hall extravaganzas (collectively known as "vaudeville"), operettas in the Viennese mold of Strauss and Lehar, and early musical comedies with pretensions to plot. The great names of the time included producer Florenz Ziegfeld, actor-songwriter-producer George M. Cohan, operetta composers such as Victor Herbert, Rudolph Friml and Sigmund Romberg, playwrights P. G. Wodehouse and Guy Bolton, and star performers such as Sophie Tucker, Al Jolson, Eddie Cantor, Fannie Brice, W. C. Fields, Fred and Adele Astaire, Irene Castle, Marion Davies, Groucho Marx and the comedy team of George Burns and Gracie Allen.

In addition to his prior exposure to the Broadway milieu, Gershwin had become extremely interested in the Yiddish theatre music of Joseph Rumshinsky and Abraham Goldfaden between 1913 and 1915. The Gershwins were not a particularly religious family, nor were they exceptionally attached to their ethnic Jewish roots, so it appears that Gershwin's interest had more to do with the potential commercial gains offered by the then-thriving Yiddish musical comedy and drama. An abortive attempt was launched for the young Gershwin to collaborate on a score with Sholom Secunda, later to become a major composer in this idiom, but the project went nowhere. However, Schwartz has pointed out that certain aspects of Gershwin's later music, both for Broadway and the concert stage, bear a close resemblance to features found in the music of Goldfaden and others. Particularly, Gershwin's penchant for melodic use of slowly tremulated major or minor thirds seems to derive from melodic traits common in

[19] Schwartz, *Gershwin: His Life and Music*, pp. 55–56.

Yiddish theatre (and possibly cantorial) music. This interval plays a prominent role in many of Gershwin's best-known melodies, such as the songs "Funny Face" and "'S Wonderful," the famous second *Piano Prelude,* the slow movement of the *Concerto in F,* and both "Summertime" and "It Ain't Necessarily So" from *Porgy and Bess.* And there are other examples of such "Jewishisms" to be found as well.[20]

Furthermore, there are a number of superficial resemblances between the melodic procedures of ethnic Jewish music and African-American blues, notably the ambiguity of the major and minor thirds mentioned and the potential thus presented for microtonal "bending" of this important coloristic tone of the scale. Such features, plus the predilection for Old Testament texts found in African-American Christian culture,[21] probably eased the way for many cultural associations between American blacks and immigrant Jews.

Equipped with this background, Gershwin set out to make his mark on Broadway. Initially he found a job as pianist at Fox's City Theater on 14th Street, but was hindered by his poorly developed ability to read music at sight. Next he was hired as a rehearsal pianist for the musical *Miss 1917,* with book by Wodehouse and Bolton, music by Kern and Herbert and choreography by the selfsame Adolph Bolm who figures prominently in the careers of Griffes and Carpenter. Apparently Gershwin's reading had improved, because Kern then hired him as rehearsal pianist for his 1918 musical *Rock-a-bye Baby.* Later in 1918, Irving Berlin (who was a virtual musical illiterate) offered young Gershwin a job as his musical secretary, which the latter respectfully declined. He also landed a job as rehearsal pianist for the *Ziegfeld Follies of 1918.*

In February of 1918, Gershwin was introduced to Max Dreyfus, the influential head of the publishing house of T. B. Harms. Dreyfus hired him as a staff songwriter, and Gershwin produced "Some Wonderful Sort of Someone," which Dreyfus published in September of that year. This marked the beginning of a decade-long relationship between Gershwin and the Harms publishing firm. Harms would remain his exclusive publisher throughout the period when he produced *Rhapsody in Blue,* the *Concerto in F* and the *Three Piano Preludes.*

"Some Wonderful Sort of Someone" was incorporated into the 1918 musical *Ladies First* by its star, Nora Bayes. When the show later went on a six-week road tour, another early Gershwin number, "The Real American

---

[20] Schwartz, op. cit., pps. 24–29, 322–325.
[21] This identification was probably as a result of antebellum slaves, after adopting Christianity, having identified with the ancient Hebrews of the period of Egyptian captivity. It is reflected in the texts of such spirituals as "Go Down Moses" and "Joshua Fit the Battle of Jericho."

Folk Song," was added to it. The significance of "The Real American Folk Song" lies in the fact that it was the first time lyrics written by George's elder brother, Ira Gershwin, appeared in a professional production. Increasingly thereafter, Ira became his brother's principal lyricist, and the two Gershwins gradually evolved into the most formidable American songwriting team of the early 20th century.

In 1919 Gershwin got his first big break when he was commissioned by Alex Aarons to write the music for the Broadway show *La, La, Lucille*. This successful musical, the first for which Gershwin composed the entire score himself, ran for more than one hundred performances during the summer of that year. During the run of *La, La, Lucille*, Gershwin and lyricist Irving Caesar had also come up with the now-famous song "Swanee," lifting both the reference to this relatively minor river and the initial harmonic sequence of the song from Stephen Foster's "Old Folks at Home." Charles Previn, late uncle of composer-conductor André Previn and premiere conductor of *La, La, Lucille*, introduced Gershwin to singer Al Jolson in Atlantic City, and Jolson became so enamored of the song that he began to program it regularly (according to Ewen, without the usual demand for "payola" and a share of the publication royalties[22]). Within a year, Jolson's rendition of "Swanee" had sold more than two million records and one million copies of sheet music, placing Gershwin's name "on the map" of famous young songwriters of the day.

After *La, La, Lucille*, the increasingly well-known Gershwin approached dancer-producer George White about writing the music for White's *Scandals of 1920*. White, who had at one time appeared in an obscure musical by the young Deems Taylor entitled *The Echo* (1910) and worked with Gershwin in *Miss 1917*, was attempting at that time to establish his *Scandals* as competition to the *Ziegfeld Follies*. The *George White Scandals of 1920* was White's second original vaudeville production, and the collaboration with Gershwin proved so successful that the composer continued providing music annually for subsequent *Scandals* through 1924. Among the most famous Gershwin songs to emerge from these productions were "Stairway to Paradise" (1922) and "Somebody Loves Me" (1924). Another significant aspect of Gershwin's professional collaboration with White was his first attempt at writing a "jazz" opera. At first entitled *Blue Monday*, and later renamed *135th Street* (by Paul Whiteman for a 1925 concert production), the opera was a dismal failure when first presented in the 1922 *Scandals*. To describe *Blue Monday* as an "opera" was stretching the label to the breaking point. What Gershwin actually created was a series of popular songs, including a reuse of the theme from his earlier *Lullaby*

---

[22] Ewen, *op. cit.*, p. 57.

for string quartet, connected by jazzlike recitatives. The issue of recitatives continued to plague Gershwin even into the creation of *Porgy and Bess* some ten years later.

Throughout the 1920s, the so called "jazz age," the white urban population of America seemed incapable of defining precisely what jazz was. The black musicians who were then creating the idiom had no such difficulty. This problem, namely of mainstream white culture keeping pace with the musical innovations of black American culture, persisted right up through the period of early rock and roll in the 1950s. It stemmed from the segregationist racism of the period.

The great black musicians of the time, such as W. C. Handy, Bessie Smith, Fletcher Henderson, Duke Ellington and Louis Armstrong, were permitted to perform for white audiences in white clubs, such as Harlem's famous Cotton Club, but were not allowed to enter as patrons of those same clubs even to hear their own music played. The real cutting edge of jazz composition was to be found in late-night jam sessions and performances in black venues to which the white populace had no access, in cities like New Orleans, New York, Chicago and Kansas City and in rural black clubs of the deep south. By the time any given innovation in jazz reached the more commercial venues and became familiar to white audiences, it was often already passé among the real jazzmen. Furthermore, such tunes were usually then "covered" by white bands, that is, rearranged for more conventional "big-band" instrumentation, watered down rhythmically and harmonically until they were more "commercial" (read, "palatable") for white audiences.

It was this diluted, commercial "jazz" that most white Americans associated with the label in the 1920s. This was the nearest thing to real jazz that bands like Paul Whiteman's ever played, and this was the only "jazz" to which Gershwin had any serious or systematic exposure. So, as Gershwin began to collect critical accolades during the early 1920s, accolades written by white music critics who praised his innovative treatment of "jazz," it was entirely in the context of jazz as the term was understood by those critics.

On November 1, 1923, the same Eva Gauthier who had stimulated Griffes to work with Asian music, gave a recital at Aeolian Hall in New York featuring a startlingly eclectic program of songs by Purcell, Bellini, Bartók, Hindemith, Schoenberg, Milhaud, Arthur Bliss, Jerome Kern, Irving Berlin and George Gershwin. Billed as a "Recital of Ancient and Modern" music, the event made history. Gauthier's genius in mixing "jazz" with concert repertoire virtually guaranteed a full house and attentive critics. Gershwin himself accompanied her in the American numbers on the program.

This concert was a critical success. Deems Taylor, writing in the New York *World,* stated that Gershwin performed "mysterious and *fascinating rhythmic* and contrapuntal stunts with the accompaniment" (emphasis mine). Gauthier later claimed that it was Paul Whiteman's attendance at this recital which led to the commissioning of *Rhapsody in Blue,* although that claim has been disputed.

Whatever the case, Gershwin became acquainted with two of the most important colleagues of his life during this period. One was the previously mentioned Whiteman, band leader and musical entrepreneur *par excellence,* who later "commissioned" the *Rhapsody.* The other was the scholarly, lanky composer-conductor, William Daly. The sober, systematic, classically trained Daly became an important consultant in Gershwin's musical decisions and one of his closest friends. By nature he presented such a contrast to the impetuous Gershwin that the two formed an alliance of opposites. Daly would continue to provide advice on orchestration and other matters for Gershwin until his death in 1936.

The story of the genesis of *Rhapsody in Blue* has been told and retold so many times by so many different persons, including Gershwin himself, that a predictable amount of uncertainty arises in knowing whose version to trust. But the broad outlines of fact seem to be fairly consistent. In late 1923, Whiteman discussed with Gershwin the prospect of writing a "jazz" work for his band. Gershwin, as usual occupied with his Broadway obligations, filed the idea away in the back of his mind and made only a few sketches of themes that might be used in such a work. Then, while Gershwin was playing billiards with lyricist Buddy DeSylva at a Broadway billiard parlor one day during the following January, Ira called George's attention to a report in the next day's issue of *New York Tribune* (January 4, 1924). This press blurb, issued by Whiteman's press agent, announced that he (Gershwin) was at work on a "jazz concerto" to be premiered by the Whiteman Band at its Aeolian Hall concert the following February 12, less than six weeks away. The article went on to state that a distinguished panel of judges, including Rachmaninoff, Heifetz and Efrem Zimbalist, Sr., would pass judgment on the question "What is American music?" after the performance. Furthermore, it stated that Victor Herbert and Irving Berlin were also composing works for the program.

No doubt surprised by this preemptive announcement on Whiteman's part, Gershwin nevertheless rose to the challenge and began work on the *Rhapsody* on January 7, a mere four days later. He was, at the time, engaged in the final revisions of his now-obscure musical, *Sweet Little Devil,* and committed to being present for its Boston tryouts. Later Gershwin would claim that the rhythm and rattle of the train on which he rode to Boston stimulated the rhythmic ideas of the opening sections of the *Rhapsody*.

Gershwin completed the composition in three weeks, and Whiteman's staff arranger, Ferde Grofé (later composer of the pops classic *Grand Canyon Suite*) orchestrated the band's part from Gershwin's two-piano manuscript. Much has been written on the issue of whether Gershwin could or could not have orchestrated the *Rhapsody* himself. The fact is that he was accustomed, up to this point in his career, to having someone else orchestrate his music for him as this was (and still is) the standard practice on Broadway. Moreover, Gershwin had never written for orchestra before nor had he ever made a systematic study of the craft of orchestration. It is doubtful, therefore, whether he possessed the requisite skills to produce a polished instrumentation for the Whiteman ensemble at the time. He certainly could not have done so in the few weeks available to him, nor could he at his best have matched Grofé's intimate knowledge of the individual capabilities of Whiteman's players. Had Gershwin chosen to orchestrate the piece himself, however, there is no doubt that he could have done so after 1925, when he had produced his *Concerto in F* with his own instrumentation. But, by that time, there was no need to improve on Grofé's work. It would merely have been a waste of Gershwin's energies to reinvent that particular wheel. Grofé later expanded his original setting for the Whiteman group to full symphonic proportions, and this is the version which is published and performed today.

Accordingly, the premiere took place on February 12, 1924. The *Rhapsody* was placed second from the end on a long and not very distinguished program that Whiteman billed as an "educational" experiment in modern music. The announced celebrities were all present in the audience, and Gershwin himself played the piano solo. Because of the length and monotony of the program, the audience had become restless and some had even surreptitiously made their exit by the time Gershwin strode out onto the stage. But from the very first sound of the long clarinet trill rising through a mixolydian scale into the famous glissando that begins the *Rhapsody*, Gershwin had their undivided attention. The performance was a tremendous success and brought a huge ovation for Gershwin and Whiteman. The critics, with one or two notable exceptions, were unanimous and effusive in their praise. Among those exceptions was Lawrence Gilman, who would play such an instrumental role in establishing Charles Ives' reputation fourteen years later (see Chapter 3). Gilman wrote: "Recall the most ambitious piece on yesterday's program and weep over the lifelessness of its melody and harmony, so derivative, so stale, so inexpressive. And then recall, for contrast, the rich inventiveness of its rhythms, the saliency and vividness of the orchestral color."[23]

One need not sacrifice one's admiration for the *Rhapsody* to understand what Gilman was talking about, nor to agree with his statements in the perspective from which they were written. The fact of the matter is that several of the most prominent tunes in the *Rhapsody* are rather pedestrian as melody writing goes. In the case of the famous "Andantino moderato" theme, the melodic structure is underdeveloped to the point of aphorism, when removed from its orchestral setting. Indeed, the complete *Rhapsody in Blue* has come as a disappointment to more than one first-time listener primed by tales of its magnificence. As a piece of concert music, it can be a decidedly acquired taste.

In the hands of a lesser musical imagination than Gershwin's such material would undoubtedly have fallen flat on its face. But the ultimate determinant of the quality of any large work has often been not so much the beauty or ingenuity of its themes, per se, but the way that the composer handles those themes. This is no less true of the *Rhapsody* than it is, for example, of Beethoven's symphonies. And, conversely, many an inferior, forgotten work has been created whose inherent melodies promised much more than their composer was ever able to realize from them.

Gershwin's good sense is also displayed in his choice of the rhapsody form as a vehicle for this first large-scale work. Rhapsodies permit a looser structure than symphonies or concertos. They tend to feature a succession of themes without much thematic development, and can easily be "cut and pasted" to fit a variety of performance occasions and resources. Gershwin quite obviously knew he was not yet up to the compositional demands of a more formal work, and history has confirmed the wisdom of his judgment in this case. A great deal of the criticism that has been heaped upon the *Rhapsody in Blue*, from the standpoint of its so-called formal deficiencies, is, therefore, rather inane and could equally well be applied to the Hungarian rhapsodies of Franz Liszt, or the rhapsodies of Enesco, Rimsky-Korsakov, Brahms and others who have worked in this particular form.

The *Concerto in F*, however, which followed the *Rhapsody in Blue* in 1925, represents a different case entirely. Here Gershwin took on one of the most demanding compositional forms of classical music. During the rest of 1924 and early 1925, George and Ira had produced their first full collaboration and first unquestioned musical comedy hit, *Lady Be Good* (which included the now-famous songs "Fascinating Rhythm" and "The Man I Love") as well as the lesser-known musicals *Primrose, Tell Me More* and *Tip Toes,* not to mention the last of the *George White Scandals* scored

---

[23]   Review in the *New York Tribune*, February 13, 1924.

by Gershwin. George was riding high in the musical whirl of New York and London, and carrying the talents of Whiteman, brother Ira, Bill Daly, friend and songwriter Vernon Duke and a number of others along with him. A few months after the premiere of *Rhapsody in Blue,* the innovative conductor of the New York Symphony, Walter Damrosch, arranged for Gershwin to be commissioned to write his first truly symphonic work. A contract was arranged that included Gershwin's commitment to appear as soloist, and he began the concerto in July of 1925. So hectic was the pace of his life in New York during 1925 that pianist Ernest Hutcheson provided Gershwin with a studio in semi-rural Chautauqua, upstate from the city, in which to compose. Gershwin also rented an apartment separate from the family home on 103rd Street to get away from the constant round of visitors to the Gershwin household.

By late September the sketch of the concerto was complete. This time Gershwin undertook the orchestration himself, as he was now more fully in command of both formal and instrumental considerations, although he was undoubtedly assisted by several of his musical mentors such as Bill Daly and Joseph Schillinger. Gershwin originally planned to call the work *New York Concerto,* and the opening themes can certainly be heard as some of the most startlingly evocative "New York" music ever written, but he later dropped the title in favor of the more abstract *Concerto in F.* The premiere took place on December 3 with Damrosch, who had also premiered Copland's first symphony only a few months earlier, conducting and Gershwin at the piano. As in the case of the *Rhapsody* the previous year, the critics were largely enthusiastic about the *Concerto,* with the stubborn exception of Gilman, who (unaccountably) found the music "conventional, trite, at its worst a little dull." Prokofiev, who heard the work later, considered it nothing more than a succession of 32-bar, Broadway-style tunes. But, criticism notwithstanding, the *Concerto in F* slowly began to make its way and has now become one the most frequently performed piano concertos in the standard repertoire.

The unique qualities that make the *Concerto in F* the masterpiece it is are more easily heard than defined. Like any Gershwin piece, it is full of rhythmic dynamism and an almost constant shifting of keys. Furthermore, Gershwin is often given less credit than he deserves for the skillful development and transformation of melodic motifs that run throughout the entire tapestry of the piece. True, there are some awkward transitions, again reminiscent of the two piano concertos of Franz Liszt. Perhaps the most radical of these occurs at the climax of the third movement, where the composer devotes a full twenty-two bars to repeating the principal motif of the movement through a succession of keys building toward the great solo cymbal (tam-tam) crash, then launches into a full orchestral reprise of the dramatic first-movement theme. This moment packs a tremendous acoustical punch, but, from only a slightly different perspective, also sounds incredibly clumsy as a transition. If poorly timed in performance, it can create the impression that Gershwin simply didn't know how to get out of the rhythmic tattoo of his third movement and end the piece. Gershwin's symphonic music is full of such paradoxes, moments that shouldn't work musically, but do. These are the kind of "crudities" that critics bemoan, but to which general audiences consistently remain sublimely indifferent—because Gershwin, with all his technical flaws, was unmatched in his ability to create a fundamental thematic idea that sweeps away virtually every other consideration. When we say "thematic idea," moreover, we are not merely talking about a tune. It has already been noted that some of Gershwin's tunes are less than brilliant melodic constructions. But he alone had the capacity to take such tunes, rhythmic gestures or motifs and to set them in an holistic texture of such stark originality that it is always and unmistakably his own.

He marshals a number of musical resources to do so. Principal among these resources is his absolutely fresh harmonic idiom. Gershwin does not just harmonize a melody (either in a conventional or unconventional fashion). He evolves each melody as an inevitable and inseparable element of a unique harmonic idea. Thus, it becomes virtually impossible to "reharmonize" a Gershwin tune without sacrificing its fundamental character. The essential outlines of the resulting phrase are always defined with crystal clarity, rarely seem pretentious, and, even when an argument can be made for antecedents in the work of some other composer, never ultimately sound like anyone but Gershwin. Furthermore, his orchestration, however unconventional, is always perfectly suited to the inherent nature of the idea.

These observations lead one to an inescapable conclusion with regard to whole overblown issue of Gershwin's command of technique. That conclusion is simply this: had Gershwin been able to force himself to conscientiously pursue the conventional training given to all his predecessors, had he actually mastered what was then considered to be the standard technique of a "serious" composer, those very features that created his unique musical voice would undoubtedly have been damaged and diluted. This view is confirmed by the comments of Henry Cowell, reflecting on Gershwin's lessons with him in the late 1920s.

> The lessons were to be once a week, but usually something would in-
> terfere, so they were nearer once in three weeks. His fertile mind
> leaped all over the place. He was exasperated at the rules—but not
> because he was incapable of mastering them. With no effort at all he
> rattled off the almost perfect exercise, but would get side tracked
> into something using a juicy ninth and altered chords that he liked

better, and would insert these into the Palestrina-style motet. The whole period lasted a little over two years.[24]

In short, Gershwin could not patently incorporate predefined classical forms and techniques into his personal style for the same reasons that Beethoven could not master the predefined fugal technique of the 18th century: it was an alien musical language offering the wrong compositional tools for the musical vision he was struggling to achieve. With such composers it is absolutely essential that they reshape the tools of their predecessors to suit their own conceptions. And whether or not those conceptions work can only finally be judged with reference to the resulting piece itself, not by analogy to the works of prior composers. Measured by this yardstick, the *Concerto in F* is one of the most strikingly original and inventive pieces in the entire 20th-century repertoire. It goes far beyond anything in the *Rhapsody in Blue,* and incorporates an *internal* musical logic, married to a wealth of original melodic conceptions, which Gershwin was never to achieve again in any single extended composition.

The mid-1920s also saw the composition of Gershwin's third "classical" instrumental works to achieve major significance in the repertoire of American music. These were his *Three Piano Preludes.* The history of these short, brilliantly conceived pieces (the second of which has become a cliché in documentary films portraying the Great Depression of the 1930s) is convoluted. As early as 1923, the period of his few abortive lessons with Goldmark, Gershwin had produced at least the first of two piano pieces he chose to call "Novelettes." Neither of these works has attracted any serious attention, and they can best be considered juvenile sketches. In an attempt to promote them, however, Gershwin arranged them for violin and piano, and it was in this form that they were premiered by violinist Samuel Dushkin at the University Club of New York in February, 1925. For this performance, the two pieces were amalgamated under the single title "Short Story," and have been subsequently published under that title. Some time later (probably in late 1925 or early 1926) Gershwin took the original piano versions of these "novelettes" and added three more, to make a total suite of five pieces. This he performed at a recital that he gave with the singer Marguerite d'Alvarez on December 4, 1926 at the Hotel Roosevelt. It was the three added pieces that became what we now know as the *Three Preludes,* and were published as such in 1927.

If Gershwin encountered certain formal obstacles which he could not overcome in his longer instrumental works, at least in the *Three Preludes* he demonstrated his mastery over the condensed form of the short piano

---

[24] Cited in Ewen, *op. cit.,* p. 115.

piece, more closely related to the song forms he was familiar with. Each of the *Three Preludes* is written in a loosely ABA pattern, with a varied return of the opening theme at the end. Moreover, the entire set reflects the same pattern, with the slow middle prelude sandwiched between two fast, rhythmically vigorous ones. The first and third bear identical tempo indications *Allegro ben ritmato e deciso* (fast, highly rhythmic and decisive), while the middle prelude is designated *Andante con moto e poco rubato* (moderately slow, but moving and with some expressive variation in speed), and betrays certain resemblances both to the slow movement of the *Concerto* and portions of the *Rhapsody in Blue*. As mentioned previously, the main theme of the third prelude is also clearly derived from the first theme of Gershwin's 1916 piano rag, *Rialto Ripples.*

Both singly and as a group, the *Three Preludes* show Gershwin at his best. Their structure is tight and flawlessly logical; not a note is wasted. Individual phrases are replete with the kind of intervallic symmetries one admires in the late works of Debussy and Bartók. The harmonic and rhythmic scheme of each is perfectly suited to the melodic material, and the sense of inevitability that always characterizes Gershwin's best work is fully present. But above all, the central idea of each prelude is unique, distinct and striking. And the thematic flow from one piece to the next is sufficiently well proportioned and interrelated that, ignoring tonal relationships, the three movements almost form a sonatina.

Between January of 1925 and December of 1926 then, a period of less than two years, Gershwin had gone from being merely a skillful and highly successful Broadway tunesmith to the role of serious composer. Within this short span, he produced his three most important instrumental works and experienced at least a decade's worth of creative development. In the remaining eleven years of his life he would go on to write *An American in Paris,* his *Second Rhapsody, Cuban Overture* and *Porgy and Bess,* each of which would represent certain advances over his earlier classical pieces. But he would never again achieve the white heat of concentrated evolution that inflamed him during the mid-1920s, nor would any of the future works in its entirety display that pairing of musical craft with unfailing melodic imagination so vividly present in the *Rhapsody, Concerto* and *Preludes.*

Between 1926 and 1931, George and Ira completed a succession of musical comedies that rank among their best work. These included, *Oh, Kay!* (1926), *Strike Up the Band* (1927), *Funny Face* (1927), *Rosalie* (1928, with additional music by Sigmund Romberg), *Treasure Girl* (1928), *Show Girl* (1929), *Girl Crazy* (1930) and *Of Thee I Sing* (1931), as well as songs and incidental music for the Fox film, *Delicious.* This remarkable succession of Broadway hits included such now-standard Gershwin favorites as "Do,

Do, Do," "Someone to Watch Over Me," "The Man I Love," "Funny Face," "'S Wonderful," "I've Got a Crush on You," "Embraceable You" and "I Got Rhythm." Perhaps the most remarkable of these shows was the last, *Of Thee I Sing*. In this play, by George S. Kaufman and Morrie Ryskind, Gershwin was at least partially able to realize his long-felt ambition to elevate the Broadway musical into a domain of art that was something more than entertainment. The story is a political satire lampooning American presidential electoral politics, and it approaches the quality of a Gilbert and Sullivan operetta in terms of sheer wit and finesse. It became the first Broadway musical to win the prestigious Pulitzer Prize, and a major feather in the cap of all its creators. Unfortunately, also like Gilbert and Sullivan, much of the material in *Of Thee I Sing* proved too topical to the time in which it was written to give the show much lasting impact. That, together with the fact that, as Gershwin's most "abstract" show score, it lacks even a single hit tune comparable to his best, resulted in increasingly poor reception of the work during subsequent revivals over the years. But, despite these problems, the great popular songs created by George and Ira Gershwin for these shows have remained staples in the American musical diet, and are heard and admired by millions even today who know nothing about George Gershwin.

On March 11, 1928, Gershwin embarked on his fifth and final visit to Europe, in company with Ira, their sister Frances and Ira's wife, Lee. Arriving in Paris on the 25th, the Gershwins settled into the Majestic Hotel. Six days later the *Rhapsody in Blue* was performed by the Pasdeloup Orchestra with the duo-piano team of Wiener and Doucet dividing the solo part between them. In April, dancer-choreographer Anton Dolin, colleague and lover of Ballet Russe impresario Serge Diaghilev, gave a ballet rendering of the *Rhapsody* at the Théâtre des Champs-Elysées. On May 29 the European premiere of the *Concerto in F* took place at the Paris Opera under conductor Vladimir Golschmann. The piano soloist was the young Dmitri Tiomkin, who would later achieve fame as a composer of Hollywood movie scores.

During this European trip, Gershwin made or renewed acquaintances with Ravel, Milhaud, Poulenc, Auric, Prokofiev, Alban Berg and William Walton. Walton became a particularly supportive friend. Ravel declined to accept Gershwin as a pupil. And, at a soiree at his Vienna apartment, Berg expressed a wholly unexpected admiration of Gershwin's music. The thirty-year-old composer also brought back with him a number of art works and other souvenirs. But perhaps the most important item in his luggage on the return trip was a draft of a new symphonic poem, *An American in Paris*.

Again Gershwin took on the orchestration himself and, by the end of the year, had completed the final version, including the famous Parisian taxi horns which he personally brought from Paris. *An American in Paris* was premiered by the New York Philharmonic, once more under the baton of Walter Damrosch, on December 13, 1928. From the very opening notes, which so aptly capture the rhythm and ambience of a bustling urban street scene, the piece was a rousing success. Critics were highly favorable, and even the recalcitrant Lawrence Gilman finally came around, writing that the piece had the "tang of a new and urgent world, engaging, ardent, unpredictable."

But, in spite of the taxi horns, there is nothing particularly Parisian about *An American in Paris,* unless it be the piece's wit and verve. Just as Dvořák had created a finely crafted but very European symphony in response to his American visit thirty-five years earlier, Gershwin had now produced a quintessentially American work stimulated by his excitement and love for Paris. The structure of the music is far more diffuse than that of the *Concerto,* and its melodic sections flow together without the abrupt shifts of the *Rhapsody.* These were elements that appealed to Gilman and others of his ilk, representing an advance in Gershwin's compositional skills. But, from the public viewpoint, these are probably the very features that weaken *An American in Paris* when compared to the vastly more popular *Rhapsody.* This is not to say that *An American in Paris* is anything like an obscure or unpopular work. It has remained in the repertoire of symphonic and pops orchestras ever since its premiere, and has been choreographed for both stage and cinema many times. The music has also been used, either directly or as a model for imitation, by many film and television composers seeking to evoke a bustling urban atmosphere. Indeed, it is reasonable to assert that, in *An American in Paris,* Gershwin finally achieved a work that was to have a direct and significant influence on the subsequent efforts of other American classical composers.

Also during the late 1920s, Gershwin became closely (and perhaps romantically) attached to the principal woman in his life, Kay Swift. Gershwin's biographers have written extensively on his difficulty in forming a close relationship with any woman. Apparently he experienced an intense sexual drive throughout his life that, like Brahms and Schubert, he often satisfied with prostitutes. But Gershwin's lifelong obsession with his work and his career clearly got in the way of romantic liaisons of any substance. His was a contradictory personality. Many perceived him as flawlessly polite, modest and ingenuous. But there is evidence that he could be equally rude, egotistical and self-obsessed. He suffered from chronic constipation throughout his adult life and was a hypochondriac. Once he began to achieve success, he became addicted to fad diets, cigars and a fast-lane lifestyle.

Kay Swift was a trained musician and skillful songwriter in her own right, and perhaps understood Gershwin better than his many non-musical girlfriends. She assisted him materially with advice about his work, and by copying parts and performing other clerical chores for him. But she was married at the time of their closest interaction and apparently happy to remain so. Whatever might have transpired between them was over by the time her husband died and she became free to consider a serious love relationship with Gershwin. Whether or not he was interested in or capable of such a relationship with her, or anyone, remains an open question. Whatever the case, he remained a bachelor until the end of his life.

Throughout the late 1920s, while George and Ira were involved in creating their unbroken string of stage hits, George was also involved in plans to convert DuBose Heyward's novel *Porgy* into an opera. Gershwin had read the book, given to him by his friends Emily and Lou Paley, in 1926 and was immediately enthused by its stage possibilities. He corresponded with Heyward only to discover that the latter's wife, Dorothy, was already engaged in making a stage adaptation with her husband's collaboration. Always the southern gentleman, Heyward felt obliged to see his wife's adaptation completed and staged before pursuing the matter with Gershwin, although he was highly excited by the prospect of the opera. Negotiations and correspondence continued for the next several years before a contract for the creation of *Porgy and Bess* was finally signed in 1933. By then the Heywards' stage version had already run for 367 performances on Broadway, in addition to a road tour. While this was certainly a respectable record for any play, it was felt by all concerned that *Porgy* could be even more impressive in Gershwin's musical setting.

In the meantime, Gershwin had turned once more to the composition of concert works. In 1931 he composed his *Second Rhapsody* for piano and orchestra, which he premiered with the Boston Symphony Orchestra under the baton of Serge Koussevitsky in January of 1932. Koussevitsky was, like Gershwin, of Russian-Jewish heritage and, from 1925 onward, began to assume a greater and greater significance in the musical life of America. He eventually founded the Tanglewood Music Festival in the Berkshires of western Massachusetts, commissioned many works (including Bartók's last great orchestral masterpiece, the *Concerto for Orchestra*) and became the musical mentor of both Aaron Copland and Leonard Bernstein. We will see more of him in subsequent chapters of this history.

Unlike the *Rhapsody in Blue,* Gershwin's *Second Rhapsody* has never achieved the status of a major "hit." This is probably attributable to the less catchy nature of the melodic writing and, as with *An American in Paris,* perhaps to the greater refinement of the work. A paradox that applies to Gershwin no less than to many another great composer is that his best works are often not his most popular, and his most popular works are often not his best from the purely musical standpoint. But despite its relative lack of popular acclaim, the *Second Rhapsody* showed very clear evidence of advances in Gershwin's technical command of form, melodic development and orchestration.

In August of the same year Albert Coates conducted the premiere of Gershwin's *Cuban Overture,* with the New York Philharmonic. If anything, the *Cuban Overture* is even less memorable melodically than is the *Second Rhapsody.* It has remained in the concert repertoire largely because it is short, can be played by a small orchestra and offers conductors a set of rhythmic challenges that are engaging but not overwhelming. Indeed, the *Cuban Overture* is very largely a rhythmic piece and exploits Gershwin's remarkable facility for cross-rhythms and polyrhythms to a greater degree than any of his other orchestral works.

Both the *Second Rhapsody* and the *Cuban Overture* can best be viewed as "warm-up" pieces for *Porgy and Bess.* While neither bears any direct musical relation to the opera, they offered Gershwin an opportunity to get back into the compositional mode of absolute music after the long string of Broadway shows. As there is evidence that he was thinking of *Porgy,* and making some sketches which might later serve as a basis for it, from at least 1929 on, it is likely that Gershwin himself viewed these orchestral works in very much the same light.

DuBose Heyward had been born in Charleston in 1885 and lived there most of his life. He died in 1940. Heyward had worked on the piers of that southern port city, become friends with many of the local black people about whose lives he later wrote and developed a genuine, if somewhat detached, appreciation for their culture and life. Where Gershwin was a brash, ambitious first-generation American, Heyward was a reserved, even courtly, Southern gentleman who traced his ancestry back to a signer of the Declaration of Independence.

Heyward's literary hero, Porgy, was based on an actual person: Samuel Smalls. Known locally as "Goat Sammy," Smalls was an ill-tempered beggar who moved about Charleston in a goat-drawn cart due to the loss of the use of his legs. While the real-life Smalls was a surly individual with a long criminal record, Heyward's transmutation of him into the courageous Porgy reflected an understanding of the deeper life buried beneath the outward appearances of his characters.

In his 1956 review of the film version of *Porgy and Bess,* James Baldwin wrote:

DuBose Heyward *(1885–1940), author and librettist of*
Porgy and Bess. (Photo courtesy of ASCAP.)

[The story] owes its vitality to the fact that DuBose Heyward loved
the people he was writing about. (By which I do not mean to imply
that he loved all Negroes; he was a far better man than that.)

Just the same, it is a white man's vision of Negro life. This means
that when it should be most concrete and searching it veers off into
the melodramatic and the exotic. It seems to me that the author
knew more about Bess than he understood and more about Porgy
than he could face—than any of us, so far, can face.[25]

With the passage of time these sentiments have become the consensus
of critical judgment on *Porgy.* They are similar to Duke Ellington's laconic
dismissal of the "lampblack Negroisms," embodied in the work and the
general lack of respect accorded to any claim that the authors might have
intended to make regarding its true-life reflection of Southern coastal
blacks. To be appreciated on its own terms, *Porgy and Bess* must be viewed
in the context of the times in which it was written, and of the men who

[25] James Baldwin, "Catfish Row," reprinted in *The Price of the Ticket: Collected Nonfiction,
1948–1985,* New York: St. Martin's/Marek, 1985, p. 179.

wrote it—all of them white. It presents not so much an accurate picture of the life of its characters as, in Baldwin's terms, a "white man's vision" from the mid-1930s. But that vision is nonetheless a sympathetic one, and the work played a historically significant role when it became the first opera that presented such a view to achieved major success. *Porgy and Bess* was at the same time more finely crafted than Harry Lawrence Freeman's earlier efforts (such as his 1928 opera *Voodoo*) and less stilted than Scott Joplin's unperformed, Sullivanesque *Treemonisha*. Whatever its flaws, it opened many doors for later works dealing with similar issues.

The plot of *Porgy and Bess* is as follows. The crippled beggar, Porgy, lives in Catfish Row, a Charleston tenement. The prostitute, Bess, comes to this place, accompanied by her pimp, Crown. Crown gets into a fight with one of the inhabitants of the Row and kills him. Crown flees, leaving Bess alone with the hostile inhabitants of the Row. She takes refuge from the police by hiding with Porgy.

Living with Porgy, Bess begins to accept and love him and is herself gradually assimilated into the Catfish Row community. Later, Crown abducts Bess during a picnic, but she escapes and returns to Porgy. There follows the great hurricane scene, during which it is assumed that Crown has been killed, but he returns to claim Bess and fights Porgy. Despite his physical handicaps, Porgy kills Crown and is detained for questioning by the police. In despair, Bess allows herself to be seduced away to New York by the amoral Sportin' Life. After being released by the police, Porgy sets out in search of her, and the story ends on this rather indefinite note.

Working from the novel and his wife's playscript, Heyward fashioned the libretto in three acts. Ira was brought in to collaborate on the lyrics, and Gershwin began serious work on the composition in February of 1934.

Over the next year and a half, Gershwin worked diligently on the opera and devoted enormous effort to the orchestration. He visited Heyward in Charleston that summer, living in a cabin at Folly Beach, about ten miles from Heyward's home. It is not certain how much of the local Gullah music Gershwin absorbed during this trip. Given his apparently casual approach to matters involving anything like systematic research, it is likely that his exposure to the local culture was at best haphazard. But Gershwin was not out to recreate a historically authentic portrait of Gullah culture. Throughout the process of composition, his own and Heyward's conception of the opera on its own terms were uppermost in his mind, despite his desire to be near the source of the scenes that inspired it.

By early 1935 the composition was largely complete and Gershwin set about the painstaking job of orchestrating the work himself. He made a good start on this while vacationing in Palm Beach at the home of Emil Mosbacher. Upon returning to New York, he redoubled his efforts in order to have the opera ready for its premiere date. He sought the advice of Joseph Schillinger on technical matters of the orchestration and was assisted in the editing of the score and copying of parts by Kay Swift and Albert Sirmay, his long-time editor for most of his publications.

By the beginning of September 1935, after hiring a "pick-up" orchestra to try out parts of the orchestration the previous July, the score for *Porgy and Bess* was finished and the opera went into rehearsal. Throughout the rehearsals, Gershwin was occupied with the necessary cuts and revisions always required during this process, and was functioning at a high peak of nervous energy. Finally, on October 10, 1935, *Porgy and Bess* opened at the Alvin Theater.

While moderately successful, the original production of *Porgy and Bess* was not an immediate hit. Many critics, perhaps expecting an attempt at traditional grand opera on Gershwin's part, were disappointed at the folk-opera quality of the result. The pacing of stage action was impeded by Gershwin's insistence on incorporating through-composed recitatives throughout the work, to create a texture of continuous singing. (In fact, apart from occasional spoken utterances by the black characters, the only speaking roles in the opera are those of white men.) Gershwin had insisted on including these recitatives against the advice of Heyward and others. They were largely removed for the heavily cut 1942 revival of the opera, supervised by Gershwin's mother, Rose, and led to a far more popular public reception of the work. Subsequently, however, Gershwin's view has prevailed, and the fully restored version of the work is now standard in performance.

In addition to the above problems, African-American musicians were virtually unanimous in condemning the opera for what they viewed as its patronizing and inauthentic portrayal of its characters. Furthermore, *Porgy and Bess* tends to be "front-end loaded" in terms of its most memorable tunes. That is to say that the best set pieces in the opera—"Summertime," "Bess, You Is My Woman Now," "My Man's Gone Now," "It Ain't Necessarily So"—all occur before the middle of the second act. The remainder of the second, and all of the third act, contain powerful and impressive music—but not the most memorable music in the show. The absence at the end of a clear resolution of the most fundamental character relationship in the plot, that of the two title figures, also probably weakens its dramatic structure. It would require several years for *Porgy and Bess* to find its place in the repertoire of American opera, and Gershwin would not live to see this happen.

With the advent of talking pictures in 1929, the American entertainment industry underwent a major upheaval. Stars of the silent films, whose voices did not sound well in the talkies, became overnight has-beens. New performers, who could speak as well as act, took their places. It also became possible for Hollywood to produce films with music, and musical plays on film, thus canceling the Broadway monopoly on this medium and bringing it to every theatre in middle America. Actors, actresses, producers, lyricists, writers, composers and stage directors fled New York for the greener pastures of Hollywood. And the Gershwin brothers were not to be left behind by the exodus. Furthermore, the economic ravages of the Great Depression had decimated Broadway. Theatres closed right and left. Great producers, such as Ziegfeld, suffered drastic economic losses. So desperate was the situation that President Franklin Roosevelt established the Federal Theater Project in 1935 to provide employment for hundreds of out-of-work theatre professionals (and, incidentally, provided the opportunity for a great many outstanding and experimental plays, which would not have been commercially viable before, to be presented).

George and Ira had created songs and incidental music for the film *Delicious,* in 1931, and some of the unused incidental music for this project eventually became the basis for Gershwin's *Second Rhapsody.* But that was

The **Gershwin** *brothers, Ira (left) and George at work on one of their final film scores in Hollywood, 1937. George was already suffering from the brain tumor that would kill him only weeks after this photo was taken.* (Photo courtesy of ASCAP.)

their only movie employment prior to 1936. In June of that year they negotiated a contract with RKO to do the songs for a Ginger Rogers–Fred Astaire musical, first entitled *Watch Your Step,* but ultimately released as *Shall We Dance.* Gershwin got less than he wanted from this deal, but the tepid reception of *Porgy and Bess,* together with its high-brow label as an "opera," had damaged his bargaining position with the Hollywood powers that were.

In August, George, Ira and Lee packed up their belongings and joined the general migration west, settling into a large mansion on Roxbury Drive in Beverly Hills. During the remaining eleven months of his life, Gershwin would deliver songs for *Shall We Dance* and two more films, *A Damsel in Distress* (1937) and *The Goldwyn Follies* (1938), including such classics as "Let's Call the Whole Thing Off," "Shall We Dance," "Nice Work If You Can Get It" and "Love Walked In." Neither of the last two films were to see theatrical release until after Gershwin's death.

In addition to his film work, Gershwin conducted and performed at the Hollywood Bowl and elsewhere during his final year. He met Arnold Schoenberg, who had joined the faculty of UCLA in 1936 after fleeing Hitler's Germany, and became a regular tennis partner of the originator of 12-tone music. Schoenberg, however, like Ravel before him, declined to accept Gershwin as a private pupil. In addition, Gershwin continued his romantic liaisons with such Hollywood stars as Paulette Goddard and Kitty Carlisle.

In February 1937, Gershwin experienced a blackout, accompanied by the sensation of the smell of burning rubber, during a performance of the *Concerto in F* with the Los Angeles Philharmonic. This was the first indication of the brain tumor that would kill him five months later. Throughout the spring he became increasingly subject to headaches and photosensitivity. Unfortunately, because he was known to be a notorious hypochondriac by all the people close to him, very few took these symptoms seriously. Edward Jablonski relates an incident where Gershwin collapsed from headache upon leaving the famous Brown Derby restaurant in Hollywood one afternoon, whereupon an unnamed female companion told the entourage to "leave him there; he just wants attention."[26] Even Ira was not fully convinced that there was anything seriously wrong with him.

Gershwin had been seeing Dr. Gregory Zilboorg, the famous psychiatrist, off and on for a number of years. This was a period when it was fashionable for the wealthy and famous to be "in analysis," and Zilboorg numbered many of them among his clientele. He consulted Zilboorg about the headaches, as well as the eminent psychoanalyst Ernest Simmel. Both

[26] Jablonski, *Gershwin,* p. 319.

suspected the trouble was organic rather than psychological, but a battery of medical tests failed to identify the problem.

Gershwin declined steadily over the next few weeks. His once robust constitution deteriorated to the point where he had to helped to and from his bed by a male nurse. His room was kept darkened because of the sensitivity of his eyes; he was sedated much of the time. There was difficulty with the studio over his inability to finish songs on schedule, and the friends who visited him, including Copland, were shocked at the sudden and radical change in a man who had been so vigorous only weeks before.

On July 9 he lapsed into a coma and was rushed to Cedars of Lebanon Hospital. After two abortive attempts to locate the best brain surgeons available, the doctors in Los Angeles agreed that emergency surgery was indicated. The five-hour operation began after midnight on July 10. A rapidly growing, cystic tumor (known as a glioblastoma) was located in the right lobe of his brain and substantially removed. But the roots of this tumor had gone deeply into Gershwin's midbrain, and hope for his recovery disappeared. He died at 10:35 the following morning without ever regaining consciousness.

With regard to American musical theatre, no serious person disputes Gershwin's contribution. Furthermore, in the light of those developments that have affected American jazz since 1935, he is not considered seriously to be a "jazz" composer anymore by anyone familiar with the idiom. But Gershwin's role in American classical music has been consistently underrated. If we judge a "great" composer by the fact that his music has influenced many other serious composers, both of his own and other nationalities, Gershwin clearly passes the test. If we judge such a composer by the fact that his song has moved millions deeply, then again Gershwin fulfills the requirement. If we insist that a great composer must capture in his music the spirit of his age and the temper of the people from which he emerged, no single figure can be more evocative of the spirit of early 20th century urban America than Gershwin.

But, in the realm of classical music, we are often prone to judge composers by their technique. If this is the sole criterion, then Gershwin belongs on the shelf labeled "Composers with great ideas but limited skills." He shares this shelf with such figures as Moussorgsky, Puccini, Glinka and others—not exactly disreputable company. On the other hand, the history of music is filled with thousands of forgotten composers who had great skills but no ideas. If given a choice, most listeners will consistently prefer the former to the latter. So the validity of this criterion by itself is open to serious question.

Part of the classical music world's hostility to Gershwin unquestionably arises from jealousy. He was one of the lucky few who acquired great wealth and fame from his music, thus breeding resentment among lesser figures who are left merely to criticize. But, above all, he was spectacularly successful in both the popular and classical worlds of music, and this is an achievement that no other American composer, including Leonard Bernstein (who came closest to it), has matched in the fifty-five years since Gershwin's death. And this, perhaps, breeds the greatest resentment of all among self-styled "serious" composers.

The flaws in Gershwin's more serious works are sometimes significant, at least by the standards of European compositional practice, but they have not in any way hindered the popularity of his music, nor its ability to express all the nuances of America and its people. Perhaps it was not so much Gershwin's failure to conform to accepted practice, but the premises of that practice itself that required a new evaluation. Whatever the case, Gershwin clearly achieved that which no other American composer before him had achieved, despite his casual musical education, namely: the creation of substantive music that found a worldwide audience in his lifetime and has remained a major part of the repertoire ever since.

After Gershwin, American classical music became focused as it had never been focused before. And the world began to sit up and listen.

6

Copland, Thomson, Harris and Their Generation

ॐ

Part I: 1900–1933

In the 1920s, musical America had finally come of age. The three major branches of the developing American musical tree—classical, jazz and musical theatre—were well established. Gone were days when a single conductor, such as Theodore Thomas, could set the pattern for all orchestral performances, or when American composers of merit had to propagandize for the need to be heard or to finance their own performances. Indeed, the world of American classical music has probably not been more active at any time this century than it was during the 1920s and 1930s. This was the period of pioneering conductors, such as Damrosch, Koussevitzky, Stokowski; of adventurous performers such as Leo Ornstein, John Kirkpatrick, Samuel Dushkin, Artur Rubinstein, Eva Gauthier; of dedicated patrons and promoters such as Elizabeth Sprague Coolidge, Alma Wertheim, Mary Curtis Bok, Chick Austin, Marian MacDowell and Claire Reis; and of brilliant American composers who spoke a language that the public was, on the whole, willing and able to hear.

Among the many important names to emerge from this generation, especially in the wake of George Gershwin's concert music successes, were Aaron Copland, Virgil Thomson, Roy Harris, Wallingford Riegger, Henry Cowell, Walter Piston, Edgard Varèse, Roger Sessions, Howard Hanson and William Grant Still. Even relative old-timers, such as Ernest Bloch, Percy Grainger and John Alden Carpenter benefited from the upsurge of interest in American art music during these decades. Still other composers, of only slightly lesser importance, included such names as Quincy Porter, Leo Sowerby, George Antheil, Douglas Moore, Randall Thompson, Marc Blitzstein and David Guion. In addition, a third string of composers who wrote a high quality of music, but, for a variety of reasons, did not make a strong impression on the public included Anis Fuleihan, Dane Rudhyar, Stefan Wolpe, Ernst Bacon, Adolph Weiss, Eliot Griffis, Robert Russell Bennett and Bernard Rogers, among others. The musical life of America flourished during the 1920s and 1930s as it had never flourished before.

Because of the sheer number and importance of the contributions to our classical music made by this generation of composers, it is impractical to deal thoroughly with all of them in a single chapter. Therefore, we will defer discussion of Bloch, Piston, Hanson and Sessions until the next chapter, when we take up the subject of American musical academia, and will discuss Cowell, Grainger, Varèse, Rudhyar and Ruggles in still another chapter on the roots of the 1960s avant-garde.

Aaron Copland (through the Piano Variations, 1932)

Apart from Gershwin's unique position, the leader of that generation of American composers born during the last decade or so of the 19th century was unquestionably Aaron Copland (1900–1990). From his earliest successes, beginning at the age of twenty-five, until his death at the age of ninety, Copland held a commanding position in American classical music through the impact of his compositions, his books, articles and lectures, his conducting, his musical embassies to foreign countries, his espousal of the works of his contemporaries and his advocacy of both North and South American music. Moreover, he played an important role in the founding of a number of important musical institutions, such as the American Composers Alliance and the Tanglewood Festival in Lenox, Massachusetts, and formed a crucial link in a generational chain of musical mentors that led from Koussevitzky to Bernstein.

Copland was born in Brooklyn, New York, on November 14, 1900. Like Gershwin (as well as Ornstein, Gruenberg, Irving Berlin, Koussevitzky, Bernstein and a number of others), he was of Russian-Jewish extraction. This fact becomes significant in context of Copland's later "Americanist" compositions, in which he achieved a sound more closely identified in the public's mind with the Anglo-Celtic musical traditions of the United States than did any of the earlier, more authentically Anglo-Celtic composers who tried, including Chadwick, MacDowell, Ives and others.

Like Griffes and Gershwin before him, Copland came from a family of no great musical distinction; his parents were merchants and business people. And his first exposure to the art appears to have been from hearing older siblings and relatives playing amateur pieces. Apparently he liked to make up songs as a child, and even attempted to compose an opera at age eleven! Predictably, the attempt lasted only for a few measures of actual music. At about the age of twelve he began piano lessons with one Leopold Wolfsohn in New York and worked on such things as C. L. Hanon's *The Virtuoso Pianist* (the bane of many a young keyboardist) and traditional European repertoire. Copland's first serious public performance occurred in 1917, when he performed Paderewski's *Polonaise in B* at Wanamaker's Department Store in Manhattan.

It was about this time that young Copland decided on the career of a musician, but was hampered in his ambitions by his haphazard musical experiences and lack of access to regular professional instruction. Throughout his long career, Copland displayed remarkable self-assurance and, once he had made up his mind to do some particular thing, set about systematically to do it, usually succeeding. Thus it was that, once he had settled on a musical career, he never wavered from 100 percent commitment to that decision.

After an unsuccessful attempt to master the study of harmony through a correspondence course, Copland was sent by his piano teacher, Wolfsohn, to the same Rubin Goldmark who was, six years later, to engage in the unsuccessful attempt to teach Gershwin harmony. Goldmark was a nephew of the highly regarded Austrian composer Karl Goldmark, and a dyed-in-the-wool musical pedant. It is a measure of the difference in temperament and musical objectives between Gershwin and Copland that, while the former found nothing to admire in Goldmark, Copland would later describe him as "an excellent teacher in the fundamentals of musical composition ... the lessons he gave were clearly presented and stayed close to the subject under discussion."[27] Although the above comment was written when Copland was in his eighties, it seems to reflect the supposition that, even at the tender age of seventeen, he was already adopting those values of clarity, objectivity and intellectual precision that were to characterize both his life and his work to come.

Copland continued to work successfully with Goldmark through the first half of 1921. He abandoned Wolfsohn to study piano with Victor Wittgenstein and, later, Clarence Adler. But all of this training was relentlessly conservative, offering the fledgling composer little exposure to modern music of the day. He was left to his own devices to seek out and study the newer works of then-contemporary composers. When Copland saw a copy of Ives' *"Concord" Sonata* in Goldmark's studio in 1921 (a copy that

---

[27] Copland and Perlis, Vol. 1, p. 27.

could only have been sent by Ives himself, as this was the year in which the composer had had the first edition privately printed), Goldmark urged him to stay away from such radical stuff. And when he was called upon to play the Ravel *Sonatine* at a recital in Adler's studio one day, Copland felt obliged to explain such a "modern" piece to his assembled fellow pupils—and was later to cite this event as the beginning of his career as a musical commentator.

After deciding not to go to college, upon graduation from Boys' High School in June of 1918, Copland looked about for new artistic and educational opportunities. In 1916 he had met and formed an intimate acquaintance with one Aaron Schaffer while spending the summer at the Fairmont Hotel in Tannersville, New York. The two young men became close companions, and Schaffer presented Copland with a book of original poems, several of which the young composer set to music. The best known of these early songs was entitled "Night" (1918). Schaffer subsequently traveled to Paris for study at the Sorbonne and yearned for the young Copland to join him there. He advised the fledgling composer, still searching for direction, to stay away from theatre music. Copland apparently took this advice, possibly to his later detriment as a dramatic composer. He made pocket money by playing for dances and playing chamber music for social events, all the while dreaming of Paris. When *Musical America* announced the formation of a summer school for American musicians at Fontainebleau in 1921, Copland saw his opportunity and took it. Over Goldmark's objections, he applied for admission and was awarded one of only nine scholarships available.

Copland departed for Paris in June of 1921. While on board ship he struck up an acquaintance with fellow passenger Marcel Duchamp, whose painting, "Nude Descending a Staircase," had created a sensation in European art circles some eight years earlier. This was only the first of many serendipitous meetings with influential artists and personalities in the world of the fine arts that Copland, and others who went to France at the time, experienced. It was largely through meetings of this type that networks of friendship were formed which enabled young and unknown composers such as Copland, Thomson, Antheil and others to get their work performed during the 1920s.

Copland had arranged with his cousin, Harold Clurman, who would later become one of the most important voices in American theatre of the 1930s, to meet in Paris and seek lodgings together. Shortly after his arrival in France, Clurman joined him and the two became roommates. Whether the attachment between Clurman and Copland was of a romantic nature remains obscure to this day, as do all of Copland's intimate relationships, about which he never expressed himself in print. But the two were constant companions for the duration of Copland's Paris years and, for several years afterward, frequently traveled together. They remained lifelong friends.

One of the teachers at Fontainebleau was the thirty-four-year-old Nadia Boulanger. Copland at first resisted the idea of attending her classes, because she was teaching harmony and he felt he had had enough of harmony under Goldmark. But a friend persuaded him to audit one session and so powerfully was Copland impressed by Boulanger's dynamic approach that by October 1921 he was studying composition with her. Thus began one of the most important relationships in modern American musical history, for Boulanger was to play a decisive role in launching Copland's American career some four years later. For his part, Copland proved to be only the first of a long succession of American composition students who made the pilgrimage to Paris to study with her over the next fifty years. The roster of Boulanger's American students would eventually include Virgil Thomson, Walter Piston, Roy Harris, Elliott Carter, Ross Lee Finney, John Kirkpatrick, Marc Blitzstein, David Diamond, Harold Shapero, Irving Fine and Philip Glass, as well as hundreds of lesser-known composers and musicians.

Boulanger was an exacting teacher who did not hesitate, when she felt it necessary, to take her students back to the most fundamental levels of musical study to relearn their craft. She held the view that a flawless technique, in every practical and theoretical aspect of music the student intended to pursue, was a prerequisite for artistic success. And, when she said "flawless," she meant precisely that. Among the many teaching tactics she used were sight-reading at the piano of full scores from all historical periods of European music, improvisation in traditional forms such as the motet and the keyboard invention, requiring students to supply contrapuntal lines with the voice while playing the other parts, and intensive analysis of the music of all the great European masters. By all accounts, she was a brilliant, inspiring and sometimes terrifying teacher. She lived modestly for most of her life and devoted most of her waking hours to teaching.

But, despite her manifest brilliance, Boulanger was entirely European in her musical values and temperament. The source material of the great bulk of her work, at least in the 1920s, was the repertoire of European music from the 12th century through the early 20th. There is little evidence that she made use of the American classical music that existed at the time, although she was probably familiar with it. And it seems clear that the predicates of the individual styles she nurtured in her American composition students, even into the 1960s, were always solidly grounded in European tradition. As an analyst of historical trends, she was convinced that American art music was about to "take off" in the '20s, just as Russian music had taken off fifty years earlier, and thus devoted special attention to developing the creative gifts of her American students.

Boulanger's Europhilic perspective posed little problem for young Copland, who had virtually no exposure to serious American music when he began his studies with her. Whether or not as a result of her influence, Copland clearly favored European symphonic and instrumental forms and techniques throughout his career. Given the stature Copland and his music eventually achieved, as well as that of the many who followed his footsteps to Boulanger's door, it may be argued that Boulanger's influence actually contributed to the problems experienced by American composers in achieving a distinctly American approach to music during the next fifty years. For all the Americanisms and the popularity of Copland's later work, no aspect of his composing, with the possible exception of the rhythmic dimension of his style, ever departed significantly from the fundamental compositional premises of European symphonic, operatic or instrumental music. Through the use of American folk material and rhythms, his music became American in content only, while remaining European in form and technique.

Given Copland's extraordinary talents for self-promotion and for selecting precisely the right *mode* of presentation that would maximize the impact of his pieces on musicians and the public alike, this duality of approach may have been the result of conscious career choices on his part. It certainly made his music congenial to conductors of American orchestras, most of whom were European in nationality and training prior to 1970. But it also prevented Copland from ever achieving the radically native conceptions of an Ives, a Gershwin, a Cowell or a Cage.

Prior to his Parisian sojourn, Copland's early works had been relatively undistinguished. These included a number of piano pieces and songs, most of which were highly derivative of French models (Ravel, Debussy, Satie). But, under Boulanger's guidance, he began to develop the beginnings of his own style. In part this was due to his more systematic exposure to the works of contemporary European masters, such as Stravinsky, Schoenberg and Milhaud. The French publisher Durand brought out his early piano piece, *The Cat and the Mouse* (composed in 1920 while he was still a student of Goldmark), in 1922, and Copland went on to compose the ballet *Grohg* later that year to a scenario by Clurman derived from Murnau's classic silent film, *Nosferatu.* Copland was never fully satisfied with *Grohg* in its original form, but would later extract orchestral movements from it to stand as separate pieces. These included his *Cortege Macabre,* premiered by Howard Hanson in Rochester, 1925, and his *Dance Symphony,* which he submitted in 1929 to a competition sponsored by the RCA Victor recording company.

During his period of study with Boulanger, Copland also composed four motets, a *Passacaglia* for piano and a *Rondino* for string quartet, as well as the song "As It Fell Upon a Day" while visiting Vienna with Clurman in the summer of 1923. But the climax came later that year when Boulanger introduced Copland to Serge Koussevitzky, who was about to take up his post as conductor of the Boston Symphony Orchestra (BSO). In the presence of the young Sergei Prokofiev, who was visiting Koussevitzky that day, Copland played the piano version of *Cortege Macabre* for the maestro, who, with Boulanger's encouragement, suggested that Copland write an organ concerto to be performed the following year in Boston with Boulanger as soloist.

Copland returned to America with Clurman in June of 1924, only a few months after the premiere of Gershwin's *Rhapsody in Blue.* While working frantically to have the organ symphony ready on schedule, he nevertheless found time to make the acquaintance of Marion Bauer. Bauer got him involved with the then-fledgling League of Composers, and arranged for him to perform his *Passacaglia* and *The Cat and the Mouse* on their first "Young Composers Concert" that November. These pieces attracted some favorable press attention.

The *Organ Symphony* received its premiere as scheduled, on January 11, 1925 at Aeolian Hall with Walter Damrosch conducting his progressive New York Symphony. The piece was successful and led to Copland's being hailed in the press as the "Stravinsky from Brooklyn." At the concert, Damrosch gave a little speech about the work in which he made the now-famous comment, "If a gifted young man can write a symphony like this at twenty-three, within five years he will be ready to commit murder!" Koussevitzky's BSO premiere followed a few days later, with equal success. And, at that point, Copland's American career was launched.

With the success of the *Organ Symphony* behind him, Copland was awarded the first Guggenheim Fellowship ever given to a composer, upon the joint recommendation of Boulanger, Damrosch and Koussevitzky in 1925. Renewed the following year, this enabled him to devote his time exclusively to music. He also lived in a notoriously frugal, even monkish style during the 1920s and 1930s, and was noted among his friends for being perpetually in search of free apartments for a few weeks or months at a time. In addition to his important contact with Marion Bauer, he had also developed a close rapport with Minna Lederman (later: Minna Daniel), editor of the then-embryonic magazine *Modern Music.* It was at Lederman's urging that Alma Wertheim also endowed Copland with an additional thousand dollars to help see him through 1925–1926.

The League of Composers commissioned *Music for the Theatre* from Copland in 1925. He worked on this important, jazz-influenced suite at the

MacDowell Colony, finishing it in September of that year. It received its premiere the following November and attracted considerable attention, not the least of the reasons being the absence, despite its title, of any dramatic scenario or program.

Copland, as much a practical musical entrepreneur as he was a composer, could not have been indifferent to the enormous successes that Gershwin was achieving at this time, right under his very nose in New York, with the *Rhapsody in Blue, Three Preludes* and *Concerto in F,* without even the benefit of Boulanger's instruction. Copland very definitely saw himself as part of the "high-brow" classical music world, as Gershwin did not, and at the age of 25 there can be little question that he hungered for similar popular success. While Copland denied any conscious influence from Gershwin to the end of his days, certain facts speak for themselves regarding his work at this period.

Gershwin, theatre composer *par excellence,* created his three concert masterpieces within the two-year span of 1924–1925. Copland's first major work after the *Organ Symphony* was his *Music for the Theatre,* followed almost immediately by his 1926 *Piano Concerto,* many of whose textures are directly reminiscent of the Gershwin *Concerto.* From discarded sketches for the *Concerto,* Copland fashioned the first two of his eventual four *Piano Blues,* a suite similar to Gershwin's *Preludes,* although the latter did not receive their first performance until December of 1926.

Even more striking evidence of Copland's direct attempt to compete with Gershwin lies in the relationship of both composers to violinist Samuel Dushkin. As was noted in Chapter 5, Gershwin had arranged two early piano pieces (from 1923) for violin and piano under the tile "Short Story," which were performed by Dushkin in New York in February 1925, only a month after the premiere of Copland's *Organ Symphony.* In March of 1926, after his return to Paris with Clurman, and just as he was beginning work on the concerto, Copland composed *Two Pieces for Violin and Piano* for the same Samuel Dushkin, who later performed them as well. Whatever role Dushkin himself may have played in the genesis of these works remains unclear to this day, but it is a virtual certainty that Copland was at least aware of the existence of the Gershwin pieces, even if he was not familiar with them. And given Copland's lifelong attention to *all* the music of his contemporaries, the possibility of his *not* knowing seems remote.

In any case, the evidence strongly favors the notion that Copland, during the mid-1920s, experienced a decided and unacknowledged influence from both Gershwin's professional success and some of his musical mannerisms. Copland's abandonment of jazz techniques after completion of his *Piano Concerto,* therefore, can be viewed not only in the context of his purely musical evolution (the terms in which he himself described it), but also as an abandonment of a particular avenue of commercial success that had outlived its potential usefulness for him as the jazz age was winding down. It should also be stated that Gershwin was probably not indifferent to Copland's early successes in classical media and may have sought to achieve comparable prestige with his own concert music. It is significant to note, in this context, that Gershwin was among the opening night audience for Virgil Thomson's *Four Saints in Three Acts* in 1934.

This tendency to follow a lead set by others would remain with Copland throughout his creative life. In Chapter 8 we will see how his turn toward "Americanism" in his great ballets of the late 1930s and early 1940s was foreshadowed in the music written by Virgil Thomson for the government-produced films, *The River* and *The Plow That Broke the Plains*, a few years earlier. Similarly, Copland's turn toward serial music in the 1950s followed the very conspicuous example of Stravinsky, after the death of Schoenberg. While Copland was never as slavish a follower of trends as was, for example, the Austrian composer Ernst Křenek—who jumped on so many stylistic bandwagons that, at the end of a long career, he found himself to be a composer without any independent identity at all—he nevertheless had a well-developed sense for which kind of music would create the greatest public impact at each epoch of his development.

After sojourning in Europe during 1926–1927, Copland returned to the United States and became a lecturer at the New School for Social Research in New York. He was to continue these lectures, interrupted by his various travels and periods of intense composition, for the next ten years. Ultimately the core of his lecture material was collected in book form, under the title *What to Listen for in Music,* first published in 1938.

It was also at this time that Copland began to discuss with his colleague, Roger Sessions, the possibility of sponsoring a joint series of new music concerts. Copland had met Sessions, a fellow Brooklynite four years his senior, in Paris in 1926. They began to discuss the concert series seriously in the summer of 1927, and finally produced their first concert in April 1928, featuring music by Theodore Chanler (another alumnus of the "Boulangerie"), Walter Piston, Mexican composer Carlos Chávez (with whom Copland had already begun to form what would become a lifelong collegial relationship) and Virgil Thomson. These concerts would continue for the next four years, finally concluding in December of 1931. Despite the fact that Sessions remained in Europe for much of that time and had only minimal participation in their actual organization, they continued to be called the "Copland-Sessions Concerts" and provided a much-needed hearing for many of the most cutting-edge composers of the time, among them: Henry Cowell, Marc Blitzstein, George Antheil, Vernon Duke, Roy Harris, Nino Rota, Henry Brant, Robert Russell Bennett, Colin McPhee,

Darius Milhaud, Paul Bowles, Israel Citkowitz and, of course, Copland and Sessions themselves.

In addition to lecturing and organizing the Copland-Sessions concerts, Copland spent much of the late 1920s composing music that began to move away from the early, jazz-influenced pieces such as *Music for the Theatre* and the *Piano Concerto*. In July of 1928 he performed the concerto to an audience of 17,000 at the Hollywood Bowl. The piece was greeted with shock and derision by some, and with enthusiasm by others—a fate it continued to experience wherever it was performed for several years thereafter. After spending a week with Henry Cowell in San Francisco, Copland returned to the MacDowell colony and immersed himself in work on his first major chamber piece, the trio *Vitebsk*. Vitebsk was the name of the birthplace of the Russian-Jewish playwright, S. Ansky, author of *The Dybbuk*. Copland was an admirer of this play, as was Gershwin, and both composers had toyed with the idea of setting it to music. However, neither pursued the matter to the point of actual composition, and it remained for Leonard Bernstein to finally bring *The Dybbuk* to the musical stage as a ballet some forty-five years later. Although, like Gershwin, Copland was not a particularly observant Jew, in *Vitebsk* he began a process of examining ethnic musical ideas that was to lead him toward works such as *El Salon Mexico* (based on Latin American music) and *Appalachian Spring* (based on American Anglo-Celtic folksong) over the next ten to fifteen years.

In 1928 Copland finally joined the League of Composers, which had helped him out so many times before, and helped to organize the Cos Cob Press. During the winter he oversaw two more Copland-Sessions concerts (on December 30, 1928 and February 24, 1929). *Vitebsk* was premiered by Walter Gieseking (piano), Alphonse Onnou (violin) and Robert Maas (cello) at Town Hall in New York on February 16, 1929. Later that year, Copland submitted a *Dance Symphony*, extracted from his discarded ballet *Grohg* to the competition, mentioned earlier, sponsored by the RCA Victor recording company. He shared the eventual prize with Louis Gruenberg, Ernest Bloch and Robert Russell Bennett. But, while all this activity had been going on, Copland the composer was moving in an even more abstract direction. In the late 1920s he had conceived the idea of writing a set of variations for piano.

The musical world, no less than America at large, had been radically altered by the stock market crash of October 1929. This ushered in the Great Depression, which lasted until World War II finally put an end to it. The crash had ruined many of the great theatre promoters on Broadway and, when combined with the invention of talking pictures, lured much of New York's finest theatrical talent to California (see previous chapter). In the "high-brow" world of serious art and music, the glamour and energy of the 1920s gave way, overnight it seemed, to a sober atmosphere of intensely intellectual works. And, later in the decade, much of the new music and theatre acquired a strong political focus as well. Performance resources were scaled down, concerts were fewer and more poorly attended, patronage dried up in many places, and the plight of the millions of people dispossessed by the Depression increasingly occupied the attention of writers, independent photographers and filmmakers, painters and composers. The American labor movement, which had been gathering momentum during the preceding three decades, shifted into high gear. And the Marxist political ideas that had succeeded, albeit with unprecedented brutality, in drawing the almost medieval Russia of the Romanovs into the 20th century, began to appear more and more attractive to young American intellectuals of the period.

It was in this social and political context that Copland began working on the piece that was to become the major item in his oeuvre for solo piano, the *Piano Variations*. He had become enamored of the young writer Gerald Sykes, whom he had met in 1925 through critic Paul Rosenfeld, and together they rented a small house in upstate Bedford, New York, where Copland went to work intensively on the new piece. He began by playing through dozens of examples of keyboard variations by great European composers of the past and gradually began to sketch out his own ideas. The emerging shape of the *Variations* was the closest Copland had come to working with Schoenberg's tone methods up to that time, and the final set of eleven (completed at the Yaddo camp in Saratoga Springs, New York the following summer) were eventually distilled from more than sixty pages of sketches. Unlike *Music for the Theatre* or the *Concerto,* the *Piano Variations* owed no discernible debt to the jazz styles of the 1920s. And, unlike *Vitebsk,* they had no reference to an extra-musical idea. In fact, the abstract character of these variations was the closest thing to "absolute" music that Copland had done since the *Organ Symphony* of 1924, from which he had subsequently excised the organ solo, converting the piece into his *First Symphony* for orchestra alone in 1926. But the *Piano Variations* were far more advanced compositionally than anything in the symphony. After thirteen years of intensive work, and equally intensive exposure to all the important ideas of his colleagues in the avant-garde, Copland had achieved the ability to concentrate his musical thinking into an economy of tonal and rhythmic gestures previously unknown in his music. This is not to say that the *Piano Variations* reflected the aphoristic style being espoused concurrently in Europe by Anton Webern, but rather that they demonstrated a mastery of musical integration, with a minimum of thematic materials, more comparable to the *Three Preludes* that Charles Griffes had left unfinished at his death ten years earlier. The *Variations* were to become the first really major work of Copland's to remain in the repertoire of serious musicians.

Virgil Thomson (to 1931)

Almost four years to the day before Aaron Copland entered the world, a very different child had been born to a long-established Southern Baptist family in St. Louis, Missouri, on November 25, 1896. This boy was to become the second most well-known American classical composer of his generation, and his name was Virgil Garnett Thomson. By contrast to the stressful, goal-directed urban childhood of Copland, Virgil Thomson's proceeded at a more leisurely southern pace. Things moved more slowly, summers were longer, roots were deeper and relatives, possibly, more numerous. Life consisted of school, church, music lessons, vacations, holidays, and lots of visiting among relations.

Unlike his urban colleagues, Thomson grew up with a strong sense of place. His natal American landscape was that of the southern Midwest, and the family traced itself back for many generations before an immigrant ancestor was to be found. While young Virgil displayed an aptitude for

Virgil Thomson *(1896–1989) as he looked in the early 1940s after replacing Lawrence Gilman as critic for the* New York Herald-Tribune. (Photo courtesy of ASCAP.)

music, there was no single point in his life where he, like Copland, resolved to become a musician and set out to do so in a hard-headed, systematic way. Rather, Thomson came to music gradually, through a process of evolving interest throughout his childhood. And his early passion was very largely focused on the monolithic tradition of American Protestant church music in all its forms.

Thomson trained as a military pilot during World War I, but the war ended before he saw any action. After leaving the military, Thomson returned home to take private organ and piano lessons and to study at the local junior college. During this period of his life, among other things, he was introduced to a short-lived habit of chewing hallucinogenic peyote by Dr. Frederick M. Smith, grandson of Mormon prophet Joseph Smith and father of one of Thomson's classmates, Alice Smith. Finally, Thomson settled on Harvard as his educational objective, hoping eventually to become an organist and choir director at a well-paying city church, which would give him the freedom to pursue his composing. So, with the financial assistance of family and friends, including Dr. Smith, Thomson set off for Cambridge, Massachusetts, in August of 1919.

At Harvard, Thomson immediately made the acquaintance of Archibald Davison, the director of the Harvard Glee Club and distinguished scholar and editor of choral music whose editions are still standard fare among many choral groups. He became Davison's assistant and substituted many times for the older man, as well as aiding in the preparation of some choral settings eventually included in Davison's anthologies.

Thomson also studied composition with the composer Edward Burlingame Hill (see Chapter 4), who would later become Leonard Bernstein's teacher as well. Both Davison and Hill had substantial French education and a strong orientation toward French music. Their combined influence opened Thomson's eyes to a more cosmopolitan view of music than he had brought with him from St. Louis and led, in 1921, to his own migration to Paris.

Harvard had established two "traveling fellowships," in honor of John Knowles Paine, to enable composition students to work in Europe for a time. One of these was held by Thomson's friend, Melville Smith. With the help of Hill and Davison, Thomson procured the other, on condition that he return to Harvard after one year and complete his degree. Accordingly, Thomson set sail for Paris during the same month of the same year that Copland embarked on his own journey into music history.

Copland and Thomson did not meet each other immediately. It was only after Melville Smith had encouraged Thomson to study with Boulanger that the two became acquainted. But Thomson's relationship with Boulanger was neither as sympathetic, nor as successful as Copland's.

Copland and Boulanger shared an almost perfect sympathy of temperaments; both were hard-working, objectivist personalities whose whole attention was focused on music, despite casual interests in art and politics. Thomson, in contrast, possessed a distinct flair for expository writing and a passion for modern literature, painting and design, in addition to his musical vocation. Moreover, in the early 1920s Copland was becoming increasingly committed to the kind of "modernist" approach to music that intrigued Boulanger, while Thomson always maintained a foothold in his conservative, midwestern Protestant origins, which held less appeal for his teacher. These differences between the two pre-eminent American composers of the early 20th century were apparent even from their student days, and developed into occasional frictions between them in later years, although each maintained a cordial, frank and mutually respectful public attitude toward the other throughout his life.

Thomson's interest in the visual arts led him into the circles of the many brilliant painters with which Paris abounded in the 1920s. He was particularly drawn to the declining school of Dadaism and absorbed the self-consciously eclectic principles of many of its exponents. Without this background, it is doubtful whether Thomson would have been sufficiently sympathetic with the works of Gertrude Stein to later complete two major operas with her. Thomson's interest in the visual arts also led him in the eventual direction of musical portraiture, a method of composing that he, for all practical purposes, invented.

Before leaving Cambridge, Thomson had been asked by the prominent critic of *The Boston Transcript,* H. T. Parker, to send periodic reviews of Parisian musical activity home for publication. One of these articles, which appeared in early 1922, was an enthusiastic report of the conducting of Serge Koussevitzky in Paris. As Pierre Monteux, conductor of the Boston Symphony Orchestra was about to depart that institution, Thomson's article spurred Boston's interest in Koussevitzky as a possible replacement. In his 1966 autobiography, Thomson claimed that these events led to Koussevitzky's appointment to the Boston Symphony in 1924. Given the important role that Koussevitzky subsequently played in launching Copland's career, with the 1925 Boston Symphony performance of the *Organ Symphony,* it is easier to understand some of the resentment Thomson came to feel a few years later, when he perceived that Copland, Koussevitzky and the modernist circle were less than enthusiastic about helping him find an audience for his neo-Romantic works.

While studying with Boulanger, Thomson completed a *Prelude* for piano and began work on a *Sonata di Chiesa,* or "Church Sonata" for chamber ensemble. He also made sketches for his *Symphony on a Hymn Tune* (completed in 1928), using the American classic, "How Firm a

Foundation," as his main theme, but did not show these sketches to Boulanger.

It was also during this first Parisian period that Thomson formed an attachment with his lifelong companion, the painter Maurice Grosser, also in France on a Harvard fellowship. Thomson's relationship with Grosser, like Griffes' with Dan Martin, Copland's with Victor Kraft (see Chapter 8), and Samuel Barber's with Gian-Carlo Menotti (see Chapter 9), was to join the long list of "best kept secrets" in American art music. In the homophobic climate of American culture, public disclosure of homosexuality could, quite literally, mean the end of one's career, even in the supposedly more tolerant fields of the fine arts. This situation is somewhat less restrictive today than it was in the early part of the century, but remains an issue, especially at the highest levels of artistic activity. It was largely for this reason that homosexual composers throughout American history, such as Griffes, Copland, Thomson, Barber, Henry Cowell, Marc Blitzstein, Leonard Bernstein, Paul Bowles and John Cage, maintained such an extraordinary silence in interviews, articles and biographies on the subject of their personal lives. Some, such as Cowell, Bernstein, Bowles and (briefly) Cage, sought protection behind the facade of conventional marriage and may have been authentically bisexual in nature. But this was certainly not the case with either Thomson or Copland.

In a culture that attaches perhaps inordinate importance to matters such as an artist's ethnic background, religion, physical health, gender, regional origins and heterosexual romantic liaisons, it is astonishing that something as central to an informed understanding of the creative personality and life experience as is a gay composer's sexual orientation could have been so consistently and facilely "blacked-out" by generations of scholars and critics. Yet that has been the case more often than not in American music history. Moreover, the conspicuous differences of attitude, temperament, esthetic objectives and style which have existed between gay composers, such as Thomson and Copland, clearly debunk the standard heterosexist assumption that all gay people in the fine arts hold similar views of the world or have identical lifestyles. And lastly, such deliberate expurgation of history deprives upcoming generations, of both homosexual and heterosexual artists, of important factual data and historical role models.

In 1922 Thomson received word that his traveling fellowship was not to be renewed, so it became clear that he would have to return to the United States, as previously agreed, to finish his Harvard degree. Davison arranged for him to be appointed organist at the historic King's Chapel in Boston (a post that has been held by numerous distinguished American musicians, including its current tenant, Daniel Pinkham). Accordingly, Thomson returned to Boston and took up his duties, finally graduating from Harvard in 1923. For the next three years he traveled between Boston and New York, continuing private studies with Hill, joining (with Grosser) the Harvard Liberal Club, and digesting some of the musical, literary and artistic stimuli he had absorbed in Paris. He also began his serious work as a music journalist in 1924, with articles for H. L. Mencken's *American Mercury* and for *Vanity Fair.* He was present for the premiere of Copland's *Organ Symphony* in 1925 and told Boulanger that he had "wept" because he hadn't been the one who wrote it.

All of the composers of the "Boulangerie" supported each other's work to some extent, but factional divisions did occur. Throughout the 1920s, Copland held the commanding position in the circle of Boulanger's current and former students, and was the best known and most often performed of the group. Neither Boulanger nor Copland favored the unique brand of neo-Romanticism that Thomson was beginning to develop, nor did the most powerful composers of "les Six," Milhaud and Poulenc. As a result, Thomson had a difficult time securing performances, either in Paris or New York. This already touchy situation was further complicated by the literary rivalry between James Joyce and Gertrude Stein, each of whom functioned as the center of a distinct literary solar system, orbited by lesser planets and satellites. Joyce was a strong promoter of Pound, George Antheil (see below), and the modernist esthetic. Stein, by contrast, whose literary style was more closely related to Dadaism and Cubism in the visual arts, grew exceptionally fond of Thomson, especially after he set her poem "Capital Capitals" as a song.

The relationship between Thomson and Stein had begun when they met in the winter of 1925–26. By early 1927, they were discussing plans for an opera. Stein, who loved Spain and was a close friend of Picasso, gravitated more and more toward the subject of Spanish saints and encouraged Thomson to visit that country, which he did. Gradually the libretto took shape, fertilized by much correspondence and exchange of ideas between Thomson and Stein. In November of 1927, Thomson was ready to begin composing what would eventually become *Four Saints in Three Acts.*

Thomson worked steadily on the opera, composing it at the piano and singing the parts. In his autobiography he claimed that his procedure was to complete each act in this manner before committing any notes to paper. When he did finally begin scoring, it was in the form of vocal lines accompanied by a figured bass, identical to the practice of Monteverdi and other early Baroque opera composers, and a technique that would have been meaningless with anything other than highly tonal music. In this form, the opera was completed in July of 1928. As it turned out, Thomson was exceptionally farsighted in not orchestrating the work until shortly before its premiere, because that left him the flexibility to adapt the final version to the very unusual staging decisions which were eventually made.

The composition of *Four Saints in Three Acts* had interrupted Thomson's work on his *Symphony on a Hymn Tune,* to which he promptly returned, finishing the sketch of the last movement during a visit to Spain in the late summer of 1928. After returning to the States later that year, he showed the symphony to Koussevitzky, who declined to perform it with the Boston Symphony, despite Thomson's assistance in having secured his position as conductor of that orchestra.

Thomson also began his lifelong practice of making musical portraits during the summer of 1928, deriving the idea from what he had observed of the working practices of Gertrude Stein. Particularly in her later work, Stein devoted much attention to interpreting external realities through the unique prism of her echolalic literary style. She often wrote quickly and from life, the way a painter does when making a portrait of an individual. Thomson adopted a similar procedure when asked to write something for a young Spanish woman who played the violin, whom he had met in the town of Ascain that summer. Written for solo violin, this *Portrait of Señorita Juanita de Medina Accompanied by Her Mother* became the first in a long, long list of such short works that Thomson would continue to produce until only days before his death. His last effort, left unfinished when he died, was a portrait of playwright Jack Larson, librettist of his third and final opera, *Lord Byron.*

In composing his musical portraits, Thomson always worked in the presence of the subject, just like a painter. Over the years he discovered that this procedure imposed a discipline on the composer that could not be duplicated precisely in any other way. He also felt that it led him to unique insights and observations about the character of the subject, which would not otherwise have come out through ordinary interaction. By the time of his death in 1989, he had completed close to 300 such musical portraits, and created a new procedure, if not a new genre of composition. Much of this work remains unpublished to this day, and we can only await the time when it becomes generally available.

Life for Virgil Thomson, after the completion of *Four Saints in Three Acts* and the *Symphony on a Hymn Tune,* continued to be a matter of seeking performance of his existing works, composing new ones, traveling in Europe and the United States and circulating among visual artists and literary people. His relationship with Copland at this time was a mixture of gratitude and resentment: gratitude for the efforts Copland made to help get his work performed, and resentment over the exclusion he still felt from the movers and shakers of the American music world due to his deliberate lack of "modernist" musical credentials.

In London, in 1931, Thomson met Everett "Chick" Austin, director of the progressive Wadsworth Atheneum art museum in Hartford, Connecticut. He began to interest Austin in the Stein opera, and was making headway with an increasing number of performances of his Stein song "Capital Capitals." He was also composing at the time his *Stabat Mater,* three early *Piano Sonatas,* his first two *String Quartets,* his *Second Symphony* and some songs and chamber pieces. When Thomson sailed for America in December of 1932, it was to be the beginning of the end of his expatriate existence. Although he would return to Europe many times in ensuing years, particularly during the prelude years of World War II, from that point on, New York became his base of operations and would remain so for the rest of his life.

Roy Harris (through the Piano Sonata, 1931)

While Copland and Thomson were growing up and growing into their musical personalities, yet a third major figure was beginning to emerge even farther west. Le Roy Ellsworth (Roy) Harris was born, according to his own none-too-reliable account, in a log cabin in Lincoln County, Oklahoma, on February 12, 1898. As there is no documentary support for his birthdate and place, one must accept on faith the extraordinary associations in Harris' mind with the memory of Abraham Lincoln created by the timing and setting of his birth. His parents were farmers with somewhat more than the usual education and, around 1903, the family moved to the then-rural town of Covina in the San Gabriel Valley of southern California (now part of the Los Angeles megalopolis). Harris was in poor health for his first ten years of life and, possibly as a result, developed somewhat greater intellectual tendencies than his few boyhood companions. His mother gave him his first music lessons on the family piano and, in high school, he took up the clarinet as well. Harris also became a very physical youngster once his health began to improve and later excelled in high school sports.

Apart from his apparently excellent high school band classes, Harris' early musical training was sporadic. Around 1916 he enlisted in the Army Training Corps but, like Thomson, missed being called to serve by the armistice that ended World War I in November of 1918. Thereafter he experimented for a while with farming, briefly fulfilling his father's wish that he continue the family tradition, but soon abandoned it in favor of courses in philosophy, sociology and economics at the University of California's Berkeley and Los Angeles campuses. He continued his practice of improvising on the piano and took some harmony lessons from a Charles Demarest, and then from one Ernest Douglas, both organists. Harris attempted a large work for chorus and orchestra at this time and succeeded

Roy Harris *(1898–1979) in late middle age. The premier American symphonist of the 1930s and 1940s, his photogenic smile belied a monumental ego and vociferous temper.* (Photo courtesy of ASCAP.)

in getting it shown to Alfred Hertz, then conductor of the San Francisco Symphony. Hertz, in turn, gave him an introduction to the prominent local composer and teacher, Albert Elkus, who declined to accept Harris as a pupil. However, Harris did meet Arthur Farwell (see Chapter 4), who was teaching at Berkeley at the time. The ever-adventurous Farwell saw something in Harris' immature work that the others, except possibly Hertz, had missed. He admired the younger man's harmonic daring and unique ways of deriving the form of his work from its melodic materials, which was to become a permanent trait of Harris' mature style.

Under Farwell's experienced tutelage, Harris completed an *Andante* for orchestra, originally conceived as part of a symphony he never finished. Harris sent this work to Howard Hanson, newly appointed director of the Eastman School of Music in Rochester, New York, in 1924. Hanson was so impressed with it that he played it with his orchestra at Eastman. The *Andante* received favorable notices from some New York critics, which

enhanced the young composer's reputation back home in California sufficiently to attract the attention of pianist Elly Ney, wife of the conductor
Willem Van Hoogstraten. At his wife's insistence, Van Hoogstraten pro-
grammed the *Andante* at a concert of the New York Philharmonic in
Lewisohn Stadium in July 1926.

Harris traveled to New York in the summer of 1925, on borrowed
money, in order to establish an East Coast base for himself before the
performance. While in the East, he was able to stay briefly at the MacDowell
Colony in Peterborough, New Hampshire. There he met Copland, who
was completing his *Music for Theatre,* as well as the elder Americanist
composer, Henry F. B. Gilbert. The two younger composers immediately
struck up a friendly acquaintance, and Copland suggested that Harris go to
Paris to study with Boulanger. This was not the first time, nor would it be
the last, that Copland exerted himself to send the most promising young
composers of his acquaintance to Boulanger for the kind of study he himself
had experienced.

Financed by the ever-amenable Alma Wertheim, patron of the Cos
Cob Press which printed so much of the early music of this generation,
Harris embarked for Paris with his second wife, Sylvia, arriving in the late
summer of 1926. By this time Virgil Thomson had also returned to Paris
and was deeply involved in the cultural scene there. Copland and Clurman
were also sojourning in Paris and Berlin during the latter part of 1926, while
Copland was working on his *Piano Concerto.* That fall marked the first time
that the three major non-academic composers of their generation, Copland,
Harris and Thomson, were together at the same time and place, and in
regular communication with each other.

By 1930, Roy Harris had completed his studies with Boulanger,
although he had done so less thoroughly than Copland or Thomson.
Boulanger called Harris her "autodidact" because he simply would not
bend his independent nature to her rigid musical discipline. Perhaps he had
been, as Copland later thought, too old when he went to her for instruction.
More likely the problem lay in Harris' extremely volatile, egocentric and
maverick nature. He exasperated Boulanger as no student prior to him had
done, and the two ultimately settled on a routine where most of their work
involved analyzing what Boulanger believed to be flaws in the work of
earlier composers. Unlike his contemporaries, Harris was magnetically
drawn to the European music of earlier centuries. Both in Paris and later in
New York he made an intensive and independent study of the works of
masters from the Medieval through Baroque periods, from organum
through the fugue. These were later to serve as important technical models
for him in his symphonies.

Harris was unhappy in his marriage to Sylvia, and Sylvia appeared to be equally unhappy in France. Through Boulanger, Harris met a young woman named Hilda, who became his copyist, friend and, later, his third wife after a divorce from Sylvia was arranged. (*N.B.*—the absence of maiden names for Harris' first three wives is due to the composer's later faulty memory and a mysterious lack of documentation.)

While studying with Boulanger, Harris had composed his *Concerto for Piano, Clarinet and String Quartet,* which was performed in Paris in the spring of 1927. The *Concerto* became Harris' first truly mature work and showed elements of the melodically expansive, polytonal style that has become identified with his name. He also began work on his only sonata for solo piano in 1928, but was hindered by his insecure command of piano technique and, according to Nicolas Slonimsky, who knew him at the time, his already formed habit of thinking in contrapuntal terms. Completed in 1930–1931, the *Piano Sonata* remains Harris' only large work for solo piano and an example of the transitional style in which he was writing during the late 1920s. Even though he would eventually marry a virtuoso pianist and compose a number of other solo pieces, his piano music remains secondary to his more important symphonic and choral works that came later.

Harris slipped and fell on the steps of the cottage he shared with Sylvia in Juziers in 1929. He injured the coccyx bone at the base of his spine and had to return to the United States for corrective surgery. During the several months of his convalescence he was, of course, unable to work at the piano. This proved to be a significant benefit to the still-developing composer, sharpening his aural imagery and opening a whole new world of non-pianistic textures to his imagination. He was at work on both his first complete symphony, entitled *An American Portrait—1929* at the time, as well as his first *String Quartet.* The enforced change in his composing procedure caused problems for him in finishing the quartet, but the symphony went on to help make his reputation.

Harris had been the recipient of Guggenheim Fellowships in 1927 and 1928, partly as a result of the success of his *Concerto,* but was now at loose ends and experiencing medical expenses associated with his treatments. In 1931, back in California, he was granted a composing fellowship from the Pasadena Music and Art Association, which eased the way for him until 1932, when he began teaching summer classes in composition at the Juilliard School in New York, a position he maintained until 1938. One of his first pupils at Juilliard to achieve later importance as a composer was the young William Schuman (see next chapter). Harris finally married Hilda in 1932, but the union was as short-lived as had been his earlier marriages. It was not until 1934 that Harris would meet and marry Beula Duffey (who later changed her name, at Harris' request, to Johanna), a brilliant pianist and sympathetic spirit, with whom he would spend the remainder of his life.

George Antheil

In addition to Copland, Thomson and Harris, the Boulanger circle of the mid-1920s included George Antheil (1900–1959), Marc Blitzstein, Roger Sessions and Walter Piston, the last three of whom will be discussed more fully in subsequent chapters. Antheil is a pivotal composer from this period of music history and was attracting the greatest public attention of any American in Paris during the 1920s. He had been born in Trenton, New Jersey, to Polish parents on July 8, 1900, but the family moved to Poland soon thereafter, where Antheil lived until the age of fourteen. After the family's return to New York, the sixteen-year-old fledgling composer commuted to Philadelphia regularly for lessons with Constantin von Sternberg, who subsequently referred him to Ernest Bloch in New York.

Antheil worked with Bloch from 1919 to 1921, completing his *Symphony No.1 "Zingareska"* under Bloch's tutelage. This was at the same time that the young Roger Sessions was studying with the Swiss composer (see next chapter), but, unlike Sessions, Antheil did not follow his teacher to the Cleveland Institute of Music when Bloch took up the directorship of that institution in 1920–21. Instead, financed by Mary Louise Curtis Bok, future founder of the Curtis Institute in Philadelphia and patron of Samuel Barber, Antheil sailed for Europe in May of 1922, intending to establish himself as a progressive concert pianist. He settled in Berlin, where he became acquainted with the music of Stravinsky and Schoenberg, and continued to develop his highly innovative musical ideas in mechanistic and percussive works such as his *Airplane Sonata* (1921) and *Sonata Sauvage* (1922).

Antheil moved to Paris in the summer of 1923 and almost immediately generated huge controversy with an October performance of his piano music at the Théâtre des Champs-Elysées. He attracted the attention of the poet and amateur composer, Ezra Pound, who found in Antheil a convenient peg on which to hang many of his own esoteric theories of harmony and form.[28] But Antheil's conception of the relationship of time and space in music, and the blocklike constructions from which he fashioned his harmonic style in the 1920s, go far beyond Pound's exposition of his work. His ideas ran parallel to many of the similar techniques that Henry Cowell had begun to develop during the previous decade, and were undoubtedly influenced by the Italian "futurist" composers Luigi Russolo (1885–1947) and Francisco Pratella (1880–1955) who had staged concerts of noise-music

---

[28] See *Antheil and the Treatise on Harmony* (1923), New York, Da Capo Press reprint, 1968.

under the label "bruitismo" as early as 1913 in Milan. Antheil also anticipated much of the later work of Edgard Varèse, John Cage and avant-garde
composers and visual artists of the 1960s. The crowning achievement of
Antheil's early work, indeed of his entire career, was his 1925 *Ballet
Mécanique,* scored for large percussion ensemble, player pianos and airplane propellers. *Ballet Mécanique* foreshadowed Varèse's more highly
regarded 1931 percussion piece, *Ionisation,* and established Antheil as the
self-described "bad boy" of modern music.

During the late 1920s and early 1930s, Antheil lived alternately in
America and Europe then settled permanently in the United States in 1933.
He continued to compose, producing many fine concert works as well as
music for radio, films and television. He also contributed a Hollywood
column to Minna Lederman's *Modern Music.* But, after *Ballet Mécanique,*
Antheil turned to eclectic and conservative styles of composition, never
truly achieving a coherent voice that could be associated with his name.

The interest in the use of "noises" in music, as H. H. Stuckenschmidt
has pointed out,[29] was nothing new at the time, having precedents as far
back as Mozart. But this idea received fresh impetus during the foreshadowing, consummation and aftermath of the mechanized brutality of World
War I. The "expressionistic" movement arose in European art and gave
birth to Dada, Cubism, atonal music and such theatrical masterpieces as
Alban Berg's *Wozzeck,* Karel Čapek's *R.U.R.* ("Rossum's Universal Ro-
bots") and Fritz Lang's silent film *Metropolis.* Expressionism, combined
with the earlier "bruitism," generated a new interest in sound for its own
sake, as distinct from the specialized timbres of traditional orchestral
instruments. During this period, composers like Cowell, Antheil and
Varèse, began to view noises as legitimate material for composition. The
interesting question for them, however, was the means of organizing such
material in compositions. Antheil's principal contribution to this area lay
in his development of harmonic and textural progression by means of
mosaic, blocklike, non-developmental sections. This procedure became so
integrated into his musical thinking that he could never fully liberate
himself from it, even in later works for which it was not appropriate.
Antheil's approach resembled Anton Webern's contemporaneously evolving treatment of detached harmonic structures (and, by extension, that of
Webern's later disciples such as Morton Feldman). As we will see in
Chapters 10 and 11, such notions also dovetailed nicely with the East Asian
(and specifically Chinese) views of music that influenced John Cage and
Lou Harrison, and led additionally in the eventual direction of early
electronic music.

---

[29] Stuckenschmidt, *Twentieth Century Music,* pp. 48–49.

While it is difficult to trace any direct influence of Antheil's music on the student works created by Copland, Thomson and Harris under Boulanger in the 1920s, his was a powerful voice at the time. There can be little question that his ideas and early works entered the minds of his more traditionally oriented colleagues, perhaps giving a sharper edge to their music than it might otherwise have had. The percussive effects found in some of Thomson's later music for theatrical and radio plays produced by John Houseman, as well as the percussive piano style of Copland (and his specialized use of drums in such works as the *Fanfare for the Common Man*) may reflect the continuing germination of bruitismic ideas in their creative thinking of later years.

During the 1920s and early 1930s, Copland, Thomson and Harris were the three principal young composers on the cutting edge of American classical music. The energy and excitement they generated spilled over into the formation of several important musical organizations (see Chapter 8) and created new opportunities for other composers as well.

While these three remained relatively aloof from the growing academic establishment in subsequent decades, other composers—for whom they paved the way—opted to make their livings via university teaching. It is to these academic colleagues of the "big three" free-lances that we turn in the next chapter.

7

The Rise of Musical Academia (Hanson, Sessions, Piston and Their Colleagues)

~❧

After the founding of music departments in the major American universities during the late 19th century, American academic music went through a period of slow consolidation. Up to the 1930s most departments remained small, and the solidly conservative curricula were oriented around theoretical and historical studies. For the highest levels of applied instrumental and vocal practice, serious students went to the venerable New England Conservatory in Boston or to one of the more newly founded conservatories: Juilliard in New York, Curtis in Philadelphia, Peabody in Baltimore and Eastman in Rochester, New York. During the early part of the 20th century, smaller state and private universities began to form music departments and acquire faculty of a serious caliber as well.

Since the late 1890s, it had been feasible for a serious American music student to receive a complete musical education in the United States, but most still preferred to travel to Europe for study, partly because European classical music was still dominant in America, and partly for the prestige of having studied abroad. During the 1920s and 1930s however, American academic music underwent a tremendous spurt of growth. Affluent patrons endowed many music schools prior to the stock market crash of 1929, and the growing reputations of composers such as Copland, Hanson, Thomson, Harris, Piston and Sessions stimulated a renewal of interest on the part of the cultural elite in indigenous compositions. During the 1930s, moreover, as fascists infiltrated and seized control of the German and Italian governments and as the Stalinist regime became more firmly implanted in the

147

Soviet Union, the trickle of contemporary European composers migrating to America became a flood. By the early days of World War II, the major European composers resident in the United States included Schoenberg, Stravinsky, Hindemith and Bartók, as well as earlier immigrants such as Rachmaninoff, Varèse and Bloch. Many of these, as well as their entourage of disciples, assumed leading chairs at major university music departments, thus reinforcing in a new and more direct way the grip of European esthetics on American composition that lasted through the 1970s. In Virgil Thomson's words, the influx of European professor-composers during the 1930s became a "Trojan horse" for American music.

Before going into the lives and works of the major native academic composers of this period—Piston, Sessions, Hanson and others—it might be worthwhile to consider some of the conditions inherent in the organization of collegiate music departments as they affected (and continue to affect) composition. One of these conditions can be illustrated with an historical anecdote.

When various former students of Ernst Křenek (Robert Erickson, Wilbur Ogden, Thomas Nee) began in the mid-1960s to organize what later became the music department at the University of California's San Diego campus, they conceived a kind of department structured upon almost Platonic academic lines: no formal classes, open seminars, unconventional evaluation techniques and so on. When presenting this plan to the university they were told to proceed as they wished, but not to expect the university to recognize the department or grant credit to its students. So the founders revised their plan to conform to the university's requirements.[30]

Universities tend to measure success by their numbers of graduates and the success of those graduates in later life. They therefore have less than total enthusiasm for students who are not pursuing a degree, or for educational methods that cannot produce quantifiable results in terms of student performance. This places the university paradigm of education in direct conflict with many aspects of teaching creative artists such as composers, painters or poets, who cannot be so conveniently quantified.

Because music, among all the fine arts, possesses the greatest potential for an organized, systematic theoretical infrastructure, it followed naturally that a great deal of compositional instruction was actually theoretical instruction in the early days. And, prior to 1925, the operative theory was that of functional and chromatic tonality based largely on Germanic models. After Schoenberg demonstrated the 12-tone system of composition in 1925, this hyper-rational approach to organizing tonal materials fed the

---

[30] Robert Erickson, conversation with the author, November, 1974.

theoretical machine of American university composition departments to an even greater degree.

Music theory is easily quantifiable: one's knowledge of its premises, techniques and methods can be lectured about, cast in the form of work-book exercises and evaluated via conventional testing methods. This made it exceptionally congenial, as an academic discipline, within the method-ological contexts of most American university classrooms. But theory and composition are not precisely the same thing. While conventional thinking asserts that composers must be thoroughly trained in traditional harmony, counterpoint, formal analysis and orchestration—despite the embarrassing examples of great composers, such as Gershwin, whose training was neither thorough nor formal—the more nebulous aspects of the composer's craft are far more difficult to teach in the university context. Such things as the shaping of melodic lines and phrases, through-composed form, the match-ing of instrumental timbres to the inherent character of the musical idea, underscoring the dramatic potential of a given moment in a song lyric or libretto, the evolution of a personal harmonic language—these and many other essential skills of a composer defy conventional teaching methods and objective evaluation. They are often only communicable via intensive private instruction and/or individual apprenticeship for which universities are poorly suited.

As a direct result, American academic music as an institution through-out its history has tended to favor the promotion of composers and styles whose approach is objective, quantifiable and non-controversial. Thus, the composers whose work has been most popular with the public, such as Copland, Thomson, Harris, Menotti, Bernstein, Glass, etc., have not, on the whole, maintained a lasting connection with any single academic estab-lishment, and have often been notoriously uncomfortable in such short liaisons as they did consent to. On the other hand, composers who have been major figures in academia, such as Piston, Sessions, Hanson, Schuman, Babbitt, Kirchner, Hiller, Druckman and Riley, have usually had a more difficult time establishing their work with a broad public.

Unlike the Europeans—composers like Hindemith and Milhaud—who were accustomed to different attitudes toward academia and took to university teaching like the proverbial fish to water, American composers have often seemed uncomfortable in the role of professor. In the case of men like Piston and Sessions, this discomfort has led to sometimes ponder-ous forays into the diversionary pathways of theory and esthetic philoso-phy, demonstrating their musical erudition to one and all, but failing to improve the public acceptance of their music. Others, like Babbitt and Hiller, have sought to reshape their music into an imitation of physical sciences, which could then compete for recognition, funding and publication on supposedly equal ground with more traditional departments of the university. The experimentalist composers, like Cage, Cowell, Partch and Harrison, found ways to use the university, in spite of itself, to provide them with resources needed for their work, but, with a few exceptions, did not become permanent fixtures at any one school for the bulk of their lives. Roy Harris also successfully resisted the lure of tenure, flitting from teaching job to teaching job throughout most of his career.

The first American composer of the 1890s generation to exert a major impact on higher musical education in the United States was Howard Hanson. Born in Wahoo, Nebraska, on October 28, 1896, Hanson studied under the pedantic theorist, Percy Goetschius, at the Institute of Musical Art (later to become the Juilliard School) during 1914 and subsequently at Northwestern University, from which he took his B.A. in 1916. After several years of teaching at various institutions, and a quick rise through the academic ranks fueled by his manifest creative energy, he was awarded the first Rome Prize given by the newly founded American Academy at Rome

Howard Hanson *(1896–1981). His predilection for a lush, post-Romantic sound won many admirers for his symphonies.* (Photo courtesy of ASCAP).

in 1920. Not to be confused with the Prix de Rome, won by Debussy and many other important French composers in earlier years, the American Rome Prize was nevertheless modeled on its French predecessor and specifically intended for young American composers residing in Rome. It would later be awarded to Sessions, among others, and has become an important item on the resumés of many academic composers.

In 1924, Hanson was appointed director of the Eastman School of Music at the University of Rochester, New York, where he would remain until 1964. He immediately undertook an energetic expansion of the Eastman curriculum, enhanced its faculty, developed its performing ensembles and offered the premieres of many works by emerging composers throughout the country. It was Hanson who gave Roy Harris his first break by performing the *Andante* for orchestra he had completed under Farwell in 1925, which led to Harris' subsequent career development. And this was only the first of many such services provided by Hanson throughout his long and distinguished career. His students included a number of American composers who achieved later importance, such as Jack Beeson, William Bergsma and Peter Mennin.

By 1929, Hanson held a place among the best known classical music personalities in America. For many years he was considered the most important (certainly the most accessible) living American composer. But his music has tended to fade with the passage of time. For one thing, he was absolutely committed to a big, post-Romantic sound, especially reflected in his symphonies, of which the most popular is still the second, subtitled the "Romantic." Hanson, preoccupied for most of his life with teaching, conducting and administrative duties, never seemed to develop either the interest or the creative acumen to explore the more experimental aspects of modernism then being developed by Copland, Cowell, Sessions, Varèse and others. Had he done so, his music might have benefitted from more intellectual or emotional substance. And, while his technique was solid, it was never sufficiently remarkable to attract the kind of respect given to Piston, Sessions or William Schuman. Moreover, his personal musical voice lacked a clear identity of its own based on distinctive stylistic elements. All too often his orchestral works sound like the Hollywood scores of European hacks like Erich Korngold or Max Steiner. These characteristics actually contributed to Hanson's popularity during his active life as a composer, but also ultimately placed him in a category of second-rate creative talents alongside such figures as Amy Beach, John Alden Carpenter, Charles Wakefield Cadman, Henry Hadley, E. B. Hill and Edgar S. Kelley.

Hanson's major contribution was not, therefore, as a composer, but as an educator and promoter of other composers. He continued this activity for forty years and earned an important place in American musical history. He died in Rochester on February 26, 1981.

Sessions, Bloch and Piston

Of all the significant American composers who have functioned largely in an academic context for the bulk of their careers, Roger Sessions (1896–1985) and Walter Piston (1894–1976) hold primacy of place in the 20th-century history of our music, both for the quality of music that they produced and for their contributions to the development of later composers. Sessions, like Copland and Gershwin, was born in Brooklyn, New York, on December 28, 1896. His parents belonged to the genteel, white middle class and were both aspiring writers. His mother maintained a student residence hall at Smith College in Northhampton, Massachusetts, while his father practiced law in New York, living with the family only during the summers. Like most successful composers, young Sessions settled on his career early in life. He began taking piano lessons at the age of four and had created a romantic opera after Tennyson's *Lancelot and Elaine* by 1910. He was a sensitive boy and, although of superior academic ability, had difficulty fitting in to the social routine of the various private and military schools to which his parents sent him. He entered Harvard in 1911 at the age of fourteen and worked, as would Virgil Thomson and Walter Piston a few years later, with Archibald Davison and Edward Burlingame Hill.

As a young man, Sessions had a passion for the music of Richard Wagner and Richard Strauss. He wrote appreciative articles on these composers and other musical subjects for the *Harvard Musical Review,* beginning in 1912. His sympathies, in contrast to Copland's and Thomson's, lay in the Germanic, not the French direction at this time. (Later, he would come to view the works of Strauss after *Der Rosenkavalier* as vastly inferior to that composer's earlier tone poems.) After receiving his B.A. from Harvard in 1915, Sessions went on to Yale, where he worked exclusively with Ives' former teacher, Horatio Parker, until receiving his Bachelor of Music degree in 1918. His relationship with Parker was much more sympathetic than Ives' had been twenty years earlier, although he sensed Parker's frustration at being left behind by the musical innovations of the early part of the century. Sessions felt that Parker had given up trying to assert his brand of post-Romantic composition. Parker was to die less than two years after Sessions graduated.

While at Yale, Sessions had won the Steinert Prize for the first movement of his unpublished *Symphony in D major*. This, together with his mother's connections, got him a job teaching music theory at Smith College in 1918. But, despite his solid Ivy League credentials, Sessions ran afoul of the chairman of Smith's music department and felt frustrated at what he considered the infantile level of music education being promulgated at the college. He was to remain at Smith until 1921 and, while there, met and married Barbara Foster in 1920. This marriage would end in divorce some seventeen years later.

It was also during his tenure at Smith College that Sessions met the teacher who was to have the greatest impact on his slow development as a composer. Ernest Bloch (1880–1959) had come to the United States in 1916 from his native Geneva, Switzerland, where he had studied with Emile Jacques-Dalcroze. Bloch was engaged at that time as conductor for the dance company of Maud Allan and stayed on to teach at Mannes College. His 1919 *Viola Suite* won a Coolidge Prize, and he devoted himself thereafter to establishing a reputation as the leading Jewish composer of his generation. Bloch's self-conscious assertion of his Jewish identity is embodied in such works as his rhapsody for cello and orchestra entitled *Schelomo* (1915), his 1916 *"Israel" Symphony* for solo voices and orchestra, the Hebrew cantata *Avodath hakodesh* (1933), and in his adaptation of Jewish melodic and articulative patterns into various of his chamber and sym-

Ernest Bloch *(1880–1959) in old age. The radically minded Swiss composer immigrated to America in 1916 and became the principal teacher of Sessions and many others.* (Photo courtesy of ASCAP.)

phonic works. While he had a solid technique that he could use with great finesse, particularly in such works as his 1925 *Concerto Grosso No.1,* he was equally capable of tasteless and superficial bombast, as, for example, that which is displayed in his overrated epic rhapsody for chorus and orchestra, *America* (1926).

Bloch was of volatile and eccentric temperament, but he was also a gifted composer, teacher and administrator, and possessed a first-rate intelligence. In 1920 he assumed the first directorship of the Cleveland Institute of Music, and later went on to become director of the San Francisco Conservatory (1925–1930) and (together with his former student, Sessions) a faculty member at the University of California, Berkeley (1940–1952). When Sessions first sought him out, in late 1919, he was living in New York.

Sessions' first meeting with Bloch has become a favorite anecdote among students of American classical music. Bloch sat the young composer down at the piano and demanded that he play some of his music. Sessions began to work his way through the early *Symphony in D* with Bloch standing behind him shouting out the names of the various older composers whose influences he detected in the work. Sessions, equally conscious of those influences, soon joined in—anticipating Bloch and announcing the names ahead of him. Bloch later insisted that he had staged this scene as a kind of test for young Sessions.

In any case, Sessions developed a strong tutorial relationship with Bloch, and followed him to Cleveland in 1921. Bloch arranged for him to join the faculty of the Cleveland Institute, together with Theodore Chanler, who also later became an alumnus of the "Boulangerie" in Paris, and the young Douglas Moore, who would go on to make his own name in American opera.

During his time at the Cleveland Institute, Sessions created his first mature work, incidental music to Leonid Andreyev's dark, Poe-esque tragedy, *The Black Maskers.* It is significant that, despite his later important contributions to the literature of piano music, cantata and symphony, Sessions inaugurated his career with music for the stage.

There is a strange parallel between the esthetic divisions of the major American composers from the early 20th century, and the European romantic composers of the 19th. In the latter case, the sober, even scholarly works of the Germans—Schumann, Mendelssohn and Brahms—contrast sharply with the more flamboyant, and sometimes more superficial works of the cosmopolitans—Chopin, Liszt, Berlioz and Wagner. In a similar manner, the deeply serious side of American musical thinking from the first part of this century is to be found in the music of Sessions, Piston, William Schuman and Elliott Carter, while the less ponderous, more popular music of Copland, Thomson, Harris and their circle has achieved a higher public profile, but not necessarily greater respect from serious listeners and scholars. Because of this phenomenon, as well as the association of Sessions' name with musical academia, his music is often thought to be difficult, dense and colorless. But, throughout his career, from *The Black Maskers* through his last completed and greatest opera, *Montezuma,* Sessions clearly showed an affinity for the theatre and for music as dramatic gesture, possibly derived from his early attachment to Wagner. The subjects of his music theatre pieces are often dark, and the issues serious, as contrasted with the sunnier efforts of Copland, Thomson or Blitzstein (see Chapter 8). But the dramatic intensity of Sessions' music never fails to marry the theme of the piece, and his rarely staged theatrical works remain among the most effective dramatic music conceived by an American.

The Black Maskers was performed, under the composer's baton, at Smith College in 1923 and eventually published by the Cos Cob Press in 1932. It is dedicated to Ernest Bloch. Although Andreyev's play is highly expressionistic in character, with many of its devices blatantly lifted from Poe, Sessions' music for it owes more to Stravinsky, with whose works he was deeply involved at the time, than to the more authentic musical expressionists Schoenberg and Berg (whose works were barely known in America then). Sessions later extracted an orchestral suite from the play, which he conducted at the Copland-Sessions concert of March 15, 1931 and which has subsequently been performed by several major orchestras. It is in this form that the music to *The Black Maskers* is best known today. Sessions would further develop his interest in Poe by attempting (like Debussy before him) an opera on "The Fall of the House of Usher." But, also like Debussy, he failed to complete this project and eventually abandoned it. "Usher" would not see life as an opera until Philip Glass finally accomplished what so many others had tried, some sixty years later.

By 1925, Ernest Bloch's excitable personality and sometimes rigid ideas had provoked open warfare with the directors of the Cleveland Institute, who fired him. Sessions resigned in protest but did not follow Bloch to San Francisco. Instead Sessions prevailed upon his father to finance a trip to Europe, possibly to study with Nadia Boulanger, whom he had met via Theodore Chanler during a brief visit to the French capital in 1924. Sessions and his wife would remain in Europe, living mostly in Florence, Rome and Berlin, until 1933, supported partly by two Guggenheim Fellowships (1926, 1927), a Rome Prize from the American Academy (1928, for which committee-head Walter Damrosch had to bend a number of rules), and a Carnegie Foundation Grant (1931). As previously mentioned, he met Copland in 1926 and soon began discussions with him which led to the formation of the Copland-Sessions concerts in 1928. Sessions had originally planned to return to the United States and take a more active role

in the management of this series. But he remained in Europe in the sympathetic company of friends like Hindemith, Ernst Toch, Artur Schnabel and
Alfredo Casella, leaving most of the actual organizational work to the New
York-based Copland, though he did provide suggestions and pieces for the
concerts. He also became more politically aware during his years abroad,
especially as he witnessed the rise of fascism first hand in Germany and
Italy. Sessions was to remain uncharacteristically (for a composer) conscious of political events for the rest of his life.

Sessions' three most important works created during his European
years were his *Symphony No.1* (premiered by Koussevitzky with the
Boston Symphony Orchestra in 1927), his first *Piano Sonata* (1930) and his
Violin Concerto (1935). All three of these are tonal, if highly dissonant,
works and reveal the composer's abiding attachment to the procedures of
late-Romantic European music, inherited from Parker, Bloch and his own
study of late-19th-century German composers. Sessions was not yet entirely sure of his personal voice as a composer, and the symphony in
particular required some revision before anyone, including Sessions, was
satisfied with it. While he never did decide to study with Boulanger in a
formal sense, he showed her the score of this work and she made several
suggestions for tightening the structure of the first movement recapitula-
tion, suggestions that he rejected at first. This, combined with Sessions'
distinct preference for the German musical milieu, became a source of
alienation between him and Boulanger. The two were never close after that.
After the Boston Symphony premiere, and similar suggestions from
Koussevitzky, however, Sessions had to acknowledge the problems with
the symphony, and extensively rewrote it.

The first *Piano Sonata*, which has become one of Sessions' best-
known works, had an equally tortured genesis. It had been intended for the
first Copland-Sessions concert in May of 1928, but Sessions was unable to
finish it in time. Like many painstaking and highly self-critical composers,
especially those obsessed with formal considerations, the young Sessions
often wrote non-linearly. In the case of the *Sonata,* the famous introduction
in B minor was actually added after the main thematic idea of the first
movement had been conceived, and then assumed a greater structural
importance in the completion of the work. Sessions returned to New York
for the first performance, by pianist John Duke, and worked himself into
exhaustion trying to finish the piece in time. But only the first two movements were played at the concert, albeit to favorable reaction from Sessions'
former teacher Hill and others. It was only after Sessions returned to
Europe, and the pressure was off him, that he was able to complete the
remainder of the work. The *First Sonata* was finally premiered in its entirety

by Frank Mannheimer at the International Society for Contemporary Music (ISCM) Festival in July of 1930.

The *Violin Concerto,* which is perhaps the most important of these three early works, had only received two major performances at the time of the composer's death in 1985. It was originally intended to be performed by the famous violinist Albert Spalding in 1937 with Koussevitsky and the Boston Symphony. But Spalding had difficulty mastering the piece, appeared to be temperamentally unsympathetic to it, and objected to the unrelieved staccato of the final movement. When he presumed to alter the notes of this movement, Sessions withdrew the piece from him, and it was not premiered until Robert Gross undertook it with the Chicago Symphony in January 1940. The *Concerto* did not receive its New York premiere until nineteen years later, when Leonard Bernstein and violinist Tossy Spivakovsky played it with the Philharmonic in 1959. Sessions' withdrawal of the piece from Spalding and, consequently, the Boston Symphony, resulted in a rift between Sessions and Koussevitzky that never healed. The Boston Symphony, as a result, played Sessions' music far less frequently than that of his contemporaries, which in turn slowed the process of public recognition already hindered by Sessions' slow pace of composition during his early and middle years.

Throughout this period, Sessions' marriage had been deteriorating. He and his wife separated in 1933 and were divorced in 1937. Shortly thereafter he remarried. In 1935, he took up his academic career in earnest when he joined the faculty of Princeton University.

Unlike Copland, Thomson or Harris, Sessions had no interest in American folk music, nor is there any evidence that he appreciated the importance of the African influence in American music generally. His perspective was entirely European, and he considered the "high" culture of America to be the extension and inheritor of what had gone before in Europe. Nor was he particularly concerned with the development of a characteristically "American" sound, as was Copland, viewing this quest as the short road to superficiality and phoney exterior mannerisms in a composer.

He shared these attitudes with his otherwise very different contemporary, Samuel Barber (see Chapter 9), and he fostered them in his students as well. He taught at Princeton from 1933 to 1944, then at the University of California, Berkeley, until 1953. Returning to Princeton that year, he remained there until his "official" retirement in 1965, and then assumed faculty chairs again at Berkeley, Harvard and Juilliard. In his more than sixty years of teaching, Sessions' students included the later-noted American composers Milton Babbitt, Edward Cone, Peter Maxwell Davies, David Del Tredici, Leon Kirchner, Donald Martino, Conlon Nancarrow, Hugo

Roger Sessions *(1896–1985) in his later years. At first a close colleague of Copland, he turned to serialism after 1950 and became the motive force in much American academic music.* (Photo courtesy of BMI.)

Weisgall, Vivian Fine, Lehman Engel, David Diamond, Eric Salzman, Earl Kim, John Harbison, John Eaton and Ellen Taaffe Zwilich.

Sessions has often been viewed as a monolithic figure in American academic music, indifferent to public acclaim, preoccupied with purely developmental questions of the art itself—in short, the quintessential "Ivory Tower" composer, especially in his later teaching years. The gradual proliferation of an innocuous style of academic composition among American students during the 1960s and 1970s has been attributed to his pervasive influence, exerted both directly and indirectly via his students, as they began to assume academic chairs themselves throughout the country.

There is undoubtedly some truth in this view. By contrast to the efforts of Copland, Hanson, Schuman and others, Sessions was notoriously indifferent to the future course of his students' careers and rarely exerted himself to assist them with such practical matters as promoting public performance of their works or finding jobs. But, the view of Sessions as a doctrinaire pedagogue—despite his published theoretical writings such as *Harmonic Practice* (1951)—seems to be exaggerated. Reactions of a broad selection of Sessions' students, summarized in Andrea Olmstead's *Roger*

Sessions and His Music,[31] emphasize that Sessions consistently sought to develop the inherent qualities of those students' individual ideas, rather than create carbon copies of himself (a criticism, for the sake of comparison, that has often and cogently been leveled at Hindemith's teaching). When the work of his students resembles Sessions' own—as, for instance, in the case of John Eaton, whose musical values and later operas bear a strong Sessions imprint and have continued to develop ideas and musical processes latent in Sessions' work from the period of *Montezuma*—it is more likely the result of the powerful personal example he set for them.

During his first Princeton period, Sessions created a number of significant works, including his *String Quartet No.1* (1936), the piano suite *Pages from a Diary* (1940) and his *Second Symphony* (completed in 1946). While his personal voice was becoming more secure, his style was also becoming more freely dissonant and less attached to the post-Romantic models of his youth. The symphony, in particular, aroused the ire of colleagues who felt he was becoming overly involved in abstruse formal issues, to the detriment of the finished sound.

Although tonality and key orientations had always been more a point of departure for Sessions, rather than the fundamental organizing principle of his pieces, with the *Piano Sonata No.2,* written for pianist Andor Foldes in 1946, after the composer's move to Berkeley, tonality had clearly ceased to become an issue for him. He was set firmly on the path that would eventually lead to full application of 12-tone methods in his later works. Sessions' adoption of the 12-tone system was arrived at through a course of internal compositional evolution, in contrast to Copland's similar stylistic transformation in the late 1950s. In Leonard Bernstein's view—and Bernstein was sufficiently intimate with Copland to know—Copland felt left behind by musical fashion and attempted to "catch up" by deliberately adopting the dodecaphonic technique.[32] Sessions, on the other hand, like his frequent model Stravinsky, moved toward dodecaphony in small, but consistent stages throughout the 1940s. This transition found its expression in his two major operas, created between 1947 and 1963, *The Trial of Lucullus* and *Montezuma.*

These operas represent a study in contrasts within Sessions' work. *Lucullus* was brief (one act), lightly scored and written in a month. *Montezuma* was three acts long, massively scored for an orchestra of Wagnerian dimensions, densely textured and composed over a period of sixteen years. Both libretti dealt with weighty issues of moral responsibility under conditions of political and military conquest and reflected Sessions' essentially

---

[31] Olmstead, pp. 93–100.
[32] Joan Peyser, *Bernstein, a biography,* p. 332.

antimilitaristic politics. But, the most important contrast lies in Sessions' compositional migration from his highly chromatic/atonal early style, in *Lucullus,* to his frank adoption of the 12-tone system in *Montezuma.* Moreover, *Montezuma,* particularly, forms an important if unintentional bridge from the expressionistic serial atonality of Alban Berg's *Wozzeck* and *Lulu* to the later stage rituals of American composers as diverse as Pauline Oliveros and Philip Glass, despite its serial organization. One of the most important features of *Montezuma* in this regard is its use of rhythmic leitmotivs, differently assigned tempi, and ostinatos to represent both ceremonial or violent action and the personal and ideological traits of characters. The framing of violent actions in ritualistic tableaux, characteristic of *Montezuma*'s second act, anticipates similar procedures in Glass's later work, especially *Akhnaten.*

During the decade-and-a-half in which he worked on *Montezuma,* Sessions also produced some of his most important works in other media, including his second *String Quartet* (1951), *Sonata for Violin* (1953) and *String Quintet* (1958). In all his chamber music, Sessions revealed his fondness for the structural elements of Beethoven's late chamber works. This period also saw the composition of his *Third* and *Fourth Symphonies,* his only *Piano Concerto,* his *Mass for Unison Choir* (1955), *Divertimento for Orchestra* (1960) and his cantata for soprano and orchestra, *The Idyll of Theocritus* (1954). In all of these works, Sessions continued to develop his personal application of the 12-tone method, which became the organizing principle of all his later music. *The Idyll of Theocritus* pursues a historical connection with Schoenberg as well in that it is very similar in concept to the latter composer's monodrama, *Erwartung.* But, unlike Schoenberg's piece, *The Idyll of Theocritus* is not practical for staged performance.

After *Montezuma,* Sessions entered a period of prolific composition, discovering a fluency he had never experienced before. It is probable that his consistent application of the 12-tone system was largely responsible for this. The long arch of his musical designs led him increasingly to large works whose movements were meant to be played without pause. Furthermore, the expanded instrumental resources Sessions had employed in *Montezuma* heightened the color of his orchestrations thereafter, especially with the use of unusual percussion instruments. Between 1963 and 1981, Sessions composed five more symphonies, a third *Piano Sonata* (1965) of which the third movement is an elegy to the assassinated president John F. Kennedy, a *Rhapsody* (1970), *Concertino* (1972) and *Concerto* (1981) for orchestra, *Six Pieces for Violoncello* (1966), written for his son John, a *Double Concerto* (1971) for violin, 'cello and orchestra (also written for John Sessions), a brief set of *Canons* for string quartet composed in memory of Stravinsky (1971), choral music including settings of *Psalm 140* (1963), *Three Choruses on*

Biblical Texts (1972) and his most famous late work, the massive 1970 cantata on Walt Whitman's *When Lilacs Last in the Dooryard Bloom'd*.

Sessions had always been unusually conscious of the global political events taking place around him and remained so to the end of his days. The *Sixth* (1966), *Seventh* (1967) and *Eighth Symphonies* (1968) reflected especially his personal reactions to the Vietnam War and the cultural changes it was bringing to the United States. But such extra-musical associations as exist in these works are never as overt as, for example, quoting the tunes of peace-movement songs—which might have been Copland's or Thomson's practice under similar circumstances. Sessions remained loyal to his personal musical values and style in all his work, and his reactions to contemporary events exist purely within the syntax of his own musical language.

In 1974, Sessions received a Pulitzer Prize for lifetime achievement in music. Between 1975 and 1978 he composed his ninth and final *Symphony*, based on reflections on the work of the English poet/engraver, William Blake. In 1981 he completed his last work, the *Concerto for Orchestra*, which was premiered by Seiji Ozawa and the Boston Symphony in October of that year, and for which he was awarded a second Pulitzer. At his death on March 16, 1985 in Princeton, he left unfinished an opera on the fairy tale "The Emperor's New Clothes" on which he had been working with librettist and then-*New Yorker* critic, Andrew Porter.

Throughout his career Sessions' music, like that of most academic composers, was largely unknown to the American public, and it remains so today. Much of his music is still unpublished (although this is less true of him than of many of his contemporaries), and his influence on the development of American classical music outside of academia has thus far been negligible. However, while Sessions' music rarely inspires affection or enthusiasm among lay listeners, he is held in great respect by most of the musicians who have made any systematic study of his oeuvre, even those few who were not his students or students-of-his-students. Sessions' relative inaccessibility is probably due to his commitment to the 12-tone methods on which all of his music after the early 1950s is based. But Sessions, unlike many serial composers, was no mere compositor of pitches. His formal designs are deserving of serious study because of their tremendous scope and ingenious structure, and his orchestration, especially after *Montezuma* is always the work of a master craftsman. While the memorability of his vocal lines is complicated by the serial method, he nevertheless had a strong sense of melody and was capable of extraordinary lyricism within the parameters he imposed on himself. Today serialism is out of fashion and, as a consequence, Sessions' music is likely to languish in oblivion for some time to come. But, once musicians have achieved a more balanced perspective on the historical role played by this unique method of composition, and serial music can be heard in the context of a historical style, there is more than enough substance in Sessions to predict a future revival of interest in his work.

Of equal importance to the history of American academic music is the work of Walter Piston. Unlike Sessions, Copland and others, Piston never adopted the 12-tone method exclusively, but remained devoted to exploration of new approaches to tonality throughout his career.

Piston was born in the fishing town of Rockland, Maine, on January 20, 1894. He was the son and grandson of Italian immigrant fishermen, and his surname was originally spelled "Pistone." Thus, his background contrasts with the Anglo-Saxon, middle-class Sessions in that he was of Med-

Walter Piston *(1894–1976). Another major student of Nadia Boulanger (with Copland, Harris, Thomson and Carter). He became the leading composer on the Harvard faculty and devoted himself to symphonic and chamber music of superb craftsmanship.* (Photo courtesy of BMI.)

iterranean descent and proletarian family. Whether these influences led him to a greater fondness for American popular music (and possibly a greater attachment to tonality) than Sessions ever displayed is arguable, but Piston began his musical life by playing the violin in theatre orchestras and dance bands after the family's move to Boston in 1905 and his subsequent graduation from the Mechanic Arts High School. Piston was also a trained draftsman and remained very finicky about the visual clarity of his scores throughout his life.

During World War I he learned the saxophone in order to play in the Navy band, then afterward continued to make his living playing in dance halls and other commercial venues. But the young Piston was dissatisfied with the intellectual limitations of popular music and enrolled as a special student at Harvard, contemporaneously with Virgil Thomson in 1919. Like Thomson and Sessions, he also worked with Archibald Davison and Edward Burlingame Hill at Harvard, as well as assisting with conducting and transcription chores. He graduated in 1924 and, again following in Thomson's footsteps, received a John Knowles Paine traveling fellowship to go to Paris for study with Boulanger and Paul Dukas (composer of *The Sorcerer's Apprentice*). In Paris he joined the remarkable collection of American composers that included Copland, Thomson, Sessions, Blitzstein, Antheil and Harris. He naturally became acquainted with the works of Satie and "Les Six"—as well as the astonishing renaissance of visual and literary arts taking place in the city during the 1920s—and, like Harris, delved deeply into strict counterpoint and the works of the early European polyphonists. While in Paris, he created his first serious composition, titled simply *Orchestra Piece* (1925), which has not been published.

In 1926, Piston returned to the United States and joined the faculty of Harvard, where he would remain for the next thirty-four years. He also composed in that year an unpublished (and later withdrawn) *Piano Sonata* and *Three Pieces* for flute, clarinet and bassoon. E. B. Hill introduced him to Koussevitzky, which led to the beginning of a long and fruitful association with the Boston Symphony even though Koussevitzky did not personally conduct a Piston premiere until 1947, when he played the *Third Symphony*.

In his early years at Harvard, Piston became increasingly uncomfortable with the hidebound, pedantic way in which music theory—and harmony in particular—was taught. His experiences in Paris had opened his eyes to new approaches, and the traditional pedagogy inherited from theorists like Paine, Goetschius and Hill was not sufficient to deal with current developments. This would ultimately lead Piston to write his own textbook on the subject, *Harmony* (first published in 1941), which would thereafter become one of the standard texts in American music education.

Piston's most significant contribution to this theoretical field was his development of the concept "harmonic rhythm," i.e., the rate and pattern of harmonic changes which underlie phrase structures and the organization of formal sections in large works, especially those in sonata form. *Harmony* was followed by two other texts of major significance: *Counterpoint* (1947) and *Orchestration* (1955). Through these influential books, Piston's ideas became ubiquitous in the education of American composers from the 1950s onward, and they are still used as standard texts in many music courses.

Between 1927 and 1937 Piston composed an unpublished *Symphonic Piece* (1927), his first *Suite for Orchestra* (1929), a *Flute Sonata* (1930), a *Suite* for oboe and piano (1931), a *Piano Trio* (1935), his first two *String Quartets* (1933, 1935), a *Concerto for Orchestra* (1933, predating works with the same title by Bartók, Sessions and Elliott Carter), a *Prelude and Fugue* for orchestra (1934), a *Concertino* for piano and chamber orchestra (1937) and his *First Symphony* (1937). Slower to develop than most of his colleagues, Piston used these works to hone and perfect his personal creative voice, heavily influenced by European Baroque and Classical models. By the time of the *First Symphony*'s premiere in Boston, April 1938, with the composer conducting, he had evolved a polished, infinitely skillful modernist tonal style. Like his fellow Mainer and Harvard predecessor, Paine, he would become noted for the perfection of musical craft above all other things in his subsequent work. Like Sessions and Harris, he had a predilection for long, archlike melodic lines and phrases. He shared Harris' love of counterpoint derived from traditional models and, throughout his work, occasionally incorporated elements of dodecaphony in a manner not unlike Sessions during the 1940s. But he differed from Sessions in never adopting the 12-tone method as the systematic foundation of his melodic/harmonic style. Piston also shared with his younger colleague at Juilliard, William Schuman, a certain affinity for jazz rhythms and other references to popular music in his symphonic works—perhaps an echo of his early experience as a professional player.

But it was the 1938 premiere of his ballet, *The Incredible Flutist*, that brought Piston into national prominence on the American musical scene. One of the paradoxes in the lives of many American composers is that their most *uncharacteristic* works are often the ones best known to and admired by the broad public. This has been the case with "The Alcotts" movement of Ives' *Concord Sonata,* with Elliott Carter's *Holiday Overture,* with Schuman's *William Billings Overture,* with Bernstein's *West Side Story,* with Sessions' *The Black Maskers,* and was also the case with *The Incredible Flutist. Flutist* was Piston's only theatre music and one of only two major works he composed that contain any extramusical referents at all. The story is a lighthearted fairy tale, reminiscent of Robert Browning's "The Pied

Piper of Hamelin," which depicts the strange effects of the arrival of a circus musician on the inhabitants of a rural village. The music has a Latin American flavor at times and is among the most immediately accessible of all Piston's work. It was premiered in its entirety by the Boston Pops Orchestra in 1938. Piston extracted an orchestral suite from it later that year, which was premiered by the Pittsburgh Symphony under Fritz Reiner in 1940 and has remained among his most frequently performed works.

As he continued his work at Harvard, Piston moved more deeply into the realm of "absolute" music, concentrating especially on symphonies, string quartets and concertos. Among his many students were Elliott Carter, Arthur Berger, Irving Fine, Leonard Bernstein, Harold Shapero and Daniel Pinkham. He composed seven more symphonies between 1943 and 1965, two concertos for violin and one each for viola (1957), two pianos and orchestra (1959), clarinet (1967), flute (1971) and string quartet and orchestra (1976), the last of these being his last completed composition. In addition, his oeuvre included a wide variety of chamber music. Perhaps the most important of his works in this medium are the five *String Quartets* (recently recorded by the Portland [Maine] SO String Quartet) written between 1933 and 1962, a 1949 *Piano Quintet*, the 1956 *Wind Quintet*, the 1964 *String Sextet* and his second *Piano Trio*, written in 1966. Furthermore, like Carter, Copland, Persichetti and others of his contemporaries, Piston composed several works for wind and percussion ensembles (concert band, brass quintet, etc.) in response to the growing importance of high school and college bands as a principal vehicle for music education in the United States during and after World War II. Piston died in Belmont, Massachusetts, on November 12, 1976.

Piston's work has always been more popular than that of Sessions and considered more serious than Hanson's. His impeccable compositional technique continues to be a subject of study and admiration for aspiring composers, but his music often fails to arouse the immediate enthusiasm of comparable works by Copland, Thomson, Harris, Still, Barber and others. Because, like Sessions, he was passed over by the changing musical fashions of the 60s and 70s, a great deal of his music is only now coming under the scrutiny of serious performers, and it is possible that his reputation as a composer, rather than as a pedagogue, will increase in years to come.

William Schuman

Several important parallels exist between Piston's development and that of his younger colleague, William Schuman (1910–1992), who also became an important force in American academic music of the mid-20th century. Both men were third generation Americans who came to music relatively late, and both turned away from training in other careers to begin by playing popular music. Of all the major American academic composers who developed a truly original style, Schuman's music remains the most accessible and popular today.

Schuman was born in New York City on August 8, 1910. Although he had some violin lessons as a child, he showed no serious interest in classical music until the age of twenty when he attended a concert of the New York Philharmonic that was to alter the course of his life. Prior to that time, from about the age of fifteen, he had formed a jazz band and composed some Tin Pan Alley songs (which were published) with his boyhood friend, Frank Loesser. Loesser would later go on to make a significant name for himself with such Broadway musicals as *Guys and Dolls, Most Happy Fella* and *How to Succeed in Business Without Really Trying.*

Schuman graduated from George Washington High School in 1928 and then enrolled in the New York University School of Commerce. On April 4, 1930, he attended the Philharmonic concert mentioned above and was swept away by the power of the music he heard. He dropped out of NYU the very next day and enrolled in Max Persin's harmony course at the little-known, but highly significant, Malkin Conservatory in Manhattan. He continued his lessons with Persin, adding the study of counterpoint with Charles Haubiel in 1931, and supported himself with odd jobs and arranging for Tin Pan Alley publishers. After taking some summer courses at Juilliard, he enrolled in Columbia University Teacher's College in 1933. That same year he attempted to write an operetta with Loesser on the life of Leonardo Da Vinci, but the two soon abandoned that project. Nevertheless, Schuman's interest in popular music continued alongside his more formal studies, and he wrote a musical entitled *Fair Enough* that was produced at the Brent Lake Camp in upstate New York during the summer of 1934. In 1935 he took part in a summer conducting program at the Mozarteum in Salzburg, then returned to the United States where he assumed a faculty position at the highly progressive Sarah Lawrence College.

Schuman taught at Sarah Lawrence from 1935 until 1945, and spent a good deal of his time there developing his philosophical positions with regard to music education. Principal among these was his concept that there is no single best way for all students to learn music, but that music education is part of a process of self-discovery that will manifest itself in different ways for each individual. This was acceptable enough at Sarah Lawrence, but, when Schuman assumed the presidency of Juilliard in 1945, his ideas turned the academic traditions of that institution upside down.

During the decade of his tenure at Sarah Lawrence, Schuman married Frances Prince and began studies with his most important teacher, Roy Harris. Harris was, at that time, at his compositional peak and was exploring the ramifications of his unique polytonal system of composition (see Chapter 8). Schuman, who would become the most important of Harris' students, worked with him closely during this period and absorbed the essential elements of Harris' technique into his own. Schuman's development and application of Harris' ideas would continue to influence his major works, especially his symphonies, for the next several years.

In the fall of 1936, J. Werner conducted the premiere of Schuman's *First Symphony* at a Works Progress Administration (WPA) Composers' Forum laboratory concert. The symphony shared the program with the premiere of Schuman's *First String Quartet* and his *Canonic Choruses* (conducted by Lehman Engel), which had been composed the previous year. The *Choruses* were successful, but both the symphony and the quartet came under harsh criticism. The consensus was that Schuman had not yet gained sufficient mastery of musical technique and materials to succeed with larger forms.

Profiting from this experience, Schuman's second attempt at a symphony was considerably more successful. His *Symphony No. 2*, premiered

William Schuman *(1910–1992). He abandoned Tin Pan Alley to become a major American symphonist as well as president of Juilliard and Lincoln Center.* (Photo by Carl Mydans. Courtesy of E. Snapp, Inc., composer's representative.)

in May of 1938 under Schenkman, was awarded a prize by the North American Committee to Aid Spanish Democracy, comprised of Copland, Sessions, and two of Schuman's former teachers: Harris and Bernard Wagenaar. Copland, especially, took up the younger composer's cause and wrote a laudatory article in the May–June, 1938 issue of *Modern Music*. The symphony was repeated by a WPA orchestra in Greenwich Village in June and later played again by the CBS Orchestra under Howard Barlow. In February 1939, Koussevitzky, at Copland's suggestion, played it with the Boston Symphony, attracting the attention of the young Leonard Bernstein. Despite a favorable review by Paul Rosenfeld in the *Musical Quarterly,* the public reaction to this performance ranged from indifference to overt hostility. Schuman was in the process of establishing modernist credentials.

Encouraged by the attention of serious musicians, but still in need of winning over the public, Schuman went on to compose his popular *American Festival Overture* later in 1939, and then yet another symphony in 1940–1941. The *Third Symphony,* premiered in October of 1941 by Koussevitzky, received a far more favorable reaction than had the previous two and won for Schuman the first New York Music Critics' Circle Award ever given. This was followed in 1943 by a Pulitzer Prize (the first awarded in music) for his secular cantata *A Free Song,* to a text by Whitman. In eight short years, Schuman had risen from a barely competent fledgling to the first rank of American classical composers. Thereafter his music was more widely performed than that of any of his academic colleagues.

In 1945, the G. Schirmer publishing company asked Schuman to become its editorial director. After some soul-searching he left Sarah Lawrence College to accept the position. But only a few weeks after taking on this job, he was invited to become president of the Juilliard School. Faced with this difficult choice between two positions, either one of which would have given him a substantial role to play in influencing the future of American serious music, he opted for Juilliard, but continued to serve in an advisory capacity with Schirmer until 1952.

At Juilliard he immediately began implementing his ideas about the reform of higher music education. He merged the Institute of Musical Art, where Hanson and others had studied, with the Juilliard Graduate School to form the present-day Juilliard School of Music. In addition, he amalgamated the separate studies of theory and music history into a single, four-year curricular program under the rubric, "Literature and Materials of Music." He founded the Juilliard String Quartet, which has since evolved into one of the most important ensembles of its kind, and revived the opera theatre, adding to it a dance division. Furthermore, over the years Schuman enhanced the Juilliard composition faculty with such dynamic personalities as William Bergsma, Vincent Persichetti, Peter Mennin, Robert Starer and Hugo Weisgall, many of whom became important teachers of the next generation of minimalist and post-modernist composers such as Steve Reich and Philip Glass.

In 1962 Schuman became president of Lincoln Center and used his office to secure commissions for many important American composers. He also lobbied successfully for the housing of Juilliard at the Lincoln Center complex and added a drama division to the school. This later became a principal forum for John Houseman and other significant directors. In short, Schuman's career and legacy as an administrator were as important as his work as a composer, and his ability to handle both roles with such energy and excellence baffled many. But Schuman had a unique capacity to work on many things at once and was one the most efficient managers of his personal time since the piano pedagogue Carl Czerny in the 1830s. If he had fifteen minutes between appointments, it was the most natural thing in the world for him to spend them adding a few notes to his latest symphony.

As a result, his compositional activity continued unabated. He completed nine of his ten symphonies prior to his retirement from Lincoln Center in 1969, and, in the remaining twenty years of his creative life, produced six major orchestral works, nine choral pieces and roughly a dozen works for other ensembles. Schuman's work is characterized by its rhythmic vigor, bold orchestration, arching melodic lines and polytonality. His penchants for layering of choirs, counterpoint and polytonality, especially as revealed in his symphonies, can be traced back to the influence of Harris. But Schuman extended and developed his teacher's ideas; he did not merely imitate them. And he was never as doctrinaire in his application of these methods as was Harris.

Perhaps his best-known orchestral work is his *New England Triptych* (1956), based on melodies of the old singing master-composer, William Billings (see Chapter 1). The most popular of these three movements is, of course, his treatment of Billings' "Chester," which has been played under the title *Chester Overture* many times. The *New England Triptych* should not be confused with Schuman's earlier *William Billings Overture* (1943), which was withdrawn by the composer after its premiere under Rodzinsky in 1944. Schuman had a special interest in Billings, and the earlier overture served more as a prototype for the later suite.

In addition, Schuman contributed to the growth of Charles Ives' reputation with his brilliant 1963 orchestration of the latter's *Variations on "America"* (see Chapter 3). This early and highly accessible work by the teenage Ives had received only limited exposure in its original setting for organ up to that time. Schuman's orchestration, and subsequent arrangement for concert band (1968), vastly expanded its audience.

Schuman's most successful work for the stage was his 1953 opera, *The Mighty Casey*, based on the popular narrative poem by E. L. Thayer. Following the pattern set by Copland with his high school opera, *The Second Hurricane* (see next chapter), Schuman chose a popular subject and gave it a treatment that could be handled by less than professional singers. *Casey* has also been performed as a cantata, without staging.

It is still too early to evaluate the ultimate fate of William Schuman's music. Of all the academics discussed in this chapter, his music is the least "professorial" and, indeed, could as easily bear inclusion in our discussions of non-academic American composers. In the last twenty years his work has been eclipsed by the greater attention given to post-modernist and minimalist composers such as Glass, Adams, Del Tredici and Corigliano. But he may yet prove to be one of the great American composers of this century, as he was certainly one of its greatest music educators.

Milton Babbitt

The most prominent of Roger Sessions' students, and his successor at Princeton, was Milton Babbitt (b. 1916). Babbitt was the fifth, and youngest, of the major American composers in this century to function primarily in academia. And he became the high priest of a view of serial music as an academic discipline that had a profound (and, some would say, pernicious) influence on young American composers throughout the middle decades.

Babbitt was born in Philadelphia on May 10, 1916, but spent most of his early life in Jackson, Mississippi. Like Piston and Schuman, he discovered an early attraction to popular music and, as a teenager, played clarinet and saxophone in jazz bands and wrote popular songs. He maintained a lifelong interest in American musical theatre and even wrote an unsuccessful musical, entitled *Fabulous Voyage*, in 1946. But Babbitt's principal musical vocation lay elsewhere. He was as gifted a mathematician as he was a musician and entered the University of Pennsylvania in 1931 to pursue a major in mathematics. Dissatisfied with UP, he transferred to New York University and studied composition with Marion Bauer (see Chapter 4), earning his B.A. in music in 1935. He then went to Princeton where he studied with Sessions, at first privately then as an enrolled graduate student. In 1942, he was awarded one of the first Master of Fine Arts degrees to be given by Princeton in music.

Babbitt had joined the Princeton faculty as a graduate student in 1938, and continued there, serving as well on the mathematics faculty, until 1945. During this first period of his academic and creative work, he developed strong interests, first in the music of Varèse and Stravinsky, then in the 12-tone methods of Schoenberg, Berg and Webern. Babbitt, drawing on his background as a mathematician, was the first to recognize and develop systematically the mathematical possibilities inherent in Schoenberg's method. Initially this took the form of applying set theory to pitch organization, which he articulated in an unpublished 1946 paper, "The Function of Set Structure in the Twelve-tone System."

Perhaps in reaction to the intense intellectual labor and profound ramifications of this kind of work, Babbitt took a two-year hiatus from Princeton between 1946 and 1948 during which he turned back to more popular modes of composition, creating the musical mentioned above. But, frustrated in any Broadway ambitions he might have had, he returned to Princeton in 1948 and would remain there for the next twenty-five years, developing the implications of his initial discoveries.

The decade from 1947 to 1957 saw the creation of a group of Babbitt's works which explored the mathematical implications of the 12-tone method, applied it to other parameters of music to create the concept of "total serialism," and established Babbitt's international reputation as the foremost exponent of mathematical composition. These works included his *Three Compositions for Piano* (1947), *Composition for Four Instruments* (1948), *Composition for Twelve Instruments* (1948), first two *String Quartets* (1948, 1954), *Composition for Viola and Piano* (1950), *Woodwind Quartet* (1953), *All Set* for saxophones, trumpet, trombone, piano, contrabass and vibraphone (1957) and *Partitions* for piano (1957). In addition to extending his application of set theory to pitch organization (and his concomitant development of such theoretical concepts as "source sets," "derived sets" and "combinatoriality" of the 12-tone row and its subsets), Babbitt applied serial procedures to the rhythmic placement of tones as well as to dynamics and the metrical organization of his pieces, frequently at multiple levels of the formal design. As a result, he created music for which the conventional theoretical vocabulary of terms such as "melody," "harmony," "motif," "tonality" and so on was not only inadequate but actually irrelevant. Thus, listeners who were unprepared for the resulting sound complexes, and unfamiliar with the premises of Babbitt's approach, were literally unable to hear the organizational principles at work in the music. To them, Babbitt's highly structured compositions sounded, ironically, like random agglomerations of unrelated tones.

The difficulties posed for *performers* by these early works of Babbitt were as unprecedented and as great as those presented to listeners. The rapid shifts of dynamics and register, as well as the meticulous rhythmic placement of articulations called for in these pieces exceeded even the demands made in the music of Schoenberg and Webern. This aroused resistance and hostility to Babbitt's works on the part of performers and, in turn, led the composer to seek means of realizing his music which neither required the coöperation of live players nor was subject to their technical limitations. This last issue led Babbitt to explore the possibilities for total control of musical materials presented by the then-emerging technology of analog synthesizers. But before discussing this later phase of his work, it may be helpful to gain a further perspective on the controversy created by Babbitt's style of total serialism and its implied socio-musical agenda, especially in view of the impact it was to have on other academic composers through the 1950s and 1960s.

The fundamental point of dispute in the 12-tone method, as postulated by Arnold Schoenberg in the 1920s, lay in his assertion that the twelve notes of the chromatic scale can be heard as relating only and equally to each other, simply because the composer says that they do when this method is applied to them. In most European and American music up to that time, the tones of the scale (and the chords built upon them) had been related in a hierarchy of importance to a central "tonic" or key tone. Seven of the twelve tones (in the conventional major, minor or modal scales) were "diatonic" and assigned an order of importance based on their functions such as preceding the tonic, following the tonic, connecting the tonic to other important chords, or serving as transitions between such secondary chords. The different harmonic functions of chords built on the diatonic notes were analogous to the various functions of pieces in a chess game, all working toward a common "tonal" goal. The five remaining, or "chromatic," tones of the scale provided opportunities for harmonic variety, inventive chord changes and modulations from one key to another.

These functions of tones were based on the supposedly fixed consonant or dissonant harmonic relationships among them, relationships derived from the relative compatibility of the overtone series generated by any given pair of notes. This traditional view of consonance and dissonance was based on acoustical studies going back to Pythagoras and the ancient Greeks. Where Schoenberg departed, and departed radically, from the practice of earlier centuries was in denying these acoustical harmonic relationships between tones. He asserted, in effect, that all intervals between pitches were equal partners in a kind of musical democracy. He attempted to substitute the absolute difference in pitch between two notes (i.e., how far apart they are in the gamut) for the tension-building properties achieved in earlier tonal music by harmonic dissonance. Thus, the original 12-tone theory led, if applied with strict consistency, to certain musically contentious propositions, such as the conclusion that a (traditionally defined) major sixth must be heard as more "dissonant" than the more closely spaced tritone. Disruptive as Schoenberg's approach was to the traditional flow of melody (and even Schoenberg acknowledged that his system worked best in melodic/contrapuntal terms), it played worse havoc with harmony, effectively demolishing the system of tonality that had been practiced in European music since the earliest stages of the Baroque period.

The 12-tone system lent itself to mathematical, and even numerological manipulation, and thus attracted composers whose interest in music was often more theoretical than practical. It also exerted a certain philosophical appeal to politically conscious composers, such as Boulez, Stockhausen and Xenakis, especially after World War II. They saw in the old tonality a metaphor for the hierarchical socio-political relationships that had led to the authoritarian, class-structured organization of European society, and in turn led to the devastating global wars of the early 20th century. Moreover, and by contrast, these same composers saw in the 12-tone, and later serial organization of music an equally potent musical metaphor for the egalitarian ideals of Marxism. Like Marxism, serialism attempted to alter, by executive fiat as it were, fundamental principles of organization established through centuries of usage. And, like Marxism, when its proponents began to discover that the new system did not, in fact, work the way it was supposed to, denial set in with a vengeance—leading them to turn the system into a theology.[33]

Babbitt, though not a Marxist, became one of the leaders of the serialist religion and, like a latter-day Thomas Aquinas, set about in a systematic way to forge a scientific rationale for it. He couched all his theoretical utterances in the complex vocabulary of pure science, and lobbied vigorously for academic music to be placed on a par with the physical sciences within the university system. His most important statement of these objectives was his 1958 essay, "Who Cares If You Listen?," originally published in *High Fidelity* and later reprinted in Gilbert Chase's anthology, *The American Composer Speaks*. The somewhat misleading title of this article was, according to Babbitt's supporters, actually imposed by the magazine editor,[34] not Babbitt himself—a not uncommon practice in publishing. Unfortunately, many people read no further than the title.

In "Who Cares If You Listen?," Babbitt argued, among other things, (a) for the dedication of university music curricula to scientific "research" in composition, (b) for publication of the resulting works by university presses in the same manner as that of other research documents, and (c) for acceptance of his view of the composer as a kind of esthetic scientist whose studies should no more be based on public opinion than was the work of

---

[33] For further discussion of related issues see Boulez, *Orientations*, p. 61 *et seq.* and Xenakis, "Toward a Philosophy of Music" in *Formalized Music*, pp. 201–208.
[34] Composer, scholar and former Babbitt student Noel Zahler, conversation with the author, Aug. 7, 1992.

physicists, chemists or biologists. Babbitt's thinking was absolutely consistent with the self-image of most American universities at the time, reflected in University of California president Clark Kerr's famous description of the university as a "knowledge factory" (see Chapter 11). It placed Babbitt's philosophy even more solidly within the university "establishment" against which so many young people, including young composers, began to react in the 1960s and early 1970s. In view of this, it is not unreasonable to assert that some of the reaction against serialism which gave birth to the post-modernist and minimalist styles of composition among the next generation of composers was as much motivated by political thinking as it was by musical thinking. And, while this may not be such an important issue in itself, it does imply that there may be more musical substance lurking in the old rejected serialism than it is currently fashionable to admit.

In any case, the degree of control over musical materials and processes that Babbitt sought, and had such difficulty achieving with live performers, led him in the late 1950s to begin working with synthesizers and other electronic means of musical realization. He began working with the RCA Mark II synthesizer at the Columbia-Princeton electronic music center that he co-founded officially with Otto Luening and Vladimir Ussachevsky (see below) in early 1959. The first fruits of this labor were realized in his 1961 *Composition for Synthesizer,* followed in that same year by his *Vision and Prayer* for soprano and synthesizer, and later by his *Ensembles for Synthesizer,* composed between 1962 and 1964.

Electronic music was not a new phenomenon in the late 1950s. As early as 1916—the year of Babbitt's birth—Edgard Varèse had called for its development, and early electronic instruments such as the Ondes Martinot, the Rhythmicon and the Theremin had been used by Cowell, Varèse and other major composers since the early 1930s. The increasing availability of the tape recorder after World War II, moreover, added yet another resource to the techniques of early electronic composers.

Unlike today's computer-controlled digital synthesizers, however, the earliest synthesizers achieved their novel effects through manipulation of electrical currents in ways that were analogous to the propagation and behavior of acoustic sound waves: hence the term "analog" synthesizer. By modern standards these machines were bulky and cumbersome to work with, requiring laborious programming with dials, switches and yards of telephone patch cords (affectionately known as "spaghetti"). The results of a programming patch were often inconsistent from one work session to the next, due to the vagaries of the vacuum tubes that powered the apparatus and the electrical currents available from wall outlets in laboratories and auditoriums. This made it difficult for composers to achieve predictable or

Milton Babbitt *(b. 1916) in old age. Sessions' fore-most pupil and an uncompromising exponent of mathematical composition who tried to elevate serial-ism into an exact science.* (Photo courtesy of C.F. Peters Corp.)

repeatable results. And, of course, there was no standardized notation yet developed for manipulating such instruments.

But, despite their difficulties, the old analog synthesizers offered the composers who worked with them a capacity to manipulate sound at its most fundamental structural levels which was superior in some respects to that available from today's generation of digital synthesizers. It was easier, for example, to create new timbres from pure wave forms, to filter the harmonic partials of such source waves in order to achieve even further timbral refinement, and it was easier to create innovative articulative patterns by causing an electronic signal or waveform to control the pitch, articulation and/or timbre of the actual sound produced. These features enabled composers literally to create new sound structures, not just new timbres—sound structures that could not be achieved easily by any non-electronic means and sound structures which had never been heard on earth before. After the development of the first practical commercial synthesizer, by Robert Moog around 1967, synthesizer technology became increasingly concerned with purely timbral issues and the attempt to create novel tone colors that could be manipulated in conventionally tonal ways. This was due in large part to the demands of pop performers and commercial composers, who formed the largest segment of the market for the new instruments, but who possessed neither the education nor the desire to depart from conventional tonal music.

Despite his own interests in popular music, Babbitt's purpose was not so much to exploit the new timbral or textural possibilities offered by the Mark II as it was to use the synthesizer's ability to precisely control dynamics, articulation and rhythm in complex serial works. After acquiring facility in the manipulation of electronic sound sources, Babbitt returned to the theoretical development of serialism in the 1970s and 1980s, producing works which integrated electronics and live performance, such as his *Concerti* for violin, small orchestra and tape (1974–1976) and *Images* for saxophone and tape (1979), as well as purely acoustic works that extended the applications of serialist theory, including his 1977 *Solo Requiem,* the orchestra piece *Ars combinatoria* (1981) and his *Concerto for Piano and Orchestra* (1986). Despite the often grim character of his music and theoretical influence (not to mention his reputation), Babbitt was capable of a dry wit that shows both in his titles and his personality. And his well-concealed interest in popular music continues to this day. His earliest works have aged sufficiently that some young musicians are willing to take a new look at them, and it is likely that his music will survive as the most polished example of early American academic serialism, for whatever degree of interest future generations might have in that genre.

George Perle

A somewhat more humanistic approach to academic serialism is found in the music of Babbitt's colleague and contemporary, George Perle, born in Bayonne, New Jersey, on May 6, 1915. Like Babbitt, Perle was a graduate of NYU and developed a strong interest in the 12-tone procedure during the 1930s. He has also served on the faculties of many prestigious music schools, though his academic career has been less stable than Babbitt's.

But, unlike his slightly younger colleague, Perle maintained an interest in integrating serial procedures with the hierarchical structure of tonality (which links him more closely to Berg than to Schoenberg or Webern) and produced a large number of works that explore this possibility. Perle was also a highly self-critical composer and was in the habit of withdrawing finished works, reworking all or parts of them and reincorporating them into subsequent compositions. In Perle's musical thinking, one idea seemed to lead to another in such a way that the next composition almost always caused him to rethink previous ones, all of which makes absorption of his oeuvre fairly problematic. Perle's music is generally more accessible than Babbitt's, and his theoretical contributions to serialist thought, while significant, have not had as innovative and uncompromising a character as the latter's. His most important book is *Serial Composition and Atonality,* and his best known works are mostly in the chamber music genres.

Otto Luening

The advent of electronic music brought to the fore a contemporary of Aaron Copland's generation who, prior to the 1950s, had made many serious contributions to American music, but failed to achieve the recognition he deserved. The composer in question is Otto Luening (b. 1900), whose name has come to be associated primarily with the early days of the Columbia-Princeton electronic studio, despite a vast amount of music in other genres that he either composed or premiered in his capacity as an accomplished flutist and conductor.

Luening was born in Milwaukee, Wisconsin, on June 15, 1900 to a musical family of German descent. When he was twelve years old, the family moved to Munich, where Luening received systematic instruction at the Staatliche Hochschule für Musik. He made his debut as a flutist at sixteen, and moved to Switzerland the following year, where he continued his studies. During this time, Luening also became acquainted with the progressive musical thinker, Ferruccio Busoni (see Chapter 10) and even spent some time as an actor and stage manager for James Joyce's English Players Company.

In the early part of his career, Luening was known primarily as a conductor, especially of contemporary opera. After returning to the United States in 1920, he conducted a number of historically important American operas during the next several decades, including Cadman's *Shanewis* (see Chapter 4) and the world premieres of Thomson's *The Mother of Us All* (see next chapter), Menotti's *The Medium* and his own *Evangeline* (1932, based on the narrative poem by Longfellow). He served as the executive director of the opera department during the first years of Hanson's tenure at Eastman (1925–1928), and, during the ensuing years, taught variously at Bennington (Vermont) College, Columbia, Barnard College and Juilliard, among other institutions. In addition, he was a co-founder, with Copland and others, of the American Composers Alliance and the American Music Center and served on many boards and committees related to the advancement of American classical music. His non-electronic works include a large number of orchestral, chamber, keyboard and vocal or choral pieces, many of which are written in the modern tonal idiom of the Copland generation and based on American vernacular music and folklore.

But, in 1952, Luening began collaborating with fellow composer Vladimir Ussachevsky in the exploration of electronic music, and it is this phase of his work that is best known today. Between 1952 and 1968 he created, either independently or with Ussachevsky, some twenty works for synthesizer, tape or acoustic instruments in combination with same. Among the most familiar of these works are his own *Gargoyles* (1960) for violin and tape, and the 1954 *Poem in Cycles and Bells* for orchestra and tape, written with Ussachevsky. Their pioneering work in this area led to the formal establishment of the Columbia-Princeton electronic music center mentioned above, the first (and for many years the most important) center of its kind in the United States.

In the late 1960s, Luening returned to working primarily with acoustic instruments and simpler styles. His music, by contrast to that of both his academic and freelance contemporaries, is refreshingly eclectic, approachable and rich in associations that can be grasped by the lay listener. However, the very scope of Luening's interests has operated against his

Otto Luening *(b. 1900). An early contemporary and colleague of Copland, he turned to the exploration of electronic music in the 1950s and collaborated with Vladimir Ussachevsky on several important synthesizer works.* (Photo by Nancy Rica Schiff, courtesy of BMI.)

reaching a broad public, because the variety of styles and genres his work encompasses has made it difficult for him to establish a highly recognizable personal voice when compared to his contemporaries. As with most recent American composers, Luening still requires several generations of critical examination before his ultimate place in American music history can be established.

During the past six decades, American academic music has become entrenched in the university system. At least three generations of American composers have arisen and faded from view, generations that functioned almost exclusively in the context of academia. As a result, much of the work of our most recent creative talents is entirely unknown to the general public, apparently by mutual consent of the composers and that public. What began as a troubled relationship between academic composers and popular culture has become a complete divorce, with very little prospect of reconciliation in the near future. Some of the better or more persistent academic composers of the mid-century have managed to make a small dent in the awareness of the musical public outside the university system. The list includes Ross Lee Finney (b. 1906, see Chapter 9), Vincent Persichetti (1915–1985), Leon Kirchner (b. 1919), Earl Kim (b. 1920), Harold Shapero (b. 1920), Andrew Imbrie (b. 1921), Daniel Pinkham (b. 1923), Gunther Schuller (b. 1925), Donald Erb (b. 1927), Jacob Druckman (b. 1928), George Crumb (b. 1929), Charles Wuorinen (b. 1938), Roger Reynolds (b. 1934), Robert Helps (b. 1928) and a few others. The works of these composers are held in high esteem by their academic colleagues and a few private connoisseurs, but many such composers have continued to pursue ever more esoteric paths into the realms of pure theory and theoretical composition of which the general public has no knowledge, and no discernible interest.

In the 1960s and early 1970s, the rarefied musical conceptions of some academic composers became so alienated from the mainstream of American music that they were collectively dubbed "honk-squeak" music in the popular media. Whether honk-squeak music has any value beyond its demonstration of purely theoretical issues is a question which cannot be answered at this point in our history. But it is abundantly clear that the rise of American academic music since 1930, despite the good intentions that fostered it, has siphoned off such a large number of young composers into the insulated world of the university that it is unlikely we will ever have an opportunity to discover what most of these people might have contributed to our national music had they been channeled in the direction of dealing with "real world" audiences—for those audiences, despite their well-earned reputation for conservatism, have always shown and continue to show symptoms of starvation for authentically moving new-music experiences.

8

Copland, Thomson, Harris and
Their Generation

෨෨

Part II (after 1933)

By the first half of the 1930s, the differences between the three
major composers of the generation circa 1900 were becoming
clear. Copland premiered his *Piano Variations* at the Yaddo (New York)
Festival, which had replaced the defunct Copland-Sessions Concerts, in the
summer of 1932. They were published by Cos Cob Press later that year,
and repeated by Victor Babin at the ISCM conference in 1933. Harris,
having been introduced to Koussevitzky by Copland in the spring of 1933,
composed his *Symphony—1933*, which Koussevitzky subsequently premiered with the Boston Symphony in early 1934. At almost the same time,
Thomson's *Four Saints in Three Acts* received its first performance at the
Wadsworth Atheneum in Hartford, using an all-black cast. In addition, the
stars of Marc Blitzstein, Piston and Sessions were rising. George Antheil
and Henry Cowell were both beginning to experience a conservative
retrenchment from their own early radicalism.

With the *Piano Variations*, Copland had consolidated those qualities
of lean texture, complex rhythm, highly colored percussive sonority and
economy of materials that were to characterize all his subsequent work,
regardless of genre. Harris, on the other hand, had begun to develop his
highly personalized theories of melody and harmony that would lead him
to become the major American symphonist of the early 20th century. And
these ideas were already playing a significant role in his *Symphony—1933*.
Thomson, in contrast to his colleagues, remained true to neo-Romantic

ideals, and continued writing in a personal tonal idiom that was perceived as simplistic (even reactionary) by his contemporaries. But, with each new piece, he increased the subtlety and sophistication of the means by which he employed his techniques, achieving by 1940 a style whose alleged simplicity was far more apparent than real. And, ultimately, Copland and his fellow "modernists" were compelled to recognize this.

Virgil Thomson

Thomson had met Everett "Chick" Austin, director of the Atheneum in Hartford, Connecticut, in London in 1931. Austin was a very progressive thinker and was interested in doing more with his gallery than just showing paintings. As Thomson's and Austin's friendship evolved, plans began to take shape for the premiere of *Four Saints* at the gallery's theatre. This non-traditional performing space offered both opportunities and limitations. It was ideally suited to the presentation of an "experimental" opera, but neither large enough nor sufficiently well-equipped to accommodate a full orchestra and traditional operatic staging. Fortunately, Thomson had not yet made the orchestration of the work, and Gertrude Stein's non-representational text allowed for a variety of interpretive options. Maurice Grosser, Thomson's lover, developed a stageable scenario, and Thomson himself conceived the idea of an all-black cast one night while visiting a nightclub in Harlem. He admired the very precise enunciation typical of educated African Americans and the unique form of energy he felt they brought to the stage. Thomson's friend, socialite Florine Stettheimer, had volunteered to take on the challenge of designing the production, despite a complete lack of prior theatrical experience, and the young John Houseman was persuaded to direct. This was to be Houseman's first directing job and the beginning of a lifelong friendship with Thomson. Frederick Ashton, who would later become a major figure in the world of dance, was secured as choreographer. It is clear that Thomson's friendships and associations with emerging talent in the visual arts, theatre and dance served him well in organizing this production.

While in Europe during the summer of 1933, Thomson completed the orchestration, choosing an unusual collection of instruments based on the space limitations and his desire for the fullest possible chord voicings. While there he engaged in a minor dispute with Stein over their respective percentages of the royalties, amicably settled in Stein's favor. He also kept company with Arnold Schoenberg who was then living in Paris to avoid the increasingly anti-Semitic policies of the German and Austrian governments.

After Thomson's return, the rehearsals were begun and the premiere took place as planned in Hartford, in February 1934. George Gershwin and Arturo Toscanini were among the audience for the first performance. Gertrude Stein remained in France.

Fours Saints quickly moved to New York, where it ran in various theatres for eight months. Alexander Smallens, the original conductor, had never imagined that the opera would be such a success, or run for so long, and had other commitments to fulfill. So Thomson himself took over conducting as the opera moved to Chicago in November 1934. Stein and her lifelong companion, Alice B. Toklas, came over from France for the Chicago premiere. Apparently the librettist was vastly pleased with the final result. As fate would have it, this was the only opportunity she had to see one of her operas with Thomson performed. She died of cancer shortly after completing the text of their second joint venture, *The Mother of Us All,* in 1946, before the premiere of that work.

Thomson continued serving his apprenticeship as a theatre and film composer throughout the 1930s. In January 1936 he was commissioned by documentary filmmaker Pare Lorentz, who had already interviewed and rejected both Copland and Harris, to compose music for a film sponsored by the United States Resettlement Administration, *The Plow that Broke the Plains.* This was Thomson's first film commission and for it he created a score based on the vernacular music of his midwestern boyhood. This was followed in 1938 by his score for Lorentz's *The River,* for which Thomson drew on southern hymnody contained in collections like *The Sacred Harp* and *Southern Harmony.* Although Thomson would go on to write other film music, it was largely in these two scores that he began to develop an orchestral sound that was extraordinarily evocative of the midwestern plains and great southwest to the ears of non-specialist listeners. Boldly orchestrated and heavily derived from folk music (including Thomson's own *Symphony on a Hymn Tune* of 1928), these film scores would later serve as models for many Hollywood composers, particularly Elmer Bernstein, who scored innumerable westerns and other American "period" films set west of the Mississippi. Indeed, Thomson's later fame with the general American public was more largely derived from the orchestral suites he extracted from these film scores, and from his later music for *Louisiana Story,* than from any of his more formalized music, including his three operas. In particular, Thomson struck gold with his adaptation of the almost forgotten hymn, "My Shepherd Will Supply My Need," which assumed a place in his oeuvre comparable to that of "Simple Gifts" in Copland's after *Appalachian Spring.*

Between his first two film scores, Thomson continued his work with John Houseman and Orson Welles in the FTP-sponsored Negro Theatre of Harlem. He created sometimes startlingly experimental music, heavily oriented toward percussion, for the seminal Houseman-Welles production of *MacBeth* in the summer of 1936, as well as the plays *Injunction Granted, Horse Eats Hat* and Shakespeare's *Hamlet*. In late 1937 he was terminated by the WPA because of an unauthorized trip to Paris the previous summer, taken while on the Federal Theatre payroll. Throughout this period, he continued sharing apartments with Houseman, who was producing Blitzstein's *The Cradle Will Rock,* while Orson Welles took on the direction of Copland's first opera, *The Second Hurricane.*

Nor was Thomson idle as World War II approached. After the success of his two films with Pare Lorentz, *The Plow That Broke the Plains* and *The River,* he was commissioned by Lincoln Kirstein to create the music for an unusual ballet entitled *Filling Station* in 1937. Kirstein was committed to American subjects of all kinds, both historical and modern. His almost simultaneous commissioning of Copland's *Billy the Kid* (see below) and Thomson's *Filling Station* reflected a deliberate strategy of expanding and "Americanizing" ballet in the United States. It was he who, with Thomson's help, had lured George Balanchine away from the Ballet Russe de Monte Carlo in 1933 to form the American School of the Ballet in New York, and he who promoted the careers of later great choreographers such as Loring, Christensen, Hawkins and Robbins.

Filling Station was unique in several ways. First of all, the principal character was male (as was Copland's *Billy* one year later) and, while this was not unprecedented in ballet at the time, it was still regarded as unusual. Secondly, it dealt with a very modern subject which was part of the everyday life of most Americans—the cheerful, uniformed gas station attendant that was a fixture on almost any street corner at the time—and a subject which was so far removed from the esoteric realms of "high art" that the very concept seemed ludicrous to many. But, in the hands of choreographer Lew Christensen, and with Thomson's uncharacteristically modernist music, the piece caught on. *Filling Station,* though rarely performed today, remains one of the most remarkable works in the American ballet repertoire.

During this same period, Thomson wrote incidental music for a production of Shakespeare's *Antony and Cleopatra,* featuring the volatile actress, Tallulah Bankhead, in the title role. This play has always been a risk because, while it contains some of Shakespeare's most movingly poetic language, it is at times seriously deficient in dramatic action. As we will see later, Samuel Barber suffered the greatest setback in his otherwise illustrious career when he crashed on the rocks of this difficult drama. Neither Bankhead's performance nor Thomson's music was successful in breathing life into this production.

In 1937 Thomson joined Copland, Blitzstein, Harris, Piston and Sessions in founding the American Composers' Alliance and Arrow Music Press and, during much of 1938, occupied himself with an abortive attempt to forge an opera from John Webster's blank verse play, *The Duchess of Malfi* (1635). Perhaps in discouragement, perhaps because he could never keep himself away from Paris for long, Thomson returned to the French capital shortly thereafter, where he remained until the early days of World War II.

While in Paris, Thomson wrote his first book, entitled *The State of Music,* which was published in 1939. Unlike Copland's 1938 *What to Listen for in Music,* Thomson's effort was less pedagogical and more in the vein of an extended critical essay. Though much of what he wrote about has been superseded by subsequent historical developments in music, his insights proved to be, as always, deeply discerning and skillfully articulated. *The State of Music* paved the way for Geoffrey Parsons' invitation, in 1940, for Thomson to replace the recently deceased Lawrence Gilman as music critic on the New York *Herald-Tribune,* a post that Thomson ultimately accepted and retained until his resignation in 1954.

Thomson remained in Paris as long as he safely could, despite entreaties from friends and colleagues, including Houseman and Copland, to return to the United States. But, he waited until the Nazis were virtually on his doorstep before making the harrowing return trip to New York, detailed in his autobiography. Assuming his post at the *Herald-Tribune* almost immediately thereafter, he just as quickly began making enemies with his often barbed and always independent criticism.

During the war, Thomson continued to compose, though at a reduced pace. He created innovative incidental music for a John Houseman radio production of *The Trojan Women,* in which he paired individual speaking voices with solo woodwind instruments, foreshadowing a similar technique used by Steve Reich in his 1993 music-video-theatre piece, *The Cave.* In 1941 Thomson was approached by twenty-nine-year-old John Cage, a recent product of Schoenberg's classes at UCLA, who had already begun writing highly experimental percussion and serial music. Cage was attracted to Thomson because of the strong connection between Thomson's esthetic and that of the French composer Erik Satie. Cage was a devotee of Satie's self-consciously simplistic compositions, and saw in Thomson a reflection of his idol. A few months later, Cage introduced Thomson to the young Lou Harrison, who was then also just beginning to test his compositional wings, and the three became fast friends. Cage would later write an extensive resume of all Thomson's music, published together with Kathleen Hoover's biographical sketch of the composer in 1954.

After the war, Thomson returned to Paris again and renewed contact with Gertrude Stein, already suffering from her fatal cancer. They began work on *The Mother of Us All* almost immediately. The plan was to create an opera that would be a pageant of 19th-century American personalities, from Daniel Webster to Andrew Johnson to Lillian Russell. Stein chose the women's suffrage leader, Susan B. Anthony, as her focal character, and the libretto was finished in March of 1946. Stein died the following July, and Thomson began the composition in October. *The Mother of Us All* was finally premiered at Columbia University on May 9, 1947, under the baton of Otto Luening. It has subsequently become the most popular of Thomson's three operas and is still often performed at universities.

While in Paris during the first post-war years, Thomson broadcast radio commentary with recordings and performances of American music. His eighteen-year-old *Symphony on a Hymn Tune* finally received its premiere under Artur Rodzinski with the New York Philharmonic in 1945, and he published his first book of *Piano Etudes* (edited in close collabora-tion with the progressive French pianist, E. Robert Schmitz) that same year. In 1948 he composed music for Robert Flaherty's Pulitzer Prize–winning film, *Louisiana Story*, in which Thomson repeated the process of adapting indigenous music—this time Louisiana Cajun (Acadian) songs—that he had pioneered in the earlier Pare Lorentz films. With the Federal Music Project now defunct, the film had been subsidized by the Standard Oil Company of New Jersey. The music was recorded by Eugene Ormandy with the Philadelphia Orchestra, and the suite Thomson extracted from the score became one of his most frequently performed and influential works.

After his retirement from the *Herald-Tribune* in 1954, Thomson reduced the pace of his compositional activity. His major late works, apart from the numerous musical portraits that he continued to compose, were his massive 1960 *Missa Pro Defunctis* and his third and final opera, *Lord Byron*. Thomson had never been the modernist that Copland and Harris were, so his work was neglected to an even greater degree than was theirs in the 1950s, 1960s and 1970s. Moreover, he devoted increasing amounts of his time and energy to expository writing, producing his autobiography, *Virgil Thomson*, in 1966 and his book *American Music Since 1910*, in 1971.

In the mid-1960s Thomson had met poet and playwright, Jack Larson, by requesting to read a copy of Larson's play, *The Candied House*. Larson, who had achieved early fame through his portrayal of Jimmy Olsen in the 1950s *Superman* television series, had turned to writing and film production after *Superman* went off the air and produced a number of his own plays off-Broadway. In him, Thomson found a sympathetic spirit and skilled poet who he felt could fill the void left by the death of Gertrude Stein in 1946. At the suggestion of writer Gore Vidal, they conceived the idea of an opera on the life of the early 19th-century English poet and rake, George Gordon, Lord Byron (1788–1824). Larson created a libretto to Thomson's liking, interweaving excerpts of Byron's own poetry with original verse, and, after completing his autobiography, Thomson set to work on the music.

As had been his practice with the earlier Stein operas, Thomson set the entire text, without changes, exactly as Larson had written it. He followed his usual practice of incorporating musical quotations from other sources, this time from appropriate English music, but also brought to bear his substantial skills as an original melodist to create a unified, if eclectic, score with conscious reference to the bel canto style of Byron's contemporary, Bellini.

The Metropolitan Opera, headed by Sir Rudolph Bing, had expressed willingness to mount the first production, despite the sometimes rough treatment they had received over the years from Thomson's critical pen. But Bing was aging and unsure of himself during the late 1960s, and the increasing indications he received that the opera dealt with such scandalous subjects as Byron's incestuous relationship with his half-sister and suggestions of his bisexuality, caused him to back the Met out of the project. Thomson, naturally enough, was furious and bitterly frustrated by this event. Convinced of the opera's viability and quality, he nevertheless made a large number of seemingly arbitrary cuts in the score (including the excision of ballet music that had been added specifically for the Met). In this pared-down form, *Lord Byron* was eventually premiered by John Houseman at Juilliard in 1972. But this performance proved a disappointment to Thomson, who would not live to see a full production of the work as he had intended it.

Lord Byron, Thomson's last major work, was finally presented in its entirety in the fall of 1991, some twenty years after its composition, under the baton of James Bolle at the Monadnock Festival in New Hampshire. The edited recording of this performance is only now in current release as a compact disc.

Unlike Copland, Thomson retained full possession of his mental faculties to the end of his life. On his 90th birthday in 1986, he was the subject of numerous radio and television interviews and features. Despite failing health, he continued to compose until only a week or so before his death, his last (uncompleted) work being the musical portrait of Larson mentioned in Chapter 6. He died in New York in 1989 at the age of ninety-three.

Roy Harris (to his death)

Of the three major non-academic American composers of the mid-century, Harris was the only one who never wrote an opera (indeed, who worked almost exclusively in "absolute" music genres). He was also the only one who systematized his theoretical ideas into a personal framework, to which he adhered with little deviation throughout his mature creative life. His need to do this may have arisen from the non-traditional nature of his formal instruction, when contrasted with that of his contemporaries. His adoption of a personal "system" clearly insulated him from the influence of other composers throughout his life, and he paid very little attention to the works of his contemporaries, especially as he grew older. Thus, while differences in his style between the 1930s and the 1960s are evident, he underwent fewer superficial changes than his contemporaries, making little or no effort to keep abreast of the times, and the public's attention to his music tended to fade during the 1950s, 1960s and 1970s.

A very detailed exposition of all Harris' theoretical ideas is given in Dan Stehman's *Roy Harris: An American Musical Pioneer* (Boston: G. K. Hall, 1984). Suffice it to say here that he evolved a unique polytonal harmonic style, later adopted and transformed by William Schuman as well. The elements of this technique involved reducing his vocabulary of chords to simple triads and their associated seventh chords, deriving the pitches of higher sonorities from the overtones of simultaneously played lower ones, and relating the roots of some triads to non-root tones of others by unconventional tonic-dominant-subdominant connections. Thus his work is tonal, but does not participate in the traditional vocabulary or syntax of European-based functional harmony. In terms of melody, Harris created synthetic modes by combining properties of various diatonic modes and made these the basis of his long, arching melodic lines. Thus, what appear to be conventionally chromatic melodies, especially in his symphonies, are actually the result of a kind of modal mutation as the line unfolds. He continued and developed his early practice of evolving the overall form of his long works from the inherent properties of their melodic and harmonic materials, especially in his famous *Third Symphony,* and maintained a lifelong attachment to the influences of Medieval *organum* and 17th- and 18th-century counterpoint that had fascinated him as a young man.

Both Thomson and Harris exerted a much more direct appeal than did Copland on the American classical music public outside of New York and Boston, at least until the early 1940s. In part, this may have been because of their Anglo-Saxon heritage, which attracted musical conservatives such as Daniel Gregory Mason (see Chapter 4) and others of his Second New England School ideology. What is abundantly clear from their music, however, is that Thomson and Harris, both midwesterners, were far more interested in American folk music from the very beginning than was the New Yorker Copland. It may, indeed, have been partly their influence, together with the growing public awareness of Charles Ives' work in the

1930s, that drew Henry Cowell away from experimentation with tone clusters and other new timbral devices, toward the exploration of fuguing tunes and similar artifacts of indigenous American music.

But Thomson and Harris approached the issue of folk music from very different perspectives. Thomson, by far the more sentimental and eclectic of the two, was prone to musical quotation, especially of lyrical hymn tunes. His use of quotation is both more direct and less contrapuntally dissonant than that of Ives, and thus had more immediate appeal at the time. Like Ives, he was also capable of synthesizing original melodies that sounded like quotations but were not. He used this technique to particular advantage in *The Mother of Us All*. Harris, on the other hand, while he made settings of American folksongs for piano, for chorus and for orchestra, was never content to leave the song in its more or less original form, but habitually took the tune in question as a starting point for a highly personal and idiomatic interpretation—sometimes to the point where the original melody became unrecognizable or of secondary importance to its "accompaniment." It is not unreasonable to surmise that part of the reason for Copland's new-found interest in American folk music, beginning with his ballet *Billy the Kid* in 1937, was a response to the public attention given to Harris and Thomson during the mid-1930s, especially after Thomson began writing scores for government sponsored documentary films that drew heavily on this vernacular material.

Harris continued to be Harris, composing another ten symphonies and numerous other works over the next forty years. He lived in increasing obscurity with his fourth wife Johanna (née Beulah Duffey) until his death in Santa Monica in 1979.

Whatever the specific reasons may have been for the sea change in the musical atmosphere from the 1920s to the 1930s, it should be noted that America, overall, underwent a rebirth of cultural conservatism during these years. True, the labor movement and the Communist party grew and found new converts, and the radical programs initiated by President Franklin D. Roosevelt after 1932 aimed at breaking the stranglehold of the Great Depression, stood American political conservatives on their ears. Moreover, the repeal of Prohibition could not exactly be viewed as conservative policy. But the imagination of America was turned inward during the decade of the Depression, toward things American, and foreign musical influences held less power then than at any previous time in our history. The Works Progress Administration (WPA), created by Roosevelt as part of his New Deal policies, sponsored both a Federal Music Project and a Federal Theatre Project in 1935. The purpose of these programs was to stimulate new, original creative efforts by American artists, to help educate and enlighten average Americans about their own heritage, and to provide jobs for the thousands who had been cast out of work by the Depression, especially in the New York theatrical community. The emphasis of both programs was toward American, not European, subjects and styles. And the security offered by government subsidy made possible the exploration of new themes and the creation of politically "conscious" works which would not have been considered commercially viable in the 1920s.

Marc Blitzstein (1905–1964)

One of the most important composers to take advantage of this situation was Marc Blitzstein. Blitzstein was born in Philadelphia on March 2, 1905. He was a child prodigy as a pianist and entered the newly founded Curtis Institute of Music in Philadelphia at the same time as his younger colleague, Samuel Barber, while commuting to New York to continue piano studies with Alexander Siloti. Like Roy Harris, he went to Paris in 1926, where he also studied with Boulanger and became acquainted with her current and former pupils. Blitzstein also took some lessons from Schoenberg in Berlin at the time. His *4 Songs for Baritone and Piano* appeared on the program of the second Copland-Sessions concert on December 30, 1928.

By 1930, Blitzstein was back in the United States and beginning to embrace the leftist political causes that shaped all his work of the Depression era. Unlike any of his non-academic colleagues except Vernon Duke[35], Blitzstein had an interest in composing for the Broadway musical theatre and created a one-act "opera," *Triple Sec,* for the Garrick Gaieties of 1930.

During 1931, two very significant groups of young composers began to coalesce in New York. One of these, the "Young Composers' Group," a discussion group focused primarily on contemporary musical concerns, included Arthur Berger, Henry Brant, Israel Citkowitz, Vivian Fine, Bernard Herrmann and Elie Siegmeister, and was led by Copland. Their deliberations culminated in a concert held on December 22, 1932. The other, focused as much on political issues as musical ones, comprised the folk music collector/composers Charles Seeger (teacher of Henry Cowell) and Earl Robinson (creator of the song "Joe Hill"), as well as Siegmeister (who also had a strong interest in American folk music), Wallingford Riegger, Stefan Wolpe, Blitzstein and others. (Copland was also involved to some extent in this second group, which called itself "The Composers' Collective," but, according to his possibly selective recollections of later

---

[35] Pop composer and friend of Gershwin, who wrote serious music under his birth name, Vladimir Dukelsky.

years, took a much less active part than some of the other members, and was by no means the leader of the group.)

The Composers' Collective published two *Workers' Songbooks,* to which Copland contributed a labor song, "Into the Streets, May First," and went on to promote the leftist labor agenda of the time. Because of covert government scrutiny of such groups, even then, many of the principal composers involved identified themselves by false names. Copland and Blitzstein were exceptions to this practice.

During the period of his participation in the Composers' Collective, Blitzstein became galvanized politically. In 1932 he composed an oratorio entitled *The Condemned* on the subject of the executions of labor activists Sacco and Vanzetti in Boston in 1927, an event that had aroused the ire of the entire progressive artistic community from Edna St. Vincent Millay to Virgil Thomson. After *The Condemned,* Blitzstein went into a period of relative compositional dormancy, concentrating his energies on political activities and developing the ideas that would give shape to his most important work, the 1938 musical *The Cradle Will Rock,* for which he also wrote the book and lyrics.

By the late 1930s, John Houseman had become the principal producer for the WPA's Federal Theatre Project. Shortly after directing the premiere of *Four Saints in Three Acts* he had made the acquaintance of the brash young directorial genius, Orson Welles, with whom he collaborated on many productions that are now considered milestones in the history of American theatre. Houseman produced and Welles directed *The Cradle Will Rock* for the WPA, but the undisguised leftist propaganda embodied in Blitzstein's script drew pressure from the government. The decision was made by WPA bureaucrats in Washington, and reportedly confirmed by Roosevelt himself, to cancel the production so as not to give the appearance that the government, through the Federal Theatre, was siding with steel-workers then on strike. The order was relayed to the company in New York only hours before the curtain was to rise on opening night. A frantic search was made for a theatre in which the play could be performed without benefit of WPA subsidy. The nearby Venice Theatre was secured, and actors, audience and composer moved en masse to it, leaving behind scenery, costumes and orchestra, all of which had been paid for with WPA funds.

The Cradle Will Rock was premiered, then, in oratorio style with Blitzstein himself accompanying at the piano and providing impromptu commentary for the audience, to make up for the absence of scenery, props and costumes. Surprisingly, the play was a critical and popular success in this form, perhaps a bigger hit than it would have been if staged according to the original plan. Blitzstein's music was universally regarded as the best he had written to date and showed a tremendous richness and variety in both the form and content of the songs. The young Leonard Bernstein mounted a production at Harvard the following year (1939), in which he assumed Blitzstein's role of accompanist-commentator. Out of curiosity, Blitzstein attended this performance and met Bernstein, of whom he became an intimate friend and adviser for the rest of his life. *Cradle* proved to be exactly the right piece for that moment in the American theatre, but, like Gershwin's *Of Thee I Sing*, was too focused on contemporaneous events ever to duplicate the impact of its first performance in subsequent revivals.

After a stint in the military during World War II, Marc Blitzstein would go on to write, among other works, a musical version of Lillian Hellman's powerful play, *The Little Foxes,* entitled *Regina,* which ran for a modest fifty-six performances on Broadway in 1949, and to adapt the definitive English version of the Brecht-Weill *Threepenny Opera.* But *The Cradle Will Rock* would remain his masterpiece. Bernstein's later musicals, *On the Town* (1944) and *West Side Story* (1957), would show considerable Blitzstein influence.

Blitzstein lived until January 22, 1964, when he died of injuries sustained after being savagely beaten by a group of young men outside a bar on the waterfront in Martinique. Because Blitzstein—like so many of his contemporaries in American music—was homosexual, it has been reported that he may have expressed some sexual interest in his assailants, or merely been suspected of being gay by them. In either case, he holds the dubious distinction of being the only significant American composer to date known to have died as a result of "gay bashing."

Copland (to his death)

In the summer of 1934, Copland and his lover, Victor Kraft, rented a cottage on Lake Bemidji, Minnesota, where Copland worked on his *Statements* for orchestra and his little-known ballet, *Hear Ye! Hear Ye!,* for the independent company of Ruth Page, ballet director of the Chicago Grand Opera. This visit to Minnesota was Copland's first protracted stay, other than a visit to Mexico in 1932 where he was hosted by Carlos Chávez, away from the influence of East Coast or European urban cultural establishments. It allowed him to come into contact with local residents of this rural area who were suffering severely from the Depression. Together with his already highly developed liberal politics, this exposure probably helped divert Copland's thinking along lines of more accessible music than he had written up to that time. But, beyond Copland's personal evolution, American composers in general were becoming increasingly concerned with the apparently growing esthetic distance between the mass audience and modern music during this period. Thus, even without the not-yet-realized

influence of Virgil Thomson's WPA film scores, Copland had begun grop-
ing for the elements of a more accessible style.

In 1933, shortly after the first Mexican trip, Copland had conceived
the idea for an orchestral piece—similar in concept to Milhaud's *Le Boeuf
sur le Toit*—based on impressions he had received from his visit to a
nightclub named "El Salon Mexico" with Chávez. As a result of all these
concerns coming together at the same time, in 1933–1934 Copland found
himself working simultaneously on *Statements for Orchestra* (in his early
modernist style) and *El Salon Mexico* (in his folkloric, middle period style).
El Salon Mexico was more closely allied to modernist techniques than was
Copland's next major work, *Billy the Kid,* but still began to develop a strain
of interest in achieving accessibility through extra-musical connotations
that had been foreshadowed in *Vitebsk.* This interest would bear its greatest
fruit in Copland's famous ballets of the late-1930s and early 1940s. *El Salon
Mexico* was eventually premiered in 1938 at the ISCM Festival in London,
but not until Copland had also begun work on *Billy the Kid* for Lincoln
Kirstein's Ballet Caravan.

In the interim, between 1935 and 1937, Copland had been busy in
New York, after a brief stint filling in for Walter Piston at Harvard, working
on his opera for high school students, *The Second Hurricane,* to a libretto
by his close friend Edwin Denby. In the progressive cultural atmosphere
of the 1930s, the idea of an opera for young people seemed completely
appropriate. The work was produced by the Henry Street Settlement
School and directed by Orson Welles, who was simultaneously directing
Blitzstein's *The Cradle Will Rock* and developing, with Houseman, the
Mercury Theatre. But, despite everything the opera had going for it, it failed
to make a strong impression and has not done so during its subsequent
revivals either. Copland's second opera, *The Tender Land,* written in the
early 1950s, proved to be equally underwhelming with the public. How the
composer of such spectacular ballets as *Billy the Kid, Rodeo* and *Appalachian Spring,* and of such intensely effective film music as his scores to *The
Red Pony* (1939) and *Our Town* (1940) could be so unimpressive in the
medium of opera is a question that has puzzled many, including Copland
himself. Perhaps the relative absence of a strong gift for vocal melody in his
work, despite a respectable number of songs composed, or his propensity
to rhythmic complexity offers a partial explanation. Perhaps if he had
ignored his friend Aaron Schaffer's advice in 1919 and, like Gershwin, spent
more time in the musical theatre during his formative years, he might have
developed a more finely honed sense of stage drama. In either case, it was
Virgil Thomson who was to claim the laurels of being the finest American
opera composer of this generation, just as Harris was its premier sympho-

nist. Copland, for his part, continued to excel in ballet music, free-form orchestral works and solo piano compositions.

In addition to his work on *The Second Hurricane,* during the middle 1930s Copland went to Hollywood, but was unable to break into commercial film music at first because he lacked prior film credits. While there he visited the ailing George Gershwin (June 1937), communed with George Antheil who was by now a Hollywood composer and reviewer, and met a number of movie stars. But the trip proved musically uneventful. It was not until he was asked to write the music for the documentary film *The City*—conceived by Pare Lorentz but produced and directed by Ralph Steiner and Willard Van Dyke and shown continuously at the 1939 New York World's Fair—that Copland acquired the credentials necessary to compose for the commercial cinema. He also created, during this period, his *Outdoor Overture,* commissioned by Alexander Richter, the head of New York's High School of Music and Art, following in the "youth music" mold of *The Second Hurricane.* This overture was performed by Alexander Smallens, also at the World's Fair, and reviewed by the young Elliott Carter for *Modern Music.*

In 1937, Copland had met the nineteen-year-old Leonard Bernstein, then a student at Harvard, at a dance recital given by Anna Sokolow, wife of film composer Alex North. Bernstein was already an enthusiast of Copland's *Piano Variations* and was commissioned to prepare the two-piano score of *El Salon Mexico* in 1939. This proved to be the beginning of a close, lifelong association between Copland and Bernstein, in which Copland served as one of Bernstein's principal mentors, just as Koussevitzky had been his own musical father figure. Linked by a passion for new music, a mission to communicate with a broad public, and a common Russian-Jewish heritage, these three men formed a musical triumvirate, spanning three generations and largely centered around Tanglewood, which would sustain public interest in American composition for at least forty years. Bernstein, as conductor, was later to play a significant role in keeping Copland's work before the American listening public throughout the middle years of the century, while that of Thomson, Harris and others of their generation began to fall into neglect.

But by far the greatest triumph for Copland in the late 1930s was his second (actually his third, if we count the early *Grohg*) ballet, *Billy the Kid,* commissioned by Lincoln Kirstein, to be choreographed by Eugene Loring. Copland composed the bulk of *Billy* in Paris during the summer of 1938. He finished the score at the MacDowell Colony, where he was staying for the fourth time, in September of that year. The ballet was premiered less than a month later, on October 6, by Ballet Caravan in Chicago, sharing the bill with Elliott Carter's *Pochahontas.* Despite his prior successes,

Copland was still too poor to afford the trip to hear his work, and his transportation had to be subsidized by the ballet company. The cast of the original production included Loring himself, as well as Erick Hawkins and Jerome Robbins, both of whom would later go on to become major choreographers. Less than a fortnight later (October 14), *El Salon Mexico* received its Boston premiere, which Copland also managed to attend while renewing acquaintances with Bernstein, Ernst Křenek and Quincy Porter.

Billy the Kid is the first work in which Copland displayed the folksy Americanisms that later became so closely identified with his name. While he retained his lean sound and rhythmic innovations, he also brought all his considerable technique to bear on the task of rendering American vernacular themes into a musically sophisticated fabric that would, at the same time, appeal to a mass audience. In this he was more successful than any of his colleagues. His form was more sharply defined than Thomson's and his harmonic language less esoteric than Harris'. *Billy* set the stylistic pattern for most of the remaining music that Copland would compose prior to the mid-1950s.

After the Mercury Theatre's notorious broadcast of H. G. Wells's *War of the Worlds* on October 31, 1938, twenty-two-year-old Orson Welles became an overnight national celebrity. This proved to be the beginning of the end of his fabulously productive partnership with John Houseman, for Welles became increasingly concerned with living up to his own press after that. The split occurred after Welles' dismal production of a play entitled *Five Kings*, for which Copland wrote the music in 1939. In *Five Kings* Welles had taken excerpts from all the Shakespeare plays that featured the character of Sir John Falstaff and assembled them into a dramatic anthology intended to serve as an actor's vehicle for himself. But the production was hastily conceived and poorly executed, and Houseman complained in a long and immensely revealing letter to Virgil Thomson of his increasing dissatisfaction with Welles' new attitudes. Shortly thereafter Welles would begin work on his cinematic masterpiece, *Citizen Kane*, for which Bernard Herrmann would be commissioned to write the music, achieving his first major success as a film composer. Although Houseman continued to work with Welles throughout the production of *Citizen Kane*, actually co-authoring the script, the film would prove to be their last significant collaboration.

Meanwhile, Copland had gone on to write the music, at Harold Clurman's request, for an unrealized Group Theatre production of the Irwin Shaw play *Quiet City* during the balance of 1939. When the production was canceled because of its too-experimental nature, Copland reworked his music into an orchestral suite that was eventually premiered by Koussevitzky at Tanglewood in February 1942. *Quiet City* showed Copland in a different compositional mode than the vigorous works that preceded it. His penchant for superficially complex rhythms was submerged into more placid textures which, in turn, enabled him to focus on the more purely harmonic and timbral aspects of his maturing style. *Quiet City* provided the final brick in the wall of Copland's middle-period technique and made possible his subsequent achievements in the *Piano Sonata, Our Town* and *A Lincoln Portrait,* as well as the pastoral sections of *Appalachian Spring.*

Apart from all the compositional work being done by our important composers during the 1930s, a great many organizational advances occurred as well, many at Copland's instigation or with, at least, his participation. The League of Composers had become a serious musical force in New York under the energetic leadership of Claire Reis, and Minna Lederman's magazine, *Modern Music,* was thriving as never before. Copland played a major role in both of these institutions. Among the other organizations founded at the time were the American Composers' Alliance (ACA) and its associated Arrow Music Press, created by Copland, Thomson, Harris, Blitzstein, Piston and Sessions in 1937. As radio broadcasting became more frequent, the collection of broadcast royalties became more of an issue. The composers' rights organization, Broadcast Music Inc. (BMI) had been founded in 1938, in direct competition with the older American Society of Composers, Authors and Publishers (ASCAP). For several years a conflict ensued between the two organizations over which would handle the royalties of the rising stars of American classical music during this period. Copland and Thomson were ASCAP members; Sessions and Otto Luening belonged to BMI. By 1944, the ACA had definitely aligned itself with BMI, which necessitated Copland's and Thomson's reluctant resignations. Later the ACA would create the important institutions: Composers' Recordings Inc. (CRI, in 1954) and the American Composers' Orchestra (ACO, in 1978). In March of 1939, Copland also organized a group for the purpose of collecting, distributing and preserving the vast amount of American classical music that was being written at the time. The participants included Howard Hanson, Marion Bauer and Quincy Porter, and the result was the American Music Center (AMC) in New York, which continues to thrive today.

But perhaps the best-known of all the institutional births at this time was that of the Berkshire Music Festival in Lenox, Massachusetts, popularly known as "Tanglewood." In 1937 the immensely wealthy Tappan family donated its western Massachusetts estate, Tanglewood, as a site for the festival that had been the dream of Serge Koussevitzky for many years. Koussevitzky envisioned a place where the greatest living composers would come to teach composition, the greatest conductors to teach conducting, and the finest young musicians to learn and play music together. Predictably, the early years were difficult and many setbacks threatened to swamp the whole project. But Koussevitzky had a will of iron hidden beneath his usually gentle exterior and saw each stage of the festival's development through to its completion. By 1940, with the opening of the Berkshire Music Center, the institution was solidly established and has since become one of the most important musical centers in the United States. During the 1940 and 1941 seasons, Copland would share composition teaching duties at Tanglewood, not always comfortably, with the German emigré composer Paul Hindemith.

Before Tanglewood entered the picture, however, Copland delivered himself of three works of major significance. The first of these is his *Piano Sonata,* composed largely during the summer of 1939 at a cottage in Woodstock, New York. The young Benjamin Britten and his lover, tenor Peter Pears, were living nearby, and Copland developed a powerful relationship of mutual respect with Britten at this time. The two remained close friends and colleagues until Britten's untimely death in 1976.

As noted above, the *Piano Sonata* enabled Copland to develop many of the newer stylistic features that had begun to enter his work with *Quiet City.* Although it is not a uniformly placid work, containing a rhythmically complex middle section, Copland's *Sonata* represents a degree of integration between his characteristic rhythmic gestures and his newer harmonic syntax that is not present in his earlier works. When producer Hal Roach and director Lewis Milestone summoned the composer to Hollywood in October of that year, to write the music for the film version of John Steinbeck's novel, *Of Mice and Men* (to be followed the next spring by music for Thornton Wilder's *Our Town*), Copland was in an excellent position to exploit the new developments in his technique for a broader audience than he had ever played to before. In both of these film scores he eschewed the typical Hollywood practice of composers such as Max Steiner and Erich Korngold, namely, of reflexively underlining virtually every significant speech or event with descriptive music derived from European Romantic models. Instead, particularly in his haunting music for the highly metaphysical *Our Town,* Copland sought to capture the inner emotional-thematic idea of the film and to find a musical parallel that would enhance it, without intruding itself between the audience and the screen. On both films he worked directly from the movieola—a device which allows the composer to view, rewind and review any portion of the film—rather than merely working from a printed cue sheet, as was often the practice of studio film composers. He also departed from tradition in making his own orchestrations to achieve the precise sound he wanted. Despite these new con-

straints and his long-established habit of composing slowly and painstakingly, Copland delivered both scores on schedule, and both have become
milestones in the history of music for the American cinema.

World War II, brought about a huge and predictable upsurge of
nationalist feeling, as well as a serious diminution of concert music activities
not connected with the war effort. The attention of many composers was
diverted either to active military service, or to projects that would contribute to maintaining morale both at home and on the front.

In 1941 Copland was asked by Carlton Sprague Smith to make a tour
of South America as a sort of cultural ambassador for Nelson Rockefeller's
Committee on Inter-American Affairs. His mission was to study and report
on musical activity in the southern continent and to identify promising
young composers who might benefit from a term of government-supported
residency in the United States. All of this was a part of Roosevelt's "good
neighbor" policy designed to shore up inter-American political solidarity

Aaron Copland *(1900–1990) in his seventies, looking
very much the dean of American music that he was at
the time, despite his dwindling output.* (Photo courtesy
of ASCAP.)

during the war and peripherally to combat the sympathetic relationships existing between certain South American regimes and the Nazis. During this tour Copland played, lectured about and disseminated much of his own music and that of his "gringo" colleagues, while developing important relationships with prominent South American composers such as Domingo Santa Cruz (Chile), Heitor Villa-Lobos (Brazil), Alberto Ginastera (Argentina) and, of course, Chávez. He recommended many to the U.S. government for sponsorship.

But the more significant event in Copland's life in 1941 was Andre Kostelanetz's commission of *A Lincoln Portrait*. Kostelanetz, one of the most commercially oriented of all the serious conductors of his day, was interested in acquiring portraits of several great Americans that he could perform with various orchestras as a contribution to wartime morale. Similar commissions went to Jerome Kern, who produced *Portrait for Orchestra (Mark Twain)*, and Thomson, who created his *Mayor La Guardia Waltzes* (portraying New York City's flamboyant mayor) and *Canons for Dorothy Thompson* in response. But Copland took the idea altogether more seriously than did Kern or Thomson. Remembering his old teacher, Rubin Goldmark, and Goldmark's attempt to set Lincoln's Gettysburg Address symphonically (see Chapter 4), Copland took on the challenge in a major way with his choice of Lincoln as a subject. He devised a text of his own, using quotations from Lincoln's writings and original, if not particularly inventive, descriptive interpolations, and cast the piece for spoken narration with orchestral accompaniment and interludes. Stylistically, *A Lincoln Portrait* continued the kind of orchestral writing developed for *Our Town* and exploited many of the same devices. However, Copland also began to adopt Thomson's technique of folk tune quotation, incorporating fragments of Stephen Foster's "Camptown Races" and the folksong "Pesky Sarpent" into his score. *A Lincoln Portrait* was premiered in May 1942, shortly after Copland had received a commission from choreographer Agnes DeMille for the piece that would become his next major ballet, *Rodeo*.

Copland spent the summer of 1942 teaching again at Tanglewood (this time sharing duties with Bohuslav Martinu) and working on *Rodeo*. By the fall, he had most of the ballet completed. While *Rodeo* represented no great technical advance over the kind of music Copland had created for *Billy the Kid*, it became by far the more popular of the two ballets, especially after Copland condensed the score into *Four Dance Episodes from "Rodeo,"* published in 1943 after the ballet's premiere. Overall the music for *Rodeo* was more melodic, more easily encapsulated into memorable phrase periods and, perhaps, more effectively orchestrated.

Copland spent the fall of 1942 working on his two-piano *Danzon Cubano* on a commission from the League of Composers. At the same time he had received a request from the English composer-conductor, Eugene Goosens, music director of the Cincinnati Symphony Orchestra, for a fanfare that would be appropriate to play at the beginning of a concert. Like the *Lincoln Portrait,* this was to be one of a series of such pieces commissioned from several prominent composers and reprised a similar project Goosens had initiated in England during World War I. In Copland's words, "The challenge was to compose a traditional fanfare, direct and powerful, yet with a contemporary sound."[36] As had been the case with *Quiet City* and *Our Town,* Copland achieved his "contemporary sound" by pairing mildly dissonant tonal harmony with rather conventional and rhythmically simplified (for him) phrase structures. With the incorporation of stark, dramatic percussion effects, these techniques projected the *Fanfare for the Common Man* into the status of an instant "classic" when it was premiered in March of 1943. In the fifty years since its creation, the *Fanfare* has probably been played, partially or completely, with and without attribution, more often than any other single work of Copland's. So significant was its success that Copland later incorporated it into his *Third Symphony.*

Also in 1943 Copland was hired to compose the score for the Samuel Goldwyn film, *The North Star,* dealing with the lives of Soviet peasants during the war. With a script by Lillian Hellman, song lyrics by Ira Gershwin, a stellar cast and an operating budget in excess of three million dollars (a fortune by the standards of the time), *The North Star* was the biggest cinematic project on which Copland had worked to date. In it he adapted some Russian folk music, as well as the Communist anthem "Internationale," without necessarily trying to sound Russian, as he had adapted Mexican and cowboy material in earlier ballets. But, despite all this, the songs fell flat. Copland's persistent inability to craft a satisfying vocal melody, without sounding naive on the one hand or pretentious on the other, tripped him up here as it had in his art songs and in *The Second Hurricane.* During the Communist paranoia of the 1950s, *The North Star* would become awkward political baggage for Copland and other leftist artists who had worked on it. It was subsequently re-edited and released for television under the title *Armored Attack.*

In 1944, Copland completed his *Sonata for Violin and Piano,* then took on a brief lecturing stint at Harvard. That summer he and Victor Kraft went once again to Mexico, where Copland received word of his mother's death. He had begun an orchestra piece, *Letter from Home,* dealing with the subject of American GI's off fighting the war, earlier that year in

---

[36]   Copland-Perlis, vol. 1, p. 368.

Cambridge. Already in a somber mood from this work, the news of his mother's death gave him additional impetus to finish this piece and return home, just in time for the premiere of another ballet, which was to prove his most enduring musical legacy.

In 1940, Copland had come across the Shaker song "Simple Gifts" in an old collection. The Shakers were a religious sect that had evolved from the Quakers and come to America with their leader, Mother Ann, in the late 18th century. Committed to a life of hard work and chastity, including strict segregation of the sexes, the Shakers numbered several thousand members at their peak. And, while the sect has died out in recent times, their settlements in New England and Appalachia have become historic sites, visited by hundreds of tourists each year.

The Shaker lifestyle produced characteristic styles of furniture making, clothing, architecture and other crafts. And their music was equally distinctive. Unlike many Christian sects, they were given to dancing as a form of devotional meditation, and their songs were usually intended to accompany patterns of repetitive movement. "Simple Gifts" is absolutely typical of Shaker melodic structure and style, but was not generally known to the public before Copland "discovered" it and incorporated it into his music for Martha Graham's ballet, *Appalachian Spring*. It has since achieved its rightful place as a classic of American folk music.

The genesis of *Appalachian Spring* is a convoluted story. Graham had choreographed Copland's *Piano Variations* under the title *Dithyrambic* in the early 1930s, and had approached Copland about a full ballet score in 1941. Copland had rejected her subject, Medea, at that time. However, after the great patron of early 20th-century American music, Elizabeth Sprague Coolidge, became acquainted with Graham's work, she agreed to sponsor a joint commission for two ballets, one by Copland and one by Carlos Chávez. *The North Star* and other projects had delayed Copland's work on the ballet, but by early 1944 he was seriously at work on the sketches.

Graham was exceptionally vague about the final choice of scenario and title throughout the entire composition process, giving Copland only general ideas about the locales, characters, feelings and situations she wished to embody in the dance. Apparently this was perfectly congenial to Copland, who enjoyed the freedom from choreographic constraints often imposed on ballet composers. Together with Leo Smit, he made a piano recording of the finished music and sent it to Graham, who used this as the basis of her choreography. Copland did not even see the finished product until just before the premiere, nor did he know until then the title Graham had given it.

Appalachian Spring was an immediate success with audience and critics alike. It was awarded the Pulitzer Prize and became one of the few authentic classics of American ballet. The symphonic suite entered the standard repertoire of all the major American orchestras, just as "Simple Gifts" entered the mainstream of American folk music. In this work, which catapulted both Copland and Graham into a national prominence that exceeded their individual prior accomplishments, Copland reached the pinnacle of his career. To be sure, he still had major works to write, including his *Third Symphony,* his *Clarinet Concerto* for Benny Goodman, *The Tender Land,* film scores for *The Red Pony* and *The Heiress,* and his two major serial compositions, *Connotations* and *Inscape,* but nothing Copland composed after 1944 ever made as great an impact on the public consciousness as his three "American" ballets, the *Lincoln Portrait* and the *Fanfare for the Common Man.*

In 1947, jazz clarinetist Benny Goodman commissioned Copland to write a concerto for clarinet and orchestra. Scored for an orchestra of strings, harp and piano, Copland composed the first movement of this *Concerto* while on yet another goodwill tour of South America in 1947 and completed it the following year. As the *Concerto* was written specifically for Goodman, Copland naturally employed jazz techniques again, harking back to his earlier *Piano Concerto* (1926). But his technique was by now much more seasoned and mature, and the *Clarinet Concerto* embodies more refined and relaxed elements than did the earlier work. It was premiered by Goodman in November of 1950.

This same period of time saw Copland's creation of two more film scores, *The Red Pony* (Republic, 1948), from which he later extracted a popular orchestral suite, and *The Heiress* (Paramount, 1949), in which Copland made extensive use of Jean Paul (Giovanni) Martini il Tedesco's[37] early 19th-century potboiler, "Plaisir d'amour." In March of 1950 he completed his only major song cycle, *Twelve Poems of Emily Dickinson.* In this work, for voice and piano, Copland exerted his greatest effort to achieve, finally, a fully satisfying vocal composition and came closer to it than in any of his other works. The more abstract medium of the art song allowed him to exploit the chromatic melodic writing that was natural to his technique at this time more effectively than had his previous attempts at labor or political songs, or the dramatic demands and vocal limitations of *The Second Hurricane.* He later orchestrated eight of these songs, which were performed at Juilliard in honor of his seventieth birthday in 1970.

---

[37] Martini (1741–1816) is an interesting, if obscure, figure in music history. Not to be confused with the earlier Giambatista "Padre" Martini (1706–1784), Martini il Tedesco was a Bavarian organist and composer. His original surname was Schwartzendorf, but he changed it to the Franco-Italian Jean Paul Égide Martini after migrating to Paris in 1764. He wrote several operas and other works under this name, including the song "Plaisir d'amour." "Il Tedesco" is the Italian term for "the German." "Plaisir d'amour" is his best-known song, and has achieved the status of an American folksong during the past one hundred and fifty years.

In 1950, Copland produced his first major 12-tone work, the *Piano Quartet*. Although organized by an 11-note series, and following the basic procedures developed by Schoenberg, it would be a mistake to categorize this work as a "serial" composition in the same sense that works contemporary to it by Babbitt, Boulez et al. are serial. The *Piano Quartet* is a serial work in terms of the organization of its pitch material only. Its formal structure, textures and overall "sound" remained very idiomatic to Copland. This, together with its highly effective writing for the instruments, is perhaps one of the reasons that it is one of the most often performed "serial" works in the current repertoire. Copland would later claim that his adoption of the serial method in the *Quartet* was a means of "freshening" his technique and opening up new sonorities that he would not have heard in his mind's ear, given his accustomed methods of composing.[38] Thus, his motive for using the technique seems very similar to Schoenberg's motive for developing it in the first place.

The *Piano Quartet* was followed by Copland's second opera, *The Tender Land,* written on a commission from Rodgers and Hammerstein to celebrate the 30th anniversary of the League of Composers. Premiered by the New York City Opera at City Center on April 2, 1954, *The Tender Land* was a flop. Copland and his librettist, Erik Johns (writing under the pseudonym "Horace Everett"), spent the next several months making revisions, performing an intermediate version at Tanglewood the following August, and yet another revision in May of 1955. But *The Tender Land* has never been fully successful. Both the music and the story, about a bucolic midwestern farm family during the Depression, attempt to achieve a sense of profound universal values hidden within an outward guise of simplicity—all too reminiscent of Steinbeck and Thornton Wilder. But Johns, who later achieved recognition as a painter and dancer, was neither a Steinbeck nor a Wilder, and Copland had already moved beyond the period in his development when this kind of music—similar to *Our Town* and *Appalachian Spring*—was at the center of his creative thinking. Despite several subsequent attempts to revive the work, including a PBS broadcast in the late 1970s, *The Tender Land* was never entirely successful. (However, during the late 1980s a new arrangement of the opera was made by Murray Sidlin for a reduced orchestra of thirteen instruments. This was produced at the Long Wharf Repertory Theatre in Connecticut and again at the University of Minnesota, with Copland's endorsement and approval. This smaller, more workshop-like production of *The Tender Land* seemed to capture more of the family intimacy demanded by the story than did its

---

[38] *Perspectives on American Composers,* B. Boretz and E. T. Cone, eds., p. 141.

earlier, full-blown operatic productions—and may yet prove to be the salvation of Copland's last attempt at opera.)

In 1953, Copland was called to testify before Sen. Joseph McCarthy's infamous Senate subcommittee investigating Communist activity in the United States. The pretext for this lay in Copland's past association with left-wing composers and intellectuals such as Lillian Hellman, Arthur Miller, Hans Eisler, Marc Blitzstein and Ralph Steiner, as well as his own prior membership in organizations such as the Composers' Collective, his work on *The North Star* and his public support of the leading Soviet composer of the day, Dmitri Shostakovich. The incident that precipitated Copland's "interview" with McCarthy occurred when *A Lincoln Portrait* was removed from the program of Dwight Eisenhower's presidential inaugural concert at Constitution Hall in Washington on January 18, 1953. Sen. Fred E. Busbey of Illinois had engineered this ban on Copland's work as a result of the composer's past political affiliations. A huge controversy erupted, fueled by the anti-Communist paranoia of the time, in which many leading figures in American life rallied to Copland's support—pointing out the absurdity of an attack on the one composer who had glorified American culture in his work more conspicuously than any of his predecessors. Nevertheless, Copland was summoned before McCarthy in secret session on May 25, 1953. Accompanied by his attorney, Oscar Cox, Copland fielded McCarthy's questions and insinuations for two hours, remaining calm and refusing to implicate any of his friends or colleagues. The question of Copland's homosexuality—a subject in which both McCarthy and his attorney, Roy Cohn, were always inordinately interested—did not come up, possibly because it was unknown to the committee.

McCarthy's hidden agenda was to use Copland to get at the United States Information Agency, which controlled such institutions as the Voice of America radio broadcasting system, and which, McCarthy was convinced, was a nest of Communists. He was unsuccessful in this effort. Copland could be a master dissembler when he wanted to be. To the end of his days he exercised tremendous control over what and how much information about his life was revealed to others, even close personal friends. And he did so in such a seamlessly affable, polite and even humorous way that many did not even realize what he was doing. As he grew older, and began to experience authentic problems with his memory during the 1980s, this provided him with even greater leverage to shape his public image through selective recall of the past. He used these skills to the utmost with McCarthy, as revealed in the transcript of his interview,[39] and played

---

[39] See Copland-Perlis, vol. 2, pp. 192–194.

the pompous, paranoid senator from Wisconsin like a musical instrument. Other composers were subjected to McCarthy investigations as well, throughout the 1950s. These included Elie Siegmeister, Blitzstein, Wallingford Riegger and Roy Harris. Overall, in the history of our classical music, as in other domains of American life, this shabby period in American politics had ramifications that lasted well into the 1960s.

In 1955, Copland produced his next major serial work, the *Piano Fantasy*. The *Fantasy* is also his third and last big work for piano, after the *Variations* and the *Sonata*. Like the *Piano Quartet*, the *Fantasy* makes use of serial techniques, but within a fundamentally tonal orientation. It exploits the extreme registers of the piano as well as its dynamic extremes, more than Copland's previous piano works, and is by far his most taxing piece for the pianist. Perhaps for this reason, as well as its length and serial organization, the *Fantasy* is played less often today than either the *Variations* or the *Sonata*. But it is by no means inferior to them musically.

Under the influences of his recent composition of the *Piano Fantasy* and his recently begun career as a conductor (as well as a commission from the Louisville Symphony), Copland orchestrated his 1930 *Piano Variations* under the title *Orchestral Variations* in 1957. From then on, Copland was to devoted more and more of his time to conducting and less and less to composing. Undoubtedly he had already begun to have the sense of having been left behind by changing musical fashions. The academic serialists were well entrenched in the university/conservatory establishment by 1957, and the avant-garde aleatorists, led by John Cage, were beginning to dominate freelance circles of American music making. In a sense, Copland's very success began to work against him as he approached the age of sixty. Increasingly he was perceived as the "Dean" of American composers, which also carried implications that he had passed his peak and that most of his important work was behind him. It is still too early to judge, in historical terms, whether or not this was a valid perception at the time.

In 1960 Copland returned briefly to a more tonal, neoclassical style of composition with his *Nonet* for three violins, three violas and three cellos, commissioned by the Dumbarton Oaks Research Library in Washington, D.C. This was followed in 1963 by another tonal work, *Dance Panels*, which was to be Copland's last music for dancers. Like the early *Music for the Theatre, Dance Panels* is abstract music without a scenario and has been choreographed by Jerome Robbins (who commissioned it) and others as they saw fit.

Copland's last two major works were both large orchestral pieces, organized along serial lines. The first of these, *Connotations*, was written in 1962 on a commission arranged by William Schuman from the New York Philharmonic for the inaugural concert of Philharmonic Hall (later Avery

Fisher Hall) in Lincoln Center. In *Connotations*, Copland allowed himself free rein to explore the musical issues that interested him. He had at his command one of the world's finest orchestras and, at that stage of his life, virtually no extra-musical or career objectives that had to be satisfied by this piece. The result is a massive, arch-like musical structure, rich in contrapuntal texture, extremely dissonant and concluding with the largest agglomeration of sheer sound that Copland ever composed. But *Connotations*, like the contrasting *Inscape* that followed it in 1967, was music heard initially only by the "uptown" cultural elite in New York. The frontline of musical thinking had moved elsewhere by then, and Copland's last major work was virtually ignored by the younger composers in whose reactions he was most interested.

Between *Connotations* and *Inscape*, Copland composed his *Music for a Great City*, derived from his score to the obscure 1961 film *Something Wild*, starring Carroll Baker. This abstract four movement suite, premiered under Copland's baton by the London Symphony in May of 1964, represents a kind of nostalgia for the New York of his younger days versus what New York had become by the 1960s.

After 1973 Copland ceased composing, with the exception of a few minor sketches and reworkings of earlier pieces. In characteristic style, he explained this as the normal slackening of the pace of professional activity for a man in his seventies.[40] But clearly there were deeper reasons. Increasingly he quoted the advice allegedly given him in earlier years to find some activity in the twilight of his life that would not compete with his achievements as a younger man. For Copland, this activity was conducting. Throughout the final two decades of his life he became a professional conductor of international standing, handling standard repertoire as well as his own works.

Conducting kept him musically active, but was no substitute for composing. As honors, awards and testimonials began to flow in on an almost daily basis in his last years, his affable exterior nevertheless betrayed signs of regret that the major portion of his creative mission was accomplished. In the summer of 1976, Copland's intimate friend of many years, Victor Kraft, died suddenly of a heart attack while vacationing in Maine. No one was permitted to view Copland's innermost reaction to this event. In recent years, he and Victor had been less close than they were during the 1930s and 1940s. Kraft had made an unsuccessful attempt at an abortive marriage, and he and Copland had not lived together on a regular basis for some time. But Victor was only one of many friends that Copland lived to mourn. Marc Blitzstein, Harold Clurman, Orson Welles, Virgil Thomson,

---

[40] Conversation with the author, spring, 1972.

Roy Harris, Roger Sessions, Walter Piston and many others preceded him to the grave.

During the last decade of his life, Copland suffered increasingly from failing memory, possibly caused by a series of minor strokes.[41] This was kept carefully concealed from the public by the composer and his circle of friends. Fortunately, the pioneering oral historian of American music, Vivian Perlis, was able to complete work with him on his massive, two-volume autobiography before his periods of mental lucidity became too infrequent to make such a project possible. In the words of the aging John Kirkpatrick,[42] "Vivian got to Aaron just in time." While conducting a filmed recording session for the PBS documentary celebrating his 80th birthday, Copland forgot that the technical crew was present and was suddenly startled by the appearance of a man with a hand-held camera under the podium. On a visit to Los Angeles to conduct the Robert Shaw Chorale in the early 1980s, he found himself stranded in LA International Airport, unable to remember why he was in Los Angeles or where he was expected to go.[43] These and other embarrassing incidents became more frequent, and Copland increasingly kept to his home in Peekskill, New York, where he died on December 2, 1990.

During the 1950s, 1960s and 1970s, Copland, Thomson and Harris continued to compose. But their heyday was over. A younger generation of composers had begun to emerge, building on their accomplishments and, frequently, reacting against the "Americanist" stylistic mode they had begun to foster. It should not, however, be assumed that the late works of these three, any more than those of their lesser-known colleagues, are necessarily inferior to their earlier ones merely because they did not receive the same degree of attention. Harris died in 1979, Thomson in 1989, and Copland in 1990. Even though Copland and Harris had ceased composing in the last years of their lives, the final works of all three are still far too new to have received the repeated hearings and evaluation by several generations of listeners necessary to render a final judgment. Indeed, several of the late works of these composers have not yet been published and/or recorded.

Other Contemporaries

Though Copland, Thomson and Harris clearly dominated the public perception of American classical music during the 1930s and early 1940s, a

---

[41] Vivian Perlis, conversation with the author, October, 1993.
[42] Conversation with the author, November, 1985.
[43] Jack Larson, conversation with the author, February, 1993.

number of other significant composers rose in their wake. The most prominent of these was the young Samuel Barber (see next chapter), whose 1936
Adagio for Strings has become an American classic on a par with Gershwin's
Concerto in F and Copland's *Appalachian Spring*. Others included Wallingford Riegger, Randall Thompson, William Grant Still, Ernst Toch, Bernard
Herrmann, Quincy Porter and Otto Luening. Some of these, like Riegger,
were actually older than Thomson (the oldest of the "big three"), but did
not achieve serious recognition until after Copland and his colleagues had
paved the way for them. Others were either contemporary with or slightly
younger than Copland. Still more obscure members of this generation
included Ernst Bacon, Adolph Weiss, Stefan Wolpe, R. R. Bennett, Bernard
Rogers, Elie Siegmeister, Hunter Johnson, Ruth Crawford Seeger, Leo
Sowerby, David Guion and Anis Fuliehan, among others, some of whom
have been mentioned previously. One of the most prominent composers
active in America and contemporary with Copland was the German, Kurt
Weill, who had collaborated with Bertolt Brecht in Germany on such
important musical theatre works as *The Threepenny Opera* and *The Rise
and Fall of the City of Mahagonny*. However, Weill's concert music is
generally inferior to his theatre music, and the extent to which he played a
significant role in American classical music, as opposed to musical theatre,
is debatable. As there are several excellent studies already devoted exclusively to him, his story is omitted here.

Perhaps the most important older composer to benefit from the
upsurge in interest in American music created by Copland and his generation was **Wallingford Riegger (1885–1961)**. Contemporary with such
popular figures as Cadman and Carpenter, Riegger had a much more serious
musical mission than they, but endured a less happy public reception during
his lifetime. The essential tragedy of Riegger's life is that he was born too
late to fit comfortably into the post-Romantic mold and too early to belong
to the Copland generation where his true sympathies lay. Yet, despite the
uneven musical quality of his work, largely engendered by the financial
necessity of accepting commissions that didn't really interest him, his music
remains several cuts above the work of all his exact contemporaries except
Griffes.

Riegger was born in Albany, Georgia, on April 29, 1885. He spent
most of his childhood in Indianapolis and began studying the violin at an
early age. In 1900 the family moved to New York, where Riegger added the
study of cello to his musical skills, eventually becoming a first-rate orchestral cellist. Around 1904 he enrolled in the newly formed Institute of
Musical Art, which later became part of the Juilliard School. As would
Howard Hanson later, Riegger also studied composition with the pedantic
theorist and author of books on sonata form, Percy Goetschius. After

graduation from the Institute in 1907, Riegger enrolled at the Berlin Hochschule für Musik, where he continued his cello studies and pursued composition with Max Bruch and the American, Edgar Stillman Kelley (see Chapter 4). He made his conducting debut with the Blüthner Orchestra in 1910, then returned to the United States for a three-year stint as principal cellist with the St. Paul (Minnesota) Symphony. He returned to Germany in 1914 and resumed his conducting career until America's entry into World War I forced him to return home.

During the 1920s, Riegger struggled to make a living at various teaching jobs, being unable to secure a regular conducting post. He began composing in a serious way at this time and produced, among other works, a *Piano Trio* (1920), a setting of Keats' poem, *La belle dame sans merci*, for soloist, female choir and chamber orchestra, and his 1922 *Triple Jazz* for orchestra. The trio won him a Paderewski Prize, and, in 1924, *La belle dame* received the first Coolidge Award given to any American composer. But his 1927 *Study in Sonority* for ten violins (or any multiple thereof) aroused hostility due to its biting dissonance. *Study in Sonority* proved to be the turning point for Riegger, and, thereafter, his essential musical interest lay with the modernist camp—although he would continue to produce conventional music in response to commissions.

Throughout the 1930s, Riegger became solidly entrenched in the world of New York's musical avant-garde, led by Copland, and participated in many of the committees and organizations that were formed to promote both musical and musico-political causes. His politics were distinctly left wing. He too was eventually hauled before the House Un-American Activities Committee and McCarthy investigations in the 1950s. Because of the difference in age between Riegger and his younger colleagues, they tended to view him as something of a senior partner in their organizations. But he was held in considerable respect by them for his musical powers nonetheless. He also became acquainted with Ives, Ruggles, Varèse and Cowell at the time, and developed collegial relationships with all of them.

Also during the 1930s, Riegger became seriously interested in composing music for the emerging field of modern dance. He produced scores for Martha Graham, Doris Humphrey, Erick Hawkins and other avant-garde choreographers, including two of his best-known works, *New Dance* (1935) and *With My Red Fires* (1936). In all he created nearly twenty dance scores between 1930 and 1941, of which only two have been published in their original form.

In the 1940s and 1950s, Riegger turned more to absolute music, composing chamber works, symphonies and original vocal music, together with some seven hundred arrangements of folksongs and anthems (both

A striking photograph of **Wallingford Riegger** *(1885–1961) and his wife battling a Chicago snowstorm. Older than the rest of the Copland generation. Riegger neverthe-less created a canon of vivid, impressive works—often in the 12-tone style.* (Photo cour-tesy of BMI.)

under his own name and various pseudonyms) for more than half-a-dozen different commercial publishers. Altogether he produced four symphonies, two string quartets, a piano quintet, a woodwind quintet, a concerto for piano and woodwind quintet, and a large number of pieces for orchestra alone and orchestra with soloist(s) during these years.

After 1930, Riegger had a distinct predilection for the 12-tone method in all his original works. He is often compartmentalized as an "American dodecaphonist" in earlier music histories. But, unlike other 12-tone com-posers, he applied the system unsystematically, as it suited his basically intuitive compositional needs in various pieces. His musical textures are, on the whole, far less dense than those of other serialists, such as Sessions. And he always exhibited a flair for colorful, highly dramatic musical gestures. By the end of his life, Riegger had received the usual shower of awards, honors and testimonials given to successful American composers, but his music remains largely unpublished and largely unplayed today. This is unfortunate, because Riegger's work is among the most colorful, imagina-tive and accessible of all atonal and 12-tone music. We may hope for a day when it receives the attention it deserves.

Another of the more obscure composers from this generation was **Randall Thompson** (1899–1984). Born in New York on April 21, 1899, Thompson, like Virgil Thomson, studied with Davison and Hill at Harvard, from which he graduated in 1920. He also spent some time working with Ernest Bloch before 1922, and, in that same year, received one of the first fellowships awarded by the American Academy in Rome. Although Randall Thompson spent most of his professional life teaching at various colleges and conservatories, he did not have the impact on academic music of a Hanson, Sessions, Piston, Schuman or Babbitt. Rather, his music remained consistently tonal and highly accessible throughout his career and found a more public audience than is usual for an academic composer.

Thompson's forte was choral composition and conducting. His best known work in this medium is his *Alleluia,* premiered at Tanglewood in 1940. This short piece has since become the traditional Tanglewood anthem, sung at its annual ceremonies, and a favorite staple in the repertoire of many amateur church choirs. But Thompson's major works for chorus are less well known. These include secular pieces such as his 1924 *Five Odes of Horace, The Testament of Freedom* (1943, after Thomas Jefferson), *Frostiana* (1959, on poems of Robert Frost), and *A Concord Cantata* (1975), as well as sacred works such as the *Mass of the Holy Spirit* (1956), the *Requiem* (1958), his 1962 setting of the *23rd Psalm* for female voices, and his 1967 cantata *A Psalm of Thanksgiving.*

Thompson also wrote three symphonies, two operas and a variety of instrumental and chamber music. His pupils included Leonard Bernstein, Lukas Foss, Leo Kraft and Ivan Tcherepnin. He died in Boston on July 9, 1984.

Of equal importance was another basically academic composer whose impact was greater on the public than it was on academia. **Quincy Porter** was born in New Haven, Connecticut, on February 7, 1897 and was associated with Yale for most of his career. He studied with Horatio Parker and Parker's successor, David Stanley Smith (see Chapter 4), taking his Bachelor of Arts in 1919 (the year of Parker's death) and his Bachelor of Music in 1921. In addition to Parker and Smith, he studied composition with d'Indy in Paris and with Bloch in Cleveland, and was appointed by the latter to the faculty of the Cleveland Institute in 1922, after the departure of Sessions and Chanler. He also taught at Vassar and was dean of the New England Conservatory from 1938 until 1946, when he returned to Yale as a full professor.

Porter was an accomplished violinist/violist and devoted most of his creative energies to chamber music for strings, following the example of his Second New England School predecessor, Arthur Whiting. Just as Thompson dominated the field of choral composition, Porter held a commanding position among mid-century American composers of chamber music, although he also wrote two symphonies (1934, 1962), a number of concertos and concertante works and an important *Piano Sonata* (1930). His most significant works are his *Viola Concerto* (1948) and his *Concerto Concertante*, which was awarded the Pulitzer Prize in 1954.

Though Porter was involved in much of the organizational work stimulated by Copland in the 1930s, especially in the founding of the American Music Center, and thus associated with avant-garde composers of the time, his style remained fundamentally tonal and conservative throughout his career. Even so, his ideas are provocative and his music is skillfully conceived for its instruments. He was not a great innovator, but his works represent a solid contribution to the literature of American classical music, and are worthy of greater attention than they currently receive. He died in Bethany, Connecticut, on November 12, 1966.

Yet a third shadowy figure to emerge in America during the mid-century is the much-neglected **Ernst Toch** (1887–1964). Like Grainger, Bloch, Varèse and others, Toch was an immigrant whose work in America superseded the importance of his earlier compositions and exerted a greater influence here than abroad. Born in Vienna on December 7, 1887, Toch was largely self-taught as a composer. He developed an early passion for the Mozart String Quartets and spent many hours copying them out in longhand, analyzing them and attempting to compose alternate developments of the thematic material in them, comparing his results with the original.

Toch was a brilliant pianist and, in 1913, was appointed teacher of composition at the Mannheim Musikhochschule. The rise of the Nazis prompted his immigration to the United States in 1933, as part of the general European artistic exodus, and he became a fellow faculty member with Copland at the New School for Social Research in New York shortly after his arrival.

In 1936, Toch moved to southern California where he became associated with University of Southern California for most of the remainder of his life. He also became involved in composing music for films and either scored or contributed to the scores for a diverse array of movies, including *Catherine the Great* (London/UA, 1934), *The Private Life of Don Juan* (London/UA, 1934), *Peter Ibbetson* (Paramount, 1935, score nominated for an Academy Award), *The General Died at Dawn* (Paramount, 1936), *The Story of Alexander Graham Bell* (20th Century–Fox, 1939), *The Cat and the Canary* (Paramount, 1939), *Dr. Cyclops* (Paramount, 1940), *The Hunchback of Notre Dame* (RKO, 1939), *Ladies in Retirement* (Columbia,

1941), *Address Unknown* (Columbia, 1944, also nominated for an Oscar) and *The Unseen* (Paramount, 1945, produced by John Houseman).

But, distinguished as Toch's film music is, the real focus of his work lay in absolute and program music, especially for chamber ensembles. He created thirteen string quartets, a *String Trio* (1936), a *Piano Quintet* (1938) and numerous other works for small ensemble. His 5×10 Etudes for piano and his *Two-Piano Sonata* (1962) are among the most challenging and interesting of modern works for keyboard, and his orchestral music, including four symphonies written between 1950 and 1957, ranks among the most accessible body of work in tonal modernism.

Toch was a serious musical intellectual, but he did not believe in the value of precompositional methods and thus resisted the lure of serialism and other experimental procedures of his time. He felt that form and substance were identical in music, and that composition must represent a process of organic growth from the material at hand. And, while Sessions' work demonstrated that these views were not necessarily inconsistent with avant-garde procedures of the time, particularly serialism, Toch could never reconcile himself to the adoption of *any* predetermined system. The result is a piquant, neoclassical chromaticism in his own work, which communicates as effectively with youth orchestras (among which his 1959 *Intermezzo* is standard repertoire) as with more mature listeners.

Despite a bevy of honors and testimonials awarded before his death, Toch justifiably felt ignored during the latter part of his life. Like so many others of his and later generations of American composers, he was passed over by the mercurial vicissitudes of musical fashion and was treated with indifference by the academic serialists. While the outward circumstances of his life were comfortable, he died basically a frustrated man on October 1, 1964 in Los Angeles. Again it is to be hoped that future generations of listeners will revive the work of this important composer.

The significant composers of Copland's generation are so numerous that it is impossible here to detail the full story of each individual's life and work without swamping the reader in a sea of interconnected biographies. Many of the lesser figures previously mentioned deserve far more attention than it is practical to give them here. But no discussion of this generation can be considered even partially complete without inclusion of William Grant Still (1895–1978). Though never on the cutting edge of modern American music, Still's work is important for two reasons: (a) it represents a substantial contribution to the more accessible styles of mid-century American classical music, and (b) he is one of the few African-American composers (Harry Lawrence Freeman and Ulysses Kay being among the others) to have made his mark primarily in the domain of concert music, as opposed to jazz.

Still was born in Woodville, Mississippi, on May 11, 1895. Both his parents were educated African Americans—the children of former slaves—and determined to make their way upward in American society during the post-Reconstruction era. Still's father died when the composer was still a small boy, and his upbringing was left entirely in the hands of his strict, iron-willed, but affectionate mother (a professional teacher) until her re-marriage some years later. After his mother went to Little Rock, Arkansas, in search of teaching employment, young William was given violin lessons. But this was the extent of his early musical training.

Still enrolled at Wilberforce College in 1913, intending (at his mother's insistence) to pursue a career in medicine. At Wilberforce, how-ever, he was captivated by the life and work of the Anglo-African composer, Samuel Coleridge-Taylor. Under the influence of Coleridge-Taylor's ex-ample, Still's interest in music blossomed, and he left Wilberforce, before taking his degree, to pursue musical studies.

In 1916, Still met W. C. Handy, the composer and trumpet player who, more than any other individual, was responsible for developing and codifying the 12-bar blues as a defined musical form. Handy managed his own band and publishing company, and enlisted Still's help with orches-trations and other musical chores. This apprenticeship gave Still some of his most valuable experience as a practical musician, as well as thorough grounding in the musical and business mechanics of early jazz.

In 1917, Still enrolled at Oberlin College and studied composition. But his studies were interrupted by military service in World War I. After the war, he relocated in New York where he studied with Varèse and received an offer of a scholarship to the New England Conservatory from George W. Chadwick. Sensing that he had reached the end of his formal studies, Still declined Chadwick's offer, but took seriously the elder composer's advice to concentrate his energies on specifically American musical subjects. During the 1920s Still began his career in earnest, produc-ing a symphonic poem, *Darker America* (1924), the orchestral suite *From the Black Belt* (1926) and the song *Levee Land* (soprano and instrumental ensemble, 1925) to his own text. Throughout this period he was working very much on his own, or within the small confines of that segment of New York's African-American community that was interested in "high brow" music. His career development was undoubtedly impeded by his lack of contact with the emerging avant-garde represented by Copland, and it is doubtful whether his haphazard musical training, combined with the socio-political context of the time, would have enabled him at that point in his

William Grant Still *(1895–1978) as a young man.*
He became the first African American to be taken
seriously as a symphonic and operatic composer.
(Photo courtesy of ASCAP.)

development to compete on common ground with his more formally European-trained white colleagues.

But, in spite of these difficulties, Still achieved his first substantive composition in 1930 with his *Symphony No. 1,* subtitled the "Afro-American." This was performed by the Rochester Philharmonic and advertised as the first symphony by an African American to be played by a major orchestra—a claim that has not yet been successfully disputed by historians. Thereafter, Still went on to compose four more symphonies, six symphonic poems, ten more orchestral suites, and numerous other songs, chamber and solo instrumental works. Among the other "firsts" in his career were his debut as the first African American to conduct a major orchestra and one of the first to write music for radio, film and television. His 1934 opera, *Blue Steel,* attracted significant attention, and his 1941 opera, *A Bayou Legend,* was broadcast forty years after its creation on PBS.

Throughout his career, Still remained a descriptively modern tonal composer. His work sometimes suffers from a lack of formal clarity and never achieved the melodic invention necessary to firmly implant it in the public mind. But his achievement is, nevertheless, substantial, and his best work is as good as that of any of his contemporaries. In later years he experimented with more modernist techniques, but never really abandoned his fundamentally neo-Romantic style. By the time of his death in Los Angeles, on December 3, 1978, he had received awards from CBS and the League of Composers, as well as Roswenwald and Guggenheim Fellowships.

The deaths of Thomson, Copland and Harris brought to an end an epoch in American music history. In the sixty-five years between 1925 and 1990, American music had indeed "taken off," as Nadia Boulanger had predicted that it would. The works of this generation of composers, performers and conductors put American music on the map of world cultural history in a way that it had never been before. But, following World War II, both American society and American music were permanently changed by the advent of mass electronic media, the Cold War and the explosion of computer technology. In the next few chapters we shall see how these changes erased many of the achievements of the Copland generation from the consciousness of the American public at large, and posed even greater challenges for subsequent generations of American classical composers— challenges that few have successfully met even yet.

9

The Generation of the Forties, Fifties and Sixties

&

World War II had devastated Europe and driven most of its prominent living composers to America. Some of the older European composers—such as Vaughan Williams, Kodály, Sibelius, Prokofiev—remained in their native countries and made various contributions to reconstructing cultural life. But, despite Nadia Boulanger's continued activity in France, by 1945 the idea that a young American *needed* to study in Europe to establish compositional credentials was basically dead. As important centers of experimental and electronic music were founded in Cologne and Darmstadt, European music in the 1950s gradually fell into the hands of a younger and more radical generation, including Boulez, Stockhausen, Berio, Dallapiccola, Nono and Xenakis. Some of these composers were doctrinaire Marxists who perceived the old post-Romanticism of their grandfathers as an integral part of the mindset that had led, as a historical inevitability, to the military and economic holocausts of the first half of the century. And they were determined that history would not repeat itself. The prophet of their new musical theology was the serialist, Anton Webern, who, ironically, had been shot to death by an American GI in occupied Germany in 1945 when he carelessly stepped out on his porch to light a cigarette during a blackout.

Simultaneously, American academic music had finally achieved respectability in the microcosm of the American university. By 1955, any American institution of higher liberal arts education that lacked a music department was viewed as a second-rate school. American academic music was dominated in the 1950s by European composers of the Schoenberg/Hindemith generations, and by native academic modernists

216

led by Sessions, Piston, Schuman and Babbitt. In the training of composers born in the 1930s, the result was an increasing preoccupation with the developing techniques of post-Webern serialism on the one hand, and of abstruse but still-tonal academic modernism on the other. Most of these younger composers chose to absorb and develop serialist ideas. A few, who later became the minimalists and post-modernists of the 1970s and 1980s, resisted them. Non-tonal electronic music and musique concrète were also beginning to emerge from the work of Varèse, Luening, Ussachevsky and Lejaren Hiller during the 1950s.

One of the results of this development was the increasing irrelevance of the kind of "Americanist" music pioneered by Copland, Thomson and Harris to the movers and shakers of contemporary musical thought. While Copland et al. remained active, musical fashion had begun to pass them by and, more and more, they were shunted off into the role of "elder statesmen." But, even as Copland's generation was beginning to fade, a younger group of their successors and disciples continued to walk a precarious line between academic modernism and the desire to appeal to a broad public. The most conspicuous of these were Elliott Carter and Leonard Bernstein. Moreover, both Bernstein and the Italian-American opera composer, Gian-Carlo Menotti, deliberately sought to harness the new medium of television in service of their musical mission. The roster of younger composers whose impact was felt during the 1940s, 1950s and 1960s also included Samuel Barber, David Diamond, Morton Gould, Bernard Herrmann, Paul Creston, Norman Dello Joio, Leon Kirchner, Daniel Pinkham, Ned Rorem, Ross Lee Finney, Gunther Schuller and others.

When discussing composers in terms of their "generation," chronological age alone is not necessarily a sufficient criterion for determining *which* generation any given composer belongs to. Prodigies—such as Ornstein, Antheil, Copland, Barber, Lukas Foss or (as we will see later) Christian Wolff—tend to exert their greatest influence early in their careers, rendering themselves effectively contemporary with the musical thinking of older colleagues. On the other hand, late bloomers—such as Ives, Ruggles, Riegger, Luening, Douglas Moore, Ross Lee Finney and others—may not begin to have a serious impact until they are well into their middle years, thus associating themselves more with a generation of younger creative minds. We will discover that the composers belonging to the "generation" after Copland, who dominated non-academic American classical music between the end of World War II and the beginning of the 1960s, were born mostly between 1906 and 1929. The most important of these were Schuman, Barber, Carter, Menotti and Bernstein. As Schuman has already been discussed in our chapter on academic music, we will concentrate here on Barber, Carter, Menotti, Bernstein and their colleagues.

Samuel Barber

Samuel Barber (1910–1981) remains one of the most difficult modern American composers to classify under any convenient label. His life, his work and his esthetics form a mass of contradictions and give him a historical profile virtually unique among his contemporaries. He was, for example, a Europhilic neo-Romanticist. But he disdained the attachment to vernacular music of his fellow Romanticist, Thomson, and steered equally clear of the abstract modernism of his fellow Europhile, Sessions. Barber was also homosexual and lived most of his adult life in a close but often troubled relationship with Gian-Carlo Menotti. However, he never indulged in the more flamboyant "gayness" of Thomson, Blitzstein or Bernstein. He established his name very early in his career, around 1932, but was never considered a part of the Copland generation, despite the many similarities between his work and theirs. The modernists championed by Copland were offended by Barber's unabashed affection for a lush Romantic sound in much of his work, and never wanted to get too close to him. As a result, his career ran parallel to theirs without his ever really joining them. Furthermore, Barber had no interest in the advocacy of new American music, per se, and did not participate in any of the organizational projects or committees fostered by the Coplandites.

Unlike most of his contemporaries, Barber was educated entirely in the United States. Born in West Chester, Pennsylvania, on March 9, 1910, he came from a genteel, upper-middle-class family and was related by marriage to the composer Sydney Homer, who became a lifelong mentor and confidant. He entered the newly founded Curtis Institute in Philadelphia in 1924, at the age of fourteen, and became a special protégé of its founder and patron, Mary Louise Curtis Bok. At Curtis, Barber was viewed as a "wunderkind" by his teachers and fellow students alike. He was a gifted pianist and possessed a professional caliber baritone voice. But it was his genius for composition and intense craftsmanship that made him the star pupil of Curtis' star composition teacher, Rosario Scalero. During his eight years at Curtis, Barber produced a number of significant works that far exceeded the quality of mere student compositions and have remained in the general repertoire. These included his *Serenade* for string quartet, Op.1 (1928), his *Three Songs,* Op.2 (1927), *Dover Beach* for low voice and string quartet, Op.3 (1931), a sonata each for violin and cello, and his orchestral overture to *The School for Scandal,* Op.5 (1933). He met Gian-Carlo Menotti, one year his junior, when the young Italian was brought to Curtis by his mother in 1928, on the advice of Toscanini, to study with Scalero. Barber had been asked to take Menotti, who spoke no English at the time, under his wing and help orient the younger student. At first the two were friendly but not especially close, communicating mostly in French. But, as time passed, the complementary personalities of Barber and Menotti caused the friendship to blossom. Where Barber was quiet and reserved, Menotti was vivacious and full of curiosity. Barber's poetic, serious nature tempered Menotti's flair for dramatic gesture, while Menotti's restless energy infused excitement into Barber's otherwise rather staid lifestyle. These qualities were to characterize their relationship for the next forty-six years during which they lived and traveled together and pursued simultaneous, but very different, careers as composers.

Throughout the early 1930s, Barber and Menotti spent their summers in Europe, visiting Menotti's extensive collection of relatives in the region of his native Cadegliano, Italy, as well as spending time in Rome, Austria and Switzerland. During this period Barber produced some of the most lyrical music in his entire oeuvre, including his *Music for a Scene from Shelley* (1933), *Symphony No.1* (1936) and his Op.11 *String Quartet* (1936) from which the famous *Adagio* was later extracted and arranged for string orchestra. The two young composers dropped in unannounced at Toscanini's Italian villa one day in 1935, and Menotti introduced Barber to the volatile maestro. Within a short time, Toscanini became an advocate of Barber's music and premiered the *First Essay for Orchestra* Op.12 (1937) in 1938 and, on the same program, the orchestral version of the *Adagio for Strings*. With these performances, and the 1941 premiere of his moving *Violin Concerto* by the same Albert Spalding who was so conspicuously unable to cope with Sessions' work (see Chapter 7), Barber's reputation soared. At the age of twenty-eight he found himself one of the most highly regarded living American composers.

In 1943, Mary Curtis Bok (who had subsequently married the violinist Efrem Zimbalist, Sr. and was now, therefore, Mary Louise Curtis Bok Zimbalist) purchased a house in Mount Kisco, New York, for Barber and Menotti. They christened the new home "Capricorn," and it would remain the two composers' base of operations until 1974, when they split from each other and sold the house. Capricorn became the scene of many a memorable party, under the influence of Menotti, at which a variety of great names in music and theatre cavorted uproariously. This kind of life became a strain on the meticulous and quiescent Barber, who was notoriously jealous of Menotti's friends. One anecdote (told in the 1978 biography of Menotti by John Gruen) has Barber locking himself in the bathroom for nine hours in order to avoid the presence of actress Tallulah Bankhead.

During the 1940s, after a brief wartime stint in the Army Air Force, Barber completed a second symphony. But, despite repeated revisions, he was never satisfied with it and eventually destroyed the score. The second movement of this work, however, was preserved under the separate title *Night Flight,* Op.19a (1964). The period of the late 1940s-early 1950s also saw the creation of most of the remaining non-operatic music for which Barber is remembered today, including his *Cello Concerto,* Op.22 (1945), the song cycle *Knoxville: Summer of 1915* for voice and orchestra to a text by James Agee (Op.24, 1947), the *Hermit Songs* for high voice and piano, Op.29 (1952), and his two major works for solo piano, the *Excursions* (Op.20, 1944) and *Sonata* (Op.26, 1949), both premiered by Horowitz.

Perhaps his most significant work from this period was the music for Martha Graham's 1946 ballet, *Medea.* Graham had approached Copland about this project some five years earlier, but he was not enthused by the subject matter. Instead, he and Graham went on to create *Appalachian Spring* together. But, in Barber, Graham finally found a composer who was receptive to the classical Greek idea, and the finished ballet was premiered in May of 1946. The following year, *Medea* was revised and premiered again under the title *The Cave of the Heart.* Later in 1947, Barber, following Copland's tactic, arranged some of the music as an orchestral suite that was premiered by Ormandy and the Philadelphia Orchestra in December. But history did not repeat itself, and the suite never achieved the popularity of Copland's similar works. In 1953, Barber adapted the music once again as *Medea's Meditation and Dance of Vengeance,* Op.23a. It is in this form that the work is most often heard today and, as such, has had a profound influence on a later generation of post-modernist composers (notably John Corigliano) whose esthetics were more compatible with Barber's than were those of any of his contemporaries.

As the years wore on, and each became a major composer, and as other young men joined the household from time to time (including the poet, Robert "Kinch" Horan, and the young conductor, Thomas Schippers), Barber and Menotti's relationship lost the idyllic romance of their early years at Curtis and abroad, and became more of a settled, professional partnership. In 1953, the two collaborated on a chamber opera, *A Hand of Bridge,* and, shortly thereafter, on the four-act opera *Vanessa,* Menotti creating the libretto and Barber the music for both of these works. Completed in 1957, *Vanessa* was premiered by the Metropolitan Opera in 1958 and has remained one of the most important, if rarely performed, American operas ever since. It was awarded the 1958 Pulitzer Prize in music. *A Hand of Bridge* has been produced mostly by universities and small opera companies since its premiere.

In the early 1960s, Barber added another significant work to his oeuvre in his 1962 *Piano Concerto,* Op. 38. Commissioned by the publishing house of G. Schirmer for its centennial and premiered by John Browning and the Boston Symphony Orchestra under Leinsdorf, the *Concerto* revealed Barber in his most mature style and earned him his second Pulitzer.

But, despite these successes, Barber found it increasingly difficult to compose. His had always been a somewhat melancholic temperament, and, as the pressure to compete with his earlier successes became more extreme, he became subject to periods of depression. The tragic turning point in his career came with the Metropolitan Opera's commission to compose an opera for the opening of the new house at Lincoln Center in 1966. As mentioned in the discussion of Virgil Thomson, Shakespeare's *Antony and Cleopatra* had always been a play full of hidden pitfalls for actors, directors and composers alike. Added to this situation now was the Met's desire for a massive spectacle, worthy of the new opera house, as well as the grandiose ideas of the erratic directorial genius, Franco Zeffirelli, who was to be the librettist. Clearly, the Met and Zeffirelli both had in mind an operatic extravaganza to exceed the dimensions of Verdi's *Aida,* and Barber unwisely committed to the project despite reservations.

By 1966, classical music activity in New York had sharply divided into "uptown" and "downtown" factions. The uptown faction, largely based around Carnegie Hall, Lincoln Center and Juilliard, was becoming increasingly conservative, self-conscious and even hostile toward American music. The downtown concerts and events in Soho and Greenwich Village were ever more oriented toward avant-garde and post-modernist music and musicians, who considered themselves to be the true cutting-edge of American musical thought, sublimely indifferent to the irrelevancies of the prestigious uptown institutions. Each faction had its own distinct audience as well, and, while concert-goers may not have been particularly sensitive to this division, critics were. The premiere of *Antony and Cleopatra* placed Barber firmly in the bosom of the uptown elite, a place where his natural sympathies had always lain in any case. But this context damaged critical reaction to his setting of the opera. His already conservative, post-Romantic style just seemed all the more out of touch with contemporary currents in American music, and the press was not hesitant to say so.

Moreover, the massive staging effects, designed by Zeffirelli to show off all the technological capacities of the new house, together with the director's dramatically weak libretto, conspired to overshadow such quality as Barber's music may have had. The opera, in short, was a monolithic flop.

Barber, accustomed to early success and world fame, was devastated by the failure of *Antony and Cleopatra.* He hid his depression with a characteristic show of outward equanimity and set to work with Menotti

The premier American neo-Romanticist, **Samuel**
Barber *(1910–1981) toward the end of his life. His*
brilliant early successes were shattered by the disas-
trous reception of his opera, Antony and Cleopatra.
(Photo courtesy of ASCAP.)

to repair the flaws in the opera, but was never able to recover from this
highly public humiliation nor to fully recover his creative powers. The
revised version of *Antony and Cleopatra* was finally presented at Juilliard
in 1975 and was far more successful than had been the premiere nine years
earlier, but, by that time, it was too late for Barber.

In 1974, after nearly half a century of constant companionship, he and
Menotti sold Capricorn and went their separate ways. Plagued by a relentless depression that he could not shake off, Barber sought relief in alcohol
and became addicted. In the late 1970s he developed cancer and died in New
York on January 23, 1981, a sad ending to an otherwise illustrious career.

Gian-Carlo Menotti

If Barber was, at best, grudgingly tolerated by the modernist camp, the
work of his lifelong companion, Gian-Carlo Menotti (b. 1911), was openly

scorned by them. Part of the reason undoubtedly lay in the fact that Menotti became one of the most frequently performed and wealthiest of living American composers, for popular success always breeds resentment. But, beneath this superficial envy lay an even deeper sense that Menotti achieved his successes at the expense of more serious, deeper composers—that he siphoned off much of the attention that might have gone to the more serious creative efforts of others by attracting it to his easily accessible, dramatically shallow operas. Whether or not Menotti's works deserve such abrupt dismissal is a point that has been hotly debated ever since he began his career with *Amelia Goes to the Ball* in 1937. There can be little question that the quality of his conceptions is very uneven, ranging from works that are held in great respect, such as *The Consul* (1949), to those which are almost entirely disregarded now, such as his neo-classical *Piano Concerto* (1945).

Menotti was born to a large family of Italian merchants in the northern Italian town of Cadegliano on July 7, 1911. He was his mother's favorite child and received early instruction and encouragement in music from her as well as a variety of hired teachers. His mother took her young prodigy to Philadelphia in 1928 to study with Scalero at Curtis, which led to the initial meeting of Menotti and Barber. Menotti had been drawn to the theatre early in life and was saturated with his national heritage of opera. He was as fluent in creating recitative as he was in his native language, and often wrote both text and music hastily, without a clear sense of where he was going with his story. Though thoroughly trained at Curtis and possessing a facile technique, Menotti was no musical scholar and lacked patience with academic forms or learned styles. Opera was his métier, and absolute music forms only a small and relatively insignificant portion of his output.

The success of the American production of *Amelia* encouraged the NBC broadcasting network to commission a radio opera from the young Menotti in 1939. This work, the first that he wrote in English, was *The Old Maid and the Thief,* for which he also created the scenario and libretto. *Old Maid* was written in the opera buffa tradition and displayed Menotti's skill at working with light, ingratiating textures and rapid dialogue. But his next effort, *The Island God,* was a failure with both the critics and the public.

The poor reception of *The Island God* brought home to Menotti the adage that a composer is only as good as his latest work. He discovered that the fickle theatrical public which had lionized him in 1939 was just as anxious to shun him in 1942. Dutifully registering as an "enemy alien" during World War II, Menotti spent the early 1940s in New York, turning to non-operatic projects with the aforementioned *Piano Concerto* and his ballet, *Sebastian.*

But success returned to Menotti in a major way when, in 1945, Columbia University asked him to write a small opera for its Brander

Matthews Theatre. The result was *The Medium,* a surrealistic drama about a demented spiritualist caught between the real and supernatural worlds. For this opera Menotti composed his most "modernistic" music up to that time, and the premiere was conducted by Otto Luening at Columbia on May 8, 1946. In *The Medium,* Menotti struck a balance between facile accessibility and dissonant modernism that enhanced his reputation among serious composers without diminishing the public popularity of the work. The intense theatricality of the action onstage further added to the opera's appeal. With an authentic success on his hands, Menotti went in search of a wider audience. He approached Lincoln Kirstein about including *The Medium* in the upcoming season of New York's Ballet Society. Kirstein suggested the composition of a contrasting, companion piece to make a full evening, and Menotti complied by composing *The Telephone. The Telephone* was, once more, in the opera buffa vein and offered a vivid contrast to the dark character of *The Medium.* These two short operas complemented each other so well that the young Efrem Zimbalist, Jr., son of the violinist and stepson of Mary Curtis, formed a partnership with Menotti and Chandler Cowles to produce the pair on Broadway.

Gershwin had set the precedent for opera production on Broadway with *Porgy and Bess* in 1935, and others had, from time to time, tried to follow suit. But the opening of *The Medium* at the Ethel Barrymore Theatre in 1947 represented the first serious opera production to achieve a major success outside of the traditional operatic venues, and the opera ran for eight months.

During the highly successful Broadway run of *The Medium,* Menotti received simultaneous invitations from MGM and David O. Selznick to write scripts and/or music for a number of Hollywood films. Shrewdly playing these two Hollywood institutions off against each other, Menotti wrote his own contractual terms, giving himself almost complete creative control over the outcome of his efforts, terms that MGM eventually bought. There followed a brief sojourn in Hollywood during which Menotti drafted two scripts, neither of which was ever to be filmed. But one of these efforts, entitled *The Bridge,* led him to the idea for his next major opera, *The Consul.*

Menotti had been inspired to create the story of *The Consul* by a newspaper account of a Polish immigrant woman who hanged herself at Ellis Island after being denied entry into the United States. His somewhat Kafkaesque libretto is basically an indictment of the inhumanity of 20th century state bureaucracy, and would later be decried by Marxist serialists, such as Luigi Nono, as anti-Soviet propaganda. The recitativo style of *The Consul* draws heavily on the Italian "verismo" pioneered by Puccini,

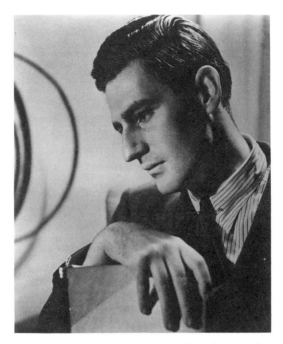

Gian-Carlo Menotti *(b. 1911) at about the time of his first opera,* Amelia Goes to the Ball. *He lived with Barber for 46 years and created a legacy of stage and television operas which made him enormously popular.* (MUSIC DIVISION, The New York Public Library for the Performing Arts. Astor, Lenox and Tilden Foundations.)

though melodically it is a bit more spartan than Puccini's gushing post-Romanticism. *The Consul,* in three acts, was Menotti's first full-length opera and was premiered under the baton of Copland's colleague, Lehman Engel, in Philadelphia on March 1, 1950. It was repeated two weeks later at the Ethel Barrymore Theatre in New York.

The Consul was a huge success; it projected Menotti to his highest point as a composer up to that time. It also brought Menotti into contact with the young conducting prodigy, Thomas Schippers, who was obliged to stand in for Engel on short notice one night. Menotti, Barber and Schippers developed an almost familial relationship over the next few years, during much of which Schippers lived at Capricorn. The young conductor became a champion of both men's work and conducted the premier of Barber's ill-fated *Antony and Cleopatra* at the Met in 1966. His premature death in 1977, at the age of forty-seven, left a void in the lives of both composers that would not easily be filled again.

In many of these early efforts Menotti showed an astute sense of the role beginning to be played in American life by the popular media. Always in search of a big audience, he turned first to radio, then to Broadway, then to Hollywood. But there was never any question that his attempt, unlike that of, for example, Kurt Weill, was to work within the established classical forms of opera. Regardless of his venues, Menotti was not writing "musicals," nor did he have any conscious intention of breaking down the stylistic barrier between opera and the musical in the manner of a Leonard Bernstein or a Stephen Sondheim. The next step in his career came with the advent of television, wherein Menotti found the way to place his name in the forefront of contemporary composers.

In early 1951, Samuel Chozinoff of NBC had commissioned Menotti to write a Christmas opera for the infant medium of television. While Menotti may have been making sketches in his mind, by Thanksgiving of that year he had still not set a note down on paper. His attention seemed to be focused more on choosing a title than on actually composing the work, and he debated this issue with Barber and Schippers endlessly. It was only after he had decided to stick with his own choice of title, *Amahl and the Night Visitors*, that the actual work was begun and completed within two or three weeks. Based on the Italian Christmas tradition of having gifts brought to children by surrogates of the three Magi (rather than Santa Claus), *Amahl* was first broadcast on Christmas Eve, 1951, and repeated every year thereafter until 1964. Despite the haste in which it was composed, Menotti astutely conceived *Amahl* so that it would be suitable for both stage and television presentation. This maximized its utility for a variety of performance venues and led to its being the single most popular chamber opera in American music history. In the six years between 1966 and 1972 alone, it received 2,187 separate performances worldwide.[44] The music is direct and among the most accessible of Menotti's highly accessible works, and the vocal roles are simple enough to be performed by amateurs. All of this has contributed to the enormous popular success of this opera, but has also led critics of a more demanding stripe, such as Joseph Kerman (writing in his 1956 book, *Opera as Drama*), to damn the work as shallow trash. While *Amahl* and others of Menotti's operas may not be the most profound musical conceptions ever to grace the stage, it cannot be denied that the success of his work at least achieved the purpose of opening the ears of post-war bourgeois Americans to the possibility of accepting modern compositions.

Amahl was followed, in 1954, by Menotti's second full-length opera, *The Saint of Bleecker Street*. In it he continued his adaptation of Puccinian

---

[44]   Gruen, *Menotti: a biography*, p. 109.

"verismo," and exposed himself to even more criticism from the exacting Kerman. But, criticism notwithstanding, *Saint* went on to win the New York Drama Critics' Circle award, the New York Music Critics' Circle award and the Pulitzer Prize in 1955.

By 1958, after the successful completion of *A Hand of Bridge* and *Vanessa,* Menotti's relationship with Thomas Schippers had begun to supplant his relationship with Barber. After *The Saint of Bleecker Street* closed, and Menotti's next two works, *The Unicorn, the Gorgon and the Manticore* and *Maria Golovin,* had been premiered, the forty-seven-year-old composer began to cast around for a new type of creative activity. Together he and Schippers conceived the idea of a "Festival of Two Worlds" and began to travel in search of a location. The Italian town of Spoleto was finally selected and, in 1958, the festival founded. From that point on, Menotti's compositional work decreased somewhat as he gradually assumed more and more responsibility for the organization of what is now known as the annual Spoleto Festival, which opened an American branch in Charleston, South Carolina in 1977 and has premiered a number of new works.

Among Menotti's more significant works after 1958 are the cantata, *The Death of the Bishop of Brindisi* (1963), the church opera *Martin's Lie* (1964), the satirical, science-fiction opera, *Help! Help! the Globolinks!* (1968), a number of children's operas, a *Triple Concerto* for nine soloists and orchestra (1970), his *"Halcyon" Symphony* (1976) and the television opera *Goya* (1986). After his separation from Barber in 1974, Menotti and his adopted son, Chip, acquired a large estate in Scotland known as "Yester" House, where the composer intends to live out his remaining years. The ultimate value of his contribution to American classical music has yet to be assessed authoritatively, but it is likely that Menotti's more popular works will continue to survive as viable operas from the 20th-century repertoire. His influence on other composers may prove to be felt more in the opportunities that the two Spoleto festivals have offered for the performance of new works than in any direct musical sense.

Elliott Carter

There is an excellent chance that future historians will view Elliott Carter (b. 1908) as the most significant of the mid-20th-century American classical composers, for Carter's achievement goes far beyond mere inventive composition with conventional methods. Like Debussy and Schoenberg before him, Carter reconceived and restructured the fundamental language of Western art music in evolving his powerful personal style, and his music has earned immense respect from colleagues of virtually every esthetic stripe, as well as three generations of performing musicians and audiences.

Carter's lifetime effort has been sharply focussed on addressing new discoveries in the developmental processes of music itself, rather than expressions of personal feelings or political events. He was born in New York City on December 11, 1908, and educated at the Horace Mann School, from which he graduated in 1926. Because his family had no particular interest in music and actively discouraged their son's growing passion for the art, young Carter was raised without absorbing any strong stylistic prejudices. Surprisingly, he found, as he began to study music on his own, that he had no interest in the European classics of the common practice era. Whether it was the music of Bach, Mozart, Schumann or Wagner, it left him equally cold. But he was fascinated by modern music and studied the works of Stravinsky, Schoenberg, Milhaud, Ives and their contemporaries with a passion. This fortuitous natural indifference to the creative practices of pre-20th-century composers played an important role in enabling Carter to free himself from the vestiges of "received" traditions in his later work, without which freedom it is doubtful he would have been able to achieve the startlingly original approach to music that characterizes all his compositions after 1948.

Possessed of one of the finest intellects among all 20th-century composers, Carter displayed an early gift for languages and learned French as a child, later pursuing advanced studies in Greek and German as well. Moreover, unlike many musicians, the field of his enquiries extended far beyond the confines of music—into the study of classics, literature, philosophy and mathematics. Like the later composer, Christian Wolff, he was as adept as a teacher of some of these other subjects as he was a musical pedagogue, and he spent a portion of his adult life teaching at various American universities, including St. John's College, Annapolis (1940–42), the Peabody Conservatory (1946–48), Columbia University (1948–50), and Yale (1960–62).

While at the Horace Mann School, Carter studied piano with Clifton J. Furness, who introduced the sixteen-year-old musician to Charles Ives in 1924. Despite Carter's youth and Ives' increasing physical infirmities, the two developed a close rapport and Carter attended many concerts of modern music in the company of Ives and Furness. Carter was deeply impressed at this early age by Ives' ideas and by his densely textured, vigorous, adventurous music. Ives would continue to exert an influence on Carter's musical thinking throughout the latter's career. But Carter's was a much more disciplined intelligence than that of Ives, and the younger composer would discover a later dissatisfaction with the looseness of some aspects of Ives' conceptions, as well as with Ives' still-controversial refusal to deal with the professional musical world as a fully participating member.

In 1926, Carter entered Harvard and took his B.A. in English in 1930, followed by an M.A. in music in 1932. During his Harvard years, he sang in the Glee Club and participated in other musical activities, but was unsympathetic to the conservatism of the music curriculum. As a result, he also took private lessons in oboe and theory at the Longy School and engaged in much independent study of music. Upon his graduation in 1932, he took the advice of Walter Piston and went to France to study with Boulanger, despite continued opposition from his family. Living on a shoestring budget in Paris—his well-heeled father had cut Carter's allowance in response to his ongoing musical studies—the fledgling composer spent three years working with Boulanger, primarily on counterpoint studies.

Although Carter, of course, continued to compose under Boulanger, "Mademoiselle" did not consider his original creative work to be his forte at the time. Characteristically, and perhaps unconsciously, Carter was even then resisting the unchallenged assumption that composers learn their craft through imitating and absorbing the techniques of other composers—an assumption that lay at the root of Boulanger's teaching no less than the Harvard faculty's. While studying with Boulanger, Carter created a string quartet, a sonata for flute and piano and a one-act comic opera entitled *Tom and Lily*. All of these works were later withdrawn and destroyed by the composer. The Paris quartet was actually Carter's second attempt in this form (following an earlier one from around 1928) and would be followed by yet another effort in 1937. All three of these early quartets would be withdrawn by Carter before he achieved the composition of what is now known as his *String Quartet No.1* in 1951. Because Carter's string quartets form such an important part of his oeuvre, it is important to avoid confusing his four published works in this form with his prior efforts of the 1930s.

An important point to grasp about Carter's relationship with Boulanger (in contrast to Copland's) is that Boulanger did not offer Carter his first serious introduction to the modernist esthetic. His experiences in the avant-garde musical world of New York during the 1920s included exposure to the music of Cowell, Antheil, Ruggles, Ornstein and Dane Rudhyar (see next chapter), in addition to his familiarity with Ives. Where Copland had been a raw youth, only sporadically acquainted with modern music when he went to Boulanger in 1920, Carter was a developed musician of twenty-four when he began his studies with her twelve years later. In the interim, Boulanger had become much more attached to the developing neo-classical style of her close friend, Stravinsky, and was fostering a more specifically Stravinskyian approach to modernism in her students than had been her practice even in the early 1920s. These circumstances created a situation where Boulanger's teaching clearly had less of a formative effect on Carter's compositional development than it had had on Copland's. The principal result of Carter's work with Boulanger, as had been the case with Harris and Piston, appears to have lain in his mastery of counterpoint, so brilliantly displayed in his mature chamber and orchestral works.

Because of his literary education and grasp of the humanities, Carter also became a penetrating prose writer on music and the role of music in contemporary life. From the mid-1930s on he produced essays, reviews and lectures at least equal in depth to the writings of Thomson and Sessions on modern music. These included a review of the 1939 premiere of Ives' *Concord Sonata* that, while less idolatrous than Lawrence Gilman's famous review, was more incisive in its perception of the limitations inherent in Ives' esthetic. The two principal collections of Carter's ideas about music available today are the composer's own *The Writings of Elliott Carter* (1977) and Allen Edward's *Flawed Words and Stubborn Sounds: A Conversation with Elliott Carter* (1971). These, together with David Schiff's lucid *The Music of Elliott Carter* (1983), are indispensable texts for the reader who wishes to acquire a full understanding of Carter's philosophical thinking and compositional methods over the span of his entire career.

In 1936, after his return from Paris, Carter produced his *Tarantella* (text by the Roman poet Ovid) for male chorus and piano, 4-hands, derived from incidental music he had written for a Harvard production of Plautus' *Mostellaria* earlier that year. The ever-attentive Lincoln Kirstein heard *Tarantella* and asked Carter to become music director of his company, the Ballet Caravan. Carter accepted the position and composed the original version of his ballet *Pochahontas* later that year for Kirstein's troupe. Carter remained music director of Ballet Caravan until 1940. It was during his tenure that Kirstein commissioned and premiered both Copland's *Billy the Kid* and Thomson's *Filling Station,* although the extent to which Carter may have influenced Kirstein to embark on these ventures remains unclear. *Pochahontas* was premiered at Keene, New Hampshire, in August of 1936, and repeated several times by the company. But Carter was still not satisfied with the work and, in 1938, began to rework it as an orchestral suite. It was premiered in this form in New York in May 1939. In 1960, it was revised again by the composer. The original ballet version that, according to Carter's later recollections, was quite different from the surviving orchestra suite was withdrawn and later destroyed by the composer, along with most of his early works.

It is worth taking a few moments, at this point, to comment on the practice indulged in by many modern American composers of withdrawing and/or destroying early works, sometimes even after their premiere, publication or recording. In addition to Carter, much of the early work of Sessions, Varèse, Perle, Partch, Hovhaness, Glass and many others is basically lost to historians because the composers themselves suppressed it, even to the point of physically destroying the scores. While no one can dispute the absolute right of any creative artist to determine which portion of his or her work should be made available to the public, the practice of destroying early works, no matter how embarrassing or unrepresentative they may seem to be at a later point in the artist's career, robs the future musicologist of vital information for the study of that composer's personal evolution. Moreover, it tends to create the impression among future generations of younger composers that their predecessors "sprang full grown from the head of Zeus," as it were, and can deprive such future composers of important models that reveal the struggles of past masters to achieve their final, definitive creative voices.

Throughout the 1940s, after *Tarantella,* Carter worked largely in the choral medium and produced three major compositions that advanced his development toward the mature style he achieved in 1948. These were *The*

Elliott Carter *(b. 1908) photographed in 1965. His fresh approach to musical organization created a powerful but difficult personal voice.* (Photo by Sylvia Salmi, courtesy of BMI.)

Defense of Corinth (1941, text by Rabelais, for speaker, male voices and piano, 4-hands), *The Harmony of Morning* (1944, text by Mark Van Doren, for female voices and small orchestra) and *Emblems* (1947, text by Allen Tate, for male voices and piano). The stylistic range and dramatic effect of these three works are enormous, running from the sunny affability of *The Harmony of Morning* to the rapier-like musical irony of *Corinth* to the dark vision of *Emblems*. To some extent, Carter was still playing out the possibilities he perceived in the ideas of colleagues such as Stravinsky and Milhaud in these three pieces, as he was playing out the influences of Ives, Copland and Boulanger in his *Symphony No.1* (1942), his *Holiday Overture* (1944) and his last ballet, *The Minotaur* (1947), all similar in concept to Copland's "populist" works of the late 1930s and early 1940s. But, more important, Carter was beginning to refine the extraordinary sense of drama that would characterize all his future work. For Carter was, above all, a dramatic composer.

This statement may sound strange applied to a composer who never wrote an opera after the juvenile *Tom and Lily* (1934), but it is nonetheless the key to understanding all of Carter's mature work. First, however, it is necessary to distinguish (in Joseph Kerman's terminology) the difference between a "dramatic" composer and a merely "theatrical" one. Menotti was, like his predecessor Puccini, a prime example of a theatrical composer—one whose music accompanies and enhances the actions and effects of the play it sets. But dramatic composers, such as Mozart, Wagner, Berg, Carter or Sessions, discover musical processes that parallel the structure of the drama and interweave these with it to form an integrated unity of effect. This goes beyond mere musical mood setting or accompaniment.

Generally speaking, merely theatrical music doesn't work without its accompanying play. But dramatic music, because of its greater structural integrity, can exert its effect even when divorced from text or stage action. Thus, the cantatas of J. S. Bach are every bit as dramatic as any opera contemporary to them, even without stage action. And the concertos and chamber works of Mozart (especially after the mid-1780s) are conceived in every sense as dramatically as were his operas, even without text. It is, therefore, no accident that Carter abandoned the composition of ballets, incidental music and choral works altogether after 1948 and turned more or less exclusively to the composition of concertos and chamber works that function as highly dramatic musical scenarios.

The fundamental technique that Carter evolved for establishing the interactive dramatic entities in his music after 1948 is the tactic of "partitioning," derived from the theoretical ideas of Milton Babbitt. Babbitt used partitioning merely to divide sets of pitches and/or rhythms. But partitioning as Carter applied it involves the assigning of a particular ambient mood, melodic texture, set of pitches, modulating rhythmic idea, tempo or other musical phenomenon to a given instrument or group of instruments. In this manner, independent musical "personalities" or "entities" are created within the total ensemble—personalities that then interact to generate the dramatic dialectic of the piece. A pivotal work in Carter's evolution toward this approach is his solo *Piano Sonata* of 1946. The *Sonata* at once summed up Carter's absorption of the influences of Ives (especially the Ives of the *First Piano Sonata*) and Copland, and pointed in the direction of abstract musical drama that would be reflected in Carter's later work. As a solo piece it does not, of course, deploy its "character" elements among different instruments but rather among different voices of its highly contrapuntal texture and in the harmonic tension established between key regions related by a semitone. A fuller realization of the dramatic dialectic was reached in Carter's *Wind Quintet* of 1948, in which each of the five instruments retains a distinct melodic texture of its own throughout the entire course of the piece.

But it was with his *Sonata for Cello and Piano* (1948) that Carter began to realize the full implications of the partitioning technique. Rather than being merely a cello piece with piano accompaniment, the *Sonata* established two absolutely equal musical entities in the two instruments, entities that pursue independent, but interrelated development throughout this crucial work. Moreover, the *Cello Sonata* begins to illustrate clearly the difference between Carter's mature approach to composition and that of Ives (and other composers who have juxtaposed dissimilar musical "personalities" within their ensemble works). Where Ives and some other modern contrapuntal composers often deliberately relied on one or more basic processes to generate contrasts among voices, choirs and other elements once those processes had been set in motion by the composer, Carter preserved precise, personal control over every detail of the contrapuntal interaction that resulted from his starting premises. Thus he was, at all times, absolutely in control of every gesture and event, no matter how minute. Where the seemingly unrelated musical events in a work by Ives or Cage can happen at times almost by themselves, in Carter's work they are always the result of meticulous craft. Carter's arrival at this style, which may sometimes be characterized by a feeling of "composed improvisation," was also influenced by his early studies of Arabic music and American jazz. By the time of his *First String Quartet* (1951), this resulted in a very difficult kind of music to study and to play.

In composing the *Cello Sonata,* Carter also began to develop a process he later termed "metric modulation." A crude form of metric modulation is sometimes seen in unmetered, written-out cadenzas of 18th- and early 19th-century concertos, where a passage beginning in 32nd notes is reduced successively to 16th notes, 8th notes and, finally, quarter notes in an attempt to convey to the performer the idea that the pace of notes should slow down in a continuous fashion. The process can also occur in the reverse, or accelerating direction. Carter developed this linear form of metric modulation to the point where the perceived tempos of individual lines can expand and contract continuously, yet always with the composer controlling the metric ratios between the lines. As a result of multiplying this process into many simultaneous lines of melodic activity, the overall meter (expressed by the conventional means of time signatures) changes periodically in response to the conglomerate metric relationships of the individual parts, but the idea of "meter" merely as a framework for a series of articulated phrases, including agogic accents such as the downbeat, becomes effectively obsolete.

Carter developed these and related ideas in all of his increasingly abstract works after 1948, including his *Eight Etudes and a Fantasy* for woodwind quartet (1950), his first two *String Quartets* (1951, 1959), his *Variations for Orchestra* (1955), his *Double Concerto* for harpsichord, piano and two chamber orchestras (1961), his 1965 *Piano Concerto*, the 1969 *Concerto for Orchestra*, and his works of the 1970s and 1980s such as the *Third String Quartet* (1971), the *Symphony of Three Orchestras* (1976) and *Night Fantasies* (1980), the last of these being his first solo piano work after the 1946 *Sonata*. In all of these pieces, except *Night Fantasies*, he continued to explore the possibilities for creating distinct, interactive musical personalities formed by solo instruments, concertino groups or other combinations of players, and he evolved a variety of non-traditional tonal and formal processes that emerge from the interaction between these entities. Thus, his music became basically independent of received traditions, including 20th-century traditions and posed unique challenges both for performers and listeners. Despite its profound technical difficulties, requiring protracted periods of study, young performers took to Carter more energetically than to many of his American contemporaries. And audiences proved to be unexpectedly enthusiastic about his music. Today, at the age of eighty-five, he is held in the highest esteem by musicians and educated listeners alike. It is probable that the passage of time will only enhance our understanding of the importance of Carter's discoveries and the role he played in American classical music of this century.

Leonard Bernstein

By far the most dynamic public *personality* in American classical music of the 1950s through the 1970s was Leonard Bernstein (1918–1990). Despite his creative limitations, Bernstein became one of the best-known and most popular composers and conductors of the century and came closer than any of his colleagues to duplicating Gershwin's extraordinary achievements.

Bernstein was born in the mill town of Lawrence, Massachusetts, on August 25, 1918. His parents, like Copland's and Gershwin's, were first-generation Russian-Jewish immigrants of middle-class merchant stock. His early life paralleled that of his famous predecessors in other respects as well. The family was not particularly musical and the young Leonard, the eldest of three offspring of Samuel and Jennie Bernstein, began to show his first serious interest in music at around the age of ten, when the family acquired an upright piano. His first lessons were with local teachers, and he later progressed to studies at the New England Conservatory in Boston. Like Carter's and Varèse's fathers, Samuel Bernstein opposed his son's musical aspirations and pressured him unsuccessfully to enter the family business.

After graduation from the Boston Latin School, Bernstein entered Harvard in 1935. There he studied with Edward Burlingame Hill, teacher of Thomson, Sessions, Carter and many other significant American composers. He also worked with Walter Piston, who was just beginning to exert a major influence on the Harvard curriculum at that time. At Harvard, Bernstein showed himself to be a prodigious practical musician. He could sight-read virtually any orchestral score at the piano, was a brilliant keyboard executant and possessed a distinct flair for conducting as well as a voracious appetite for good music of all kinds. He became acquainted with Copland in 1937 and was commissioned to arrange the two-piano version of *El Salon Mexico* in 1939. This proved to be the beginning of a close and lifelong association between Copland and Bernstein, in which Copland played the role both of mentor and colleague, while Bernstein used his later conducting and media powers to serve as an advocate. Despite the almost twenty-year difference in their ages, these two foremost musical Americanists and intimate friends were to die within three months of each other in late 1990, bringing to a decisive end an unprecedented era of accomplishment in American music.

While at Harvard, Bernstein also created incidental music for a performance of Aristophanes' play, *The Birds.* But, more significantly, he mounted the Harvard production of Blitzstein's *The Cradle Will Rock,* which led to his important creative and personal friendship with that composer. As Bernstein began to compose Broadway musicals in the 1940s, culminating in the revolutionary concept that became *West Side Story* (1957), Blitzstein's influence became increasingly prominent in his work. It is a sad irony in American music history that Bernstein's meteoric rise to the pinnacle of musical celebrity was inversely paralleled by Blitzstein's downward spiral into obscurity and a sordid death in 1964. It fell to

Bernstein to perpetuate many of Blitzstein's best ideas after transmuting them through the prism of his own compositional style in the 1950s.

During his sophomore year at Harvard, Bernstein also made the acquaintance of Dmitri Mitropoulos, soon to become permanent conductor of the Minneapolis Symphony. Mitropoulos was so impressed by the enthusiastic and capable young man that he took Bernstein under his wing, shaping his conducting style and musical attitudes. During the winters in 1940 and 1941, Bernstein also worked with Fritz Reiner at the Curtis Institute, but his relationship with Reiner was less agreeable.

Bernstein's most important apprenticeship began in the summer of 1940, when he joined Koussevitzky's conducting class at the newly founded Berkshire Music Festival at Tanglewood. This enabled him to maintain a close connection both with Koussevitzky and Copland, who was sharing composition faculty duties with Hindemith that year. During the 1940s, Koussevitzky, Copland and Bernstein formed an intimate and mutually supportive musical family, spanning three generations, linked by their common Russian-Jewish roots, their shared passion for new American music and their sheer determination to carve out a major role for the highest caliber of classical music in American life. It is no exaggeration to state that the entire modern history of American symphonic music would have been vastly different (and probably vastly poorer) had these three men never existed or never formed the powerful team that they eventually became. Koussevitzky appointed Bernstein his assistant conductor at Tanglewood in 1942, and Bernstein succeeded him as head of the orchestral and conducting departments when Koussevitzky died in 1951.

In 1943, Bernstein made his spectacular professional conducting debut with the New York Philharmonic. He had been appointed an assistant conductor by Artur Rodzinski earlier that year and, as a consequence, was obliged to familiarize himself with all the music being performed in case an emergency should require him to stand in. Such an emergency arose on November 14, when guest conductor Bruno Walter was suddenly taken ill before a concert that was to be broadcast nationwide over the radio. The twenty-five-year-old Bernstein took over and so electrified both the concert and radio audience that he received that rarest of accolades, a front-page review in the *New York Times*. From that point on, his name began to become a household word in American life, even among people who had no other connection with serious music.

During the early 1940s, Bernstein continued his conducting apprenticeship and began to develop as a serious composer. In 1942 he finished a *Clarinet Sonata*, which was to become his first published composition, followed in 1944 by the premiere of his *"Jeremiah" Symphony* (Symphony No.1), which won the New York Music Critics' Circle Award. Under the continued influence of Blitzstein, he preserved his attachment to Broadway and popular genres as well, creating the ballet *Fancy Free* with Jerome Robbins in 1944. This proved to be the beginning of a significant career partnership between Bernstein and Robbins that would lead through a second ballet, entitled *Facsimile* (1946) and eventually to *West Side Story*.

In partnership with the Broadway team of Betty Comden and Adolph Green, Bernstein reworked *Fancy Free* into the musical *On the Town*, which opened on Broadway in December 1944. *On the Town* became Bernstein's first unqualified popular success as a composer and elevated him, at the age of twenty-six, into even greater national celebrity. In 1953 he would again join with Comden and Green to create the musical *Wonderful Town* which, despite the similarity of its title and setting, is a work entirely separate from its predecessor. Like Gershwin, Bernstein's career and persona were inseparably tied to New York City, and his most popular music helped to create an almost mythic image of New York, often belied by current reality, in the minds of many Americans. This association was further reinforced by Bernstein's stark, evocative music for Elia Kazan's 1954 film, *On the Waterfront*, which starred three of America's most formidable acting talents of the time: Marlon Brando, Rod Steiger and Lee J. Cobb.

From the earliest period of his adult life, Bernstein was actively homosexual and became involved in erotic liaisons with a great many young men, including the youthful Ned Rorem, who was just beginning his own compositional career. However, Bernstein's flamboyant homosexuality posed a serious threat to his budding career as a conductor. As Joan Peyser has pointed out in her revealing and sometimes harsh biography of Bernstein, conducting orchestras had always been, up to that time, a male dominated profession and one in which "machismo" tended to be highly valued. After Koussevitzky's death in 1951, when Bernstein assumed the elder conductor's role at Tanglewood, both he and his close friends were increasingly concerned about the difficulties he would face if his private life ever became public. So, like many gay men in similar circumstances, Bernstein chose to marry. His new, naive bride was a Chilean actress named Felicia Montealegre. The couple remained together until Felicia's death from cancer in 1978 and produced three children. But the relationship was a troubled one during which Felicia was frequently humiliated and outraged by Bernstein's continued relationships with young men.

During the late 1940s and early 1950s, Bernstein continued to compose, producing a number of his most important works, including his *Symphony No.2: "The Age of Anxiety"* in 1949, his *Prelude, Fugue and Riffs* for clarinet and jazz ensemble that same year, the opera *Trouble in Tahiti* in 1952, the *Serenade* for violin, strings, harp and percussion in 1954, and, in addition to *Wonderful Town* and *On the Waterfront,* the operetta *Candide* (after Voltaire) in 1956. But 1957 was the banner year of the decade for Bernstein, inaugurated when his old mentor, Mitropoulos, appointed him assistant director of the New York Philharmonic and crowned when *West Side Story* opened in Washington, D.C. on August 19, then moved on to Broadway.

West Side Story has become an American classic and continues to be Bernstein's best-known and most admired work. More than any other musical in the history of the American theatre, and even perhaps more than *Porgy and Bess,* it began to break down the categorical division between opera and musical theatre. Subsequent works, such as Mitchell Leigh's *Man of La Mancha* and Stephen Sondheim's *Sweeney Todd* continued the process set in motion by *West Side Story,* and Bernstein was eventually to assert the philosophical position that the musical as an art form was, in effect, the only truly American replacement for the fundamentally European form of opera, all the American "operas" composed before or since notwithstanding.

But distinctions of this kind can pose problems for the analyst of musical styles and forms. Some creative figures, such as the Englishman Andrew Lloyd Webber, have taken the position that the definition "opera" resides principally in the fact that all of a play's dialogue is sung, rather than spoken: hence the classification of The Who's *Tommy* and even Webber's own early works as "rock operas." But such simplistic categorization fails to account not only for the works of earlier composers, including Mozart, who wrote operas with some spoken dialogue, but even more for avant-garde works, such as Philip Glass's *The Photographer,* which is an "opera" with no singing roles at all.

More germane is the question of musical style, regardless of how much or how little singing is built into the structure of the piece. What distinguished *West Side Story* from all the Broadway shows that preceded it—from the time that Romberg-style operettas ceased to be performed regularly—was the symphonic dimensions of the instrumental writing, the inventiveness of its approach to rhythm (particularly in the "Symphonic Dances" that Bernstein later extracted as a suite and the song "America") as well as the sometimes "classical" character of its musical themes. In it, Bernstein reached the expressive, if not the technical, peak of his melodic writing, and he was never again to achieve a comparable success with any single work.

In 1958, Bernstein took over from Mitropoulos as music director of the New York Philharmonic and immediately launched a series of progressive, educational programs aimed at increasing the broad public's acceptance and understanding of art music from all genres, but especially that of the 20th century. The most dramatic of his successes in this area were his "Young People's Concerts," televised from 1958 to 1973. Previously, Bernstein had scored similar hits with his appearances on the 50s TV show "Omnibus," but, in the Young Peoples' Concerts, he honed to a fine pitch of perfection his genius for making complex music understandable to lay audiences. Like his mentor, Copland, Bernstein had the gift of language in addition to his musical abilities and used it to maximum effect. Unlike Copland, his was a magnetic, hugely charismatic presence that dominated both stage and television screen. The American passion for public music education is a tradition that goes back to William Billings, Lowell Mason and William Henry Fry. But, via the medium of television, and with all the resources of the modern New York Philharmonic at his disposal, Bernstein wrote an entirely new chapter in the history of such efforts. It is impossible to estimate how many professional musicians today were inspired to pursue their studies, or received their first exposure to serious music through the "Young Peoples' Concerts," and the surviving tapes of these broadcasts, despite their primitive video quality by contemporary standards, are ripe for rebroadcast.

The early 1960s were something of a golden age for classical music in America. The new Lincoln Center complex was being built on Manhattan's Upper West Side (replacing the very tenement neighborhoods that were the setting of *West Side Story*) and soon would house both the Metropolitan Opera and, thanks to William Schuman's efforts, the Juilliard School. The young administration of Bernstein's Massachusetts compatriot, John F. Kennedy, encouraged new efforts toward promoting the arts, culminating in the formation of the National Endowment for the Arts under Kennedy's successor, Lyndon Johnson, in 1965. Virtually all of the recognized American masters were alive and composing during this period, and Bernstein became their principal advocate.

But, as in Edgar Allan Poe's "The Haunted Palace": " . . . evil things, in robes of sorrow, assailed the monarch's high estate." After the assassination of President Kennedy in November 1963, and the escalation of the Vietnam War under Johnson, most of the luster of this brief golden age was lost. Bernstein's impact, along with that of many of his colleagues, diminished proportionally as the nation became obsessed with darker issues. In 1969, Bernstein retired from the Philharmonic with the title of conductor laureate. Like MacDowell's acceptance of the teaching job at Columbia in 1896, this proved to be a tragic mistake for, while it removed some of the stress from Bernstein's hectic life, it also deprived him of his principal rostrum from which to make an impact on American cultural life.

Almost immediately both his temperament and the quality of his compositions began to deteriorate. Stories of his arrogance, rudeness and

brusque treatment of musicians proliferated. Despite continued guest conducting and lecturing positions throughout the world, and an especially
congenial relationship with the Vienna Philharmonic that developed during
the ensuing years, Bernstein suffered from a persistent sense of having lost
his creative equilibrium. In 1971 he created his last major work, the poly-
stylistic *Mass.* Though intensely committed to his Jewish identity, Bernstein took the Ordinary of the Roman Catholic Mass, with additional verse
by Stephen Schwartz, as his text and produced a controversial multi-media
theatre piece which combined an enormous variety of musical styles into a
tenuous work that barely holds together. While the *Mass* contained some
genuinely moving moments, and certainly demonstrated Bernstein's virtu-
osic command of virtually every current style of composition, both popular
and classical, it was also written in great haste and under intense pressure
to meet its premiere deadline; it has been subject to justifiable criticism for
its hyper-eclecticism.

Bernstein's life was further darkened by his wife's illness during the
1970s. He became increasingly involved with liberal political causes and,
with Felicia, hosted a famous cocktail party for the radical Black Panthers
at his Manhattan apartment in the early 1970s, inspiring novelist and social
critic, Tom Wolfe, to coin the term "radical chic." He composed a ballet on

Leonard Bernstein *(1918–1990) as he looked around
1970.* (Photo courtesy of ASCAP.)

S. Ansky's supernatural tale, *The Dybbuk,* in 1974, followed by the musical *1600 Pennsylvania Avenue* in 1976, and an operatic sequel to *Trouble in Tahiti* entitled *A Quite Place* in 1983. *The Dybbuk* is probably the best of these works. Its complex musical style explores aspects of modernist technique that promised to break new ground for Bernstein the composer. But audiences accustomed to Bernstein's earlier works found it disappointing and, so far, it has received too few performances to evaluate its ultimate place in the American repertoire. In any case, Bernstein failed to follow up *The Dybbuk* with further developments in the direction to which it seemed to point.

After Felicia's death in 1978, Bernstein found himself a bachelor again. His children were grown and pursuing lives of their own, and his position in the musical world was as well established as it was ever going to be. He was, therefore, free to pursue his personal interests and to return to an openly gay lifestyle—which he did. His political interests now included support for those groups that were actively lobbying for increased governmental resources to be devoted to the AIDS epidemic, and he eventually turned down a prestigious award from President George Bush in protest of the Bush administration's failure to provide adequate funding for AIDS research and education. He also continued to teach, especially at Tanglewood, and became a father figure to many of the rising conductors of the 1980s.

Bernstein had always been a heavy cigarette smoker and, by the late 1980s, was suffering visibly from emphysema. Despite the ravages to his health, he continued to smoke and finally reached the point where he had to leave the stage between pieces on his concert programs to receive oxygen infusions. During the last weeks of his life, he was forced to curtail his conducting activities altogether. This proved to be the final defeat for Bernstein, and he died unexpectedly of a heart attack in his New York apartment on the evening of October 24, 1990, at the age of seventy-two.

While no one can dispute the profound impact of Leonard Bernstein's career on the status of symphonic music as an institution in American life, nor the importance of *West Side Story* in the history of American musical theatre, it is still too early to render any final evaluation of Bernstein's legacy as a "serious" composer. He remained persistently tonal throughout all his creative work and went farther than anyone since George Gershwin toward integrating polished jazz techniques into his scores—and his works have received a degree of popular acclaim that few serious composers have matched. Like Gershwin's, Bernstein's symphonic music is still a reliable "draw" for any orchestra in need of increasing its gate receipts. But its ultimate quality is certainly uneven, and while works like *Wonderful Town* may recede into oblivion, it is equally possible that those such as *The Dybbuk* will assume greater importance as time passes. Nevertheless, even if he had never written a single note, American classical music would still owe an incalculable debt to Bernstein for his conducting, for his promotion of other composers and for his brilliance as our most articulate teacher to date of musical professionals and laymen alike.

Other American Composers of the Mid-20th Century

Among the other important American composers of the mid-20th century are Paul Creston, Alan Hovhaness, David Diamond, Morton Gould, Ross Lee Finney, Norman Dello Joio, Leon Kirchner, Bernard Herrmann, John LaMontaine, George Crumb, Vincent Persichetti, Lukas Foss and Gunther Schuller, to name only a few. While none of these men wrote music that has yet achieved the consistent public status of the diverse works of Schuman, Carter, Barber, Menotti or Bernstein, each made important contributions to the literature of American classical music, as did many of their colleagues too numerous to detail. The remainder of the present chapter will, therefore, present a comparative and, unfortunately, all to sketchy survey of the work of some of these.

Ross Lee Finney is the oldest of this assorted group, born in Wells, Minnesota, on December 23, 1906. Like many of his contemporaries, he studied with Hill at Harvard and Boulanger in Paris, but his most significant teacher was Alban Berg, with whom he studied from 1931 to 1932. Berg is probably the most accessible of the three major composers of the second Viennese school, and maintained that group's connection to its German Romantic antecedents, especially in his two great operas, *Wozzeck* and *Lulu*. Finney is the only well-known American composer to have studied intensively with Berg.

Finney's work covers a broad spectrum of 20th-century techniques, ranging from early "Americanist" pieces in the Thomson–Copland mold, such as his 1943 *Hymn, Fuguing and Holiday* for orchestra (homage to Billings), to later 12-tone works such as his *String Quartet No.6* (1950) and *Variations on a Theme of Berg* for piano (1952). Though always piquant and interesting, Finney's music does not display a strongly personal style. He has avoided the awesome complexities of a Carter or a Sessions, and as late as 1980, was still interested in composing instructional music for piano. Among his contributions to this neglected genre are his 1968 *32 Piano Games,* his 1970 *24 Inventions* and the 1980 *Youth's Companion* (five short pieces). He has a particular predilection for exploring the technique of variation, and has integrated this with his personal applications of the 12-tone method, as well as with the systematic exploration of the listener's short-term memory as a compositional factor. Among his major works are

Ross Lee Finney *(b. 1906) with ever-present pipe and pencils. An accessible serialist, he was the only major American to study with Alban Berg. He later taught Crumb, Reynolds and others.* (Photo courtesy of ASCAP.)

four symphonies, two violin concertos, two piano concertos, two dance pieces composed for the Erick Hawkins Company, concertos for percussion, alto saxophone and strings, eight string quartets and a variety of solo sonatas for various instruments.

Though not a major figure in forging the academic styles of American music, Finney spent a great deal of his life teaching at a number of universities, especially the University of Michigan. Among his more prominent students are George Crumb (see below) and Roger Reynolds.

Finney's most successful student was **George Crumb**. Born in Charleston, West Virginia on October 24, 1929, Crumb evolved a highly distinctive style of composition that became a major influence on young composers of the late 1960s and 1970s. Like Finney, with whom he studied at Michigan in the 1950s, Crumb worked largely within a basically 12-tone harmonic context in most of his mature writing, but has been more concerned with the didactic and psychoacoustic dimensions of his music than

George Crumb *(b. 1929) in the 1980s. His darkly mystical visions became a major influence on composers of the 1960s and 1970s.* (Photo courtesy of C.F. Peters Corp.)

with its purely abstract theoretical structure. His orchestral work, *Echoes of Time and the River* was awarded a Pulitzer Prize in 1968.

Crumb's most influential works to date, however, have been in smaller genres: either for solo piano, piano with voice, or other chamber groups. Building on the ideas of Henry Cowell, Crumb vastly expanded the repertoire of internal piano techniques[45] and other unconventional timbral devices in such highly effective works as his *Five Pieces for Piano* (1962), *Makrokosmos, Books I–IV* (1972–1979) and *Gnomic Variations* (1981). His related ensemble pieces include the celebrated *Black Angels: 13 Images from the Dark Land* for electronic string quartet (1970), *Vox balaenae (Voice of the Whale)* for electrified piano, flute and cello with prerecorded whale song (1971) and his *Ancient Voices of Children* (1970).

---

[45] I.e., new ways of playing the piano by directly manipulating the strings, frame and sounding board.

Among Crumb's other vocal music are four books of highly innovative *Madrigals* and the requiem *Lux aeterna* for soprano, bass flute/tenor recorder, sitar and two percussionists. In this last work, as in others of Crumb's chamber pieces, a theatrical element is added by asking the musicians to wear masks.

Crumb's penchant for mystical and Latin titles emphasizes the dramatic and philosophical aspects of his musical mission. His work is always darkly colored but also displays an enormous timbral imagination. He is extremely precise in his notational practice and succeeds in investing a structural significance into timbre, dynamics, texture and register that goes beyond the ideas of many of his contemporaries. However, by the late 1970s Crumb's unique personal voice had become so distinctive that he found himself virtually trapped by his too well-defined style. As a result, his output diminished somewhat during the 1980s. It is still too soon, however, to predict what future efforts might emerge from Crumb's fertile imagination.

A composer who shares some traits with both Finney and Crumb is **Lukas Foss**. Foss was born in Berlin on August 15, 1922, but migrated to the United States with his family in 1937. In Germany he had worked with the great pedagogue of German choral music, Julius Herford (né Goldstein, who also joined the migration forced by the Nazis), and acquired a strong technical foundation. After moving to America, Foss studied at the Curtis Institute with the same Rosario Scalero who taught Barber and Menotti. In addition, he joined Leonard Bernstein as one of the most prominent pupils in Koussevitzky's conducting classes during the early years of Tanglewood (1939–1943). Like Finney's, Foss' music divides into two broad categories: a body of early, more-or-less conventionally modern compositions, and a body of later, sometimes highly progressive pieces.

Foss was a prodigy who found an audience for his works almost immediately. As early as 1938 the sixteen-year-old composer's *Grotesque Dance* was published by G. Schirmer in New York and anthologized beside the music of older composers such as Farwell, Griffes, Grainger and Harris. His cantata on Carl Sandburg's *The Prairie* won the New York Music Critics' Circle award in 1944, and, in the following year he became the youngest composer ever awarded a Guggenheim Fellowship. His small works from this early period were often more harmonically and stylistically adventurous than his larger ones, such as his 1949 opera *The Jumping Frog of Calaveras County* (after Twain) or his 1955 *Psalms* for chorus and orchestra or pianos.

In the mid-1950s Foss joined the faculty of UCLA and founded the Improvisation Chamber Ensemble. This became the principal vehicle for the ensuing experimental phase of his composition, when he focussed on

Cagean-style techniques of indeterminacy and graphic notation (see Chapter 11), and became deeply interested in the dynamics and mechanics of group improvisation. His best known work from this period is *Time Cycle* for soprano and orchestra (1960), which won for him his third Critics' Circle Award (his second having been received for the 1953 version of his *Piano Concerto No.2*). In addition to indeterminacy and improvisation, Foss' music from 1956 through the 1960s explored unconventional uses of serialism and electronic techniques. During the 1970s and later, Foss' mature musical thinking reverted to more conventional pieces that integrated the diverse elements of his earlier works.

Foss' work as a conductor has been as influential as his composition, and he has served as music director for many prestigious orchestras. He is as at home with traditional repertoire as with new music on the podium and, while never as flamboyant nor as famous as Leonard Bernstein, has made solid contributions to the presentation of newer works by American and European composers over the years.

Among the more traditional of American (and "Americanist") composers from the mid-century, the names of Paul Creston (1906–1985),

Paul Creston *(1906–1985) in later life. A gifted composer, enchanted with rhythm. Like his colleague, Norman Dello Joio, he studied with Pietro Yon and remained true to his tonal language throughout the serialist period.* (Photo courtesy of ASCAP.)

Morton Gould (b. 1913), David Diamond (b. 1915), and Norman Dello Joio (b. 1913) stand out conspicuously, as does their lesser known contemporary John La Montaine (b. 1920). **Paul Creston**, a second-generation Italian native of New York, was largely a self-taught composer who had studied organ with Pietro Yon (composer of the Christmas song "Gesu Bambino"). Throughout his career he was preoccupied with the study of rhythm and produced, among other things, a ten-volume set of piano studies entitled *Rhythmicon*. His harmonic style was conservative and uncomplicated, and he is perhaps best known for his 1940 *Marimba Concerto*, which has also frequently been played on the xylophone.

Morton Gould, the past president of ASCAP, has been an eclectic composer who works as facilely with Coplandish Americanisms and Broadway musicals as with the 12-tone method. He was a child prodigy and gave piano recitals in and around his native New York from his teenage years. After studies at the Institute for Musical Art (later: Juilliard), he spent the late 1930s and early 1940s working in radio as both a broadcaster and composer. His musical *Billion Dollar Baby* was produced on Broadway in 1945 and his ballet, *The Fall River Legend* attracted considerable attention in 1947. But Gould is best known for his energetic orchestral works, including the *American Salute* (1943, on the folk song "When Johnny Comes Marching Home"), his 1976 *Symphony of Spirituals* and his three numbered symphonies. He has also produced a number of scores for television.

David Diamond is best known today as a symphonist and the youngest member of Copland's immediate circle during the 1940s and 1950s. He was born in Rochester, New York, on July 9, 1915 and studied with Copland's colleague, Bernard Rogers, at the Eastman School during the early 1930s. In 1934 he began to study with Sessions and continued as one of that composer's most promising students for about three years. Afterward, he went to Paris for further study with Boulanger and became closely acquainted with that segment of the Parisian intellectual elite that continued to function during the late 1930s.

Today, Diamond is viewed as the principal inheritor of the modernist tradition developed by Copland, Harris, Carter and Sessions during the 1930s. His style has remained closely allied with theirs from this period, and his works have been mainly in the standard symphonic and chamber music genres. Like Sessions and Barber, he possessed a strong affinity for Europe and chose to live in Italy from 1953 to 1965. Diamond has composed nine symphonies and numerous sonatas and chamber works. Throughout his career, the strongest intellectual influences on his work have been drawn

A soulful portrait of the young **David Diamond** *(b. 1915). An early follower of Copland, he developed a remarkable modernist classicism expressed in nine symphonies, among other works.* (Photo by Christian Steiner, courtesy of Peer-Southern.)

from the early Copland-Sessions esthetic, including the music of Satie, Stravinsky and Roussel, and the poetry of e e cummings.

While Diamond has maintained a sufficiently original voice to keep his music before the public, he has not made substantial contributions toward developing new ideas about music or new stylistic premises. His work represents a well-crafted addition to the literature of mid-century American classicism, but it remains to be seen whether it will survive.

Another New Yorker of Italian descent, **Norman Dello Joio,** like his colleague Creston, received his first serious instruction from Pietro Yon. He later proceeded to Juilliard, where he worked with Bernard Wagenaar. From 1941 to 1943 he was music director for Eugene Loring's dance company, and he succeeded William Schuman on the faculty of Sarah Lawrence College in 1945.

Dello Joio is another inheritor of the Copland tradition, but has brought a more uniquely personal flavor to it than did Diamond and relates better to a later phase of Copland's work. Where Diamond's music flows from the modernist esthetic of the 1920s and 1930s, Dello Joio's draws more from the period of the 1940s and can be compared to Copland's thinking in such works as *Our Town,* the *Lincoln Portrait,* the *Piano Sonata* and the *Fanfare for the Common Man.* Moreover, Dello Joio's music possesses a strongly monastic religious streak, reminiscent of John J. Becker, which is almost wholly lacking in that of his contemporaries. His major works—such as the 1942 orchestral *Magnificat,* the 1956 *Meditations on Ecclesiastes* or the opera *The Triumph of St. Joan*—all have religious themes and draw heavily on Gregorian chant, integrated with more modernist techniques. The ecclesiastical element in Dello Joio's music gives it its frequently haunting character and contributes to its strongly individual stamp. This is apparent even in his secular compositions, such as his highly regarded music for a 1965 NBC television documentary on the Louvre, which won Dello Joio one of the few Emmy Awards ever given to a serious composer and was later adapted into compelling orchestral and band suites.

John LaMontaine, the youngest of this group of mid-century classicists, studied with Diamond's teacher, Bernard Rogers, at Eastman and with Dello Joio's teacher, Bernard Wagenaar, at Juilliard. After the almost obligatory sojourn with Boulanger in Paris, he returned to the United States and served as pianist with the NBC Symphony under Toscanini, then went on to teach at Juilliard and elsewhere. LaMontaine won the Pulitzer Prize for his extraordinarily lyrical *Piano Concerto,* premiered by Jorge Bolet in 1959, but has attracted little attention since. Nevertheless, his work remains among the most accessible and effective of his generation's and, in some respects, foreshadowed the later school of post-modernism created by composers such as Rochberg, Schwantner, Del Tredici and Corigliano.

Many of the alumni of Copland's "Young Composers' Group"—such as Vivian Fine, Elie Siegmeister and Bernard Rogers—went on to greater or lesser accomplishments as composers and teachers. But none achieved a higher profile than **Bernard Herrmann,** whose strikingly original music for many of Hollywood's finest films established his reputation as perhaps the first great film composer America has produced. Herrmann was born on June 29, 1911, in New York City and studied with Grainger (New York University) and Wagenaar (Juilliard). During the mid-1930s he worked as an arranger and rehearsal conductor at CBS and developed an extraordinary ability to create impressions of various sound effects through the use of conventional instruments. Herrmann did not try so much to duplicate the acoustical signature of the effects he was after as to mirror their psychological impact through music. This ability served him well in radio, but most conspicuously in the terrifying music he eventually created for Alfred Hitchcock's 1960 film, *Psycho.*

Herrmann began his film career auspiciously enough when Orson Welles tapped him to create the score for *Citizen Kane* in 1940, followed by *The Magnificent Ambersons* the following year. During the next thirty-five years he produced a continuous succession of distinguished scores for great films, together with some for films whose music was their only distinguished trait. Among the former group were such cinematic master-pieces as *The Ghost and Mrs. Muir* (1947), *The Day the Earth Stood Still* (1951), *The Five Fingers* (1952), *The Kentuckian* (1955), *Prince of Players* (1955), *The Man Who Knew Too Much* (1956), *Vertigo* (1958), *North by Northwest* (1959), *Psycho* (1960), *Cape Fear* (1962), *Fahrenheit 451* (1966) and *Taxi Driver* (Herrmann's last work, 1976). Brilliant directors, such as Welles, Hitchcock, Truffaut and Scorsese, found in Herrmann a composer who could match the originality of their conceptions without either intrud-ing the music between the film and its audience, or drawing upon the hackneyed musical clichés so common in the work of other professional film composers.

Herrmann also produced music for a number of lesser films—such as *The Snows of Kilimanjaro* (1952), *White Witch Doctor* (1953), *The 7th Voyage of Sinbad* (1958), *Jason and the Argonauts* (1963), *Marnie* (1964), *Twisted Nerve* (1968) and *It's Alive* (1974)—but, even when working with second-rate horror, suspense or adventure movies, he managed to bring his characteristic originality to bear, despite increasing disillusionment with Hollywood during the late 1960s and 1970s. Herrmann was a domineering, temperamental figure whose explosions of rage were as notorious as they were short-lived. But this never seriously interfered with his working relationships with those directors who respected his extraordinary craft. Almost single-handedly, Herrmann transformed the traditions of first-rate film scoring from the trite conventions of Steiner and Korngold (about which Copland complained so bitterly) to the more imaginative and inte-grated approach that Copland tried to demonstrate in his own commercial film music. His work set a standard of which later, occasional film compos-ers—such as Bernstein—were conspicuously aware. As a well-paid Holly-wood composer, he lived a comfortable life and indulged his epicurean tastes in art, furnishings and food to the fullest. He died in his sleep on Christmas Eve of 1975, only hours after completing the final recording session of his music to Scorsese's *Taxi Driver.*

Among the other composers of the mid-century generation, at least four require special attention from any serious student of American music.

These are Alan Hovhaness (b. 1911), Vincent Persichetti (1913–1985), Leon Kirchner (b. 1919) and Gunther Schuller (b. 1925).

Alan Hovhaness, born Alan Chakmakjian on March 8, 1911, in Somerville, Massachusetts, has been one of the most prolific composers of this century after Henry Cowell. Having spent his early life in Boston and New Hampshire, he studied with Frederick Converse at the New England Conservatory during the 1930s and experienced some early exposure to Hindustani music in the Boston area. But his early music was undistinguished and reflected a post-Romantic esthetic.

In 1943, Hovhaness went through a major period of self-reevaluation, after which he destroyed a vast quantity of early compositions (including no less than seven symphonies). He had been roughly handled by Copland at Tanglewood and felt that his work, up to that point, was without either individual character or musical value. He began to delve into the folk music

Alan Hovhaness *(b. 1911) during the 1960s. A gifted contrapuntalist and immensely prolific composer, his symphonic and instrumental works explore many facets of non-Western music.* (Photo courtesy of C. F. Peters Corp.)

of his ancestral Armenia, as well as that of other regions of the Near East and central Asia. Always a facile contrapuntalist, who can write fugues as easily as most people can write a letter, Hovhaness integrated his Western musical skills with the tonalities, modalities, textures and formal procedures of this music, adapting it to Western instruments and ensembles. He later expanded his study of non-Western music to encompass the music of China, Japan and other regions of the Far East, incorporating these into his pieces as well. Thus, Hovhaness became the first American composer after Eichheim to focus in a serious way on "Orientalism." His works foreshadowed the later obsession with Eastern music developed by Lou Harrison and others.

By 1990, Hovhaness' mature compositions numbered upward of four hundred and fifty titles, including sixty-five symphonies. Despite periodic bouts of illness, he has continued to compose without interruption since. The sheer volume and uniform quality of his music makes it difficult to single out any particular works, but his *Prayer of St. Gregory* for solo trumpet and strings or organ has remained a favorite with audiences for many years. Like the Italian Baroque master, Vivaldi, Hovhaness has tended to work in an easily accessible style and to repeat himself in many compositions. A deeply humanistic and spiritual composer, his esthetic is not so much concerned with the creation of a small number of masterpieces as it is with articulating a fluent musical "ethos" through a large number of similar-sounding works.

Though a native of Brooklyn, New York, **Leon Kirchner** spent most of his youth in southern California, where he became acquainted with Ernst Toch and studied with Schoenberg at UCLA. After taking his degree in 1940, he went on to graduate studies at Berkeley and then further studies with Sessions in New York. After serving in the army during World War II, he returned to New York and began to establish his name with his 1948 *Piano Sonata*. He went on to teach at University of Southern California and Mills College, then succeeded Piston at Harvard when the latter retired in 1966. Kirchner's work owes more to Harris, Sessions and Carter than it does to the the influence of Copland's Americanist phase. He has remained something of an academic serialist while adopting Carter's technique of partitioning musical elements to create a dramatic dialectic within his pieces. His relatively small output includes two piano concertos, three string quartets, an opera and various solo and chamber works, including his 1949 *Little Suite* for piano, similar in concept to Harris' work of the same title. Kirchner has achieved a higher public profile than most of his academic colleagues due to the originality and effectiveness of his conceptions.

Another well-known composer who made his mark principally in academia was **Vincent Persichetti**. Born in Philadelphia on June 6, 1915, Persichetti spent his life closely connected to his native city, its educational institutions and publishing houses. He graduated from the Combs Conservatory (Philadelphia) in 1936 and the Philadelphia Conservatory (1945), while studying conducting with Fritz Reiner at the Curtis Institute. In 1952 he became publications director for the Elkan-Vogel music publishing company, and later the chief music editor for the Theodore Presser Co., of which Elkan-Vogel is a subsidiary. He served in these capacities until his death in 1987 and was largely responsible for Presser's ongoing commitment to keeping the music of contemporary composers in print.

Persichetti also taught at Juilliard from 1947 through the 1970s. He, together with William Bergsma, was one of the principal teachers of both Steve Reich and Philip Glass, as well as many other prominent living American composers. Though neither as prolific nor as arcane as Hovhaness, Persichetti produced a large amount of very accessible music during his lifetime. His music tends to be bright, rhythmically vigorous and frequently easy enough for young students to play. Of particular note are his works for high school and college symphonic bands, including the 1950 *Divertimento*, the 1953 *Pageant*, his 1956 *Symphony for Band* (Symphony

Vincent Persichetti *(1915–1987) in later life. A prolific and versatile composer who made major contributions to the modern repertoire for band and harpsichord, among other genres.* (Photo by Clarence E. Premo, courtesy of ASCAP.)

No.6) and his 1960 *Serenade*. He also produced a large quantity of keyboard music, including a provocative *Piano Concerto* (1962), and turned increasingly toward the composition of music for the neglected harpsichord during his later years. While Persichetti's music is probably not of the first rank in American composition, it maintains fresh interests nonetheless and is worthy of continued attention.

One of the most original minds in mid-century American music was that of Gunther Schuller. Born in New York on November 22, 1925, Schuller was the son of a violinist in the Philharmonic and became a virtuoso horn player early in life. He has been a prolific composer, conductor and teacher and is one of the few American classical composers to have made a systematic study of jazz while attempting to integrate it into his own work. In addition to many other academic posts, Schuller was associated with Boston's New England Conservatory throughout the late 1960s and 1970s, where he founded the New England Ragtime Ensemble in response to the revival of interest in Scott Joplin's work provoked by the 1973 film, *The Sting*.

Schuller's earliest works, naturally enough, revolved around the horn and included a well-received *Concerto* (1944) for that instrument as well as one for cello, and a variety of other orchestral pieces. In the 1950s he became increasingly interested in jazz, both in its historical and practical aspects. Working with John Lewis and the Modern Jazz Quartet, he made a serious effort to integrate jazz procedures with the 12-tone music that dominated academia at the time, thus creating what is generally labeled "third stream" music today. At the same time, Schuller pursued music of a more abstract character, and attempted to find musical parallels for formal processes occurring in the visual arts. His work in this area anticipated the later concerns of his contemporary, Morton Feldman. Schuller's most influential piece from this other dimension of his composition is his 1959 *Seven Studies on Themes of Paul Klee*, which has remained his best-known single composition.

Despite being a self-taught composer (or perhaps because of it), Schuller's creative interests have ranged over the entire spectrum of 20th-century music. He is a composer with a strong sense of the historical roles played by various vernacular traditions and has written extensively on the subject. Though his activities as a conductor, teacher and administrator have reduced the time and energy available for composition, it is likely that his works will continue to interest future generations of American musicians.

Throughout the 1940s, 1950s and 1960s, mainstream American composers, such the ones discussed in this chapter, continued to build on the foundations laid by Copland and his generation in the 1930s and 1940s. The institutions of American musical life expanded rapidly and, for a brief period, music education blossomed at the secondary and collegiate levels, attracting the attention of major composers not only to the survival occupation of college teaching, but to serious creative work with younger musicians as well. The technological marvel that was television in the 1950s opened up new avenues for the dissemination of contemporary classical music, and significantly advanced the careers of Bernstein, Menotti, Dello Joio and others. The work of Bernard Herrmann raised the standards of film music to unprecedented heights of sophistication and set forth both a model and a challenge for subsequent film composers. While composers like Samuel Barber continued to advance the European traditions in symphony, chamber music and opera, Bernstein and others breathed new life into the Broadway musical, while Hovhaness expanded public awareness of non-Western musics. And, in the midst of it all, Elliott Carter continued to break new ground in setting music free from received traditions while simultaneously demonstrating the endless possibilities that could be achieved by applying some truly original thinking to the form and fabric of music itself.

Overall, despite both American's growing political paranoia and the icy grip of academic serialism on post-secondary music education during the 1950s, those of our composers who worked in the trenches of real-world audiences and institutions made significant, energetic strides toward making the musical vision of their predecessors a permanent reality in America life. In the process, they generated a vast and diverse treasure of mid-20th-century American composition, much of which has not yet been digested or promoted sufficiently to be as familiar to the general public as it should be.

But, even while this expansion of public, mainstream music-making unfolded, there continued to develop an underground experimental tradition that had its roots in the music of Ives, Ruggles, Varèse and Cowell. This experimental tradition would ultimately find its greatest realization in the musical revolution wrought by John Cage in the 1960s, a revolution that profoundly challenged the tacit assumptions behind the music of even our most publicly successful composers. However, before that revolution took hold, the musical world had to be prepared for it by the work of several erratic American geniuses, whose outré conceptions caused them to be ostracized by the established musical and social institutions in the United States. These figures included Conlon Nancarrow, Harry Partch, Lou Harrison, Dane Rudhyar and their followers. In the next chapter, we turn our attention to an examination of the works of these men and their antecedents.

10

The Roots of Dissatisfaction: Foundations of the '60s Avant-Garde

ॐ

Throughout the entire first half of the 20th century, while composers like Ives, Gershwin, Copland, Sessions, Piston, Carter, Barber and Bernstein were forging a truly American tradition in concert music, an independent, iconoclastic and only somewhat related tradition of American experimental music was growing from the works of Henry Cowell, Edgard Varèse, Conlon Nancarrow, Harry Partch, John Cage, Lou Harrison and others. This experimental tradition developed in response to the confluence of several streams of historical and musical events during the first two decades of this century, and led, in turn, to Cage's specific development of aleatoric music in the late 1950s and 1960s.

Around the turn of the century, Western music itself was in one of its periodic states of radical ferment. Such transitional epochs had occurred before in the history of European music: such as the period at the turn of the 12th–13th centuries that saw the birth of polyphony in the works the Notre Dame composers, Leonin and Perotin; such as the beginnings of the functional tonality of the diatonic system and the related revolution in opera brought about by Palestrina and Monteverdi respectively at the dawn of the Baroque era; such as the deliberate reconstruction of compositional procedures engineered by the Mannheim composers during the mid-18th century, which bore fruit in the Classical masterpieces of Haydn, Mozart and Beethoven. The revolution of 1900 was only the most recent in a series of periodic metamorphoses in the way Western civilization wrote, performed, listened to and defined art music itself.

Among the many factors that brought about the post-1900 crisis were: (1) the increasing awareness on the part of European composers like Debussy and Americans like Griffes of non-Western musics and their seemingly alien systems of organization, (2) the ongoing development of instrument technology and acoustics, stimulated by the research of Helmholtz and other physicists, (3) the inevitable playing-out of the finite harmonic possibilities embodied in sonata form, tonal modulation and post-Wagnerian chromaticism, and (4) the overall climate of political and social changes occurring in European and American culture, reflected in the consolidation of industrial and colonial empires, the decay of the last remaining European monarchies, and the increasing influence of socialist ideology, all of which were to result in the devastating world wars, revolutions and economic upheavals of the period 1914–1945.

In addition, American artistic thinking from the time of Poe, Whitman, Gottschalk, and the Hudson Valley painters had often been independent, iconoclastic, irreverent and determined to follow its own course of development—despite the ongoing inferiority complex of our developing cultural institutions and their slavish adherence to European art, manifested in American music by the attitudes of Mason, Fry, Paine and the Second New England School. When paired with the transitional state of turn-of-the-century artistic thought in Europe, the fundamentally maverick quality of certain American artists yielded a rich harvest of new ideas and working modes.

Unbeknownst to anyone, except his son Charles and a few skeptical Danburyites, the American experimental tradition had been born in the fantastic musical imaginings of George Ives after the Civil War. Charles Ives later developed these notions and brought them to magnificent fruition in his works written after 1902. And, while Ives' music did not begin to be generally known until about 1930, he himself was not without influence during the intervening thirty years.

Carl Ruggles (1876–1971)

Many strange parallels exist between Ives and his Yankee friend and contemporary, Carl Ruggles. Born in East Marion, Massachusetts, on March 11, 1876, Ruggles was only two years younger than Ives, but outlived him by nearly two decades. Like Ives, Ruggles was born into a long-established New England family, saturated with Yankee tradition and ideology. Also like his elder colleague, he displayed an early and avid interest in music, constructing his own "violin" from a cigar box at the age of six and later taking lessons from the town bandmaster (who was not, however, his father). But, unlike Ives, Ruggles was steered into the career of a professional musician and functioned as such throughout his early life. Ruggles studied violin and composition privately with a number of distinguished teachers in the Boston area, including John Knowles Paine, and, after ten years of conducting and teaching in Winona, Minnesota (1907–1917), settled in New York. There he made the acquaintance of Varèse and Cowell, who assisted him in procuring early performances and publication of his music. His first published work in his characteristic idiom was a song entitled *Toys* (1919), written for the fourth birthday of his son.

In the early 1920s, Ruggles entered a period of intense musical activity that saw the creation of most of his major works, including *Angels* (for muted brass, 1921), *Vox clamans in deserto* (soprano and orchestra, 1923), *Men and Mountains* (orchestra, 1924) and *Portals* (string orchestra, 1925), as well as initial work on his tone poem, *Sun-Treader*. The publication of *Men and Mountains* and *Portals* in Cowell's *New Music Edition* in 1927 brought Ruggles' work to Ives' attention, and the two became close friends shortly thereafter—a friendship founded on their extraordinary similarity of musical styles and personal ideals. This friendship lasted until Ives' death in 1954.

It would not be correct to state that Ives influenced Ruggles, or, for that matter, that Ruggles influenced Ives in terms of either man's compositions. There is no evidence of contact between the two prior to 1927, and, by that time, each had composed virtually all of his important music. Ives wrote nothing new after 1933, and Ruggles, who completed *Sun-Treader* in 1931, produced only two significant pieces during the rest of his life: the piano suite *Evocations* in 1943 and the orchestral piece *Organum* in 1947. Both spent much of their later years revising earlier scores, and Ruggles, who had also been a professional artist from his early adulthood, turned to painting as his principal vocation after 1950. Moreover, Ruggles' music is much more in the mainstream of European avant-garde thinking of the time. He worked explicitly and systematically with pitch series, although he did not apply precisely the same principles as Schoenberg, Berg or Webern, and was more concerned than was Ives with his music's connection to polyphonic tradition.

Ruggles' small output was largely the result of an intensely, even obsessively, self-critical attitude. He is reputed to have spent hours playing a single chord at the piano before convincing himself that he was satisfied with it. All his major works underwent several revisions during his later years before achieving their final form. In this respect he presents something of a contrast to Ives, who often wrote hastily and sometimes carelessly, and was rarely able to come to definitive editorial decisions. As a result, unlike Ruggles, many of Ives' compositions have several different "final forms."

Moreover, Ives had what we might describe as a "mystical bent," which sought expression in certain of his works (*The Unanswered Question,* the *"Concord" Sonata,* the unfinished *"Universe" Symphony*). Ruggles' mysticism was the constant theme of his work and makes Ives' look positively mundane by comparison. While neither developed a coherent metaphysical "system" in any published writings, both were deeply involved in that same profound sense of spirituality, linked to place (and specifically to New England), which permeates the work of so many New England artists and that is the prototype for much of the later attachment to specific spiritual geographies in American art. Both were also deeply attached to the metaphysics of certain English and American poets, including Browning, Whitman, Keats and Blake.

Like Ives (and many others), Ruggles only began to receive serious recognition late in life, after he had ceased composing. He did not even have an opportunity to hear his *Sun-Treader* until 1965 (in a recording made by

Carl Ruggles *(1876–1971) at the age of 91. This feisty New Englander was a close friend of Ives and distinguished himself as both a composer and painter.* (Photo courtesy of Marilyn Ziffrin.)

Zoltan Rozsnyai), some thirty-four years after its creation. Growing increasingly deaf and garrulous with the passage of time, he nevertheless was revered by younger composers in his last years as the sole survivor of the Ives generation. He died in Bennington, Vermont, on October 24, 1971.

One of the central arguments in the redefinition of music that began around 1900 (and still continues today) hinges on the role of melody in serious composition. Throughout the centuries, melody had been handled in different ways by different composers, but it was always present and was almost always the main feature that defined any given piece. Without the crucial functions served by melody in the music of the so-called "common practice era," it would be difficult to delineate the important structural sections of pieces and impossible to identify the "great themes" of the masters. Indeed, the music of the common practice era is so ineluctably married to the concept of the melodic line that it is impossible to imagine what this music might have been like without it.

Melody derives, originally, from folksong and is usually the first aspect of any traditional piece heard, recognized or remembered by the lay listener. And the more sharply defined melodic structures, commonly referred to as "tunes", in the works of all the great European composers, often overshadow those other aspects of the music that actually go farther toward defining the individual composer's skill and style.

Despite the other progressive features of their work, most early-20th-century composers (Debussy, Stravinsky, Bartók, Schoenberg, Ravel, Berg, Copland, Prokofiev, Milhaud, etc.) continued to use the parameter of melody in its accustomed place, as the centerpiece of most of their compositions. And they continued to use the standard orchestral instruments which had evolved between the Renaissance and the 19th century to produce music that, while timbrally imaginative, did not depart radically from the standard orchestral palette of available tone colors.

But, beginning around 1910, other composers began to challenge the tacit assumptions that the melodic dimension of music was of primary importance, or even necessary, and also that "music" as such was necessarily comprised of only the specialized timbres available to conventional instruments. The growth of mechanized urban industry and the increasing dependence of Westerners on such machines as the telephone, typewriter, automobile, train, airplane and electric light stimulated composers, like the Italian futurists and George Antheil, to compose works using "noise" as the primary acoustic material. Unfortunately, but inevitably, these early experiments were often arbitrary and poorly organized as expressions of creative thought.

But the upshot of these and related debates was a new emphasis in the work of the radical avant-garde, both in Europe and America between

1910 and 1930. This emphasis was on such previously underexploited resources as texture, unconventional timbres and "non-musical" sounds, polyrhythms, the aggregate or "compound rhythm" of extreme dynamic fluctuations, and variable form. While much of this was presaged in the as-yet-unknown work of Ives, the primary public exponents of such radically new approaches to music, both in the United States and Europe, were Henry Cowell and Edgard Varèse.

Henry Cowell (1897–1965)

Henry Cowell, the first of what would later be called the "West Coast School" of American composers, was born in Menlo Park, California, on March 11, 1897. His parents, like those of his southern California contemporary, Roy Harris, were free-thinking agriculturalists who allowed the boy to pursue musical studies as it suited him. As a result, Cowell grew up in a remarkably unprejudiced musical environment, permeated as much by the Asian music of California immigrants and the Irish folk music of his ancestors as it was by European classical models.

Cowell's parents were divorced in 1903, and he spent several years with his mother in the Midwest before returning to the Menlo Park homestead in 1910. Despite his later energetic musical activities in New York and elsewhere, he would continue to treat the family cottage as his home base until 1936.

In 1912, the fifteen-year-old Henry bought a piano and began experimenting with different ways of playing it. He studied with a variety of local private teachers, but this did nothing to inhibit his passion for composing with unusual techniques, such as tone clusters played with fists and/or forearms, directly manipulating the internal harp of the instrument and other innovative devices. He used some of these in his early piano work, *The Tides of Manaunaun,* dating from around 1917, and also explored the various possibilities of atonal pitch sets.

In 1914, Cowell began to study with Charles Seeger at the University of California, Berkeley. After a brief and unsuccessful term at the Institute of Musical Art in 1916, he returned to California and resumed his work with Seeger, who was a pioneer of American folk music collection and composition. Together, they evolved the theory that has since become known as "dissonant counterpoint."

Seeger encouraged Cowell's ongoing compositional experimentation, but also saw to it that the young composer acquired a thorough traditional training. More importantly, he insisted that Cowell embody the fruits of his musical experiments in a systematic theoretical document, which led to the first version of Cowell's book, *New Musical Resources* (1919). *New*

Henry Cowell *(1897–1965), photographed by his wife Sidney six years before his death. One of the great experimentalists in American music, he was instrumental in bringing Ives into public prominence as well.* (Photo courtesy of C.F. Peters Corp.)

Musical Resources dealt with the organization of tonal and timbral materials, new approaches to the treatment of rhythm and meter, and the exploration of new ways to play old instruments. In its revised and published form (1930), it was to become one of the most influential books in modern American music history.

The advent of World War I saw Cowell enlisting in the Army (February 1918–May 1919), where he played the flute in military bands. Shortly after his discharge, he staged a concert of his own works in New York, then embarked on a series of European tours as a composer-pianist that would occupy him intermittently between 1923 and 1933. These concerts, as well as his ongoing New York performances, brought him to the forefront of public attention as an exponent of radically new musical techniques and placed him on a collegial basis with the most important composers of the day.

Predictably, his concerts generated outrage from some and enthusiasm from others. His exploration of new musical techniques continued unabated, and he became involved in a wide variety of organizational and promotional efforts on behalf of the new music of the time. He founded the New Music Society in 1925 and created the quarterly publication *New Music,* in which he published Ruggles' *Men and Mountains* in 1927, thus leading to the association between Ives and Ruggles. He edited the important collection of essays, *American Composers on American Music,* in 1933 and was directly responsible for the American publication and promotion of many works by Ives, Schoenberg, Webern and Varèse. In 1928, he joined with Varèse, Carlos Chávez and harpist-composer Carlos Salzedo in founding the Pan American Association of Composers, which became the principal rival to the more conservative Bauer-Reis-Copland League of Composers until about 1932.

From late 1927 onward, Cowell became the principal champion of Ives' music and served as Ives' most important link to the musical world in general. Cowell idolized the elder composer and, quite rightly, viewed him as the first truly great creative figure America had produced in the domain of classical composition. This would eventually lead to his book, co-authored with his wife Sidney, *Charles Ives and His Music* (1955), which became the first comprehensive study of Ives and led, inevitably, to a number of distorted ideas about him that have not yet been fully dispelled.

But before that book came into being, Cowell's relationship with Ives, indeed Cowell's whole life, took a tragic turn that altered the entire future course of his development. In 1936, Cowell was accused of having sex with a male student who was below the age of consent. Whether or not he was guilty of this charge has remained a debated point among scholars. But, in any case, Cowell was brought to trial, convicted and sentenced to the penitentiary at San Quentin, where he was imprisoned until 1940.

Understandably, Cowell was never willing to discuss publicly his years as an inmate, nor has any historian yet succeeded in uncovering any useful information about his experiences there. He did, however, continue composing during his imprisonment. While a few composers and other figures in the world of the fine arts made appeals on his behalf, most (including many who had benefited from Cowell's energetic advocacy) dropped him like the proverbial hot potato—possibly to avoid the danger of attracting attention to their own homosexuality. A notable exception to these was the Australian-born pianist and composer Percy Grainger.

Grainger, prior to 1940, had built his reputation as a free-spirited Romantic pianist, arranger of English and American folksongs for piano and sometime composer and conductor. He had worked extensively with the Norwegian Edvard Grieg, during the last few years of that composer's life, in preparing the definitive edition of the A minor *Piano Concerto,* but his contributions to American avant-garde music had been minimal.

Australian-born pianist and composer **Percy Aldridge Grainger** *(1882–1961), at about the time he came to Henry Cowell's defense and assisted in securing his parole.* (Photo courtesy of ASCAP.)

Grainger, to his credit, came strongly to Cowell's defense and exerted himself in print and in person on the younger composer's behalf. As he had unimpeachable heterosexual credentials and was safely married, it was perhaps easier for him to do so than for some others. But, whatever Grainger's motives, it was largely due to his influence that Cowell was paroled in 1940. After Cowell had atoned for his sins by marrying the writer, folksong collector and photographer Sidney Hawkins Robertson in 1941, he was pardoned by the governor of California. Grainger further supported Cowell by giving him a job as his personal secretary after his release from prison.

As might be imagined, this incident strained Cowell's relationship with the sexually conflicted, homophobic Ives to the breaking point. John J. Becker and Harmony Ives at first took great pains to conceal the facts of

Cowell's arrest from Ives. But this pretense could not be continued indefinitely and, after Mrs. Ives was finally able to break the news to him, Ives resolved never to have anything to do with Cowell again. It was only after Ives had been partially persuaded that Cowell was wrongfully accused, and after Cowell had made a successful demonstration of heterosexual respectability via his marriage to Sidney, that Ives resumed his friendship with him, which blossomed thereafter into the Cowells' book.

The period of Cowell's incarceration proved a setback in the continuing progress of Ives' career as well. Cowell had been his closest advisor in matters relating to his dealings with professional musicians and musical institutions, and, without Cowell's more reality-based perspective and mediation, Ives' vitriolic temperament was apt to alienate many who would otherwise have been willing supporters. But Ives' reputation received a much-needed shot in the arm with Kirkpatrick's 1939 premiere of the "Concord" Sonata, before Cowell's parole. Perhaps a more serious consequence of Cowell's enforced removal from the musical scene was the deterioration of the New Music Society and its publications.

Cowell had turned over the management of New Music to composer Gerald Strang when he entered San Quentin. But Strang lacked Cowell's enormous energy and administrative skills. Despite efforts by Ives and others to impose a greater level of business sense on Strang, the organization's finances fell into disarray and publications diminished. Copland's organizations, the American Composers' Alliance and Arrow Music Press, as well as the American Music Center, stepped in to fill part of the void, but it was not until Cowell resumed editorial leadership of New Music after his release that the primary alternative to the Copland camp's view of American composition became fully functional again.

Cowell had always had a strong streak of interest in American folk music. He partly inherited this from his Irish ancestors, but was undoubtedly reinforced in it by his studies with Seeger. And it formed an additional point of connection between him and Ives. Up to 1940, however, the part of his compositional work oriented toward folk music was overshadowed by the importance and innovativeness of his explorations of new instrumental resources. After his release from prison, he turned increasingly toward music based on American vernacular sources, notably the fuguing tunes of William Billings and his generation of 18th-century New England singing-school masters as well as William Walker's Southern Harmony. This personal transition in Cowell's work was consistent with the generally more conservative and "Americanist" styles of composition that arose during the mid-1930s. But the experience of his scandalous arrest, trial and imprisonment cannot have failed to have had a traumatic effect on the basically guileless composer.

Cowell could be almost childlike in his innocence and enthusiasms. Unlike many of his colleagues, he didn't have a mean bone in his body and was constitutionally incapable of organizing or executing schemes and plots against composers whom he may have perceived as professional rivals. On the contrary, his history shows nothing but an uninterrupted succession of whole hearted support for new music during the first half of this century. Thus, it is difficult for the average person, as it was difficult for Cowell, to reconcile the paradox of public reaction to the outward appurtenances of his sexual behavior with the fundamentally non-exploitative, and emotionally chaste approach to human relationships from which it grew.

Given this context, it is all the more remarkable that Cowell recovered from the scandal so quickly and restored himself to the position in American music that he had occupied before his arrest. If retrenchment showed, it showed only in his marriage to Sidney and the more traditional orientation of his music after 1940, such as the eighteen *Hymns and Fuguing Tunes* for various instrumental combinations that he produced between 1944 and 1964.

But, despite the increased occurrence of works of this kind in his output, especially in the Thomsonesque symphonies and chamber music that he began to compose, Cowell continued to be an exponent of new techniques and new approaches in composition to the end of his career. As early as his *Third String Quartet* (1935), Cowell had begun to explore what he referred to as "mosaic" or "elastic" form. In its earliest manifestations, this consisted of Cowell's instructions for the performer to play the various movements of the work in an order determined by themselves, rather than prescribed by the composer. It is likely that Cowell's ideas about this indeterminate ordering of formal sections influenced Grainger who, in 1943,[46] produced an ensemble piece entitled *Random Rounds,* based on similar principles. As both Cage and Lou Harrison studied with Cowell during the 1930s, it is equally probable that Cowell's initial ideas about indeterminate structure either set Cage on the path toward full-blown aleatory, or reinforced similar ideas Cage had already arrived at independently. In either case, Cowell's thinking in the above-mentioned quartet and other works, such as his *26 Simultaneous Mosaics* (1963), forms a direct precursor of the aleatoric school.

Henry Cowell was one of the most prolific composers the United States has produced. In all, he created close to a thousand separate compositions, and the catalogue of his works that appeared in the 1985 edition of *Grove's Dictionary of American Music* fills five double-column pages of fine print. Yet, despite its quantity, the bulk of Cowell's varied music has

---

[46] Some authorities have erroneously given the date as 1913.

not found a permanent place in the modern repertoire of performers. His innovative piano works, such as *Tiger* (1930), *Aeolian Harp* (1923) and *The Banshee* (1925) have received, perhaps, the greatest exposure due to their relative ease of performance and availability in print. But, given the massive indifference of the American listening public even to indigenous works that are far more accessible and easy to program than Cowell's, it should not be inferred from this neglect that Cowell's music is second-rate. Much of it is highly experimental in nature, and requires far more study, practice and interpretive thinking than many professional performers are willing to bestow upon it. What is needed, and has not yet appeared, is a comprehensive analytical study of all the many phases of Cowell's immense compositional output, and the issuance of authoritatively edited print versions of the bulk of his scores. A promising beginning has been made toward filling this void with W. Lichtenwanger's *The Music of Henry Cowell: a Descriptive Catalogue* (1986), but much more is needed before the musical public will even be in a position to render anything like a final judgment.

Edgard Varèse (1883–1965)

Of equal importance to the history of the early 20th-century American avant-garde is the Franco-American composer, Edgard Varèse. Born in Paris on December 22, 1883, the infant Varèse was entrusted to the care of an aunt and uncle in the Piedmont village of Villars only a few weeks after his birth. He grew up adoring his rustic maternal grandfather and grew to detest his hard-bitten, bourgeois businessman father.

In 1893, the father moved the family to Turin and forced young Edgard to study mathematics and engineering as preparation for a career in business. When he realized that his son was beginning to display an early and unwelcome interest in music, Varèse's father locked the family piano and covered it with a heavy drape. Despite his early passion for the rural environs of his grandfather's village, Varèse was attracted by the more urban atmosphere of Turin, with its industrial sounds, its conservatory and its opera house. He was able to hear performances of some of the great post-Romantic French and German music there, and was especially enamored of Debussy's *Prelude to the Afternoon of a Faun*. He composed a juvenile opera for the amusement of his friends on Jules Verne's *Martin Paz* around 1895, and, after a particularly violent argument with his father, moved to Paris in 1903.

Varèse had managed to acquire some musical training from Giovanni Bolzoni in Turin after 1900, but, when the twenty-year-old fledgling musician arrived in the City of Light, he was still in need of serious study. He enrolled in the Schola Cantorum, where he studied composition with

Roussel and conducting with d'Indy, but he experienced an uncomfortable relationship with the paternalistic and authoritarian d'Indy that triggered all his pent-up hostility toward his father. Varèse therefore sought admission to the Conservatoire, then headed by Gabriel Fauré. He was duly admitted and enrolled in Charles-Marie Widor's composition class, supporting himself, like Schoenberg, as a music copyist. During this time he became acquainted with such figures as Erik Satie, Max Jacob, Picasso, Apollinaire, Modigliani and other denizens of the bohemian Montmartre neighborhood. Varèse also developed a lifelong interest in certain aspects of science and para-science, especially the notebooks of Leonardo Da Vinci and the mysticism of the Hermetic philosopher, Paracelsus. He was obsessed with subjects such as wave motion, currents and electricity, and saw parallels for these in the movement of sound in musical composition. He was particularly taken with the analogy between river currents and musical polyphony, which would play a significant role in his approach to form and texture in his later works. He also began to view all types of sound, not just specialized tones, as legitimate material for composition and began to speak in terms of "organized sound" rather than "music."

As a result of his early training and predilections, Varèse's musical tastes in his formative years encompassed primarily the works of Medieval polyphonists and the French and German post-Romantics, especially Debussy and Richard Strauss. The only Romantic composer for whom he felt any real affinity was Berlioz, because of the latter's innovative orchestral conceptions and wildly mystical temperament.

In 1907, shortly after his first marriage (to the actress Suzanne Bing), Varèse and his wife moved to Berlin, where he became a close friend of Ferruccio Busoni. Busoni, who also played a significant role in the career of Charles Griffes, had recently published his seminal essay, *Sketch of a New Esthetic of Music,* in which he prophesied many of the developments that were soon to take place in the 20th century.

Busoni was something of a paradox himself. A brilliant romantic pianist, his own compositions included conventional salon music and bombastic piano arrangements of the music of Bach as well as operas and chamber pieces that have since fallen into obscurity. But, despite the nature of his own creative output, Busoni was a radical visionary in the esthetics of music and was in the habit of supporting younger composers whom he felt were likely to advance the art in new directions. And he had enormous prestige in the international musical world at the turn of the century. His support alone could and did open doors for young composers, doors that might otherwise not be approached.

Busoni became Varèse's principal mentor in Berlin, and encouraged the young Frenchman to seek out Richard Strauss. But Varèse at the time was so much in awe of the composer of *Salomé* and *Elektra* that he avoided a direct request for an interview. This kind of emotional contradiction was to become characteristic of Varèse throughout his life. On the one hand, he could be enormously egotistical and domineering—convinced of his absolute, exclusive rightness and authority, especially as a musical prophet. This would later bring him into conflict with Henry Cowell, Ives and others and would act to the detriment of the Pan American Association they organized together. On the other hand, Varèse was also subject to long periods of depression, shyness and creative block in which he seemed to doubt both the validity of his mission and his personal ability to carry it off. This resulted in a long period during the 1940s in which he completed virtually nothing.

In any case, he actually did meet Strauss in a chance encounter, and Strauss also became a supporter of Varèse's early music. Strauss used his influence to compel conductor Josef Stransky to program Varèse's *Bourgogne* with the same Blüthner Orchestra of which the young Wallingford Riegger was later to serve as conductor. *Bourgogne,* the manuscript of which Varèse would destroy in a fit of despair in 1962, was an early symphonic work reflecting the young composer's attachment to his ancestral connections with the Burgundy region of France. Its premiere, on December 15, 1910, in Blüthner Hall, was the first performance of any work by Varèse and raised a scandal comparable to Stravinsky's later premiere of *The Rite of Spring.* Busoni, though ill, attended the performance and praised the work, as did one or two critics. With this performance, Varèse began to attract serious attention.

During the three years between his arrival in Berlin and the premiere of *Bourgogne,* Varèse had made frequent return visits to Paris and had become a close friend of Debussy, who admired both the younger composer's music and his personal dynamism. At this time Varèse cut a striking figure, tall, exceptionally handsome, muscular and graced with piercing black eyes that could fix people in a disconcertingly intense stare. Varèse and Debussy carried on an extensive correspondence, interspersed with numerous visits, until the latter's death from cancer in 1917. It was Varèse who first brought to Debussy's attention the early works of Schoenberg, which he had acquired and studied in Berlin. Theirs was a relationship founded on mutual respect and a commonality of musical goals, despite the great differences in their personal styles as composers. In addition to Debussy, Varèse was on close terms with Hugo von Hofmannsthal, Romain Rolland and Jean Cocteau, and participated in various projects with each of these writers. Between 1909 and 1913, Varèse composed an opera on Hofmannsthal's *Oedipus and the Sphinx* which, together with most of his extant manuscripts to that time, was destroyed in a fire in the Berlin warehouse in which they were stored during World War I.

Despite his growing reputation in European musical circles, and his having conducted the premiere performance of the suite from Debussy's *The Martyrdom of St. Sebastian* in 1914, Varèse was unable to find enough work to support himself in Europe during the early war years. His wife, Suzanne, had returned to Paris from Berlin in 1913 in order to resume her acting career, and the couple had divorced amicably, leaving their infant daughter, Claude, in the care of an aunt in Berlin. Having nothing to tie him to Europe then, Varèse decided to immigrate to America. He embarked for New York on December 18, 1915.

Varèse had two important friends who saw him through his early days in America. One was the conductor Karl Muck, soon to be driven out of his post at the Boston Symphony in favor of Monteux as a result of anti-German sentiment during the war. The other was the harpist and progressive composer Carlos Salzedo. Muck helped introduce Varèse to the important musicians active in the United States at the time, and Salzedo gave him entree into the circles of avant-garde composers. Varèse wasted no time trying to establish himself in America and was giving interviews to major newspapers within three months of his arrival.

Varèse found it necessary to articulate his esthetic for the American press in a more precise way than had been necessary in Europe, where he was surrounded by musicians more in touch with the various streams of European musical evolution. In particular, he began to re-emphasize the need for new instruments to encompass a vastly wider variety of sounds than those available to traditional ensembles, and to refine his conception of the composer's role in shaping organized sound structures. He publicly rejected the earlier experiments of the Italian futurists for their absence of a controlling intellectual force behind the work (the same reason for which he was later to reject the aleatorists) and resisted the idea that any kind of "system," including Schoenberg's not-yet-fully-defined 12-tone approach to atonality, could substitute for the organizing power of the composer's individual creative intelligence. This was to remain a part of Varèse's credo throughout his life. It rendered him unsympathetic to some, and highly sympathetic to other later experimenters, all of whom looked to him as a father figure. But Varèse did not possess the kind of temperament that could allow him to yield the traditional composer's dictatorial control over the musical outcome to any extra-musical or pre-compositional "process," despite the innovative character of his forms and orchestration. It was also for this reason that, while he was on friendly terms with the group of expatriate Dadaists centered around Marcel Duchamp and Francis Picabia in New York, he never accepted their esthetic principles in his own work.

Varèse first established himself as a freelance conductor in America with such performances as the Berlioz *Requiem,* in New York's mammoth

Hippodrome in 1917, and with concerts of new music. Later in 1917 he met poet and translator Louise McCutcheon Norton, and, shortly thereafter, the two were married. Louise was to become the mainstay of Varèse's life. She saw him through his depressions, supported and collaborated in his work and, like Harmony Ives, displayed an unshakable faith in her husband's genius that was not diminished by long periods of lack of public recognition. Louise Varèse wrote an important and revealing biography of the composer after his death, which is one of the most valuable contributions to our current understanding of Varèse.

In 1921, Varèse and Salzedo founded the International Composers' Guild for the performance of new music. During the next six years, until the organization disbanded, they produced music by Ruggles, Cowell and contemporary European composers such as Schoenberg and Stravinsky. The ICG also provided a forum for the performance of Varèse's own early mature works, including *Offrandes* (1922), *Hyperprism* (1923), *Octandre* (1924) and *Intégrales* (1925). Like Ruggles, Varèse finished only a small number of pieces during his creative lifetime, but the significance of each work more than compensates for this lack of quantity. In the case of both these composers it can truthfully be said that there are no *unimportant* extant compositions, if only for the fact that so few remain to us. In addition to the above-named pieces, Varèse's short catalogue includes *Amériques* (orchestra, 1921), *Arcana* (orchestra, 1927), *Ionisation* (percussion ensemble, 1931), *Ecuatorial* (voices, brass, percussion, keyboards and ondes martinots, 1934), *Density 21.5* (solo flute, 1936), *Etude pour Espace* (chorus, piano, percussion, 1947), *Déserts* (winds, piano, percussion and 2-track tape, 1954) and *Poème électronique* (3-track tape, 1958). In addition to these, there is a song on a poem of Verlaine dating from 1906, a 1955 tape of music for a film about the artist Joan Miró, and the unfinished *Noctournal* for chorus and orchestra on which Varèse was still at work when he died. The bulk of his reputation as a composer rests on this collection of a dozen or so pieces. All his other music is either incomplete or lost (by accident or by design).

Varèse returned to Paris in 1928 and remained there until 1933. During this period, he occupied himself with an abortive attempt to create a theatre piece (entitled *The One-all-alone*) on a text by his wife, Louise. This project later evolved into the unfinished work, *L'astronome*. In a similar vein, he also began work on a massive project that he called *Espace,* but the only finished result of this work was his 1947 *Etude* noted above. Like his mentor Debussy, Varèse always projected more pieces than he could actually complete in a satisfactory way, and, in the case of both composers, much of their later music actually represents sketches, studies or by-products of larger creative efforts that never materialized. But it should not be inferred from this observation that either Debussy or Varèse lacked industry, or didn't know what they were about. Rather, in both cases, these composers were "feeling" their way toward new discoveries and the application of new principles throughout their mature works, and this resulted in a degree of trial and error in their actual composing procedures.

During his Paris sojourn, Varèse also began to see the realization of the kind of collaboration he had called for between composers and (electro) acoustical engineers in his 1916 manifesto. He worked with Jean Bertrand, inventor of the electronic proto-instrument, the "dynaphone," and incorporated parts for Theremin's early synthesizer and the ondes martinot in *Ecuatorial* and *Amériques,* respectively. Upon returning to the United States in 1933, Varèse was commissioned by flutist George Barrère (who had commissioned Griffes' *Poem* in 1919, along with many other progressive works) to create a piece for a platinum flute Barrère was using at the time. The number 21.5 represents the molecular density of platinum, hence the title Varèse chose for his only solo work: *Density 21.5.*

The period of the late 1930s was a frustrating one for Varèse. The Depression had reduced the availability of financial and performance resources needed for extremely avant-garde music or electroacoustic research, and he had difficulty convincing sponsors of the viability of his work. Furthermore, the growing Americanist modernism reflected in the work of Copland and his native-born colleagues during the late 1930s left little room for an outsider (and a foreigner) like Varèse. As a result, Varèse found himself sharing the fate of other composers not in line with the Copland esthetic (including Barber, Hovhaness and, to some extent, Ives, Cowell and Thomson), namely: he was left to fend for himself. Relations with the Copland camp had also not been helped by Cowell and Varèse's frank attempt to establish the Pan American Association's concerts in direct competition with first the Copland-Sessions concerts and later the Yaddo Festival.

As a result of these conditions, Varèse went into a protracted depression, resulting in a period of creative sterility that lasted for fourteen years. With the exception of the *Etude pour Espace,* noted above, he completed nothing between *Density 21.5* in 1936 and his next major work, *Déserts* (1950–1954). He spent the entire decade of the 1940s principally occupied in teaching and lecturing, and was often viewed as a wild-eyed revolutionary whose work had no practical value.

The turning point came when Varèse received an Ampex tape recorder from an anonymous donor in 1953. Working without the institutional support enjoyed by Luening and Ussachevsky at Columbia during the same period, Varèse started collecting sounds (to be used in *Déserts*)

The passionate visionary, **Edgard Varèse** *(1885–1965). His early work with noise sources and electronic music laid the foundation for many 20th-century composers, both in America and Europe.*

and almost singlehandedly began to evolve what came to be generally known as "musique concrète." During the 1930s, composers such as Toch, Hindemith and Honegger had experimented with manipulating noises on the sound tracks of films, but musique concrète as we know it today was initiated (and labeled as such) by Pierre Schaeffer. In 1948, Schaeffer, working at the RTF national radio studios in Paris, produced an *Étude aux chemins de fer* (or "Study of Trains") based on locomotive sounds recorded and manipulated on phonodisc. But, as the technology of recording on magnetic tape began to replace the old-fashioned wire recorders of World War II, the physical material of the tape itself allowed for kinds of manipulation that were not available either to wire, film or phonodisc. Although he did not yet exploit the sophisticated splicing, stretching and echoing techniques common to later musique concrète, five years after Schaeffer's *Étude,* Varèse took Schaeffer's ideas one step farther by imposing a structured montage on the tape segments he prepared as interludes between the instrumental sections of the work. Varèse was not yet equipped to integrate tape techniques directly with the performance of the instrumental portions of *Déserts* (the bulk of which had already been composed by the time he received the recorder), but instead used the prerecorded musique concrète segments as intermezzi, articulating the sectional divisions of the piece.

Déserts, as its title suggests, had been Varèse's response to the wilderness years he experienced during the 1940s and was intended to reflect broadly the total range of geographical and metaphysical images evoked by the word "desert." After its premiere in France on December 2, 1954, it became his best known and most innovative single composition after the percussion "symphony" *Ionisation* of 1931. As usual, it reflected his preoccupation with rhythm, timbral mixing and the spatial aspect of music, as well as his non-developmental, blocklike approach to sound organization based on small, self-contained musical cells. In this latter respect his work is remarkably similar to the early pieces of George Antheil. Both he and Antheil were, of course, influenced by the experiments of the Italian futurists dating from around 1913—although, as previously noted, Varèse emphatically rejected the futurists' uncontrolled approach to the manipulation of sound materials.

Varèse completed only two other major works after *Déserts*. These were his *La procession de Vergès* for the previously mentioned film about Miró, and his epochal *Poème électronique*, composed for the Phillips Pavilion (designed by the architect Le Corbusier) at the 1958 Brussels Exposition. In *Poème électronique*, Varèse extended both the range of source sounds and the degree to which he manipulated them electronically. Moreover, he designed the piece to be played over a variety of loudspeakers deployed throughout Corbusier's building, thus actualizing ideals about the direct spatiality of music that had obsessed him since his early study of the Berlioz *Requiem*. His early exploration of the means by which electronic music can be integrated with spatial design presaged the work of Xenakis and other later composers.

Varèse died in New York City on November 6, 1965, only a month before Henry Cowell's death in Shady, New York (December 10). The loss of these two great musical innovators, just as the United States was entering a period of counterculture, revolutionary violence, political assassination and protracted warfare in Vietnam, represented the completion of the first great era in American experimental music, an era that began with the work of Ives after 1902. In tandem with the factionalism that plagued American society during the 1960s and 1970s, their legacy of controlled, systematic music experimentation soon fragmented into a variety of separate exploratory paths in the work of the next generation of the radical avant-garde. The range of these seemingly diverse, but subtly related schools of thought will be seen in the balance of this chapter and the next one.

Other Experimental Composers (1930–1990)

The primary exponents of American experimental music, after Ives, Ruggles, Cowell and Varèse, were Harry Partch (1901–1974), Conlon Nancarrow (b. 1912), Dane Rudhyar (1895–1985), Lou Harrison (b. 1917), John Cage (1912–1992), Richard Maxfield (1927–1969), Morton Feldman (1926–1987), Earle Brown (b. 1926), Christian Wolff (b. 1934) and Pauline Oliveros (b. 1932). Because Cage, Maxfield, Feldman, Brown, Wolff and Oliveros all played a significant role in the development of aleatoric and later electronic music, discussion of their work will be found in the next chapter. It is to Partch, Nancarrow, Rudhyar and Harrison that we turn our attention now.

Harry Partch represents an extreme example of a fundamental change in society's definition of art music, indeed, of the creative arts themselves, that has begun to emerge in the 20th century. By the very nature of his work, more than through any philosophical manifesto, he challenged several of Western culture's most basic assumptions about what an artist is, what that artist's goals should be in terms of addressing an audience and what role music itself should play in society. His means of raising these questions gave birth to an approach to music that was later extended in other directions by other composers, notably Pauline Oliveros and LaMonte Young.

Partch was born in Oakland, California, on June 24, 1901. Together with Cowell, Cage and Harrison, he is one of the original creators of what is sometimes called the "West Coast School" of modern American classical music. He was basically a self-taught musician and never associated himself with the faculty of any major academic institution, although he did work in a research or resident composer capacity at several schools, especially San Diego State University where, in his final years, he developed his own performing ensemble and housed his unique collection of instruments. He began his musical career as a violist and introduced the first of his many instrumental innovations when he lengthened the fingerboard of his viola to allow for easier performance of microtonal passages.

For the reader unfamiliar with the concept of "microtones," it might be helpful at this point to detour into a brief explanation. The standard diatonic/chromatic scales discussed in Chapter 7 developed in European music during the Middle Ages, Renaissance and Baroque eras, based on what scholars of the time believed to have been the tuning systems of the ancient Greeks. Many instruments of the time, especially brass and woodwinds, were limited by their primitive technology in the number and range of tones they could play, and their tuning was based on the fundamental acoustical properties of the pipes or tubes from which they were constructed. As a result, any given wind instrument could only play in tune over a certain limited range of major, minor or modal keys. The reason why, for example, most Baroque trumpet music is pitched in the key of D major is that the trumpet itself was usually built to play in that key, or in keys closely related to it on the circle of fifths. String and keyboard instruments were similarly limited by the corresponding tuning theories of the time.

In the late 17th century, instrument builders and musicians began to demand more, and improvements were made to broaden the chromatic range of most wind and keyboard instruments. A system of tuning was devised for keyboard instruments that divided the acoustically pure octave into twelve equidistant "half-steps" or "semitones." Each semitone was rendered approximately equal to every other semitone in terms of its vibration ratio. As a result, the so-called perfect consonances (such as the perfect 5th and the perfect 4th) defined by Pythagoras, were no longer quite "perfectly" in tune by acoustical standards. But, this minor disadvantage (inaudible to most listeners) was offset by a tremendous compensating advantage, namely: most instruments could now be built and tuned to play equally well in any of the twelve major or twelve minor keys, and could move freely from one to another. It was this newfound advantage, dubbed "equal temperament" that J. S. Bach was demonstrating in his *Well-Tempered Clavier.* The ability to change key at will gave rise to the harmonic technique called "modulation." Harmonic modulation became a powerful tool in the musical arsenal of mid-18th-century composers and evolved into the principal musical foundation of sonata form, which then replaced the Baroque fugue as the pre-eminent formal vehicle for serious composition.

But the human ear is actually capable of discriminating between far more subtle differences of pitch than those represented in the equal-tempered half-steps of the chromatic scale. It is entirely possible to hear quarter-tones (which lie midway between the notes of a semitone), or sixth tones, or third-tones and so on. These intervals smaller than a semitone are referred to generically as "microtones." Many non-Western musical systems have made extensive use of microtones in their tuning systems for centuries, which is one reason why Western instruments can only give an approximation of the actual tonality of such instruments as the Indian sitar or Indonesian gamelan instruments. The interest in non-Western musics which began to grow in the United States after the work of Eichheim, Griffes (see Chapter 4) and the Canadian Colin McPhee, dovetailed with a corresponding interest in the exploration of microtones that emerged from the more experimental work of Ives, Cowell and others.

The problem for composers such as Ives and Cowell, who were interested in exploring microtones, was that the instruments available to them, with the possible exception of strings and trombones, were inherently unsuited by their design for microtonal tunings. Ives found an ingenious, if only partial solution to this problem by having two pianos tuned a quarter-tone apart from each other, then placing them at right angles so the performer could play with one hand on each keyboard. Later composers exploited the ability to program electronic synthesizers to play microtones. But, even when the problems associated with instrument design were overcome, or sidestepped, there still remained the problem of performers who were trained to hear in terms of semitones. This problem was particularly acute for instrumentalists (especially string players) possessing so-called "perfect pitch" or a highly developed sense of "relative pitch," that is, the ability to identify any note by its letter name merely by listening to it, even without reference to any other note. Such performers, because of their training, tended to hear microtones as if they were merely conventional notes played "out of tune." For them to cope with microtonal music required a complete reorientation of their listening and aural monitoring reflexes. And if the problem was acute for performers, one need only imagine how difficult it was for untrained audiences to grasp the *intent* of microtonal music.

Partch began to grapple with these issues very early in his career and adopted the radical solution of building his own instruments, devising his own notation and training his own performers to perform the music he wrote for them. In addition to the theoretical and performance practices of a huge variety of non-Western music and theatre traditions, he studied carpentry and acoustics. Among the many instruments he designed and built were microtonal reed organs that he christened "Chromelodeons," fantastically complex microtonal harps named after the ancient Greek "Kithara," and a family of marimbas that extended both the pitch range and tuning sensitivity of the standard marimba prototype. He also created a large number of idiophones[47] to extend the timbral range of percussion instruments. Among these are his "Cloud Chamber Bowls" made from unseamed, oversize glass bottles suspended from a wooden framework, and his "Spoils of War," made from precisely cut, tuned and polished artillery shell casings similarly suspended.

Moreover, Partch was not merely concerned with the new sounds he could create with these instruments, but also with their visual appearance.

---

[47]   An idiophone is any instrument, such as a triangle, gong, cymbal or woodblock, carved or molded into a single, resonating object.

Harry Partch *(1901–1974). An independent and iconoclastic composer who built his own instruments, devised his own scales and evolved a unique kind of performance art.* (Photo by Malcom Lubliner, courtesy of BMI.)

Throughout history, instrument builders have striven to integrate form and function in their designs, succeeding to the degree that traditional instruments such as the violin or the bassoon are as interesting as objets d'art as they are for their musical capacities. Partch was no exception. He devoted great care and skill to the sculptural design and ornamentation of all his instruments, which enabled him to use them onstage as part of a visually fascinating performance set.

The theatrical elements in Partch's work stemmed both from his innate sense of biting social criticism—he spent much of the Depression riding the rails throughout America with a host of other "hobos"—and from his study of the classical music drama of East Asian cultures. He possessed an acerbic wit that permeates most of the texts he wrote for his ensemble pieces and was a master of parody, irony, satire and other rhetorical devices.

The music and music theatre pieces that Partch composed from 1932 onward have a sound unlike anything else in the literature of Western music. Unlike—for example—Elliott Carter, who gradually freed himself from "received" tonal, rhythmic and melodic practices while continuing to work in traditional forms with traditional instruments, Partch divorced himself from the entire context of Western music before the age of thirty-five and literally created a music culture of his own. As a result, many listeners have found it necessary to make a study of Partch's ideas and procedures before being able to comprehend, if not to enjoy, his work. In addition, the extraordinary nature of his instruments, of the acoustical principles embodied in their design and of the music he wrote for them, makes it almost impossible to get any comprehensive idea of what Partch was about merely from recordings, no matter how sophisticated the sound-reproduction technology. If there ever was a kind of music that only displays its full range of effect in live performance, that music is the music of Harry Partch.

It is in this last point that Partch's fundamental departure from the assumptions of Western art resides. Partch's music can only be performed on the instruments he himself created, and only by performers trained in the unique skills required to manipulate those instruments. Moreover, no one outside of Partch's immediate circle of disciples has written any other significant music for those instruments, nor have the instruments been reproduced or manufactured for distribution beyond San Diego, where they are housed. In short, Partch's work is unique to himself and his locale. It cannot effectively approach the listener; the listener must approach it. This is a position without precedent in Western music history of the past several centuries. And yet Partch was no mere local crank, tucked away in some obscure corner of the world, doing his own "thing." His is a major voice and a major influence in the American experimental music tradition, one that must be understood by anyone who seeks to gain a complete perspective on that tradition.

The implications of Partch's approach to music challenge a number of "givens" in the way composers see themselves and their work. For one thing, the Occidental cult of personality that has characterized the ambitions of all major composers since Beethoven is negated by a kind of music which cannot be notated or published in the traditional manner, replayed by standard ensembles or standard instruments, or understood by reference to any established style. Partch was indeed the center of his own musical universe, surrounded by a small corps of dedicated disciples, but in this he was more akin to an Eastern guru than a modern composer seeking to establish an international reputation. Furthermore, the idea of standardized music education, involving absorption of a common set of practices and procedures broadly accepted by all composers of a given epoch is rendered irrelevant by Partch's approach. If every composer were to adopt Partch's fundamentally independent manner of evolving his own musical language, all music education would ultimately have to be a matter of private study with individual masters. In both these respects, the underlying ideology of

Partch's example relates more to an Asian or pre-Medieval European concept of what an artist is and what his relationship to his pupils is, than to our modern systems of cultural education. Similarly, the conception of music as being created for individual performers, with unique skills (and sometimes uniquely modified instruments), music not admitting of performance by others—an idea that was further developed in the works of Oliveros—implies a view of music as an individualized art, painstakingly crafted for a specific, nonreproduceable set of circumstances. This idea stands in diametric opposition to the ambitions of artists who seek the broadest possible exposure or who go in search of a mass market audience.

In the late 20th century, when mass electronic media have given birth to a worldwide popular culture that is often viewed as representing the lowest common denominator of human greed, selfishness, ignorance and indifference to the spiritual values embodied in the humanities, Harry Partch's model for the societal role of the creative artist may yet prove to be prophetic. As will be demonstrated before the conclusion of this history, the contemporary period of American classical music is characterized by an unprecedentedly large number of obscure composers, competing for an ever-shrinking pool of performance resources and audiences. It may be that Partch and his ideological successors point the way for future generations of composers by abandoning the quest for an illusive and irrelevant personal fame, whether in the public arena or the academic establishment, in favor of many isolated, localized, independent and unique ways of conceiving and practicing musical art. It may even come to pass that generations one or two centuries hence will view the history of our present era as a "tradition" (whose coherence escapes us at present) comprised of the collective product of many such individual iconoclasts.

Only somewhat less radical than Partch in his departure from received traditions, is **Conlon Nancarrow.** Born in Texarkana, Arkansas, on October 27, 1912, Nancarrow played both jazz and classical trumpet as a young man and studied first at the Cincinnati College-Conservatory, then later in Boston with Slonimsky, Piston and Sessions. Like many composers of his generation, Nancarrow was a political leftist whose exercise of his constitutional right to hold and express dissenting views provoked harassment from the federal government during the 1930s. As a result, he immigrated to Mexico in 1940 where he has lived since, apart from a few brief visits to the United States.

Although Nancarrow composed music for chamber ensemble, piano and orchestra between 1930 and 1945, after World War II he began to work exclusively with music for player piano. Nancarrow had always been interested in the rhythmic dimension of music and found it impossible to get live performers to execute his increasingly complex rhythmic counterpoint. He found that programming a player piano by punching holes on the paper roll that controls its mechanism gave him virtually unlimited freedom to explore multiple levels of rhythmic complexity. In 1947 he commissioned the building of a machine that enabled him to punch the paper directly by hand, rather than using the conventional roll-recording piano keyboard.

From 1945 to the mid-1980s, Nancarrow devoted himself to exploring the possibilities created by this means of composing. He studied and absorbed Cowell's ideas relating to rhythm and pitch found in *New Musical Resources,* and adopted procedures for partitioning tempos and pitch sets among different voices and registers of the piano analogous to the work of Babbitt and Carter. But Nancarrow's rhythmic counterpoint, freed from the limitations of live performers, achieved a degree of complexity that exceeds anything found in the work of these composers, and did so without resorting to electronics. His music is structured largely in canonic form, with several lines of activity imitating or duplicating each other at different pitch levels and in differing rhythmic ratios, and his early training in jazz is reflected in the rhythmic vitality of his root ideas. Moreover, he also used graphic, geometric and mathematical procedures to plot some of his scores, which anticipated the later work of Xenakis (especially the latter's *Metastasis* [1955]).

Nancarrow achieved a sound that, like Partch, is absolutely unique to himself. Unlike Partch, however, Nancarrow's ideas are theoretically duplicatable and extendable by other composers (given the availability of the necessary equipment). In the mid-1980s, Nancarrow finally achieved a measure of recognition from the world of serious music. He returned to the composition of pieces for other instrumental combinations and has made numerous visits to the United States for performances of his work. But it is impossible to determine at this point what influence he may yet have on younger generations of composers.

A third independent figure in the roster of American experimentalists is **Dane Rudhyar.** Rudhyar was born Daniel Chennevière in Paris on March 23, 1895 and died in San Francisco on September 13, 1985. During his youth he studied at the Sorbonne and Conservatoire in Paris, immigrating to the United States (like Varèse) in 1916. Shortly thereafter he moved to California, which became his base of activities for the rest of his life.

Rudhyar was involved with Cowell's work very early, assuming leadership of the California branch of Cowell's New Music Society and serving as a member of the International Composers' Guild. But his interests extended beyond the musical sphere. He became a devotee of the mystical school known as Theosophy, which had been founded by the Russian mystic, Helena Blavatsky, and incorporated elements of Hindu theology with the European spiritualism of the late 19th century. He adopted his pseudonym, Rudhyar, as a result of these studies.

Rudhyar was also an astrologer and devoted much of his energy between 1930 and 1970 to this and other Hermetic researches. Where his countryman, Varèse, had had only a superficial, if important, interest in Hermetic philosophers such as Paracelsus, Rudhyar pursued the mystical path to a much greater degree.

In 1970 he returned to composing in a serious way and produced a large number of works during the remaining years of his life, primarily for solo piano and for orchestra, which transmuted the early influences of Scriabin and Varèse into an integrated, coherent stylistic language. His ideas tend to proceed by "fits and starts," but avoid percussive effects. Most of his late work is characterized by contemplative melody (clearly influenced by his love for Asian music) over a richly evocative tonal ground of slowly changing chords.

Rudhyar was not a radical musical innovator, but his work combined elements of non-Western music and 20th-century music experiment in unique ways. As a result of his parallel musical and metaphysical studies, he has become a significant influence on the school of contemporary commercial composition known as "New Age Music."

Similar in some respects to Rudhyar's is the highly influential life and musical thinking of **Lou Harrison.** Though born in Portland, Oregon, on May 14, 1917, Harrison has lived most of his life in northern California, and is the pre-eminent living figure of the so-called "West Coast School." Harrison studied with Cowell in San Francisco during the mid-1930s and later with Schoenberg at UCLA. Around this time he became acquainted with John Cage and formed a professional and personal friendship that would link these two very different composers until the latter's death in 1992.

At the time of their first acquaintance, Cage was involved in a brief marriage to his wife, Xenia. Though both Harrison and Cage were homosexual, Harrison eventually came out of the closet and devoted significant energy to public support of the gay rights movement in the 1970s. In contrast, after his divorce from Xenia, any reference to Cage's personal life and homosexuality was carefully excluded from all his interviews and public documents—remaining known only to his circle of friends and collaborators. (Cage would later develop a lifelong primary relationship with his choreographer/collaborator, Merce Cunningham.) Harrison and Cage worked closely together during the 1930s and 1940s and shared an obvious affinity of interests in experimental music, Asian culture and personal lifestyle. They staged many concerts together in California and New York, taught at many of the same institutions, notably Black Mountain College, and both became closely acquainted with Cowell and, later, Virgil Thomson. Neither of them was in a position to offer Cowell any significant assistance during the period of his trial and imprisonment (1936–1940).

But, where Cage went on to pursue an uncompromising commitment to the philosophical view of music he developed, Harrison remained eclectic throughout his career, maintaining a diverse array of activities and compositional styles. His music runs the gamut from Thomsonesque Americanism, to serial works in sonata form, to indeterminate experimental pieces, to a later intense involvement with Asian music. Possessed of a high-strung, sensitive nature, Harrison found himself unable to live and work in the environment of New York and suffered a nervous breakdown after a period of intense activity there in the 1940s. During that period he wrote reviews for many significant publications, helped organize the manuscripts of Charles Ives and conducted the first complete performance of

A recent portrait of **Lou Harrison** *(b. 1917). An early colleague of Cage, his music has sampled an enormous range of styles and ideas.* (Photo by David Harsany, courtesy of C. F. Peters Corp.)

Ives' *Third Symphony* in 1947, which netted Ives his Pulitzer Prize later that year.

Harrison also developed a passion for the internationalist ideal represented by the creation of the phonetic, pan-national language, Esperanto. He mastered this language himself and composed many works using it as the textual language of the piece, including his 1955 *Four Strict Songs* for voice and orchestra.

In 1962, Harrison traveled to the Far East on a Rockefeller Grant, studying Korean court music with Lee Hye-Ku and Chinese classical music with Liang Tsai-Ping. This marked the beginning of his obsessive interest in Asian classical music that would lead him, by 1985, to adopt a radical posture which viewed the Pacific Rim as the pre-eminent domain of world culture. Much of his later work is based on Asian musical concepts, just intonation, the integration of non-Western instruments into Western ensembles and the physical construction of Western duplicates of various Asian instruments. Thus, his work combines elements of all the major branches of American experimental music, from Ives through Partch. Just as Elliott Carter today occupies the position of the surviving "grand old man" of the mid-century American modernist esthetic, Harrison is the surviving master of the entire range of our experimental traditions.

Throughout the 20th century, American classical music pursued at least three parallel lines of development. The most conspicuous of these was the Americanist modernism stimulated by Gershwin and Ives, and developed in the music of Copland and his generation. A second stream was the academic modernism founded by Sessions that led to the domination of academic serialism in the work of his and others' students. The third, experimental stream of American musical thought, also rooted in the work of Ives, as well as that of Ruggles, Cowell and Varèse, received much less attention from either the public or the academic establishment. Certain conventional modernists, such as Lukas Foss, became enamored of it in the mid-1950s, but, on the whole, the experimental school was treated with indifference or outright contempt by more established composers, performers, patrons and audiences. It was not until 1960 that the experimental tradition evolved into a serious challenge to our complacent thinking about modern music, a challenge so cogent in its form and so profound in its implications that American composers were forced either to confront it head-on or to hide from it altogether. This challenge emerged from the work and ideas of John Cage.

11

John Cage and the Aleatoric Revolution

≥∿

The end of World War II gave rise to an unprecedented period of prosperity in the United States, accompanied by a paranoid obsession with Communism, especially after the development of the hydrogen bomb. The far-reaching consequences of the early post-war period profoundly transformed every aspect of American life, including its music.

Most of the old super-wealthy arts patrons had been swept away by the Great Depression, and the newly emerging potentates of multinational commerce had not yet acquired a sense of their role in supporting the fine arts. The infant technology of television would lead to increasing sponsorship by corporate entities of "cultural" programming for the masses during the 1950s and early 1960s, but it took some time for corporate sponsorship to gear up—and it has never yet fully replaced the loss of the old-style private patrons in its ability to generate new works.

With the wholesale construction of single-family housing developments, the unprecedented availability of higher education via scholarship programs and the GI Bill and the growth of a burgeoning consumer economy, the United States transformed itself after the war from a society that was predominantly either urban or rural, to a society that was predominantly *suburban*. The extended family living group of the 19th and early 20th centuries gave way to the mid-century concept of the "nuclear" family.

As the two pre-eminent "classical" composers living in the United States, Stravinsky and Copland, both turned toward 12-tone composition following the death of Schoenberg in 1951, new music became a much less public art than it had been before the war. Classical music broadcasts on radio and television became increasingly centered on the repertoire of dead

European masters. Serious composers, unable to make a living in the outside world, gravitated more and more toward the narrow confines of academia. Those interested in the exploration of electroacoustic music, such as Otto Luening and Lejaren Hiller, were virtually forced into academic partnerships, due to the enormous cost and technical requirements of acquiring and maintaining the necessary equipment.

Popular culture exploded during this period. The advertising media fostered a conformist consciousness among the public based on automobiles, household appliances, cosmetics, cigarettes and sex. Increasingly, the intellectual and artistic life of America became narrower and duller, aided by McCarthyist paranoia on one hand, and the economic complacency of the Eisenhower era on the other.

As for academia itself, the last hoped-for refuge of the serious musical artist, colleges and universities in the 1950s grew ever more closely intertwined with the military-industrial-educational complex, as evidenced by the growth of ROTC programs, expanding corporate recruitment on college campuses and joint research ventures by the military, private industry and university science departments. By the early 1960s the president of the University of California, Clark Kerr, was openly defining his institution as a kind of factory, a leader of the burgeoning "knowledge industry."

Above all, Americans seemed to care less and less with each passing year about the latest ideas and works of their greatest literary, musical and visual artists. The ephemera of electronic media culture began to displace serious artistic efforts, and those composers who chose to remain aloof from the university or conservatory found themselves concentrated in tiny urban enclaves, principally in New York City. While composers such as Leonard Bernstein, Norman Dello Joio, Elliott Carter, Lukas Foss, Gian-Carlo Menotti and others managed to continue working in this new social environment, even on occasion making use of the new media to disseminate their work, many others began to chafe against the spiritual and intellectual repression of the era.

In the mid-1930s a young man from Los Angeles named John Cage enrolled in Schoenberg's theory course at UCLA. Prior to this, Cage had already developed an interest in musical experiment and Asian philosophy and art, but his experiences with Schoenberg focused Cage's thinking about music and sowed the seeds of a revolution that would prove to be the antithesis of the total control advocated by more conventional disciples of the Schoenberg/Webern axis such as Milton Babbitt.

Like many California intellectuals, including Harry Partch, Henry Cowell and Lou Harrison, Cage was always an unconventional thinker. He was born in Los Angeles on September 5, 1912, and was from the very earliest a brilliant, endlessly inquisitive student of life, nature and the arts.

His father, not unlike George Ives in many respects, was a social iconoclast and inventor who nurtured an inquiring spirit in his son. Cage graduated from Los Angeles High School in 1928 with the highest academic record in the school's history up to that time.

He began his compositional work in earnest in the 1930s. After two years at the progressive Pomona College (now part of the Claremont Colleges east of Los Angeles), he traveled in Europe and became connected with the ongoing work of the Dadaists and Marcel Duchamp, as well as John Kirkpatrick's Parisian performances of avant-garde American music. After returning to the United States, Cage sought out the progressive pianist Richard Buhlig, an early exponent of Schoenberg in America, and took some lessons with him in 1933. These gave him his first systematic exposure to the still-new technique of serialism and resulted in the composition of Cage's first published work, the serial *Sonata for Clarinet* (1933). Buhlig encouraged Cage to send this piece to Henry Cowell. Further encouraged by Cowell's favorable reaction, Cage traveled to New York the following year to study with him at the New School for Social Research. Cage's early works from the 1930s explored unconventional applications of the serial technique and extended the principle to rhythm as well as pitch relationships. However, unlike Milton Babbitt, who would apply serialism to rhythm fifteen years later by serializing the *durations* of tones and the time intervals between attacks, Cage—influenced by his encounter with Varèse's *Ionisation* (1931) at a Hollywood Bowl performance of that work in the summer of 1933—deployed small rhythmic cells in serialized patterns of repetition to form a rhythmic counterpoint. Cage's principal compositions from the early 1930s, in addition to the clarinet sonata, include *Three Stein Songs* (before 1933), the *Sonata for Two Voices,* the *Composition for Three Voices* and the fantastically-titled *Solo with Obbligato Accompaniment of Two Voices in Canon, and Six Short Inventions on the Subjects of the Solo.* His specific application of serial ideas to percussion is most vividly revealed in the starkly contrasting *Quartet* for unspecified percussion instruments (1935) and the precisely notated *Trio* for percussion (1936). Both Varèse and Cowell were to become profound formative influences on Cage's musical thinking, and he would continue to develop ideas expressed or implied in their work throughout his life. The first evidence of this is in Cage's 1937 lecture, "The Future of Music," in which he articulated his fundamental belief (derived from Varèse and even harking back to the Italian futurists) that *any* sound is legitimate material for music.

In 1935, having already explored many unconventional applications of serialism, Cage began studies with Schoenberg himself in Los Angeles. The Viennese master was attracted by Cage's extraordinary intellectual facility in music, his ability to quickly realize all possible conventional harmonizations of a given chorale or to abstract the permutations of a 12-tone row in his head. Cage, in turn, was powerfully impressed by Schoenberg's uncompromising dedication to his work and the seemingly unrealistic demands he made upon his students to extend their thinking beyond the ordinary reflexes of received traditions. Cage worked with Schoenberg for two years, finally moving to Seattle in 1937 where he became increasingly involved in collaborating with choreographers. It was during this period that he met his lifelong companion and professional collaborator, Merce Cunningham.

Cage's music from the late 1930s began to reflect a deep sensitivity to Asian concepts of rhythm as well as linearity and transparency of texture. Other composers have, of course, achieved transparent, linear textures in serial music, but more often as a by-product of their compositional objective in a given piece. Cage's early music was distinguished by a clear Asian influence, possibly acquired during his California upbringing as a result of the vigorous Asian cultural presence in that state. Perhaps the most obvious example of this influence was Cage's early and lifelong insistence that each sound is a complete event, in and of itself, without any necessary correlation to sounds that precede it or sounds that follow it. MacDowell had noted this as a feature of Chinese music as early as his Columbia lecture on "Suggestion in Music" (ca. 1896). The composer Chou Wen-chung has pointed out as well that this is a very ancient premise of Chinese music, and the connection between this point of view and Cage's later extensive use of both the philosophy and divinatory methods of the Taoist scripture *I Ching* in his composition is unlikely to be an accident or coincidence. This denial of the inherent psychological relationship between sounds (or, if you prefer, Cage's insistence that all such relationships are imposed by the cognition of the listener) is at once a logical extension of Schoenberg's treatment of the twelve chromatic tones and a basis of all Cage's subsequent discoveries and theories.

Understanding Cage's music, and the theoretical ideas he developed after 1948, requires an understanding of the ways in which Asian philosophies and world views differ from those of the West, because this Asian sensibility permeates all periods of Cage's later composition. Without such understanding, performing or listening to Cage's work can be a confusing and frustrating experience.

Perhaps the most important aspect of this issue is the different view of the ego held in most East Asian cultures. China, India, Japan, Indonesia and Southeast Asia are all very ancient cultures that have sustained enormous populations for centuries, sometimes in very limited geographic areas. Moreover, they have been the parent cultures of Hindu, Buddhist and Taoist teaching, all of which de-emphasize the importance of individual desires, cravings and ambitions in a material universe that is thought to be an illusion in the mind of God. In part, this de-emphasis on individuality and the personal ego has been a sociological necessity brought about by overcrowding of populations; in part it is a deliberately adopted philosophical view. But, in either case, it is directly antithetical to the Western concept of individual rights, freedom and expression, of Western personal ambition and cult of the individual.

Nowhere is the Western cult of the individual more obvious than in European classical music. After 1800 the personality of the individual composer became an artistic issue as it had never been before. Beethoven in particular fostered this attitude, and individual expression at any price was the cornerstone of the whole Romantic movement of the 19th century. Not only composers, but performers as well, carefully nurtured their public images and still do. It has been noted by some critics, such as Harold Schonberg, that the personalities of performers such as Liszt, Paderewski, dePachman, Paganini, and Anton Rubinstein were as important an element in their public success as was their actual music-making. And this is self-evidently true of multitudes of popular music performers today as well. By contrast, the Asian artist is much closer in spirit to those hundreds of anonymous monks and troubadours who dominated European music in the Middle Ages, caring more for the quality of their work than for the personal fame or future immortality it might bring them.

If a group of performers approaches the kind of piece Cage later developed—such as *Cartridge Music* for instance, which consists of nothing more than scratching the needles of phonograph cartridges over a variety of objects according to a variable set of graphic patterns—with the Western idea of giving vent to one's individual creativity, to "showing off" in other words, the piece quickly becomes an horrendous cacophony of high decibel noises that invariably alienate its audience. If, on the other hand, the ensemble adopts a cooperative, interactive mode of performance in which the players exercise their most sensitive judgment in determining when and what to play, *Cartridge Music* can become a fascinating vehicle of acoustic contrasts and insights. This latter approach often feels alien and uncomfortable to Western-trained musicians, unless they have a strong chamber music background, but it is as essential a prerequisite to a good performance of Cage as practicing scales is to a good performance of Mozart.

In the late 1940s Cage and Cunningham migrated east and began a series of teaching engagements and concerts throughout New York state. During this time Cage developed what he called the "prepared" piano, in which a variety of materials are inserted at nodal points between the piano strings in order to alter the sound of the instrument. The effects produced by the prepared piano vary from high, clear harmonics to metallic twangs to percussive thumps not unlike African pitched drums or Indonesian gamelan instruments. Many people have been so horrified at the idea of inserting furniture bolts or rubber erasers between the strings of a Steinway concert grand, that they have dismissed the resultant music out of hand, often before they have even heard it. In fact, Cage's prepared piano produced a plethora of marvelously subtle effects and his principal work for this instrument, the seventy-minute *Sonatas and Interludes* (1948), exploited those effects with great delicacy and finesse. *Sonatas and Interludes* followed a period of study of Hindustani and Indonesian music on Cage's part, and its distinctly East Asian flavor reflects that as well. The prepared piano is, in fact, probably the closest equivalent to the Indonesian gamelan orchestra that can be achieved with a Western instrument.

In 1951 Cage experienced an anechoic chamber at Harvard University. An anechoic chamber is a room rendered as silent as technologically possible. Inside the chamber, Cage heard only the sounds of his own blood

The irrepressible **John Cage** *(1912–1992), father of the 1960s avant-garde. The musical world has not yet fully dealt with the implications of his ideas.* (Photo by Susan Schwartzenberg, The Exploratorium, 1987. Courtesy of C. F. Peters Corp.)

circulating and of his nervous system firing millions of bio-electric signals. He realized that, even in such an environment, there is no such thing as absolute silence but only relative degrees of noiselessness that approach a purely theoretical concept of absolute silence. The ramifications of this realization for Cage's subsequent work were profound. It became clear to him then that listening to music, as traditionally defined, is entirely a matter of selecting certain acoustical events to which one attends, and attempting to ignore others. Thus, in a concert hall, one tries to listen only to the music, while ignoring the sounds of the air conditioner or heating system, audience coughing and shuffling, traffic outside, the 60-cycle hum of electrical fixtures and other ambient sounds. Over time Cage began to view this selective listening as symptomatic of the narrow, smug view of life so prevalent in America during the 1950s. He reacted against the assumption that a definition of reality based on such selective perceptions is, in fact, a total or satisfactory description of the reality of any given moment, in life or in music. He surmised that a large part of the traditional European idea of separation between the experience we term "art" and the experience we term "life" was due to such unconscious, selective perception. And he concluded that our proneness to believe in the literal reality of such selective perceptual categories was a major contributor to the stultifying and repressive cultural conditions that prevailed at the time.

In 1952 Cage created a piece he called *4'33"* (*Four Minutes, Thirty-Three Seconds*). Although usually performed by a pianist, the piece is actually played upon a socio-musical situation, and can be done with any instrument or combination. In *4'33"* the player simply comes out onto the stage, as if about to perform something, and sits at or stands with his/her instrument for various specified time segments, usually indicated by opening or closing the piano key cover, for the total duration indicated by the title. Audiences at first had no idea what to make of such a piece. Cage's intention was that, sooner or later, they would have no choice but to hear the ambient sounds around them. His supposition was that, by focusing their attention on expected music which never actually materializes, they would spontaneously become aware of the myriad subtle environmental sounds present at any moment, and that hopefully this would lead to an awakening of their awareness of the ongoing dynamic complexity of life at every moment: living in the "now" as a child of the '60s might express it.

Whether or not *4'33"* works depends upon a great many factors beyond the control of the composer or the performer. In fact, the audience plays a serious role in determining its own reaction, as there is virtually nothing given in the situation for them to react to other than their own attitudes and assumptions. This understanding of the important role played by the audience itself in any musical event led to Cage's principal theoretical contribution to modern music, a concept he termed "indeterminacy."

Certain indeterminate elements are, of course, present in any musical performance. The acoustical conditions of the hall, the individual interpretation of the performer, the quality of the instruments, the sensitivity of the listeners' hearing, the presence or absence of memory lapses or other errors in the performance—all these are elements that vary widely from performance to performance of even the most precisely notated traditional piece of music. When we consider improvised music, the range of variables expands enormously. But, even in the case of improvisation, there is generally still a controlling musical intelligence—either the composer of the initial subject or the performer, or both—which largely determines the outcome. John Cage extended this idea of indeterminacy to include the composer as well, and *that* was an innovation that was too radical even for many of the most progressive composers of the day.

Basically, Cage's theory of indeterminacy works like this: it assumes that any individual composer's personal taste, technique or intention is not necessarily any better or worse than that of any other person (including performers and listeners). Therefore, it becomes "politically undesirable" (in Cage's terminology) that a single individual, such as the composer, should dictate on the one hand what the musicians should or should not play, and what the audience on the other hand may or may not hear. This is a degree of control that none of us would accept in our daily lives. Why, therefore, Cage argued, should we be asked to accept it in music? To the obvious answer, namely: that the "great composers" were far more creative, musically knowledgeable and inspired than the rest of us, Cage replied, "Nonsense," citing the fact that even the greatest composers were mere human beings like you and me. And he extended the argument to claim that what one human being can do, any other human being can probably do as well with some effort and practice. If one accepts the validity of these arguments, the question then arises: what is the appropriate role for one who wishes to compose music, but has no desire to be a dictator?

"Indeterminacy," sometimes called "aleatoric" composition, is Cage's personal answer to that question. The vast majority of his compositions after 1951 were devoted to demonstrating ways and means by which a composer can invent performance paradigms that not only allow, but actually require the performer and listener to participate in creating the resulting musical perception.

Many writers on Cage and his movement, and many composers who sought to imitate him, concentrated on the specific means used by Cage to construct his performance designs. Principal among these techniques was the tossing of coins as part of the Taoist divination ritual that uses the *I*

Ching. The *I Ching,* or "Book of Changes" uses eight graphic trigrams, formed from patterns of three broken and/or unbroken lines, to generate sixty-four possible hexagrams, each of which is associated with a metaphorical description used to give insight into the conditions of everyday life. This unique approach to philosophy and divination appealed at once to Cage's affinity for Asian mysticism and the precociously mathematical bent of his thinking. Among his other radically new "notational" devices were the random superimposition of transparent plastic sheets, each of which contains some markings, to create an aggregate performance diagram; and the selection of random imperfections woven into the paper on which the music is written as part of the notational symbols. The point that is missed in focusing on the these and other Cagean techniques is that the techniques themselves were merely means to an end, that end being the esthetic liberation of all participants in the music-making process. It is possible to take any of Cage's notational devices and use them in such a way that the resultant piece is as totally predetermined as any conventional sonata or string quartet. This of course frustrates the whole philosophical purpose behind Cage's approach.

The use of such "chance" operators was Cage's way of forcing his own preconceptions out of the way of the creative process. Composers throughout history have experienced similar needs to free themselves from old habits, unchallenged assumptions and the technical conventions of received tradition that threaten to rob new music of its spontaneity and originality. This is partly what Schoenberg was doing when he developed the 12-tone method and imposed it on himself; it is partly what Ives was doing when he turned to the collagistic quotation of folk material as a creative resource; it is partly what Haydn did in the 1760s when he deliberately purged his style of its residual Baroque mannerisms. Thus, the *nature* of Cage's approach to solving his creative dilemma was no different than that of earlier composers. The difference lay in the *degree* to which Cage permitted processes outside of his own intuition to control the resulting work. As with any composer, certain of Cage's pieces are more effective than others. But, in the case of aleatoric music, effectiveness is not judged by the beauty or emotional colors of the finished music. It is judged by whether the piece or performance design "works" in the sense of making it possible for performers and listeners to achieve the social, philosophical and musical experience Cage hoped to give them: an experience generated within themselves with the aid of the performance vehicle, not an experience forced on them by the expressive moods of the composer.

Because a great many audiences reacted negatively to Cage's work, many have assumed that his effort was a failure. Today the attitude of most general audiences who have experienced a Cage piece from the 1950s or later is that he was a wild-eyed revolutionary clown, a flash in the pan of music history that is now, mercifully, behind us. But it is also clear that most of Cage's audiences in the mid-1960s and 1970s, even among musicians, had at best a very poor understanding of what Cage was trying to do. It may be a flaw in his work that it did not communicate its esthetic premises more clearly, but that was certainly not for lack of effort on Cage's part. In addition to the lectures he gave regularly throughout the world during his lifetime, the two major collections of Cage's writing and thinking on these subjects were his books, *Silence* (1961) and *A Year From Monday* (1967), the first of which became a major influence on Philip Glass and other composers of the minimalist school (see Chapter 13). It is entirely possible that the full significance of Cage's ideas and experiments has not yet been felt, that he has been passed over by musical fashion and must await the time when a deeper understanding of all the ramifications of indeterminacy emerges from the work of other composers.

Because John Cage achieved greater public recognition as a composer than any other figure of the 1960s, he was envied and imitated by a great many musicians. However, very few of these displayed much understanding of Cage's real purpose, and many used their imitations as part of a perfectly conventional attempt to promote their own careers. An additional reason that indeterminate music fell into disrepute in the 1970s, apart from the difficulty of getting audiences to grasp what was going on, was the avalanche of imitators who cleverly used the theoretical jargon of aleatory and superficially Cagean compositional techniques to disguise their insistence on maintaining absolute creative control over every aspect of the final piece.

Among the composers who seem to have genuinely understood and been in sympathy with Cage's ideas were Christian Wolff (b. 1934), Morton Feldman (1926–1987) and Earle Brown (b. 1926). Of the three, Wolff and Brown were probably closest to Cage in temperament and intentions. Wolff, the prodigy of the group, began to achieve recognition at the tender age of eighteen. His early pieces focused especially on the interactive element between the players, as did Cage himself. Since 1970, the Dartmouth-based Wolff, who, like Elliott Carter, is also an outstanding scholar of classic literature and languages, has turned more toward pieces that he hopes will communicate with a broader audience, and especially pieces with an overtly political message. Brown, in turn, focused much of his compositional attention on exploring indeterminate works with graphic notation, often producing pieces whose scores are more interesting as visual art than as performable sound structures.

Morton Feldman has become the most influential of Cage's immediate circle, and his work has received renewed attention since his untimely

Morton Feldman *(1926–1987). An unreconstructed modernist, he combined the influences of Cage, Webern and others into a passionately quiescent style and remains one of the most original figures in American music.* (Photo courtesy of C.F. Peters Corp.)

death in 1987. Feldman remained much more closely allied with the modernist tradition of Anton Webern and with real or hypothetical analogies between music and the literary and visual arts. He was also unable to commit himself fully to the uncompromising loss of composer control implied by Cage's thinking, and this became a major stimulus to creative exploration for most of his career. Like Brown, Feldman worked extensively with graphic notation in the early 1950s, but was dissatisfied with the often bizarre interpretations that performers placed on his graphic symbols. He attempted to reconcile the competing demands of plasticity in the musical structure with clarity in his instructions to performers by returning to traditional notation in the late 1950s, but was equally unhappy with the result. Eventually he reached a workable compromise by notating the linear direction of pitches but allowing the rhythmic counterpoint to occur more or less at random, a concept not unlike Elliott Carter's more determinate approach to constructing independent musical "personalities" from various instrumental groupings. Feldman termed this solution, "race-course" notation. In the 1960s and 1970s, he became interested in working with sound structures that minimized overt musical motion and isolated events from each other. The pieces he produced as a result of this preoccupation—including the orchestral work *On Time and the Instrumental Factor* (1969)—

created a link, in the textural if not the tonal dimension, between the late music of Webern and the early works of the minimalist composers.

Yet another significant follower of Cage was the relatively obscure Richard Maxfield. Maxfield was born in Seattle on February 2, 1927, and committed suicide in Los Angeles on June 27, 1969 for reasons which remain unclear. In his early years he had studied with Sessions, Babbitt, Křenek, Copland and Dallapiccola, but his relationship with Cage was the strongest formative influence on his musical thinking.

Maxfield's contribution lay principally in the domain of electronic and tape music, although he also wrote for acoustical instruments. He succeeded Cage as principal composition teacher at the New School for Social Research in 1959 and spent the early 1960s in New York, developing his ideas about electronic music studio techniques as a systematic branch of musical study. He was one of the first prominent American teachers of such techniques, despite a relative lack of institutional support, and made many contributions to the ongoing exploration of new ways to manipulate electronic instruments and tape recorders. His 1960 *Night Music* initiated the technique of modulating sound with very high-pitched and/or very low-pitched electronic frequencies, which soon became a standard technique for composing with analog synthesizers and has become a textbook procedure for creating pre-programmed sounds in the more recent digital synthesizers. In 1966 he became the director of the electronic music studio at San Francisco State College, and remained based in California until his death.

The music of Wolff, Brown, Feldman and Maxfield has remained largely and undeservedly unknown outside of academic circles. Other composers associated with the Cagean movement included David Tudor, Alvin Lucier, Gordon Mumma, Robert Ashley, La Monte Young, and the Englishman Cornelius Cardew. But, perhaps the most significant, if equally non-public, living composer to emerge in the wake of Cage's efforts to open up the ears and minds of Western listeners is Pauline Oliveros. Born in Houston, Texas on May 30, 1932, Oliveros studied piano, violin, accordion and French horn as a child. After further studies at the University of Houston, she eventually took her degree from San Francisco State College in 1957, then continued to study privately with Robert Erickson. Oliveros began her career as an "avant-gardist" in San Francisco in the early 1960s. She was co-director (with Morton Subotnik and Ramon Sender) of the San Francisco Tape Music Center in the early 1960s until she joined the faculty of the highly progressive music department at the University of California, San Diego (UCSD) in 1967.

Oliveros attracted favorable critical attention in the Bay Area with performances of her post-Webernesque *Variations for Sextet* (1960) and was awarded the Foundation Gaudeamus (Holland) prize for her 1961 choral work, *Sound Patterns*. But, from an early age, her interests gravitated toward the human aspect of music-making as well as its acoustical dimension. This resulted in several early theatre pieces, including *Pieces of Eight* for wind octet and tape (1965) and her 1966 *Theatre Piece* composed for avant-garde trombonist, Stuart Dempster. The latter work sparked derisive comment from Slonimsky (in *Baker's Biographical Dictionary of Music and Musicians*) for its use of garden hose segments as part of the instrumental resources.

After she joined the faculty of UCSD, Oliveros began to explore the deeper ramifications of music as an interactive and meditative activity. Like Harry Partch, who was based in San Diego at the same time, she pursued the creation of pieces that were designed exclusively for specific performance situations, and even specific performers. Unlike Partch, however,

Pauline Oliveros *(b. 1932), who has come closer than anyone to date in defining the special consciousness of the American woman composer.* (Photo courtesy of Pauline Oliveros.)

Oliveros did not carry this over into the creation of specialized, permanent instruments. Instead she concentrated on innovative uses of the voice and body, as well as the integration of human performance with existing electronic instruments in various ways. She was a founder of UCSD's Center for Music Experiment and a women's ensemble for the exploration of sonic meditations.

Much of this work was paralleled in the similar experiments of Oliveros' former San Francisco colleague, Morton Subotnik, and others at the California Institute for the Arts in Valencia, UCSD's principal rival as a hotbed of cutting-edge experimentation on the West Coast during the 1960s and 1970s.

Oliveros is a feminist and possesses an abiding interest in certain non-Western approaches to music as well, particularly those of Native Americans. These facts, together with her gender-identity as a woman composer, have given her a highly individual profile in the musical world and raised a significant philosophical issue concerning the relationship of the composer to the public—an issue that was foreshadowed in the work of Partch and that is likely to become even more significant during the next century.

Within the past decade or so, an idea has gained currency among certain feminist artists, as well as a number of psychologists, that there are distinct, inherent, definable differences between the fundamental ways in which females and males perceive reality, experience emotion, communicate ideas and feelings, and react to the changing circumstances of everyday life, and that these differences are biological in origin and tend to withstand and/or adapt to social and cultural conditioning. As a result, the specific manifestations of "female consciousness" versus "male consciousness" may vary somewhat from culture to culture, but will always show certain common traits.

While this is not exactly a new idea in anecdotal terms, its status as a testable behavioral-science hypothesis is still controversial. If valid, it holds profound ramifications for the world of serious music—for unlike literature, poetry or dance, the creative aspect of the arts of music, painting and sculpture, architecture and drama have been almost exclusively dominated by males for centuries in both the Eastern and Western worlds. If there is, then, a distinctively male consciousness at work in the way the Western world (not just the United States) views classical music, it is not unreasonable to conclude that virtually the entire history of Western music, including the ways in which composers define themselves and their creative mission, represents an exclusively male perspective. In some circles of musical thinking today, it is not unusual to encounter the idea that normally unquestioned assumptions about the artist's mission—such as the quest for personal fame, the ambition to move audiences on a massive scale through the emotional power of one's work, the passion to create large works such as operas and symphonies, the desire for the composer to preserve dictatorial control over the outcome of the performance, even the desire to develop a highly personal style associated with one's creative identity—are all characteristically *male* attitudes. If, indeed, there is a contrasting *female* sensibility to which these assumptions have no relevance, then Oliveros' work provides the most cogent illustration of such a sensibility to be delivered by any woman composer, American or otherwise, to date.

The principal vehicle of Oliveros' ideas during the late 1960s and early 1970s was a group of pieces she called *Sonic Meditations.* These represented a diverse array of experimental music situations, in which the consistent focus was inward, toward the performer's private relationship with sound and the perceptible effects on his/her conscious state produced thereby. In one experiment, she even went so far as to wire her own electroencephalograph to a synthesizer in order to produce sound with her brain waves while in a meditative state.

As often as not, Oliveros' work does not require any prior musical training on the part of its performers, and the term "performer" itself loses much of its applicability. The word "participant" would more aptly characterize anyone involved in the realization of many of Oliveros' works. Moreover, the non-traditional nature of her documentation, as well as her unaggressive attitude toward publication, have prevented much of her work from becoming available to the public in printed form. Several of her earlier works, especially those for electronic resources or extended vocal techniques, have been recorded. But as sound is only one of many elements that enter into the bulk of Oliveros' compositions, such recordings offer only a minimal introduction to her esthetic.

In 1975, Oliveros combined elements of prior *Sonic Meditations* with several new ideas into a stage work entitled *Crow Two,* performed in March of that year at UCSD. The central focus of the audience's attention in *Crow Two* is the "Crow Poet," a female shaman who sits meditating in the center of several large concentric circles of performers for the forty-five minute duration of the piece. Other participants include four players of the aboriginal Australian instrument, the digeridu, who maintain a constant low-pitched drone via circular breathing while various performers mime mirror-imitation movements, play percussion instruments or chant. An important dramatic function is performed by the "heyokas," the trickster deities of Amerindian and other mythologies who attempt to distract the Crow Poet from her vision.

Crow Two represented an approach to music-theatre that was unprecedented for its time and has since been reflected, consciously or otherwise, in the works of various performance artists as well as the early portrait operas of Philip Glass. As a piece of theatre, it appears absolutely static. There is no plot, no overt character interaction, no libretto—and yet a great deal is happening in this work. It can perhaps best be compared to a theatrical mobile sculpture in which sound-producing as well as silent human performers form the objects of our perception. It is filled with subtly changing sonic and spatial relationships, and evocative of a kind of religious ritual that harks back to our racial memory of the earliest periods of human prehistory.

After leaving UCSD in 1981, Oliveros became consulting director of the short-lived Creative Music Foundation in West Hurley, New York, where she formed a woman's ensemble group to pursue further development of her ideas. She has also created the Pauline Oliveros Foundation (A Program for the Arts) based in Kingston, New York. Unlike other American women composers, from Amy Beach to Joan Tower to Ellen Taaffe Zwilich, who have pursued conventional careers as "composers who happened to be women as well," Oliveros represents a unique approach to her work that is hard to visualize having emerged in its totality from any male artist. With Partch, she constitutes another conspicuous example of the locally based musical "guru" who eschews a public career in favor of exploring a radically independent set of musical interests. Neither of these composers made serious efforts to promote their music on a national, commercial scale. In both cases, the composers have created circumstances where students and devotees must come to them instead. And, as will be discussed in the final chapter, there is some reason to believe that this emerging definition of what a serious composer is may prove to be one "wave of the future" in the 21st century.

The question of the place of the Cagean movement in the overall history of American classical music is a difficult one. Aleatoric music, because of its extreme admixture of philosophical ideals with acoustic phenomena, does not partake of any obviously nationalistic style as does, for instance, the music of Ives or Copland. But, by its very nature, the multi-cultural ideology and freshness of musical thinking embodied in aleatory is reflective of the American propensity for exploration and unconventional thinking. It is difficult to imagine a John Cage emerging from any of the hidebound European national traditions, despite the debt that he himself acknowledged to Erik Satie, Schoenberg and other European influences. And European composers who have been associated with his movement, such as Cardew or the Italian Sylvano Bussotti, were clearly followers, not leaders.

Furthermore, as has often been the case with movements in contemporary music, the aleatoric period of the 1950s and 1960s was allied to similar movements in literature, visual arts, theatre and dance. Cage's work was paralleled in the dramatic arts by the experimental productions of the Polish director Jerzy Grotowski and by the French theatre of the absurd. But it was the Living Theater, founded by Julian Beck and Judith Malina in the late 1950s, that displayed the closest affinity with Cagean ideals and practices. The two most significant productions of this group were their highly original versions of *Frankenstein* and *The Brig*. The Living Theater explicitly advocated a leftist political agenda, which was not true of Cage or most other major artists of the time, but, more importantly, attempted to utilize techniques such as audience participation, non-narrative plots, discontinuous time sequence and linguistic distortion of text, to achieve a fundamentally new kind of theatre. Many of their techniques were indeterminate and form a precise analogy to Cage's work in music. Moreover, the Living Theater exerted a profound influence on the next generation of artists such as Robert Wilson and Philip Glass, most of whom were students at the time, and made a major contribution toward the development of later music theatre and opera.

In the visual arts, the aleatoric movement was reflected in a host of abstract modernists and in the growing trend toward multimedia productions (drawing upon the earlier Dadaist movement that existed in Germany and France between the world wars). In the United States, Cage served as an influence on the works of many visual artists, and was in turn influenced by them. Among these were architects Buckminster Fuller and Richard Halprin, painter Robert Rauschenberg, sculptors Claes Oldenberg and Harry Bertoya, and media artist Andy Warhol. Many of the ideas and experiments of these 1960s artists have led into the modern forms of minimalist music and performance art, and the Cagean influence continues to be felt there, combined with a general return to the idea of a single controlling creator.

In the area of dance, Cage's influence can be seen in the works of choreographers such as Ann Halprin, Erick Hawkins and Lucinda Childs. But it was his extended personal relationship and professional collaboration with choreographer Merce Cunningham, with whom he lived for almost fifty years, that forms the most important body of musical theatre work produced by Cage. His "accompaniments" for Cunningham's dance company were generally derived from already created pieces of his own, such as *Aria, Fontana Mix, Cheap Imitations* (based on the music of Erik Satie), and others. The music was never composed to the dance, nor the dance to the music. Each was created independently, and the two elements were only combined in actual performance, without any overt attempt to relate them to each other.

The works of John Cage can also be identified as the first branch of American classical music to integrate the mass electronic media, however tentatively, into itself as a structural element. This is particularly apparent in his *Imaginary Landscape No. 4* (1951) for twelve radios. In this radically innovative piece, Cage instructed the performers how to manipulate the tuning dials of the radios, but the musical content was a random by-product of whatever various local stations happened to be broadcasting at the time of the performance. This propensity to form collages from pre-existing music or sound, and to connect with whatever emotional, collocative psychological associations the audience might have with that music, was further developed in Cage's last major works, which he titled *Europeras 1–4* (1989). These music-theatre pieces made use of fragments of the repertoire of European operas in stark juxtaposition with Cage's own compositional devices.

In the mid-1960s the age of music experiment reached its zenith worldwide. Two opposing trends had characterized this musical revolution: the movement toward minimizing the composer's personal control over the resulting piece, and the countermovement toward maximizing that control. John Cage, who died of a stroke in New York on August 12, 1992, a month short of his eightieth birthday, was the apostle of the former position. Composers such as Milton Babbitt, the Frenchman Pierre Boulez and the Greek Iannis Xenakis were the leaders of the latter. Boulez and Babbitt remained ideologically in the camp of Anton Webern throughout the bulk of their careers. Xenakis however, who was much more directly influenced by Varèse, displayed a more far-ranging imagination, particularly in the use of computers—he is generally considered the father of computer generated music—and multi-media.

A paradox arises from the demonstrated fact that most lay audiences, who have not devoted intense study to the ideas and works of either Cage or Xenakis, perceive virtually no difference in the final product of either composer. While we may attempt to explain this away by claiming the audience is ignorant, unperceptive or unimportant, the fact remains that the broad musical public found both the total freedom of Cage and his followers and the total control of Xenakis and his followers to sound equally chaotic in the end. The lesson in this phenomenon seemed to be that whether one seeks to liberate music from the taste, intention and technique of the composer, or to concentrate control over literally every aspect of it in the composer's hand via technology, the end result is the same: effective perceived acoustical chaos. Both paths led to the same perceptual end.

This observation became of crucial importance in determining the influence Cage's music had on the generation that immediately succeeded him, including some of his own devotees such as La Monte Young, and younger composers such as Steve Reich and Philip Glass. These composers, while admiring Cage's innovative spirit (and adapting some of his ideas and techniques) were not willing to suffer the same alienation from the mass audience that resulted from most aleatoric music. In this regard, they saw aleatory and total serialism as equally unacceptable alternatives. Although the minimalist composer Terry Riley made some attempt to apply explicitly indeterminate techniques to some of his early, jazz-influenced improvisations, none of the other composers born in the late 1930s chose to pursue the implications of indeterminacy to their logical conclusions. But Cage and his school did not exhaust the possibilities implied by indeterminacy, as is illustrated by the struggles of Feldman to achieve a middle ground between it and fully notated music. On the contrary, they merely opened the door to those possibilities. It will remain for later generations of composers to develop the potential for interactive music to its logical conclusion, once the tides of changing musical fashion have moved on and the aleatoric period can be viewed in a more sober historical perspective.

12

Post-modernism

෭

The label "post-modernism" is a nebulous term that acquires slightly different meanings according to who is using it and/or the field of art to which it is applied. Unlike other musical labels, such as "post-Romanticism," "academic serialism," "aleatory" or "minimalism," "post-modernism" tends to be a sort of catchall category for those recent American composers (and some Europeans—such as Arvo Part or Nick Bicât) whose music reflects a general return to tonal organization and a backing off from radical experimentation. But, post-modernist composers are not merely musical Luddites who have denied the influence of recent musical thought and pursued a reactionary retrenchment to the style of Beethoven as is often assumed. On the contrary, the contemporary post-modernists constitute the first generation of American composers who have had full access, during their education, to the complete range of early-to-mid-20th-century techniques, including European, American and non-Western art music. Their music is informed by a vastly greater comprehension of the works of all their predecessors than was the case with any previous generation, and this is at once both an advantage and a curse for them: an advantage because it has made available a world of musical thinking far more diverse than anything that preceded it in Western music history; a curse because it has forced the post-modernists into a position of having to invent their own musical languages through conscious selection, adaptation and development of the many different approaches to music received from their teachers. As a result, the music of the American post-modernists incorporates an eclectic array of modern musical devices into styles rooted in what their creators regard as fundamental principles of Western classical music itself: such things as (a) fundamental consonances whose effect cannot be erased at the whim of the composer, (b) traditional formal patterns (such as fugue or sonata) whose structural paradigms are ingrained into the listening habits of Western audiences (even when those audiences are not consciously aware of the fact), and (c) deliberate references to the characteristic textural, harmonic, timbral and stylistic procedures of earlier music.

Although post-modernist thinking was always present to some degree in the work of certain older 20th-century Americans, such as Barber, Hovhaness, Rudhyar, Creston and even Virgil Thomson, its birth as a new category of contemporary worldwide music began essentially when George Rochberg turned from a career in academic serialism to a type of composition that incorporated collagistic quotations of earlier European tonal music into a kind of musical "stream of consciousness" around 1960. After Rochberg, the major American post-modern composers active today include David Del Tredici, John Corigliano, Ellen Taaffe Zwilich, Jacob Druckman, Joan Tower, John Harbison, William Bolcom, Bernard Rands and Joseph Schwantner. To this list must be added the late Stephen Albert, whose career was cut short by his death in an automobile accident in December 1992.

The post-modernist esthetic can be divided into two somewhat differing approaches to music, depending on the degree to which the composer makes conscious reference to pre-existing musical styles. Rochberg, Del Tredici, Corigliano, Druckman and Bolcom, among others, have devoted a considerable portion of their music to the integration of 20th-century techniques with earlier classical and popular styles, including at times ragtime, jazz and rock music. Zwilich, Albert, Rands and Schwantner have each, on the other hand, pursued a more independent path toward discovering new ways to make use of older approaches to music without much deliberate, specific quotation of music of the past. In the case of all these composers, however, the resultant sound of the music has offered performers and audiences alike a much-needed relief from the harshness of total serialism as well as from the perceived chaos of aleatoric and electronic music. And conservative, contemporary audiences have rewarded them with a greater degree of attention and appreciation than was given to those composers whose work dominated the 1960s and 1970s.

The founder of post-modernism in music, as noted above, was **George Rochberg.** Rochberg was born in Paterson, New Jersey, on July 5, 1918. He took his B.A. from Montclair (New Jersey) State Teachers College and studied at the Mannes College in New York from 1939 to 1942. After serving in the armed forces during World War II, he began studies with Rosario Scalero and Menotti at Curtis, from which he received a Bachelor of Music degree in 1947. He later received his M.A. from the University of Pennsylvania.

Rochberg began his compositional career as a somewhat conventional modernist, typical of the period of the late 1930s. His early music follows the paths begun by Bartók, Stravinsky and Hindemith in the early 20th century. But, after an encounter with Sessions' friend and colleague, the uncompromising serialist Luigi Dallapiccola, while studying in Rome in 1950, Rochberg became increasingly involved with serialist methods and began producing serial works. He taught at the Curtis Institute until 1954, when he joined Persichetti as a music editor for the Theodore Presser publishing firm. In 1960, he joined the faculty of the University of Pennsylvania and spent the bulk of his remaining academic career there.

During his early teaching years, Rochberg followed the conventional serialist line in his own music and his work with this students. This is revealed in such typical works from the period as his *Second Symphony* and *Cheltenham Concerto*. But, beginning in the mid-1960s, he began to incorporate quotations from other composers into his work. The first product of this new approach was his *Contra mortem et tempus,* which quotes Boulez, Berio, Varèse and Ives. After experiencing an intense period of self-reevaluation, following the premature death of his son at about this time, Rochberg began to seek what he viewed as more universal musical values, and to write in a language that at times openly returned to traditional tonal principles. He went farther back into music history for sources of his musical quotations, even to Mozart and Beethoven, and began to create works that featured startling juxtapositions of diverse musical styles. Eventually he arrived at a philosophical position which frankly repudiated serialism and asserted that the traditional forms and principles of earlier composers were more closely in touch with eternal values in Western music.

Rochberg's rebellion against the serialist theology created a furor in American academic music. Many viewed him as a sort of traitor to his class, but others admired his courage. His supporters applauded him for pointing out the fact, which most of them had believed privately but not been willing to state publicly, that the serialist emperor was naked and had always been so. Despite the protests of his critics, the damage had been done. For such a prominent figure in American academic music to turn against the prevailing mode of thought created a sufficient crack in the academic serialist armor for a host of young composers to flow into the breach, citing Rochberg as their model. From this emerged a full-scale revolution against the repressive influence of Babbitt, Sessions and other 12-tone composers in the training of American serious composers, a revolution that was then expanded by Rochberg's successors.

George Rochberg *(b. 1918). In the late 1960s he turned from academic serialism to an eclectic neo-tonalism, and founded the contemporary school of Post-Modernism in the process.* (Photo courtesy of ASCAP.)

After the 1960s, Rochberg continued to develop his ideas about reshaping the values of American classical music, and began to incorporate elements of jazz and non-Western styles into his works as well. His late music, as a result, tends to be highly eclectic and often questionably organized, although he occasionally breaks through into a work of consistent appeal. But the importance of his contribution in opening new avenues of musical exploration remains unchallenged.

The young composers of the 1960s were born in the late 1930s. Between 1935 and 1939, almost all of the currently prominent minimalists and post-modernists were born, including Terry Riley and La Monte Young (both 1935); Steve Reich (1936); Philip Glass and David Del Tredici (both 1937); William Bolcom, John Corigliano and Joan Tower (1938); and Ellen Taaffe Zwilich (1939). These were the young composers who were weaned on academic serialism. And all of them benefited from Rochberg's revolution.

The first post-modernist of this generation to attract significant attention was **David Del Tredici.** Born in Cloverdale, California, not far from San Francisco, Del Tredici intended at first to become a concert pianist and made his debut at the age of sixteen with the San Francisco Symphony. But, in 1958, he met Darius Milhaud, who taught at the Aspen (Colorado) Music Festival during the summers. Milhaud recognized Del Tredici's talent for composition and encouraged him to develop it. So Del Tredici went on to study composition at University of California, Berkeley and then at Princeton with Roger Sessions and Earl Kim.

Typically enough, given his teachers, Del Tredici's earliest music was founded on post-Webern serialist principles. But he was never comfortable with the dogmatic positions of American musical academia and, even in these early works, most of which were settings of the poetry of James Joyce, achieved an expressiveness that was closer to the post-Romantic model than to the more objectivist approach of academic serialism. Thus, from the very beginning, Del Tredici displayed the romantic leanings that were to make his later works so popular with the public.

In the mid-1960s, Del Tredici converted to an openly tonal style when he began to make settings of the literary works of Lewis Carroll, *Alice in Wonderland* and *Through the Looking Glass. Alice* had been an inspiration for several American composers at an earlier period of history, notably Deems Taylor and Edgar Stillman Kelley. Del Tredici, however, developed something of an obsession with the subject and devoted most of his writing for the next eighteen years to "Alice"-derived pieces. The first of these was his 1968 *Pop-pourri* for amplified soprano, chorus, rock group and orchestra, premiered in La Jolla, California, in July of that year. In 1969, he went on to compose *An Alice Symphony* in five movements for similar instrumental resources. Each of the movements of *An Alice Symphony* is separately titled: (1) "Speak Gently/Speak Roughly," (2) "The Lobster Quadrille," (3) "'Tis the Voice of the Sluggard," (4) "Who Stole the Tarts?" and (5) "Dream-Conclusion." The second movement was premiered under Aaron Copland's baton in London in late 1969 and attracted considerable attention. *An Alice Symphony* has also been performed as two separate compositions, the first (sometimes called *Illustrated Alice*) comprised of movements 1, 4 and 5; the second (sometimes called *In Wonderland*) comprised of movements 2, 3 and 5. This is often a more practical arrangement because of the extraordinary length of the work (about an hour and a half), engendered by Del Tredici's highly repetitious style.

An Alice Symphony was followed in 1971 by the two-movement orchestral suite, *Adventures Underground,* then in 1972 by *Vintage Alice: Fantascene on a Mad Tea Party.* Del Tredici intended to finish his attachment to this subject with his 1976 *Final Alice,* premiered in Chicago that year under Sir George Solti, but was enticed into yet another "Alice" work by the tremendous success of this performance. The result was his massive *Child Alice*, completed in 1980. *Child Alice* again divides into two parts: *In Memory of a Summer Day* and *Quaint Events, Happy Voices, All in the Golden Afternoon*. This was followed by yet another "Alice" piece in 1986, *Haddock's Eyes* for soprano and chamber ensemble. *In Memory of a Summer Day* was awarded the Pulitzer Prize in 1980, which substantially increased Del Tredici's public recognition.

Despite the great success of his works, Del Tredici's music is no more frequently performed today than that of most of his contemporaries. In part, this is due to the massive, Straussian orchestra he calls for (which is so large as to require amplification of the solo voice). But he has also aroused controversy in the musical world for his blatantly romantic style, which appears to cater to the lowest common denominator of reactionary attitudes on the part of the listening public. In this he goes even farther than did, for example, Samuel Barber—for, while Barber's music is decidedly post-Romantic in its sensibility, Del Tredici's style is based on heavy-handed, invariant, seemingly endless repetition of even more atavistic orchestral ideas. As will be seen in the next chapter, repetition is also a cornerstone of minimalist technique, but Del Tredici's use of repetition contrasts sharply with that of Steve Reich or Philip Glass. Where the minimalist composers repeat and vary small melodic/rhythmic cells to generate a contrapuntal fabric that is constantly changing in subtle ways, Del Tredici almost continuously repeats large segments of material intact, apparently to achieve a kind of hypnotic dulling of the senses consistent with the psychological ambience of Alice's hazy summer afternoon. This more ponderous approach to the use of repetition, which, if nothing else, at least succeeds in driving Del Tredici's themes into the memory of his listeners, also forms a point of connection between his work and that of John Adams (see next chapter). While Adams is generally viewed as a minimalist, his manner of repeating ideas cyclicly, without significant alteration in the basic material, is very reminiscent of Del Tredici.

Despite the criticisms to which Del Tredici's music has been subjected, his work always displays consummate craft in orchestration and melodic conception and tends to be less derivative than that of his friend and colleague, John Corigliano. Whether it will survive remains to be seen.

John Corigliano, in contrast to Del Tredici, has been much less obsessive in his style and choice of subjects. Born in New York on February 16, 1938, he was the son of violinist John Corigliano, Sr., the first American-born concertmaster of the New York Philharmonic, and studied with both Otto Luening and Paul Creston.

David Del Tredici *(b. 1937) [left] and* **John Corigliano** *(b. 1938) on a visit to Trinidad. Two of the foremost exponents of post-modernism.* (MUSIC DIVISION, The New York Public Library for the Performing Arts. Astor, Lenox and Tilden Foundations).

Like Del Tredici, Corigliano has worked in exclusively tonal idioms for the bulk of his career. He attracted early attention when his *Violin Sonata* was premiered at Menotti's Spoleto Festival in 1964 and devoted much of the 1960s and early 1970s to the composition of instrumental concertos and a trilogy of songs on poems of Dylan Thomas: *Fern Hill* (chorus and orchestra, 1961), *Poem in October* (tenor and orchestra, 1970) and *Poem on his Birthday* (baritone, chorus and orchestra, 1976).

Corigliano has also been more attracted to work in the electronic media and film than have most of his contemporaries. He served as a music programmer and producer for various FM radio stations and for CBS television, and it was his Academy Award-nominated score for Ken Russell's 1980 film, *Altered States,* that made his name familiar to the lay musical public. The script for *Altered States*—about a precocious young scientist who uses isolation tank experiments, of the kind pioneered by John Lilly, and hallucinogenic drugs to regress to a primitive stage of humanoid evolution—allowed Corigliano to exploit extraordinary orchestral effects in a variety of interesting, but still tonal ways. Despite certain obvious debts to Barber's *Medea's Meditation and Dance of Vengeance* (see Chapter 9), Corigliano managed to produce a startling work and to deepen his command of orchestra technique in this music.

Prior to 1990, Corigliano's position in the world of classical music was somewhat uncertain. His forays into media and popular music had caused him to be viewed with suspicion by some "serious" composers and audiences, in spite of his early works. But, with the premieres of his *Symphony No.1* (1990) and his opera *The Ghosts of Versailles* (1991), he began to establish more credentials as a classical composer. The symphony, dedicated to various of the composer's friends who had died of AIDS, was especially successful and has been replayed frequently in the short time since its premiere. The early critical consensus was that this is a very moving work which reflects a return to more humanistic values in contemporary composition. However, removed from the context of its political message, laudable as that message may be, the symphony has also been criticized as a bombastic and superficial piece in which no new musical ground is broken.

The Ghosts of Versailles, which was one of the most successful contemporary operas premiered by the Met in recent years, displayed Corigliano's superb command of style-imitation, ranging from pseudo-Arabic music to neo-Mozartean ensemble writing, but also resorted to an almost slapstick level of theatrical gimmickry to please its audience. On the surface, it is a modern sequel to Mozart's *La Nozze di Figaro*, but, even in its choice of subject, displays the same tendency to cater to the conservatism of modern audiences for which Del Tredici has been criticized.

Perhaps the best, though certainly not the best known, of those of our contemporary post-modernist composers who deliberately use pre-existing styles in their work is **William Bolcom.** Bolcom represents a tradition of non-specialization that has become rare in recent classical music history, as he is not only a distinguished composer but a brilliant professional pianist as well. Born in Seattle on May 26, 1938, Bolcom, like Del Tredici, began studies with Milhaud in 1958 and later traveled to Paris to study with Olivier Messiaen as well. Living in New York in the late 1960s, Bolcom became enamored of the ragtime music of Scott Joplin and his contemporaries, and developed a distinctive style as a ragtime pianist. When ragtime underwent a nationwide revival in 1973, after release of the film *The Sting* for which Marvin Hamlisch adapted the music of Joplin, Bolcom was in an excellent position to join the front rank of ragtime specialists. Later in the 1970s, he started touring with his wife, mezzo-soprano Joan Morris, in programs devoted to historical examples of American art songs and popular music.

By turning his back on the idea that composers only compose and performers only perform, Bolcom, like his younger colleague, guitarist-composer David Leisner, placed himself in diametric opposition to the 20th-century division of labor in serious music which, in part, had contributed so perniciously to the separation of compositional thinking and public taste. But, in addition to rejecting the rigid categorical division between specialist composer and specialist performer, he also rejected what he viewed as the artificial division between classical and popular music, noting the historical fact that older European composers (such as Mozart, Handel or Verdi) were as much in the popular mainstream of their day as they were in the classical. In this respect, Bolcom's philosophical attitudes are closer to those of the minimalists than they are to any of his post-modernist colleagues.

Bolcom's connection to Rochberg is demonstrated by his having edited Rochberg's collected writings, published in 1984 as *The Aesthetics of Survival: a Composer's View of Music in the 20th Century*. Like Sessions, he has also been a devotee of the English poet, engraver and mystic, William Blake (1757–1827). His passion for Blake's work culminated in settings of forty-six Blake poems under the title *Songs of Innocence and Experience*, premiered in Stuttgart in January of 1984.

The other Blake in Bolcom's life is the African-American ragtime composer-pianist, Eubie Blake (1883–1983). In 1973 he co-authored a book

Pianist-composer **William Bolcom** *(b. 1938), who mixes popular and classical techniques in everything from string quartets to symphonies to operas.* (Photo by Pach Brothers, courtesy of Shaw Concerts, Inc., New York.)

with Robert Kimball entitled *Reminiscing with Sissle and Blake,* which focused especially on Blake's 1921 musical, *Shuffle Along,* a work that firmly established ragtime and syncopation on Broadway. (*N.B.*—The "Sissle" referred to was Noble Sissle, Blake's collaborator who later became a bandleader and honorary "Mayor of Harlem.")

Bolcom's music usually makes specific reference to pre-existing styles, integrated with a very effective flair for dramatic, dissonant textures of his own. This is most clearly heard in his theatre music, beginning with the "cabaret" opera, *Dynamite Tonite* (1963) right up through his most recent work, an operatic setting of Frank Norris' grim American novel, *McTeague* (1992). He has also composed numerous works for piano and chamber ensembles as well as five symphonies, and concertos for piano (1976), violin (1983), clarinet (1988), and flute (1993), as well as ten string quartets. His use of references to (more than quotations of) earlier music is always deliberate and, though well integrated into his personal style, has caused him to be superficially described as an "eclectic" composer by some writers. But Bolcom's work goes beyond mere eclecticism. He is neither as reactionary as Del Tredici, nor as gimmicky as Corigliano, and has created one of the most original voices of any composer active today.

Yet another post-modernist who has achieved significant recognition is **Jacob Druckman.** Druckman's work is better known among musicians than the general public, and his profile among the lay audience is somewhat less conspicuous than those of Rochberg, Del Tredici, Corigliano or Bolcom. This is because, like Ellen Taaffe Zwilich (see below), he writes mainly for orchestra and, like both Zwilich and Bernard Rands, has preserved a closer connection to the more formalist works of his 20th-century predecessors.

Born in Philadelphia on June 26, 1928, Druckman began composing at about the age of fifteen and studied with Copland at Tanglewood in 1949. He also had some early experience as a jazz player, and later went on to Juilliard where he studied with Peter Mennin, Vincent Persichetti and Bernard Wagenaar. After taking his Master's Degree at the École Normale de Musique in Paris (1956), he returned to the United States and taught at Juilliard, City University of New York (CUNY) in Brooklyn and Yale. Like Rochberg and many of the American composers born in the 1920s, Druckman began his creative life with personal applications of serialist ideas and explorations of the newly emerging field of electronic music. But, unlike many others, he also possessed an affinity for the large orchestral works of turn-of-the-century composers such as Mahler, Stravinsky and Schoenberg, as well as the musical thinking of Debussy and Ravel. As a result, the mature works of Druckman have been almost entirely in the orchestral medium, beginning with his Pulitzer Prize winning *Windows* (1972), and extending through later compositions such as *Incenters* (1973), *Mirage* (1976), the *Violin Concerto* (1978), *Aureole* (1979), *Prism* (1980), *Athanor* (1985) and *Brangle* (1988). Druckman has also composed provocative works for chorus and chamber ensembles, sometimes employing tape and other electronic resources as well. His exploration of electronic music in the late 1960s probably had an influence on his treatment of *textures* and *orchestration* in the large works cited above, for Druckman frequently achieves a plasticity of sound in these parameters that is unlike anything produced by his contemporaries. His orchestral music has had a serious influence on composers born in the 1950s and later. Like Bolcom, Druckman has also made extensive use of references to pre-existing works/styles in his music. But he is more prone to literal quotation, and his sources are less obvious, ranging over a broader spectrum of European and American music history.

Though somewhat younger than his other post-modernist colleagues, the late **Stephen Albert** also studied with Milhaud at Aspen during the summer of 1958, when he was a mere seventeen years old. This had been preceded by two years of study with Elie Siegmeister in New York, and was followed by further studies with Bernard Rogers and Rochberg. Born in New York on February 6, 1941, Albert received numerous awards from the mid-1960s to the late 1970s, including Guggenheim Fellowships, two Rome Prizes, Rockefeller, NEA and Alice M. Ditson Fund fellowships. His propensity for winning awards was climaxed when he received the Pulitzer Prize in 1985 for his symphony subtitled *River Run*.

As a young man, Albert had explored neo-tonal applications of electronic music and sought means of integrating these with live performance in ways other than those used by the avant-garde of earlier generations. But it was his skill as a vocal composer that attracted the most significant critical attention. The bulk of his catalogue was devoted to works for solo or multiple voices with chamber ensemble or orchestra, and included many settings of Greek classics and the works of James Joyce, among other poets.

Albert served as composer-in-residence with the Seattle Symphony from 1985 to 1987, and shortly thereafter joined the faculty of Juilliard. In his later work, he explicitly rejected what he described as both "the unrelieved dissonance of serialism and the unrelieved consonance of minimalism,"[48] placing himself squarely at odds with those academic composers of

---

[48] Keynote address, New Hampshire Music Festival composers conference (August 1990).

his generation, such as Wuorinen or Eaton, who continued to pursue post-Webernesque modernism.

Albert's promising career was cut tragically short when he died at the age of fifty-one in an automobile accident in Truro, Massachusetts, on December 29, 1992. But he left behind a substantial canon of post-modernist works that, after the passage of time, may prove to be among the more effective contributions to the literature of American music to emerge in recent years.

Among the post-modernist composers who have rejected deliberate quotation of pre-existing styles and, instead, pursued the development of independent, personal idioms, **Bernard Rands** stands out conspicuously. Like his friend and colleague Druckman, Rands has tended to pursue a more conservative and more European-oriented exploration of post-modernist techniques than have Del Tredici, Bolcom, Albert or Corigliano. In Rands' case, this is partly attributable to his European birth and musical education. Born in Sheffield, England, on March 2, 1934, Rands studied both music and English literature at the University of Wales in Bangor, and later moved to Italy, where he worked closely with the avant-garde serialist Luigi Dallapiccola, Bruno Maderna and the aleatoric modernist Luciano Berio. Moreover, Rands did not merely study with Berio but actually lived in the composer's home as an apprentice for a time. In addition, he attracted the early attention of Pierre Boulez at Darmstadt, and was at the center of Boulez's doctrinaire serialist collective during the late 1950s. But, while Rands was capable of producing music that not only pleased his teachers but actually garnered their active sponsorship, he never really accepted the serialist doctrine.

During the late 1960s he migrated to the United States, where he taught at Princeton and the University of Illinois. He returned to England to teach at York University from 1970 to 1975, then once again moved to the United States, this time to join the faculty of the University of California, San Diego (UCSD). Rands became the first major post-modernist composer to join the UCSD faculty, and his influence moderated much of that school's musical radicalism which, by 1975, had frequently degenerated into nonsensical projects posing as music experiment. At UCSD, Rands founded the contemporary performance group, SONOR, which did much to revitalize and elevate the performance standards of new music and has since gone on to become one of the most respected ensembles of its kind in the world. Rands has also established a significant reputation as a skilled and sensitive conductor of contemporary works.

After receiving the Pulitzer Prize in 1984 for his 1982 *Canti del sole*, Rands joined the faculty of Boston University and was later invited to replace the retiring Leon Kirchner at Harvard, where he remains today as the principal composition professor. In selecting Rands, who became a naturalized United States citizen in 1983, Harvard departed from its century-long tradition of awarding its principal composition chair only to native-born composers, a tradition that began with Paine and extended through Hill, Piston and Kirchner. But Rands' most significant work has all been done in the United States, and, like Gruenberg, Varèse, Toch, Menotti and others born overseas, he is rightly viewed as an American composer today.

But, for all of that and despite his studies in Italy, much of Rands' ethos resides in a uniquely Celtic world-view, especially the earthy, passionate, poetic, somewhat mystical and highly musical culture of Wales. In this his esthetic, if not his music is somewhat reminiscent of an earlier Boston composer, the French-born Charles Martin Loeffler (see Chapter 4). But, where Loeffler was merely a pallid and sometimes incoherent imitator of impressionist styles, Rands' music possesses a distinctively original voice, meticulously crafted, neo-tonal, highly lyrical and filled with subtle dramatic gestures. This is best revealed in his pair of song cycles, *Canti Lunatici* (1980) and *Canti del Sole*. In each of these works, Rands assembled a diverse selection of poems relating to the moon and sun, respectively. The range of texts reflects the composer's own far-reaching literary interests, as well as his grasp of languages, and includes poems in Spanish, English, Italian, French and translations of ancient Gaelic. The authors include Salvatore Quasimodo, Blake, Lorca, Joyce, Whitman, Plath, Artaud, Shelley, Rimbaud, D. H. Lawrence, Dylan Thomas, Wilfred Owen, Baudelaire and others. More recently, Rands has turned for inspiration to the poetry of Irish playwright Samuel Beckett, a disciple of James Joyce and author of such absurdist masterpieces as *Waiting for Godot* and *Endgame*. The composer's 1991 "*... in the receding mist ...* ", written as a sixtieth birthday present for Druckman, is a purely instrumental work that reflects Beckett's poetic image through a complex and delicate network of neo-tonal counterpoint.

The cosmopolitan character of Rands' life, ideas and music is consistent with a contemporary trend toward pan-nationalism in American music. The heritage of Cage, Harrison, Berio, Oliveros and others of the 1960s avant-garde contributed significantly to breaking down traditional barriers between "nationalistic" styles, both in music and in Western thinking generally, and has led, in modern times, to a more open musical world where the works of composers of both sexes and all national origins can be given an equal chance for acceptance. The explosion of modern communications technology has facilitated this process as well, and we will have more to discover about the probable effects it will continue to exert during the next century in the final chapter of this history.

One of the benefits of this more open attitude toward musical style has been the emergence of a greater number of women composers, conductors and musical scholars during the past thirty years. Amy Beach was the first to make serious headway in gaining for women a respected position among American composers. Her work was ably followed by that of the Canadian-born Gena Branscombe, and the Americans Ethel Glenn Hier, Mary Carr Moore, Vivian Fine, Ruth Crawford Seeger, Peggy Glanville-Hicks and, especially, Marion Bauer during the early part of this century. And the tradition appears to be continuing on the work of more recent composers such as Marilyn Ziffrin, Judith Lang Zaimont and Augusta Read Thomas, among others. In the field of conducting, figures such as Fiora Contino, Sarah Caldwell and JoAnn Falletta have made major strides, as did Natalie Curtis, Donna K. Anderson, Vera Brodsky Lawrence, Andrea Olmstead, Barbara Tischler, Barbara Zuck and Vivian Perlis in the area of historical musicology. Apart from the unique position of Pauline Oliveros, however, the most prominent American women composers active today are Joan Tower and Ellen Taaffe Zwilich, both of the post-modernist stripe.

Tower, born in New Rochelle, New York, on September 6, 1938, studied with Otto Luening and Chou-Wen Chung, and began her career in the academic serialist mode of some her contemporaries such as John Eaton or Charles Wuorinen. But, in the mid-1970s she began to move away from serialism and to write in a more lyrical vein. Her preoccupations have always been the temporal and rhythmic dimensions of music and even in her earlier serialist period the vigorous rhythmic element of her work was conspicuous. Within the last ten to fifteen years, her titles and subjects have acquired a more frankly feminist character, reflected in such works as *Amazon III* (1983) and *Fanfare for the Uncommon Woman* (1989). But her work has remained musically complex and somewhat limited in its appeal to a mass audience.

Greater attention has been given in recent years to **Zwilich,** especially after her receipt of the Pulitzer Prize in 1983. She was the first woman composer to receive that award, as she had earlier been the first woman graduated from the Doctor of Musical Arts in Composition program at Juilliard (1975). Zwilich was born in Miami, Florida, on April 30, 1939 and studied initially at Florida State University. During her student days she became both an accomplished violinist and trumpet player, and later played violin for several years under Stokowski in the American Symphony Orchestra in New York. It was during her tenure as an orchestral violinist that

Zwilich became interested in composition and successfully gained admission to the Juilliard program. Once there, she studied extensively with Sessions and briefly with Elliott Carter. Her first significant recognition came when her orchestral piece *Symposium* (1973) was performed by Pierre Boulez with the Juilliard Orchestra in 1975. This was soon followed by critical acclaim for her *String Quartet* (1974), which was premiered in Boston for the ISCM "World Music Days" festival in November, 1976.

Zwilich's string writing has always been among her best work, and her 1973 *Sonata in Three Movements,* written for her husband, violinist Joseph Zwilich, attracted favorable attention when the latter took it on tour in Europe. The *Sonata* was later awarded the gold medal in the G. B. Viotti composition competition in Italy (1975). But it was her 1979 *Chamber Symphony* that projected Zwilich into serious national attention as a composer. Zwilich's husband, Joseph, had died unexpectedly during the composition of this work and, without the composer necessarily intending it, an extraordinary lyrical poignancy found its way into this piece and moved audiences wherever it was heard.

Like Albert and Rands, Zwilich has been one of the most conservative, as well as one of the most musically independent, post-modernists and her works often flow as a natural development from the melodic material she takes as her starting point. She has not articulated any special theory or method of composition and appears to be a wholly intuitive composer.

Also in 1979, the Minnesota Orchestra premiered her 1977 *Clarino Quartet,* in which she drew on her experience as a trumpet player to produce one of the brightest and most interesting works for brass to appear in recent years. The *Quartet* is scored for Bb piccolo trumpet, and three others in D, C and Bb respectively.

After receiving the Pulitzer for her first symphony, Zwilich went on to compose a second in 1985, as well as a *Piano Concerto* (1984), a *Double Quartet* for strings (1984) and a *Flute Concerto* (1990) for longtime Boston Symphony Orchestra principal flutist Doriot Anthony Dwyer on the occasion of her retirement from that orchestra. Zwilich's other works include the 1971 song cycle *Einsame Nacht* on poems of Hermann Hesse, a *Divertimento* for flute, clarinet, violin and cello (1983), and her 1984 *Celebration for Orchestra.*

Taken as a whole, the works of our most important post-modernist composers are as diverse as the vague nature of this category might suggest. In fact, there is no single constellation of stylistic traits that can be consistently associated with the label "post-modernism," and theorists, such as Paul Paccione or Dilo Mook, who have tried to define it have run into serious trouble accounting for this extraordinary diversity of styles and ideals. Paccione, in particular, has argued that post-modernism is at once a reaction against and an extension of certain features in the modernism of Webern, Feldman and others of that ilk, sublimely indifferent to the inherent contradiction in such a statement.

Almost all of the composers born after 1932, however, have abandoned serialism, as well as the early 20th-century modernism pioneered by Stravinsky and Bartók. While they still acknowledge their debt to their comprehensive study of these earlier styles, they are also clearly attempting to strike out in a different, neo-tonal direction. Whether or not their different solutions to this problem will coalesce into a coherent style period remains to be seen.

In contrast to the so-called post-modernists, another group of neo-tonal composers born in the 1930s, however, shows very clear similarities of style and intention—at least in their early work. It is to this last group of contemporary American composers, the "minimalists," that we turn in the next chapter.

13

Minimalism

ॐ

E ver since the mature works of Charles Ives, American classical music has pursued multiple lines of development. This raises a certain ambiguity in attempting to define precisely what makes American music characteristically "American." Some American works, such as those of Copland and his colleagues, sound American because they draw on idiomatic melodic, harmonic and rhythmic traits of American folk or vernacular music. That is, these works are American in *content* while remaining rooted in the technical and formal procedures of European classical music. Other American works, such as the music of Varèse, Cage or Nancarrow, reflect an adventurous, multi-cultural attitude toward music itself, which stems from the iconoclastic, practical, entrepreneurial spirit on which Americans pride themselves. This music might be considered *ideologically* American, without its displaying any folkloric or nationalistic content.

But, as varied as the differing musical values of Cowell, Griffes, Gershwin, Copland, Babbitt, Carter, Cage and others have been, it is still possible to discern three broad streams of evolution in that body of classical music that can be called distinctly American. One of these might be called the "Americanist" mode, drawing heavily on vernacular styles and themes, and operating within the essentially stable universe of the traditional symphonic, choral, vocal and instrumental forms. The second might be described as the "experimental" mode, seeking to explore new timbral resources, organizational methods and performance styles. Certain composers, such as Ives, Cowell, Grainger or Foss, kept one foot in each of these camps. Others adhered mainly to one or the other. Thus, it is possible to speak in terms of the MacDowell-(Ives)-Griffes-Gershwin-Copland-Thomson-Harris-Schuman tradition, on the one hand, and the Ives-

C owell-Varèse-Partch-Cage-Oliveros tradition on the other. The third, more academically oriented, tradition includes such figures as Howard Hanson, Elliott Carter, Roger Sessions, Milton Babbitt and Walter Piston, and traces its historical, if not its musicological, roots back as far as John Knowles Paine, Edward MacDowell and Horatio Parker. Important as the works of these more academically oriented composers are, however, there is little evidence to suggest that they have caught the imagination of the broad American public with the same fervor as either the "Americanists" or the "experimentalists."

One thing is absolutely clear, however, whether one argues for three or more main streams of American art music outside of jazz: that the latest phase of development in American music, somewhat loosely called "minimalism," has been created by a collection of composers whose training, like that of the post-modernists, involved thorough study of all these American musical trends, and whose music builds to some extent on each of them, including jazz.

The term "minimalism" comes from the world of painting and sculpture, and refers to an approach to art (and music) that, while it has attracted considerable attention and financial support from abroad, was primarily based in the United States. Minimalist visual art has been viewed by some art historians as the last stage in the evolution of Abstract Modernism, and was a predominant style of the 1960s. After a period of dormancy during the 1970s, minimalism resurfaced in the 1980s, although it never achieved the immediacy and excitement it had generated two decades earlier. Among the more famous exponents of minimalism were the sculptors Sol DeWitt and Donald Judd, and the painter Frank Stella.

Minimalist art acquired its label because the works generally avoided conspicuous figural images, compositional maneuvering, rounded forms or sharp contrasts of hue. Minimalist sculpture makes extensive use of simple geometric forms, such as the right angle and cube, while minimalist painting often tends to explore subtle gradations of single hues on monochrome canvases as well as geometric designs extended over large spaces. From the viewer's standpoint, the thrust of the minimalist esthetic resides in the fact that reacting to such works often requires extended periods of time while the subtle inflections of the works in question gradually permeate one's awareness.

As with all esthetic labels, there are serious problems with the term "minimalism," whether applied to visual art or to music. Almost none of the artists or composers to whom the label has become attached accept it as any kind of useful description of their work, and in fact it is often confusing and contradictory in the face of the actual pieces it purports to describe.

This is only one of the many parallels between "minimalism" and the label "impressionism," which was similarly adapted from the world of visual arts and applied to the music of Debussy, Ravel and others in the early 20th century.

In a very real sense, it is misleading even to speak of musical minimalism as a distinct style, because its roots are ancient and are found in more than just American or European music history. If minimalism is defined as gradual, rather than sudden change in the tonal, rhythmic, timbral, textural and other parameters of music, the term can be as well applied to a great deal of early European polyphony, to aspects of Indonesian gamelan music, to a variety of Middle Eastern and European religious chant styles, to indigenous Amerindian and West African music, to Hindu and Tibetan Buddhist vocal meditation techniques, to some of the preludes and toccatas of J. S. Bach and other European Baroque composers, and to certain works of Anton Webern, Morton Feldman and other modernists wherein all the musical events are reduced to the merest gestural signatures or aphorisms. These are only a few of the terminological quagmires one risks becoming stuck in if the label is taken too seriously.

But, for better or for worse, the label is in common usage and provides the most generally recognizable handle for discussing this style of American music. So, for the sake of convenience, this chapter will continue to use it—as long as we bear in mind its manifest limitations.

There are five major composers currently associated with the development of that constellation of stylistic traits which is called minimalism today. They are La Monte Young (b. 1935), Terry Riley (b. 1935), Steve Reich (b. 1936), Philip Glass (b. 1937) and John Adams (b. 1947). None of these refers to himself as a "minimalist," and the music of each is recognizably the product of a distinctly different creative personality finding different solutions to a set of related musical issues and challenges.

During the 1950s, academic serialism became the predominant style of composition, even for such previously tonal composers as Stravinsky, Copland and Sessions. The triggering event seems to have been the death in 1951 of Arnold Schoenberg, creator of the 12-tone method. Whether or not major composers consciously felt freer to explore Schoenberg's methods, after he (along with Berg and Webern) was no longer around to critique their efforts, remains unclear to this day. But after 1951 serialism decidedly expanded into an almost religious movement, especially in American universities and European musical centers such as Darmstadt, West Germany. The high priests of this method of composing—men like Sessions, Babbitt, Boulez, Perle, Stockhausen, Dallapiccola—were not content to let the musical results speak for themselves, but founded journals, associations and educational consortia exclusively devoted to promulgation of the post-Webern gospel. In many respects the serialist movement resembled the dogmatic, totalitarian organization of a Communist state, and, in fact, a good many of the composers involved imported overtly Marxist political agendas and dialectic into their musical utterances. In Germany especially, this was partly attributable to an overreaction to the excessive Wagnerian nationalism and romanticism that had made possible the trauma of the Nazi holocaust. In America, however, it was somewhat harder to explain.

Overall, the attitude of American musicians and audiences toward serialism contrasted markedly with that of their European counterparts. Western Europe, of course, possessed a much longer tradition of support for avant-garde movements in classical music, and this enthusiasm for new developments arose not only from the wealthy patrons of European composers, but from the universities and bourgeois intelligentsia as well. On the whole, European audiences were far more tolerant of music that was intellectually stimulating, even if it sounded bizarre or hyper-dissonant. Americans, on the other hand, have tended since colonial times to view music as a form of entertainment first and only secondarily, if at all, as a fine art. As a result, Americans were far less willing to put up with music whose sound repelled them, no matter how brilliant its conception might be. Thus, in Europe, the serialist movement gained more widespread support among lay audiences. In America, it tended to gravitate toward the rarefied intellectual atmosphere of universities and conservatories.

It is also likely that the more highly objective and methodic approach to composition represented by serialism made it easier to teach, evaluate and demonstrate within the educational paradigm of the typical American university, and thus the very structure of university music education favored such pseudo-scientific means of composition over the more nebulous questions of "personal expression" or "inspiration." But, whatever the case, composition students born in the late 1930s took the full brunt of the serialist storm when they entered college or conservatory in the 1950s. It is no accident, therefore, that four of the five premier minimalist composers were born between 1935 and 1937, because, in many important respects, the so-called "minimalist" movement was and is a specific, conscious reaction against dogmatic serialism, and the repellent effect 12-tone music had on audiences and performers throughout the 1940s, 1950s and 1960s.

La Monte Young and Terry Riley

La Monte Young is credited today as the founder of minimalism. Born in Bern, Idaho, on October 14, 1935, he began studying clarinet and saxophone as a child. He attended Los Angeles City College, Los Angeles State

College and UCLA during the 1950s, graduating from the last of these in 1958. That same year he created his *Trio for Strings,* probably the first identifiable minimalist composition. He did graduate work at University of California, Berkeley from 1958 to 1960, then went to Darmstadt for further study with Stockhausen. In 1960–1961 he also studied electronic music with Richard Maxfield in New York and to this day preserves documents of Maxfield's career that are available nowhere else.

From an early age, Young was fascinated by steady-state sounds such as wind, electrical hums and geographic resonances. After encountering recordings of Indian and Japanese music at UCLA he began to use sustained tones as a primary structural element in his music. This is most obvious in his 1957 *For Brass* and the previously mentioned trio. His use of sustained tones led to later work that experimented with just-intonation and other aspects of tuning. In 1970 he began studying the Kirana style of Hindustani classical vocal music and became a disciple of the Indian master Pran Nath.

Terry Riley, born in Colfax, California, in 1935 is only a few months older than Young and was a fellow graduate student with the latter at UC Berkeley during the late 1950s. Young introduced Riley to serialist techniques, with which he was deeply involved at the time, but the latter soon

A contemporary photograph of **Terry Riley** *(b. 1935), whose early work with "pattern fields" laid the groundwork for minimalism.* (Photograph courtesy of the composer.)

rejected these as the foundation of a viable personal style. Under Young's influence however, and drawing on his interest in jazz improvisation as well, Riley began to experiment with the same sort of sustained-tone ideas. By 1963, he had evolved a theory of what he calls "pattern fields," the simultaneous sounding of identical tonal, highly rhythmic musical phrases that shift against themselves in a pulsating field of sound.

After taking his M.A. in 1961 he went to Paris and worked at the ORTF recording studios. He returned to the Bay Area in 1964, and, in that same year, achieved the first culminating application of his idea of pattern fields in the seminal work, *In C* for unspecified instruments. He encountered the young Steve Reich, who had recently completed studies with Luciano Berio and Darius Milhaud at Mills College. *In C* exerted a profound influence on Reich's developing ideas about pulse and phase shifting (see below). At about the same time, Riley produced his *A Rainbow in Curved Air,* which further developed his unique approach to musical texture and would later influence the popular music of the late 1960s and early 1970s as well. He pioneered the practice of holding all-night improvisation concerts, and placed himself in the forefront of the trend toward marathon performances that later found theatrical expression as well in the works of Robert Wilson.

Like Young, Riley became a disciple of Pran Nath in 1970, then proceeded to an academic career at Mills College in 1971. His work has concentrated heavily on improvisational schemata, with strong influences of both American jazz and Hindustani classical music. During the 1980s he produced a series of nine string quartets, in collaboration with the adventurous San Francisco–based Kronos Quartet. These works extended the integration of Riley's varied techniques and ideas into a new realm of mature compositions that have yet to be fully evaluated by the musical world.

Neither of the two senior minimalists, Young and Riley, has pursued public careers to the same extent as their slightly younger colleagues, Reich and Glass, although both remain active. This is probably due to the powerful effect of their experiences with Pran Nath and Hindu theology in general, which is less oriented toward the achievement of the individual artist as such. Young, in particular, has created a number of continuously evolving composition projects (such as his *The Tortoise: his Dreams and Journeys,* begun in 1964, or his *The Well-Tuned Piano,* whose creation spanned the years 1964–1981) which cannot exactly be called "pieces," but serve more as a vehicle for ever-changing musical experience over time, thus acquiring a fluidity analogous to Walt Whitman's ever-unfinished *Leaves of Grass.* He has also recently begun to amalgamate his earlier ideas into various traditions of American jazz, and has formed an avant-garde blues band that is currently performing both in the United States and abroad.

As striking as are the parallels between the careers of La Monte Young and Terry Riley, those between Steve Reich and Philip Glass are even more so. Reich is the elder of the two and received recognition for his work somewhat earlier than Glass, but both were students at Juilliard at the same time, both later worked with Milhaud, and, in the late 1960s, they worked and performed together in New York. It has been said of Debussy and Ravel that they were too similar, and, in some respects, too different to remain friends for very long. Although the age difference between Reich and Glass is much smaller than between the two impressionist masters, a similar principle appears to be operating in their relationship as colleagues. Since 1974, when Glass began to achieve a substantive personal style and to create operas, these two foremost contemporary American composers' paths have diverged significantly, and their personal relationship has assumed a more competitive character.

Steve Reich

Steve Reich was born in New York on October 3, 1936. After receiving some piano instruction as a child, he developed an interest in jazz drumming and became a devotee of Kenny Clarke. At the age of fourteen he began formal instruction in Western percussion styles with Roland Kohloff, then proceeded to studies in philosophy and music (with William Austin) at Cornell University. Reich graduated with honors in philosophy from Cornell in 1957, then began private composition lessons with Hall Overton in New York. During his work with Overton he devoted extensive study to the *Mikrokosmos* of Béla Bartók, particularly with regard to Bartók's unique application of contrapuntal methods, which played an important role in the evolution of his personal style. In 1958 he enrolled at the Juilliard School and began further study with Vincent Persichetti and William Bergsma.

After leaving Juilliard, Reich went on to Mills College for further study with Darius Milhaud and Luciano Berio. He remained in the Bay Area until 1965, producing early tape pieces such as *It's Gonna Rain*, in which he explored the polyrhythmic results of manipulating multiple pre-recorded voices. This was also the period in which he met and was influenced by Terry Riley. In addition, Reich collaborated with experimental filmmaker Robert Nelson on soundtracks for the films *The Plastic Haircut* and *Oh Dem Watermelons.*

Steve Reich *(b. 1936) whose early work with phase-shifting and polyrhythm laid the foundations of minimalism.* (Photo by Linda Alaniz, c. 1989 by Martha Swope Associates, courtesy of Outward Visions Inc.)

The technique known as "phase shifting" became something of an obsession in Reich's work between 1968 and 1970, after his return to New York. Phase shifting, as Reich applied it, works essentially like this:

Two identical musical or acoustic activities, whether recorded on tape or performed by musicians, are begun at the same time and repeated. As repetitions accumulate, the events become slightly disconnected in time, i.e., "out-of-phase" with each other. As more time and repetitions pass, the discontinuities become more extreme and new perceptual relationships begin to emerge, seemingly at random, but always as a result of the continual shifting of phase relationships. This might be represented graphically in the following way.

In phase
1 ′ ′ ′ ′ ′ ′ ′ ′ ′
2 ′ ′ ′ ′ ′ ′ ′ ′ ′

Shifting phase
1 ′ ′ ′ ′ ′ ′ ′ ′ ′
2 ′ ′ ′ ′ ′ ′ ′ ′ ′

After returning to New York, Reich developed (in collaboration with electronic engineer Larry Owens) a device that they christened the "Phase-Shifting Pulse Gate" to channel electronic impulses into a phase-shifted sound complex. In 1968–1969 he created *Pulse Music,* using eight electronic oscillators, and performed it with the pulse gate. This was followed by *Four Log Drums,* which used acoustic instruments via microphones to explore further possibilities of the device. But Reich was becoming disenchanted with the musical passivity involved in merely sitting at a table and turning dials.

In 1966, he formed his first ensemble, "Steve Reich and Musicians," and began to give concerts in venues such as the Park Place Gallery (1967) and Town Hall (1971). In 1969 he followed a precedent set by many of America's most significant composers (including Copland, Toch, Cowell, Cage, Maxfield and others) in joining the faculty of New York's New School for Social Research, and, in 1970, traveled to Ghana where he studied African drumming at the University of Ghana in Accra.

Reich had been interested in African, Balinese and other non-Western music since his years in California, especially the rhythmic aspects of such music. In the early 1960s he had read A. M. Jones' seminal *Studies in African Music* and also been later impressed by Colin McPhee's fundamental text, *Music in Bali.* While Reich had (and has) no interest in attempting to create "Westernized" versions of such ethnic musics, in the late 1960s and early 1970s he began to incorporate rhythmic and polyrhythmic *processes* derived from these studies into an original style of composition that was driven by a central, articulated, sometimes changing pulse.

After he returned to New York from Ghana in 1970, he began work on one of the key compositions of his oeuvre, *Drumming.* In *Drumming* Reich began to move away from the interest in shifting phase relationships that characterized his earlier work, and concentrated more exclusively on the purely rhythmic dimension. He became particularly interested in polymetric processes, derived from African drumming techniques, which implied simultaneous but contradictory metric bases. This is particularly germane when rhythmic units of 3, 4, 6 (and less symmetrical groupings) occur simultaneously within a compound meter such as 12/8 time. This principle lies at the root of much African drumming and is presaged in American music as early as the "Alcotts" movement (1912) of Ives' *Concord Sonata.* It also plays a significant role in Balinese gamelan music, and can be found in motets and madrigals of the English Renaissance composers as well—all of which have entered into Reich's study and musical thought at various times.

This second phase of Reich's ongoing concern with rhythmic processes at many different levels of musical organization enabled him to compose works that could be performed by live musicians, rather than electronic devices, and thus preserve those more humanistic qualities in live performance that Reich values highly. Later, both his experience with phase shifting and with pulse-driven structures would combine to produce pieces such as his *Vermont Counterpoint* (1982) and *New York Counterpoint* (1985).

Throughout the early 1970s Reich continued developing these and other ideas, and gave more performances with his ensemble, both in the United States and abroad. He spent the summers of 1973 and 1974 studying Balinese gamelan music with Balinese teachers at the American Society for Eastern Arts in Seattle, and also in Berkeley. This period culminated in the *Music for 18 Musicians,* which premiered at Town Hall in New York in April of 1976. *Music for 18 Musicians* is identified as a minimalist piece by John Adams (writing in *Grove's Dictionary of American Music,* 1985) and represented perhaps Reich's most complex application of all his techniques developed up to that time. It was scored for larger instrumental resources than any of his prior works, and did more than any previous piece to establish his reputation. This was followed by major works such as his *Octet* (1979), *Tehillim* (based on Hebrew psalms and reflecting Reich's growing interest in his Jewish heritage), *The Desert Music* (1984), and *Sextet* (1985).

After the premier of Philip Glass' first opera, *Einstein on the Beach,* in 1976, Reich became increasingly estranged from his former colleague and fellow graduate student. Glass' approach to opera is often highly ceremonial. His early works often harked back to the pageantry of ancient Greek and Hindu religious drama and, especially after 1984, made use of conventional styles of singing and acting. When John Adams joined the revival of interest in contemporary opera with his even more conventional *Nixon in China* (1986), Reich began to object to what he perceived as a neo-conservative trend in these and similar works. For one thing, Reich asserts that the conception of any music theatre piece must begin with a definition of its vocal style, and considers the highly cultivated vocal style of traditional opera to have already served its purpose in music history. In contrast to Glass and Adams, his work has called for a generally wider variety of singing-voice types and is also more deeply involved in the manipulation of speech rhythms. Reich's interest in speech rhythms dates from his earliest tape pieces based on recorded speech, such as *It's Gonna Rain* and *Come Out,* and was further developed in his 1986 *Different Trains*—a work that also explored the psychological and musical associations in the composer's mind relating both to the frequent train journeys he experienced as a child being shuttled back and forth between divorced parents living in different cities, and the final, fatal train journeys of European Jews being driven to concentration camps by the Nazis in the 1930s and 1940s.

In 1989 Reich began a collaborative work with his wife, video artist Beryl Korot, on which he worked exclusively for three years and which was to become his first fully staged foray into music/video theatre, or "intermedia," as it has come to be called in the 1990s. Entitled *The Cave,* this piece further develops Reich's overriding interests in speech rhythm and rhythmic organization, and in articulating the psychological landscape of his personal Jewish heritage. Furthermore, it is intended to represent in actual practice (as opposed to mere verbal critique) his view of the direction that musical theatre should be going. The title refers to the cave at Hebron, Israel, legendary site of the grave of Abraham, and the work deals with interpretations of characters in the biblical patriarch's life as expressed in pre-compositional interviews that Reich recorded with individuals from three distinct cultural groups: Israelis, Palestinians and contemporary Americans. In *The Cave,* Reich incorporates live performance by actors and musicians as well as the recorded voices of the non-performers previously interviewed on the subject of the piece, all integrated with oversized video projections. Its American premiere at the Brooklyn Academy of Music in October 1993 was heralded with much discussion in the press of ways in which this work contrasts with the operas of Glass and Adams. But whether Reich's view will prevail in contemporary music theatre remains to be seen.

Philip Glass

The music of Philip Glass has received much wider exposure than that of any of his minimalist colleagues. This is partly due to Glass' talent for self-promotion and partly due to the music's greater intersection with popular music styles. But there is also an inherent craftsmanship and calculated plan behind each of Glass' pieces that his critics often miss. It has been said of Glass that "anyone can write that stuff," a comment that also often greeted the music of Schoenberg and Webern in earlier decades. In their case, this reaction was prompted by the high degree of dissonance and seeming motivic chaos of early 12-tone music. In Glass' case, it is prompted by the deceptive simplicity of his harmonic and rhythmic constructions. His many imitators have discovered to their chagrin that it is anything but easy to duplicate the fine line Glass treads between sheer monotony and subtle musical tension in both his large and small works.

Glass was born in Baltimore on January 31, 1937. His father, Ben Glass, ran a radio repair shop which carried phonograph records as a sideline. The senior Glass would, on occasion, bring home records that were not selling well and play them for his children, hoping to divine the reasons for their poor commercial appeal. Among these recordings were sonatas by

Schubert, symphonies by Shostakovich, the late Beethoven string quartets and other masterworks slightly askew of the classical mainstream. Thus, the young Glass acquired an early exposure to some of the more interesting and esoteric works of the classical repertoire. It was not until he entered college that he encountered the core symphonic, instrumental and operatic literature.

Glass took up study of the violin at the age of six, and the flute at eight. In 1946 he became the youngest student ever admitted to Baltimore's prestigious Peabody Conservatory. After his second year of high school, he was admitted to the University of Chicago where he majored in philosophy and mathematics. While pursuing his undergraduate studies, Glass continued to devote a major portion of his attention to piano and composition. At that time, like all academic composers of his generation, he was under the sway of the serialist movement represented by Babbitt and Boulez. Although it then appeared that the future of all art music lay in the serialist direction, Glass was no exception to the tendency of students born in the 1930s to resist the serialist dogma. He gradually became disaffected with serialism and gravitated more and more toward the "Americanist" works of Ives, Copland and Schuman.

Philip Glass *(b. 1937) in 1983, a lyrical minimalist who has become the only fully committed opera composer of his generation.* (Photo by Richard Pasley, courtesy of International Production Associates.)

After graduating from Chicago in 1956, Glass went on to Juilliard, where he, like Reich, studied with William Bergsma and Vincent Persichetti. He was still writing in the 12-tone idiom, not yet having synthesized his growing dissatisfaction into an independent style, and, with Persichetti's support, he succeeded in having some of his early, conventional works from this period published by the Theodore Presser Co. But, while Juilliard gave him its usual first-class training in musicianship (and a Master's Degree in Music), Glass still failed to find the new creative direction he was seeking there.

In the summer of 1961, Glass, like so many of his generation, studied with Darius Milhaud in Aspen. Whether or not Milhaud's influence led Glass to approach Nadia Boulanger is unclear—but approach her he did and, by 1964, Glass found himself in Paris on a Fulbright scholarship working with the same creative force that had shaped the talents of Copland, Thomson, Piston, Carter and a host of others.

While in Paris, Glass was commissioned by filmmaker Conrad Rooks to translate the music of the great Indian sitarist, Ravi Shankar, into Western notation for recording by French musicians. The young composer's encounter with the Indian master, whose work was just then beginning to influence musicians as diverse as Yehudi Menuhin and George Harrison, proved to be the long-sought catalyst which set Glass on the path that led to his mature style. Working with Shankar and his associate, tablaist Alla Rakha, Glass encountered for the first time the extended rhythmic cycles of Hindustani classical music, its sophisticated system of modal scales (called "ragas") and its propulsive improvisational techniques. This opened the young composer's eyes (and ears) to a whole new vista of possibilities. He spent the next six months traveling in India, the Himalayas and the Middle East, absorbing the varied approaches to music indigenous to those regions.

It was also during his Paris years that Glass met and married actress/director JoAnne Akalaitis. A veteran of Herbert Blau and Jules Irving's Actors Workshop in San Francisco, Akalaitis fostered Glass' developing interest in modern theatre. Together they regularly attended Jean-Louis Barrault's Théâtre Odeon where they saw the works of Beckett and Genet, directed by Roger Blin, as well as the plays of Bertolt Brecht at the Théâtre Nationale Populaire. In addition, the young couple made theatre excursions to England and Germany, and associated with a group of young actor/directors with whom Glass co-founded what was later to be called the Mabou Mines theatre company in New York City. While working with the Mabou Mines collective in Paris, Glass functioned as music director and/or resident composer for a number of original productions of modern repertoire.

In 1967, Glass returned to New York and began systematically to build the foundation of his musical style. He uses the terms "repetitive" and "reductive" to describe that style, but there is more to it than is conveyed by these simple words. Like Reich and others, Glass often works with cycles of musical events. But where Reich's cycles tend to focus on polyrhythmic and polymetric patterns, Glass' are most audible in the harmonic dimension. While returning to traditional triadic and other ternary chord structures in his harmony, Glass eschewed conventional harmonic progressions and modulations. Instead of producing chromatic sequences by altering individual chord tones, in the manner of a Wagner or a Franck (two composers whose chromaticism began the evolution toward the very serialism that "minimalists" reacted against), Glass' principal mode of harmonic movement is the abrupt shift between chords that are *related*, but not *sequential* in the traditional manner of functional harmony. That is to say, his harmonic sequences are based largely on the spatial proximity of close position chords on the keyboard (or staff), rather than their harmonic proximity on the circle of fifths. This has enabled him to "short-circuit" the ear's conventional harmonic expectations and produce a kaleidoscopic array of non-traditional harmonic shifts, which are then frequently delegated to repetitive cycles, both long and short depending on the context of the piece. In his lighter works, such as those in his early *Glassworks* album, the repetitive harmonic patterns tend to be shorter and more directly audible. In longer pieces, such as the operas, the harmonic designs may stretch out over the length of entire acts, or even the entire opera.

Glass' harmonic procedures, by their very nature, require protracted stretches of time to play themselves out. He shares with all "minimalists" the proneness to let the *process* take over at times, reflecting the aleatoric influence of Cage. But, like his colleagues (and contrary to Cage's approach), he always maintains direct control over the length and variability of those processes. Thus, a major portion of his craft resides in knowing just how much repetition is too much, and when to introduce the subtle variations that will hold the listener's attention.

Rhythmically, Glass' music is deliberately less sophisticated than that of Reich. Where Reich often establishes a separately articulated rhythmic "core" at the center of his total sound structure (as, for instance, in his *Desert Music*), Glass more often deploys separate rhythmic patterns among the individual tonal voices in his minimalist counterpoint, similar in certain respects to the more complex (and less audible) technique of creating separate rhythmic entities in the work of Carter and Sessions during the 1950s and 1960s. Overall his music tends to be more traditionally contrapuntal than that of other minimalists, and he uses both the alternating slow tremolo and repeated close-position arpeggios to the point where they have become signatures of his style.

After his return to New York in 1967, Glass created a piano duet entitled *In Again, Out Again,* which explored the intersections between the early minimalism of Young, Riley and Reich with the non-Western techniques he had studied in India. He also attempted to arouse local interest in a *String Quartet* he had composed while in Paris, but the quartet was not to see major distribution until it was recorded some twenty-three years later by the progressive Kronos Quartet. He performed once or twice with Reich's ensemble, then began to form his own. Throughout this period, minimalist ideas were beginning to influence many of the avant-garde composers based in lower Manhattan, and both Reich and Glass functioned as part of a minimalist "community" that included such lesser-known figures as Meredith Monk, Terry Jennings, Tom Johnson, James Tenney and Charlemagne Palestine. Glass had some experimental works performed in gallery concerts in SoHo and other downtown Manhattan locations, but devoted a major portion of his time to continued development of his theatre music and work with the Mabou Mines company. He encountered and was influenced by Joseph Chaikin's "Open Theater" and Richard Schechner's "Performance Group" as well as the "Living Theater" founded by Julian Beck and his wife, Judith Malina (see Chapter 11). From its embryonic days in Paris through the early 1980s (a period of almost twenty years) Glass composed more than a dozen scores for the Mabou Mines troupe.

In 1969 Glass, Akalaitis and other members of the Mabou Mines company began work on the culminating production of their period of collaboration: *Red Horse Animation.* To stage this piece it became necessary to construct a special floor that would act as a sounding board—amplified by contact microphones—for the dancers' feet. Working together at Glass' recently purchased summer home in Nova Scotia, the creative team of Glass, Akalaitis and painter Power Boothe designed a system of modular sections to pull off this effect.

Red Horse Animation also provided the vehicle that enabled Glass to develop his personal application of "additive" rhythm, where the rhythmic underpinnings of a piece are organized in an arithmetical manner. This technique became a cornerstone of Glass' mature style and is characterized by the continuous addition of notes and rests to the repetitive rhythmic patterns of his melodic phrases. The additive process provided Glass another means of spinning out melodic phrases in the absence of conventional tonal modulation.

The last big work Glass created before turning to opera was *Music in 12 Parts,* a four-hour piece amalgamating and summarizing all the aspects of his style as it had developed during the period from 1967 to 1974. It is from *Music in 12 Parts* that one can reliably date the beginning of Glass' mature style.

In 1973, came one of the most significant meetings in Glass' career. Glass attended a Brooklyn Academy of Music performance of writer/director Robert Wilson's *The Life and Times of Josef Stalin,* and his reaction to this eleven-hour meditation in movement and images was immediate and profound. In Wilson, Glass felt he had found the sympathetic spirit with whom he could realize the vision of a new musical theatre that had been forming in his imagination over the past several years with Mabou Mines. In the spring of 1974 the two began to meet on a regular basis to explore ideas for a joint project. Sharing an interest in historical personalities, they alternately proposed and rejected such diverse figures as Charlie Chaplin, Mahatma Gandhi and Adolf Hitler as subjects for a piece. When Wilson suggested Albert Einstein, in Glass' words, "that immediately clicked." From these beginnings emerged the revolutionary opera that put Glass' name on the map of major living composers, *Einstein on the Beach.*

Capitalizing on the resources offered by the performance ensembles and administrative contacts that each of them had established by this time, and with the help of a Rockefeller Grant secured for Wilson by Virgil Thomson's librettist, Jack Larson, Wilson and Glass began to rough out the structure of the opera during the summer and fall of 1974. After two and a half years' work, *Einstein* officially premiered at the Avignon Festival in France in August of 1976. This was followed by a European tour and subsequent performances at the Metropolitan Opera House and Brooklyn Academy of Music in New York City.

Einstein brought together a multitude of movements, trends, theories and techniques that had been evolving in the worlds of avant-garde theatre and music since the days of John Cage and Julian Beck. The authors view it as a "portrait" opera, as distinct from a biographical piece, and dispensed with plot entirely in favor of a series of images that bear greater or lesser relationship to Albert Einstein as a 20th-century cultural icon. Trains form one of the central images of the piece, as does the symbolism of a courtroom trial (history passing judgment on science and technology run amok?). The figure of Einstein himself acts as a unifying presence onstage, kind of a Greek chorus, but does not participate directly in the tableaux. Many of these ideas stem from roots laid down in the 1960s by the Living Theatre, but were developed and refined by Wilson through his formidable history of pre-*Einstein* productions, which made innovative use of special lighting, linguistic distortions of text, and juxtaposition of images that are historically locatable but displaced from any ordinary time sequence.

Glass' music, on the other hand, with its abstract, non-descriptive properties of extended repetition and very gradual harmonic change, could not be viewed as "scoring" in any conventional sense of the term. That is, his textures, rhythms and melodies do not overtly represent musical parallels to the stage action or meaning of the text. In this regard he followed the tradition established by Cage and Cunningham in their joint productions of the 1960s and 1970s, wherein the music bore no intentional relationship to the dance whatsoever.

As a young man, Glass had been powerfully affected by Cage's book, *Silence* (1961). Glass' special way of articulating the Cagean principal of "indeterminacy," vis-a-vis *Einstein*, lies in his assertion that "the audience completes the work." That is to say, the opera provides a vehicle, not unlike a psychiatrist's ink-blot test, into which each audience member projects his or her own meaning, relevance, emotion and perceptions, stimulated by the visual and sonic images of the piece. Although this notion is not always as explicit in Glass' later operas, it continued to influence his approach to the shaping of all his subsequent music theatre pieces.

The success of *Einstein* led to further operas: *Satyagraha* (1980), a more historically conventional portrait of Mahatma Gandhi, and *Akhnaten* (1984), a portrait of the monotheist Egyptian pharaoh. But the definition of opera itself began to change in Glass' hands, and this change aroused a predictable amount of controversy from all sides of the operatic community.

Operatic conservatives were put off by Glass' seeming indifference to chronological time sequences of events in the plot, when he used plot at all. Furthermore, the apparent disconnection between much of the emotional evocations of Glass' "minimalist" music and the drama flies in the face of conventional European practice from the time of Gluck, if not earlier.

From the other side, composers such as Reich criticized Glass' increasing use of the highly trained voices and highly specific vocal style of opera singers, as opposed to singing actors or other kinds of voices. As stated earlier, in Reich's view, the conception of any work of music theatre begins with the vocal style, and he sees Glass as having contributed nothing new in this department.

Following his first trilogy of large-scale "portrait" operas, Glass collaborated with Wilson again on the "Rome Section" of Wilson's twelve-hour, multi-national, multi-composer epic, *the CIVIL warS*, created for the Olympic Games of 1984. As with the earlier Wilson-Glass collaboration on *Einstein*, the "Rome Section" is non-narrative, filled with temporal discontinuities and peopled by an eclectic group of characters ranging from Hercules to Garibaldi to Mary Todd Lincoln.

Although Glass lists his 1980 mixed-media theatre piece, *The Photographer*, in his opera catalogue, this work challenges the conventional definition of opera more radically than anything in his output between *Einstein* and *the CIVIL warS*. Based on the scandalous life of photographer Eadward Muybridge, this three-act performance utilizes drama, dance and slides of Muybridge's photos, but has no singing roles at all.

In 1986, Glass turned to yet another kind of subject, the fairy tale, in his collaborative opera *The Juniper Tree* based on the story by the Brothers Grimm. The music was composed jointly by Glass and Robert Moran, to a libretto by Arthur Yorinks. The composers divided their labors in such a way that each produced half the scenes, a Glass scene alternating with a Moran scene throughout the piece. Although reviews of this short (ninety minute) work were mixed, most critics agreed that Glass and Moran achieved a startling consistency of stylistic focus, despite their risky composing method.

In 1988, Glass created *The Making of the Representative for Planet 8,* to a libretto by Doris Lessing derived from her allegorical novel of the same name. *Representative* followed a more conventional dramatic format than the earlier operas and used a standard orchestra. That same year saw the completion and premiere of *The Fall of the House of Usher,* to a libretto by Yorinks based on Poe. This particular short story has been a consistent temptation to opera composers in the century and a half since it was written and generated incomplete attempts at "operafication" by both Debussy and Sessions. The Glass-Yorinks piece focuses on the psychological ambiguities of the tale, rather than its horror-movie kitsch, leaving the audience uncertain as to whether the characters are real or merely products of their own fantasy.

The four latest operas that Glass has created include *Hydrogen Jukebox,* on which the composer collaborated with poet Allen Ginsberg, premiered at the Spoleto U.S.A. Festival in 1990; *The Voyage,* premiered by the Metropolitan Opera in October 1992; *Orphée,* a chamber opera based on the film by Jean Cocteau, composed in Brazil in 1991; and *White Raven,* another collaboration with Robert Wilson, dealing with the history of Portuguese explorers. He has also created music for two important films, *The Thin Blue Line,* an exploration of the series of events that led to the wrongful conviction of a man for murder, and *Mishima,* a somewhat surrealistic biography of the great Japanese novelist who committed ritual suicide in 1970.

Of the later operas, *The Juniper Tree, Usher* and *Orphée* were all conceived for the small performing space of the American Repertory Theatre in Cambridge, Massachusetts and, as a result, have a more chamber-like quality than Glass' larger works. Moreover, as his style has matured over the years, the signature elements that were associated with the "minimalist" label during his early works—elements such as his repetitive use of slowly tremulated melodic intervals, tonally and/or modally shifting triadic chords, and repeated arpeggios—have receded increasingly into the background textures of his work. By the time he composed the unclassifiable theatre piece, *1000 Airplanes on the Roof* (1989), the motion of the bassline had assumed more prominence in Glass' style, and, by 1991, during the period of the composition of *The Voyage* and *Orphée,* solo contrapuntal lines between the voices and various instruments began to emerge significantly. Glass' recent works have focussed more tightly on the internal logic of musical and dramatic construction, in traditional operatic terms, and, for the time being at least, abandoned the use of arias and other set pieces—leading to the kind of greater dramatic continuity achieved by Menotti in *The Medium, The Consul* and *Martin's Lie.*

Of all the minimalist composers, Glass has become the best known. His music is generally more accessible to untrained listeners than is that of Reich, Young or Riley, and it is perhaps not unreasonable to describe his style as somewhat more lyrical than that of his contemporaries. He is also the only fully committed dramatic composer to emerge from the "minimalist" generation. His musical language has become almost too distinctive, and the composer himself admits that, after having struggled for twenty years to achieve his highly individual voice, he is now struggling to expand it and avoid becoming trapped by it.

John Adams

John Adams is the youngest of the five principal minimalist composers, having been born in Worcester, Massachusetts, on February 15, 1947. Unlike Young, Riley, Reich and Glass, Adams did not play a personal role in the formation of the aggregate minimalist style, but came to it more or less as a fully developed composer when Reich's ensemble gave him his first break by presenting the string sextet version of *Shaker Loops* in a New York concert in 1978.

Furthermore, Adams has not always functioned so exclusively as a composer as have his elder colleagues and did little performing of his own work prior to 1985. Adams studied principally with Leon Kirchner at Harvard University, from which he received both his B.A. and M.A. (1971) degrees. Thereafter he served as composer-in-residence with the Marlboro (Vermont) Festival and the San Francisco Symphony Orchestra. A great deal of his time was, therefore, spent in examining and evaluating the works of other composers, as well as overseeing the commissioning and premieres of other new works, both with these orchestras and with the San Francisco Conservatory, where he taught for several years.

During the late 1970s and early 1980s, Adams achieved significant recognition, primarily for his orchestral works such as *Shaker Loops* (revised version), *Harmonielehre* and *Harmonium.* The influences he acknowledges are eclectic, including jazz, Cagean aleatory and American vernacular music. He differs from the four senior minimalists in that his music tends to be more conservatively written, along more traditional theoretical lines and for more traditional performance resources. His style is something of a bridge between the experimental rhythmic approach of Reich, and the repetitiveness of Glass, to the post-modernist romanticism of Del Tredici or Corigliano (see Chapter 12).

In 1983, Adams was introduced to impresario Peter Sellars by conductor James Bolle. This meeting led to their subsequent collaboration on the operas *Nixon in China* (1985) and *The Death of Klinghoffer* (1991), both with libretti by Alice Goodman. Adams' approach to opera as a theatrical form is even more conservative than the conservatisms Reich has criticized in the works of Glass, though not as atavistic as Corigliano's. In both operas he worked with conventional voices, orchestra and plot structures. *Nixon in China* still betrays the obsessive repetitiveness associated with minimalism, even though the composer describes it as a "post-minimalist" work. *Klinghoffer,* however, largely repudiates even this level of intersection with minimalist traditions and comes much closer in effect to the kind of through-composed opera of Benjamin Britten, Menotti and Barber. The use of topical subjects from recent American history, rather than existing literary works or librettos dealing with more classical themes, has helped arouse public interest in the Adams-Goodman-Sellars operas, but whether or not Adams' reputation will ultimately rest on his musical theatre work or other aspects of his composition remains to be seen.

So-called "minimalism" constitutes the latest definable phase in the evolution of American classical music. As each of the composers associated with the label struggles to shake it off, and to pursue his unique course of development, we can only speculate on what kind of music will emerge from the next generation of composers: those born in the 1950s, 1960s and 1970s, who are just now beginning to have an impact on our national musical life. The academic icons that were held up as models to music students in the 1950s, Stravinsky, Schoenberg and Webern, were replaced in the 1960s by Cage, Crumb, Xenakis, Penderecki, Boulez, Berio and others. If it is often the fate of music students to react against their models, as Ives reacted against Parker and Chadwick, and as Reich and Glass reacted against Webern and Stravinsky, then it is reasonable to expect that younger composers will react against the post-modernists and minimalists—leading to yet a new synthesis of ideas and techniques. Moreover, the infusion of popular music, and especially of rock music created after 1964, into the musical environment of younger composers cannot fail to have some influence on their work. It may be that the next wave of American classical composers outside of academia will attempt a synthesis of popular and "serious" styles analogous to that achieved by George Gershwin in the context of the popular music of the 1920s, or Leonard Bernstein in the context of the 1950s. There are some preliminary indications of a growing tendency toward what seems like hyper-conservatism in the concert music of these younger composers, but it is too early, at this writing, to form any firm judgments about the shape this music might take.

Finally, the sociological and technological conditions that must be faced by younger composers at the close of the present century are very different than those dealt with by previous generations, and this is bound to have an effect on what gets written and what gets played in the late 1990s and afterward. In the final chapter, we will discuss some of those conditions as they are now emerging in the world of American classical music.

14

"The Shape of Things to Come" (Where We Have Come; Where We Are Going)

&

H. G. Wells, finishing his monolithic *Outline of History* shortly after the end of World War I, experienced the dangers of predicting the future based on the lessons of the past when he assured us that another worldwide conflict of such devastating proportions was not possible. He then had the unenviable luck to live through World War II. Having reviewed the lives and works of the most significant American composers to date—and some of the cultural conditions, auxiliary persons and institutions that made them possible—the purpose of this concluding chapter is not so much to offer predictions about the future of American classical music as to examine those forces at work in the contemporary world that seem to be having an impact on it, and that may reasonably be expected to continue exerting such influence as we approach the end of the millennium. This examination will include a survey of the major problems facing contemporary composers of serious art music today and will point out certain possibilities for new opportunities which seem to be present. In addition, it will seek to uncover a few false assumptions about American music that may exist in the minds of laypersons, assumptions based on historical conditions which no longer exist in any meaningful way.

Summary of the Recent History of American Classical Music

One often hears older composers saying today that this is an exciting time to be a composer. Such comments represent, perhaps, a kind of sigh of relief now that the death-grip of academic serialism on American classical music seems to have been broken once and for all. The demise of serialism has undoubtedly permitted composers in their sixties and seventies, who have formed the uniquely academic habit of keeping a sharp eye on all their colleagues' works before committing to a new piece, to experience a renewed sense of stylistic freedom. But the comment is dangerously naive.

The layman, no doubt, sometimes imagines that composers (and other artists) live in a perpetual state of free-spirited iconoclasm, a universe of total artistic self-determination where fashions, trends and pressures to conform hold no sway. But, if the history of music demonstrates nothing else, it demonstrates that *all* composers, past and present, have existed in a historical context where speaking in the broad musical syntax of the current era, or something reasonably close to it, whatever that syntax may be, is a prerequisite for even the most minimal recognition of one's efforts by one's peers. This is because music itself is continually evolving. To describe this evolution as "progress"—in music no less than in, for example, paleontology—implies the presence of some ultimate, conscious purpose to be achieved by it. And such a view has long and rightly been dismissed by serious scholars. But, even if there is no specific ideal toward which the entire history of musical development strives, there can be no question that each generation of composers has traditionally attempted to build on the discoveries and innovations of its predecessors. The popular image of the composer as a law unto him- or herself, even with such radicals as John Cage and Harry Partch, remains the purest sort of romantic fantasy.

During the course of this book, we have seen that the absence of a surviving indigenous American classical tradition prior to 1910 forced American composers from William Henry Fry through Edward MacDowell to seek their stylistic context in European forms and practices. This held true even for those later composers who sought to incorporate American folk music elements into their symphonic and operatic works—with the possible exceptions of Farwell, Ives, Cowell and Gershwin. After 1910, as a uniquely American classical music literature began to take shape, composers of William Schuman's and subsequent generations had the *option* of basing their studies on the works of purely American antecedents, but the musical traditions of Europe continued to exert such power in American music that none chose to avail him/herself of this option. Moreover, the rise of musical academia—and the self-conscious efforts of composers like Babbitt to transform academic composition into something akin to an experimental science—created a conformist atmosphere from the late 1940s onward, an atmosphere of intense pressure on American composers to work within theoretical concepts developed from the music of contemporary European masters such as Schoenberg, Webern, Bartók and Stravinsky. Not even such established freelancers as Copland or Foss were wholly immune to this pressure.

During the middle decades of this century, those American composers who remained dedicated to nurturing their own personal voices—such as Barber, Harris or Still—found themselves basically shut out of any venues in which the academic establishment exerted any measure of control, even while they remained more popular with the public than their academic contemporaries. Such authentic individualists gradually lost ground and even began to doubt themselves as the austere, mathematical and increasingly technological product of "precompositional methods" took over that portion of the musical world supported by universities and foundations.

Inevitably, audiences grew increasingly alienated from indigenous American composition during these years, despite the efforts of composers like Bernstein and Menotti to harness television in service of more humanistic types of music. Sources of funding dried up; serious, well-trained performers began to lose interest and reverted to the more or less exclusive study of ancient European masterpieces; pre-collegiate educators found themselves without the time or the means to integrate the increasingly outré conceptions of any composers more progressive than a Vincent Persichetti or a Vaclav Nelhybel into their curricula, with the result that students received ever-smaller exposure to contemporary music—indeed began to perceive classical music itself as a relic of a former age. And the return to more accessible styles in the music of the post-modernists and minimalists of recent years has not yet succeeded in restoring the public's interest in American music to anything like what it was in the 1920s, 1930s and early 1940s.

Some Problems Facing Composers and Others in the World of American Classical Music Today

A. Proliferation of Composers The growth of indigenous American classical music throughout the past century and a half has also been accompanied by a corresponding proliferation of composers. In the days of Anthony Philip Heinrich, serious American composers were viewed as freaks. By the time of John Knowles Paine, they had become mere oddities. Fifty years later—during the period of young Gershwin and Copland—serious American composers were a new, exciting cultural development. And, by the end of World War II, they had become esoteric specialists demanding a serious place in academia and major funding from public and private agencies. Each stage of this development was accompanied by a corresponding increase in the number of composers competing to be heard. But there is little evidence that a serious listening public for these voices has grown proportionally.

Today, with literally thousands of American composers striving in almost complete public oblivion, our situation is not unlike someone trying to make a speech in a room filled with several hundred people, each of whom is also trying to deliver his or her own oration. And the room was originally built to accommodate only a few dozen.

B. Public Arts Agencies and the Definition of Categories Faced with this Babel of contradictory, competitive, demanding creative voices—as well as the decline in private patronage after World War II—governments, corporations and groups of individuals have tried to respond through the formation of public arts agencies such as the National Endowment for the Arts (NEA), created by act of Congress in 1965, and individual state arts councils. In addition, large performance organizations, such as opera companies and symphony orchestras, have attempted to institutionalize their commissioning programs as well, placing them in the hands of committees rather than single managers or conductors.

But such agencies have had to make hard decisions. With limited funds available, they have had to decide whether (a) to try to offer a little support to the greatest possible number of qualified artists, or (b) to single out a select few for more comprehensive promotion. Because the committees charged with making these choices are often comprised of a cross section of the fine arts "community," each member bringing his or her own agenda to the task, the decision-making process favors the former approach over the latter.

Compounding the problems of such agencies is a total lack of agreement on what constitutes "art" in the late 20th century. Attempts to formulate objective criteria for awarding grants have been met with charges of elitism, often by individuals working within specific ethnic, experimental or folk art traditions who fear that the resulting criteria will not be applicable to their own work, or who simply fear a loss of financial support. The argument has extended to seemingly absurd lengths, even to the point of rejecting such an apparently obvious and desirable feature as "quality" in setting criteria.

But, in fact, objective standards in the arts can only be defined within established and relatively stable traditions. A master African drummer can define relative degrees of "quality" within the drumming of his students. A jazz improviser can discriminate between competent and incompetent improvisation. A teacher of European functional harmony can tell when an exercise does or does not conform to the "rules." An orchestral conductor can assess the playability, if not always the effect, of a given score. But, beyond this level of evaluation, no one can determine what distinguishes great art from mediocrity before the fact. The only historically reliable standard for making such judgments is whether or not a given work or style has survived and continued to have an impact on people after several generations of critical audiences have had a chance to digest it. History demonstrates that not even the artist himself is ultimately able to assess the "quality" of his own work with any final degree of assurance. So it is rather difficult to see how an agency such as the National Endowment proposes to define such a nebulous term as "quality," given the enormous range of styles and media (some of them quite experimental) that it seeks to support.

Such debates would be insignificant if today's artists, including composers, were not so dependent on arts councils and other public funding. This dependency, which has grown ever larger since the establishment of the NEA, is largely the result of the absence of a commercial market for "advanced" works, especially in the performing (as opposed to the visual and literary) arts. It is well worth examining why that commercial market does not seem to exist.

The categorical division between "classical" and "popular" music is a relatively recent phenomenon and largely a product of American music history. The preface to this volume defined "classical" music as that which is written to be listened to for its own sake, apart from any utilitarian, extra-musical function, and noted that no classical music culture has ever emerged in any part of the world without having been preceded by the development of a body of religious and folk music, and of a literate society with well-defined institutions. Furthermore, it put forth the proposition that any given "national" classical music must somehow embody in its broadly characteristic style a reflection of the spirit, values and emotional character common to more or less *all* the people native to that national culture. From this flowed the assertion that jazz, and other subcultural or region-specific musics, cannot lay claim to being THE American "classical" music, but may reasonably be considered one among many strains of American "art" music. The inescapable conclusion is this: if the unique nature of American society compels us to accept that each ethnic subgroup possesses its own "classical music," then THE American classical music simply has not yet evolved and may never evolve.

The effort to define these categories is not merely an academic issue. It affects the serious American composer's creative mission and ability to survive in the modern world in major ways. Commercial record companies, for example, very definitely distinguish between such categories and evaluate the sales performance of any given album or CD based on the expectation that "popular" music is going to perform better than "classical" music in the commercial marketplace. A composer or performer who sells ten thousand copies is considered a solid proposition under the classical label, but would not even be kept in circulation under the popular label.

Conversely, a composer or performer who sells a hundred thousand copies in the pop category would be considered a modest success, but in the classical category would be seen as a superstar.

Performing rights/royalty distribution organizations such as ASCAP and BMI must also wrestle with this issue in real economic terms on a daily basis. Both of these organizations have institutionalized the theoretical division between classical and popular music, and pay a different rate of royalties based on the category to which any given composer is assigned. Operating on the assumption that classical music is less commercially viable than popular music, both societies pay a far better rate of royalty on classical performances in order to equalize the discrepancy—a fact that is not lost on pop performers, many of whom have ventured into symphonic or other "crossover" adaptations of their pop styles in an attempt to cash in on the higher rates.

But, important as these questions are, they merely *acknowledge* the difference in size between the commercial audience for popular and classical musics—they do not *explain* it. Further insight can be gained when we consider that "classical" music is sometimes referred to as "formal" music (presumably in distinction to the "informality" of popular music). What makes it "formal" is a general preoccupation with theoretical issues relating to the structure of music itself, such as we have seen reflected in the work of composers from Ives, to Carter, to Crumb. The theoretical issues of formal music have often been derived from developments in European music of the past two centuries, but are not always so (*vide* the works of Cage, Partch, Oliveros and other experimentalists). Formal music in this century has tended toward the exploration of new tonalities, complex rhythmic phenomena and the timbral and textural innovations made possible by synthesizer and computer technology. As a result, it generally lacks the regular metric pulse characteristic of *all* American popular music, as well as the clearly defined sense of tonality, melody and symmetrical phrase structure present in popular music. The bottom line here is that formal music is more difficult to listen to and to comprehend. It often requires a serious effort on the listener's part to educate him- or herself regarding the composer's esthetic and intentions. Without this prior education, it may even be impossible to hear what the music is driving at.

But Americans, on the whole, don't want to be bothered by such things; they don't want to have to take a night school course in order to get some enjoyment out of a piece of music, especially in the age of mass musical media. If we have to read the collected works of Emerson, Hawthorne, Alcott and Thoreau to come to terms with Ives' *Concord Sonata*, for example, we'll just put on a recording of Beethoven's Fifth or the William Tell Overture.

The distinction between "formal" and "informal" music probably goes much farther toward explaining the difference in size between the audience for classical and the audience for popular music than do any of the elaborate theories about what actually constitutes "classical" music, or "quality" music, or THE American music tradition. The minimalist (and to a lesser extent, the post-modernist) composers have obviously recognized this point and deliberately removed many of the formalist elements so dear to the hearts of their immediate predecessors, with the result that their music has achieved a much higher public profile and, in the case of the minimalists, aroused the interest of several pop performers as well. A large segment of the potential audience for classical music today, conditioned by years of unheard, easy-to-listen-to, environmental Muzak, seems to want music that relaxes, music that does not intrude, music that allows the ears and the emotions to take a warm and fuzzy acoustical bath. Perhaps this is merely the latter-day extension of the auditory laziness that Charles Ives raged against throughout his lifetime. In any case, it would seem that his ideals about the rugged musical individualist seeking the "rough way up" the mountain are no closer to realization now than they were in 1910. And this is an issue that composers, performance institutions, arts agencies and performing rights organizations will probably continue to have to grapple with for the foreseeable future.

C. Censorship In addition to the problems of distributing funds and defining categories outlined above, institutions that exert an impact on contemporary music must deal with issues of both active and passive censorship in today's social and political climate. The arts councils and public funding agencies that have been created during the last thirty years have tried insure that some kind of formal, contemporary classical music tradition at least has a fighting chance for survival amid the tidal wave of popular culture. But it is the very pluralism of American art that tends to defeat them in this worthy effort. Certainly no peer evaluation panel member, charged with weighing the relative merits of this or that grant proposal, can hope to possess a comprehensive grasp of all the esthetic premises represented in any single set of application forms. Nor can any overworked political appointee, charged with administering a state or federal arts agency, expect to have an expert's knowledge of the total range of artistic disciplines supposedly serviced by that agency. The result has been that, over the past twenty years or so, different public arts agencies have developed different predilections, and all such agencies have gravitated more toward those arts whose demonstrable product is fairly easy to touch or see. This means that the visual arts, the folk arts and dance have established a strongly preferential position in public arts funding, while serious music, drama, poetry and literature, whose less-tangible products require more time between conception and realization, have been relegated to secondary consideration generally. The result is that more and more composers, willingly or not, have gravitated toward mixed-media or intermedia projects simply because such projects have a better chance of being funded.

This has often led to a kind of "passive" censorship in contemporary American composition. Motivated by well-intentioned, if naive, attempts to encourage what they perceive to be all the branches of American art equally, public funding administrators have frequently overstepped the bounds of their role by concocting specific programs that encourage certain modes of creation while suppressing others (via the mechanism of not funding them). In recent years, for example, administrators at the NEA and New England Foundation for the Arts, among others, have taken it upon themselves to decide that interdisciplinary creative ventures, collaborative efforts and projects that utilize non-Western traditions in obvious ways are "better" (or, at least, more worthy of support) than works by a single artist working within a single discipline. This, of course, enables them to spread their limited funds around among a larger number of artists, but also effectively prevents any single artist dependent upon public grants from exploring purely internal developments within his or her own work or discipline. It is hard to imagine, for instance, any contemporary arts council giving Elliott Carter a grant to develop the applications of partitioning and metric modulation within a work like his 1948 *Cello Sonata*. Such a work is neither collaborative nor interdisciplinary, nor does it make use of cross-cultural or non-Western influences in any way that would be obvious to a layman. And yet Carter's work in this area is one of the most significant musical developments in American music history of the mid-century, one whose ramifications have not yet been fully explored.

Within the past decade, moreover, the question of "active" censorship has become a serious issue in public funding of the arts. In the wake of the politically conservative ideology that dominated the 1980s, certain politicians have sought to make political capital out of controversial, experimental works whose creation or presentation was supported with public monies. Most conspicuous among these efforts was that of Sen. Jesse Helms of North Carolina in 1989 to abolish the National Endowment or, at least, limit its budget because of support given to the photographic works of Robert Mapplethorpe, Andres Serrano and others. Inevitably, then, the question arises as to *who* is in a position to decide which themes, subject matters, styles or attitudes are "appropriate" and which are not—a question that is only engaged when the artist has become dependent upon "taking Caesar's coin."

D. Audience Development In addition to the above problems, public arts agencies and large performance institutions alike share the endemic American tendency to associate the concept of classical music with European music. There is no substantial requirement, for example, either in the mandate of the National Endowment or any of the individual state arts agencies, that grants given to symphony orchestras or opera companies depend upon those organizations' willingness to program indigenous works more often than foreign products. Indeed, while American composers beg for opportunities to be heard, American taxpayers' money is largely devoted in the musical domain to propping up the very institutions that *exclude* those composers from their standard repertoire. And, while a small number of annual commissions are generally expected from institutions like the New York Philharmonic, apart from the ongoing success of the NEA's "Meet the Composer" project, there is no realistic requirement that the major portion of their programming be devoted to American music, or that those commissioned works receive more rehearsal time than standard repertoire, or that they be presented in such a way that the audience has a chance to grasp the composer's specific intentions, or that they be repeated, once premiered.[49]

When challenged on these issues, American musical performance institutions habitually reply that their audiences will not tolerate such a high proportion of American music programming. But no requirement has ever been placed on those institutions by their funding sources to engage in any meaningful market development or audience education vis-a-vis contemporary American music. In the absence of any external compulsion to engage in professional audience development, some orchestras have nevertheless created innovative outreach programs to schools and other community resources. But there is evidence to suggest that such efforts may have been too little, too late to have any meaningful impact. The calendar year 1993 has seen numerous strikes by orchestral musicians demanding more work and higher wages from orchestras that have drastically cut both outreach programs as well as the commissioning of new works.

It would be nice to imagine that audiences for classical music of any kind just spring into being spontaneously out of a collective sense of cultural obligation. In fact, the classical music market requires deliberate development as surely as does the popular music market, and audience tastes are just as responsive to professional promotion of the music in question. If those audiences are exclusively oriented toward the music of dead European masters today, it is as much due to the collective failure of teachers,

---

[49] *Vide* NEA, *Guide to Music Fellowships for Composers, Jazz and Solo Recitalists,* Washington, D.C.: The National Endowment for the Arts, 1993.

conductors, producers and composers to promote new American classical music effectively as it is to the "quality" of the old masters.

E. The Double-Edged Sword of Electronic Sound Reproduction Compounding the difficulties of audience development is the double-edged sword of electronic sound reproduction. When recordings and radio broadcasts of new American music first got started, during the early 1930s, composers such as Copland and Barber, who benefitted therefrom, naively imagined that a whole new vista had opened up for the dissemination of important new works. But these composers could not have foreseen the total range of effects that the new media would have on Americans' listening habits.

Prior to the age of electronic sound reproduction, the only way to hear music of any kind was to attend a performance, or to learn to play or sing. Concerts may have been more rare then, in purely statistical terms, but they were also more special. A major artist visiting a relatively small town to give a recital would be received with considerable press attention and much public anticipation. Compare this to our modern ability to have, at the push of a button, the finest performances by the greatest artists of the past one hundred years performing in the privacy of our own homes, at any hour of the day or night. It is crystal clear that the ready availability of recorded music has both diminished the importance of live classical performances for the mass audience, and (as any teacher can attest) not only reduced that audience's understanding of the time and effort needed to produce a good performance of any piece, even one of only moderate difficulty, but also reduced their tolerance for anything less than a perfect rendition.

But, perhaps the single greatest problem created by electronic sound reproduction is a gradual erosion of the lay audience's ability to listen, critically and discriminatively. The mass reproduction of sounding music (as opposed to notation) has deprived the experience of music itself of any qualities of rarity or uniqueness that it might have possessed in earlier ages. Far from being rare, music of all kinds is ubiquitous in today's society. It is as often something one tries to get away from as something one seeks out. And a great deal of this music not only goes unheard, in any conscious way, but is specifically created *not* to be listened to. It serves as environmental background. Inevitably, even works that *were* originally conceived to be listened to intensively, the classical masterpieces of the past (whose rough edges have worn off with time), have been appropriated as environmental music—at dinner parties, in supermarkets, in doctor's offices and other workplaces, as soundtracks for films and television commercials, as acoustic "filler" for the phone caller who has been put on hold, and in a hundred other ways.

Subtly and gradually, over a period of several decades, the infiltration of environmental music has coarsened the public's sensitivity to the melodic, rhythmic, timbral, harmonic and stylistic features of all music, until one can observe consistently, if anecdotally (hard research in this area being scant), that a vast portion of the lay public has trouble discriminating between one classical melody and another, much less between the sounds of different instruments or the characteristics of different historical styles. A probable majority of casual listeners today responds only to the most superficial features of complex music, such as whether it "has a beat," "is repetitious" or "puts me to sleep," and will often not remember from one hearing to the next whether they have even heard a given piece before.

There can be no question that modern recording technology has placed in the hands of composers, performers and educated listeners a superior tool for study, critical evaluation and deep penetration of the musical thought of all ages. But, like all sophisticated tools, it has posed a serious danger of weakening those fundamental skills that must be mastered before the tool can be used to its best advantage. Contemporary American classical composers, whose training has usually given them virtually reflexive command of such basic listening and auralizing skills, often fail to grasp how truly deficient in these specialized skills the mass audience has become, largely as a result of the easy availability of recorded music. As a result, such composers often *assume* a far greater level of musical sensitivity in their target audiences than is actually present.

Given the presence of public radio and television stations in all fifty states today, one might think that partnerships could be developed between composers, publishers, record and CD producers and non-profit broadcast media to utilize this resource to address the problems of public musical illiteracy and lack of support for new music. Why such partnerships have not emerged, apart from a few short-lived experiments, is a question that deserves (and has not yet been given) serious study. Anecdotal evidence suggests that perhaps a majority of broadcast station managers and music programmers themselves are seriously deficient in both their knowledge of American contemporary art music as well as their appreciation of the importance of the potential role they might play in keeping it alive.

Furthermore, while certain publishers (such as the Theodore Presser Co.) maintain private endowments that allow them to continue publishing commercially non-viable new classical music, many are reluctant to commit serious financial resources to promoting this part of their catalogues until there is *a priori*, external evidence of expansion in the sheet-music market, evidence that is obviously not going to present itself in the absence of professional promotion. At present, the efforts of even the most committed major publishers of new music, such as Presser, Peer-Southern or C. F.

Peters, are limited to occasional mailings of catalogue lists and biographical brochures on a select few contemporary composers. But these efforts still rely largely on the willingness of conductors and performers to explore, on their own time, the actual performance demands and actual sound of the works in question. The major publishers of classical music have not, as yet, engaged in the systematic distribution of sample recordings on a broad scale or the exploration of the previously mentioned partnerships with public radio and television to promote their product to the general public. And a similar attitude pervades many of the largest record producers.

In short, it appears that no party to the above equation wants to make the first move. Rather than aggressively develop their dwindling classical music markets, they are all too often content to allow their classical music divisions to exist as charity cases, while supporting themselves via their pop music categories. This, in turn, contributes to the disillusionment of young classical composers today, many of whom have given up entirely the effort to seek publication or broadcast of their works on a broad scale and are devoting their energies instead to self-publication and local performance.

F. Some Problems of American Music Education and Their Impact on Contemporary Classical Composition By the mid-1970s, most public secondary schools in American cities had lost their student orchestras and downsized their music programs to include only a marching/concert band, perhaps a small chorus and/or jazz band, and maybe an occasional class in elementary theory or "general" music. In part this may have been due to the increasing sophistication of commercial popular music during the Vietnam War era and radical cost-cutting measures imposed by large states such as California and New York in the mid-1960s. But there is no way to avoid the conclusion that a large portion of the declining interest in serious music on the part of young Americans during the 1960s and 1970s was also due to the increasing indifference of serious American composers toward any music that sought to make itself accessible to a broad public. The only major composer of the time who even espoused the ideal of shaping public attitudes on a large scale was John Cage, but his methods were too radical and too lacking in referents to established practice to be comprehensible to a mass audience. It bears noting, however, that many of Cage's values have, ironically, become the actual compositional, rehearsal and performance practice of an entire generation of contemporary rock musicians. These values include the idea of a piece created collectively by its performers, without a single controlling composer; music "written" without notation and which cannot, in many cases, be notated by traditional means; the incorporation of noise elements into the total sound complex; indeterminate structure, where the same song may have a different realization at each performance; audience participation in the concert milieu (currently known as the "mosh pit"); and music that functions merely as one element in a holistic environmental sound collage, without any necessary requirement that the song be listened to in an intensive way. Thus Cage has proved to be as much a prophet of the popular music of today as he was a revolutionary in classical music.

But, by far the worst result of the deterioration in public music education during the serialist era was the loss of momentum in the drive toward public music literacy, an effort in which America had led the world since the days of Lowell Mason. It only required one generation of American youth raised without even minimal ability to read notation or to recognize the fundamental themes of the major classical composers (both European and American) for the entire context of public musical literacy to be lost. And the ramifications of that loss are profound.

For one thing, as those Americans who were secondary school students during the 1970s and 1980s become parents themselves, they are left with little or no appreciation of the importance of serious music to pass on to their children. The result is often that such adults perceive classical music (whether ancient or modern) as the specialized province of a few divinely gifted individuals, lacking any relevance to the "real" concerns of daily life. While not entirely a new phenomenon in American life, in recent years this attitude has translated into even further funding cuts for a system of music education in the public schools that such parents perceive to be outmoded and frivolous. As the range and depth of course offerings in music diminishes in the public schools, the bulk of such music education available to young people is from private teachers. Unfortunately, despite the laudable efforts of such organizations as the Music Teachers National Association, America has not yet succeeded in establishing the kind of quality assurance, via teacher training and certification, in the private sector that it has in the public schools. Therefore, local private instruction tends to be a hit or miss proposition. Inevitably, some private teachers are very good and others are grossly incompetent. While one might assume that market forces alone would eliminate the hacks, it is often the case that neither the students nor parents are equipped to make such judgments. Even with today's superior teaching methodologies and computer-assisted instruction, it is not unheard of for an earnest student to have spent thousands of dollars on years of instruction with an unqualified private music teacher, with no tangible result to show for it in terms of skill or knowledge.

Second, with the disappearance of orchestras (as opposed to bands) in most American schools, the teaching of string instruments at the primary and secondary levels has virtually ceased. Stocks of inexpensive school-owned instruments have been liquidated or discarded, and string players who might have become teachers have chosen or been guided toward other options. Composition of new works for student string ensembles and orchestras has diminished to the vanishing point. And, considering the protracted time it takes to achieve basic proficiency on a bowed string instrument (as opposed to keyboard, guitar, percussion or wind instruments), it seems highly unlikely that regular, systematic string instruction in the public schools is going to resume in the foreseeable future. While this situation may or may not have diminished the supply of aspiring professional string players seeking admission to conservatories and universities (a determined student usually finds a competent private teacher somewhere), it has unquestionably diluted the number of amateur adult players or listeners who have some firsthand experience of string music. This has resulted in a consequent drop in audience attendance by young adults at orchestral concerts and less of a demand for such concerts in the mass electronic media.

Third, because people *will* have music, whether it is taught to them or not, the decline of public school music education has thrown the musically gifted (or at least the musically interested) young person back on his/her own resources. Deprived of access to the musical riches of prior generations and of the skills needed to comprehend same, they have sought models for their creativity in such music as is readily available to them. This usually means the latest creation of some heavy-metal band or the sentimental pop theme of a current hit movie. The rise of rap music in the decade immediately past has further diminished the specifically musical value of such "pop" models by shifting the thematic emphasis away from melody, harmony, and rhythmic patterns other than those dependent upon a relentlessly regular meter, onto the purely semantic content of the lyrics. Thus the bulk of the current generation of young Americans consistently relates to and defines any given popular song first in terms of its *verbal* message, rather than its tune (when it has a tune). This is confirmed by the fact that recent controversies over the "moral" content of rock and rap music (in contrast to the controversies over "rock 'n' roll" in the 1950s) have never even addressed the purely musical content of the songs in question, but have focused entirely on the lyrics.

New Developments and Opportunities

The above discussion reflects only some of the difficulties faced by contemporary American composers of classical music. But, lest we be discouraged by the gloomy side of this picture, it is important to examine some of the positive aspects of the current situation as well.

A. New Technologies   One of these positive aspects is the ongoing development of electronic instrument technology. The new availability of inexpensive, user-friendly, portable synthesizers, samplers, sequencers, recording devices and personal computer software for notation and composition has initiated a revolution in music—a revolution whose effects are only beginning to be felt. In addition to the enhancement of elementary music education via the creation of instructional computer software and the addition of computer labs both to public schools and private studios, a very specific benefit, brought about by acoustic sampling technology, lies in the teaching of orchestration and the student composer's corollary process of mastering form and texture.

In the past, the study of orchestration consisted of learning the unique capacities of each instrument, applying them to textbook exercises and studying the practices of earlier composers whose works could be heard in concert or recordings. It was a rare opportunity for a student to get a chance to actually *hear* one of his or her own orchestrations played by the specific kind of ensemble for which it was written, so a great deal depended upon that student's ability to mentally auralize the probable sound of the timbral combinations and articulated textures he or she was using. Now, with the ready availability of samplers, students are able to create a very close, if not perfect, "mock up" of even the most bloated orchestration, and to manipulate its internal features in an infinite number of ways without ever having to ask even a single live instrumentalist to take the trouble to try something out. If sampling technology is put to wise uses on a broad scale in our universities and conservatories, it is very likely that generations of virtuoso orchestrators might result. One only hopes that there will still be orchestras willing and able to play their music.

Unfortunately, the "downside" of sampling and related technologies is a reduced need for live performers. In recent decades, the demand for live instrumentalists has diminished significantly, and it is much harder for a professional instrumentalist to make even a marginal living today than it was in the past.

Professional and student musicians have also contributed to their own decline by their reluctance to promote new music. Admittedly, a great deal of the new music, both of the academic serialists and the aleatorists, written in the 1950s, 1960s and 1970s trivialized the training and artistry of serious performers, or presented them with technical demands that frankly exceeded the musical value of the resulting piece. But modern performers as a class have departed from the tradition established by their predecessors, such as Artur Rubinstein, Albert Spalding, Walter Gieseking or Serge Koussevitzky, and been all too willing in recent years to tar *all* new music with the brush created by a relatively few incompetent or offensive pieces.

Contemporary performers' overall reluctance to support the work of emerging or modern composers, and to make their audiences come to terms with it, has tended to drive composers toward technological resources which do not require the participation of live performers. Given this situation, it was only a matter of time until instrumental engineers created machines that possess the literal potential to replace live performers altogether, and the sampler is only the most recent step in this evolutionary process. Further developments are certain to follow.

B. New Ways of Finding Audiences: the Self-Sufficient Composer

Both the advance of musical technology and the decline of live performances are likely to lead toward an even greater increase in the number of *self-sufficient* composers in the future. Unless, for some reason, the market for such composers' music suddenly expands, it is equally likely that their music-making will become a much more local affair, limited to the practice and self-fulfillment of themselves and a small collection of friends or colleagues. This, in turn, opens up the potential for further development of the kind of specialized, geographically localized genres created in the Americas by Harry Partch, Pauline Oliveros, Conlon Nancarrow and others, as well as the proliferation of small local publishing and recording enterprises. The age of the Western classical composer as a cultural icon and international superstar may end within our lifetimes, and, while this may seem a dismal prospect to the young composer whose head is filled with fantasies of setting the world afire, it also implies the creation of a vastly greater range of musical options.

A statement one often hears from environmentalists and other social activists these days is: "Think globally. Act locally." The underlying rationale of this admonition seeks to address that well-known sense of futility experienced by individuals, living in a massively overpopulated society, when confronted with the need to take action to remedy social ills—a sense of futility that often becomes an excuse for apathy and inertia. It is true that one cannot solve the problem of global hunger by feeding a single starving child. But one can, at least, remedy the immediate need of that particular child. If such proactive individual efforts are copied by a gradually increasing number of other individuals, eventually even the global problem might yield to the accumulation of such individual efforts, with or without the support of governments. In effect, this is merely a contemporary application of the "categorical imperative" framed by the philosopher Immanuel Kant over two hundred years ago, namely: seek to act in such a way that your action might become universal law.

As we move into the 21st century, and it becomes increasingly likely that the bulk of individual artistic efforts will have, at best, only a local following, the above maxim becomes especially relevant to composers. It may not be possible, in the future, for any more than a handful of creative musical artists to achieve a lasting international reputation on the scale of an Aaron Copland, a Leonard Bernstein or a Philip Glass. But the local opportunities for serious creative work are manifold. Partch, Oliveros, Nancarrow, Young and others have each demonstrated ways in which this might occur. Other opportunities might include the creation of original works for local and/or regional theatre or dance companies, the development of locally based ensembles devoted to specific "schools" of composition based on the work of one or more local composers, and the development of fully automated compositions in the home studio that can then be recorded and distributed as widely as the energies and resources of the producers permit. Within the past ten years, during which the world has seen satellite communications and cable television come of age, it has become fully possible for a composer to reach a worldwide audience from virtually any local base of operations, even those far outside of the major urban centers. This specifically musical application of "think globally; act locally" should provide some comfort for those who are not content with a purely regional audience.

C. Interactive Music Yet another area of music that, at this writing, remains almost wholly undeveloped is the growing potential for "interactive" music, supported by new advances in computer and sound reproduction technology. Certain home entertainment software has already begun to explore interactive composition at a very elementary level in children's games. But its application to serious works of art music is, for all practical purposes, still a virgin field. The ideas and works of Cage provided an initial theoretical framework for the development of pieces that can have multiple or infinite specific realizations as well as for compositions whose specific internal progress can be made responsive to manipulation by the listener, but, to date, no major composer has risen to the challenge of carrying these ideas through to their logical conclusion.

Two Possible Scenarios for the Future

Based on the history that we have seen unfold in the course of this book, it is possible to project current trends forward into time and to venture both a "worst case" and a "best case" scenario. Despite the manifest risks—remembering Wells—and the virtual certainty that any such projection will fall wide of its mark as a prophecy of things to come, this exercise might prove useful nonetheless.

At worst, we might expect our current situation to continue to deteriorate. Serious composers of contemporary classical music will continue to "hide out" in academia, where they are assured of a regular income, as well as captive audiences of sycophantic students and colleagues who give them a false impression of their work's ability to communicate. If the most creative minds in American music remain clustered at the university level, the elementary training of young American musicians will remain in the hands of lower-paid and often less-qualified private and public school teachers, resulting in the perpetuation of the chauvinistic emphasis on European music, at the expense of American—a situation more often than not created merely by the primary teacher's ignorance or indifference to new ideas and methods.

Audiences for classical music will continue to age and shrink. As a result, the large orchestras and opera companies will become even more atavistic in their programming, or convert to the "pops concert" format, or both. Standards of musical literacy will continue to decline, in a self-perpetuating downward spiral, and generations of American listeners will be born, grow old and die without any grasp of their native classical musical heritage. In such a public environment, academia itself must inevitably move ever closer to the model articulated in Hermann Hesse's prophetic novel, *The Glass Bead Game* (published in America as *Magister Ludi,*) where theory and technique gradually supplant original creative efforts until no more new music is composed at all. Or, if composition does continue, it will become the esoteric domain of a handful of specialists, communing with their computers, who can neither perform the music that they themselves write, nor get anyone else to do so.

On the other hand, serious musicians might wake up to the fact that American classical music is still in a serious state of crisis, despite the advances of the past one hundred years. If so, perhaps the best creative talent will come out of its academic closet and begin to seek ways to survive in the "real" world, bringing their talents, their teaching skills, their creativity and their music to a public so starved for authentically moving new-music experiences that it must be force fed in small doses before it can even become fully aware of its own hunger. Following the example of Glass, Reich, Schwantner and others, new music might find new ways to make itself accessible to untutored ears, perhaps by demanding and acquiring equal access to the mass electronic media—following the lead set by Leonard Bernstein in his Young People's Concerts.

Students of a pre-professional caliber might consider demanding more from their teachers than a mere rehash of what those teachers were themselves taught. If this were to happen, both the teaching and the learning of professional performance skills would require original research of repertoire and non-traditional performance techniques, as well as the study of unfamiliar composers and non-Western music. In short, instrumentalists and singers will learn to become original musical *thinkers* as well, not just highly skilled mimics of each other. Competitions and festivals might begin to acknowledge, or even reward, original interpretations instead of conformity.

If these things were to take place, the public's understanding of new classical music, and its appetite for the same, might increase. Commissions would not lead merely to single performances, but to active, sustained promotion of the best emerging composers by major artists, performance institutions, publishers and record companies—recognizing their own vital, vested interests in keeping art music itself at least one step outside of the museum door. The symphony orchestra might resume the process of evolving its instrumentation, a process that was arrested around the time of Hector Berlioz, one hundred fifty years ago. Composers will feel free to experiment with new instrumental and timbral combinations, and the economic management policies of orchestras will somehow find a way to adjust to this.

Furthermore, if vitality is restored to American classical music, new kinds of music and performance paradigms might be created to meet the conditions of 21st-century life. These might include music specifically designed for post-CD sound reproduction technology, or interactive compositions that utilize advanced computer technology, or music designed for the special needs of space travelers.

With greater participation of creative artists in elementary and secondary music education, curricula might expand beyond the idea of getting Johnny or Susie to toot a second-rate clarinet in an out-of-tune concert for the local PTA, and start focusing on why Johnny is afraid to sing in public, or why Susie doesn't know who Amy Beach was, or getting Johnny or Susie to write their own music or build their own instruments. Moreover, the development of sophisticated application software will slice years off the time needed to master the fundamentals of traditional musical practice—transforming what was once a nightmare of drudgery and terror, presided over by a ruler-wielding autocrat, into a dynamic and exciting educational adventure in the hands of a new breed of imaginative teachers. And the years thus saved can then be devoted to even more exploratory projects by the students of the future.

As that educational reform whose necessity is acknowledged by all in the field today gains a foothold, music and the other fine arts may come to be perceived as a primary motivating factor in teaching children other essential skills of life, not merely as expendable frills to be dumped when the budget gets tight. We might rediscover the axiom that, given the necessary resources, education tends to take care of itself once the student's curiosity and enthusiasm have been sufficiently aroused. After a few decades of art-centered education in American schools, a new adult public might arise and begin to demand something better than worn-out commercial clichés from their everyday music. We might even begin to see an "arts-cast" in addition to the regular sportscast on the nightly television news.

Which, if either, of these scenarios will prove to be the face of things to come? Who knows? The history of American classical music in the 21st century will probably contain elements of both. But, of one thing we can be sure, and that is that American classical music does indeed exist, thanks to the efforts of those who have exerted their energies to the fullest on its behalf during the past two hundred years. Whether or not it continues to thrive, whether we keep faith with and fulfill the promise of our predecessors, rests squarely in our own hands and the hands of those future generations for whom we prepare the way.

Appendix *A*

A Timeline of American Music History (with Other Historical Events)

ટ**
*

1562 to 1993

**Note: A person's name set in boldface indicates
his or her birth or death.**

16th Century

1562   Sternhold and Hopkins's edition of "Englished" psalms for use by Protestants printed by John Day of London. Calvinists publish the *Genevan Psalter* with melodies composed/adapted by Louis Bourgeois.

1579   Damon's psalter published in England.

1592   Psalter published in England by Michael East (Este).

1599   Richard Alison's psalter published.

17th Century

1607   Colony of Jamestown, Virginia, established (first English colony of the North American mainland).

1612   The *Ainsworth Psalter,* principal psalm-book used by Pilgrims, published at Amsterdam (includes the tune "Old Hundredth").

1619   Dutch ships land the first African slaves in Virginia.

1620   Pilgrims land at Plymouth Rock on the coast of Massachussetts.

1621   Thomas Ravenscroft's psalter published at London.

1623   New Netherland (New York) founded by Dutch West India Company.

1630   Massachusetts Bay Colony established.

1640   First edition of the *Bay Psalm Book* (without music).

1647   Community at Merry Mount (near Boston) destroyed by Puritans.

1677   Playford's *The Whole Book of Psalms* published at London.

1683   First Mennonite settlement in Germantown, Pennsylvania.

1689   Beginning of the French and Indian Wars, which will continue until 1783.

1692   Infamous witch trials at Salem, Massachusetts begin.

1694   Johannes Kelpius, self-taught composer and leader of German Pietists, lands in America, settles in Pennsylvania.

1698   Ninth edition of the *Bay Psalm Book* (the first with music) printed at Boston.

18th Century

1700–1720   Growth of early New England psalmody in rural areas, development of heterophonic and improvisational practices.

1701   British take most of eastern Canada from the French in Queen Anne's War. Acadians expelled from Canada, begin migration toward Louisiana.

1707   Issac Watts, in England, publishes *Hymns and Spiritual Songs,* advocating use of hymns rather than psalms in Protestant worship.

1712   27-year-old Georg Friedrich Handel takes up residence in London, begins to dominate both English and colonial art music tastes for the next forty years.

1714 (approx.)   Rev. John Tufts publishes *A Very Plain and Easy Introduction to the Singing of Psalm Tunes,* at Boston (?), using fa-sol-la-mi system of notation then prevalent.

1720   Rev. Thomas Symmes of Bradford, Mass., publishes *The Reasonableness of Regular Singing* advocating the practice of singing by note "to divert young people . . . from learning idle, foolish, yea, pernicious songs and ballads." Conrad Beissel founds the Ephrata Cloister in Lancaster County, Pennsylvania, establishes singing school based on his own idiosyncratic musical principles outlined in his *Dissertation on Harmony.*

1721   Rev. Thomas Walter of Roxbury, Mass., publishes *The Grounds and Rules of Musick Explained,* printed by James Franklin, the first music book printed with bar lines in the colonies. John Tufts's *An Introduction to the Singing of Psalm Tunes* certifiably published.

1722 (approx.)   Boston's "Society for Promoting Regular Singing" founded.

1725   *Born:* Moravian composer **Jeremias Dencke** in Langenbilau, Silesia (October 10).

1728   John Gay's *The Beggar's Opera* produced with great success at London, ushers in the period of the ballad opera.

1730   In London, Handel turns to the composition of oratorios as an alternative to opera seria.

1732   First Moravian immigrants land at the West Indies.

1734   *Born:* Moravian composer **Jeremias Herbst** in Kempton, Germany (July 23).

1735   *Born:* Composer **James Lyon** in Newark, New Jersey (July 1).

        Events: The "Great Awakening": John and Charles Wesley, founders of Methodism, sail for Savannah, Georgia, at the invitation of the colony's founder, James Oglethorpe. On board with them are twenty-six Moravian missionaries led by Bishop Nitschmann and Peter Boehler.

1736   Charles Theodore Pachelbel, son of Johannes Pachelbel, gave the first concert in New York of which a written record exists.

1737   *Born:* Composer **Francis Hopkinson** in Philadelphia (September 21).

        Events: John Wesley publishes *A Collection of Psalms and Hymns,* including his first translations of German hymns, at Charleston, South Carolina.

1739   First American edition of Watts's *Hymns and Spiritual Songs.* Hymnody begins to replace psalmody as the dominant mode of religious singing in America.

1740   *Born:* Moravian composer **John Antes** in Bethlehem, Pennsylvania, (March 24).

1741   John Cennick publishes *Hymns for the Children of God* (second edition) at London, begins movement toward "folksy" hymn singing. Moravians become firmly established at Bethlehem.

1742   Wesley publishes *The Foundry Collection* of hymns in England, first printed examples of embellished, evangelical hymnody. First American edition of Mennonite hymnbook, *Der Ausbund: Das ist Etliche Schoene Christliche Lieder.*

1746   *Born:* **Johann Friedrich Peter,** principal musical figure of the Moravian enclave at Bethlehem, in Heerendijk, Holland (May 16). Composer **William Billings,** leader of the "First New England School" (hereafter: FNES) in Boston (October 7).

1747   *Born:* Composer and horse-breeder **Justin Morgan** (FNES) in West Springfield, Massachusetts (February 28).

        Events: Conrad Beissel publishes *The Song of the Lonely and Forsaken Turtle Dove, namely the Christian Church* (collection of sacred choral pieces) at Ephrata Cloister, Pennsylvania.

1749   *Born:* **Andrew Law** (FNES), developer of shape notes, in Milford, Connecticut (March 21).

1750   *Died:* **Charles Theodore Pachelbel** in Charleston.

        Events: Gay's *The Beggar's Opera* produced in New York. Boston enacts an anti-theatre ordinance.

1751   *Born:* Composer **Supply Belcher** (FNES), called the "Handel of Maine," in Stoughton, Massachusetts (April 9). Moravian composer **David Moritz Michael** in Keinhausen, Germany (October 21).

1753   Thomas Butts publishes *Harmonia Sacra,* including hymns in florid style. Wesley begins to react against frivolous singing.

1754   *Born:* Composer **Jacob French** (FNES) in Stoughton, Massachusetts (July 15).

1756   *Born:* Composer **Alexander Reinagle** in Portsmouth, England (April 23).

1756–57 Students at the College of Philadelphia present *The Masque of Alfred the Great,* including a song attributed to Francis Hopkinson.

1757   *Born:* Composer **Daniel Read** (FNES) in Attleboro, Massachusetts (November 16).

1758   *Born:* Composer **Timothy Swan** (FNES) in Worcester, Massachusetts (July 23).

1759   Hopkinson begins compiling his manuscript anthology of music common to his day, including his song "My Days Have Been So Wondrous Free," and several other original works. James Lyon graduates from the College of New Jersey (Princeton), ceremonies included the singing of an ode written by him.

1760   In England, Rev. Martin Madan publishes his *Lock Hospital Collection* of hymns and psalms, which had considerable influence in New England.

1761   *Born:* Composer **Jacob Kimball** the younger (FNES) in Topsfield, Massachusetts (February 22).

        Events: Benjamin Franklin develops improved version of musical glasses, which became known as the "Glassychord" (glass harmonica). Music by James Lyon and Francis Hopkinson sung at commencement ceremonies for the College of Pennsylvania (May 23).

1762   *Born:* Composer **Samuel Holyoke** (FNES) in Boxford, Massachusetts (October 15).

        Events: St. Cecilia Society founded in Charleston. James Lyon's first collection of psalms and hymns, *Urania,* published at Philadelphia.

1763   Moravians publish a collection of hymns in the Delaware Indian language. *A Collection of Psalm Tunes, with a few Hymns and Anthems* published at Philadelphia for the United Churches of Christ and St. Peter's Church, compilation attributed to Hopkinson.

1764   *Born:* Composer **Jeremiah Ingalls** (FNES) in Andover, Massachusetts (March 1).

        Events: Josiah Flagg's *Collection of the Best Psalm Tunes* published at Boston.

1765   *Born:* Composer **Oliver Holden** (FNES) in Shirley, Massachusetts (September 18).

Events: Benjamin Franklin outlines the theory of melodic and harmonic consonance in a letter to Lord Kames. In another letter to his brother Peter he critiques the arias of Handel's *Judas Maccabeus.*

1768   *Born:* Composer-publisher **Benjamin Carr** in London (September 12).

1770   *Born:* Composer and publisher **John Wyeth** (FNES), advocate of the shape-note system, in Cambridge, Massachusetts (March 31). Composer **James Hewitt** in Dartmoor, England (June 4).

Events: Billings' first book, *The New England Psalm Singer,* published at Boston. Gathering of idlers provokes British troops to fire upon them in Boston, five killed. The event is turned into propaganda by Sam Adams and others as: The "Boston Massacre."

1772   *Born:* Composer **Stephen Jenks** (FNES) in Gloucester, Rhode Island (March 17).

1773   Colonists dressed as Indians throw crates of tea into Boston Harbor to protest British tea tax: the "Boston Tea Party."

1774   Mother Ann, founder of the Shakers, migrates to America with eight followers.

1775   Battles of Lexington and Concord begin the American Revolution (April 19).

1776   Declaration of Independence signed at Philadelphia (July 4). Among the signers is composer Francis Hopkinson.

1778   Billings' *The Singing Master's Assistant* published.

1779   Former slave trader John Newton, author of lyrics of "Amazing Grace," publishes three volumes of *Olney Hymns,* culminating the radical tendencies of evangelical hymnody. Billings' *Music in Miniature* published. Moravian John Antes begins composing three string trios in Egypt while serving as a missionary.

1780   *Born:* Composer **Ananias Davisson,** advocate of shape-note singing, in Virginia (February 2).

1781   *Born:* Composer **Anthony Philip Heinrich** in Krasny Buk, Bohemia (March 11).

Events: Billings' *The Psalm Singer's Amusement* published. Corwallis' surrender at Yorktown (October 19) ends the American Revolution. Hopkinson's oratorio. *The Temple of Minerva,* produced by the French ambassador in Philadelphia for George and Martha Washington (December 11).

1784   *Born:* Composer and educator **Thomas Hastings,** author of "Rock of Ages," in Washington, Connecticut (October 15).

1785   Daniel Read (FNES) publishes *The American Singing Book. The Federal Harmony* (attributed to Timothy Swan) published at Boston.

1786   *Born:* Composer **Charles Edward Horn,** an eventual co-founder of the NY Philharmonic, in London (June 21).

      Events: Alexander Reinagle arrives in New York (summer), soon moves to Philadelphia and assumes management of the "City Concerts." Daniel Read begins publishing *The American Musical Magazine.* Billings' *The Suffolk Harmony* published. Moravian composer Johannes Herbst arrives in Pennsylvania.

1787   *Born:* **James P. Carroll** (Carrell), compiler of *Virginia Harmony* in Lebanon, Virginia (February 13).

      Events: A Compilation of the Litanies and Vesper Hymns and Anthems . . .^O, first American Catholic hymnbook, published at Philadelphia. U.S. Constitution drafted and signed at Philadelphia. George Washington attends concert given by Alexander Reinagle that includes two original works by Reinagle.

1788   Francis Hopkinson dedicates his *Seven Songs for the Harpsichord* to George Washington in a letter in which he claims to be the first native composer of the United States. Ratification of the Constitution by New Hampshire provides necessary majority for it to take effect.

1789   *Works:* Six string quintets composed by J. F. Peter, Moravian composer, at Salem, North Carolina.

      Events: George Washington elected first president of the United States. Oliver Holden's "Ode to Columbia's Favorite Son" sung for Washington at Boston, later published in *The Massachusetts Magazine* (October); Philip Phile's *The President's March* played for Washington at New York and Trenton.

1790   Daniel Read publishes *An Introduction to Psalmody.* John Antes believed to have completed his *Three String Trios* in this year.

1791   *Died:* Composer and patriot **Francis Hopkinson,** in Philadelphia (May 9).

      Events: First ten amendments to the Constitution, the "Bill of Rights," ratified.

1792   *Born:* Composer and educator, **Lowell Mason** in Medfield, Massachusetts (January 8).

      Events: James Hewitt arrives in New York from his native England. Oliver Holden publishes *The American Harmony.* Virtuoso organist, Raynor Taylor, former teacher of Reinagle, arrives in America.

1793   *Died:* Composer **Philip Phile** in Philadelphia. (?)

      Events: Composer Benjamin Carr arrives in New York, begins founding his music publishing enterprise, which later brings out *The Musical Journal, Carr's Musical Miscellany in Occasional Numbers,* and Philip Phile's *The President's March.* Jacob Kimball's *The Rural Harmony* published at Boston. Daniel Read publishes *The Columbian Harmonist.*

1794   *Died:* Composer **James Lyon** in Machias, Maine (October 12).

Events: The New Theatre opens on Chestnut Street in Philadelphia with a performance of Samuel Arnold's ballad opera, *The Castle of Andalusia,* Alexander Reinagle managing director. Supply Belcher publishes *The Harmony of Maine* at Boston. Billings' *The Continental Harmony* published.

1795   *Died:* Moravian composer **Jeremias Dencke** in Bethlehem (May 28).

1796   Benjamin Carr's opera, *The Archers* produced at New York. Together with his brother Joseph, Carr publishes *Evening Amusement,* a collection of instrumental pieces for amateurs (Philadelphia and New York), also publishes *A New Assistant for the Pianoforte or Harpsichord.*

1797   James Hewitt's *The Battle of Trenton* published. *The Pocket Hymn Book,* earliest collection of revival hymns, published at Philadelphia.

1798   *Died:* Composer **Justin Morgan** (FNES) in Randolph, Vermont (March 22).

        Events: Joseph Hopkinson sets the words of "Hail! Columbia" to Phile's *President's March.* Thomas Paine composes the words of "Adams and Liberty," set to the air "To Anacreon in Heaven" by John Stafford Smith (tune later used for "The Star-Spangled Banner"); Little and Smith copyright *The Easy Instructor,* forerunner of Law's shape-note system of singing notation.

1799   Music for Reinagle's *Columbus* copyrighted at Philadelphia. Score lost.

1800   *Born:* **Benjamin Franklin White,** compiler of the *Sacred Harp,* in Spartanburg, South Carolina.

        Died: Composer **William Billings** (September 26), founder of the First New England School, buried in an unmarked grave on Boston Common.

        Events: Benjamin Carr founds *The Musical Journal.* Jacob Kimball's *The Essex Harmony* published at Exeter, New Hampshire. Period of religious revival meetings begins in the South and West.

19th Century

1801   *Born:* Poet and songwriter **John Hill Hewitt,** son of James Hewitt, in New York (July 12).

        Events: Timothy Swan's *The New England Harmony* published at Suffield, Massachusetts.

1802   *Born:* **Ureli Corelli Hill,** another eventual co-founder of the NY Philharmonic, in Hartford, Connecticut.

        Events: First known edition of Little and Smith's *The Easy Instructor* published at New York.

1803   Fourth edition of Andrew Law's *The Musical Primer,* introducing shape-note notation, published at New Haven. United States acquires vast tract of the central North American continent from France (including the city of New Orleans) for $15 million: the "Louisiana Purchase."

1804   Alexander Hamilton, first Secretary of the Treasury, mortally wounded in a duel with his former law partner and Jefferson's vice-president, Aaron Burr. Lewis and Clark expedition begins.

1805   Jeremiah Ingalls' *The Christian Harmony* published at Exeter, New Hampshire.

1807   Robert Fulton makes the first successful steamboat trip between New York City and Albany.

1808   *Born:* **Thomas D. ("Jim Crow") Rice,** the father of blackface minstrelsy, in New York City (May 20).

1809   *Born:* **William Walker,** compiler of *Southern Harmony,* in Cross Keys, South Carolina (May 6).

          Died: Composer **Alexander Reinagle** in Baltimore (September 21).

          Events: Lock Hospital Collection published at Boston. John C. Totten's *A Collection of the Most Admired Hymns and Spiritual Songs . . . ,* important revivalist hymnbook, published at New York City.

1810   Wyeth's *Repository of Sacred Music* published at Harrisburg, Pennsylvania.

1811   *Born:* Composer **Henry C. Timm,** another founder of the NY Philharmonic, in Hamburg, Germany (July 11).

          Died: Moravian composer **John Antes** in Bristol, England (December 17).

          Events: David Moritz Michael conducts a performance of Haydn's *The Creation* in America.

1812   *Died:* Moravian composer **Jeremias Herbst** in Salem, North Carolina, (January 15).

          Events: The War of 1812 begins as U.S.S. *Constitution* sinks a British frigate.

1813   *Born:* Composer **William Henry Fry** in Philadelphia (August 10).

          Died: **J. F. Peter,** Moravian composer, in Bethlehem (July 13).

          Events: John Wyeth issues Part II of his *Repository of Sacred Music.* Padre Narciso Duran compiles choir book of Spanish missionary music at Mission San Jose, California.

1814   Francis Scott Key composes the words to "The Star-Spangled Banner" to the tune of Smith's "To Anacreon in Heaven" (September).

1815   *Born:* Minstrel **E. P. Christy** in Philadelphia. Minstrel **Daniel Decatur Emmett** in Mt. Vernon, Ohio (October 29).

          Events: Boston's Handel and Haydn Society organized by Gottlieb Graupner.

1816   *Born:* Composer **William B. Bradbury** in York, Maine (October 6).

          Events: Thomas Hastings' *Musica Sacra* published.

1817   *Died:* Composer **Jacob French** (FNES) in Simsbury, Connecticut (July 15).

Events: Davisson's *Kentucky Harmony* copyrighted. Anthony Philip Heinrich settles in Kentucky, conducts a performance of Beethoven's *Symphony No. 1.*

1819   *Born:* Composer **Issac B. Woodbury** in Beverly, Massachusetts (October 23). Pianist and editor, **William Scharfenberg,** another founder of the NY Philharmonic.

Events: Oliver Shaw's *Melodia Sacra* published at Providence.

1820   *Born:* Composer **George Frederick Root** in Sheffield, Massachusetts (August 30).

Died: Composer **Samuel Holyoke** (FNES) in East Concord, New Hampshire (February 7).

Works: Heinrich's *The Dawning of Music in Kentucky* composed.

Events: Davisson's *Supplement to the Kentucky Harmony* published. Allen Carden's *Missouri Harmony* published.

1821   *Born:* **John Gordon McCurry,** compiler of the *Social Harp,* in Hart County, Georgia (April 26). Minstrel **John Hodges "Cool" White** in Philadelphia (July 28).

Died: Shape-note composer **Andrew Law** in Cheshire, Connecticut (July 13).

Events: Lowell Mason's *Boston Handel and Haydn Society Collection of Church Music* published at Boston.

1823   The Monroe Doctrine promulgated in North America.

1825   *Born:* Composer **George Frederick Bristow** in Brooklyn, New York (December 19).

Died: Composer/organist **Raynor Taylor.**

Events: William Moore publishes his *Columbian Harmony* at Cincinnati.

1826   *Born:* **Stephen C. Foster** in Lawrenceville, Pennsylvania (July 4).

Died: Composer **Jacob Kimball** (FNES) at the Topsfield, Massachusetts almshouse (February 6). Former Presidents **John Adams and Thomas Jefferson** (July 4).

1827   *Died:* Moravian composer **David Moritz Michael** in Neuwied, Germany (February 26). Composer **James Hewitt** in Boston (August 1).

Events: Lowell Mason elected president of the Boston Handel and Haydn Society. Blackface minstrel shows begin appearing throughout the country.

1829   *Born:* Pianist **William Mason,** son of Lowell Mason, in Boston (January 24). Composer-pianist **Louis Moreau Gottschalk** in New Orleans (May 8).

Events: Publisher W. C. Peters opens his music store in Louisville.

1830   Joel Walker Sweeney (1813–1860) credited with inventing the five-string banjo in this year (some doubt remains).

1831   *Died:* Composer/publisher **Benjamin Carr** in Philadelphia (May 24).

       Events: Lowell Mason begins introducing arranged tunes from the European masters with the tenth edition of the *Boston Handel and Haydn Society Collection.* James P. Carroll's *Virginia Harmony* published.

1832   *Born:* Songwriter **Henry C. Work** in Middletown, Connecticut (October 1).

       Events: Lowell Mason founds the Boston Academy of Music, following publication of his first three song collections for children.

1834   Mason publishes the *Manual of the Boston Academy of Music, for Instruction in the Elements of Vocal Music, on the System of Pestalozzi,* codifying his pedagogical methods. Charles Babbage in England invents his "analytical machine," forerunner of the computer.

1835   William Walker's *Southern Harmony* published at New Haven.

1836   *Died:* Composer **Supply Belcher** (FNES) in Farmington, Maine (June 9). Composer **Daniel Read** (FNES) in New Haven (December 4).

       Events: Texas garrison under William Travis at the Alamo (San Antonio) wiped out by Mexican forces under Santa Ana.

1837   *Works:* Heinrich's *Columbiad* composed.

       Events: William Caldwell's *Union Harmony* published at Maryville, Tennessee. Gottschalk gives his first public concert.

1838   *Died:* Composer **Jeremiah Ingalls** (FNES) in Hancock, Vermont (April 6).

       Events: John Jackson's *Knoxville Harmony* published.

1839   *Born:* Composer **John Knowles Paine** in Portland, Maine (January 9). Organist-composer **Dudley Buck** in Hartford, Connecticut (March 10).

       Events: Hutchinson Family Singers organized in Milford, New Hampshire.

1840   *Works:* Heinrich composes his *Jubilee.*

       Events: First National Music Convention of American music teachers organized.

1842   *Born:* Poet and composer **Sidney Lanier** in Macon, Georgia (February 3).

       Died: Composer **Timothy Swan** (FNES) in Northfield, Massachusetts (July 23).

       Events: New York Philharmonic Society founded by C. E. Horn, Henry C. Timm, William Scharfenberg and U. C. Hill. Gottschalk sent to school in France.

1843   Norwegian violinist Ole Bull makes concert tour of America. The Virginia Minstrels, led by Daniel Decatur Emmett, debut at the Bowery Amphitheater, New York.

1844   *Died:* Composer **Oliver Holden** (FNES) in Charlestown, Massachusetts (September 4).

        Events: B. F. White and E. J. King's *Sacred Harp* published, included the song "Wayfaring Stranger." Minstrel Cool White composes "Lubly Fan" ("Buffalo Gals"). Stephen Foster's first published song, "Open Thy Lattice, Love" (words by G. P. Morris) printed by George Willig at Philadelphia.

1845   *Works:* Gottschalk: *La Bamboula* (played before Chopin at the Salle Pleyel in Paris). William Henry Fry: *Leonora* (received twelve performances at the Chestnut Street Theatre, Philadelphia).

        Events: Pianist Henri Herz tours the United States. Hutchinson Family Singers tour England and Ireland espousing abolition and other causes. Southern Musical Convention organized (B. F. White president). Stephen Foster moves to Cincinnati, is exposed to Negro singing at the steamboat docks and to minstrel shows. U.S. annexes Texas, leading to the Mexican War of 1846–48.

1846   *Born:* Composer **William W. Gilchrist** in Jersey City (January 8). Composer Silas G. Pratt in Addison, Vermont (August 4).

        Events: *The Negro Singer's Own Book* published. Jesse Aiken's *The Christian Minstrel* published at Philadelphia, incorporating conventional solfege syllables. William Walker publishes his *Southern and Western Pocket Harmonist.* Huge benefit concerts staged for Heinrich in New York (May 5) and Boston (June 13) by poet Lydia Child and others.

1847   E. P. Christy's minstrel show begins a ten-year run at Mechanics Hall in New York. G. F. Bristow's *Concert Overture* Op. 3, performed by the New York Philharmonic.

1848   *Born:* Composer **Frederick G. Gleason** in Middletown, Connecticut (December 17).

        Events: Southern composer William Hauser publishes the *Hesperian Harp* at Philadelphia. Stephen Foster sells all rights to "Oh, Susanna" to W. C. Peters for $100. Tennessee hymnbook *The Harp of Columbia* published at Knoxville.

1849   *Died:* **Charles E. Horn,** a founder of the NY Philharmonic, in Boston (October 21). Poet and author **Edgar Allan Poe** in Baltimore.

        Events: Discovery of gold at Sutter's Mill sets off the California Gold Rush.

1850   P. T. Barnum brings soprano Jenny Lind to the U.S. for a concert tour.

1851   *Works:* Gottschalk composes "The Banjo" in Spain.

        Events: Uncle Tom's Cabin (Harriet Beecher Stowe) and *Moby Dick* (Herman Melville) published.

1852   William H. Fry inaugurates a lecture series on music history at New York's Metropolitan Hall (November 30).

1853   *Born:* Composer **Arthur Foote** (Second New England School, hereafter: "SNES") in Salem, Massachusetts (March 5).

   Events: Gottschalk's official American debut in New York (February 11), begins concertizing extensively throughout the United States and Latin America. William H. Fry upbraids the NY Philharmonic for not having performed music by American composers in a letter to *The Musical World* after December 24 premiere of his *Santa Claus Symphony:* beginning of controversy that will involve Bristow and Timm, extending into 1854.

1854   *Born:* Minstrel composer **James Bland** in Flushing, NY (October 22). Composer **George Whitefield Chadwick** (SNES) in Lowell, Massachusetts (November 13).

   Died: Composer **James Carroll** in Lebanon, Virginia (October 28).

   Events: G. F. Bristow temporarily resigns post as violinist with NY Philharmonic in the wake of Fry controversy, becomes supervisor of music for New York's public schools. Thoreau's *Walden* published.

1855   Bristow's opera *Rip Van Winkle* opens in New York for a four-week run. First edition of Whitman's *Leaves of Grass* published.

   Works: Paine: *String Quartet in D.*

1856   *Died:* Composer **Stephen Jenks** (FNES) in Thompson, Ohio, (June 5).

   Events: Gottschalk moves to Havana, begins six-year period of wandering throughout the Caribbean. Pianist Sigismond Thalberg tours the U.S.

1857   *Born:* Composer **Edgar Stillman Kelley** in Sparta, Wisconsin (April 14).

   Died: Composer **Ananias Davisson** (FNES) in Rockingham County, Virginia (October 21).

   Events: Dan Bryant's minstrels organized in New York. John Knowles Paine travels to Germany to study. U.S. Supreme Court rules that a slave is not a citizen in famous "Dred Scott" decision.

1858   *Died:* Composer/publisher **John Wyeth,** last of the New England Singing Masters, in Philadelphia (January 23). Composer **Issac Woodbury** in Columbia, South Carolina (October 26).

   Events: Fry's *Leonora* revived in New York.

1859   *Born:* Composer **Victor Herbert** in Dublin, Ireland (February 1).

   Works: Paine: *Piano Sonata No.1.*

   Events: McCurry's *The Social Harp* published at Philadelphia. Daniel Decatur Emmett composes "Dixie," and claims authorship of "Turkey in the Straw," for Bryant's Minstrels. Abolitionist John Brown stages fatal raid on Harper's Ferry.

1860   *Died:* Minstrel **Thomas "Jim Crow" Rice** in New York (September 19).

   Events: Lincoln elected 16th President of the United States.

1861   *Born:* Composer **Charles Martin Loeffler** in Alsace, France (January 30). Composer **Arthur B. Whiting** (SNES) in Cambridge, Massachusetts (June 20). Composer **Edward MacDowell** in New York City (December 18).

Events: Civil War begins with shots fired on Fort Sumpter. John Knowles Paine returns to America, becomes director of music at Harvard the following year.

1863   *Born:* Composer **Horatio Parker** (SNES) in Auburndale, Massachusetts (September 15).

Events: G. F. Root's "The Battle Cry of Freedom" published.

1864   *Died:* **Stephen Foster** in Bellevue Hospital, New York (January 13). Composer **William Henry Fry** in Santa Cruz, West Indies (September 21).

Works: Fry: *Notre Dame de Paris* (opera after Victor Hugo).

Events: G. F. Root's song "Tramp! Tramp! Tramp!" published.

1865   *Born:* Composer **Harvey Worthington Loomis** in Brooklyn (February 5).

Works: Paine: *Mass in D.*

Events: H. C. Work's "Marching Through Georgia" published. Civil War ends with surrender of Robert E. Lee at Appomattox Court House. Abraham Lincoln assassinated (April 14). Lewis Carroll's *Alice's Adventures in Wonderland* published in England.

1866   William Walker publishes his *Christian Harmony*, converts to seven-shape vocal notation.

1867   *Born:* Composer **Amy Cheney Beach** (SNES) in Henniker, New Hampshire (September 5).

Events: The New Harp of Columbia, incorporating seven-shape notation, published. *Slave Songs of the United States* published.

1868   *Born:* Composer **Henry F. B. Gilbert** in Sommerville, Massachusetts (September 26). Composer **Scott Joplin** in Texarkana, Texas (November 24).

Died: Composer **W. B. Bradbury** in Montclair, New Jersey (January 7).

Events: Gottschalk settles in Brazil, organizes concerts for the emperor.

1869   *Died:* **Louis Moreau Gottschalk** in Tijuca (near Rio de Janeiro, December 18).

1870   *Born:* Composer **Henry Eichheim,** pioneer student of Asian music, in Chicago (January 3).

1871   *Born:* Composer **Frederick Converse** in Newton, Massachusetts (January 5). Composer **Bertram Shapleigh** in Boston (January 15). Composer/conductor **Henry K. Hadley** in Somerville, Massachusetts (December 20).

Events: Great fire kills 250 and levels most of Chicago, allegedly started by Mrs. O'Leary's cow.

1872   *Born:* Composer **Arthur Farwell** in St. Paul, Minnesota (April 23). Composer and teacher **Rubin Goldmark** in New York (August 15). Composer **Edward Burlingame Hill** in Cambridge, Massachusetts (September 9).

Died: Composer **Thomas Hastings** in New York (May 15). Composer and educator **Lowell Mason** in Orange, New Jersey (August 11).

Events: Composer **G. F. Root** awarded Doctor of Music degree from University of Chicago.

1873   *Born:* Composer **Mary Carr Moore** in Memphis, Tennessee (August 6). Blues composer **W. C. Handy** in Florence, Alabama (November 16). Composer and polemicist **Daniel Gregory Mason,** grandson of Lowell Mason, in Brookline, Massachusetts (November 20).

Events: J. K. Paine's oratorio *St. Peter* performed at Portland.

1874   *Born:* Composer **Charles E. Ives** in Danbury, Connecticut (October 20).

Works: Paine: *Piano Trio.*

Events: William Hauser publishes *The Olive Leaf* hymnbook.

1875   *Died:* **U. C. Hill,** co-founder of the NY Philharmonic, by swallowing morphine, Paterson, New Jersey (September 2). Composer **William Walker** in Spartanburg, South Carolina (September 24).

Works: Paine: *Symphony No. 1.*

Events: John Knowles Paine appointed full professor at Harvard over strenuous opposition from historian Francis Parkman. Arthur Foote graduates from Harvard, establishes himself as private teacher in Boston.

1876   *Born:* Composer **John Alden Carpenter** in Park Ridge, Illinois (February 28). Composer **Carl Ruggles** in Marion, Massachusetts (March 11).

Works: Paine: *Centennial Hymn.*

Events: Theodore Thomas conducts premiere of J. K. Paine's *First Symphony* in Boston. Paine's *Hymn* performed at the Centennial Exposition in Philadephia. Edward MacDowell sails for Europe to study. United States celebrates its first century of existence and votes the corrupt administration of President Ulysses S. Grant out of office. Alexander Graham Bell patents the telephone. In the Black Hills of South Dakota, an expeditionary force of the U.S. 7th Cavalry is annihilated by the Lakota and other Sioux tribes under Crazy Horse and Sitting Bull.

1877   *Born:* Composer **David Stanley Smith** in Toledo, Ohio (July 6).

Events: Chadwick travels to Berlin to study with Jadassohn. Thomas A. Edison patents the phonograph.

1878   Foote becomes organist at First Unitarian Church in Boston, where he will remain until 1910.

1879   *Born:* Composer **Mabel Wheeler Daniels** in Swampscott, Massachusetts (November 27).

Died: Composer and editor **Benjamin Franklin White** in Atlanta (December 5).

Works: Chadwick: *Rip Van Winkle* overture. Paine: *Symphony No.2.*

Events: MacDowell begins studies with Raff in Germany.

1880   *Born:* Composer **Arthur Shepherd** in Paris, Idaho (February 19). Composer **Ernest Bloch** in Geneva, Switzerland (July 24).

Events: J. K. Paine's *Second Symphony* premiered with great success in Boston. J. P. Sousa appointed leader of the U.S. Marine Band. Chadwick returns to the U.S., establishes himself as private teacher in Boston. President James Garfield assassinated.

1881   *Born:* Composer **Gena Branscombe** in Ontario, Canada (November 4). Composer **Charles Wakefield Cadman** in Johnstown, Pennsylvania (December 24).

Died: Poet/composer **Sidney Lanier** in Lynn, North Carolina (September 7).

Events: Paine's incidental music to *Oedipus Tyrannus* performed at Cambridge, Massachusetts.

1882   *Born:* Composer **Mary Howe** in Richmond, Virginia (April 4). Composer/pianist **Percy Grainger** in Melbourne, Australia (July 8).

Events: MacDowell receives encouragement from Liszt in Wiemar. Chadwick begins teaching at the New England Conservatory. Horatio Parker goes to Germany to study with Rheinberger. Rockefeller's Standard Oil Trust becomes the first industrial monopoly in America.

1883   Chadwick composes *Thalia* overture. Brooklyn Bridge and Metropolitan Opera House completed.

1884   *Born:* Composer **Louis Gruenberg** near Brest Litovsk, Russia (August 3). Composer **Emerson Whithorne** in Cleveland, Ohio (September 6). Composer **Charles T. Griffes** in Elmira, New York (September 17).

Died: Songwriter Henry C. Work in Hartford, Connecticut (June 8).

Works: Chadwick: *The Miller's Daughter* overture.

Events: MacDowell returns to America, marries Marian Nevins; they sail for Europe almost immediately.

1885   *Born:* Composer-harpist **Carlos Salzedo** in Archanon, France (April 6). Composer **Wallingford Riegger** in Albany, Georgia (April 29). Composer **Deems Taylor** in New York City (December 22). Composer **Edgard Varèse** in Paris (December 22).

Works: MacDowell: *Piano Concerto No. 2.* Parker: *Symphony in C.*

Events: Scott Joplin settles briefly in St. Louis, becomes a professional barroom pianist. Breitkopf and Haertel publish MacDowell's *First Concerto.*

1886   *Born:* Composer **John J. Becker** in Henderson, Kentucky (January 22).

Died: Composer **John G. McCurry** in Georgia (December 4).

Works: Foote: *The Farewell of Hiawatha.*

Events: Statue of Liberty dedicated. Surrender of Geronimo to federal troops ends Apache Wars.

1887   *Born:* Composer **Marion Bauer** in Walla Walla, Washington (August 15). Composer **Ernst Toch** in Vienna (December 7).

1888   *Works:* Ives (age 15): *Holiday Quickstep* (performed at Danbury Opera House). Foote: *The Wreck of the Hesperus.* Parker: *String Quartet.*

Events: MacDowell returns to America from his extended honeymoon in Europe; his *First Piano Concerto* premiered in Boston. Historic blizzard in northeastern U.S. kills hundreds, property damage exceeds $25 million.

1889   *Born:* Composer **Ethel Glenn Hier** in Cincinnati (June 25).

Events: MacDowell premieres his *Second Piano Concerto* in New York (March), later at a concert in Paris also including works by Buck, Chadwick, Foote and Paine. Thousands die in historic flood at Johnstown, Pennsylvania (home of 8-year-old Charles Wakefield Cadman).

1890   *Works:* Beach: *Mass in Eb.*

1891   *Born:* Composer **Adolph Weiss** in Baltimore (September 12).

Died: Minstrel **"Cool" White** in Chicago (April 23).

Works: Chadwick: *Melpomene* overture.

1892   *Born:* Composer **Ferde Grofé** in New York (March 27). Composer **David Guion** in Ballinger, Texas (December 15).

Died: Composer **Henry C. Timm,** co-founder of the NY Philharmonic, in Hoboken, New Jersey (September 5).

Works: Ives: *Variations on "America".* Paine: *Columbus March and Hymn* (premiered by Theodore Thomas at Chicago World's Fair). Parker: *Hora Novissima.*

Events: Antonin Dvořák arrives in America at the invitation of the National Conservatory (New York). Sousa forms his own band. Sensational murders of Andrew and Abigail Borden at Fall River, Massachusetts, make international headlines: their daughter Lizzie is arrested for the crime.

1893   *Born:* Composer **Bernard Rogers** in New York (February 4). Composer **Douglas Moore** in Cutchogue, Long Island (August 10).

Works: Dvořák: *New World Symphony* (premiered in New York). Harry Lawrence Freeman: *The Martyr* (produced in Denver, first known opera by an African-American composer). Foote: *The Skeleton in Armor.*

Events: Parker leaves National Conservatory. Arthur Farwell graduates from MIT determined to make music his career.

1894   *Born:* Composer **Walter Piston** in Rockland, Maine (January 20). Composer **Robert Russell Bennett** in Kansas City, Missouri (June 15).

Works: Beach: *"Gaelic" Symphony.* Ives: *Circus Band March.*

Events: Horatio Parker becomes professor of music at Yale, among his first class is Charles Ives.

1895   *Born:* Composer **Dane Rudhyar** (Daniel Chennevière) in Paris (March 23). Composer **Leo Sowerby** born in Grand Rapids, Michigan (May 1). Composer **William Grant Still** in Woodville, Mississippi (May 11). Composer/pianist **Leo Ornstein** in Kremenchug, Ukraine (December 11).

   Died: **William Scharfenberg,** co-founder of the NY Philharmonic. Composer **G. F. Root** in Bailey Island, Maine (August 6).

   Works: Ives: *First Symphony* (begun).

   Events: Dvořák publishes article on American music in *Harper's,* then returns to Europe. Ben Harney's song "You've Been A Good Old Wagon . . . " published (first recognized example of published ragtime).

1896   *Born:* Composer **Howard Hanson** in Wahoo, Nebraska (October 28). Composer **Virgil Thomson** in Kansas City, Missouri (November 25). Composer **Roger Sessions** in Brooklyn, New York (December 28).

   Works: Beach: *Violin Sonata.* Ives: *First String Quartet.* MacDowell: *Woodland Sketches.*

   Events: Edward MacDowell appointed professor of music at Columbia University, buys his summer home in Peterborough, New Hampshire (which will become the MacDowell Colony after his death).

1897   *Born:* Composer **Quincy Porter** in New Haven, Connecticut (February 7). Composer **Henry Cowell** in Menlo Park, California (March 11).

   Events: J. P. Sousa composes "The Stars and Stripes Forever." Tom Turpin's "Harlem Rag" published. John Alden Carpenter graduates from Harvard after study with Paine. Farwell studies in Germany with Pfitzner and Humperdinck.

1898   *Born:* Composer **Roy Harris** in Lincoln County, Oklahoma (February 12?). Composer **Ernst Bacon** in Chicago (May 26). Composer **George Gershwin** in Brooklyn, New York (September 26).

   Died: Composer **George Frederick Bristow** in New York (December 13).

   Works: Ives: *First Symphony* (completed). Paine: *Azra* (opera).

   Events: Charles Ives graduates from Yale, moves into "Poverty Flat," takes a job with the Mutual Life Insurance Co. The magazine *Musical America* begins publishing.

1899   *Born:* Composer **Randall Thompson** in New York City (April 21).

   Works: Beach: *Piano Concerto.* Chadwick: *Adonais Overture.* Joplin: *Maple Leaf Rag.* Ives: *The Celestial Country.*

   Events: Horatio Parker's *Hora Novissima* performed with great success at Worcester, England. Farwell returns to the U.S., teaches at Cornell.

1900 *Born:* Composer **Kurt Weill** in Dessau, Germany (March 2). Composer **Anis Fuleihan** on the Isle of Cyprus (April 2). Composer **Otto Luening** in Milwaukee, Wisconsin (June 15). Composer **George Antheil** in Trenton, New Jersey (July 8). Composer **Aaron Copland** in Brooklyn, New York (November 14).

Works: Farwell: *American Indian Melodies* (piano).

20th Century

1901 *Born:* Composer **Harry Partch** in Oakland, California (June 24). Composer **Ruth Crawford (Seeger)** in East Liverpool, Ohio (July 3).

Died: Songwriter **Ethelbert Nevin** in New Haven (February 17).

Events: President William McKinley assassinated at Buffalo, New York. Farwell leaves Cornell, founds the Wa-Wan Press at Newton Center, Massachusetts.

1902 *Born:* Composer **Stephan Wolpe** in Berlin (August 28).

Works: Scott Joplin composes *The Entertainer.* Ives's *The Celestial Country* premiered at Central Presbyterian Church in New York; completes *Second Symphony* and *From the Steeples and the Mountains.* Parker: *Organ Concerto.*

1903 *Born:* Composer **Vernon Duke (Vladimir Dukelsky)** in Pskov, Russia (October 10).

Died: Composer **Frederick G. Gleason** in Chicago (December 6).

Events: Joplin's lost first opera, *A Guest of Honor,* copyrighted. Young Charles Griffes sails for Europe to study with Humperdinck (August 13). Wright brothers demonstrate the first successful airplane at Kitty Hawk, North Carolina. Henry Ford organizes the Ford Motor Company.

1904 *Died:* Minstrel **Daniel Decatur Emmett** in Mt. Vernon, Ohio (June 28).

Works: Farwell: *Symbolistic Study No. 2* (piano and orch.). Gilbert: *Riders to the Sea* (orch.). Ives: *Third Symphony* and *Thanksgiving.*

Events: MacDowell resigns from Columbia after controversy with President Nicolas Butler. Riegger begins studies at Institute for Musical Art.

1905 *Born:* Composer **Marc Blitzstein** in Philadelphia (March 2).

Works: Farwell: *Impressions of the Wa-Wan Ceremony* for piano. Ives: *Three Page Sonata.*

Events: Edward MacDowell exhibits first signs of brain lesion that would kill him.

1906 *Born:* Composer **Paul Creston** in New York City (October 10). Composer **Ross Lee Finney** in Wells, Minnesota (December 23).

Died: Composer **John Knowles Paine** in Cambridge, Massachusetts (April 25).

Works: Chadwick: *Euterpe Overture.* Ives: *Set for Theatre Orchestra* and original version of *The Unanswered Question.*

Events: John Alden Carpenter studies briefly with Elgar in England. Five hundred killed in San Francisco after earthquake and ensuing three-day fire.

1907   *Works:* Beach: *Piano Quintet.* Chadwick: *Symphonic Sketches.* Ives: *Central Park in the Dark.*

Events: Griffes returns from Germany, begins teaching at Hackley School in Tarrytown, New York; G. Schirmer publishes some of his early songs. Emerson Whithorne becomes critic for London's *Pall Mall Gazette* (until 1915). Riegger goes to Berlin for study with Max Bruch.

1908   *Born:* Composer **Elliott Carter** in New York (December 11).

Died: Composer **Edward MacDowell** in New York City (January 23). Pianist **William Mason,** son of Lowell Mason, in New York (July 14).

Works: Ives: *The Unanswered Question* (revised) and *First Violin Sonata.* Parker: *Organ Sonata.* Varèse: *Bourgogne.*

Events: Lawrence Gilman publishes a penetrating study of MacDowell. Ives marries Harmony Twichell, forms insurance partnership with Julian Myrick. In France, Debussy composes *Golliwog's Cakewalk,* modeled after Joplin.

1909   *Born:* Composer **Elie Siegmeister** in New York City (January 15).

Died: Organist/composer **Dudley Buck** in West Orange, New Jersey (October 6).

Works: W. C. Handy: *The Memphis Blues.* Ives: *First Piano Sonata* (completed) and *Washington's Birthday.* Joplin: *Treemonisha* (begun).

Events: Charles Wakefield Cadman spends summer collecting music on Omaha and Winnebago reservations. American explorers Robert Peary and Matthew Henson reach the North Pole.

1910   *Born:* Composer **Samuel Barber** in West Chester, Pennsylvania (March 9). Composer **William Schuman** in New York City (August 8). Composer **Paul Bowles** in Jamaica, New York (December 30).

Works: Converse: *The Pipe of Desire* (first opera by an American premiered at the Met). Ives: *Second Violin Sonata.* Sessions (age 14): *Lancelot and Elaine.*

Events: Black musicians begin using the term "blues" to describe the established 12-bar form. Walter Damrosch reads through sections of Ives' *First Symphony* with his orchestra, reacts unfavorably. Amy Beach returns to active composing/concertizing after death of her husband. Wallingford Riegger makes his conducting debut with Blüthner Orchestra in Berlin.

1911   *Born:* Composer **Alan Hovhaness** in Somerville, Massachusetts (March 8). Composer **Bernard Herrmann** in New York City (June 29). Composer **Gian-Carlo Menotti** in Cadegliano, Italy (July 7).

Died: Minstrel composer **James Bland** (May 5).

Works: Carpenter: *Violin Sonata.* Henry F. B. Gilbert: *Comedy Overture on Negro Themes.* Ives: *Piano Trio.* Joplin: *Treemonisha* (published at his own expense in piano score).

1912   *Born:* Composer **John Cage** in Los Angeles (September 12). Composer **Conlon Nancarrow** in Texarkana, Arkansas (October 27).

Works: Ives: *Three Places in New England* (in progress) and *Decoration Day.*

Events: Horatio Parker's opera *Mona* produced by the Metropolitan Opera, New York (March 14). Henry Cowell begins experimenting with tone-clusters. Ives purchases farm in Redding, Connecticut. Farwell turns Wa-Wan Press over to G. Schirmer. Ocean liner *Titanic* sinks off Newfoundland (April 15), 1,500 drown.

1913   *Born:* Composer **Norman Dello Joio** in New York City (January 24). Composer **Henry Brant** in Montreal (September 15). Composer **Vivian Fine** in Chicago (September 28). Composer **Morton Gould** in Richmond Hill, New York (December 10).

Works: Gilbert: *Negro Rhapsody.* Ives: *The Fourth of July* and *Second String Quartet.*

1914   *Born:* Composer **Irving Fine** in Boston (December 3).

Works: Carpenter: *Adventures in a Perambulator.* Harry Lawrence Freemen: *Voodoo* (opera). W. C. Handy: *The St. Louis Blues.* Ives: *Three Places in New England* (completed), *General William Booth Enters Into Heaven* and *Third Violin Sonata.* Rudhyar: *Poèmes ironiques.*

Events: World War I begins after the assassination of the Austrian Archduke at Sarajevo, Bosnia. Sixteen-year-old George Gershwin becomes a "piano pounder" at Remick's publishing company on Tin Pan Alley. Hanson studies with Percy Goetschius at Institute for Musical Art in New York. Panama Canal officially opened.

1915   *Born:* Composer **George Perle** in Bayonne, New Jersey (May 6). Composer **Vincent Persichetti** in Philadelphia (June 6). Composer **David Diamond** in Rochester, New York (July 9).

Works: Bloch: *Schelomo.* Carpenter's *Adventures in a Perambulator* premiered in Chicago, composes *Concertino* for piano and orchestra. Ives: *Concord Sonata* (first complete draft).

Events: Joplin stages a demonstration performance of *Treemonisha* in Harlem, the opera's only performance prior to 1972. Henry F. B. Gilbert's article "The American Composer" published. G. Schirmer publishes Griffes' *Three Tone Pictures* and *Fantasy Pieces* at urging of Busoni. Henry Eichheim begins travels in the Far East. Gershwin begins theory lessons with Edward Kilyeni in New York. Sessions graduates from Harvard, proceeds to study with Parker at Yale. D. W. Griffiths' film *Birth of a Nation* premiered at Riverside, California.

1916   *Born:* Composer **Milton Babbitt** in Philadelphia (May 10).

Died: Composer **Silas G. Pratt** in Pittsburgh, Pennsylvania (October 30). Composer **William W. Gilchrist** in Easton, Pennsylvania (December 20).

Works: Bloch: *Israel* (soloists and orch.). Gershwin: *Rialto Ripples* (with Will Donaldson). Griffes: *The Kairn of Koridwen, Wai Kiki.* Ives *Fourth Symphony* (in progress) and *Fourth Violin Sonata* (completed). Loeffler: *Hora Mystica.*

Events: William Grant Still becomes assistant to W. C. Handy. Ernest Bloch immigrates to U.S.

1917   *Born:* Composer **Ulysses Kay** in Tucson, Arizona (January 7). Composer **Richard Yardumian** in Philadelphia (April 5). Composer **Lou Harrison** in Portland, Oregon (May 14).

Died: **Scott Joplin** in New York (April 1).

Works: Carpenter: *The Birthday of the Infanta.* Chadwick: *Tam O'Shanter* (orchestral ballad). Cowell: *The Tides of Manaunaun* (piano). Griffes: *The Pleasure Dome of Kubla Khan, Sho-Jo* (ballet).

Events: United States enters World War I. Russian Revolution establishes the Soviet Union.

1918   *Born:* Composer-conductor **Leonard Bernstein** in Lawrence, Massachusetts (August 25).

Works: Cadman: *Shanewis* (opera). Cowell: *Symphony No.1.* Griffes: *Piano Sonata, Three Poems of Fiona MacLeod.*

Events: World War I ends with armistice signed at Versailles. Griffes begins making arrangements for Schirmer under pseudonym "Arthur Tomlinson." Charles Ives suffers serious heart attack in October. Copland begins theoretical studies with Rubin Goldmark. Henry F. B. Gilbert's *Dance in Place Congo* performed at the Metropolitan Opera House. Sessions graduates from Yale, begins teaching at Smith College. Worldwide influenza epidemic begins, will kill nearly twenty million people in the U.S. by 1920.

1919   *Born:* Composer **Leon Kirchner** in Brooklyn, New York (January 24).

Died: **Horatio Parker** in Cedarhurst, New York (December 18).

Works: Gershwin: *La, La Lucille* (his first musical) and the song "Swanee." Griffes: *Three Javanese Songs* and his *Poem for Flute.* Ives: *Essays Before a Sonata* (prose). Ruggles: *Toys.* Deems Taylor: *Through the Looking Glass.*

Events: David Stanley Smith takes Parker's place at Yale. Varèse immigrates to America. Virgil Thomson and Walter Piston matriculate at Harvard, become students of Archibald Davison and E. B. Hill. Cowell studies with Charles Seeger at Berkeley, writes first draft of *New Musical Re-*

sources. Antheil and Sessions begin studies with Bloch in New York. 18th amendment to the Constitution prohibits sale and consumption of alcohol in the U.S.

1920   *Born:* Composer **Earl Kim** in Dinuba, California (January 6). Composer **Harold Shapero** in Lynn, Massachusetts (April 29). Composer **John LaMontaine** in Chicago (March 17).

Died: Composer **Charles T. Griffes** in New York (April 8).

Works: Carpenter: *Krazy Kat* (ballet). Gershwin: *Lullaby* (string quartet). Riegger: *Piano Trio.* Ruggles: *Men and Angels* (completed). David Stanley Smith: *Fête Gallante* (flute and orch.).

Events: Gershwin begins working with George White's annual "Scandals".

1921   *Born:* Composer **Ralph Shapey** in Philadelphia (March 12). Composer **William Bergsma** in Oakland, California (April 1). Composer **Andrew Imbrie** in New York (April 6).

Died: Composer and musicologist **Natalie Curtis (Burlin),** after being struck by a car in Paris (October 23).

Works: Antheil: *Airplane Sonata.* Varèse: *Amériques* and *Offrandes.*

Events: Ives publishes first edition of *Concord Sonata* at his own expense. Copland travels to Paris for study with Boulanger and Ricardo Viñes (June). Thomson travels to Paris on John Knowles Paine Fellowship from Harvard, begins studies with Boulanger, meets Satie, Cocteau and "Les Six". Bloch appointed director of Cleveland Institute; Sessions follows him to Cleveland and joins faculty. Sacco-Vanzetti case rocks Boston and the nation.

1922   *Born:* Composer **Lukas Foss** in Berlin (August 15).

Works: Antheil: *Piano Concerto No.1.* Copland: *Grohg* (ballet). Eichheim: *Oriental Impressions.* Gershwin: *Blue Monday* (opera for the George White Scandals). Hanson: *Symphony No.1: "Nordic".* Riegger: *Triple Jazz.*

Events: Ives publishes *114 Songs* (at his own expense). Durand publishes Copland's *The Cat and the Mouse.* Thomson calls attention to Koussevitzky's conducting in article in *The Boston Transcript.* Antheil sails for Europe. Quincy Porter appointed to faculty of Cleveland Institute by Bloch.

1923   *Born:* Composer **Peter Mennin** in Erie, Pennsylvania (May 17). Composer **Daniel Pinkham** in Lynn, Massachusetts (June 5). Composer **Ned Rorem** in Richmond, Indiana (October 23).

Works: Antheil: *Symphony No.1 "Zingareska"* and *Sonata Sauvage.* Cowell: *Aeolian Harp* (piano). Hanson: *String Quartet.* Leo Ornstein: *Piano Concerto.* Quincy Porter: *String Quartet No.1.* Ruggles: *Vox clamans in deserto.* Sessions: *The Black Maskers* (opera). Varèse: *Hyperprism* and *Octandre.*

Events: Nicolas Slonimsky immigrates to America. Gershwin studies briefly with Rubin Goldmark, accompanies Eva Gauthier's eclectic New York recital (reviewed by Deems Taylor). Roy Harris begins studies with Farwell at Berkeley. Antheil creates sensation in Paris; Ezra Pound publishes an essay on him. Sessions conducts premiere of *The Black Maskers.*

1924   *Died:* Composer **Victor Herbert** in New York (May 26).

Works: Carpenter: *Skyscrapers.* Cowell: *Ensemble for String Quartet and Thunder Sticks.* Gershwin: *Rhapsody in Blue.* E. B. Hill: *Jazz Studies* (begun) and *Scherzo for 2 pianos and orchestra.* Ives: *Three Quarter-Tone Pieces.* Riegger: *La belle dame sans merci.* Ruggles: *Men and Mountains.* Still: *Darker America* (symphonic poem).

Events: Rhapsody in Blue premiered at Aeolian Hall (February 12). Koussevitzky becomes conductor of the BSO. Roy Harris begins studies with Farwell at Berkeley, completes *Andante* for orchestra. Young Elliott Carter introduced to Charles Ives by Clifton J. Furness. Hanson appointed director of Eastman School of Music. Piston graduates from Harvard, sails for Europe to study with Boulanger and Dukas. Barber enters Curtis Institute. Nation outraged by the Teapot Dome scandal and sensational Leopold and Loeb murder case.

1925   *Born:* Composer **Gunther Schuller** in New York (November 22).

Works: Antheil: *Ballet mécanique,* using mechanical piano and electrical appliances. Bloch: *Concerto Grosso (No.1)* (strings and piano). Cadman: *The Garden of Mystery* (opera after Hawthorne's "Rappaccini's Daughter"). Copland: *Music for the Theatre.* Cowell: *The Banshee* (piano). Gershwin: *Concerto in F* (premiered with Damrosch and New York Symphony, December 3). Hill: *Flute and Clarinet Sonatas.* Luening: *Symphonic Fantasia I.* Piston: *Orchestra Piece.* Porter: *String Quartet No.2.* Ruggles: *Portals.* Varèse: *Intégrales.*

Events: Copland's *First (Organ) Symphony* premiered by Boulanger and Damrosch in New York, receives Guggenheim Fellowship, spends summer at MacDowell Colony with Roy Harris and Henry F. B. Gilbert. Thomson meets Gertrude Stein in France. Hanson premieres Harris' *Andante* at Eastman. Bloch assumes directorship of San Francisco Conservatory. William Jennings Bryan (prosecution) and Clarence Darrow (defense) battle over the teaching of evolution in the classroom during the trial of John Scopes in Tennessee.

1926   *Born:* Composer **Morton Feldman** in New York City (January 12). Composer **Earle Brown** in Lunenberg, Massachusetts (December 26).

Works: Bloch: *America.* Cadman: *The Witch of Salem* (opera). Copland: *Piano Concerto.* Gershwin: *Three Preludes for Piano* (premiered December 4). Ives: *Third Orchestral Set.* Piston: *Three Pieces for Flute, Clarinet and Bassoon.* Porter: *Violin Sonata No.1.* Ruggles: *Sun-Treader* (begun). Still:

From the Black Belt. Taylor: *The King's Henchman* (opera). Thomson: *Sonata di Chiesa.*

Events: W. C. Handy's *Blues: an Anthology* published at New York. Charles Ives ceases composing. Gershwin reads the novel *Porgy* by DuBose Heyward. Roy Harris and Marc Blitzstein travel separately to Paris for study with Boulanger. Piston returns to U.S. and joins Harvard faculty. Willem Van Hoogstraten performs Harris' *Andante* with New York Philharmonic. Sessions moves to Europe, meets Copland. Elliott Carter enters Harvard.

1927   *Born:* Composer **Richard Maxfield** in Seattle (February 2).

Works: Converse: *Flivver Ten Million* (using Ford horns, anvils and factory whistles in the orchestra). Farwell: *Violin Sonata.* Harris: *Concerto for Piano, Clarinet and String Quartet.* Hill: *Symphony No.1.* Porter: *Piano Quintet.* Riegger: *Study in Sonority,* begins his shift in modernist direction. Varèse: *Arcana.* Whithorne: *Poem for Piano and Orchestra* (premiered by Gieseking and Chicago Symphony).

Events: Thomson and Stein begin discussing plans for an opera, libretto to *Four Saints in Three Acts* finished by November, composition begins. Henry Bellamann's article "The Music of Charles Ives" appears in *Pro Musica* (March). Harris receives Guggenheim Fellowship. Copland appears as one of ten pianists in American premiere of Antheil's *Ballet mècanique,* becomes regular lecturer at New School for Social Research in New York, begins discussing joint concert series with Roger Sessions. Koussevitzky premieres Sessions' *Symphony No.1* with BSO. John Kirkpatrick, studying in Paris with Boulanger, receives copy of *Concord Sonata* from Ives. Cowell publishes Ruggles' *Men and Mountains* in *New Music,* attracts the attention of Ives. Sacco and Vanzetti executed. Lindbergh makes first successful non-stop flight from New York to Paris. First talking picture: *The Jazz Singer* with Al Jolson.

1928   *Born:* Composer **Jacob Druckman** in Philadelphia (June 26).

Died: Composer **Henry F. B. Gilbert** in Cambridge, Massachusetts (May 19).

Works: Copland: *Vitebsk.* Cowell: *Sinfonietta.* Gershwin: *An American in Paris.* Harris: *Piano Sonata.* Luening: *String Quartet No.3.* Sessions: *Piano Sonata No.1* (begun). Thomson: *Four Saints in Three Acts* (completed) and *Symphony on a Hymn Tune.*

Events: Harry Lawrence Freeman's opera, *Voodoo,* produced on Broadway. Henry Cowell's article "Four Little-Known Modern Composers" appears in *The Aesthete* magazine (August). First "Copland-Sessions Concert" in New York (April 22). Thomson begins practice of making musical portraits. Copland performs his *Piano Concerto* at Hollywood Bowl, visits Cowell in San Francisco. Menotti enters Curtis Institute, meets Barber.

Cowell, Varèse, Chávez and Salzedo form Pan American Association of Composers.

1929   *Born:* Composer **George Crumb** in Charleston, West Virginia (October 24).

Died: Ballet Russe impresario **Serge Diaghilev** in Monte Carlo (August 19).

Works: Barber: *Serenade for String Quartet, Op.1.* Beach: *String Quartet.* Becker: *Third Symphony.* Bloch: *Helvetia.* Cowell: *Concerto for Piano and Orchestra.* Eichheim: *Java.* Harris: *Symphony-American Portrait 1929* and *String Quartet No.1.* Hill: *Symphony No.2.* Porter: *Violin Sonata No.2.*

Events: Philadelphia Orchestra performs Eichheim's *Java* using a forty-five instrument gamelan section. Copland's *Vitebsk* premiered at Town Hall by Gieseking, Onnou and Maas. Harris injures spine in accident, returns to U.S. from Paris. New York Stock Market crash in October ushers in the Great Depression.

1930   *Died:* Composer **Harvey Worthington Loomis** in Boston (December 25).

Works: Blitzstein: *Triple Sec.* Converse: *Flight of the Eagle* (cantata). Copland: *Piano Variations.* Cowell: *Synchrony, Tiger* (piano). Farwell: *The Vale of Enitharmon.* Hanson: *Symphony No.2: "Romantic".* Piston: *Flute Sonata.* Porter: *Piano Sonata* and *String Quartet No.3.* Taylor: *Peter Ibbetson* (opera). Sessions: *Piano Sonata No.1* (completed). Still: *Afro-American Symphony.*

Events: Ives retires from the insurance business (January 1). Nicolas Slonimsky conducts premiere of Ives' *Three Places in New England* for ISCM (Feb. 16). William Schuman decides to study music after concert by New York Philharmonic. Elliott Carter graduates from Harvard after studies with Piston and Holst. Harold Clurman, Lee Strasberg and others form the "Group Theatre" in New York City. Cowell's book *New Musical Resources* published.

1931   *Died:* Composer **George Whitefield Chadwick** in Boston (April 4).

Works: Blitzstein: *The Harpies.* Cowell: *Concerto for Rhythmicon and Orchestra.* Gershwin: *Second Rhapsody* and *Cuban Overture.* Grofé: *Grand Canyon Suite.* Gruenberg: *Jack in the Beanstalk* (opera). Harris: *Toccata for Orchestra.* Hill: *Piano Concertino.* Porter: *String Quartet No.4.* Ruggles: *Sun-Treader* (completed). Varèse: *Ionisation.* Whithorne: *The Dream Pedlar.*

Events: Copland and Paul Bowles visit Gertrude Stein and Alice B. Toklas in France; Copland later assumes leadership of young composers group in New York City, including Siegmeister, Brant, V. Fine, Herrmann. "Composers' Collective" formed in New York City, includes Copland, Blitzstein, Riegger, Earl Robinson, Siegmeister, Charles Seeger. In London, Thomson begins to interest museum curator Everett "Chick" Austin in producing *Four Saints.* Gershwin's musical *Of Thee I Sing* opens on

Broadway, later wins the Pulitzer Prize. Ross Lee Finney studies with Alban Berg in Vienna. Gangster Al Capone sentenced to federal prison for tax evasion.

1932   *Born:* Composer **Pauline Oliveros** in Houston, Texas (May 30).

Works: Barber: *Cello Sonata.* Beach: *Cabildo* (chamber opera). Blitzstein: *The Condemned* (oratorio on Sacco-Vanzetti case). Bloch: *Sacred Service.* Carpenter: *Patterns.* Hanson: *Merrymount* (opera from the story by Hawthorne, libretto by Richard Stokes). Harris: *Concerto for String Sextet.* Herrmann: *String Quartet No.1.* Riegger: *Dichotomy* (orch.), *Four Tone Pictures* (piano) and *Evocation* (ballet).

Events: Carter graduates from Harvard, begins three years of study with Boulanger in Paris. Koussevitzky performs Copland's *Symphonic Ode* (revised version) in Boston and New York. Copland premieres his *Piano Variations* at Yaddo, takes his first trip to Mexico. Thomson's *Stabat Mater* performed at Yaddo. Cowell demonstrates Theremin's "rhythmicon" device in New York. Seven of Ives' *114 Songs* published by Cos Cob Press at Copland's instigation. Harris begins teaching summer sessions at Juilliard. Otto Luening conducts premiere of his opera *Evangeline* (Longfellow). Young Composers' Group (Copland, Berger, Brant, Citkowitz, V. Fine, Herrmann, Siegmeister) presents concert in New York (December 22). Amelia Earhart becomes first woman to fly the Atlantic alone.

1933   *Born:* Composer **Mel Powell** in New York City (February 12).

Works: Barber: *Overture to "The School for Scandal"* and *Dover Beach.* Becker: *Obongo.* Cage: *Sonata for Clarinet.* Carpenter: *Sea Drift.* Eichheim: *Bali.* Finney: *Violin Concerto No.1.* Gruenberg: *The Emperor Jones* (opera). Harris: *Symphony No.1: 1933* and *String Quartet No.2.* Piston: *First String Quartet* and *Concerto for Orchestra.* Schuman: *Canonic Choruses.* Whithorne: *Moon Trail.*

Events: Thomson's *Second String Quartet* performed in New York City. With Thomson's help, Lincoln Kirstein lures George Balanchine away from Ballet Russe de Monte Carlo to found School of the American Ballet in New York City. Harris' *Concerto for Piano, Clarinet and String Quartet* commercially recorded. Sessions begins teaching at Princeton. William Schuman attempts an abortive musical with Frank Loesser. Antheil returns to the U.S. Franklin D. Roosevelt inaugurated into his first term as President. Prohibition repealed.

1934   *Born:* Composer **Christian Wolff** in Nice, France (March 8).

Works: Farwell: *Rudolph Gott Symphony.* Gould: *Chorale and Fugue in Jazz.* Harris: *Symphony No.2* and *Piano Trio.* Hill: *Violin Concerto.* Porter: *First Symphony.* Varèse: *Ecuatorial.*

Events: *Four Saints in Three Acts* premieres at Hartford and New York (February), moves to Chicago with Thomson conducting in November, Stein and Toklas present for Chicago premiere. Howard Hanson's opera

Merrymount premiered by the Metropolitan Opera (February 10). Composer Ernst Toch immigrates to the U.S., begins teaching at New School for Social Research. Chavez premieres Copland's *Short Symphony* at Mexico City. Koussevitzky premieres Harris' *Symphony 1933* with BSO. Gershwin begins work on *Porgy and Bess* (February). Schuman begins teaching at Sarah Lawrence College. Babbitt studies with Marion Bauer at NYU. Louisiana Governor Huey Long assassinated in his statehouse.

1935   *Born:* Composer **Terry Riley** in Colfax, California (June 24). Composer **La Monte Young** in Bern, Idaho (October 14).

Died: Composer **Charles Martin Loeffler** in Medfield, Massachusetts (May 20).

Works: Antheil: score for the Paramount film *The Plainsman*. Bloch: *Piano Sonata*. Cage: *Quartet for Percussion*. Carter composes a later-withdrawn "String Quartet." Copland: *Statements* for orchestra. Finney: *String Quartet No.1*. Hill: *Jazz Studies* (completed) and *String Quartet*. Nancarrow: *Blues for Piano*. Piston: *Second String Quartet* and *Piano Trio No.1*. Porter: *String Quartet No.5*. Riegger: *New Dance* for Doris Humphrey. Schuman: *First Symphony* (first draft). Sessions: *Violin Concerto*.

Events: Gershwin's *Porgy and Bess* premiered (October 10). Copland organizes five one-composer concerts for New School of Social Research: himself, Thomson, Sessions, Harris, Piston. Kurt Weill immigrates to the U.S. Federal Theatre project and Federal Music project established by WPA. Houseman, Welles and Thomson organize first federal theatre in Harlem. Bernstein enters Harvard, studies with Hill and Piston. Barber records *Dover Beach*. Cage begins studies with Schoenberg.

1936   *Born:* Composer **Steve Reich** in New York City (October 3).

Died: Composer **Rubin Goldmark** in New York (March 6). Composer **Arthur B. Whiting** in Beverly, Massachusetts (July 20).

Works: Barber: *String Quartet, Op.11* including *Adagio for Strings*. Cage: *Trio* for percussion. Carpenter: *Violin Concerto*. Carter: *Mostellaria*, *Pochahontas* (ballet) and *Tarantella*. Copland: *El Salon Mexico* (begun). Harris: *Piano Quintet*. Hill: *Symphony No.3*. Ornstein: *Noctourne and Dance of the Fates*. Riegger: *With My Red Fires* for Doris Humphrey. Schuman: *String Quartet No.1*. Sessions: *String Quartet No.1*. Thomson: music for the film *The Plow That Broke the Plains* and Welles-Houseman production of *MacBeth*. Ernst Toch: *String Trio*. Varèse: *Density 21.5*.

Events: Federal Music Project initiates "Composers' Forum" series with Thomson and Harris sharing first program. Elliott Carter becomes music director of Kirstein's Ballet Caravan. Henry Cowell imprisoned at San Quentin on morals charge. Schuman begins studying with Roy Harris; his *First Symphony*, *First String Quartet* and *Canonic Choruses* premiered by the WPA. Toch moves to southern California, begins teaching at USC and writing music for film. Antheil moves to Los Angeles. Spanish Civil War begins.

1937   *Born:* Composer **Robert Moran** in Denver (January 8). Composer **Philip Glass** in Baltimore (January 31). Composer **David Del Tredici** in Cloverdale, California (March 16).

Died: Composer **Arthur Foote** in Boston (April 8). Composer **George Gershwin** in Los Angeles (July 11) after emergency surgery for a brain tumor. Composer/conductor **Henry K. Hadley** in New York (September 6).

Works: Barber: *First Essay for Orchestra, Op.12.* William Bergsma: *Paul Bunyan* (ballet). Blitzstein: *The Cradle Will Rock.* Cadman: *American Suite.* Carpenter: *Danza.* Carter: second withdrawn "String Quartet." Copland: *El Salon Mexico* (completed). Farwell: *Piano Quintet.* Finney: *String Quartet No.2.* Gruenberg: *Green Mansions.* Harris: *Third Symphony* and *String Quartet No.3.* Hill: *Piano Quintet.* Luening: *Prelude to a Hymn Tune by Billings* (orch.). Menotti: *Amelia Goes to the Ball* (his first opera). Piston: *First Symphony* and *Concertino for Piano and Orchestra.* Porter: *String Quartet No.6.* Schuman: *Symphony No.2* and *String Quartet No.2.* Still: *Symphony No.2.* Thomson: *Filling Station* (ballet) and music for the film *The River.*

Events: Virgil Thomson fired by WPA after unauthorized trip to Paris. Tappan family donates estate "Tanglewood" in Lenox, Massachusetts for Koussevitzky's Berkshire Music Festival. Copland meets young Leonard Bernstein who prepares the 2-piano score of *El Salon Mexico.* Copland, Thomson and others form American Composers' Alliance. Lukas Foss immigrates to America.

1938   *Born:* Composer **John Corigliano** in New York City (February 16). Composer/pianist **William Bolcom** in Seattle (May 26). Composer **Charles Wuorinen** in New York City (June 9). Composer **Paul Chihara** in Seattle (July 9). Composer **Joan Tower** in New Rochelle, New York (September 6).

Works: Beach: *Piano Trio.* Bloch: *Violin Concerto.* Copland: *Billy the Kid* (ballet) and *The Second Hurricane* (opera). Cowell: *Symphony No.2* and *Symphonic Set.* Foss: *Grotesque Dance* (piano). Gould: *Piano Concerto.* Hanson: *Symphony No.3.* Douglas Moore: *The Devil and Daniel Webster* (opera after S. V. Benét). Piston: *The Incredible Flutist.* Schuman: *Piano Concerto.* Toch: *Piano Quintet.*

Events: Blitzstein's *The Cradle Will Rock* premiered after controversy with WPA. Copland's book *What to Listen for in Music* published. Broadcast Music Inc. (BMI) founded. Stephan Wolpe immigrates to the U.S. Piston's ballet *The Incredible Flutist* premiered by the Boston Pops. Schuman's *Second Symphony* premiered. Copland publishes favorable article on Schuman in *Modern Music* (May–June). Orson Welles creates national panic with Halloween radio broadcast of *War of the Worlds*.

1939   *Born:* Composer **Ellen Taaffe Zwilich** in Miami, Florida (April 30).

Works: Antheil: *Symphony No.3*. Barber: *Violin Concerto*. Cage: *Imaginary Landscape No.1*. Copland: *Piano Sonata, Quiet City*, music for the film *Of Mice and Men*. Carter: extracts revised orchestra suite from *Pochahontas*. Creston: *Sonata for Saxophone and Piano*. Harris: *Symphony No.3* and *Little Suite* (piano). Harrison: *Concerto for flute and percussion*. Menotti: *The Old Maid and the Thief*. Persichetti: *Piano Sonatas Nos.1 and 2*. Piston: *Violin Concerto No.1* and *Violin Sonata*. Riegger: *String Quartet No.1*. Schuman: *American Festival Overture* and *String Quartet No.3*.

Events: Thomson publishes his first book, *The State of Music*, while living in Paris. John Kirkpatrick premieres Ives' *Concord Sonata* at Town Hall, New York, January 20 (reviews by Gilman and Carter). Leonard Bernstein graduates from Harvard after study with Piston and E. B. Hill. Koussevitzky premieres Harris' *Third Symphony*. American Music Center founded by Copland, Quincy Porter, Hanson and Bauer. Berkshire Music Festival organized by Koussevitzky. World War II begins as England and France declare war on Germany after Hitler's invasion of Poland.

1940   *Died:* Composer **Frederick Converse** in Westwood, Massachusetts (June 8). Composer **Bertram Shapleigh** in Washington, D.C. (July 2).

Works: Copland: music for the film *Our Town*. Cowell: *Pastorale and Fiddler's Delight*. Creston: *Marimba Concerto*. Finney: *String Quartet No.3*. Harris: *Folksong Symphony (Symphony No.4)*. Herrmann: *String Quartet No.2* and score for Orson Welles's *Citizen Kane*. Nancarrow: *Septet*. Thomson: music for Houseman's radio version of *The Trojan Women*.

Events: Virgil Thomson leaves Paris in path of advancing Nazi troops, succeeds Lawrence Gilman as critic for the *New York Herald-Tribune*. Copland spends summer teaching at Tanglewood with Paul Hindemith. Bernstein begins studies with Koussevitzky at Tanglewood. Stravinsky moves to Hollywood. Cowell released from prison, becomes secretary to Percy Grainger and resumes editorship of *New Music*. Randall Thompson's *Alleluia* premiered at Tanglewood.

1941   *Born:* Composer **Stephen Albert** in New York City (February 6).

Works: Carter: *The Defense of Corinth*. Diamond: *Symphony No.1*. Herrmann: music for Welles' *The Magnificent Ambersons*. Partch: *Barstow: 8 Hitchhiker Inscriptions*. Porter: *Music for Strings*. Riegger: *Pilgrim's Progress* (ballet). Schuman: *Symphonies Nos. 3* and *4*. Still: *A Bayou Legend* (opera).

Events: United States enters World War II after Japanese attack on Pearl Harbor (December 7). Copland's second book *Our New Music* published, sets out on first South American tour. John Cage and Lou Harrison become acquainted with Virgil Thomson in New York. Piston publishes his textbook *Harmony*. Koussevitzky premieres Schuman's *Third Symphony*.

1942   *Died:* Composer **Henry Eichheim** in Montecito, California (August 22).

Works: Barber: *Second Essay for Orchestra*. Bernstein: *Jeremiah Symphony* and *Clarinet Sonata*. Carter: *Symphony No.1*. Copland: *Lincoln Portrait, Rodeo* and *Danzon Cubano*. Cowell: *Symphony No.3: Gaelic*. Dello Joio: *Harmonica Concerto* and *Magnificat*. Diamond: *Symphony No.2*. Finney: *Symphony No.1*. Harris: *Fifth Symphony* and *Concerto for Piano and Band*. Persichetti: *Symphonies Nos.1 and 2*. Schuman: *A Free Song* (cantata). Thomson: *Mayor LaGuardia Waltzes* and *Canons for Dorothy Thompson*.

Events: Bernstein becomes assistant to Serge Koussevitzky at Tanglewood. Koussevitzky premieres Copland's *Quiet City* at Tanglewood. Babbitt graduates from Princeton after studies with Sessions.

1943   *Works:* Bernstein: *Seven Anniversaries* (piano). Cage: *Amores* (prepared piano). Carpenter: *The Anxious Bugler*. Blitzstein: *Airborne Symphony* (begun). Copland: music for the film *The North Star* and *Fanfare for the Common Man* (later incorporated into *Symphony No.3*). Cowell: *Fire and Ice* (R. Frost). Finney: *Hymn, Fuguing and Holiday*. Gould: *American Salute* and *Symphony No.1*. Hanson: *Symphony No.4: "The Requiem"*. Nancarrow: *Suite for Orchestra*. Partch: *U.S. Highball, San Francisco* and *The Letter*. Persichetti: *Piano Sonata No.3*. Piston: *Symphony No.2*. Porter: *String Quartet No.7*. Ruggles: *Evocations* (piano). Schuman: *William Billings Overture* (prototype of *New England Triptych*) and *Symphony No.5*. Randall Thompson: *Testament of Freedom*.

Events: Leonard Bernstein makes his conducting debut at Carnegie Hall standing in for Bruno Walter with New York Philharmonic on national broadcast (November 14). Barber and Menotti purchase house "Capricorn" at Mt. Kisco, New York. Hovhaness destroys his early work after harsh criticism from Copland, begins studying Armenian and other ethnic musics.

1944   *Died:* Composer **Edgar Stillman Kelley** in New York City (November 12). Composer **Amy Cheney Beach** in New York City (December 27).

Works: Barber: *Excursions* for piano. Bernstein: *On the Town* (musical) and *Fancy Free* (ballet). Carter: *Holiday Overture*. Copland: *Appalachian Spring* and *Violin Sonata*. Cowell: *Hymn and Fuguing Tune Nos.1–4*. Creston: *Symphony No.2*. Farwell: *Indian Suite* (orch.). Foss: *Piano Concerto No.1* and *The Prairie*. Gould: *Symphony No.2*. Harris: *Sixth Symphony* and *Piano Concerto No.1*. Herrmann: music for the film *Jane Eyre*. Partch: *Yankee Doodle Fantasy*. Riegger: *Symphony No.1*. Gunther Schuller (age 18): *Concerto No.1* for horn and orchestra.

Events: Harris elected to National Institute of Arts and Letters. Foss' *The Prairie* receives NY Music Critics Circle Award. Antheil's *Symphony No.4* premiered by Stokowski (February).

1945 *Works:* Barber: *Cello Concerto.* Carter: *The Harmony of Morning.* Diamond: *Symphonies Nos.3 and 4.* Finney: *Pilgrim Psalms* (from the *Ainsworth Psalter,* chorus). Morton Gould: *Billion Dollar Baby* (produced on Broadway) and *Concerto for Orchestra.* Harris: *American Ballads* (piano). Richard Maxfield: *Suite for Orchestra.* Menotti: *The Medium* and *Piano Concerto.* Nancarrow: *44 Studies for Player Piano(s)* (begun). Riegger: *Symphony No.2.* Schuller: *Cello Concerto.* Still: *Symphony No.3.* Thomson: first book of *Piano Etudes.*

Events: Harris appointed Director of Music for U.S. Office of War Information. Thomson returns to Paris after the war, begins to work with Stein on *The Mother of Us All;* his *Symphony on a Hymn Tune* premiered by NY Philharmonic, seventeen years after it was written. Schuman leaves Sarah Lawrence to become president of Juilliard, is replaced by Norman Dello Joio. President Franklin D. Roosevelt dies suddenly of a brain hemorrhage in Warm Springs, Georgia. United States explodes first atomic bombs over Hiroshima and Nagasaki, Japan, ending World War II.

1946 *Died:* Composer **Charles Wakefield Cadman** in Los Angeles (December 30). Writer **Gertrude Stein,** in France (July) after completing libretto to *The Mother of Us All.*

Works: Antheil: *Symphony No.5* and music for the film *The Spectre of the Rose.* Babbitt: *Fabulous Voyage* (musical). Barber: *Medea* (with Martha Graham). Bernstein: *Facsimile* (with Jerome Robbins). Blitzstein: *Airborne Symphony.* Carter: *Piano Sonata.* Copland: *Third Symphony.* Cowell: *Hymn and Fuguing Tune No.5* and *Symphony No.4.* Harris: *Concerto for Two Pianos and Orchestra.* Menotti: *The Telephone.* Partch: *11 Intrusions* (begun). Persichetti: *Symphony No.3.* Porter: *Horn Sonata.* Sessions: *Piano Sonata No.2* and completes *Symphony No.2.* Toch: *String Quartet No.12.*

Events: Nine-year-old Philip Glass admitted to the Peabody Conservatory. Babbitt writes his first paper on serialism. Porter becomes professor at Yale. Menotti's *The Medium* premiered at Columbia under Otto Luening (May 8).

1947 *Born:* Composer **John Adams** in Worcester, Massachusetts (February 15).

Works: Babbitt: *Three Compositions for Piano.* Barber: *Knoxville: Summer of 1915.* Cage: *Music for Marcel Duchamp.* Carter: *The Minotaur* (his last ballet) and *Emblems.* Finney: *String Quartet No.4.* Foss: *String Quartet No.1.* Gould: *Fall River Legend* (ballet) and *Symphony No.3.* Herrmann: music for the film *The Ghost and Mrs. Muir.* Perle: *Solemn Procession* (band). Piston: *Symphony No.3* and *String Quartet No.3.* Riegger: *Symphony No.3.* Ruggles: *Organum.* Schuman: *Violin Concerto.* Sessions: *The*

Trial of Lucullus (completed), *Montezuma* (begun). Still: *Symphony No.4.*
Thomson: *The Mother of Us All.* Varèse: *Etude pour Espace.*

Events: Ives receives Pulitzer Prize for his *Third Symphony.* The magazine
Modern Music suspends publication. Koussevitzky conducts premiere of
Piston's *Third Symphony.* Piston publishes *Counterpoint* (prose).
Menotti's *The Medium* opens on Broadway.

1948   *Works:* Antheil: *String Quartet No.3.* Babbitt: *Composition for Four In-
struments, Composition for Twelve Instruments* and *First String Quartet.*
Cage: *Sonatas and Interludes* for prepared piano and *Suite for Toy Piano.*
Carter: *Cello Sonata* and *Woodwind Quintet.* Copland: *Clarinet Concerto*
(for Benny Goodman). Cowell: *Symphony No.5.* Finney: *Piano Concerto
No.1.* Foss: *Oboe Concerto.* Hanson: *Piano Concerto.* Hill: *Bassoon So-
nata.* Kirchner: *Piano Sonata.* Piston: *Suite No.2* (orch.). Porter: *Viola
Concerto.* Riegger: *String Quartet No.2.* Schuller: *Symphonic Study.* Schu-
man: *Symphony No.6.* Thomson: *Louisiana Story* (music for the film by
Robt. Flaherty).

Events: Carter begins to develop metric modulation and other original
compositional means. Babbitt resumes teaching career at Princeton. Former U.S. State Dept. official, Alger Hiss, indicted for espionage.

1949   *Died:* Composer **David Stanley Smith** in New Haven (December 17).

Works: Barber: *Piano Sonata, Op.26.* Bernstein: *Symphony No.2: The Age
of Anxiety* and *Prelude, Fugue and Riffs* for clarinet and jazz combo.
Creston: *Piano Concerto.* Dello Joio: *The Triumph of Joan* (opera).
Farwell: *Piano Sonata, Op.113.* Finney: *String Quartet No.5.* Foss: *The
Jumping Frog of Calaveras County* (opera) and *Piano Concerto No.2.*
Harris: *Violin Concerto* and *Toccata for Piano.* Kirchner: *Little Suite* and
String Quartet No.1. Luening: *Symphonic Fantasia II.* Menotti: *The Con-
sul.* Persichetti: *Piano Sonatas Nos.4 and 5.* Piston: *Piano Quintet.*

Events: Blitzstein's *Regina* receives 56 performances on Broadway.

1950   *Died:* Composer **Kurt Weill** in New York City (April 3).

Works: Carter: *8 Etudes and a Fantasy* for woodwind quartet. Copland:
Twelve Poems of Emily Dickinson and *Piano Quartet.* Farwell: *Cello
Sonata.* Feldman: *Projections I.* Finney: *String Quartet No.6.* Harris: *Toccata* for piano. Partch: *11 Intrusions* (completed). Persichetti: *Divertimento
for Band* and *Piano Sonatas Nos.6–8.* Piston: *Symphony No.4.* Porter:
String Quartet No.8. Schuller: *Symphony for Brass and Percussion.* Schuman: *String Quartet No.4.* Toch: *First Symphony.*

Events: Menotti's *The Consul* premiered under Lehman Engel in Philadelphia (March 1). Korean War begins.

1951   *Died:* Composer **John Alden Carpenter** in Chicago (April 26). Conductor
Serge Koussevitzky (June 6). Viennese composer and originator of the
12-tone system, **Arnold Schoenberg,** in Los Angeles (July 13).

Works: Cage: *Music for Piano I, Imaginary Landscape No.4* and *Music of Changes.* Carter: *First String Quartet.* Dello Joio: *Triumph of St. Joan* (symphony). Diamond: *Symphony No. 5.* Feldman: *Projections II–V* and *Intersections I–II.* Harris: *Cumberland Concerto* (orch.). Herrmann: *Wuthering Heights* (opera) and music for film *The Day the Earth Stood Still.* Luening: *Kentucky Concerto.* Menotti: *Amahl and the Night Visitors.* Persichetti: *Symphony No. 4* and *Harpsichord Sonata No. 1.* Piston: *String Quartet No. 4.* Riegger: *Piano Quintet.* Sessions: *Second String Quartet.* Toch: *Symphony No.2.*

Events: Leonard Bernstein conducts Ives' *Second Symphony* at Carnegie Hall (February). Sessions publishes his book *Harmonic Practice.* Bernstein replaces Koussevitzky at Tanglewood. Cage experiences anechoic chamber at Harvard.

1952   *Died:* Composer **Arthur Farwell** in New York City (January 20).

Works: Antheil: *Volpone* (opera). Barber: *Hermit Songs.* Bernstein: *Trouble in Tahiti* (opera). Blitzstein: *The Threepenny Opera* (adaptation). Cage: *Music for Piano I* and *4'33".* Cowell: *Symphonies Nos. 6–8.* Farwell: *23 Polytonal Etudes* (completed). Finney: *Variations on a Theme of Alban Berg.* Harris: *Symphony No.7* and *Symphony for Band: "West Point".* Luening: *Fantasy in Space* (electronic). Menotti: *Violin Concerto.* Partch: *Plectra and Percussion Dances* and *Oedipus.* Persichetti: *Piano Sonata No.9.* Riegger: *Nonet for Brass.* Rochberg: *String Quartet No.1.*

Events: Virgil Thomson becomes acquainted with Pierre Boulez while touring in Paris with *Four Saints in Three Acts* (revised). Luening and Ussachevsky begin experimenting with electronic music. Persichetti becomes music editor for Elkan-Vogel (Theodore Presser).

1953   *Died:* Composer **Ruth Crawford Seeger** in Chevy Chase, Maryland (November 18). Composer **Daniel Gregory Mason,** last of the Second New England School, in Greenwich, Connecticut (December 4).

Works: Babbitt: *Woodwind Quintet.* Barber: *A Hand of Bridge* (studio opera). Bernstein: *Wonderful Town.* Earle Brown: *Folio.* Cowell: *Symphonies Nos.9–11.* Feldman: *Intersections III–IV.* Finney: *Piano Quintet No.1.* Harris: *Piano Concerto No.2.* Kirchner: *Piano Concerto No.1.* Persichetti: *Symphony No.5.* Porter: *Concerto Concertante* (two pianos and orch.). Riegger: *Variations for Piano and Orchestra, Suite for Younger Orchestras* and *Concerto for Piano and Woodwind Quintet.* Schuman: *The Mighty Casey* (opera) and *Voyage* (piano). Sessions: *Violin Sonata.*

Events: Early electronic music being created in Germany. Sen. Fred Busbey bans Copland's *Lincoln Portrait* from Eisenhower's inauguration, Copland summoned before McCarthy subcommittee. Barber adapts *Medea's Meditation and Dance of Vengeance* from his ballet score. Foss joins faculty of UCLA, begins work with improvisation, receives Music Critics Circle award for *Piano Concerto No.2.* Gunther Schuller begins working with Modern Jazz Quartet, develops concept of "third stream" music. Soviet dictator Joseph Stalin and composer Sergei Prokofiev die on the same day, March 5.

1954   *Died:* Composer **Harry Lawrence Freeman** in New York (March 21). Composer **Charles Ives** in New York (May 19).

Works: Babbitt: *String Quartet No.2.* Bernstein: music for the film *On the Waterfront.* Copland: *The Tender Land.* Diamond: *Symphony No.6.* Hanson: *Symphony No.5: "Sinfonia Sacra."* Herrmann: music for the film *Garden of Evil.* Sessions: *The Idyll of Theocritus.* Luening and Ussachevsky: *Poem in Cycles and Bells* for orch. and tape. Maxfield: *Structures* (woodwinds). Menotti: *The Saint of Bleecker Street.* Partch: *Two Settings from Lewis Carroll.* Piston: *Symphony No.5.* Rudhyar: *Syntony No.5* (orch.). Toch: *String Quartet No.13.* Varèse: *Déserts.*

Events: Thomson resigns post at *New York Herald-Tribune.* Composers' Recordings Inc. founded by ACA. Porter's *Concerto Concertante* receives Pulitzer Prize.

1955   *Died:* Composer **Marion Bauer** in South Hadley, Massachusetts (August 9).

Works: Barber: *Summer Music* (woodwinds). Carter: *Variations for Orchestra.* Copland: *Piano Fantasy.* Finney: *String Quartet No.7.* Foss: *Psalms* for chorus and orch. or pianos. Herrmann: music for the film *The Man Who Knew Too Much.* Persichetti: *Piano Sonata No.10.* Piston: *Symphony No.6.* Sessions: *Mass for Unison Choir* and *Piano Concerto.* Toch: *Symphony No.3.*

Events: Piston publishes his textbook *Orchestration.*

1956   *Died:* Composer **Felix Borowski** in Chicago (September 6).

Works: Bernstein: *Candide.* Bolcom: *Songs of Innocence and Experience* (begun). Cowell: *Symphony No.12.* Dello Joio: *Meditations on Ecclesiastes.* Hiller: *Illiac Suite* for computer (with Leonard Issacson). Menotti: *The Unicorn, the Gorgon and the Manticore.* Persichetti: *Symphony No.6* (band). Piston: *Wind Quintet.* Riegger: *Symphony No.4.* George Rochberg: *Symphony No.2.* Schuman: *New England Triptych* on themes of Wm. Billings. Wuorinen: *Music for Orchestra.*

Events: Harris awarded Naumburg Foundation prize for *Symphony No.7.* Foss begins working with indeterminate techniques.

1957   *Died:* Composer **Mary Carr Moore** in Inglewood, California (January 9).

Works: Antheil: music for the film *The Pride and the Passion.* Babbitt: *All Set* and *Partitions.* Barber and Menotti complete *Vanessa.* Bernstein: *West Side Story* (book by Arthur Laurents and lyrics by Stephen Sondheim). Cowell: *Ongaku* (orch.). Piston: *Viola Concerto.* Terry Riley: *Trio* (violin, clarinet, cello). Sessions: *Symphony No.3.* Thomson: music for Paddy

Chayevsky's *The Goddess*. Toch: *Fourth Symphony*. Wuorinen: *Concertante I*.

Events: Riegger summoned before HUAC.

1958   *Died:* Composer **Arthur Shepherd** in Cleveland (January 12). Composer **Emerson Whithorne** in Lyme, Connecticut (March 25).

Works: Cage: *Aria* and *Fontana Mix*. Cowell: *Symphony No.13* and *Hymn and Fuguing Tune No.12*. Finney: *Symphony No.2*. Herrmann: music for Hitchcock's *Vertigo*. Kirchner: *String Quartet No.2*. Menotti: *Maria Golovin*. Moore: *The Ballad of Baby Doe* (opera). Persichetti: *Symphony No.7*. Porter: *String Quartet No.9*. Rochberg: *Cheltenham Concerto*. Schuller: *Contours* (chamber orch.). Sessions: *String Quintet* and *Symphony No.4*. Still: *Symphony No.5*. Varèse: *Poème électronique*. Wuorinen: *Symphony No.1*. La Monte Young: *Trio for Strings*.

Events: Babbitt publishes essay "Who Cares if Your Listen?" in *High Fidelity*. Menotti and Thomas Schippers found "Festival of Two Worlds" in Spoleto, Italy. Bernstein becomes music director of New York Philharmonic, launches Young People's Concerts.

1959   *Died:* Composer **George Antheil** in New York (February 12). Composer **Ernest Bloch** in Portland, Oregon (July 15).

Works: Carter: *Second String Quartet*. Del Tredici: *Two Songs* (Joyce). Diamond: *Symphony No.7*. Feldman: *Last Pieces*. Herrmann: music for Hitchcock's *North by Northwest*. Piston: *Concerto for Two Pianos*. Porter: *Concerto for Wind Orchestra* and *Harpsichord Concerto*. Schuller: *Seven Studies on Themes of Paul Klee* and *Concertino for Jazz Quartet and Orchestra*. Toch: *Intermezzo* for orchestra. Wuorinen: *Concertante IV* and *Symphonies Nos.2 and 3*.

Events: Columbia-Princeton Electronic Music Center established by Luening, Ussachevsky and Babbitt. George Crumb graduates from University of Michigan after studies with Finney. John LaMontaine receives Pulitzer for his *Piano Concerto*. Richard Maxfield succeeds John Cage at the New School for Social Research.

1960   *Died:* Composer **Edward Burlingame Hill** in Francestown, New Hampshire (July 9).

Works: Bolcom: *12 Etudes for Piano*. Cage: *Cartridge Music*. Copland: *Nonet* for strings. Cowell: *Symphonies Nos.14–15*. Del Tredici: *Fantasy Pieces* (piano). Diamond: *Symphony No.8*. Feldman: *Structures* (orch.). Finney: *Symphony No.3* and *String Quartet No.8*. Foss: *Concerto for Five Improvising Instruments* and *Time Cycle* for soprano and orchestra. Herrmann: music for Hitchcock's *Psycho*. Luening: *Gargoyles* for violin and tape. Maxfield: *Perspectives* (violin and tape) and *Night Music*. Oliveros: *Variations for Sextet*. Partch: *Revelation in the Courthouse Park*. Perle: *Three Movements for Orchestra*. Piston: *Symphony No.7* and *Violin*

Concerto No.2. Riley: *Concert for 2 Pianos and Tape* and *String Quartet*. Rochberg: *Time Span I.* Schuman: *Symphony No.7.*

Events: Thomson conducts premiere of his *Missa Pro Defunctis* in Potsdam, New York. John F. Kennedy elected 35th President of the United States.

1961   *Died:* Composer **John J. Becker** in Wilmette, Illinois (January 21). Composer/pianist **Percy Grainger** in White Plains, New York (February 20). Composer **Wallingford Riegger** in New York (April 2). Composer/harpist **Carlos Salzedo** in Waterville, Maine (August 17).

Works: Babbitt: *Composition for Synthesizer* and *Vision and Prayer* for soprano and synthesizer. Carter: *Double Concerto* for harpsichord, piano and two orchestras. Corigliano: *Fern Hill* (D. Thomas). Cowell: *Concerto for Percussion and Orchestra.* Finney: *Piano Quintet No.2* and *Sonata quasi una fantasia* (piano). Harrison: *Symphony on G, Mooqunkwha* (orch.) and *Concerto in slendro* (violin, cello, tack piano, perc.). Porter: *Harpsichord Quintet.* Riley: *String Trio.* Rochberg: *String Quartet No.2.* Varèse: *Nocturnal.*

1962   *Died:* Composer **Irving Fine** in Boston (August 23).

Works: Barber: *Piano Concerto.* Cage: *Atlas Elipticalis* (orch.). Cowell: *Symphony No.16* and *Harmonica Concerto.* Crumb: *Five Pieces for Piano.* Harris: *Symphonies Nos.8 and 9.* Herrmann: music for the film *Cape Fear.* Luening: *Sonority Canon* (multiple flutes) and *Synthesis* (tape and orch.). Maxfield: *Toy Symphony.* Perle: *Serenade No.1* (orch.). Oliveros: *Sound Patterns* (voices). Persichetti: *Piano Concerto.* Piston: *String Quartet No.5.* Porter: *Symphony No.2.* Rochberg: *Time Span II.* Schuller: *Piano Concerto No.1.* Schuman: *Symphony No.9.* Toch: *Two Piano Sonata* and *The Last Tale* (opera).

Events: William Schuman becomes president of Lincoln Center. Copland's *Connotations* for orchestra premiered there, but attracts little attention from younger composers.

1963   *Works:* Bernstein: *Symphony No.3: Kaddish.* Bolcom: *Dynamite Tonite* (opera). Copland: *Dance Panels* (his last dance piece). Corigliano: *Violin Sonata.* Cowell: *Symphony No.17* and *26 Simultaneous Mosaics.* Crumb: *Night Music.* Druckman: *Antiphonics I–III* (chorus). Feldman: *Vertical Thoughts I–IV.* Foss: *Echoi.* Harrison: *Pacifika Rondo.* Kirchner: *Piano Concerto No.2.* Menotti: *The Death of the Bishop of Brindisi* (cantata). Schuller: *Composition in Three Parts.* Sessions: *Montezuma* (completed) and *Psalm 130.* Toch: *Symphony No.6.*

Events: President John F. Kennedy assassinated at Dallas, November 22.

1964   *Died:* Composer **Marc Blitzstein,** after being beaten in a bar in Martinique, (January 22). Composer **Louis Gruenberg** in Beverly Hills, California (June 10). Composer **Mary Howe** in Washington, D.C. (September 14). Composer **Ernst Toch** in Los Angeles (October 1).

Works: Babbitt: *Ensembles for Synthesizer.* Barber: *Night Flight.* Cowell: *Symphony No.18.* Creston: *Metamorphoses* (piano). Harris: *Cello Sonata.* Harrison: *At the Tomb of Charles Ives.* Maxfield: *Electronic Symphony.* Menotti: *Martin's Lie.* Piston: *Piano Quartet* and *String Sextet.* Riley: *In C* (first "minimalist" music, written at Berkeley, California). Thomson: music for John Houseman's short film *Journey to America.* Toch: *Symphony No.7.* Young: *The Tortoise, his Dreams and Journeys* (begun).

Events: Copland conducts premiere of his *Music for a Great City* in London. Schuman arranges Ives' *Variations on America* for orchestra. Annual TV broadcasts of *Amahl and The Night Visitors* cease after dispute between Menotti and NBC. Gulf of Tonkin Resolution (August 7) marks beginning of U.S. major involvement in Vietnamese civil war.

1965   *Died:* Composer **Edgard Varèse** in New York City (November 6). Composer **Henry Cowell** in Shady, New York (December 10).

Works: Bernstein: *Chichester Psalms.* Bolcom: *String Quartet No.8.* Carter: *Piano Concerto.* Corigliano: *Elegy* for orchestra. Cowell: *Symphonies Nos.19–20* and *Concertos for Koto and Orch,* and *for Harp and Orchestra.* Crumb: *Madrigals: Book I.* Finney: *Concerto for Percussion and Orchestra.* Harris: *Tenth Symphony* (Abraham Lincoln Symphony). Oliveros: *Pieces of Eight.* Persichetti: *Piano Sonata No.11.* Piston: *Symphony No.8.* Rochberg: *Contra Mortem et Tempus.* Ned Rorem: *Miss Julie* (opera). Schuller: *Symphony.* Sessions: *Piano Sonata No.3* (elegy to JFK). Wuorinen: *Piano Concerto No.1.*

Events: Ives' *Fourth Symphony* premiered by Stokowski. Philip Glass collaborates with sitarist Ravi Shankar in Paris. National Endowment for the Arts created by act of Congress. Dello Joio wins Emmy for his music to the TV documentary *The Louvre.* Rev. Martin Luther King, Jr. and 2,600 others arrested after March on Selma, Alabama. Black nationalist leader, Malcolm X, assassinated at rally in Harlem (February 21).

1966   *Died:* Composer **Deems Taylor** in New York (July 3). Composer **Quincy Porter** in Bethany, Connecticut (November 12).

Works: Crumb: *Madrigals: Book II.* Del Tredici: *Syzygy* (Joyce). Herrmann: music for François Truffaut's film *Fahrenheit 451.* Kirchner: *String Quartet No.3.* Oliveros: *Theatre Piece.* Partch: *And on the Seventh Day Petals Fell in Petaluma* and *Delusion of the Fury.* Perle: *Cello Concerto.* Piston: *Piano Trio No.2.* Porter: *Oboe Quintet.* Schuller: *The Visitation* (opera). Sessions: *Symphony No.6.*

Events: Disastrous premiere of Barber's *Antony and Cleopatra* at the Met. Thomson completes autobiography, begins work on *Lord Byron.*

1967   *Works:* Copland: *Inscape* for orchestra. Foss: *Concert for Cello and Orchestra.* Hanson: *Symphony No.6.* Harris: *Symphony No.11.* Persichetti: *Symphony No.8.* Piston: *Clarinet Concerto.* Reich: *Piano Phase* and *Violin*

Phase. Riley: *Poppy Nogood and the Phantom Band.* Sessions: *Symphony No.7.*

Events: Glass and Reich become reacquainted at Reich's concerts in the Park Place Gallery (New York City). Beginning of the use of the term "minimalism" applied to music.

1968   *Died:* Composer **Bernard Rogers** in New York (May 24). Composer **Leo Sowerby** in Ft. Clinton, Ohio (July 7).

Works: Corigliano: *Piano Concerto.* Del Tredici: *Pop-pourri.* Finney: *Piano Concerto No.2.* Menotti: *Help! Help! The Globolinks!* (science-fiction opera using electronic music). Oliveros: *Double Basses at Twenty Paces.* Perle: *Serenade No.2.* Schuller: *Double Bass Concerto.* Schuman: *Symphony No.9.* Sessions: *Symphony No.8.*

Events: Walter Carlos' album *Switched on Bach* demonstrates timbral possibilities of the Moog synthesizer to the public. Crumb's *Echoes of Time and the River* receives Pulitzer Prize. Martin Luther King, Jr. assassinated in Memphis (April 4). Robert F. Kennedy assassinated in Los Angeles (June 5). Richard Nixon elected 37th President of the United States.

1969   *Died:* Composer **Vernon Duke (Vladimir Dukelsky)** in Santa Monica, California (January 16). Composer **Richard Maxfield** in Los Angeles (June 27). Composer **Douglas Moore** in Greenport, New York (July 25).

Works: Carter: *Concerto for Orchestra.* Crumb: *Madrigals: Books III and IV.* Del Tredici: *An Alice Symphony.* Dello Joio: *Homage to Haydn.* Feldman: *On Time and the Instrumental Factor.* Rochberg: *Symphony No.3.*

Events: Bernstein resigns as conductor of New York Philharmonic.

1970   *Died:* Composer **Ingolf Dahl** in Frutigen, Switzerland (August 6). Composer **Anis Fuleihan** in Palo Alto, California (October 11).

Works: Babbitt: *String Quartet No.4.* Corigliano: *Poem in October* (D. Thomas). Crumb: *Black Angels* and *Ancient Voices of Children.* Finney: *24 Inventions* for piano. Hanson: *The Mystic Trumpeter* (Whitman). Menotti: *Triple Concerto.* Oliveros: *To Valerie Solanis and Marilyn Monroe in Recognition of their Desperation.* Persichetti: *Symphony No.9.* Sessions: *When Lilacs Last in the Dooryard Bloom'd* (Whitman).

Events: Steve Reich travels to Ghana to study African drumming. Reprint of Wa-Wan Press publications issued by *New York Times* and Arno Press. Four students shot to death by National Guardsmen during peaceful demonstration at Kent State University, Ohio (May 4).

1971   *Died:* Composer **Ethel Glenn Hier** in Winter Park, New York (January 14). Composer **Mabel Wheeler Daniels** in Boston (March 10). Composer **Carl Ruggles** in Bennington, Vermont (October 24).

Works: Bernstein: *Mass.* Carter: *Third String Quartet.* Crumb: *Vox balaenae* and *Lux aeterna.* Del Tredici: *Adventures Underground.* Harrison: *Young Caesar* (puppet opera). Piston: *Flute Concerto.* Sessions: *Double Concerto* and *Canons in Memory of Stravinsky.* Ellen Taaffe Zwilich: *Einsame Nacht* (Hesse).

Events: New York Public Library issues collected piano rags and collected works for voice of Scott Joplin. Slonimsky publishes updated edition of *Music Since 1900.* Cowell's 1931 *Concerto for Rhythmicon and Orchestra* realized on computer.

1972   *Died:* Composer **Ferde Grofé** in Santa Monica, California (April 3). Composer **Stefan Wolpe** in New York City (April 4).

Works: Earle Brown: *Time Spans.* Crumb: *Makrokosmos* (begun). Del Tredici: *Vintage Alice.* Druckman: *Windows* (orch.). Oliveros: *Sonic Meditations.* Rands: *Mesalliance* (piano and orch.). Riley: *Happy Ending.* Rochberg: *String Quartet No.3.* Rorem: *Last Poems of Wallace Stevens* (song cycle). Schuman: *Voyage* (orch.). Wuorinen: *Piano Concerto No.2.*

Events: Virgil Thomson's *Lord Byron* premiered at Juilliard. Scott Joplin's only surviving opera, *Treemonisha,* premiered. Jacob Druckman receives Pulitzer for his *Windows.* Watergate scandal begins as five men are apprehended attempting to bug the Democratic National Committee headquarters at Washington's Watergate hotel/office complex. Nixon makes unprecedented 8-day trip to communist China.

1973   *Works:* Crumb: *Makrokosmos I and II.* Druckman: *Incenters* (orch.). Finney: *Violin Concerto No.2* and *Symphony No.4.* Harris: *Folksong Suite* (harp and orch.). Harrison: *Concerto for organ, percussion and orchestra* and *Suite for violin and American gamelan.* Zwilich: *Symposium* (orch.).

Events: Aaron Copland ceases composing. Broadcast of Bernstein's Young People's Concerts ceases after fifteen years.

1974   *Died:* Composer **Harry Partch** in San Diego (September 3).

Works: Bernstein: *The Dybbuk.* Crumb: *Makrokosmos III.* Finney: *Saxophone Concerto* and *Symphony No.4.* Foss: *Percussion Concerto.* Oliveros: *Crow II* (theatre piece). Rochberg: *Violin Concerto.* Zwilich: *Violin Sonata* and *String Quartet.*

Events: Barber and Menotti separate, sell Capricorn. Newspaper heiress, Patricia Hearst, kidnapped by Symbionese Liberation Army. Nixon become first U.S. president to resign (August 8).

1975   *Died:* Composer **Bernard Herrmann** after completing score for Scorsese's *Taxi Driver* in Los Angeles (December 24).

Works: Corigliano: *Oboe Concerto.* Foss: *String Quartet No.3.* Harris: *Bicentennial Symphony.* Rochberg: *Piano Quintet.* Schuman: *Symphony No.10.*

Events: Revised version of Barber's *Antony and Cleopatra* performed at Juilliard. Vietnam War ends with victory by Communist forces of the north.

1976   *Died:* Composer **Walter Piston** in Belmont, Massachusetts (November 12).

Works: Babbitt: *Concerti for violin, small orchestra and tape.* Bolcom: *Piano Concerto.* Carter: *A Symphony of Three Orchestras.* Corigliano: *Poem on His Birthday* (D. Thomas). Del Tredici: *Final Alice.* Glass: *Einstein on the Beach* (premiered at Avignon). Gould: *Symphony of Spirituals.* Harris: *Symphony No.13 "Bicentennial."* Kirchner: *Lily* (opera). Menotti: *Halcyon Symphony.* Persichetti: *The Sibyl* (opera). Piston: *Concerto for String Quartet and Orchestra.* Reich: *Music for 18 Musicians.* Rochberg: *Symphony No.4.* Rudhyar: *Theurgy: Tone Ritual No.2* (piano). Schuller: *Violin Concerto* and *Horn Concerto No.2.*

1977   *Died:* Composer **Gena Branscombe** in New York City (July 26). Conductor **Thomas Schippers,** advocate of Barber and Menotti, in New York City (December 16).

Works: Albert: *To Wake the Dead* (Joyce). Babbitt: *Solo Requiem.* Corigliano: *Clarinet Concerto.* Creston: *Rhythmicon.* Foss: *Music for Six.* Persichetti: *English Horn Concerto.* Rands: *Madrigali.* Rochberg: *String Quartet No.4.* Rudhyar: *Cosmic Cycle* (orch.). Zwilich: *Clarino Quartet.*

Events: Menotti founds American version of Spoleto Festival in Charleston, South Carolina.

1978   *Died:* Composer **William Grant Still** in Los Angeles (December 3).

Works: Druckman: *Viola Concerto.* Gould: music for the TV miniseries *The Holocaust.* Rochberg: *String Quartets Nos.5 and 6.* Sessions: *Symphony No.9.*

Events: Reich's ensemble premieres John Adams' sextet version of *Shaker Loops* in New York. American Composers' Orchestra created by ACA. President Jimmy Carter mediates Camp David peace accords between Israel and Egypt.

1979   *Died:* Composer **Roy Harris** in Santa Monica, California (October 1).

Works: Crumb: *Makrokosmos IV* (completed). Druckman: *Aureole* (orch.). Feldman: *String Quartet No.1.* Luening: *Short Symphony.* Perle: *Concertino* (piano, woodwinds, percussion). Rochberg: *String Quartet No.7.* Joan Tower: *Amazon II.* Zwilich: *Chamber Symphony.*

1980   *Works:* Adams: *Harmonium.* Carter: *Night Fantasies* (solo piano). Corigliano: music for the film *Altered States.* Del Tredici: *Child Alice.* Druckman: *Prism.* Feldman: *Piano Trio.* Foss: *Night Music for John Lennon.* Glass: *Satyagraha* (opera) and *The Photographer* (mixed media). Harrison: *Scenes from Cavafy* (voices and Javanese gamelan). Perle: *Short*

Symphony. Persichetti: *Piano Sonata No.12.* Rands: *Canti lunatici.* Reich: *Octet* and *Music for Large Ensemble.* Riley: *Chorale of the Blessed Day.*

Events: Del Tredici receives Pulitzer for first part of *Child Alice, In Memory of a Summer Day.* Iranian militants seize American embassy in Tehran. Ronald Reagan elected 40th President of the U.S., ushering in a new wave of political and cultural conservatism.

1981   *Died:* Composer **Samuel Barber** in New York City (January 23). Composer **Howard Hanson** in Rochester, New York (February 26). Composer **Robert Russell Bennett** in New York City (August 17). Composer **David Guion** in Dallas (October 17).

Works: Babbitt: *Ars combinatoria.* Bolcom: *Songs of Innocence and Experience* (Blake) completed. Corigliano: *Flute Concerto.* Creston: *Symphony No.6.* Crumb: *Gnomic Variations.* Finney: *Heyoka* (ballet). Harrison: *Four Gendings (Alexander, Demeter, Hermes, Hephaestus).* Persichetti: *Harpsichord Sonatas Nos.2 and 3.* Reich: *Tehillim.* Schuller: *Piano Concerto No.2.* Sessions: *Concerto for Orchestra* (last completed work). Wuorinen: *Short Suite.* Young: *The Well-Tuned Piano.*

1982   *Works:* Adams: *Grand Pianola Music.* Babbitt: *String Quartet No.5.* Harrison: *Symphony No.3.* Luening: *Symphonic Fantasia IV.* Persichetti: *Harpsichord Sonatas Nos. 4–6.* Rands: *Canti del sole.* Reich: *Vermont Counterpoint.* Tower: *Amazon III.* Zwilich: *String Trio* and *Symphony No.1.*

1983   *Died:* Composer **Peter Mennin** in New York City (June 17).

Works: Adams: *Shaker Loops* (string orchestra). Bernstein: *A Quiet Place* (operatic sequel to *Trouble in Tahiti*). Bolcom: *Violin Concerto.* Feldman: *String Quartet No.2.* Menotti: *Contrabass Concerto.* Perle: *Serenade No.3.* Persichetti: *Harpsichord Sonata No.7.* Rochberg: *Oboe Concerto.*

Events: Terrorist explosion kills 237 U.S. Marines in Beirut, Lebanon.

1984   *Works:* Finney: *Weep Torn Land* (opera). Glass: *Akhnaten* (opera). Oliveros: *Spiral Mandala.* Rands: *Suites Nos.1 and 2* (orch.). Reich: *The Desert Music* and *Sextet.* Tower: *Cello Concerto.* Zwilich: *Celebration for Orchestra, Chamber Concerto* and *Double String Quartet.*

1985   *Died:* Composer **Roger Sessions** in Princeton, New Jersey (March 16). Composer **Richard Yardumian** in Bryn Athen, Pennsylvania (August 15). Composer **Paul Creston** in San Diego (August 24).

Works: Adams: *Harmonielehre.* Albert: *River Run.* Carter: *Penthode* (five quartets). Diamond: *Symphony No.9.* Druckman: *Athanor* (orch). Foss: *Renaissance Concerto* (flute and orch.). Harrison: *Piano Concerto.* Kirchner: *Music for 12.* Libby Larsen: *Coming Forth Into Day* (chorus and orch.). Luening: *Symphonic Fantasias V–VI.* Nancarrow: *44 Studies for Player Piano(s)* completed. Perle: *Wind Quintet No.4.* Persichetti: *Harpsichord Sonata No.8.* Rands: *Ceremonial for Orchestra.* Reich: *Three Movements for Orchestra* and *New York Counterpoint.* Rorem: *Organ*

Concerto. Tower: *Piano Concerto.* Wuorinen: *Piano Concerto No.3.* Zwilich: *Piano Concerto* and *Symphony No.2.*

Events: Stephen Albert awarded Pulitzer for symphonic poem *River Run.* PLO terrorists hijack Italian cruise ship, *Achille Lauro,* and murder American tourist Leon Klinghoffer.

1986   *Works:* Adams: *Nixon in China* (opera). Albert: *Violin Concerto: In Concordiam.* Babbitt: *Concerto for Piano and Orchestra.* Carter: *String Quartet No.4.* Anthony Davis: *The Life and Times of Malcolm X* (opera). Del Tredici: *Haddock's Eyes.* Foss: *Tashi* (string sextet). Glass: *Violin Concerto* and *The Juniper Tree* (opera). John Harbison: *The Flight into Egypt* (cantata). Harrison: *Varied Trio.* Karel Husa: *Concerto for Orchestra.* Wm. Kraft: *Contextures II: The Final Beast.* Menotti: *Goya.* Nancarrow: *Piece No.2 for Small Orchestra.* Perle: *Wind Quintet No.4.* Riley: *Salome Dances for Peace* (string quartet). Schwantner: *Toward Light.*

Events: Slonimsky publishes supplement to 1971 edition of *Music Since 1900.* George Perle awarded Pulitzer for his *Wind Quintet No.4.* Space shuttle Challenger explodes after takeoff at Cape Canaveral, killing all on board.

1987   *Died:* Composer **Vincent Persichetti** in Philadelphia, Pennsylvania (August 15). Composer **Morton Feldman** in Buffalo, New York (September 3).

Works: Albert: *Anthems and Processionals.* Cage: *Europeras 1 and 2.* Carter: *Oboe Concerto.* Vivian Fine: *After the Tradition* (orch.). Glass: *The Fall of the House of Usher.* Kirchner: *Five Pieces for Piano.* Rands: *Hiraeth* (cello and orch.). Reich: *Electronic Counterpoint* and *The Four Sections* (orch.). Jay Reise: *Rasputin* (opera).

Events: United States torn by Iran-Contra scandal.

1988   *Works:* Adams: *Fearful Symmetries.* Bolcom: *12 New Etudes for Piano.* Carter: *Enchanted Preludes* (flute and cello) and *Remembrance* (orch.). Druckman: *Brangle* (orch.). Glass: *Itaipu* (orch.) and *The Making of the Representative for Planet 8* (opera). Nancarrow: *String Quartet No.3.* Reich: *Different Trains.* Schuller: *Flute Concerto.*

Events: William Bolcom awarded Pulitzer for *12 New Etudes.*

1989   *Died:* Composer **Virgil Thomson** in New York City (September 30).

Works: Adams: *The Word Dresser.* Babbitt: *Emblems* (piano). Bolcom: *Symphony No.5.* Stewart Copeland: *Holy Blood and Crescent Moon* (opera). Mario Davidovsky: *Concertante* (string quartet and orch.). Foss: *American Landscapes* (guitar and orch.). John Harbison: *The Natural World.* Mel Powell: *Duplicates* (two pianos and orch.). Siegmeister: *Symphony No.8.* Tower: *2nd Fanfare for the Uncommon Woman.*

Events: Reich begins work on *The Cave.* Cold War ends as communism collapses in Russia and Eastern Europe.

1990   *Died:* **Leonard Bernstein** in New York City (October 24). **Aaron Copland** in Peekskill, New York (December 2).

Works: Albert: *The Flower of the Mountain* and *Cello Concerto.* Bolcom:
The Mask (chorus and piano) and *Cello Sonata.* Henry Brant: *Prisons of
the Mind* (orch.). Carter: *Violin Concerto.* Corigliano: *Symphony No.1.*
Diamond: *Kaddish* (cello and orch.). John Eaton: *The Cry of Clytemnestra*
(opera). Schuller: *Trio for violin, clarinet and piano.* Robt. Starer: *Apollonia*
(opera). Francis Thorne: *Piano Concerto No.3.* Zwilich: *Flute Concerto.*

Events: Short-lived Persian Gulf War begins as President George Bush
orders American troops to expel invading Iraqi forces from Kuwait.

1991   *Died:* Composer **Elie Siegmeister** in Manhasset, New York (March 10).

Works: Adams: *The Death of Klinghoffer* (opera). Meredith Monk: *Atlas*
(opera). Perle: *Sinfonietta No.2.* Zwilich: *Oboe Concerto.*

Events: First complete recording and concert performance of Thomson's
Lord Byron under James Bolle at Monadnock Festival (New Hampshire).
Corigliano's *The Ghosts of Versailles* premiered at the Met (December 19).

1992   *Died:* Composer **William Schuman** in New York City (February 15).
Composer **John Cage** in New York City (August 12). Composer **Stephen
Albert** in Truro, Massachusetts (December 29).

Works: Bolcom: *McTeague* (opera after Frank Norris).

Events: Philip Glass' opera *The Voyage* premiered at the Metropolitan
Opera. The magazine *Musical America* suspends publication after 94 years
of continuous operation. Bill Clinton elected 42nd President of the United
States.

1993   *Died:* Composer **Kenneth Gaburo** in Iowa City, Iowa (January 26).
Songwriter and Gershwin mentor **Kay Swift** in Connecticut (January 28).

Works: Glass: *White Raven.* Reich: *The Cave* (premiered at Vienna [May]
and Brooklyn [October]).

Events: Glass' *Orphée* (opera after the film by Cocteau) premiered at
Cambridge, Massachusetts (May 16). Historic floods in the Mississippi
River valley devastate the Midwest.

Appendix *B*

245 Significant American Composers Listed by State (Country) of Origin

Foreign-Born Composers Identified Principally as Americans

Argentina

Mario Davidovsky (Buenos Aires, 1934–)

Australia

Percy Grainger (Melbourne, 1882– 1961)

Austria

Ernst Toch (Vienna, 1887–1964)

Robert Starer (Vienna, 1924–)

Canada

Gena Branscombe (Ontario, 1881– 1977)

Henry Brant (Montreal, 1913–)

China

Vladimir Ussachevsky (Hailar, Manchuria, 1911–1990)

Cyprus, Isle of

Anis Fuleihan (1900–1970)

Czechoslovakia

Anthony Philip Heinrich (Krasny Buk, 1781–1861)

Vaclav Nelhybel (Polanka nad Odrou, 1919–)

Karel Husa (Prague, 1921–)

England

George K. Jackson (Oxford, 1745–1823)

Raynor Taylor (London, 1747–1825)

Alexander Reinagle (Portsmouth, 1756– 1809)

Benjamin Carr (London, 1768–1831)

James Hewitt (Dartmoor, 1770–1827)

John Bray (Leeds, 1782–1822)

Henry Russell (Sheerness, 1812–1900)

Felix Borowski (Kendal, 1872–1956)

Bernard Rands (Sheffield, 1934–)

France

Charles Martin Loeffler (Alsace, 1861– 1935)

Edgard Varèse (Paris, 1885–1965)

Carlos Salzedo (Archanon, 1885–1961)

Dane Rudhyar (Paris, 1895–1985)

Christian Wolff (Nice, 1934–)

Germany

Jeremias Dencke (Langenbilau, 1725– 1795)

Jeremias Herbst (Kempton, 1734–1812)

David Moritz Michael (Keinhausen, 1751–1827)

Kurt Weill (Dessau, 1900–1950)

Stephan Wolpe (Berlin, 1902–1972)

Ingolf Dahl (Hamburg, 1912–1970)

Hugo Weisgall (Eibenschutz, 1912–)

Lukas Foss (Berlin, 1922–)

Holland

Johann Frederick Peter (Heerendijk, 1746–1813)

Bernard Wagenaar (Arnhem, 1894–1971)

Ireland

Victor Herbert (Dublin, 1859–1924)

Italy

Gian-Carlo Menotti (Cadegliano, 1911–)

Peru

Meredith Monk (Lima, 1942–)

Russia

Louis Gruenberg (Brest Litovsk, 1884–1964)

Leo Ornstein (Kremenchug, Ukraine 1895–)

Vernon Duke/Vladimir Dukelsky (Pskov, 1903–1969)

Switzerland

Ernest Bloch (Geneva, 1880–1959)

United States Composers

Arkansas

Conlon Nancarrow (Texarkana, 1912–)

Arizona

Ulysses Kay (Tucson, 1917–)

California

Henry Cowell (Menlo Park, 1897–1965)

Harry Partch (Oakland, 1901–1974)

John Cage (Los Angeles, 1912–1992)

Earl Kim (Dinuba, 1920–)

William Bergsma (Oakland, 1921–)

Leslie Bassett (Hanford, 1923–)

Lawrence Moss (Los Angeles, 1927–)

Morton Subotnik (Los Angeles, 1933–)

Terry Riley (Colfax, 1935–)

David Del Tredici (Cloverdale, 1937–)

Colorado

Robert Moran (Denver, 1937–)

Connecticut

Andrew Law (Milford, 1749–1821)

Thomas Hastings (Washington, 1784–1872)

Dudley Buck (Hartford, 1839–1909)

Frederick G. Gleason (Middletown, 1848–1903)

Charles Ives (Danbury, 1874–1954)

Quincy Porter (New Haven, 1897–1966)

Delaware

Libby Larsen (Wilmington, 1950–)

Florida

Ellen Taaffe Zwilich (Miami, 1939–)

Georgia

John Gordon McCurry (Hart County, 1821–1886)

Sidney Lanier (Macon, 1842–1881)

Wallingford Riegger (Albany, 1885–1961)

Ben Johnston (Macon, 1926–)

Idaho

Arthur Shepherd (Paris, 1880–1958)

La Monte Young (Bern, 1935–)

Illinois

Henry Eichheim (Chicago, 1870–1942)

John Alden Carpenter (Park Ridge, 1876–1951)

Ernst Bacon (Chicago, 1898–1990)

Vivian Fine (Chicago, 1913–)

John LaMontaine (Chicago, 1920–)

William Kraft (Chicago, 1923–)

Marilyn Ziffrin (Moline, 1926–)

Joseph Schwantner (Chicago, 1943–)

Indiana

Ned Rorem (Richmond, 1923–)

Kansas

Steven Stucky (Hutchinson, 1949–)

Kentucky

John J. Becker (Henderson, 1886–1961)

Louisiana

Louis Moreau Gottschalk (New Orleans, 1829–1869)

David Ward-Steinman (Alexandria, 1936–)

Maine

William B. Bradbury (York, 1816–1868)

John Knowles Paine (Portland, 1839–1906)

Walter Piston (Rockland, 1894–1976)

Maryland

Adolph Weiss (Baltimore, 1891–1971)

Philip Glass (Baltimore, 1937–)

Christopher Rouse (Baltimore, 1949–)

Massachusetts

William Billings (Boston, 1746–1800)

Justin Morgan (West Springfield, 1747–1798)

Supply Belcher (Stoughton, 1751–1836)

Jacob French (Stoughton, 1754–1817)

Daniel Read (Attleboro, 1757–1836)

Timothy Swan (Worcester, 1758–1842)

Jacob Kimball (Topsfield, 1761–1826)

Samuel Holyoke (Boxford, 1762–1820)

Jeremiah Ingalls (Andover, 1764–1838)

Oliver Holden (Shirley, 1765–1844)

John Wyeth (Cambridge, 1770–1858)

Lowell Mason (Medfield, 1792–1872)

Issac B. Woodbury (Beverly, 1819–1858)

George Frederick Root (Sheffield, 1820–1895)

Arthur Foote (Salem, 1853–1937)

George W. Chadwick (Lowell, 1854–1931)

Arthur B. Whiting (Cambridge, 1861–1936)

Horatio Parker (Auburndale, 1863–1919)

Henry F. B. Gilbert (Somerville, 1868–1928)

Henry K. Hadley (Somerville, 1871–1937)

Frederick Converse (Newton, 1871–1940)

Bertram Shapleigh (Boston, 1871–1940)

Edward Burlingame Hill (Cambridge, 1872–1960)

Daniel Gregory Mason (Brookline, 1873–1953)

Carl Ruggles (Marion, 1876–1971)

Mabel Wheeler Daniels (Swampscott, 1879–1971)

Eliot Griffis (Boston, 1893–1967)

Alan Hovhaness (Somerville, 1911–)

Irving Fine (Boston, 1914–1962)

Leonard Bernstein (1918–1990)

Harold Shapero (Lynn, 1920–)

Daniel Pinkham (Lynn, 1923–)

Earle Brown (Lunenberg, 1926–)

Gordon Mumma (Framingham, 1935–)

Frederic Rzewski (Westfield, 1938–)

John Adams (Worcester, 1947–)

Michigan

Leo Sowerby (Grand Rapids, 1895–1968)

Robert Ashley (Ann Arbor, 1930–)

Roger Reynolds (Detroit, 1934–)

Russell Peck (Detroit, 1945–)

Minnesota

Arthur Farwell (St. Paul, 1872–1952)

Ross Lee Finney (Wells, 1906–)

Mississippi

William Grant Still (Woodville, 1895–1978)

Missouri

Robert Russell Bennett (Kansas City, 1894–1981)

Virgil Thomson (Kansas City, 1896–1989)

Nebraska
Howard Hanson (Wahoo, 1896–1981)

New Hampshire
Amy Cheney Beach (Henniker, 1867–1944)

Alvin Lucier (Nashua, 1931–)

New Jersey
James Lyon (Newark, 1735–1794)

William Gilchrist (Jersey City, 1846–1916)

George Antheil (Trenton, 1900–1959)

George Perle (Bayonne, 1915–)

George Rochberg (Paterson, 1918–)

Kenneth Gaburo (Somerville, 1926–1993)

Robert Helps (Passaic, 1928–)

Eric Stokes (Haddon Heights, 1930–)

Donald Martino (Plainfield, 1931–)

John Harbison (Orange, 1938–)

Stephen Paulus (Summit, 1949–)

New Mexico
James Tenney (Silver City, 1934–)

New York
John Hill Hewitt (NYC, 1801–1890)

George Frederick Bristow (Brooklyn, 1825–1898)

Edward MacDowell (NYC, 1861–1908)

Harvey Worthington Loomis (Brooklyn, 1865–1930)

Rubin Goldmark (NYC, 1872–1936)

Charles T. Griffes (Elmira, 1884–1920)

Deems Taylor (NYC, 1885–1966)

Ferde Grofé (NYC, 1892–1972)

Douglas Moore (Cutchogue, 1893–1969)

Bernard Rogers (NYC, 1893–1968)

Roger Sessions (Brooklyn, 1896–1985)

George Gershwin (Brooklyn, 1898–1937)

Randall Thompson (NYC, 1899–1984)

Aaron Copland (Brooklyn, 1900–1990)

Paul Creston (NYC, 1906–1985)

Elliott Carter (NYC, 1908–)

Elie Siegmeister (NYC, 1909–1991)

William Schuman (NYC, 1910–1992)

Paul Bowles (Jamaica, 1910–)

Bernard Herrmann (NYC, 1911–1975)

Norman Dello Joio (NYC, 1913–)

Morton Gould (Richmond Hill, 1913–)

David Diamond (Rochester, 1915–)

Leon Kirchner (Brooklyn, 1919–)

Andrew Imbrie (NYC, 1921–)

Francis Thorne (Bay Shore, 1922–)

Lejaren Hiller (NYC, 1924–)

William Mayer (NYC, 1925–)

Gunther Schuller (NYC, 1925–)

Morton Feldman (NYC, 1926–1987)

Meyer Kupferman (NYC, 1926–)

Seymour Shifrin (NYC, 1926–1979)

Mel Powell (NYC, 1933–)

Steve Reich (NYC, 1936–)

Elliott Schwartz (NYC, 1936–)

John Corigliano (NYC, 1938–)

Joan Tower (New Rochelle, 1938–)

Charles Wuorinen (NYC, 1938–)

Stephen Albert (NYC, 1941–1992)

Tod Machover (NYC, 1953–)

Augusta Read Thomas (Glen Cove, 1964–)

North Carolina
William Hauser (Bethania, 1812–1880)

Hunter Johnson (Benson, 1906–)

Ohio
Harry Lawrence Freeman (Cleveland, 1869–1954)

David Stanley Smith (Toledo, 1877–1949)

Emerson Whithorne (Cleveland, 1884–1958)

Ethel Glenn Hier (Cincinnati, 1889–1971)

Ruth Crawford (Seeger) (East Liverpool, 1901–1953)

Donald Erb (Youngstown, 1927–)

Oklahoma

Roy Harris (Lincoln County, 1898–1979)

Oregon

Lou Harrison (Portland, 1917–)

Pennsylvania

Philip Phile (Philadelphia ?, died ca. 1793)

Francis Hopkinson (Philadelphia, 1737–1791)

John Antes (Bethlehem, 1740–1811)

William Henry Fry (Philadelphia, 1813–1864)

Stephen C. Foster (Lawrenceville, 1826–1864)

Ethelbert Nevin (Edgeworth, 1862–1901)

Arthur Nevin (Edgeworth, 1871–1943)

Charles Wakefield Cadman (Johnstown, 1881–1946)

Marc Blitzstein (Philadelphia, 1905–1964)

Samuel Barber (Westchester, 1910–1981)

Vincent Persichetti (Philadelphia, 1915–1987)

Milton Babbitt (Philadelphia, 1916–)

Richard Yardumian (Philadelphia, 1917–1985)

Ralph Shapey (Philadelphia, 1921–)

Peter Mennin (Erie, 1923–1983)

David Tudor (Philadelphia, 1926–)

Jacob Druckman (Philadelphia, 1928–)

David Amram (Philadelphia, 1930–)

John Eaton (Bryn Mawr, 1935–)

Keith Jarrett (Allentown, 1945–)

Joan LaBarbara (Philadelphia, 1947–)

Rhode Island

Stephen Jenks (Glocester, 1772–1856)

South Carolina

Benjamin Franklin White (Spartanburg, 1800–1879)

William Walker (Cross Keys, 1809–1875)

Carlisle Floyd (Latta, 1926–)

Tennessee

Allen Carden (1792–1859)

Mary Carr Moore (Memphis, 1873–1957)

Judith Lang Zaimont (Memphis, 1945–)

Texas

Scott Joplin (Texarkana, 1868–1917)

David Guion (Ballinger, 1892–1981)

Pauline Oliveros (Houston, 1932–)

Vermont

Silas G. Pratt (1846–1916)

Virginia

Ananias Davisson (1780–1857)

James P. Carroll (Lebanon, 1787–1854)

Mary Howe (Richmond, 1882–1964)

John Powell (Richmond, 1882–1963)

Washington

Marion Bauer (Walla Walla, 1887–1955)

Barney Childs (Spokane, 1926–)

Richard Maxfield (Seattle, 1927–1969)

William Bolcom (Seattle, 1938–)

Paul Chihara (Seattle, 1938–)

West Virginia

George Crumb (Charleston, 1929–)

Wisconsin

Edgar Stillman Kelley (Sparta, 1857–1944)

Otto Luening (Milwaukee, 1900–)

Lester Trimble (Bangor, 1920–1986)

Lee Hoiby (Madison, 1926–)

Alphabetical Cross-Reference

৵

Adams, John (Massachusetts)
Albert, Stephen (New York)
Amram, David (Pennsylvania)
Antes, John (Pennsylvania)
Antheil, George (New Jersey)
Ashley, Robert (Michigan)

Babbitt, Milton (Pennsylvania)
Bacon, Ernest (Illinois)
Barber, Samuel (Pennsylvania)
Bassett, Leslie (California)
Bauer, Marion (Washington)
Beach, Amy Cheney (New Hampshire)
Becker, John J. (Kentucky)
Belcher, Supply (Massachusetts)
Bennett, Robert Russell (Missouri)
Bergsma, William (California)
Bernstein, Leonard (Massachusetts)
Billings, William (Massachusetts)
Blitzstein, Marc (Pennsylvania)
Bloch, Ernest (Switzerland)
Bolcom, William (Washington)
Borowski, Felix (England)
Bowles, Paul (New York)
Bradbury, William B. (Maine)
Branscombe, Gena (Canada)
Brant, Henry (Canada)
Bray, John (England)
Bristow, George Frederick (New York)
Brown, Earle (Massachusetts)
Buck, Dudley (Connecticut)

Cadman, Charles Wakefield (Pennsylvania)
Cage, John (California)

Carden, Allen (Tennessee)
Carpenter, John Alden (Illinois)
Carr, Benjamin (England)
Carroll, James P. (Virginia)
Carter, Elliott (New York)
Chadwick, George W. (Massachusetts)
Chihara, Paul (Washington)
Childs, Barney (Washington)
Converse, Frederick (Massachusetts)
Copland, Aaron (New York)
Corigliano, John (New York)
Cowell, Henry (California)
Creston, Paul (New York)
Crumb, George (West Virginia)

Dahl, Ingolf (Germany)
Daniels, Mabel Wheeler (Massachusetts)
Davidovsky, Mario (Argentina)
Davisson, Ananias (Virginia)
Del Tredici, David (California)
Dello Joio, Norman (New York)
Dencke, Jeremias (Germany)
Diamond, David (New York)
Druckman, Jacob (Pennsylvania)
Duke, Vernon (Russia)

Eaton, John (Pennsylvania)
Eichheim, Henry (Illinois)
Erb, Donald (Ohio)

Farwell, Arthur (Minnesota)
Feldman, Morton (New York)
Fine, Irving (Massachusetts)
Fine, Vivian (Illinois)
Finney, Ross Lee (Minnesota)

Floyd, Carlisle (South Carolina)
Foote, Arthur (Massachusetts)
Foss, Lukas (Germany)
Foster, Stephen C. (Pennsylvania)
Freeman, Harry Lawrence (Ohio)
French, Jacob (Massachusetts)
Fry, William Henry (Pennsylvania)
Fuleihan, Anis (Cyprus)

Gaburo, Kenneth (New Jersey)
Gershwin, George (New York)
Gilbert, Henry F. B. (Massachusetts)
Gilchrist, William (New Jersey)
Glass, Philip (Maryland)
Gleason, Frederick G. (Connecticut)
Goldmark, Rubin (New York)
Gottschalk, Louis Moreau (Louisiana)
Gould, Morton (New York)
Grainger, Percy (Australia)
Griffes, Charles T. (New York)
Griffis, Eliot (Massachusetts)
Grofé, Ferde (New York)
Gruenberg, Louis (Russia)
Guion, David (Texas)

Hadley, Henry (Massachusetts)
Hanson, Howard (Nebraska)
Harbison, John (New Jersey)
Harris, Roy (Oklahoma)
Harrison, Lou (Oregon)
Hastings, Thomas (Connecticut)
Hauser, William (North Carolina)
Heinrich, Anthony Philip (Czechoslo-
    vakia)
Helps, Robert (New Jersey)
Herbert, Victor (Ireland)
Herbst, Jeremias (Germany)
Herrmann, Bernard (New York)
Hewitt, James (England)
Hewitt, John Hill (New York)
Hier, Ethel Glenn (Ohio)
Hill, Edward Burlingame (Massachu-
    setts)
Hiller, Lejaren (New York)
Hoiby, Lee (Wisconsin)

Holden, Oliver (Massachusetts)
Holyoke, Samuel (Massachusetts)
Hopkinson, Francis (Pennsylvania)
Hovhaness, Alan (Massachusetts)
Howe, Mary (Virginia)
Husa, Karel (Czechoslovakia)

Imbrie, Andrew (New York)
Ingalls, Jeremiah (Massachusetts)
Ives, Charles (Connecticut)

Jackson, George K. (England)
Jarrett, Keith (Pennsylvania)
Jenks, Stephen (Rhode Island)
Johnson, Hunter (North Carolina)
Johnston, Ben (Georgia)
Joplin, Scott (Texas)

Kay, Ulysses (Arizona)
Kelley, Edgar Stillman (Wisconsin)
Kim, Earl (California)
Kimball, Jacob (Massachusetts)
Kirchner, Leon (New York)
Kraft, William (Illinois)
Kupferman, Meyer (New York)

LaBarbara, Joan (Pennsylvania)
LaMontaine, John (Illinois)
Lanier, Sydney (Georgia)
Larsen, Libby (Delaware)
Law, Andrew (Connecticut)
Loeffler, Charles Martin (France)
Loomis, Harvey W. (New York)
Lucier, Alvin (New Hampshire)
Luening, Otto (Wisconsin)
Lyon, James (New Jersey)

MacDowell, Edward (New York)
Machover, Tod (New York)
Martino, Donald (New Jersey)
Mason, Daniel Gregory (Massachusetts)
Mason, Lowell (Massachusetts)
Maxfield, Richard (Washington)
Mayer, William (New York)
McCurry, John Gordon (Georgia)

Mennin, Peter (Pennsylvania)
Menotti, Gian-Carlo (Italy)
Michael, David Moritz (Germany)
Monk, Meredith (Peru)
Moore, Douglas (New York)
Moore, Mary Carr (Tennessee)
Moran, Robert (Colorado)
Morgan, Justin (Massachusetts)
Moss, Lawrence (California)
Mumma, Gordon (Massachusetts)

Nancarrow, Conlon (Arkansas)
Nelhybel, Vaclav (Czechoslovakia)
Nevin, Arthur (Pennsylvania)
Nevin, Ethelbert (Pennsylvania)

Oliveros, Pauline (Texas)
Ornstein, Leo (Russia)

Paine, John Knowles (Maine)
Parker, Horatio (Massachusetts)
Partch, Harry (California)
Paulus, Stephen (New Jersey)
Peck, Russell (Michigan)
Perle, George (New Jersey)
Persichetti, Vincent (Pennsylvania)
Peter, Johann Frederick (Holland)
Phile, Philip (Pennsylvania)
Pinkham, Daniel (Massachusetts)
Piston, Walter (Maine)
Porter, Quincy (Connecticut)
Powell, John (Virginia)
Powell, Mel (New York)
Pratt, Silas G. (Vermont)

Rands, Bernard (England)
Read, Daniel (Massachusetts)
Reich, Steve (New York)
Reinagle, Alexander (England)
Reynolds, Roger (Michigan)
Riegger, Wallingford (Georgia)
Riley, Terry (California)
Rochberg, George (New Jersey)
Rogers, Bernard (New York)

Root, George Frederick (Massachusetts)
Rorem, Ned (Indiana)
Rouse, Christopher (Maryland)
Rudhyar, Dane (France)
Ruggles, Carl (Massachusetts)
Russell, Henry (England)
Rzewski, Frederic (Massachusetts)

Salzedo, Carlos (France)
Schuller, Gunther (New York)
Schuman, William (New York)
Schwantner, Joseph (Illinois)
Schwartz, Elliott (New York)
Seeger, Ruth Crawford (Ohio)
Sessions, Roger (New York)
Shapero, Harold (Massachusetts)
Shapey, Ralph (Pennsylvania)
Shapleigh, Bertram (Massachusetts)
Shepherd, Arthur (Idaho)
Shifrin, Seymour (New York)
Siegmeister, Elie (New York)
Smith, David Stanley (Ohio)
Sowerby, Leo (Michigan)
Starer, Robert (Austria)
Still, William Grant (Mississippi)
Stokes, Eric (New Jersey)
Stucky, Steven (Kansas)
Subotnik, Morton (California)
Swan, Timothy (Massachusetts)

Taylor, Deems (New York)
Taylor, Raynor (England)
Tenney, James (New Mexico)
Thomas, Augusta Read (New York)
Thompson, Randall (New York)
Thomson, Virgil (Missouri)
Thorne, Francis (New York)
Toch, Ernst (Austria)
Tower, Joan (New York)
Trimble, Lester (Wisconsin)
Tudor, David (Pennsylvania)

Ussachevsky, Vladimir (China)

Varèse, Edgard (France)

Wagenaar, Bernard (Holland)
Walker, William (South Carolina)
Ward-Steinmann, David (Louisiana)
Weill, Kurt (Germany)
Weisgall, Hugo (Germany)
Weiss, Adolph (Maryland)
White, B. F. (South Carolina)
Whithorne, Emerson (Ohio)
Whiting, Arthur B. (Massachusetts)
Wolff, Christian (France)
Wolpe, Stephan (Germany)

Woodbury, Issac B. (Massachusetts)
Wuorinen, Charles (New York)
Wyeth, John (Massachusetts)

Yardumian, Richard (Pennsylvania)
Young, La Monte (Idaho)

Zaimont, Judith Lang (Tennessee)
Ziffrin, Marilyn (Illinois)
Zwilich, Ellen Taaffe (Florida)

Appendix C

The Fundamental Repertoire of American Classical Music

❧

(A Roughly Chronological List of Works of Major Musical or Historical Importance by American Composers)

Note: The following does not represent a complete listing of the works of these composers, nor have all the composers discussed in this history been included here. This is merely an initial reference and sampling of the tremendous volume of American classical music that has been composed during the past two hundred years.

—JWS

Hopkinson, Francis (1737–1791)
"My Days Have Been So Wondrous Free" (song)
Seven Songs for the Harpsichord
The Temple of Minerva (oratorio)

Billings, William (1746–1800)
The New England Psalm Singer
The Singing Master's Assistant
The Continental Harmony
The Suffolk Harmony
The Psalm Singer's Amusement

Peter, Johann Friederich (1746–1813)
Six String Quintets

Swan, Timothy (1758–1842)
The Federal Harmony

Phile, Philip (died ca. 1793)
The President's March ("Hail, Columbia")

Hewitt, James (1770–1827)
The Battle of Trenton

Walker, William (1809–1875)
The Southern Harmony

Fry, William Henry (1813–1864)
Leonora (opera)
"Santa Claus" Symphony

Bristow, George Frederick (1825–1898)
Concert Overture, Op. 3
Rip Van Winkle (opera)

Gottschalk, Louis Moreau (1829–1869)

413

La Bamboula
The Banjo (Nos. 1–2)
The Union
The Dying Poet

Paine, John Knowles (1839–1906)
Piano Sonata No.1
Mass in D
Piano Trio
Symphonies Nos. 1–2
String Quartet
Centennial Hymn
Columbus March and Hymn
St. Peter (oratorio)
Azra (opera)
Island Fantasy (orch.)

Foote, Arthur (1853–1937)
The Farewell of Hiawatha (orch.)
The Wreck of the Hesperus (orch.)
The Skeleton in Armor (orch.)

Chadwick, George Whitefield (1854–1931)
Six Concert Overtures:
 "Rip Van Winkle"
 "Thalia"
 "The Miller's Daughter"
 "Melpomene"
 "Adonais"
 "Euterpe"
Symphonic Sketches
Tam O'Shanter
Symphonies Nos. 1–3
String Quartets Nos. 1–5

Kelley, Edgar Stillman (1857–1944)
The Pit and the Pendulum (orch.)
"Gulliver" Symphony
Alice in Wonderland (orch.)

MacDowell, Edward (1861–1908)
Modern Suites Nos. 1–2
Wood Idylls
Orchestral Suite in A minor
Woodland Sketches
Scotch Poem
New England Idylls
Piano Sonatas Nos. 1–4

Piano Concertos Nos. 1–2
Indian Suites Nos. 1–2

Loeffler, Charles Martin (1861–1935)
Pagan Poem (orch.)
Hora Mystica (orch.)
Canticum Fratris Solis (orch.)

Parker, Horatio (1863–1919)
Hora Novissima (oratorio)
Mona (opera)
Organ Concerto

Beach, Amy Cheney (1867–1944)
Piano Concerto
"Gaelic" Symphony
Mass in Eb
Piano Quartet

Gilbert, Henry F. B. (1868–1928)
Comedy Overture on Negro Themes
Negro Rhapsody (orch.)
Dance in Place Congo (orch.)

Joplin, Scott (1868–1917)
Treemonisha (opera)

Freeman, Harry Lawrence (1869–1954)
The Martyr (opera)
Voodoo (opera)

Eichheim, Henry (1870–1942)
Oriental Impressions (orch.)
Bali (orch.)
Java (orch.)

Converse, Frederick (1871–1940)
The Pipe of Desire (opera)
American Sketches (orch.)
Flivver Ten Million (orch.)
The Flight of the Eagle (cantata)

Farwell, Arthur (1872–1952)
Violin Sonata
American Indian Melodies (piano)
Symbolistic Studies (piano and orch.)
Impressions of the Wa-Wan Ceremony
 of the Omahas (piano)
The Vale of Enithharmon (piano)
"Rudolph Gott" Symphony
Piano Quintet

Indian Suite (orch.)
Twenty-Three Polytonal Etudes
  (piano)
Piano Sonata

Hill, Edward Burlingame (1872–1960)
Jazz Studies
Scherzo (2 pianos and orch.)
Symphonies Nos. 1–3
Violin Concerto
Bassoon Sonata

Ives, Charles (1874–1954)
Country Band March
Variations on "America"
114 Songs
Piano Sonata No.1
Piano Sonata No.2, "Concord, Mass.,
  1840–1860"
Symphonies Nos. 1–4
String Quartets Nos. 1–2
Violin Sonatas Nos. 1–4
Three Places in New England (orch.)
"Holidays" Symphony
Central Park in the Dark (orch.)
Calcium Light Night (orch.)
The Unanswered Question (orch.)
The Celestial Country (cantata)
Piano Trio
Largo Risoluto
Three-Page Sonata
General William Booth Enters Into
  Heaven
From the Steeples and the Mountains
Sets for Theatre Orchestra Nos. 1–3
Three Quarter-Tone Pieces (2 pianos)

Carpenter, John Alden (1876–1951)
Piano Concertino
Adventures in a Perambulator (orch.)
Krazy Kat (orch.)
Skyscrapers (orch.)
Patterns (orch.)
Sea Drift (orch.)
The Anxious Bugler (orch.)
Violin Concerto

Ruggles, Carl (1876–1971)

Men and Mountains (orch.)
Vox clamans in deserto
Evocations (piano)
Men and Angels
Portals
Sun-Treader
Organum

Smith, David Stanley (1877–1949)
Fête Gallante (flute and orch.)

Bloch, Ernest (1880–1959)
Concerto Grosso No.1
Schelomo
Sacred Service
Enfantines (piano)
Poems of the Sea
Piano Sonata
Violin Concerto

*Cadman, Charles Wakefield (1881–
  1946)*
Shanewis (opera)
The Witch of Salem (opera)
The Garden of Mystery (opera)

Grainger, Percy Aldridge (1882–1961)
American Folk Song Settings (piano)
Random Rounds (mixed instruments)

Griffes, Charles T. (1884–1920)
The White Peacock (orch.)
Roman Sketches (piano)
Piano Sonata
Poem for Flute and Orchestra
The Pleasure Dome of Kubla Khan
Three Tone Pictures (piano)
Three Preludes (piano)
Three Songs of Fiona MacLeod
Wai Kiki (song)
The Kairn of Koridwen (theatre piece)

Whithorne, Emerson (1884–1958)
New York Days and Nights (orch.)
Poem for Piano and Orchestra
The Dream Pedlar (orch.)
Moon Trail (orch.)
Fata Morgana (orch.)
Marco's Millions (orch.)

Gruenberg, Louis (1884–1964)
The Emperor Jones (opera)
Jack in the Beanstalk (opera)
Green Mansions (opera)
The Daniel Jazz (voice and orch.)
The Creation (voice and orch.)

Riegger, Wallingford (1885–1961)
With My Red Fires (ballet)
Symphonies Nos. 1–4
Study in Sonority (violins)
Piano Trio
Triple Jazz
La belle dame sans merci
Four Tone Pictures (piano)
Evocation (ballet)
New Dance (ballet)
String Quartets Nos. 1–2
Pilgrim's Progress (ballet)
Piano Quintet
Nonet for Brass
Variations for Piano and Orchestra
Suite for Younger Orchestras
Concerto for Piano and Woodwind
    Quintet

Taylor, Deems (1885–1966)
The King's Henchman (opera)
Peter Ibbetson (opera)

Varèse, Edgard (1885–1965)
Ionisation
Density 21.5
Etude pour Espace
Amériques
Offrandes
Poeme electronique
Hyperprism
Octandre
Intégrales
Arcana
Ecuatorial
Déserts
Noctournal

Becker, John J. (1886–1961)
Obongo
Symphonies Nos. 1–3

Toch, Ernst (1887–1964)
String Quartets Nos. 1–13
Piano Quintet
Symphonies Nos. 1–7
Intermezzo (orch.)
Two-Piano Sonata
5×10 Etudes (piano)
The Last Tale (opera)

Grofé, Ferde (1892–1972)
The Grand Canyon Suite (orch.)

Moore, Douglas (1893–1969)
The Devil and Daniel Webster (opera)
The Ballad of Baby Doe (opera)

Piston, Walter (1894–1976)
The Incredible Flutist (orch.)
String Quartets Nos. 1–5
Symphonies Nos. 1–8
Three Pieces for Flute, Clarinet and Bas-
    soon
Flute Sonata
Concerto for Orchestra
Concerto for Viola
Concerto for Two Pianos
Concerto for Clarinet
Concerto for Flute
Concerto for String Quartet and Or-
    chestra
Concertino for Piano and Orchestra
Woodwind Quintet
Piano Quartet
String Sextet

Still, William Grant (1895–1978)
Afro-American Symphony
From the Black Belt
Bayou Legend (opera)
Darker America

Hanson, Howard (1896–1981)
Symphonies Nos. 1–6
Merrymount (opera)
Piano Concerto

Sessions, Roger (1896–1985)
The Black Maskers (opera, suite)
Violin Concerto

Piano Sonatas Nos. 1–3
Symphonies Nos. 1–9
The Trial of Lucullus (opera)
The Idyll of Theocritus (oratorio)
Montezuma (opera)
Mass for Unison Choir
When Lilacs Last in the Dooryard Bloom'd (cantata)
Piano Concerto
Double Concerto (violin, cello, orch.)
Concerto for Orchestra

Thomson, Virgil (1896–1989)
Symphony on a Hymn Tune
Sonata di chiesa (chamber ensemble)
Piano Sonatas Nos. 1–4
String Quartets Nos. 1–2
Symphonies Nos. 1–4
Four Saints in Three Acts (opera)
The Mother of Us All (opera)
Lord Byron (opera)
ca. 300 musical portraits for various instruments
Filling Station (ballet)
The Plow That Broke the Plains (film score)
The River (film score)
Louisiana Story (film score)
Piano Etudes Books 1–2
Mayor LaGuardia Waltzes
Canons for Dorothy Thompson
Missa pro defunctis (chorus and orch.)

Cowell, Henry (1897–1965)
The Aeolian Harp (piano)
Tiger (piano)
The Banshee (piano)
The Tides of Manaunaun
Symphonies Nos. 1–20
Variations for Orchestra
26 Simultaneous Mosaics
Piano Trio (1965)
Hymn and Fuguing Tunes Nos. 1–17 (various combinations)

Porter, Quincy (1897–1966)
Violin Sonatas Nos. 1–2

Piano Quintet
Piano Sonata
Symphonies Nos. 1–2
String Quartets Nos. 1–9
Viola Concerto
Horn Sonata
Concerto Concertante (2 pianos and orch.)
Concerto for Wind Orchestra
Harpsichord Concerto

Gershwin, George (1898–1937)
Rialto Ripples (piano)
Rhapsody in Blue
Concerto in F (piano and orch.)
Lullaby (string quartet)
Short Story (violin and piano)
Ten Song Transcriptions (piano)
Three Preludes for Piano
An American in Paris (orch.)
Second Rhapsody (piano and orch.)
Cuban Overture (orch.)
Porgy and Bess (opera)

Harris, Roy (1898–1979)
Andante for Orchestra
Concerto for Piano, Clarinet and String Quartet
Piano Sonata
Symphonies Nos. 1–13
Piano Toccata
Little Suite (piano)
Toccata for Orchestra
Concerto for String Sextet
Piano Trio
Piano Quintet
Piano Concertos Nos. 1–2
Concerto for Piano and Band
Concerto for Two Pianos and Orchestra
Violin Concerto

Thompson, Randall (1899–1984)
Alleluia (chorus)
Testament of Freedom (chorus)
Frostiana (chorus)

Antheil, George (1900–1959)
Symphonies Nos. 1–6

Ballet mécanique
Airplane Sonata
Sonata Sauvage
The Spectre of the Rose (film score)
Volpone (opera)

Copland, Aaron (1900–1990)
Symphonies Nos. 1–3
Piano Concerto
Music for the Theatre
Four Piano Blues
Statements for Orchestra
Vitebsk (piano trio)
Piano Variations
Quiet City (orch.)
Piano Sonata
El Salon Mexico (orch.)
Billy the Kid (ballet)
Rodeo (ballet)
An Outdoor Overture
The Second Hurricane (opera)
Appalachian Spring (ballet)
Fanfare for the Common Man
A Lincoln Portrait (speaker and orch.)
Danzon Cubano (2 pianos)
Our Town (film score)
The Red Pony (film score)
Clarinet Concerto
The Tender Land (opera)
Piano Quartet
Twelve Songs of Emily Dickinson
Nonet for Strings
Dance Panels (ballet)
Connotations (orch.)
Inscape (orch.)

Luening, Otto (b. 1900)
Evangeline (opera)
Gargoyles (electronic)
Poem in Cycles and Bells (with V.
    Ussachevsky, electronic)
Fantasy in Space (electronic)
Sonority Canon (flutes)
Kentucky Concerto (piano and orch.)
Prelude to a Hymn Tune by Billings
Short Symphony

Partch, Harry (1901–1974)
Barstow: 8 Hitchhiker Inscriptions
U.S. Highball
San Francisco
The Letter
Yankee Doodle Fantasy
11 Intrusions
Plectra and Percussion Dances
Oedipus
Two Settings from Lewis Carroll
Revelation in the Courthouse Park
And on the Seventh Day the Petals Fell
    in Petaluma
Delusion of the Fury

Blitzstein, Mark (1905–1964)
The Cradle Will Rock (musical)
The Condemned (oratorio)
Airborne Symphony

Creston, Paul (1906–1985)
Sonata for Saxophone and Piano
Marimba Concerto
Rhythmicon (piano)
Symphonies Nos. 1–6
Piano Concerto
Metamorphoses (piano)

Finney, Ross Lee (b. 1906)
Violin Concertos Nos. 1–2
Piano Concertos Nos. 1–2
Symphonies Nos. 1–4
Concerto for Percussion and Orchestra
Alto Saxophone Concerto
Piano Sonatas Nos. 1–4
Variations on a Theme by Alban Berg
    (piano)
String Quartets Nos. 1–8

Carter, Elliott (b. 1908)
A Holiday Overture
String Quartets Nos. 1–4
Pochahontas (ballet)
The Defense of Corinth (chorus)
The Harmony of Morning (chorus)
Emblems (chorus)
Tarantella
Symphony No. 1

The Minotaur (ballet)
Piano Sonata
Sonata for Cello and Piano
Woodwind Quintet
Eight Etudes and a Fantasy (woodwind quartet)
Piano Concerto
Double Concerto (piano, harpsichord and orch.)
Night Fantasies (piano)
Variations for Orchestra
Concerto for Orchestra
Symphony of Three Orchestras
Penthode (for 5 string quartets)
Oboe Concerto
Remembrance (orch.)
Violin Concerto

Barber, Samuel (1910–1981)
Overture to "The School for Scandal"
Dover Beach (voice)
Adagio for Strings
Essays for Orchestra Nos. 1–2
Violin Concerto
Excursions (piano)
Cello Concerto
Medea's Meditation and Dance of Vengeance (orch.)
Knoxville: Summer of 1915 (voice)
Piano Sonata
Hermit Songs (voice)
A Hand of Bridge (opera)
Summer Music (woodwinds)
Vanessa (opera)
Piano Concerto
Night Flight (orch.)
Antony and Cleopatra (opera)

Schuman, William (1910–1992)
The Mighty Casey (opera)
Voyage (piano)
Symphonies Nos. 1–10
Canonic Choruses
Piano Concerto
String Quartets Nos. 1–4
American Festival Overture
A Free Song (cantata)

New England Triptych (orch.)
Violin Concerto

Herrmann, Bernard (1911–1975)
String Quartets Nos. 1–2
Citizen Kane (film score)
The Magnificent Ambersons (film score)
The Ghost and Mrs. Muir (film score)
Wuthering Heights (opera)
Psycho (film score)
Fahrenheit 451 (film score)
Taxi Driver (film score)

Menotti, Gian-Carlo (b. 1911)
Amelia Goes to the Ball (opera)
The Old Maid and the Thief (opera)
The Medium (opera)
Piano Concerto
The Telephone (opera)
The Consul (opera)
Amahl and the Night Visitors (opera)
The Saint of Bleecker Street (opera)
The Unicorn, the Gorgon and the Manticore (opera)
Maria Golovin (opera)
The Death of the Bishop of Brindisi (cantata)
Martin's Lie (opera)
Help! Help! The Globolinks! (opera)
Goya (opera)

Cage, John (1912–1992)
Sonata for Clarinet
Quartet for Percussion
Trio for Percussion
Imaginary Landscapes
Amores (prepared piano)
Music for Marcel Duchamp
Sonatas and Interludes (prepared piano)
Suite for Toy Piano
Music of Changes
Music for Piano
4'33"
Aria
Fontana Mix
Cartridge Music
Atlas Elipticalis (orch.)

Europeras 1–4

Nancarrow, Conlon (b. 1912)
Blues for Piano
Septet
Suite for Orchestra
Forty-Four Studies for Player Piano
Pieces Nos. 1–2 for Small Orchestra
String Quartets Nos. 1–3

Dello Joio, Norman (b. 1913)
Harmonica Concerto
Magnificat
The Triumph of St. Joan (opera, symphony)
Meditations on Ecclesiastes
The Louvre (television score)

Gould, Morton (b. 1913)
Piano Concerto
American Salute (orch.)
Fall River Legend (ballet)
Symphonies Nos. 1–3
Concerto for Orchestra
Symphony of Spirituals
The Holocaust (television score)

Persichetti, Vincent (1915–1987)
Divertimento for Band
Symphonies Nos. 1–9
Harpsichord Sonatas Nos. 1–8
Piano Sonatas Nos. 1–11
String Quartets Nos. 1–4
Piano Concerto

Diamond, David (b. 1915)
Symphonies Nos. 1–9

Babbitt, Milton (b. 1916)
Three Compositions for Piano
Composition for Four Instruments
Composition for Twelve Instruments
String Quartets Nos. 1–5
Woodwind Quintet
All Set
Partitions
Composition for Synthesizer
Vision and Prayer (soprano and synthesizer)

Ensembles for Synthesizer
Concerti for Violin, Small Orchestra and Tape
Solo Requiem
Ars combinatoria
Piano Concerto

Harrison, Lou (b. 1917)
Concerto for Flute and Percussion
Symphony on G
Moogunkwha (orch.)
Concerto in slendro
Pacifika Rondo
At the Tomb of Charles Ives
Young Caesar (puppet opera)
Concerto for Organ, Percussion and Orchestra
Suite for Violin and American Gamelan
Scenes from Cavafy
Four Gendings
Symphonies Nos. 1–3
Piano Concerto

Bernstein, Leonard (1918–1990)
Clarinet Sonata
Prelude, Fugue and Riffs (clarinet, jazz combo)
Seven Anniversaries (piano)
On the Town (musical)
Fancy Free (ballet)
Trouble in Tahiti (opera)
On the Waterfront (film score)
Candide (operetta)
West Side Story (musical)
Chichester Psalms (chorus)
Mass
The Dybbuk (ballet)
A Quiet Place (opera)

Rochberg, George (b. 1918)
String Quartets Nos. 1–7
Cheltenham Concerto
Time Span I–II
Contra Mortem et Tempus
Symphonies Nos. 1–4
Violin Concerto
Piano Quartet

Oboe Concerto

Kirchner, Leon (b. 1919)
Piano Sonata
String Quartet Nos. 1–3
Piano Concertos Nos. 1–2

LaMontaine, John (b. 1920)
Piano Concerto (1959)

Foss, Lukas (b. 1922)
Piano Concertos Nos. 1–2
The Prairie (cantata)
Oboe Concerto
The Jumping Frog of Calaveras County
    (opera)
Psalms (chorus and orch.)
Time Cycle (soprano and orch.)
Echoi
Concerto for Cello and Orchestra
Percussion Concerto
Night Music for John Lennon

Schuller, Gunther (b. 1925)
Horn Concertos Nos. 1–2
Symphonic Study
Symphony for Brass and Percussion
Contours (chamber orchestra)
Seven Studies on Themes of Paul Klee
Piano Concertos Nos. 1–2
Composition in Three Parts
Double Bass Concerto
Violin Concerto

Feldman, Morton (1926–1987)
Projections I–V
Intersections I–IV
Last Pieces
Vertical Thoughts
Structures (orch.)
On Time and the Instrumental Factor
String Quartets Nos. 1–2
Piano Trio

Maxfield, Richard (1927–1969)
Suite for Orchestra
Structures (woodwinds)
Perspectives (violin and tape)
Night Music

Toy Symphony
Electronic Symphony

Druckman, Jacob (b. 1928)
Antiphonies I–III (chorus)
Windows (orch.)
Incenters (orch.)
Viola Concerto
Aureole (orch.)
Prism (orch.)
Athanor (orch.)
Brangle (orch.)

Crumb, George (b. 1929)
Five Pieces for Piano
Night Music
Madrigals Books 1–4
Echoes of Time and the River
Black Angels
Ancient Voices of Children
Vox balaenae
Lux aeterna
Makrokosmos
Gnomic Variations

Oliveros, Pauline (b. 1932)
Variations for Sextet
Sound Patterns (voices)
Pieces of Eight
Double Basses at Twenty Paces
Sonic Meditations
Crow II
Spiral Mandala

Rands, Bernard (b. 1934)
Mesalliance (piano and orch.)
Madrigali
Canti Lunatici
Canti del Sole
Canti eclissi
Suites Nos. 1–2 (orch.)
Ceremonial for Orchestra

Riley, Terry (b. 1935)
Trio (violin, clarinet, cello)
Concert for Two Pianos and Tape
String Quartets Nos. 1–9
In C
Poppy Nogood and the Phantom Band

Happy Ending
Chorale of the Blessed Day
A Rainbow in Curved Air
Salomé Dances for Peace

Young, La Monte (b. 1935)
Trio for Strings
The Tortoise, his Dreams and Journeys
The Well-Tuned Piano

Reich, Steve (b. 1936)
Piano Phase
Violin Phase
Drumming
Music for 18 Musicians
Octet
Music for Large Ensemble
Tehellim
Vermont Counterpoint
The Desert Music
Sextet
New York Counterpoint
Three Movements for Orchestra
Different Trains
The Cave

Del Tredici, David (b. 1937)
Two Songs (Joyce)
Fantasy Pieces (piano)
Pop-pourri (orch.)
An Alice Symphony
Adventures Underground
Vintage Alice
Final Alice
Child Alice (including "In Memory of
a Summer Day")

Glass, Philip (b. 1937)
Music in 12 Parts
Einstein on the Beach (opera)
Satyagraha (opera)
Glassworks (mixed instruments)
The Photographer (opera)
Akhnaten (opera)
Violin Concerto
The Juniper Tree (opera)
The Fall of the House of Usher (opera)

The Making of the Representative from
Planet 8 (opera)
1,000 Airplanes on the Roof (theatre
piece)
The Voyage (opera)
Orphée (opera)

Bolcom, William (b. 1938)
Songs of Innocence and Experience
Twelve Etudes for Piano
Twelve New Etudes for Piano
Dynamite Tonite (opera)
String Quartets Nos. 1–8
Piano Concerto
Violin Concerto
Symphonies Nos. 1–5
McTeague (opera)

Corigliano, John (b. 1938)
Fern Hill (Dylan Thomas, voice)
Violin Sonata
Piano Concerto
Poem in October (D. Thomas, voice)
Oboe Concerto
Poem on His Birthday (D. Thomas,
voice)
Clarinet Concerto
Altered States (film score)
Flute Concerto
Symphony No. 1
The Ghosts of Versailles (opera)

Tower, Joan (b. 1938)
Amazon I–III
Piano Concerto
Fanfare for the Uncommon Woman

Zwilich, Ellen Taaffe (b. 1939)
Symposium (orch.)
Violin Sonata
String Quartet
Clarino Quartet
String Trio
Symphonies Nos. 1–2
Celebration (orch.)
Chamber Concerto
Double String Quartet
Piano Concerto

Flute Concerto
Oboe Concerto

Albert, Stephen (1941–1992)
To Wake the Dead
River Run (orch.)
Violin Concerto
Anthems and Processionals
The Flower of the Mountain
Cello Concerto

Adams, John (b. 1947)
Shaker Loops
Harmonium
Grand Pianola Music
Harmonielehre
Nixon in China (opera)
Fearful Symmetries
The Word Dresser
The Death of Klinghoffer (opera)

Selected Bibliography of Readings in American Classical Music

Anderson, Donna K. *Charles T. Griffes: A Life in Music.* Washington and London: Smithsonian Institution Press, 1993.

Armitage, Merle. *George Gershwin: Man and Legend.* New York: Duell, Sloane and Pearce, 1958.

Arvey, Verna. *In One Lifetime* (biography of William Grant Still). Fayetteville: University of Arkansas Press, 1984.

Austin, William W. *Music in the 20th Century: from Debussy through Stravinsky.* New York: W.W. Norton and Company, 1966.

———. *"Susanna," "Jeanie," and "The Old Folks at Home": The Songs of Stephen C. Foster from His Time to Ours.* New York: MacMillan Publishing Co., Inc., 1972.

Barbour, J. Murray. *The Church Music of William Billings.* East Lansing: Michigan State University Press, 1960.

Barzun, Jacques. *Music in American Life.* Bloomington: Indiana University Press, 1962.

Bauer, Marion. *20th Century Music.* New York: G. Putnam's, 1933.

Berger, Arthur. *Aaron Copland.* New York: Oxford University Press, 1953.

Bernard, Jonathan W. *The Music of Edgard Varèse.* New Haven, Conn.: Yale University Press, 1987.

Bernstein, Leonard. *Findings.* New York: Simon and Schuster, 1982.

Boatwright, Howard (ed.). *Essays Before a Sonata, The Majority and Other Writings by Charles Ives.* New York: Oxford University Press, 1955.

Boretz, B. and E. T. Cone. *Perspectives on American Composers.* New York: W.W. Norton, 1971.

Boulez, Pierre. *Orientations.* Cambridge, Mass.: Harvard University Press, 1986.

Briggs, John. *Leonard Bernstein: The Man, His Work and His World.* Cleveland, Ohio: The World Publishing Co., 1961.

Broder, Nathan. *Samuel Barber.* New York: G. Schirmer, Inc., 1954.

Brown, Abbie Farrell. *The Boyhood of Edward MacDowell.* New York: Frederick A. Stokes Co., 1924.

Burkholder, J. Peter. *Charles Ives: the ideas behind the music.* New Haven, Conn.: Yale University Press, 1985.

Butterworth, Neil. *The Music of Aaron Copland.* New York: Universe Books, 1986.

Cage, John. *For the Birds* (conversation with Daniel Charles). Boston, London: Marion Boyars, 1981.

———. *Silence.* Cambridge, Mass.: The MIT Press, 1966.

———. *A Year From Monday.* Middletown, Conn.: The Wesleyan University Press, 1967.

———. *I–VI, The 1988–89 Norton Lectures.* Cambridge, Mass.: The Harvard University Press, 1990.

Carter, Elliott. *The Writings of Elliott Carter.* Bloomington: Indiana University Press, 1977.

Chase, Gilbert. *America's Music from the Pilgrims to the Present.* New York: McGraw-Hill, 1955.

Chase, Gilbert, ed. *The American Composer Speaks: a historical anthology, 1770–1965.* Baton Rouge: Louisiana State University Press, 1966.

Copland, Aaron. *Our New Music.* New York: McGraw-Hill, 1941.

Copland, Aaron and Vivian Perlis. *Copland: 1900 through 1942.* New York: St. Martin's/Marek, 1984.

———. *Copland Since 1943.* New York: St. Martin's/Marek, 1989.

Cowell, Henry. *New Musical Resources* (1930). New York: Something Else Press, 1969.

Cowell, Henry and Sidney. *Charles Ives and his music.* New York: Oxford University Press, 1955.

Curtis, Natalie. *The Indians' Book.* New York: Dover Publications, Inc., 1968.

Daniel, Oliver, ed. *Jacob Kimball: Down East Spirituals.* New York: C.F. Peters Corporation, 1973.

Davis, Ronald. *A History of Music in American Life.* (3 vols.) Huntington, N.Y. and Malabar, Fla.: Robert Krieger Publishing Co., 1980, 1981, 1982.

Durham, Frank. *DuBose Heyward: the Man Who Wrote Porgy.* Port Washington, NY: Kennikat Press, Inc., 1965.

Edwards, Allen. *Flawed Words and Stubborn Sounds: a Conversation with Elliott Carter.* New York: W.W. Norton and Company, Inc., 1971.

Ellinwood, Leonard. *The History of American Church Music.* New York: Morehouse-Gorham Co., 1953. Reprint. Da Capo, 1970.

Elson, Louis. *The History of American Music.* New York: The MacMillan Company, 1904. Revised 1915.

Ewen, David. *George Gershwin: his journey to greatness.* Englewood Cliffs, N.J.: Prentice-Hall, Inc., 1970.

———. *The Life and Death of Tin Pan Alley.* New York: Funk and Wagnall's, 1964.

Fisher, William Arms. *Ye Olde New England Psalm Tunes (1620–1820).* Boston: Oliver Ditson Company, 1930.

————. *The Music That Washington Knew (With an Historical Sketch)*. Boston: Oliver Ditson Company, 1931.

Fleming, Richard. *John Cage at Seventy-Five*. Cranbury, NJ: Bucknell University Press, 1990.

Floyd, S. A. and M. Reisser. *Black Music in the United States: an annotated bibliography*. Millwood, New York and London: Kraus International Publications, 1983.

Foster, Stephen C. *A Treasury of Stephen Foster*. Foreword by Deems Taylor; historical notes by John Tasker Howard. New York: Random House, 1946.

Gillespie, Don. *George Crumb, Profile of a Composer*. New York: C.F. Peters Corporation, 1986.

————. *Ross Lee Finney, Profile of a Lifetime,* New York: C.F. Peters Corporation, 1992.

Gilman, Lawrence. *Edward MacDowell: A Study* (1908). New York: Da Capo Press, 1969.

Glass, Philip. *Music by Philip Glass*. New York: Harper and Row, 1987.

Glazer, Tom. *Songs of Peace, Freedom, and Protest*. Greenwich, Conn.: Fawcett Publications, Inc., 1970.

Gleason, H. and W. Becker. *Music Literature Outlines Series III: Early American Music (Music in America from 1620 to 1920)*. Bloomington, Ind.: Frangipani Press, 1981.

————. *Music Literature Outlines Series IV: 20th Century American Composers*. Bloomington: Frangipani Press, 1980.

Gottschalk, Louis Moreau. *Notes of a Pianist*. New York: Da Capo Press, 1962.

Gradenwitz, Peter. *Leonard Bernstein: the Infinite Variety of a Musician*. Hamburg and New York: Berg Publishers Ltd., 1987.

Gray, John. *Blacks in Classical Music*. Bibliography. New York: Greenwood Press, 1988.

Griffiths, Paul. *Cage*. London: Oxford University Press, 1981.

Grout, Donald Jay. *A History of Western Music*. 3rd edition with Claude V. Palisca. New York: W.W. Norton and Company, 1980.

Gruen, John. *Menotti: a biography*. New York: MacMillan Publishing Co., 1978.

Haas, Robert B., ed. *William Grant Still and the Fusion of Cultures in American Music*. Collection of essays, analyses and biography. Los Angeles: Black Sparrow Press, 1972.

Hall, Charles J. *A 20th Century Musical Chronicle: Events 1900–1988*. New York: Greenwood Press, 1990.

Hamm, Charles. *Music in the New World*. New York: W.W. Norton, 1983.

Heyman, Barbara. *Samuel Barber, the Composer and His Music*. New York: Oxford University Press, 1992.

Hipsher, Edward Ellsworth. *American Opera and Its Composers*. Philadelphia: Theodore Presser Co., 1927.

Hitchcock, H. Wiley. *Music in the United States: a Historical Introduction*. Englewood Cliffs, N.J.: Prentice Hall, Inc., 1969.

Hixon, Donald. *Music in Early America*. Metuchen, N.J.: Scarecrow Press, 1970.

Horn, David. *The Literature of American Music.* Bibliography with supplement. Metuchen, N.J.: Scarecrow Press, 1977.

Hoover, Kathleen and John Cage. *Virgil Thomson—his life and music.* Freeport, N.Y.: Books for Libraries Press, 1970.

Howard, John Tasker. *Our American Music: A Comprehensive History from 1620 to the Present.* 4th ed. New York: Thomas Y. Crowell Company, 1965.

———. *Our Contemporary Composers.* New York: Thomas Y. Crowell Company, 1941.

———. *Stephen Foster, America's Troubadour.* New York: Thomas Y. Crowell Company, 1934, 1953.

Hutchinson, John Wallace. *The Story of the Hutchinsons.* 2 vols. New York: Da Capo Press, 1977.

Ives, Charles E. *Memos.* Edited by John Kirkpatrick. New York: W.W. Norton and Company, Inc., 1972.

———. *Essays Before a Sonata, The Majority and Other Writings.* New York: W.W. Norton and Co. Inc., 1962.

Jablonski, Edward. *Gershwin.* New York: Doubleday, 1987.

Jezic, Diane Peacock. *The Musical Migration and Ernst Toch.* Ames: The Iowa State University Press, 1989.

Johnson, Roger, ed. *Scores: An Anthology of New Music.* New York: Schirmer Books, 1981.

Jordan, Philip D. *Singin' Yankees.* Minneapolis: The University of Minnesota Press, 1946.

Kaufman, Helen L. *From Jehovah to Jazz: Music in America from Psalmody to the Present Day.* Port Washington, N.Y.: Kennikat Press, 1937, 1969.

Kearns, William K. *Horatio Parker, 1863–1919: His Life, Music and Ideas.* Metuchen, N.J.: Scarecrow Press, 1991.

Kendall, Alan. *George Gershwin.* New York: Universe Books, 1987.

Kerman, Joseph. *Opera as Drama.* New York: Vintage Books (a division of Random House), 1956.

Kingman, David. *American Music: A Panorama.* New York: Schirmer Books, 1979.

Kostelanetz, Richard. *John Cage.* New York: Praeger Publishers, 1970.

———, ed. *John Cage: Writer (Previously Uncollected Pieces).* New York: Limelight Editions, 1993.

———. *On Innovative Musicians.* New York: Limelight, 1990.

Lang, Paul Henry. *One Hundred Years of American Music.* Essays on various aspects of American musical life. New York: G. Schirmer, Inc., 1961.

Lawrence, Vera Brodsky. *Strong on Music: The New York Music Scene in the Days of George Templeton Strong, Vol. I, Resonances, 1836–1850.* New York: Oxford University Press, 1988.

Lawrence, Vera Brodsky, ed. *The Wa-Wan Press.* Reprints of scores published by the Wa-Wan Press, complete in 5 volumes. New York: Arno Press and the New York Times, 1970.

Lowens, Irving. *Music and Musicians in Early America.* New York: W.W. Norton, 1964.

Luening, Otto. *The Odyssey of an American Composer.* Autobiography. New York: Charles Scribner's Sons, 1980.

LePage, J. W. *Women Composers, Conductors and Musicians of the 20th Century.* 2 vols. Metuchen, N.J.: Scarecrow Press, 1980, 1983.

McCue, George. *Music in American Society, 1776–1976.* Essays by William Schuman, Austin Caswell, John Eaton et al. New Brunswick, N.J.: Transaction Books, 1977.

Machlis, Joseph. *American Composers of Our Time.* New York: Thomas Y. Crowell Co., 1963.

McKay, David P. and R. Crawford. *William Billings of Boston.* Princeton, N.J.: The Princeton University Press, 1975.

Malm, William P. *Music Cultures of the Pacific, the Near East and Asia.* Englewood Cliffs, N.J.: Prentice-Hall, Inc., 1977.

Maisel, Edward. *Charles T. Griffes: The Life of an American Composer.* New York: Alfred A. Knopf, 1943, 1984.

Mason, Daniel Gregory. *Contemporary Composers.* New York: AMS Press, 1973. Reprint of the 1918 MacMillan edition.

Mason, Lowell. *Musical Letters from Abroad.* New York: Da Capo Press, 1967. Orig., 1854.

Matthews, W. S. B. *A Hundred Years of Music in America.* Chicago: 1889. AMS reprint edition, 1970.

Mellers, Wilfred. *Music in a New Found Land.* New York: Hillstone (a division of the Stonehill Publishing Company), 1964, 1975.

Moore, MacDonald Smith. *Yankee Blues: Musical Culture and American Identity.* Bloomington: Indiana University Press, 1985.

Morgenstern, S., ed. *Composers on Music.* New York: Pantheon Books, 1956.

Mussulman, Joseph A. *Music in the Cultured Generation: A Social History of Music in America, 1870–1900.* Evanston, Ill.: Northwestern University Press, 1971.

Nathan, Hans. *Dan Emmett and the Rise of Early Negro Minstrelsy.* Norman: The University of Oklahoma Press, 1962.

Nicholls, David. *American Experimental Music, 1890–1940.* Cambridge, England: Cambridge University Press, 1990.

Olmstead, Andrea. *Conversations with Roger Sessions.* Boston: Northeastern University Press, 1987.

——. *Roger Sessions and His Music.* Ann Arbor, Mich.: UMI Research Press, 1985.

Ouellette, Fernand. *Edgard Varèse.* Translated by Derek Coleman. New York: Orion Press, 1968.

Page, Tim and Vanessa W., eds. *Selected Letters of Virgil Thomson.* New York: Summit Books, 1988.

Palmer, Christopher. *The Composer in Hollywood.* London and New York: Marion Boyars Publishers, 1990.

Perle, George. *The Listening Composer.* Berkeley: The University of California Press, 1990.

Perlis, Vivian. *Charles Ives Remembered: an Oral History*. New Haven, Conn., and London: Yale University Press, 1974.

Perry, R. S. *Charles Ives and the American Mind*. Kent, Ohio: Kent State University Press, 1974.

Peyser, Joan. *Bernstein, a biography*. New York: Beech Tree Books, 1987.

Pollack, Howard. *Harvard Composers: Walter Piston and his students from Elliott Carter to Frederic Rzewski*. Metuchen: Scarecrow Press, 1992.

Pound, Ezra. *Antheil and the Treatise on Harmony*. New York: Da Capo Press, 1968.

Reich, Steve. *Writings About Music*. Halifax, Nova Scotia and New York: The Press of the Nova Scotia College of Art and Design and New York University Press, 1974.

Reis, Claire R. *Composers in America*. New York: The MacMillan Co., 1947.

Revill, David. *The Roaring Silence (John Cage: A Life)*. New York: Arcade Publishing, 1992.

Ritter, Frédéric Louis. *Music in America*. New York and London: Johnson Reprint Corporation, 1970. Orig. 1883

Rockwell, John. *All American Music: Composition in the Late 20th Century*. New York: Alfred A. Knopf, 1983.

Root, G. F. *The Story of a Musical Life*. Cincinnati, Ohio: 1891. Reprint Da Capo, 1970.

Rorem, Ned. *The New York Diary*. New York: George Braziller Inc., 1967.

———. *The Paris Diary*. New York: George Braziller Inc., 1966.

Rossiter, Frank R. *Charles Ives and His America*. New York: Liveright, 1975.

Rublowsky, John. *Music in America*. New York: Crowell-Collier Press, 1967.

Rushmore, Robert. *The Life of George Gershwin*. New York: Crowell-Collier Press, 1966.

Sablosky, Irving. *American Music*. Chicago: University of Chicago Press, 1969.

Schiff, David. *The Music of Elliott Carter*. London: Eulenberg Books, 1983.

Schonberg, Harold C. *The Great Pianists from Mozart to the Present*. New York: Simon and Schuster, Inc., 1963.

Schrader, Barry. *Introduction to Electro-Acoustic Music*. Englewood Cliffs, N.J.: Prentice-Hall, Inc., 1982.

Schreiber, F. R. and V. Persichetti. *William Schuman*. New York: G. Schirmer Inc., 1954.

Schuller, Gunther. *Musings: The Musical Worlds of Gunther Schuller*. Collection of his writings. New York: Oxford University Press, 1986.

Schwartz, Charles. *Gershwin: his life and music*. New York: Bobbs-Merrill, 1973.

Schwartz, E. and B. Childs. *Contemporary Composers on Contemporary Music*. New York: Holt, Rinehart and Winston, 1967.

Scott, John Anthony, ed. *The Ballad of America: The History of the United States in Song and Story*. New York: Bantam Books, Inc., 1966.

Sessions, Roger. *Roger Sessions on Music: Collected Essays*. Edited by Edward T. Cone. Princeton, N.J.: Princeton University Press, 1979.

Slonimsky, Nicolas. *Music Since 1900.* New York: Coleman-Ross (Charles Scribner's Sons), 1971. *Supplement* to same, New York: Charles Scribner's Sons, 1986.

Sonneck, Oscar G. T. *Early Opera in America.* New York: Benjamin Blom, 1963.

———. *Francis Hopkinson and James Lyon.* Washington, D.C.: 1905. Reprint. Da Capo, 1967.

———. *Miscellaneous Studies in the History of Music.* New York: AMS Press, 1970. Original 1921.

Starr, Larry. *A Union of Diversities: Style in the Music of Charles Ives.* New York: Schirmer Books, 1992.

Stuckenschmidt, H. H. *Twentieth Century Music.* Translated from the German by Richard Deveson. New York: McGraw-Hill Book Company (World University Library), 1969.

Thomson, Virgil. *American Music Since 1910.* New York: Holt, Rinehart and Winston, 1971.

———. *Virgil Thomson* (autobiography). New York: Alfred A. Knopf, 1966. Reprint. Da Capo, 1977.

Tischler, Barbara L. *An American Music: the search for an American musical identity.* New York: Oxford University Press, 1986.

Upton, William Treat. *Anthony Philip Heinrich: a 19th century composer in America.* Reprint of the 1939 Columbia University Press Edition. New York: AMS Press, 1967.

Varèse, Louise. *Varèse—a looking-glass diary.* New York: W.W. Norton, 1972.

Xenakis, Iannis. *Formalized Music.* Bloomington: Indiana University Press, 1971.

Yellin, Victor F. *Chadwick: Yankee Composer.* Washington and London: Smithsonian Institution Press, 1991.

Ziffrin, Marilyn. *Carl Ruggles.* Baltimore: University of Illinois Press, 1994.

Zuck, Barbara A. *A History of Musical Americanism.* Ann Arbor, Mich.: UMI Research Press, 1980.

Index

This index is arranged alphabetically letter-by-letter. Musical compositions are followed by the composer's last name in parentheses. Italic page numbers indicate illustrations or captions.